W9-CFQ-335

The
African American
Experience

THE
AFRICAN AMERICAN
EXPERIENCE

An Historiographical and Bibliographical Guide

Edited by
ARVARH E. STRICKLAND
and
ROBERT E. WEEMS, JR.

GREENWOOD PRESS
Westport, Connecticut • London

Library of Congress Cataloging-in-Publication Data

The African American experience : an historiographical and bibliographical guide /
edited by Arvarh E. Strickland and Robert E. Weems, Jr.

    p. cm.

   Includes bibliographical references and index.

   ISBN 0–313–29838–6 (alk. paper)

   1. Afro-Americans—Historiography. 2. Afro-Americans—History—Bibliography. I.
Strickland, Arvarh E. II. Weems, Robert E., 1951–

E184.65.A37   2001

973.0496073—dc21   00–025148

British Library Cataloguing in Publication Data is available.

Library of Congress Catalog Card Number: 00–025148
ISBN: 0–313–29838–6

First published in 2001

Greenwood Press, 88 Post Road West, Westport, CT 06881
An imprint of Greenwood Publishing Group, Inc.
www.greenwood.com

Printed in the United States of America

The paper used in this book complies with the
Permanent Paper Standard issued by the National
Information Standards Organization (Z39.48–1984).

10 9 8 7 6 5 4 3 2 1

Contents

Preface   vii

I   African American Migration and Urbanization   1
Arvarh E. Strickland and Robert E. Weems, Jr.

II   The African American Worker in Slavery and Freedom   23
Joe William Trotter, Jr.

III   African American Families: Historically Resilient   55
Aaron Thompson

IV   African American Women   71
Wilma King

V   The African American Educational Experience   93
Carolyn A. Dorsey

VI   The African American Literary Tradition   116
Clenora Hudson-Weems

VII   The African American Musical Experience: There's a Story in the Song   144
John A. Taylor

VIII   African American Intellectual and Political Thought   166
Robert L. Harris, Jr.

IX   The African American Political Experience   189
Sharon D. Wright and Minion K. C. Morrison

X   The African American Press   216
     Julius E. Thompson

XI   African Americans in the Military of the United States   231
     John F. Marszalek and Horace D. Nash

XII The African American Athletic Experience   255
     David K. Wiggins

XIII Constructing an Historiography of African American Business   278
     Juliet E. K. Walker

XIV Sexuality and Race   315
     Stanley O. Gaines, Jr.

XV   African American Consumerism   336
     Robert E. Weems, Jr.

XVI The Civil Rights Movement   352
     John Dittmer

XVII African American Religion in the United States   368
     Charles H. Long

Index   395

About the Editors and Contributors   445

Preface

Three decades ago, the volume of scholarly writing was such that a careful student of the field could have a detailed knowledge of the major works treating African American life and history. Outside the topics of slavery, Reconstruction, and African American migration, there was a dearth of scholarly publication. Aside from Monroe N. Work's voluminous *Bibliography of the Negro in Africa and America*, first published in 1928 and reprinted in 1966, two or three relatively slim bibliographies were about all the aspiring student needed to survey the basic books and journal articles available.

Beginning in the 1960s, this situation changed radically. The civil rights and black power movements brought increased demands for the study and teaching of African American history. University presses and commercial publishers responded to this sentiment by publishing an increasing number of works related to African American life and history. In fact, compared to the first decades of the twentieth century, the last thirty years has featured a literal (and ongoing) explosion of published works related to the African American experience.

This volume is intended to help fill the need for a comprehensive bibliographical work to serve as a guide in the use of this growing body of sources. Moreover, this purpose requires not only a listing of key books and articles but also analysis of how the study of African Americans has changed. Consequently, scholars from the fields of history, literature, religion, political science, sociology, psychology, music, and religion have contributed essays that spotlight the historiographical trends associated with the evolving study of African American life and history. Students and scholars, as well as general readers, should find this guide useful as a tool in identifying secondary materials for study, class use, and scholarly research.

It is evident that this, like all bibliographies, is a compilation of selected works, and also that while the authors and editors were at work and while the book was in press, important new works on these and additional topics were written and published. Moreover, although the authors and editors exercised due diligence, inevitably in works of this type, errors of spelling and even errors of citation are inadvertently overlooked. For these, we apologize in advance and will correct such errors subsequently discovered.

I

African American Migration and Urbanization

Arvarh E. Strickland and Robert E. Weems, Jr.

By the 1990s migration and urbanization as a subtopic in African American history had come of age. Scholars in African American history and migration studies have long recognized the dramatic movement of southern blacks to northern and western cities during the early to mid-twentieth century as a significant phenomenon, and thus this period has received extensive study. Yet black America's entire history has been profoundly influenced by the mass movement of people—both voluntary and involuntary.

Before the twentieth century, there existed a wide range of movement linked with the mobility of African Americans. In the pre–Civil War years these included the transatlantic slave trade, the subsequent forced movement of slaves based upon the whims of their white masters, runaway slaves and such support groups as the "Underground Railroad," and organized movements that promoted blacks returning to Africa. Moreover, while there is a tendency to view African American urbanization as primarily a twentieth-century phenomenon, as early as the colonial period, African Americans were present, in a variety of capacities, in American cities. Before the Civil War, most African American city-dwellers were free persons, yet there also existed a considerable number of urban slaves.

Between 1865 and 1900, African American migration and urbanization intensified as former slaves graphically demonstrated their freedom by moving about freely, often to nearby cities. Moreover, as the promise of Reconstruction descended into the nightmare of "Jim Crow," a considerable number of late-nineteenth-century African Americans resurrected the emigrationist sentiment of their forebears. Although physically returning to Africa essentially remained the elusive "impossible dream" of many southern blacks, some did, in the short term, solve the dilemma posed by southern white racism by moving to such western locales as Kansas and Oklahoma. In fact, this late-nineteenth-century westward movement of southern blacks resulted in, among other things, the establishment of a number of all–African American towns. Moreover, other southern blacks, during this period, began what would subsequently become a massive movement to northern urban areas.

In 1860, 94.9 percent of the black population lived in the South, and only 5.1 percent lived in the North and West. By 1910, the percentage living in the North and West had risen to 10.4 percent, in 1940 this proportion stood at 23.8 percent, and in 1970 it had risen to 46.8 percent. In other words, the percentage of the black population in the North and West doubled each generation from 1860 to 1970. After 1970, however, these proportions stabilized at about 47 percent in the North and West.

There exist a number of important works that chronicle pre-twentieth-century African American migration and urbanization from the transatlantic slave trade to the late-nineteenth-century dispersal of southern blacks. In fact, the historiography of this expansive chronological period has grown dramatically in recent years.

Despite ongoing research examining the dynamics of the transatlantic slave trade, Elizabeth Donnan's four-volume *Documents Illustrative of the History of the Slave Trade to America* (1930–1935) still provides the best overall depiction of this phenomenon. Major historiographical issues related to the transatlantic slave trade include estimating the number of Africans taken to the Western Hemisphere, the nuances of the Middle Passage and the subsequent dispersal of Africans in Europe's "New World," and the linkage of the transatlantic slave trade with the development of capitalism. Phillip D. Curtin's *Atlantic Slave Trade: A Census* (1969), which critics maintain is an undercount, remains, perhaps, the most discussed book associated with estimating the number of Africans taken to the Western Hemisphere. There exist a number of important studies related to the actual dynamics of the transatlantic slave trade and its aftermath, including W.E.B. Du Bois's *Suppression of the African Slave Trade to the United States, 1638–1870* (1896); Daniel R. Mannix's *Black Cargoes: A History of the Atlantic Slave Trade, 1518–1865* (1962); and Herbert S. Klein's *Middle Passage: Comparative Studies in the Atlantic Slave Trade* (1978). Finally, Eric Williams's *Capitalism and Slavery* (1944) remains the starting point for any inquiry into the broader economic ramifications of the transatlantic slave trade.

An overview of the historiography of slavery during the colonial and antebellum periods provides insight into the involuntary movement of transplanted African slaves at the whim of their white owners. Important sources include Lorenzo J. Greene's classic, *The Negro in Colonial New England* (1942); Edgar J. McManus's *History of Negro Slavery in Colonial New York* (1966); Peter Wood's *Black Majority: Negroes in Colonial South Carolina from 1670 through the Stono Rebellion* (1974); Betty Wood's *Slavery in Colonial Georgia, 1730–1775* (1984); Frederick Bancroft's *Slave Trading in the Old South* (1931); Kenneth M. Stampp's *Peculiar Institution* (1956); John W. Blassingame's *Slave Community: Plantation Life in the Antebellum South* (1972); Leslie Howard Owens's *This Species of Property: Slave Life and Culture in the Old South* (1976); and Peter Kolchin's *American Slavery, 1619–1877* (1993).

Although a significant amount of African American movement before 1865 was involuntary, many blacks, both slave and free, did exercise a degree of residential self-determination. Moreover, there exists a burgeoning historiography detailing this aspect of African American history.

Historically, most discussions of slave runaways have centered around the Underground Railroad. Over time, a number of studies have chronicled the activities of this legendary entity. Some of the more important studies include Levi Coffin's 1876 book, *Reminiscences of Levi Coffin: The Reputed President of the Underground Railroad*; Henrietta Buckmaster's *Let My People Go* (1941); Larry Gara's *Liberty Line: The Legend of the Underground Railroad* (1961); Horatio T. Strother's *Underground Railroad in Connecticut* (1962); Robin Winks's *Blacks in Canada: A History* (1971); and Charles L. Blockson's *Underground Railroad* (1987). Benjamin Quarles's 1969 classic *Black Abolitionist* deserves special mention for its groundbreaking documentation of African Americans' far-reaching activities within the Underground Railroad.

Although the Underground Railroad indeed deserves the attention it has generated among scholars and students, other subjects associated with the fugitive slave phenomenon also merit special consideration. Gerald W. Mullin's 1972 book, *Flight and Rebellion: Slave Resistance in 18th Century Virginia*, represents one such effort. Mullin's seminal work surveyed the different strategies for freedom employed by skilled artisan and semiskilled agricultural worker runaways during the colonial period. Daniel Littlefield's *Africans and Seminoles: From Removal to Emancipation* (1977) and *Africans and Creeks: From the Colonial Period to the Civil War* (1979) further expanded our perception of fugitive African American slaves by focusing upon those who settled with Native Americans.

The movement of blacks before the Civil War encompassed international, as well as domestic, dimensions. One of the least-appreciated aspects of the African American experience has been an undercurrent of interest in physically returning to the African continent. A number of studies have highlighted this aspect of pre–Civil War black America. Floyd J. Miller's 1975 book, *The Search for a Black Nationality: Black Colonization and Emigration, 1783–1863*, represents the most thorough depiction of "back-to-Africa" sentiment during this time. Paul Cuffee, the era's most noteworthy Pan-Africanist, is capably examined in Lamont D. Thomas's *Rise to Be a People: A Biography of Paul Cuffe* (1986). Philip J. Staudenraus's 1961 study, *The African Colonization Movement, 1816–1865*, provides a detailed examination of the controversial American Colonization Society (ACS). Although the majority of contemporary African Americans decried the ACS as a black deportation organization, a significant minority of African Americans welcomed the opportunity to leave this country for Liberia. Tom W. Shick's 1980 study, *Behold the Promised Land: A History of Afro-American Settler Society in Nineteenth-Century Liberia*, provides the best examination of their experiences.

Before the Civil War, most African Americans toiled as slaves in rural settings. Thousands of other transplanted Africans, however, especially the "quasi-free," lived their lives in urban settings. Moreover, a number of studies have chronicled the nuances of the pre–Civil War black urban experience.

Works examining the experiences of free urban blacks in the South include Letitia Woods Brown's *Free Negroes in the District of Columbia, 1790–1846* (1972); Ira Berlin's *Slaves without Masters: The Free Negro in the Antebellum South* (1975); James L. Roark and Michael P. Johnson's *No Chariot Let Down: Charleston's Free People of Color on the Eve of the Civil War* (1984); Suzanne Lebsock's *Free Women of Petersburg: Status and Culture in a Southern Town* (1984); and Bernard E. Powers, Jr.'s *Black Charlestonians: A Social History, 1822–1885* (1994).

Studied likewise were the experiences of free urban blacks in the North, featured in such works as Leon Litwack's *North of Slavery: The Negro in the Free States, 1790–1860* (1961); Carol George's *Segregated Sabbaths: Richard Allen and the Rise of Independent Black Churches, 1760–1840* (1973); James and Lois Horton's *Black Bostonians: Family Life and Community Struggle in the Antebellum North* (1979); Leonard P. Curry's *Free Black in Urban America, 1800–1850* (1981); Robert Cottroll's *Afro-Yankees: Providence's Black Community in the Antebellum Era* (1982); and Gary B. Nash's *Forging Freedom: The Formation of Philadelphia's Black Community, 1720–1840* (1988).

Not all African American city-dwellers before the Civil War were free of course. Richard C. Wade's *Slavery in the Cities: The South, 1820–1860* (1964) and Claudia D. Goldin's *Urban Slavery in the American South, 1820–1860: A Quantitative History* (1976) survey the institution of slavery in urban settings. Whereas Wade asserted that urban slavery differed considerably from slavery practiced in rural areas, Goldin demonstrated that whether urban or rural, slaves shared a similar degraded experience.

After 1865, with the dawn of universal "freedom" for African Americans, personal mobility became one of the former slave population's most-prized possessions. Contrary to contemporary white beliefs that post–Civil War black movement represented an aimless, childlike response to their new status, several studies have clearly demonstrated the rational motivations for this phenomenon. William Cohen's *At Freedom's Edge: Black Mobility and the Southern White Quest for Racial Control, 1861–1915* (1991) provides a comprehensive look at post–Civil War black mobility. Herbert G. Gutman's more focused 1976 study, *The Black Family in Slavery and Freedom, 1750–1925*, reveals that a significant number of post–Civil War African American migrants were searching for family members who had been separated under slavery. Also, many former slaves, who wanted to get as far away as possible from their previous place of "employment," gravitated toward urban areas in the South. Howard N. Rabinowitz's

Race Relations in the Urban South, 1865–1890 (1978) remains the best general overview of this aspect of African American history.

There also exist a number of studies that chronicle the experiences of African Americans in specific southern cities between 1865 and 1900. These works include John Blassingame's *Black New Orleans, 1860–1880* (1973); William Ivy Hair's *Carnival of Fury: Robert Charles and the New Orleans Race Riot of 1900* (1976); Leon H. Prather, Sr.'s *We Have Taken a City: Wilmington Racial Massacre and the Coup of 1898* (1983); Peter J. Rachleff's *Black Labor in the South: Richmond, Virginia, 1865–1890* (1984); George C. Wright's *Life behind a Veil: Blacks in Louisville, Kentucky, 1865–1930* (1985); Robert P. Ingalls's *Urban Vigilantes in the New South: Tampa, 1882–1936* (1988); and Eric Arnesen's *Waterfront Workers in New Orleans: Race, Class, and Politics, 1863–1923* (1991).

Southern cities may have indeed offered black migrants a relatively better lifestyle than that of their still-rural counterparts. Nevertheless, the complete reascendancy of former Confederates to political and social power after 1877 prompted a number of African Americans to explore residential options outside the region. The most dramatic black response to the rise of "Jim Crow" was a resurgence of interest in emigration to Africa, and Edwin S. Redkey's *Black Exodus: Black Nationalist and Back-to-Africa Movements, 1890–1910* (1969) remains the definitive work on this subject. A significant number of late-nineteenth-century southern black migrants chose to go to Kansas. Nell Irvin Painter's 1977 *Exodusters: Black Migration to Kansas after Reconstruction* is a classic depiction of this movement. Robert G. Athearn's *In Search of Canaan: Black Migration to Kansas, 1879–1880* (1978) and Thomas C. Cox's *Blacks in Topeka, Kansas, 1865–1915: A Social History* (1982) provide additional information about the early African American experience in Kansas.

Another popular western destination of late-nineteenth-century southern black migrants was Oklahoma. Jimmy Lewis Franklin's *Journey toward Hope: A History of Blacks in Oklahoma* (1982) represents a superb overview of this migration. William E. Bittle and Gilbert Geis's 1964 book, *The Longest Way Home: Chief Alfred C. Sam's Back-to-Africa Movement*, is another excellent source of information about the early African American experience in Oklahoma.

An important offshoot of late-nineteenth-century southern black migration to the West was the proliferation of all-black towns in the region. Norman L. Crockett's *Black Towns* (1979) is a useful survey of this occurrence. Significantly, Crockett's belief that black towns were in part established as concrete manifestations of racial pride and uplift differed from that put forward in Kenneth M. Hamilton's 1991 study of the black town phenomenon, *Black Towns and Profit: Promotion and Development in the Trans-Appalachian West, 1877–1915*. According to Hamilton, black capitalism, rather than black pride or black nationalism, represented the primary impetus for black town development during this period.

At the same time that some late-nineteenth-century southern blacks sought relief by migrating to Kansas and Oklahoma, others went to northern cities. Pre-1900 African American migration to the North appeared minuscule compared to later movements. Still, the experience of these individuals represents an important part of the total African American northern urban experience. Among the books that chronicle pre-1900 black life in northern urban centers are David M. Katzman's *Before the Ghetto: Black Detroit in the Nineteenth Century* (1973); Kenneth L. Kusmer's *A Ghetto Takes Shape: Black Cleveland, 1870–1930* (1976); Elizabeth Pleck's *Black Migration and Poverty: Boston, 1865–1900* (1979); and Roger Lane's *Roots of Violence in Black Philadelphia, 1860–1900* (1986).

Finally, two classic works remain extremely useful to students of late-nineteenth-century black migration and urbanization. W.E.B. Du Bois's 1899 study, *The Philadelphia Negro*, showcased Du Bois's skills as both a historian and a sociologist. Carter G. Woodson's 1918 book, *A Century of Negro Migration*, documented a historic tradition of black movement that, significantly, reached monumental proportions during the first decades of the twentieth century.

The 1991 publication of *The Great Migration in Historical Perspective: New Dimensions of Race, Class, and Gender*, edited by Joe William Trotter, Jr., attested to the coming of age of migration and urbanization studies. Trotter's insightful introduction and conclusion in this volume—"Black Migration in Historical Perspective: A Review of the Literature" and "Black Migration Studies: The Future"—provided both an excellent analysis of the development and status of migration studies and a framework for understanding the developing historiography of the topic. The *Journal of Urban History* also marked the coming of age of African American urban history with the publication of special issues in March and May 1995.

The conceptual framework for the historiographical analysis of migration and urbanization studies has, like the scholarly studies themselves, undergone development and refinement. August Meier and Elliott Rudwick in their 1986 volume, *Black History and the Historical Profession, 1915–1980*, pointed to the contributions that sociological community studies, beginning with W.E.B. Du Bois's *Philadelphia Negro*, made to migration and urbanization studies. They labeled the model followed in the community studies a "race relations approach." Meier and Rudwick also described the changes in interpretation in works by historians who examined how American racism created residential segregation and ghetto "pathology" and how blacks coped with their predicament by establishing racial self-help and advancement organizations.

Trotter adopted the "race relations" and the "ghetto model" as a part of his analytical framework. To these interpretative models he added the concept of the race-class or "proletarian" approach based upon the interpretative framework he used in his own seminal studies on migration and urbanization. In the late 1980s and the 1990s, works appeared that do not fit neatly under the traditional headings. Building on the accumulating body of scholarly works, old and new bodies of source materials, and using interdisciplinary historical models and approaches, scholars of migration and urbanization are making this a dynamic subfield in African American history.

Following the pattern set by Du Bois's *Philadelphia Negro*, pre–World War II studies of the General Migration emphasized causation and the resulting effect on race relations of the movement of African Americans to northern cities. These authors used the "push" and "pull" model of causation, and they emphasized the primacy of economic forces. The race relations approach led to viewing the African American as a social problem, at the same time viewing them as victims of racism and viewing their condition as pathological. Du Bois and other scholars using this model saw it as a way to expose the evil of racism and as a means of promoting reform.

Before the first wave of World War I migrants could clean the southern clay from their shoes, investigators had begun thorough examinations of their activities and their motives. Journalists, representatives of organizations, researchers for governmental agencies, and scholars began studying and writing about the volume and causes of black migration. The prevailing verdict reached by the authors of the early studies was that the motives of African American migrants were economic.

That so disparate a group of writers—northerners and southerners; journalists, sociologists, historians, and social workers; blacks and whites—agreed on causation was indeed unusual. On the surface, it seems that such a preponderance of testimony only confirms the validity of the economic interpretation. Nevertheless, reasons for this unanimity made for rather strange bedfellows. Southerners realized quite early that by emphasizing economic forces, attention could be diverted away from the South's racial policies. Moreover, inferences could be drawn to support southern contentions about black inferiority and to reinforce stereotyped descriptions of African American character traits. With few exceptions, however, scholars have also agreed that the causes of black migration were fundamentally economic. Black intellectuals found the economic interpretation useful. They could use generally accepted economic and sociological principles to support their premise that there was nothing peculiarly racial about the migrations. The weight of this opinion, though, did not completely drown out the voices of those who contended that more than inexorable economic laws were at work, that the movement of black people was, to a great extent, a response to oppression, a protest by flight.

Economic causationists found self-evident economic arguments readily available. Beyond question, the boll weevil and floods, low wages, and the crop lien system were major causes of suffering among southern blacks. Equally evident were the effects of World War I on the supply of immigrant labor in the North and the increased need for labor occasioned by the expansion of industry to meet wartime demand.

Writing during the first two years of the Great Migration, Carter G. Woodson in his *Century of Negro Migration* (1918) produced the first work to place

African American migration in historical perspective. Concern about the effects of migration on the labor supply during wartime led to migration studies sponsored by the U.S. Department of Labor. The result of the investigations appeared in *Negro Migration in 1916–17* (1919). Studies carried on under the auspices of the Carnegie Endowment for International Peace furnished the material for Emmett J. Scott's *Negro Migration during the War* (1920). In his study of agricultural conditions in Georgia, *Negro Migration: Changes in Rural Organization and Population of the Cotton Belt* (1920), Thomas J. Woofter, Jr., found that areas of Georgia into which black people had moved earlier in search of greater opportunities were the areas hardest hit by the boll weevil and by outmigration in 1916–1917. Woofter found that discontent with agricultural conditions was largely responsible for movement among rural people in the pre–World War I period, and he concluded that the wartime movement during 1916–1917 had the same causes as the earlier movement. The research conducted in connection with the wartime studies provided valuable source materials for later studies written from different conceptual models.

Clyde Vernon Kiser's 1969 study, *Sea Island to City: A Study of St. Helena Islanders in Harlem and Other Urban Centers*, like that of Woofter, came out of empirical investigations of African Americans through the University of North Carolina. The migration of St. Helena islanders did not fit the general pattern of black migration studied by other scholars using the race relations model. These migrants did not experience the push that African Americans on the mainland felt. The residents of St. Helena lived in a black environment, and they were largely independent landowners. Consequently, Kiser used a case study method and devoted more attention to social, cultural, and economic forces. His work, however, was more descriptive than interpretative. Even so, his study foreshadowed the empirical studies later conducted by E. Franklin Frazier and Charles S. Johnson, products of the University of Chicago school of sociologists.

The "push" and "pull" concepts were used in most works written before World War II. These included the study of migration contained in the report of the Chicago Commission on Race Relations, *The Negro in Chicago: A Study of Race Relations and a Race Riot* (1920); Louise V. Kennedy, *The Negro Peasant Turns Cityward: Effects of Recent Migrations to Northern Cities* (1930); and Edward E. Lewis, *The Mobility of the Negro: A Study in the American Labor Supply* (1931). The studies by Kennedy and Lewis extended the study of migration and urbanization into the post–World War I years.

Historians dealing with migration and urbanization, writing in the 1960s and 1970s, emphasized the formation of segregated black communities in northern cities. The authors of these ghetto studies owed much to the social scientists, beginning with Du Bois, who conducted the empirical research upon which the community studies were based. St. Clair Drake and Horace R. Cayton based their study of African American life and institutions in Chicago, *Black Metropolis* (1945), on empirical investigations conducted under the auspices of the

Works Projects Administration (WPA). Also influential was Gunnar Myrdal's study of African American life on the eve of World War II, *An American Dilemma: The Negro Problem and Modern Democracy* (1944).

Historians added historical perspective to the largely one-dimensional community studies. Prominent among such studies are Gilbert Osofsky, *Harlem: The Making of a Ghetto: Negro New York, 1890–1930* (1968); Allan H. Spear, *Black Chicago: The Making of a Negro Ghetto, 1890–1920* (1967); Constance McLaughlin Green, *The Secret City: A History of Race Relations in the Nation's Capital* (1967); William M. Tuttle, Jr., *Race Riot: Chicago in the Red Summer of 1919* (1974); Florette Henri, *Black Migration: Movement North 1900–1920* (1975); Kenneth L. Kusmer, *A Ghetto Takes Shape: Black Cleveland, 1870–1930* (1976); and David A. Gerber, *Black Ohio and the Color Line, 1860–1915* (1976).

These scholars traced the roots of northern black urban communities to the pre–World War I years. Early proponents of this approach continued to treat African American migrants as passive victims of white oppression and to focus on the pathology of life in urban black communities. As historians of African American migration and urbanization began to place greater reliance on African American sources, they modified their interpretations of the black urban experience. Gerber analyzed institutions, leadership, and class structure in Ohio black communities; and Kusmer uses the papers of Cleveland blacks to gain insights into the social, cultural, and economic lives of blacks in Cleveland. Henri's synthetic study followed the pattern of those who understood the dynamics of urban African American communities. Tuttle tried to capture something of the dynamic nature of the Chicago black community in his study of the 1919 race riot.

Historians using the race-class or proletarian approach concentrated on the plight of the migrant as a worker. Joe William Trotter, Jr.'s study of migrants to Milwaukee, *Black Milwaukee: The Making of an Industrial Proletariat, 1915–45* (1985) examined the process by which African American workers moved upward from sharecropping and lower-level urban occupations into jobs in industry. In concentrating on the economic adjustment to urban life, Trotter neglected other significant elements of the urbanization process.

Somewhat out of step with the interpretative trend followed by historians in the 1980s, sociologist Carole Mark's *Farewell—We're Good and Gone: The Great Black Migration* (1989) posited an economic interpretation based upon neo-Marxist theories. Her model again places African Americans at the mercy of inexorable economic forces. Marks argued that the African American migrants were urban workers, not farmers, who had been displaced in fledgling southern industries by white workers. This surplus black labor was attracted north through deliberate plans by northern industrialists. These workers did not become a part of the industrial proletariat; rather they sank into an exploited underclass.

Both Trotter in *Black Milwaukee* and Mark's new economic interpretation neglected important aspects of the migration and urbanization process. Trotter remedied this deficiency in his study of West Virginia coal miners, *Coal, Class, and Color: Blacks in Southern West Virginia, 1915–32* (1990). In this book, he explored the role of social and cultural forces in the migration process. This is also true of Peter Gottlieb's study of Pittsburgh, *Making Their Own Way: Southern Blacks' Migration to Pittsburgh, 1916–1930* (1987).

Richard W. Thomas's *Life for Us Is What We Make It: Building Black Community in Detroit, 1915–1945* (1992) and James R. Grossman's *Land of Hope: Chicago Black Southerners, and the Great Migration* (1989) add important interpretative concepts to the earlier works. Building on the works of the "ghetto" scholars who came to recognize that urban black communities were dynamic and often vibrant places and looking anew at African American sources, these authors carried the race-class model a step farther. Grossman analyzes the cultural backgrounds of African American migrants to Chicago. He reexamined many of the stereotypes found in the works using the race relations and ghetto models. Grossman found that migration was not, in general, an impulsive act; on the contrary, it was deliberate on the part of the migrants. Moreover, African American migrants brought cultural traits and skills with them to Chicago that facilitated their economic, social, political, and cultural adjustment to urban life.

African American migration and urbanization in the period from World War II to the present remains, curiously understudied by historians. Compared to similar studies focusing upon the dynamics and implications of the World War I Great Migration, the historiography of more recent black migration and urbanization is limited. This, despite the quantitative fact that many more African Americans participated in the second Great Migration that began during World War II and accelerated dramatically during the 1950s. Joe W. Trotter has provided a partial explanation for this phenomenon. His introductory essay in *The Great Migration in Historical Perspective* asserted that the cold war, which minimized U.S. domestic issues, made scholars wary about focusing upon massive post–World War II black migration and its possible impact upon American society. Significantly, the timidity of researchers in the years immediately following World War II would haunt the United States during the 1960s.

Kenneth Kusmer's insightful May 1995 *Journal of Urban History* article entitled "African Americans in the City since World War II: From the Industrial to the Post-industrial Era" categorized recent black urban history into three distinct phases: (1) 1942 to the early 1960s, (2) the middle and late 1960s, and (3) 1970 to the present. These categories will be used to assess the evolving historiography of post-1940 African American migration and urbanization.

The most dramatic aspect of the period from World War II to the early 1960s was the massive movement of rural southern blacks to northern, western, and southern cities. The increasing mechanization of southern agriculture, which forced black sharecroppers off the land, and the existence of better-paying jobs in urban centers, especially in the North and West, contributed to what Daniel M. Johnson and Rex R. Campbell described in their 1981 book, *Black Migration in America: A Social Demographic History*, as "the relocation of Black America" during the 1950s, Moreover, by 1960, for the first time in U.S. history the proportion of African Americans who resided in urban areas exceeded that of whites (73.2 percent versus 65.5 percent).

Consistent with historical precedent, this increased African American presence in northern cities contributed to increased racial tensions in the region. Dominic J. Capeci's 1977 book, *The Harlem Riot of 1943*, and his 1991 coauthored work with Martha Wilkerson, *Layered Violence: The Detroit Rioters of 1943*, provide in-depth case studies of these dramatic instances of racial discord. Arnold Hirsch's 1983 classic, *Making the Second Ghetto: Race and Housing in Chicago, 1940–1960*, revealed, among other things, that white resistance to black residential mobility remained as virulent during the second Great Migration as it had been during the first.

In southern cities an increased African American presence between World War II and the early 1960s contributed to the development of the civil rights movement. In Montgomery, Alabama, for instance, where blacks represented nearly 70 percent of the city bus line's consumer base, local African Americans protested against discriminatory treatment by waging a successful bus boycott between 1955 and 1956. Martin Luther King, Jr.'s *Stride toward Freedom: The Montgomery Story* (1958) represents a valuable firsthand account of this watershed event. Other books that provide in-depth accounts of the civil rights movement in specific southern cities include William Chafe's 1980 study, *Civilities and Civil Rights: Greensboro, North Carolina and the Black Struggle for Freedom*, and Robert J. Norrell's 1985 work, *Reaping the Whirlwind: The Civil Rights Movement in Tuskegee*.

Even though the southern-based civil rights movement stood center-stage during the early 1960s, the consequences of the recent massive migration of southern blacks to northern and western cities would by decade's end command the nation's attention. Despite the optimism that many southern blacks carried with them to their new residences, adverse structural changes in the U.S. economy—which would become more obvious in later decades—along with ongoing white racism, relegated many of these newcomers to lives of desperation in expanding "ghetto" areas. Among the works that documented the nuances of 1960s urban black deprivation, before the term "underclass" entered the national vocabulary, were Kenneth Clark's important 1965 study *Dark Ghetto: The Dilemma of Social Power*; Elliot Liebow's *Tally's Corner: A Study of Negro Streetcorner Men* (1967); Lee Rainwater's *Behind Ghetto Walls: Black Families in a Federal Slum* (1970); and Richard J. Meister's edited 1972 book *The Black Ghetto: Promised Land or Colony?* Nicholas Lemann's 1992 work *The Promised Land: The Great Black Migration and How It Changed America* provides a later assessment of the dynamics of post–World War II black migration to northern cities (and its consequences). Lemann's work suggested that southern black migrants, victimized by the exploitative system of sharecropping, brought with them a "culture of poverty" and an "ethic of dependency." Moreover, these characteristics set the stage for today's "underclass" phenomenon. Significantly, Lemann's thesis is convincingly critiqued in Gretchen Lemke-Santangelo's 1996 work *Abiding Courage: African American Migrant Women and the East Bay Community*. She argues that recent black migrants brought with them such positive—southern black—characteristics as self-help and community mindedness and they were not traumatized victims of sharecropping who transported their malaise to the North and West. Moreover, *Abiding Courage*, like Grossman's *Land of Hope*, treats cultural, social and economic factors, as well as race, class, and gender considerations in black migration.

The disillusionment spawned by northern-style "Jim Crow" led to a series of urban racial disorders in the mid-1960s. Sidney Fine's 1989 book *Violence in the Model City: The Cavanaugh Administration, Race Relations, and the Detroit Riot of 1967* provides an exhaustive account of the decade's most violent urban rebellion. *The Report of the National Advisory Commission on Civil Disorders*—the Kerner Commission—issued in 1968, and still the best overall resource related to 1960s urban disorders, recommended that the federal government undertake a "massive" and "sustained" program to improve the plight of African Americans, especially those in urban areas. Unfortunately, an examination of the African American urban experience since 1970 clearly suggests that the Kerner Commission's recommendations fell on deaf ears.

The ongoing and worsening plight of many black city-dwellers since 1970 illuminates, perhaps, the most profound contradiction of recent African American urban history. On one hand, black political power has dramatically increased in many cities. On the other, this proliferation of individual black elected officials has not translated into tangible gains for the masses of black urbanites. Despite the best intentions of urban black politicos, meaningful efforts to ameliorate the plight of the urban African American poor have been thwarted by shrinking federal subsidies to American cities, accelerated export of industrial jobs overseas since 1970, and white resistance to black political power.

Included in a growing body of works examining the recent trials and tribulations of urban black elected officials are Edward Greer's *Big Steel: Black Politics and Corporate Power in Gary, Indiana* (1979); Paul Kleppner's *Chicago Divided: The Making of a Black Mayor* (1985); William J. Grimshaw's *Bitter Fruit: Black Politics and the Chicago Machine*, 1931–1991 (1992); and George C. Galster and Edward W. Hill's edited work *The Metropolis in Black and White: Place, Power and Polarization* (1992).

Notwithstanding attention given to contemporary black politicians, the burgeoning urban black poor have all but dominated the attention of many historians, sociologists, and other researchers—if not public policy makers. Moreover, no scholar examining the underclass has generated as much controversy and debates as William Julius Wilson. Although his books *The Declining Significance of Race* (1978) and *The Truly Disadvantaged: The Inner City, the Underclass, and Public Policy* (1987) incorrectly minimize racism as an ongoing factor in U.S. society, Wilson's discussion of class differences in the contemporary African American community is especially useful.

Among other books examining the plight of the contemporary urban black poor are the following edited works: Fred R. Harris and Roger W. Wilkins's *Quiet Riots: Race and Poverty in the United States* (1988); Christopher Jencks and Paul E. Paterson's *The Urban Underclass* (1991); Bill E. Lawson's *Underclass Question* (1992); and Michael B. Katz's *Underclass Debate: Views from History* (1993). One of the most discussed non-edited books related to the urban black poor is Douglas S. Massey and Nancy A. Denton's provocatively titled 1993 work *American Apartheid: Segregation and the Making of the Underclass.*

If Massey and Denton are correct in their contention that the current plight of the urban underclass represents a manifestation of ongoing racial discrimination—or apartheid—urban policy makers in particular, and the American public in general, must totally reassess their perception of recent American history. Contrary to the Civil Rights Act of 1964 and notions of "the declining significance of race," the United States remains a place where having African ancestral roots can be both life inhibiting and life threatening.

In closing, this chapter has attempted to demonstrate that the subtopic of migration and urbanization within the realm of African American history represents an exciting and dynamic field of inquiry. Moreover, an ever-increasing number of studies in this area ensures that it will remain vibrant and important well into the twenty-first century.

BIBLIOGRAPHY

Anderson, Elijah. *Life Behind a Veil: Blacks in Louisville, Kentucky, 1865–1930.* Baton Rouge: Louisiana State University Press, 1985.

———. *Streetwise: Race, Class, and Change in an Urban Community.* Chicago: University of Chicago Press, 1990.

Anderson, Jervis. *This Was Harlem: A Cultural Portrait, 1900–1950.* New York: Farrar Straus Giroux, 1982.

Arnesen, Eric. *Waterfront Workers in New Orleans: Race, Class, and Politics, 1863–1923.* New York: Oxford University Press, 1991.

Athearn, Robert G. *In Search of Canaan: Black Migration to Kansas, 1879–80.* Lawrence: Regents Press of Kansas, 1978.

Bancroft, Frederick. *Slave Trading in the Old South.* Baltimore: J. H. Furst Company, 1931.

Bauman, John F. *Public Housing, Race, and Renewal: Urban Planning In Philadelphia, 1920–1974.* Philadelphia: Temple University Press, 1987.

Beeth, Howard, and Cary D. Wintz, eds. *Black Dixie: Afro-Texan History and Culture in Houston.* College Station: Texas A&M Press, 1992.

Berlin, Ira. *Slaves without Masters: The Free Negro in the Antebellum South.* New York: Pantheon Books, 1975.

Berndt, Harry Edward. *New Rulers in the Ghetto: The Community Development Corporation and Urban Poverty.* Westport, CT: Greenwood Press, 1977.

Bigham, Darrel E. *We Ask Only a Fair Trial: A History of the Black Community of Evansville, Indiana.* Bloomington: Indiana University Press, 1987.

Bittle, William E., and Gilbert Geis. *The Longest Way Home: Chief Alfred C. Sam's Back-to-Africa Movement.* Detroit: Wayne State University Press, 1964.

Blassingame, John W. *Black New Orleans, 1860–1880*. Chicago: University of Chicago Press, 1973.

————. *The Slave Community: Plantation Life in the Antebellum South*. New York: Oxford University Press, 1972.

Blockson, Charles L. *The Underground Railroad*. New York: Prentice Hall, 1987.

Bodnar, John, Roger Simon, and Michael Weber. *Lives of Their Own: Blacks, Italians, and Poles in Pittsburgh, 1900–1960*. Urbana: University of Illinois Press, 1982.

Bontemps, Arna, and Jack Conroy. *Anyplace but Here*. American Century Series ed. New York: Hill and Wang, 1966.

————. *They Seek a City*. Garden City, N.Y.: Doubleday, 1945.

Boskin, Joseph. *Urban Racial Violence in the Twentieth Century*. London: Collier Mac-Millan Publishers, 1976.

Brossard, Albert S. *Black San Francisco: The Struggle for Racial Equality, 1900–1954*. Lawrence: University Press of Kansas, 1993.

Buckmaster, Henrietta. *Let My People Go: The Story of the Underground Railroad and the Growth of the Abolitionist Movement*. 1st ed. New York: Harper and Brothers, 1941.

Buni, Robert. *Robert L. Vann of the Pittsburgh Courier*. Pittsburgh: University of Pittsburgh Press, 1974.

Capeci, Dominic J., Jr. *The Harlem Riot of 1943*. Philadelphia: Temple University Press, 1977.

————. *Race Relations in Wartime Detroit: The Sojourner Truth Housing Controversy of 1942*. Philadelphia: Temple University Press, 1984.

Capeci, Dominic J., Jr., and Martha Wilkerson. *Layered Violence: The Detroit Rioters of 1943*. Jackson: University of Mississippi Press, 1991.

Chafe, William. *Civilities and Civil Rights: Greensboro, North Carolina and the Black Struggle for Freedom*. New York: Oxford University Press, 1980.

Chicago Commission on Race Relations. *The Negro in Chicago: A Study of Race Relations and a Race Riot*. Chicago: University of Chicago Press, 1920.

Clark, Kenneth. *Dark Ghetto: The Dilemma of Social Power*. New York: Harper and Row, 1965.

Coffin, Levi. *Reminiscences of Levi Coffin: The Reputed President of the Underground Railroad*. Cincinnati: Western Tract Society, 1876.

Cohen, William. *At Freedom's Edge: Black Mobility and the Southern White Quest for Racial Control, 1861–1915*. Baton Rouge: Louisiana State University Press, 1991.

Coles, Robert. *Farewell to the South*. Boston: Little, Brown, 1972.

Connolly, Harold X. *A Ghetto Grows in Brooklyn*. New York: New York University Press, 1977.

Cottrol, Robert. *The Afro-Yankees: Providence's Black Community in the Antebellum Era*. Westport, CT: Greenwood Press, 1982.

Cox, Thomas C. *Blacks in Topeka, Kansas, 1865–1915: A Social History*. Baton Rouge: Louisiana State University Press, 1982.

Crockett, Norman L. *The Black Towns*. Lawrence: Regents Press of Kansas, 1979.

Cronon, E. David. *Black Moses: The Story of Marcus Garvey and the UNIA*. Madison: University of Wisconsin Press, 1955.

Curry, Leonard P. *The Free Black in Urban America, 1800–1850*. Chicago: University of Chicago Press, 1981.

Curtin, Phillip D. *The Atlantic Slave Trade: A Census*. Madison: University of Wisconsin Press, 1969.

Darden, Joe T., Richard Child Hill, June Thomas, and Richard W. Thomas. *Detroit: Race and Uneven Development*. Philadelphia: Temple University Press, 1987.

Delaney, Martin R. *The Condition, Elevation, Emigration and Destiny of the Colored People of the United States*. New York: Arno Press and the New York Times, 1969.

Deskins, Jr., Donald R. *Residential Mobility of Negroes in Detroit, 1837–1965*. Ann Arbor: Department of Geography, University of Michigan, 1972.

Donnan, Elizabeth, ed. *Documents Illustrative of the History of the Slave Trade to America*. Vols. 1–4. Washington, DC: Carnegie Institution of Washington, 1930–1935.

Drake, St. Clair, and Horace R. Cayton. *Black Metropolis: A Study of Negro Life in a Northern City*. Torchbook ed. Vol. 1. New York: Harper & Row, 1945/1962.

———. *Black Metropolis: A Study of Negro Life in a Northern City*. Torchbook ed. Vol. 2. New York: Harper & Row, 1945/1962.

Drotning, Phillip T., and Wesley W. South. *Up from the Ghetto*. New York: Washington Square Press, 1971.

Du Bois, W.E.B. *The Philadelphia Negro: A Social Study*. 1st ed. New York: Schocken Books, 1899/1967.

———. *Suppression of the African Slave Trade to the United States, 1638–1870*. Cambridge, MA: Harvard University Press, 1896/1970.

Epstein, Abraham. *The Negro Migrant in Pittsburgh*. Pittsburgh: University of Pittsburgh Press, 1919.

Fine, Sidney. *Violence in the Model City: The Cavanaugh Administration, Race Relations, and the Detroit Riot of 1967*. Ann Arbor: University of Michigan Press, 1989.

Fish, John Hall. *Black Power/White Control: The Struggle of the Woodlawn Organization in Chicago*. Princeton, NJ: Princeton University Press, 1973.

Fligstein, Neil. *Going North*. New York: Academic Press, 1981.

Forman, Robert E. *Black Ghettos, White Ghettos, and Slums*. Englewood Cliffs, NJ: Prentice-Hall, 1971.

Formissano, Ronald P. *Boston against Busing: Race, Class, and Ethnicity in the 1950s and 1970s*. Chapel Hill: University of North Carolina Press, 1991.

Fox, Stephen R. *The Guardian of Boston: William Monroe Trotter*. 1st ed. New York: Atheneum, 1970.

Franklin, Jimmie Lewis. *Journey toward Hope: A History of Blacks in Oklahoma*. Norman: University of Oklahoma Press, 1982.

Galster, George C., and Edward W. Hill, eds. *The Metropolis in Black and White: Place, Power and Polarization*. New Brunswick, NJ: Center for Urban Policy Research, 1992.

Gara, Larry. *The Liberty Line: The Legend of the Underground Railroad*. Lexington: University of Kentucky Press, 1961.

George, Carol. *Segregated Sabbaths: Richard Allen and the Rise of Independent Black Churches, 1760–1840*. New York: Oxford University Press, 1973.

Gerber, David A. *Black Ohio and the Color Line, 1860–1915*. Urbana: University of Illinois Press, 1976.

Glasgow, Douglas G. *The Black Underclass*. San Francisco: Jossey-Bass, 1980.

Glazer, Nathan, and Daniel Patrick Moynihan. *Beyond the Melting Pot*. Cambridge, MA: MIT Press and Harvard University Press, 1963.

Goldin, Claudia D. *Urban Slavery in the American South, 1820–1860: A Quantitative History*. Chicago: University of Chicago Press, 1976.

Goodwin, E. Marvin. *Black Migration in America from 1915–1960: An Uneasy Exodus*. Lewiston, NY: E. Mellen Press, 1990.

Gottlieb, Peter. *Making Their Own Way: Southern Blacks' Migration to Pittsburgh, 1916–1930*. Urbana: University of Illinois Press, 1987.

Grant, Robert B. *The Black Man Comes to the City: A Documentary Account from the Great Migration to the Great Depression 1915–1930*. Chicago: Nelson-Hall Company, 1972.

Green, Constance McLaughlin. *The Secret City: A History of Race Relations in the Nation's Capital*. Princeton, NJ: Princeton University Press, 1967.

Greenberg, Cheryl Lynn. *Or Does It Explode: Black Harlem in the Great Depression*. New York: Oxford University Press, 1991.

Greene, Lorenzo J. *The Negro in Colonial New England*. New York: Columbia University Press, Atheneum, 1942/1969.

Greer, Edward. *Big Steel: Black Politics and Corporate Power in Gary, Indiana*. New York: Monthly Review Press, 1979.

Gregg, Robert. *Sparks from the Anvil of Oppression: Philadelphia's African Methodist and Southern Migrants, 1890–1940*. Philadelphia: Temple University Press, 1993.

Grimshaw, William J. *Bitter Fruit: Black Politics and the Chicago Machine, 1931–1991*. Chicago: University of Chicago Press, 1992.

Groh, George W. *The Black Migration: The Journey to Urban America*. New York: Weybright and Talley, 1972.

Grossman, James R. *Land of Hope: Chicago, Black Southerners, and the Great Migration*. Chicago: University of Chicago Press, 1989.

Gutman, Herbert G. *The Black Family in Slavery and Freedom, 1750–1925*. 1st ed. New York: Pantheon Books, 1976.

Hair, William Ivy. *Carnival of Fury: Robert Charles and the New Orleans Race Riot of 1900*. Baton Rouge: Louisiana State University Press, 1976.

Hamilton, Kenneth M. *Black Towns and Profit: Promotion and Development in the Trans-Appalachian West, 1877–1915*. Urbana: University of Illinois Press, 1991.

Harding, Vincent. *There Is a River: The Black Struggle for Freedom in America*. New York: Harcourt Brace Jovanovich, 1981.

Harris, Fred R., and Roger W. Wilkins, eds. *Quiet Riots: Race and Poverty in the United States*. 1st ed. New York: Pantheon Books, 1988.

Harrison, Alferdteen, ed. *Black Exodus: The Great Migration from the American South*. Jackson: University Press of Mississippi, 1991.

Haynes, George E. *The Negro at Work during the War and Reconstruction*. Washington, DC: Government Printing Office, 1921.

———. *The Negro at Work in New York City: A Study in Economic Progress*. New York: Columbia University Press, 1912.

———. *Negro Migration in 1916–1917*. Washington, DC: U.S. Department of Labor, Division of Negro Economics, Government Printing Office, 1919.

Henderson, Alexa Benson. *Atlanta Life Insurance Company: Guardian of Black Economic Dignity*. Tuscaloosa: University of Alabama Press, 1990.

Henri, Florette. *Black Migration: Movement North, 1900–1920.* 1st ed. Garden City, NY: Anchor Press/Doubleday, 1975.

Hill, Daniel G. *The Freedom Seekers: Blacks in Early Canada.* Agincourt, Canada: Book Society of Canada, 1981.

Hirsch, Arnold. *Making the Second Ghetto: Race and Housing in Chicago, 1940–1960.* Cambridge: Cambridge University Press, 1983.

Honey, Michael K. *Southern Labor and Black Civil Rights: Organizing Memphis Workers.* Urbana: University of Illinois Press, 1993.

Horton, James Oliver, and Lois E. Horton. *Black Bostonians: Family Life and Community Struggle in the Antebellum North.* New York: Holmes and Meier, 1979.

Ingalls, Robert P. *Urban Vigilantes in the New South: Tampa, 1882–1936.* Knoxville: University of Tennessee Press, 1988.

Jencks, Christopher, and Paul E. Paterson, eds. *The Urban Underclass.* Washington, DC: Brookings Institution, 1991.

Johnson, Daniel M., and Rex R. Campbell. *Black Migration in America: A Social Demographic History.* In *Studies in Social and Economic Demography*, ed. George C. Myers, No. 4. Durham, NC: Duke University Press, 1981.

Jones, Marcus E. *Black Migration in the United States with Emphasis on Selected Central Cities.* Saratoga, CA: Century Twenty One Publishing, 1980.

Katz, Michael B., ed. *The Underclass Debate: Views from History.* Princeton, NJ: Princeton University Press, 1993.

Katzman, David M. *Before the Ghetto: Black Detroit in the Nineteenth Century.* In *Blacks in the New World*, ed. August Meier. Urbana: University of Illinois Press, 1973.

Katznelson, Ira. *Black Men, White Cities: Race, Politics, and Migration in the United States, 1900–30, and Britain, 1948–68.* London: Oxford University Press, 1973.

Kennedy, Louise V. *The Negro Peasant Turns Cityward: Effects of Recent Migrations to Northern Centers.* New York: Columbia University Press, 1930.

King, Martin Luther, Jr. *Stride toward Freedom: The Montgomery Story.* 1st ed. New York: Harper, 1958.

Kiser, Clyde Vernon. *Sea Island to City: A Study of St. Helena Islanders in Harlem and Other Urban Centers.* In *Studies in American Negro Life*, ed. August Meier. 1st ed. New York: Atheneum, 1969.

Klein, Herbert S. *The Middle Passage: Comparative Studies in the Atlantic Slave Trade.* Princeton, NJ: Princeton University Press, 1978.

Kleppner, Paul. *Chicago Divided: The Making of a Black Mayor.* DeKalb: Northern Illinois University Press, 1985.

Kolchin, Peter. *American Slavery, 1619–1877.* New York: Hill and Wang, 1993.

Kusmer, Kenneth. "African Americans in the City since World War II: From the Industrial to the Post-industrial Era." *Journal of Urban History* 21 (May 1995): 458–504.

———. *A Ghetto Takes Shape: Black Cleveland, 1870–1930.* Urbana: University of Illinois Press, 1976.

Lane, Roger. *Roots of Violence in Black Philadelphia, 1860–1900.* Cambridge, MA: Harvard University Press, 1986.

Lawson, Bill E., ed. *The Underclass Question.* Philadelphia: Temple University Press, 1992.

Lebsock, Suzanne. *The Free Women of Petersburg: Status and Culture in a Southern Town.* 1st ed. New York: W. W. Norton, 1984.

Lemann, Nicholas. *The Promised Land: The Great Black Migration and How It Changed America.* 1st ed. New York: Vintage Books, 1992.

Lemke-Santangelo, Gretchen. *Abiding Courage: African American Migrant Women and the East Bay Community.* Chapel Hill: University of North Carolina Press, 1996.

Levine, David Allen. *Internal Combustion: The Races in Detroit, 1915–1926.* Westport, CT: Greenwood Press, 1976.

Lewis, Earl. *In Their Own Interests: Race, Class, and Power in Twentieth Century Norfolk, Virginia.* Berkeley: University of California Press, 1991.

Lewis, Edward Erwin. *The Mobility of the Negro: A Study in the American Labor Supply.* New York: Columbia University Press, 1931.

Ley, David. *The Black Inner City as Frontier Outpost: Images and Behavior of a Philadelphia Neighborhood.* Washington, DC: Association of American Geographers, 1974.

Liebow, Elliot. *Tally's Corner: A Study of Negro Streetcorner Men.* Boston: Little, Brown, 1967.

Littlefield, Daniel. *Africans and Creeks: From the Colonial Period to the Civil War.* Westport, CT: Greenwood Press, 1979.

———. *Africans and Seminoles: From Removal to Emancipation.* Westport, CT: Greenwood Press, 1977.

Litwack, Leon. *North of Slavery: The Negro in the Free States, 1790–1860.* Chicago: University of Chicago Press, 1961.

Lynch, Hollis R. *The Black Urban Condition.* New York: Thomas Y. Crowell Co., 1973.

Mannix, Daniel R. *Black Cargoes: A History of the Atlantic Slave Trade, 1518–1865.* New York: Viking Press, 1962.

Marks, Carole. *Farewell—We're Good and Gone: The Great Black Migration.* Bloomington: Indiana University Press, 1989.

Massey, Douglas S., and Nancy A. Denton. *American Apartheid: Segregation and the Making of the Underclass.* Cambridge, MA: Harvard University Press, 1993.

McManus, Edgar. *A History of Negro Slavery in Colonial New York.* 1st ed. Syracuse, NY: Syracuse University Press, 1966.

Meier, August, and Elliot Rudwick. *Black History and the Historical Profession, 1915–1980.* Urbana: University of Illinois Press, 1986.

Meister, Richard J., ed. *The Black Ghetto: Promised Land or Colony?* Lexington, MA: D.C. Health and Company, 1972.

Miller, Floyd. *The Search for a Black Nationality: Black Colonization and Emigration, 1787–1863.* Urbana: University of Illinois Press, 1975.

Miller, Randall M., and George E. Pozzetta, eds. *Shades of the Sunbelt: Essays on Ethnicity, Race, and the Urban South.* New York: Greenwood Press, 1988.

Moore, Jesse Thomas, Jr. *A Search for Equality: The National Urban League, 1910–1961.* University Park: Pennsylvania State University Press, 1981.

Mullin, Gerald W. *Flight and Rebellion: Slave Resistance in 18th Century Virginia.* New York: Oxford University Press, 1972.

Myrdal, Gunnar, and with the assistance of Richard Sterner and Arnold Rose. *An American Dilemma: The Negro Problem and Modern Democracy.* 2 vols. New York: Harper and Brothers, 1944.

Naison, Mark. *Communists in Harlem during the Depression.* Urbana: University of Illinois Press, 1983.

Nash, Gary B. *Forging Freedom: The Formation of Philadelphia's Black Community, 1720–1840*. Cambridge, MA: Harvard University Press, 1988.

Norrell, Robert J. *Reaping the Whirlwind: The Civil Rights Movement in Tuskegee*. New York: Knopf (distributed by Random House), 1985.

Osofsky, Gilbert. *Harlem: The Making of a Ghetto: Negro New York, 1890–1930*. Harper Torchbooks ed. New York: Harper and Row, 1968.

Ottley, Roi, and William J. Weatherby, eds. *The Negro in New York: An Informal Social History, 1626–1940*. New York: Praeger Publishers, 1969.

Ovington, Mary White. *Half a Man: The Status of the Negro in New York*. American Century paperback ed. New York: Hill and Wang, 1969.

Owens, Leslie H. *This Species of Property: Slave Life and Culture in the Old South*. New York: Oxford University Press, 1976.

Painter, Nell Irvin. *Exodusters: Black Migration to Kansas after Reconstruction*. New York: Knopf, 1977.

Parris, Guichard, and Lester Brooks. *Blacks in the City: A History of the National Urban League*. Boston: Little, Brown, 1971.

Perdue, Robert E. *The Negro in Savannah, 1865–1900*. New York: Exposition Press, 1973.

Perlmann, Joel. *Ethnic Differences: Schooling and Social Structure among the Irish, Italians, Jews, and Blacks in an American City*. Cambridge: Cambridge University Press, 1988.

Philpott, Thomas Lee. *The Slum and the Ghetto: Immigrants, Blacks, and Reformers in Chicago, 1880–1930*. Belmont, CA: Wadsworth Publishing Company, 1978/1991.

Pleck, Elizabeth. *Black Migration and Poverty: Boston, 1865–1900*. In *Studies in Social Discontinuity*, ed. Charles Tilly and Edward Shorter. New York: Academic Press, 1979.

Powers, Bernard E., Jr. *Black Charlestonians: A Social History, 1822–1885*. Fayetteville: University of Arkansas Press, 1994.

Prather, Leon H. *We Have Taken a City: Wilmington Racial Massacre and the Coup of 1898*. Rutherford, NJ: Fairleigh Dickerson University Press, 1983.

Price, Daniel O. *Changing Characteristics—Negro Population*. Washington, DC: Department of Commerce, 1965.

Price, Daniel O., and Melanie Sykes. *Rural-Urban Migration Research in the United States*. Washington, DC: Center for Population Research, Government Printing Office, 1979.

Quarles, Benjamin. *Black Abolitionists*. New York: Oxford University Press; DaCopa Press, 1969/1991.

Rabinowitz, Howard N. *Race Relations in the Urban South, 1865–1890*. New York: Oxford University Press, 1978.

Rachleff, Peter J. *Black Labor in the South: Richmond, Virginia, 1865–1890*. Philadelphia: Temple University Press, 1984.

Rainwater, Lee. *Behind Ghetto Walls: Black Families in a Federal Slum*. Chicago: Aldine Publishing Company, 1970.

Ralph, James R., Jr. *Northern Protest: Martin Luther King, Jr., Chicago, and the Civil Rights Movement*. Cambridge, MA: Harvard University Press, 1993.

Redkey, Edwin S. *Black Exodus: Black Nationalist and Back-to-Africa Movements, 1890–1910*. New Haven, CT: Yale University Press, 1969.

Roark, James L., and Michael P. Johnson, eds. *No Chariot Let Down: Charleston's Free People of Color on the Eve of the Civil War*. New York: W. W. Norton, 1984.

Rogers, Kim Lacy. *Righteous Lives: Narratives of the New Orleans Civil Rights Movement*. New York: New York University Press, 1993.

Rosenberg, Daniel. *New Orleans Dockworkers: Race, Labor, and Unionism, 1892–1923*. Albany, NY: SUNY Press, 1988.

Ross, Alexander Frank, and Louise Venable Kennedy. *A Bibliography of Negro Migration*. New York: Columbia University Press, 1934.

Rudwick, Elliot M. *Race Riot at East St. Louis*. Carbondale: Southern Illinois University Press, 1964.

Sandburg, Carl. *The Chicago Race Riot*. New York: Harcourt, Brace and Rowe, 1919.

Scheiner, Seth M. *Negro Mecca: A History of the Negro in New York City, 1865–1920*. New York: New York University Press, 1965.

Scott, Emmett J. *Negro Migration during the War*. In *Preliminary Economic Studies of the War*, ed. David Kinley, No. 16. New York: Oxford University Press, 1920.

Sherman, Richard B., ed. *The Negro and the City*. Englewood Cliffs, NJ: Prentice-Hall, 1970.

Shick, Tom W. *Behold the Promised Land: A History of Afro-American Settler Society in Nineteenth-Century Liberia*. Baltimore: Johns Hopkins University Press, 1980.

Shogan, Robert, and Tom Craig. *The Detroit Race Riot: A Study in Violence*. Philadelphia: Chilton Books, 1964.

Small, Stephen. *Racialised Barriers: The Black Experience in the United States and England in the 1980s. Critical Studies in Racism and Migration*, ed. Robert Miles. London: Routledge, 1994.

Spear, Allan H. *Black Chicago: The Making of a Negro Ghetto, 1890–1920*. Chicago: University of Chicago Press, 1967.

Stampp, Kenneth, M. *The Peculiar Institution*. New York: Vintage Books, 1956.

Staudenraus, Phillip J. *The African Colonization Movement, 1816–1865*. New York: Columbia University Press, 1961.

Stein, Judith. *The World of Marcus Garvey: Race and Class in Modern America*. Baton Rouge: Louisiana State University Press, 1986.

Strickland, Arvarh E. *History of the Chicago Urban League*. Urbana: University of Illinois Press, 1966.

Strother, Horatio T. *The Underground Railroad in Connecticut*. Middletown, CT: Wesleyan University Press, 1962.

Suggs, Henry Lewis, ed. *The Black Press in the South, 1865–1979*. Westport, CT: Greenwood Press, 1983.

Taeuber, Karl, and Alma Taeuber. *Negroes in Cities*. Chicago: Aldine, 1965.

Tate, Thad W. *The Negro in Colonial Williamsburg*. Charlottesville: University of Virginia Press, 1965.

Taylor, Henry L., Jr., ed. *African Americans and the Rise of Buffalo's Post-industrial City, 1940 to Present*. Buffalo: State University of New York at Buffalo, 1990.

Taylor, Henry Louis, ed. *Race and the City: Work, Community, and Protest in Cincinnati, 1820–1970*. Urbana: University of Illinois Press, 1993.

Taylor, Quintard. *The Forging of a Black Community: Seattle's Central District from 1870 through the Civil Rights Era*. Seattle: University of Washington Press, 1994.

Thomas, Brinley. *Migration and Economic Growth*. 2nd ed. Cambridge: Cambridge University Press, 1973.

Thomas, Lamont D. *Rise to Be a People: A Biography of Paul Cuffee*. Urbana: University of Illinois Press, 1986.

Thomas, Richard W. *Life for Us Is What We Make It: Building Black Community in Detroit, 1915–1945*. Bloomington: Indiana University Press, 1992.

Thornbrough, Emma Lou. *T. Thomas Fortune*. Chicago: University of Chicago Press, 1972.

Trotter, Joe William, Jr. *Black Milwaukee: The Making of an Industrial Proletariat, 1915–45*. Urbana: University of Illinois Press, 1985.

———. *Coal, Class, and Color: Blacks in Southern West Virginia, 1915–32*. Urbana: University of Illinois Press, 1990.

———, ed. *The Great Migration in Historical Perspective: New Dimensions of Race, Class, and Gender*. In *Blacks in the Diaspora*, ed. Darlene Clark Hine, John McCluskey, Jr., and David Barry Gaspar. Bloomington: Indiana University Press, 1991.

Tuttle, William M., Jr. *Race Riot: Chicago in the Red Summer of 1919*. New York: Atheneum, 1974.

United States. Kerner Commission. *Report of the National Advisory Commission on Civil Disorders*. New York: Bantam Books, 1968.

U.S. Department of Labor. *Negro Migration in 1916–17*. Washington, DC: Government Printing Office, 1919.

Vickery, William. *The Economics of the Negro Migration, 1900–1960*. New York: Arno Press, 1977.

Vose, Clement E. *Caucasians Only: The Supreme Court, the NAACP and the Restrictive Covenant Case*. Berkeley: University of California Press, 1967.

Wade, Richard C. *Slavery in the Cities: The South, 1820–1860*. New York: Oxford University Press, 1964/1972.

Watts, Jill. *God, Harlem, U.S.A.: The Father Divine Story*. Berkeley: University of California Press, 1992.

Weare, Walter B. *Black Business in the New South: A Social History of the North Carolina Mutual Insurance Company*. Durham, NC: Duke University Press, 1973/1993.

Weaver, Robert C. *The Negro Ghetto*. New York: Russell and Russell, 1948.

Weems, Robert E., Jr. *Black Business in the Black Metropolis: The Chicago Metropolitan Assurance Company, 1925–1985*. Bloomington: Indiana University Press, 1996.

Weiss, Nancy J. *The National Urban League, 1910–1940*. New York: Oxford University Press, 1974.

White, Shane. *Somewhat More Independent: The End of Slavery in New York City, 1770–1810*. Athens: University of Georgia Press, 1991.

Widick, B. J. *Detroit: City of Race and Class Violence*. Chicago: Quadrangle Books, 1972.

Williams, Eric. *Capitalism and Slavery*. Chapel Hill: University of North Carolina Press, 1944/1994.

Wilson, William Julius. *The Declining Significance of Race: Blacks and Changing American Institutions*. Chicago: University of Chicago Press, 1978.

———. *The Truly Disadvantaged: The Inner City, the Underclass, and Public Policy*. Chicago: University of Chicago Press, 1987.

Winch, Julie. *Philadelphia's Black Elite: Activism, Accommodation, and the Struggle for Autonomy*. Philadelphia: Temple University Press, 1988.

Winks, Robin. *The Blacks in Canada: A History*. New Haven, CT: Yale University Press, 1971.

Wood, Betty. *Slavery in Colonial Georgia, 1730–1775*. Athens: University of Georgia Press, 1984.

Wood, Peter. *Black Majority: Negroes in Colonial South Carolina from 1670 through the Stono Rebellion*. 1st. ed. New York: Knopf, 1974.

Woods Brown, Letitia. *Free Negroes in the District of Columbia, 1790–1846*. New York: Oxford University Press, 1972.

Woodson, Carter G. *A Century of Negro Migration*. Washington, DC: Association for the Study of Negro Life and History, 1918.

———. *Free Negro Heads of Families in the United States in 1830*. Washington, DC: Association for the Study of Negro Life and History, 1925.

Woofter, Thomas Jackson, Jr. *Negro Migration: Change in Rural Organization and Population of the Cotton Belt*. New York: W. D. Gray, 1920.

Wright, George C. *Life behind a Veil: Blacks in Louisville, Kentucky, 1865–1930*. Baton Rouge: Louisiana State University Press, 1985.

II

The African American Worker in Slavery and Freedom

Joe William Trotter, Jr.

Twenty-five years ago, *Labor History* published a special issue titled "The Negro and the American Labor Movement." In a historiographical survey of the field, James A. Gross concluded that black labor history had "virtually the same faults and virtues" as white labor history. Written from the vantage point of organized labor unions, it largely ignored unorganized workers, lacked a convincing theoretical framework, and showed little creativity in the location and use of new sources. Perhaps most importantly, it failed to produce comprehensive studies that integrated African American labor history into the larger story of national development.

Fortunately, over the past two and a half decades, African American labor history has changed considerably. Studies of black workers have not only proceeded apace, but have supplemented and even transcended the old labor history. Historians no longer perceive the experiences of black workers narrowly through the lens of the organized labor movement. African American workers are increasingly examined within the overlapping contexts of work, culture, politics, and community. Covering the impact of commercial as well as industrial capitalism, recent studies illuminate the transformation of Africans into African American slaves, the transition of slaves to free wage earners and sharecroppers during the emancipation era, and the rise of a new urban-industrial proletariat

This chapter and bibliography are adapted from an article I previously published. See special "Race and Class" edition of *Labor History* 35, no. 4 (Fall 1994): "African American Workers: New Directions in U.S. Labor Historiography," by Joe William Trotter, Jr.

during the twentieth century. Moreover, some scholars are beginning to integrate black labor history into the history of the nation.

Reviewing changes in scholarship over the past twenty-five years, this essay analyzes the shift from what we may call the "old" to the "new" African American labor history, identifies areas for future research, and suggests the need for a new synthesis. A new African American synthesis would seek to achieve two basic objectives: (1) to fuse earlier emphases on the relationship between black workers and organized white labor with recent understandings of African American workers' culture, politics, and communities; and (2) to identify gaps in our understanding that require additional research, fresh theoretical perspectives, and new methodologies as we approach the twenty-first century.

AFRICAN AMERICAN WORKERS AND THE
OLD LABOR HISTORY

African American labor history has deep roots in the "old" labor history, which emphasized the primacy of labor unions in the struggle of workers for industrial democracy. It also builds upon an older race relations model developed by sociologists, economists, and public policy experts as well as historians. The old African American labor history emerged in the teeth of white supremacy. During the Jim Crow era, mainstream popular and scholarly accounts described black workers as innately inferior, inefficient, and lazy; as incapable of adapting to the requirements of the machine; and/or as disloyal to their class interests. In 1909, for example, the Yale University geographer George T. Surface conducted a study of black miners in Kentucky, Tennessee, Virginia, and West Virginia. The "great majority," he said, were irregular in labor and "unstable in residence." Moreover, he argued that "the efficiency of this class would be increased by a lower scale of wages." "The Negro's moral weakness," he concluded, "is in reality more pronounced than his economic capacity." Charles H. Wesley quoted another contemporary analyst, A. H. Stone, who wrote for the publications of the University of Virginia. He reinforced Surface's interpretation of black workers, describing "slave" labor as deficient because it was "Negro" labor. "In truth," according to Stone, "it was not slave labor but Negro labor which was, at bottom, responsible" for the low productivity of the South compared to the North. "The contrast between the North and South was not the contrast between free and slave labor, but that between white and Negro labor." Stone, Surface, and their white scholarly contemporaries ignored the exploitative practices of American industry, the role of racial discrimination in the labor movement, and the specific responses of black workers to these phenomena.

To counteract prevailing racial stereotypes, the first generation of scholarship of African American labor history often employed a race relations framework. Emphasizing the discriminatory attitudes and behavior of white workers, employers, and the state, the first generation rejected racist perceptions of black workers as inefficient, lazy, incompetent, and "incapable of filling a place in modern industrial organization." According to W.E.B. Du Bois, the tyranny of slave masters, and later employers, combined with the enmity of white workers, reinforced slavery and the economic subordination of the free black proletariat. *The Negro Artisan* traced conflict between black and white workers to the era of slavery. "There appeared too," Du Bois exclaimed, "in early times that same opposition to Negro working men, with which we are so familiar today." In the South, most of the opposition occurred in the border states, where free black mechanics came in contact and conflict with white mechanics. In the North, as white workers organized the first trade unions, then local general trade organizations, and finally national labor bodies, African Americans were "either tacitly or in plain words excluded from all participation." In the era of emancipation, Du Bois defended black workers against charges that they "carelessly threw away their" monopoly of the southern labor market and allowed the white mechanic to supplant them. Lack of political rights—through "social protection"—white worker competition, and the development of new industrial processes had undermined the position of black artisans in the emancipation era. As Du Bois put it, "The result was of course that he was enabled to maintain himself only by accepting low wages and keeping at all hazards the good will of the community."

Historian Charles Wesley surveyed black workers' experience from slavery through the mid-1920s in *Negro Labor in the United States*. Describing capitalism as "human bondage" and "debasing wage slavery," he emphasized how it made possible "the continual exploitation of black workers," who struggled against the usual obstacles of American workers as well as against "the special handicaps of race and color." Wesley also emphasized the vital role that slaves played not merely as "gang" or "task" labor in the production of cotton, tobacco, rice, and sugar commodities but also as specialized artisans who built houses, manufactured and repaired agricultural equipment, made clothing, and met a variety of other demands requiring skill in the plantation economy. Moreover, as industrialization and new machinery gradually reached the South, slaves slowly learned new skills and took on new jobs in the industrial sector. Such experiences, Wesley concludes, helped to prepare the black worker for freedom. "Although shackled by the past, and hampered by contemporary southern labor ideals, the former slaves rapidly seized the new opportunities and within a few years after the war they were working more earnestly than when they were mere units in the slave regime."

Through the Great Depression and World War II, scholars of black labor continued to combat racist portrayals. They repeatedly called attention to the negative impact of slavery and the early emancipation years, when black workers faced an increasingly organized and racially exclusive white labor movement. In *The Black Worker*, Sterling Spero and Abram Harris argued that the subordination of the black worker was rooted deeply in the slavery experience, but it was also "kept alive and aggravated within the ranks of organized labor by the structure and politics of American trade unionism." In *Negro Labor*, Robert

Weaver examined the status of black workers as they entered the Great Depression and World War II, relating the poor position of black workers in the economy to a set of historical and contemporary conditions involving the complicated interaction of government, employer, and white labor attitudes in the context of a defective capitalist economy. The subordination of black workers, Weaver believed, had its origins in the unfavorable position of "poor whites" in the slave era, intense competition for employment in the South during Reconstruction, and employers' repeated use of blacks as strikebreakers in the North and West during the industrial era. Strikebreaking, he argued, was "instrumental in spreading the white fear of black workers geographically and infecting organized labor with its germ." By the end of World War II, the black worker had become "a symbol of a potential threat to the white worker" and the black worker's occupational advancement was "consciously or unconsciously feared." As late as 1965, Ray Marshall pinpointed the persistent problem of racism in shaping the economic and social position of black workers. In *The Negro and Organized Labor*, he wrote that the race problem "is one of the most important facing organized labor."

Even as the old labor history attacked racism among white workers, it affirmed the common interests of all workers and advocated an improved pattern of race relations as a means of uniting black and white labor. As racism escalated at the turn of the century, the first generation pondered: "What, then, should be the black man's attitude toward white laborers and the labor movement?" Invariably, they answered in the affirmative. As Du Bois and Dill put it, "The salvation of all laborers, white and black, lies in the great movement of racial uplift known as the labor movement. . . . Let us black men fight prejudice and exclusion in the labor world and fight it hard; but do not fight the labor movement." Similarly, Wesley concluded that the "successful solution of the Labor problem . . . lies largely in the worker's cooperation without regard to race. . . . The tradition of the absolute racial inferiority of the Negro should be examined by all workers, and the open-minded attitude should be adopted." Spero and Harris not only affirmed the unity of interests among black and white workers but also believed that black workers could play a key role in bringing about working-class unity even when they formed their own independent unions, such as the Brotherhood of Sleeping Car Porters, among others.

As scholars accented the common class interests of black and white workers, they also acknowledged the great variability in labor and race relationships. Early studies showed how black membership in predominantly white longshoremen, miners, and garment workers unions deviated from most craft unions of the American Federation of Labor (AFL) and admitted black and white workers on an equal footing; how the Knights of Labor and the Industrial Workers of the World (IWW) offered even greater egalitarian possibilities; and how the Railroad Brotherhoods represented the most extreme instances of black exclusion. Such emphasis on variability gained perhaps its clearest expression in Herbert R. Northup's *Organized Labor and the Negro*. Northup examined policies in eleven industries and concluded that the racial policies of American trade unions varied not only from union to union but also within the same union from region to region, "depending upon local customs and the type of leadership that is selected."

Although the scholarship of the first generation was held together by its common assault on white racism in the larger political economy as well as within the house of labor, it was by no means monolithic. It varied considerably in chronology, sources, methodology, interpretation, and specific emphases. Whereas in 1902 Du Bois had emphasized the role of training, higher education, and black business and professional people in his policy suggestions for the advancement of the black workers' cause, Spero and Harris were suspicious of such suggestions, arguing that such emphases were little more than the lever by which a black middle class would lift itself. In their view, the increasing labor union consciousness of black workers would reveal weaknesses in the notion of a "self-contained black capitalist economy." An organized black working class, they believed, would soon learn that the enrichment of a few blacks would do little to improve the lot of the rank and file. Whereas pre-1930s studies stressed the anti-black attitudes of white workers as barriers to a unified labor movement, studies of the 1930s and 1940s also emphasized the need to create a favorable climate for interracial unionism within the black community. Horace Cayton and George Mitchell analyzed economic, labor, and race relations in the iron and steel, meat packing, and railroad car shops of the 1930s. Under the impact of the Great Depression, the New Deal, and the Congress of Industrial Organizations (CIO), they noted the readjustment of organized white labor's attitude toward black workers and stressed the need to "increase and strengthen favorable union sentiment" in the black community alongside efforts to "break down the racial prejudice of white workers and union officials." Northup was especially pointed: "The Negro community owes its friends in the labor movement greater support than has been forthcoming."

Despite significant variations in chronology, sources, and methodology, the old labor history was informed by efforts to delineate the debilitating impact of white racism on black workers' lives. The race relations school defended black labor history from prevailing racist treatments of the late nineteenth and early twentieth century. It not only salvaged the image of black workers as productive participants in the changing economy but also placed the onus of racism and the fragmentation of the working class squarely on the shoulders of white employers, white workers, and the state. Such studies strongly indicted white workers for their racism but did not exonerate employers and their political allies who used the state to reinforce the elite's class and racial dominance. Emphasizing the fallacy of race in depictions of black workers, the old labor history illuminated the impact of race and class on the black working class. By focusing on the complex interaction of race and class, early scholars not only exploded dangerous myths about the inferiority of black workers but also laid essential groundwork for placing the lives of black workers within the context of larger socioeconomic and political change. Although they were primarily interested in the early emancipation and industrial eras, they also acknowledged slavery as a backdrop for the emergence of the free wage-earning black working class and helped to establish important temporal connections in the ongoing making and remaking of the black working class.

Unfortunately, even as the old African American labor history made its important contributions, it exhibited significant shortcomings. It overplayed the role of organized labor in the history of African American workers, particularly before the organizing drives of the CIO during the 1930s. Moreover, although such studies offered extensive documentation on the attitudes of black workers as well as employers and white workers, few systematically analyzed the experiences of black workers (particularly unorganized or unskilled workers) from the vantage of their own institutional, cultural, and political perspectives. In short, the old labor history paid insufficient attention to the interrelationship between the development of the black working class and changes in the larger African American community. When these shortcomings in the intellectual perspectives of the old labor history met the powerful political, socioeconomic, and cultural currents of the modern civil rights movement, a new African American labor history would gradually emerge. The new history, however, would owe a great deal to its earlier predecessor.

AFRICAN AMERICAN WORKERS AND THE
NEW LABOR HISTORY

Spurred by the dynamics of the modern civil rights movement as well as by the intellectual currents of the new social history "from the bottom up," historians of the late 1960s and early 1970s took a new look at the black working class. Heartened by growing evidence of black activism and interracial cooperation in the present, the new writers hoped to uncover the extent of interracial working class harmony and black self-assertion in the past. In 1968, in his now-classic essay on the career and letters of Richard L. Davis, a coal miner and leader in the United Mine Workers of America, the late historian Herbert Gutman largely set the new research agenda. Based on Davis's letters to the *United Mine Workers' Journal* and the *National Labor Tribune*, a labor paper published in the city of Pittsburgh, Gutman documented the black miner's commitment to working-class unity across racial lines, at a time when African Americans faced growing restrictions on their civil rights, witnessed the meteoric ascent of Booker T. Washington to prominence, and turned increasingly toward the ideology of racial solidarity and self-help. Gutman stressed how black and white workers joined the United Mine Workers of America, how Davis was elected to the organization's Executive Board at the district and later at the national levels, and how his life symbolized the complicated intertwining of black workers' class and racial identities at the turn of the twentieth century. Following

Gutman's lead, the new African American labor history fully emerged during the 1970s and 1980s.

The new agenda unfolded in three overlapping parts. First, Gutman called for a new look at the often-forgotten tradition of interracial unionism, which character-ized much of American labor history during the late nineteenth and early twentieth centuries. In efforts to uncover early patterns of interracial unionism, a variety of scholars turned their attention to the history of the United Mine Workers of Amer-ica, the Knights of Labor, and the role of blacks in radical interracial movements like the Communist Party. Pioneering essays on the United Mine Workers of America soon addressed this concern. Second, despite his plea for more research on hidden aspects of labor unionism, Gutman also criticized labor historians for overemphasizing the role of labor unions in the history of black and white workers before 1940, when few American workers belonged to permanent labor unions. He warned that the excessive attention given to labor unions camouflaged the es-sential interplay of class, ethnicity, and race in the development of American so-ciety. As such, Gutman urged historians to focus on the workers' community and culture. Recent studies analyzing the lives of African American workers within the larger framework of communities cover a wide variety of topics as well as tem-poral, regional, and local settings: slavery and freedom; North and South; urban and rural; and increasingly, women as well as men. Finally, Gutman urged histo-rians to conduct research on the careers of more working-class blacks like Richard L. Davis, as opposed to the usual focus on black elites like Booker T. Washington and W.E.B. Du Bois. Groundbreaking biographical and institutional studies of black workers soon responded to this agenda. Over the next twenty-five years, the new labor history would bring the development of the African American working class into sharper focus.

SLAVERY AND EARLY EMANCIPATION STUDIES

The rise of the new African American labor history was closely intertwined with the emergence of the new scholarship on slavery and emancipation. Under the growing impact of the civil rights and black power movements, historians overturned an earlier image of slaves as culturally impoverished, stripped of family life, isolated from community, and essentially quiescent in the face of dehumanizing conditions. Some of the earliest and most insightful studies of black workers' culture and community focused on the pre-emancipation era. Emphasizing slave culture and community life, historians John Blassingame, Eugene Genovese, Lawrence Levine, Sterling Stuckey, and Herbert Gutman ad-vanced a new portrait of African Americans as an enslaved working class. The new scholars used not only sources left by the planters and slave owners but also those left by the slaves themselves. Slave narratives and oral recollections revealed the development of unique African American work, family, and reli-gious practices; music, songs, and dances; folklore and oral traditions. Such studies illuminate how slaves responded to their subordinate status by advocating group solidarity, building self-esteem, and supporting covert and sometimes open resistance to bondage. As historian John Blassingame put it, "However oppressive or dehumanizing the plantation was, the struggle for survival was not severe enough to crush all of the slave's creative instincts."

Through the mid-1980s, scholars continued to elaborate upon the community and culture perspective. At the same time, they extended our understanding of slaves as laborers into new chronological, regional, and topical areas, including slave religion, women, work, and the process of emancipation and community development in the antebellum North. As Blassingame, Genovese, Gutman, and others pushed the study of black workers backward into the antebellum years, Peter Wood, Daniel Littlefield, and Edmund Morgan, among others, illuminated the initial transformation of Africans into an enslaved African American working class. While these scholars expanded our understanding of the making and re-making of black agricultural laborers—involving movement from Upper South to Deep South, and from tobacco, rice, and sugar to cotton—others offered insights into the initial growth of a black urban and rural-industrial proletariat. Building upon the earlier scholarship of Robert Starobin, Richard Wade, and Leon Litwack, studies by Ira Berlin, Ronald Lewis, and Gary Nash, to name a few, all enhanced our knowledge of the urban and industrial aspects of black workers' lives, slave and free, North and South, before the onset of the Civil War.

By the late 1980s, however, the slave culture and community framework came under growing scrutiny. Scholars increasingly complained that such studies, despite their acknowledgments of slaves as workers, ignored the centrality of work in the lives of bondsmen and women. To be sure, Genovese examined what he considered to be the preindustrial work habits of African American slaves and concluded that slave work "patterns remained bound to the rhythms of nature and to traditional ideas of work, time, and leisure." In their controversial quantitative study of slavery, *Time on the Cross* (1974), historians Robert Fogel and Stanley Engerman disagreed, emphasizing the system of incentives—access to family life, garden plots, better jobs in the slave workforce, and even manumission—that spurred some slaves to render productive and efficient service that made the plantation a profitable enterprise. Although Gutman's study, *The Black Family in Slavery and Freedom. 1750–1925* (1976), responded to the controversial Moynihan Report (1965), which blamed African American poverty on the breakdown of the black family, it also reinforced efforts to tie the history of slaves to the history of the American working class. According to Gutman, this book was "a special aspect of American labor history: those men and women who labored first in bondage and then mostly as half-free rural workers." Deborah Gray White's study of slave women was even more on the mark. She used slave work as the pivot around which slave social networks developed. As she put it, "Female domestic work sealed the bonds of womanhood that were forged in the fields and other work places." Still, most studies tended to accept, even if implicitly, Blassingame's argument that the slave quarters represented the slave's "primary" environment, whereas the slave's work constituted a "secondary" influence on the culture, community, and personalities of slaves.

In recent years, scholars have turned toward work as the primary rather than secondary experience of slaves. Such studies stress the centrality of slave work and its impact on other facets of slave life. In their recent collection of essays on slavery in the Americas, Ira Berlin and Philip D. Morgan emphasize the centrality of work in the lives of slaves. They conclude that slaves worked and that "when, where, and especially how they worked determined, in large measure, the course of their lives. . . . After all, slavery was first and foremost an institution of coerced labor. Work necessarily engaged most slaves, most of the time." In his comparative study of American slavery and Russian serfdom, Peter Kolchin makes the same point: "It is appropriate to begin with the bondsmen's work, for slavery and serfdom remained most fundamentally, systems of labor exploitation. Work constituted the primary experiences of the slaves and serfs." Other scholars are beginning to push work to the forefront of studies of slaves in pre-emancipation cities and industrial settings. In a recent essay on black workers in antebellum Richmond, Suzanne Schnittman explores the transformation of slave labor in the tobacco industry. She documents the growing use of hired rather than "personally owned" slaves and concludes that the increasing use of such practices as cash payments to slaves and independent lodging arrangements allowed tobacco slaves to approximate the development of an urban-commercial, if not industrial, working class. Patricia Schechter illuminates the same process in her study of the 1847 strike at Richmond's Tredegar iron works, which resulted in the increasing displacement of free white by slave labor. Likewise, T. Stephen Whitman broadens our knowledge of the same process in his study of the heretofore little understood chemical industry of antebellum Maryland.

No less than slavery studies, the new African American labor history is closely related to the emergence of new emancipation and Reconstruction studies. Recent scholarship on emancipation and Reconstruction has turned increasingly toward the history of black agricultural workers during the first two generations of freedom. Thomas Holt, Peter Kolchin, and Nell Irvin Painter, among others, shifted the focus from an earlier preoccupation with economic and political elites to a close examination of the lives of ordinary black workers. According to Nell Irvin Painter, the "Exodusters" who fled the lower Mississippi Valley following the downfall of Reconstruction were members of the ordinary black working class, whose "immediate history as slaves" was "practically as important as their race" in shaping the course of their lives during the early years of freedom. As Peter Kolchin put it in his first book, not governmental political action but the transformation of African Americans from slave to a free labor system was key to the social changes of the emancipation years. For his part, as late as 1986, Armstead Robinson concluded that "the Civil War origins of the post-war labor system constitute the first line of inquiry that demands attention" in emancipation research.

Recent scholarship reveals how ex-slaves made the transition from slaves to free sharecroppers and members of a rural wage-earning proletariat. Such studies emphasize the dynamic role that ex-slaves played in the emergence of the new postbellum economic system, involving sharecropping, crop lien, and wage labor. Rather than a system of unilateral domination, sharecropping involved a tug of war between ex-slaves and ex-masters, with former slaves extracting a promise of access to land and a measure of independence in its cultivation in exchange for their labor. Moreover, scholars are now sensitive to the ways that ex-slaves built upon their cultural experiences in the slave community and developed a broad range of institutions—especially churches, fraternal orders, and social clubs—to address their own needs. Such institutions, in turn, facilitated the rise of small business, professional, and civil rights organizations in which black workers often supported the efforts of black elites while simultaneously articulating their own distinct class-based goals and aspirations.

The rise of a free wage-earning and sharecropping proletariat entails a variety of controversies and complexities. These receive careful attention in Gerald David Jaynes's *Branches without Roots* (1986). Jaynes documents the transition of African Americans from slave to free labor in the rural South and illuminates several areas of disagreement. While stressing the impact of capitalist landowners and merchants in the development of the new labor system, he shows that the new system of kin-based sharecropping and wage labor was mediated by the state and influenced by the ex-slaves themselves. Noting how family-based sharecropping arrangements tended to predominate in cotton and tobacco areas and that cash-wage labor predominated in the sugar and rice areas, *Branches without Roots* also seeks to reconcile Genovese's emphasis on preindustrial work habits and Fogel and Engerman's focus on the acquisitive "Protestant work ethic" among black rural workers. On this controversy, Jaynes concludes that ex-slaves were not Calvinists but "a group well endowed with attitudes toward work for wages consonant with the characteristics of any contemporary working class." At the same time, he takes a middle course in the debate between economic historians—namely, the "monopoly" school of Roger Ransom, Richard Sutch, and others who emphasize the extraordinary ability of black workers to change the basis on which they lived and labored—and the "competition" school of Robert Higgs and his associates, who argue that the existence of stiff labor competition among planters enabled ex-slaves to create a better employment package for themselves by moving from one employer to the next in a highly competitive labor market. According to Jaynes, the "black power" argument of the "monopoly school" overestimated the ability of black workers to overcome the authority of landowners, whereas the competition scholars ignored convict labor, lien laws, and other coercive features of the southern rural economy.

Under the editorship of Ira Berlin, the latest volume of *Freedom: A Docu-*

mentary History of Emancipation, 1861–1867 suggests the growing emphasis on black workers in emancipation scholarship. The study is not only a collection of documents but also a careful examination of the process by which African Americans made their first tentative steps from a predominantly slave to a free labor force from the Civil War years through the beginning of radical Reconstruction. Nearly 250,000 former slaves and free blacks had participated in federal government controlled free labor arrangements. Based largely upon these documents, Julie Saville's study, *The Work of Reconstruction: From Slave to Wage Labor in South Carolina, 1860–1870*, reveals that the initial rise of a free African American working class was a complicated and "contested" process. The creation of a free black proletariat pitted the slave's conception of freedom—as access to land and freedom to work it according to deeply held notions of subsistence—against that of triumphant northern capitalists, who increasingly viewed freedom as "the unfettered sale of one's labor power." In other words, according to Saville, emancipation entailed a dual struggle for ex-slaves: (1) against the prior sovereignty that masters and mistresses exercised over their lives as bondsmen and women; and (2) against the ascendant efforts to subject them to "landowners management and to the discipline of an abstract market," which northern Republican proponents and their southern white allies defined as "freedom."

Growing emphasis on the centrality of labor in slavery and emancipation studies reveals the significance of these formative experiences for fully comprehending the larger proletarianization process. The study of slavery and Reconstruction have too often been treated as two separate subfields, but recent scholarship suggests that both are crucial to any effort to document the emergence of a free African American rural proletariat in the wake of massive migration, industrialization, and urbanization in the nation as a whole. Expanding scholarship in these areas also shows how scholars fought, and largely won, the struggle to treat African American slaves and sharecroppers not only as blacks with a racial identity but as workers with class identities. Finally, by arguing the significance of class as well as race and "color caste" in the creation of the black working class under a variety of conditions, ranging from slavery to freedom, the new slavery and emancipation studies enable us to understand better the emergence of a black industrial proletariat during the twentieth century. Before this understanding could take hold, however, scholars of the twentieth century had to lay claims to the urban industrial era as a pivotal moment alongside slavery and emancipation in the history of the African American working class.

BLACK WORKERS IN THE INDUSTRIAL AGE

The urban-industrial era represent perhaps the most prolific area of recent scholarship on black workers. Such studies responded to three interrelated tendencies in American labor and African American history. First, until the 1960s and 1970s, African American history was conceptualized primarily as the history of slavery and Reconstruction. Few studies examined the urban industrial phases of black life. Accordingly, the new urban labor history responded to this hiatus in our knowledge. Second, when scholars did take up the urban question, they turned overwhelmingly to northern cities. Thus, recent studies also seek to address the imbalance between research on the urban North and South by bringing the latter under increasing scrutiny. Finally, recent scholarship on black workers during the industrial era not only responded to temporal and geographical concerns but to theoretical ones as well. During the 1960s and early 1970s, the ghetto synthesis emerged at the core of research on urban blacks. Focusing on the making of the black "ghetto" within major northern cities, scholars like Allan Spear, Gilbert Osofsky, and Kenneth Kusmer subordinated the study of black workers to explorations of the dynamics of ghetto formation, which emphasized the role of racism and the institutional and political responses of black elites thereto. Hence, in order to rectify some of these shortcomings, recent scholars also responded to various facets of the Gutman agenda, namely, the call for more research on interracial unionism, working-class black leaders, and workers and their communities.

The first wave of new scholarship focused on the issue of interracial unionism within the rural-industrial and urban South. Building upon Gutman's suggestions were essays by Paul B. Worthman, "Black Workers and Labor Unions in Birmingham, Alabama, 1897–1904" (1969); Stephen Brier, "Interracial Organizing in the West Virginia Coal Industry" (1977); and Daniel P. Jordan, "The Mingo War" (1977). Unlike previous studies, which acknowledged exceptions but emphasized the primacy of racial antagonisms within the working class, these scholars highlighted patterns of interracial working-class solidarity. In his study of class and race relations in the Birmingham District of Alabama, Paul Worthman focused on the late 1890s and early twentieth century, thereby pushing the story of interracial cooperation beyond the somewhat better known stories of the Knights of Labor and the Populists of the 1880s and early 1890s. He argued that historians' emphasis on "the racial hostility of white workers, and the exclusionary and racially restrictive policies of various trade unions" had "obscured the complex relationships which existed among black workers, white workers, and trade unions" and had led to "the neglect of tensions and conflicts in the labor movement and in the South which helped shape those relationships." Based on evidence of labor and race relations in the Birmingham District, Worthman concluded that "despite the rapid spread of racial conflict at the beginning of the twentieth century, the heritage of interracial cooperation in the Knights of Labor and in Populist campaigns lingered among many white and black workingmen." With the exception of the Amalgamated Association of Iron and Steel Workers, the Alabama Federation of Labor and the United Mine Workers continued to mount organizing efforts across racial lines. Moreover, according to Worthman, though he overstates the case, the failure of the Amalgamated was as much a consequence of its restrictive craft as of racial orientation. Nonetheless, Worthman convincingly shows how Alabama's labor movement momentarily overcame craft union exclusiveness and racial conflict, organized thousands of black workers, and "challenged the industrialists' ability to use racial hostility to discipline the class antagonisms of the New South." Focusing on developments in the West Virginia coal fields during the 1890s and during the 1919–1922 period, historians Stephen Brier and Daniel Jordan drew essentially the same conclusions.

Brier examined the growth of the Knights of Labor and the early United Mine Workers of America in the Pocahontas coal field of West Virginia between 1880 and 1894. Some scholars had examined the efforts of the national coal mine unions to bring West Virginia miners into the fold, but as Brier demonstrated, few had examined the "more significant" growth of "militant, interracial local unions" among southern West Virginia miners, particularly "the active participation of black mine workers in local and district trade union organizations." More specifically, he concluded that "perhaps the most striking aspect of this episode in American working class history is the fact that Southern West Virginia black miners, many recently migrated from the cities and farms of Eastern Virginia, came to view interracial union organization as the vehicle through which they could fight for their liberation both as workers and as black people." For his part, Daniel Jordan analyzed the outbreak of violence during the United Mine Workers' effort to unionize the unorganized bituminous miners in the coal fields of Mingo, Logan, and other southern West Virginia counties. Only the use of federal troops put down the violence, as the number of armed miners increased to well over 5,000 and assaulted a major citadel of non-union operators in the "Mingo War." Although Jordan, unlike Brier, was more interested in interclass than in interracial relations, he reached the same conclusions. According to Jordan, the Mingo conflict was "distinctive among contemporary labor disorders for what failed to happen." As he put it, "The postwar era was among the nation's worst in race relations. The color line had been rigidly drawn, the Ku Klux Klan had reemerged, and several bloody riots had occurred. The frequent use of Negroes as strikebreakers inevitably provoked violence. The Mingo War, however, was an interracial affair, unmarked by the racially inspired lawlessness common to many other industrial disturbances. . . . The Mingo War was neither conducted along racial lines nor marked by racial violence; and as such, for the times, it was certainly atypical."

As scholars like Worthman, Jordan, and Brier uncovered neglected traditions of interracial unionism, others pursued a related but different theme. In his essay on Davis, Gutman had also advocated more research on the careers of working-class blacks as opposed to the usual focus on black elites. Pioneering studies of black workers by Theodore Rosengarten, Nell Irvin Painter, and William H. Harris addressed this hiatus in our knowledge. Taken together, Rosengarten's *All God's Dangers: The Life of Nate Shaw* (1974), Painter's *Narrative of Hosea Hudson: His Life as a Negro Communist in the South* (1979), and Harris's *Keeping the Faith: A. Philip Randolph, Milton P. Webster, and the Brotherhood of Sleeping Car Porters, 1925–1937* (1977) provide lucid accounts of working-class black life in both the rural and urban America during the late nineteenth and early twentieth centuries. By using the workers' own language and story-telling skills and traditions, Painter and Rosengarten give to workers' lives a certain agency and coherence, despite the ambiguity, contradictions, and confusion that often marked their life histories. *All God's Dangers* uses the share-cropper Nate Shaw's (Ned Cobb's) own words to describe how he joined the sharecroppers union and fought the system that oppressed him. The book reveals how ordinary rural black workers forged ideas, beliefs, and behaviors designed to hasten their own liberation. As Shaw put it, he had participated in a shoot-out with local officials because he had labored "under many rulins, just like the other Negro, that I knowed was injurious to man and displeasin to God and still I had to fall back." For his part, Hosea Hudson, as revealed in Painter's biography, joined the Communist Party and fought racial and class oppression for a similar reason and in similar language. In his study of the Brotherhood of Sleeping Car Porters, Harris reinforced efforts to study heretofore neglected working-class black leaders. Randolph, unlike Hudson and Shaw, was a high school graduate who had taken classes at the City College of New York, but he was a "charismatic" leader who clearly articulated the "porters" grievances. Perhaps more importantly, in order to advance the cause of porters, Randolph depended upon district organizers like Milton P. Webster and Ashley Totten, who had fewer educational credentials than himself. As Harris put it, Randolph relied heavily "upon his associates, individuals who by and large have remained in obscurity, but without whom the BSCP [Brotherhood of Sleeping Car Porters] could not have succeeded."

The new biographical and institutional studies not only addressed the need for more detailed studies of working-class blacks but also foreshadowed a growing body of research on the interplay of work, culture, and community in the lives of black workers. Since the early to mid-1980s, studies focusing on the interplay of work, culture, community, and power have gradually expanded. Yet, this new scholarship is quite diverse. Some studies treat black workers within the larger framework of black communities; others offer sophisticated versions of interracial unionism; and still others analyze specific aspects of working-class black life: the migration process, resistance and the development of oppositional culture, and, increasingly, the gender question. As labor historian Robert Zieger suggests in another context, African American labor history, like southern and U.S. labor history, appears to be in transition between an "old new labor history and an even newer gender-conscious labor history."

From the mid-1980s through the early 1990s, several studies brought the study of black workers more fully within the framework of community. They examined not only the lives of black workers but also their persistent interactions with black elites in the larger social, political, cultural, and institutional life of African Americans. In his *Black Labor in the South: Richmond. Virginia, 1865–1890* (1984), Peter Rachleff pioneered in establishing a larger community-based black labor history. He emphasized how Richmond's black workers built a variety of indigenous religious and fraternal orders. These organizations helped to lay the foundations for the black worker's highly race-conscious participation in the militant Knights of Labor. Still, Rachleff retained a keen interest in the possibilities of interracial working-class solidarity. The history of the Knights of Labor in Richmond, Virginia, he concludes, demonstrates that black and white workers could act together and that they could pose a viable political challenge to the status quo. In his 1991 book, *In Their Own Interests: Race, Class, and Power in Twentieth-Century Norfolk, Virginia*, Earl Lewis urges historians to "consider the culture that blacks constantly recreated, a culture that bound blacks to one another, even while it distinguished the working class from the elite." Lewis shows how Norfolk blacks, workers and elites alike, created extensive kin and friendship networks, built a variety of institutional responses to inequality, and sustained close links with the nearby countryside, other southern cities, and the urban North. Although some black workers "manifested a semblance of worker consciousness," particularly through the formation of unions like the Coal Trimmers Union and the Transport Workers Association, Lewis concludes that their "consciousness was so embedded in the perspective of race that neither blacks nor whites saw themselves as equal partners in the same labor movement." For my part, in *Coal, Class, and Color: Blacks in Southern West Virginia, 1915–1932*, I focused on the rise of the black coal-mining working class and its resulting impact on the larger community life of blacks in coal-mining towns. *Coal, Class, and Color* emphasizes how the rise of the black coal-mining proletariat stimulated the gradual transformation of African American culture and consciousness, as indicated by the growth of the black middle class and the development of multiclass black religious, fraternal, civil rights, and political organizations.

Reinforcing research on black workers in the industrial South are a growing number of studies on the Great Migration and resettlement of black workers in the urban North and West. If studies of southern black workers responded to excessive emphasis on the urban North, studies of black workers in the urban North responded to the prevailing emphasis on the process of ghetto formation in such studies. In *Black Milwaukee: The Making of an Industrial Proletariat, 1915–1945*, for example, I aimed to shift the focus from the making of an African American urban ghetto to the transformation of rural blacks into a new urban industrial proletariat. As I suggested in that study, "ghettoization" was indeed a significant development, but urban blacks "were not only ghetto dwellers; they were also workers, who moved increasingly out of agricultural, domestic, and personal service jobs into urban-industrial pursuits." Although he recently abandoned the effort in his new book on Detroit, Richard Walter Thomas helped to pioneer emphases on the development of a black industrial working class in the urban North. In the doctoral version of his study, Thomas forcefully argued that the most important development in Detroit's black history was the formation and organization of a black proletariat.

Focusing on black steelworkers in western Pennsylvania, Dennis Dickerson offers the most ambitious study of black workers in the industrial North. Covering the period 1875–1980, *Out of the Crucible* (1986) carefully documents the persistence of racial discrimination in hiring, promotion, and job assignments in the steel industry. According to Dickerson, "Race, not class" fundamentally shaped the experiences of black workers over a long period of time. Still, the experiences of black steelworkers were not static. The first generation of black steelworkers occupied "an impressive array of skilled positions" but failed to gain the necessary security to effectively advance the position of succeeding generations. The second generation of black steelworkers faced hostile "native whites and foreign-born" laborers who heightened racial barriers in the workplace. For their part, according to Dickerson, the third generation of black steelworkers faced the disproportional ravages of deindustrialization and technological change, despite the emergence of a vigorous interracial labor movement, an increasingly activist and pro-labor state, and a militant modern civil rights movement. Dickerson's book not only examines the patterns of persistence and change in the socioeconomic status of black steelworkers, but illuminates the interplay between changes in the labor market and the larger community life of blacks in Pittsburgh, Homestead, Braddock, and other steel towns in western Pennsylvania. The study includes, for example, illuminating analyses of black steelworker preachers, baseball teams, churches, and chapters of the Garvey movement, NAACP, and Urban League.

Studies of northern black workers nonetheless failed to provide ample insight into the southern rural roots of the northern black proletariat. Research on the Great Migration to northern cities soon addressed this gap in our knowledge. Studies by Peter Gottlieb, *Making Their Own Way: Southern Blacks Migration to Pittsburgh. 1916–1930* (1987), and James Grossman, *Land of Hope: Chicago, Black Southerners, and the Great Migration* (1989), begin with detailed analyses of black life and labor in the South. Placing ordinary rural southern black workers at the center of the process, Gottlieb and Grossman treat black migration as a multidimensional phenomenon that black workers influenced through their elaborate networks of kin, friends, and communities. Specifically, Gottlieb's study illuminates the dual themes of black migration and proletarianization, each rooted deeply in the rural world of southern blacks as well as changing conditions in the industrial environment. Much like peasant migrants to industrial cities throughout the world, Gottlieb argues that black migrants sought northern wages to reinforce a southern traditional way of life. According to Gottlieb, although he overstates the case, even African Americans who settled permanently in Pittsburgh, "in fact lived, worked, socialized, and worshiped primarily among other blacks from the South." Thus, only subsequent generations of southern black workers would become "wholly" northern urban-industrial men and women. For his part, Grossman also locates the imperatives of black migration and working-class formation in the rural South and reveals how African Americans substituted their traditional faith in land ownership with a new faith in wage labor in the industrial sector. Denied economic and political citizenship in the South, many black workers perceived migration to Chicago as an entrée into the "perquisites of American citizenship." This new southern-based movement had its leaders, but "they were not the disciples of Booker T. Washington who dominated the Southern black press, who occupied whatever positions of political influence whites offered blacks, and who were the recognized spokesmen of black America." Even as African Americans moved to Chicago to share in the promise of American democracy and industrialism, Grossman concludes, they did so through the prism of race and not class consciousness.

As migration and urban studies moved the focus deeper and deeper into the home, family, and community life of black workers, other scholars worked to sharpen our understanding of the workplace, biracial unionism, and labor politics. These studies moved beyond the "class or race" perspective of the initial studies of interracial unionism in the United Mine Workers of America. In *Waterfront Workers of New Orleans*, historian Eric Arnesen illuminates the work hierarchy, jobs, and pay arrangements for skilled elite screwmen as well as common laborers and "roustabouts." At the same time, he explores the development of a highly organized and politically influential biracial movement. Rather than arguing class over race consciousness or vice versa, he concludes that black and white dock workers developed complex identities: "At the workplace and in the union hall, their behavior, their goals, and their agendas seldom could be reduced to either labor or racial identity." As such, Arnesen also elaborates upon a key theme in the old labor history. For him, trade unions (especially the Cotton Men's Executive Council and its successor the Dock and Cotton Council), interunion alliances, and the creation of a biracial union structure on the New Orleans waterfront were keys to the lives of waterfront workers. The union mediated racial and occupational disputes, developed strategy, and established work rules to regulate on-the-job behavior, limited employer exploitation, and increased wages.

Research on African American workers and labor politics during the Great Depression, World War II, and the early civil rights movement also gradually expanded. This scholarship provides fresh insights into the role of black workers and the new CIO unions in the increasing political mobilization of the African American community. It also reflects growing disagreement over the precise impact that the new labor radicals had on the actual status of black workers. In their comparative essay "Opportunities Found and Lost," Robert Korstad and Nelson Lichtenstein examine the relationship between the expansion of the black industrial working class and the early rise of the modern civil rights movement in Winston-Salem, North Carolina, and Detroit, Michigan. Specifically, they document the transition from an old middle-class black leadership to a new working-class one with close ties to CIO unions—Local 22 of the Food, Tobacco, Agricultural, and Allied Workers in the South and the United Auto Workers, especially Local 600, in the North. According to Lichtenstein and Korstad, the new leadership was nurtured by a new working-class culture that transcended the workplace and cut across neighborhood, job, and institutional affiliations and played a key role in pushing civil rights to the top of labor's war and postwar agenda. Although the radical labor-based civil rights movement would decline in the wake of the postwar offensive against radicals, increasing mechanization, and resurgence of conservative American Federation of Labor (AFL) unionism, the authors conclude that black workers and the new unions played a key role in the early emergence of a new political movement to end racial inequality in American society.

A similar story emerges from scholarship on other cities. In his 1993 prize-winning study of Memphis, Tennessee, Michael Honey emphasizes how the "conflicting forces of conservatism and change" in the city's labor, class, and political relations gave rise, in the late 1930s and early 1940s, to "one of the most successful industrial union movements in the South." The movement involved a growing African American union-based civil rights effort that resisted the discriminatory treatment of employers, unions, and municipal authorities. In short, like Korstad and Lichtenstein, Honey reinforces the connection between black CIO unionism and the rise of a vigorous new civil rights movement, which also foundered on the shoals of resurgent racism and anti-radicalism in the post-war years. Rick Halpern and Judith Stein tell similar stories for packinghouse workers in Fort Worth, Texas, and steelworkers in Birmingham, Alabama.

Recent emphasis on the very positive role of interracial unionism in the early emergence of the modern civil rights movement has been contested. Some studies stress the persistence of racial antagonisms from the early rise of the CIO onward. In their study of blacks and the United Automobile Workers (UAW) in Detroit during the Depression and World War II, August Meier and the late Elliott Rudwick stressed the ambivalence of the relationship between blacks and the new unions from the outset. Despite the UAW's growing support of the civil rights cause and efforts to upgrade African Americans in the labor force, rank-and-file white unionists repeatedly challenged and hampered the implementation of such policies. Other scholars are even more emphatic in their indictment of the new unions for their role in the perpetuation of racial inequality. Based upon a close analysis of the historical relationship between race, work, and labor law, Herbert Hill concludes that organized labor failed to use its growing influence over federal labor policy (as reflected in agencies like the National Labor Relations Board) to address racial inequities in the workforce. In an influential essay on the Birmingham steel industry during the depression, war, and postwar years, Robert J. Norrell also underscores the "centrality of race" and racial discrimination in the experiences of the city's black steelwork-ers. Based upon extensive oral interviews with black workers, Norrell documented the persistence of racial discrimination despite the rise of the CIO in the years after 1936. The reaction against radicals and the resurgence of racism in the postwar years, Norrell convincingly argues, were not as dramatic breaks with the experiences of the late depression and early war years as we have been led to believe. In his essay "Organized Labor and the Struggle for Black Equality in Mobile during World War II," Bruce Nelson also paints a complex picture of labor and race relations in the era of the CIO. According to Nelson, most white shipyard workers resisted "concessions to their black coworkers' demands for greater equality, but whites were not a monolith." Older white shipyard craftsmen accepted blacks in subordinate positions as helpers, but newer migrants from the rural South resisted black employment with a vengeance, as reflected in the Alabama Dry Dock and Shipbuilding Company riot of 1943.

As black labor history expanded under the impact of the new scholarship, some analysts sought to move beyond the narrow chronological and regional boundaries of most studies. In a sense, Dennis Dickerson's important study of steelworkers in western Pennsylvania, discussed above, helped to initiate this process by covering the experiences of black workers in a large number of steel towns over more than a century of time. But the most ambitious and successful of these books is Ronald Lewis's *Black Coal Miners in America: Race, Class, and Community Conflict, 1780–1980* (1987). Lewis explores the experiences of black workers from their antebellum beginnings to their demise during the mid- to late twentieth century. He not only covers the role of the better-known labor leader Richard L. Davis of the United Mine Workers, but also offers crucial new insights into the lives of lesser-known black coal mine leaders, including George Edmunds of Iowa, William Prentice of Illinois, and Frank Ingham of West Virginia. Perhaps most important, Lewis adopts a "comparative regional approach" and documents several distinct patterns of "race, class, and community conflict" in the bituminous coal fields of the United States—what he calls "expropriation" and "exploitation" in the ante-and postbellum South, racial "exclusion" in the North, relative "equality" in the central Appalachian fields, and "elimination" from all fields with the onset of massive technological changes in the post–World War II years. Lewis carefully reconstructs the extent of black participation in the coal-mining workforce; the racial attitudes and behavior of white employers; and the activities of black miners in their own behalf, particularly their role in the United Mine Workers of America. In explaining the devastating impact of technological changes on black miners' lives in the postwar years, Lewis not only accents the persistence of racism in the coal regions but also stresses the racially destructive mechanization policies of the United Mine Workers. Unfortunately, as he describes it, such policies were difficult for black workers to counteract, partly because the organization's tradition of interracial unionism made it less willing to admit and address racial inequality in practice.

At the same time that Lewis stretched the boundaries of black labor history, other scholars pursued more specialized topics. Studies of black women, gender, labor violence, strikebreaking, and radicalism, all gained attention in a growing body of essays and books. The question of resistance and the development of a black working-class oppositional culture is the subject of Robin D. G. Kelley's award-winning study *Hammer and Hoe: Alabama Communists during the Great Depression* (1990). Informed by literary and cultural theory, *Hammer and Hoe* unveils the deep underground sources of southern black radicalism. In poor black communities and among "tiny circles of white rebels," Kelley documents the development of a radical political movement in the Jim Crow South. Racial division in the South, he demonstrates, was "far more fluid" and working-class consciousness "far more complex than most historians have realized." Tracing men and women from the farms, factories, mines, kitchens, and city streets into the party, Kelley shows that these people were "loaded down with cultural and ideological baggage molded by their race, class, gender, work, community, region, history, upbringing, and collective memory."

Black women's labor history is also emerging as a vibrant new area. The systematic study of the interplay of class, race, and gender is the pioneering province of a growing number of women historians. These include established as well as younger scholars: Jacqueline Jones, Dolores Janiewski, Elizabeth Clark-Lewis, Evelyn Brooks Higginbottham, Sharon Harley, Darlene Clark Hine, Tera Hunter and Elsa Barkley Brown. In her groundbreaking essay "Womanist Consciousness: Maggie Lena Walker and the Independent Order of St. Luke," Elsa Barkley Brown articulates an important aspect of the emerging agenda. Reacting against dichotomous sex-race thinking in feminist theory and writing, which often "assume the separability of women's struggle and race struggle," Barkeley Brown concludes that for black women like Maggie Lena Walker, "There are no necessary contradictions between the public and domestic spheres; the community and the family; male and female; race and sex struggle—there is intersection and interdependence." Similarly, in another influential essay, "African-American Women's History and the Metalanguage of Race," Evelyn Brooks Higginbottham urges historians to recognize the impact of race on "the construction and representation" of such power relations as gender, class, and race. For her part, Tera Hunter focuses on the role of Atlanta's black women in the creation of a collective working-class culture. By exploring the lives of household workers at work, at home, and in leisure time, she shows how class consciousness was the product of complicated socioeconomic, political, and cultural interactions at different sites in the larger urban political economy. Hunter convincingly demonstrates that domestic workers not only helped to fuel the growth of the industrial city but also developed a variety of strategies for resisting its exploitative encroachment upon their lives. In *The Afro-American Woman*, Sharon Harley and Rosalyn Terborg-Penn offer a fuller treatment of recent developments in black women's labor history.

Although black women's labor history is expanding as perhaps the most illuminating recent area of research, other specialized studies also warrant our close attention. Much of the specialized scholarship is unfolding within the larger framework of black urban history. Over the past twenty-five years, a new black urban history emerged in tandem with the new African American labor history. Like black labor history, urban studies covered an expanding range of chronological units, regions, and topics: comparative group experiences, rise of new black business and professional elites, new social movements and politics, and racial violence and social conflict. Since William Tuttle's study of the 1919 Chicago race riot, first published in the special African American issue of *Labor History*, studies of racial violence have proliferated. Historical studies of racial violence now cover several southern as well as northern cities: Atlanta, Houston, New Orleans, Tulsa, Detroit, and Springfield. Whereas Tuttle emphasized competition among black and white workers as the key to the Chicago conflict, recent studies suggest some movement away from that model. In her study of the Springfield riot, for example, Roberta Senechal concludes that white hostility had built up against the presence of blacks before their numbers increased to a sizable proportion of the labor force. Thus, for her the shortage of jobs and black residential expansion in the city were less significant than prior studies have led us to believe. Similarly, in their analysis of the 1911 lynching of the black worker Zachariah Walker in the small industrial town of Coatesville in eastern Pennsylvania, Dennis Downey and Raymond Hyser downplayed labor conflict in favor of emphasis on the role that lynching sentiment and the lynching played in cementing a sense of "community" among white residents. Although such emphases have not displaced the role of labor conflict, they do require us to take seriously the broad range of factors that may have played a part in fomenting racial violence.

AFRICAN AMERICAN LABOR HISTORY: TOWARD THE TWENTY-FIRST CENTURY

African American labor history is an expanding, vibrant, and exciting field of scholarship. The emergence of the new labor history not only reveals progress in closing the gap between work and community but also suggests that a full understanding of the development of the black working class will require much more work. Our knowledge of the role of black workers in the development of pivotal industries like coal, iron, steel, auto, meatpacking, and tobacco grows, for example, but we know little about black workers in other industries like building and construction, apparel, railroads (except porters), and a host of establishments employing common laborers in the formal and informal urban economy. Even for industries that have received growing attention, there are significant blindspots on questions of work and the work process. Although we know a great deal about how rural blacks entered urban industrial jobs and faced new forms of discrimination and exploitation, we know far less about the precise ways in which they built upon their southern rural work culture and developed new skills and work practices in meatpacking plants, in steel mills, in automobile factories, and in a whole range of so-called unskilled labor jobs. Take coal mining, for example.

Like most miners, black men entered coal mines primarily as unskilled coal loaders. They worked mainly in underground positions, called "inside labor." Yet, coal loading required knowledge as well as muscle power. First and foremost, the miner learned to pace his work. As one black southern West Virginia miner recalled, "[My father] taught me to load the coal . . . after all you could do it the wrong way and get broke down and you couldn't do business. . . . There is a little art to it." Coal loading, however, involved more than merely pacing the work. It took over an hour of preparation before the miner lifted his first shovel of coal. The miner deployed an impressive range of skills: the techniques of dynamiting coal, including knowledge of various gases and the principles of mine ventilation; the establishment of roof-supports in order to prevent dangerous cave-ins; and the persistent canvassing of mines in order to spot potential hazards. The transformation of African American work experiences under industrialism also had important cultural dimensions. As one black miner recalled, he took the dangerous brakeman job because it was a "status symbol" and allowed him to "show off" in the pool halls. He even developed an anecdote to describe the skills he deployed as well as the pride he took in his work. "Few black men can do what I do, but no whites at all." We need to probe more deeply these dimensions of black workers' lives in a wide variety of work settings that were marked by class and racial inequality.

We need not only a sharper focus on how black workers used their prior cultural resources and adapted to new work environments but also a much better sense of the varieties of strategies that they employed to combat exploitation and to change the impact of the larger socioeconomic and political system on their lives. As historian Robin D. G. Kelley informs us in "We Are Not What We Seem," it is time "to render visible hidden forms of resistance, examine how class shapes political consciousness, and bridge the gulf between the social and cultural worlds of working class African Americans and political struggle." What Kelley describes as quotidian forms of resistance—including theft, work slowdowns, and destruction of property—would repeatedly test the ability of middle-class and elite black leaders to discipline the political behavior of blacks into acceptable channels. When black workers turned toward transiency, theft, and violence (individual and collective) as forms of redress, they challenged the stability and feasibility of cross-class alliances within the black community. The Garvey movement of the 1920s is an excellent illustration of how a major political movement appealed to African American workers and disrupted the fragile alliance between black workers and black elites. These issues—including middle- and working-class variants of black nationalism and radicalism—require much greater attention as well.

Education, health, leisure, technological change, and many other facets of the black workers' experience also warrant additional research. In each industry and region of the country, black workers faced recurring bouts with technological change, health hazards, and inadequate access to training, educational opportunities, and new forms of leisure activities. Yet, these issues are weakly addressed in the new African American labor history, and few studies follow the lead of Ronald Lewis to treat such issues comparatively across regions as well as racial and ethnic lines. Economist Warren Whatley's recent essay on the black strikebreaking phenomenon is a good example of potential comparative scholarship.

Focusing on the incidence of black strikebreaking in American labor history from the Civil War through the 1920s, Whatley offers fresh insights into a little-understood topic in black labor history. Based upon a variety of existing secondary accounts, he carefully examines the extent of strikebreaking, the special role of race, and the impact of general labor market conditions on the phenomenon. According to Whatley, black strikebreaking concentrated in periods of declining European immigration, suggesting that African Americans served as partial replacements for declining sources of immigrant strikebreakers. It would be quite useful to know precisely how this phenomenon unfolded among other racial and ethnic groups. Finally, whereas gender and African American women's labor history is receiving increasing attention, we know little about the construction of male identities and changes therein among African American workers. As historian Earl Lewis suggests in his essay on Charles N. Hunter, who was alternately a schoolteacher and a common laborer, gender as well as racial and class aspects of black workers' lives is indispensable to a fuller understanding of American and African American labor history. Thus, given these remaining gaps in our knowledge, over the next several years we will need to retain our commitment to systematic research on neglected aspects of black workers' lives.

The future growth of black labor history demands more than simply pinpointing substantive gaps in our knowledge. It also requires setting priorities and thinking deeply about appropriate theoretical and methodological issues. While future research will undoubtedly continue to move in a variety of directions, we might place gender studies, the transformation of black rural work culture under industrialism, and comparative research high on our list of priorities. Until we understand much better the ways that gender, like class and race, shaped the lives of black workers, our grasp of black labor history is only partial. Likewise, only by attending to the precise ways that black workers built upon their southern rural work culture in the new industrial environment will we be able to fully comprehend the development of the African American urban community—its institutions, culture, and politics. Finally, without systematic comparative research on black workers in different settings, it will be exceedingly difficult to establish fruitful lines of comparison with white and nonwhite workers in other national and international contexts.

Despite remaining gaps in our knowledge, the new African American labor history offers the intellectual foundation for a new synthesis. Existing evidence suggests that the development of the black working class was an exceedingly complex process, which changed under the impact of commercial as well as industrial capitalism and varied from industry, region to region, and city to city and by sex, age, and a host of other variables. Developing a theoretical framework that will capture the uneven development of the African American working class—over time and across a broad range of variables—is the key to a new synthesis. As suggested above, current studies illuminate numerous overlapping socioeconomic, political, and cultural dimensions of the black workers' experience. Studies of migration, work, interracial unionism, oppositional culture, cross-class alliances, and gender consciousness, all enable us to comprehend the development of the black working class as a dynamic, multifaceted, historical process, but we need a broader and more explicit conceptual framework for integrating the disparate results into a new synthesis.

The notion of working-class formation—proletarianization—seeks to systematically integrate the various facets of black workers' experience. It suggests the transformation of southern rural and semirural blacks into a new national rather than regional urban wage-earning working class, which involved not only the attitudes and behavior of white employers, workers, and the state but also the dynamic self-activity of African Americans themselves. In short, black workers would help to transform themselves into a new urban proletariat—characterized by substantial geographical mobility, intraracial working-class solidarity, multiclass alliances, gender consciousness, and interracial unionism.

As suggested above, the growth of the black proletariat was by no means a uniform process. Proletarianization would mean different things to different groups of black workers depending on the specific backgrounds from which they came and the particular structure of the local economy. Some African Americans made the transition from landowners or skilled craftsmen to common labor in southern industries, following the classical Marxist path of downward mobility of workers from former positions of autonomy rooted in highly valued skills and access to property. However, most African Americans entered the industrial system from backgrounds as landless sharecroppers or farm laborers. They often improved their socioeconomic and political status over prior conditions, making proletarianization, from their perspective, a less-debilitating process than it might have been. They moved temporarily or seasonally—into sawmills, lumber camps, rail centers, coal mines, and even some urban occupations—before making a final break with the farm. In each case, black workers built upon their rural work culture while acquiring new skills in the industrial environment. Employment in steel mills, coal mines, tobacco plants, building and construction, railroading, and shipping firms required the acquisition of new skills and knowledge.

The changes that black workers experienced went beyond skills and material conditions, however. They entailed significant shifts in attitudes, culture, and worldview. The spiritual and communalistic traditions of rural blacks would face new challenges under the impact of the individualistic, impersonal, and bureaucratic ethos of the new industrial order. The confrontation would be more intense in some settings than in others; it would also proceed farther for blacks who moved directly from farm to city than for those who gradually made the transition through a series of jobs in the industrial system. Still, the persistence of racial antagonisms and the need to combat them reinforced the mutualistic ethic.

Although the process of proletarianization varied from place to place and across time, it was nonetheless an experience that black workers shared with other workers in a variety of settings. Therefore, a synthesis of the African

American working class would also acknowledge the persistent link between the experiences of workers across ethnic, racial, and nationality lines. Although tentative and limited by existing scholarship, the synthesis here proposed will deepen our understanding of the African American working class and illuminate the ways that class and race have profoundly shaped the nation's history.

BIBLIOGRAPHY

Anderson, Jervis. *A. Philip Randolph: A Biographical Portrait.* Berkeley: University of California Press, 1986.

Arnesen, Eric. *Waterfront Workers of New Orleans: Race, Class, and Politics, 1863–1923.* New York: Oxford University Press, 1991.

———. "Following the Color Line of Labor: Black Workers and the Labor Movement before 1930." *Radical History Review* 55 (Winter 1993): 54–87.

Berlin, Ira. *Slaves without Masters: The Free Negro in the Antebellum South.* New York: Oxford University Press, 1974.

Berlin, Ira, Thavolia Glymph, Steven F. Miller, Joseph P. Reidy, Leslie S. Rowland, and Julie Saville, eds. *Freedom: A Documentary History of Emancipation, 1861–1867.* Series 1. Vol. 3, *The Wartime Genesis of Free Labor: The Lower South.* New York: Cambridge University Press, 1990.

Berlin, Ira, and Ronald Hoffman, eds. *Slavery and Freedom in the Age of Revolution.* Urbana: University of Illinois Press, 1983.

Berlin, Ira, and Philip D. Morgan, eds. *Cultivation and Culture: Labor and the Shaping of Slave Life in the Americas.* Charlottesville: University Press of Virginia, 1993.

Billias, Athan, and Gerald N. Grob, eds. *American History: Retrospect and Prospect.* New York: Free Press, 1971.

Blassingame, John W. *The Slave Community: Plantation Life in the Antebellum South.* New York: Oxford University Press, 1979.

Boles, John B., and Evelyn Thomas Nolen, eds. *Interpreting Southern History: Historiographical Essays in Honor of Sanford W. Higginbotham.* Baton Rouge: Louisiana State University Press, 1987.

Borchert, James. *Alley Life in Washington: Family, Community, Religion, and Folklife in the City, 1850–1970.* Urbana: University of Illinois Press, 1980.

Bracey, John, and August Meier. "Allies or Adversaries" (based on papers presented at the 1989 Annual Meeting of the Organization of American Historians, St. Louis, Missouri).

Bracey, John H., Jr., August Meier, and Elliot Rudwick, eds. *Black Workers and Organized Labor.* Belmont, CA: Wadsworth Publishing Company, 1971.

Brier, Stephen. "Interracial Organization in the West Virginia Coal Industry: The Participation of Black Mine Workers in the Knights of Labor and the United Mine Workers, 1880–1894." In Gary M. Fink and Merle E. Reed, eds., *Essays in Southern Labor History.* Westport CT: Greenwood Press, 1977, 18–43.

Brody, David. "The Old Labor History and the New: In Search of an American Working Class." *Labor History* 20, no. 4 (Winter 1979): 111–26.

Brooks, Evelyn. "The Feminist Theology of the Black Baptist Church, 1880–1900." In Amy Swerdlow and Hanna Lessinger, eds., *Class, Race, and Sex: The Dynamics of Control.* Boston: G. K. Hall, 1983, 31–59.

Brown, Elsa Barkley. "Womanist Consciousness: Maggie Lena Walker and the Independent Order of St. Luke." *Signs* 14, no. 3 (Spring 1989): 610–33.

———. "Uncle Ned's Children: Richmond, Virginia's Black Community, 1890–1930." Ph.D. dissertation, Kent State University.

Cantor, Milton, ed. *Black Labor in America.* Westport, CT: Negro Universities Press, 1970.

Cayton, Horace R., and George S. Mitchell. *Black Workers and the New Unions.* Chapel Hill: University of North Carolina Press, 1939.

Clark-Lewis, Elizabeth. " 'This Work Had a End': African American Domestic Workers in Washington, D.C., 1910–1940." In Mary Beth Norton and Carol Groneman, eds., *"To Toil the Livelong Day": America's Women at Work, 1780–1980.* Ithaca, NY: Cornell University Press, 1987.

Cohen, William. *At Freedom's Edge: Black Mobility and the Southern White Quest for Racial Control, 1861–1915.* Baton Rouge: Louisiana State University Press, 1991.

Corbin, David A. *Life, Work, and Rebellion in the Coal Fields: The Southern West Virginia Miners, 1880–1922.* Urbana: University of Illinois Press, 1981.

Cox, LaWanda. "From Emancipation to Segregation: National Policy and Southern Blacks." In John B. Boles and Evelyn Thomas Nolen, eds., *Interpreting Southern History: Historiographical Essays in Honor of Sanford Higginbotham.* Baton Rouge: Louisiana State University, 1987, 199–253.

Creel, Margaret Washington. *"A Peculiar People": Slave Religion and Community-Culture among the Gullah.* New York: New York University Press, 1988.

Darity, William, Jr., ed. *Race, Radicalism, and Reform: Selected Papers of Abram L. Harris.* New Brunswick, NJ: Transaction Publisher, 1989.

Davis, David Brion. "Slavery and Post–World War II Historians." *Daedalus* 103 (1974): 7–16.

Dickerson, Dennis. *Out of the Crucible: Black Steelworkers in Western Pennsylvania, 1875–1980.* Albany: State University of New York Press, 1986.

Downey, Dennis B., and Raymond M. Hyser. *No Crooked Death: Coatesville, Pennsylvania, and the Lynching of Zachariah Walker.* Urbana: University of Illinois Press, 1991.

Du Bois, W.E.B., ed. *The Negro Artisan.* Atlanta: Atlanta University Press, Conference Publications no. 7, 1902.

———. *Black Reconstruction in America, 1860–1880.* New York: A Meridian Book, 1935; reprinted, 1964.

Du Bois, W.E.B., and Augustus Dill, eds. *The Negro American Artisan.* Atlanta: Atlanta University, Conference Publications no. 14, 1912.

Dunning, William A. *Essays on the Civil War and Reconstruction*, 1908.

Elkins, Stanley. *Slavery: A Problem in American Institutional Life.* Chicago: University of Chicago Press, 1959.

Faue, Elizabeth. "Gender and the Reconstruction of Labor History: An Introduction." *Labor History* 34, nos. 2–3 (Spring–Summer 1993): 169–78.

Fields, Barbara. *Slavery and Freedom on the Middle Ground: Maryland during the Nineteenth Century.* New Haven, CT: Yale University Press, 1985.

Fink, Gary M., and Merle E. Reed. "In Defense of Gutman: The Union's Case." *International Journal of Politics, Culture, and Society* 2, no. 3 (Spring 1988): 383–95.

———. *Race, Class, and Community in Southern Labor History.* Tuscaloosa: University of Alabama Press, 1994.

Fink, Gary M., and Merle E. Reed, eds. *Essays in Southern Labor History*. Westport, CT: Greenwood Press, 1977.

Fogel, Robert W., and Stanley L. Engerman. *Time on the Cross: The Economics of American Negro Slavery*. Boston: Little, Brown, 1974; New York: W. W. Norton, 1989.

Foner, Eric. *Reconstruction: America's Unfinished Revolution, 1863–1877*. New York: Harper and Row, 1988.

Foner, Philip S. *Organized Labor and the Black Worker, 1619–1973*. New York: Praeger Publishers, 1974.

———. *American Socialism and Black Americans: From the Age of Jackson to World War II*. Westport, CT: Greenwood Press, 1978.

Franklin, John Hope. *Race and History: Selected Essays, 1938–1988*. Baton Rouge: Louisiana State University Press, 1989.

———. "Mirror for Americans: A Century of Reconstruction History" In John Hope Franklin, *Race and History: Selected Essays, 1938–1988*, 1989, 384–98.

Genovese, Eugene. *Roll. Jordan. Roll: The World the Slaves Made*. 1974. New York: Vintage Books, 1976.

Greene, Lorenzo J., and Carter G. Woodson. *The Negro Wage Earner*. 1930. New York: Russell and Russell, 1969.

Goldfield, David. "Race and the CIO: Possibilities for Racial Egalitarianism during the 1930s and 1940s." *International Labor and Working-Class History* 44 (Fall 1993): 1–44.

Gottlieb, Peter. *Making Their Own Way: Southern Blacks Migration to Pittsburgh, 1916–1930*. Urbana: University of Illinois Press, 1987.

Grob, Gerald. "Organized Labor and the Negro Worker, 1865–1900." *Labor History* 1, no. 2 (1960): 164–67.

———. "Reconstruction: An American Morality Play." In George Athan Billias and Gerald N. Grob, eds. *American History: Retrospect and Prospect*. New York: Free Press, 1971, 191–231.

Gross, James A. "Historians and the Literature of the Negro Worker." *Labor History* 10, no. 3 (Summer 1969): 536–46.

Grossman, James. *Land of Hope: Chicago, Black Southerners, and the Great Migration*. Chicago: University of Chicago Press, 1989.

Gutman, Herbert. "The Negro and the United Mine Workers of America: The Career and Letters of Richard L. Davis and Something of Their Meaning, 1890–1900." In Julius Jacobson, ed., *The Negro and the American Labor Movement*. Garden City, NY: Anchor Books/Doubleday and Company, 1968, 49–127.

———. *The Black Family in Slavery and Freedom, 1750–1925*. 1976. New York: Vintage Books, 1977.

———. *Work, Culture, and Society in Industrializing America: Essays in American Working-Class History*. New York: Vintage Books, 1977.

Halpern, Rick. "Interracial Unionism in the Southwest: Fort Worth's Packing-house Workers, 1937–1954." In Robert Zieger, ed., *Organized Labor in the Twentieth-Century South*. Knoxville: University of Tennessee Press, 1991, 158–82.

Harley, Sharon, and Rosalyn Terborg-Penn, eds. *The Afro-American Woman: Struggles and Images*. Port Washington, NY: Kennikat Press, 1978.

Harris, Robert. "Coming of Age: The Transformation of Afro-American Historiography." *Journal of Negro History* 57 (1982): 107–21.

Harris, William H. *The Harder We Run: Black Workers since the Civil War*. New York: Oxford University Press, 1982.

———. *Keeping the Faith: A. Philip Randolph, Milton P. Webster, and the Brotherhood of Sleeping Car Porters, 1925–37*. Urbana: University of Illinois Press, 1977.

Higginbotham, Evelyn Brooks. "African-American Women's History and the Metalanguage of Race." *Signs* 17, no. 2 (1992): 251–74.

———. *Righteous Discontent: The Women's Movement in the Black Baptist Church, 1880–1920*. Cambridge MA: Harvard University Press, 1993.

Higgs, Robert. *Competition and Coercion: Blacks in the American Economy, 1865–1914*. Chicago: University of Chicago Press, 1980.

Hill, Herbert. "Myth-Making as Labor History: Herbert Gutman and the United Mine Workers of America." *International Journal of Politics, Culture and Society* 2, no. 2 (Winter 1988): 132–200.

———. *Black Labor and the American Legal System*. Madison: University of Wisconsin, 1985.

Hill, Robert A., ed. *The Marcus Garvey and Universal Negro Improvement Association Papers*. Vols. 1–3. Berkeley: University of California Press, 1983–84.

———. "Racial and Radical: Cyril J. Briggs, *The Crusader* Magazine, and the African Blood Brotherhood, 1918–1922." *The Crusader, September 1918–August 1919*. New York: Garland Publishing, 1987.

Hine, Darlene Clark, ed. *The State of Afro-American History: Past, Present, and Future*. Baton Rouge: Louisiana State University, 1986.

———. "Black Migration to the Urban Midwest: The Gender Dimension, 1915–1945." In Joe Trotter, ed. *The Great Migration in Historical Perspective: New Dimensions of Race, Class, and Gender*. Bloomington: Indiana University Press, 1991.

———. *Black Women in White: Racial Conflict and Cooperation in the Nursing Profession, 1890–1950*. Bloomington: Indiana University Press, 1989.

Holt, Thomas. *Black over White: Negro Political Leadership in South Carolina during Reconstruction*. Urbana: University of Illinois Press, 1977.

Honey, Michael. *Southern Labor and Black Civil Rights: Organizing Memphis Workers. 1929–1955*. Urbana: University of Illinois Press, 1993.

———. "Industrial Unionism and Racial Justice in Memphis." In Robert Zieger, ed., *Organized Labor in the Twentieth-Century South*. Knoxville: University of Tennessee Press, 1991, 135–57.

Horton, James Oliver, and Lois E. Horton. *Free People of Color: Inside the African American Community*. Washington DC: Smithsonian Institution, 1993.

Huggins, Nathan. "Herbert Gutman and Afro-American History." *Labor History* 29, no. 3 (Summer 1988): 323–35.

Hunter, Tera. "Domination and Resistance: The Politics of Wage Household Labor in New South Atlanta." *Labor History* 34, nos. 2–3 (Spring–Summer 1993): 205–20.

———. *To 'Joy My Freedom: Southern Black Women's Lives and Labors after the Civil War*. Cambridge: Harvard University Press, 1997.

Isserman, Maurice. " 'God Bless Our American Institutions': The Labor History of John R. Commons." *Labor History* 17, no. 3 (Summer 1976): 309–28.

Jacobson, Julius, ed. *The Negro and the American Labor Movement*. Garden City, NY: Anchor Books/Doubleday and Company, 1968.

Janiewski, Dolores. *Sisterhood Denied: Race, Gender, and Class in a New South Community*. Philadelphia: Temple University Press, 1985.

Jaynes, Gerald David. *Branches without Roots: Genesis of the Black Working Class in the American South, 1862–1882*. New York: Oxford University Press, 1986.

Jones, Jacqueline. *Labor of Love, Labor of Sorrow: Black Women, Work and the Family from Slavery to the Present*. New York: Basic Books, 1985.

Jordan, Daniel P. "The Mingo War: Labor Violence in the Southern West Virginia Coal Fields, 1921–1922." In Gary M. Fink and Merle E. Reed, eds. *Essays in Southern Labor History*. Westport, CT: Greenwood Press, 1977.

Joyner, Charles. *Down by the Riverside: A South Carolina Slave Community*. Urbana: University of Illinois Press, 1984.

Kelley, Robin D. G. " 'We Are Not What We Seem': Rethinking Black Working-Class Opposition in the Jim Crow South." *Journal of American History* 80, no. 1 (June 1993): 75–112.

———. *Hammer and Hoe: Alabama Communists during the Great Depression*. Chapel Hill: University of North Carolina Press, 1990.

Kolchin, Peter. *Unfree Labor: American Slavery and Russian Serfdom*. Cambridge: Belknap Press of Harvard University Press, 1987.

———. *After Freedom: The Responses of Alabama's Blacks to Emancipation and Reconstruction*. Westport, CT: Greenwood Press, 1972.

Korstad, Robert, and Nelson Lichtenstein. "Opportunities Found and Lost: Labor, Radicals and the Early Civil Rights Movement." *Journal of American History* 75, no. 3 (December 1988): 786–811.

Kusmer, Kenneth L. *A Ghetto Takes Shape: Black Cleveland, 1870–1930*. Urbana: University of Illinois Press, 1976.

Levine, Lawrence W. *Black Culture and Black Consciousness: Afro-American Folk Thought from Slavery to Freedom*. New York: Oxford University Press, 1977.

Lewis, Earl. *In Their Own Interests: Race, Class, and Power in Twentieth-Century Norfolk, Virginia*. Berkeley: University of California Press, 1991.

———. "Invoking Concepts, Problematizing Identities: The Life of Charles N. Hunter and the Implications for the Study of Gender and Labor." *Labor History* 34, nos. 2–3 (Spring–Summer 1993): 292–308.

Lewis, Ronald L. *Black Coal Miners in America: Race, Class, and Community Conflict, 1780–1980*. Lexington: University Press of Kentucky, 1987.

———. *Coal, Iron, and Slaves: Industrial Slavery in Maryland and Virginia*. Westport, CT: Greenwood Press, 1979.

Littlefield, Daniel. *Rice and Slaves: Ethnicity and the Slave Trade in Colonial South Carolina*. Urbana: University of Illinois Press, 1981.

Litwack, Leon. *North of Slavery: The Negro in the Free States, 1790–1860*. Chicago: University of Chicago Press, 1961.

———. *Been in the Storm So Long*. New York: Vintage Books, 1979.

Mandle, Jay R. *Not Slave, Not Free: The African American Economic Experience since the Civil War*. Durham, NC: Duke University Press 1992.

Marshall, Ray. *The Negro and Organized Labor*. New York: John Wiley and Sons, 1965.

Martin, Tony. *Race First: The Ideological and Organizational Struggles of Marcus Gar-*

vey and the Universal Negro Improvement Association. Westport, CT: Greenwood Press, 1976.

Meier, August, and Elliot Rudwick. *Black Detroit and the Rise of the UAW.* New York: Oxford University Press, 1979.

———. *Black History and the Historical Profession, 1915–1980.* Urbana: University of Illinois Press, 1986.

Montgomery, David. "To Study the People: The American Working Class." *Labor History* 21, no. 4 (Fall 1980): 485–512.

———. "Gutman's Agenda for Future Historical Research." *Labor History* 29, no. 3 (Summer 1988): 299–312.

Morgan, Edmund. *American Slavery, American Freedom: The Ordeal of Colonial Virginia.* New York: W. W. Norton, 1975.

Naison, Mark. *Communists in Harlem during the Great Depression.* Urbana: University of Illinois Press, 1983.

Nash, Gary B. *Forging Freedom: The Formation of Philadelphia's Black Community, 1720–1840.* Cambridge: Harvard University Press, 1988.

Nelson, Bruce. "Organized Labor and the Struggle for Black Equality in Mobile during World War II." *Journal of American History* 80, no. 3 (December 1993): 952–88.

Neverdon-Morton, Cynthia. *Afro-American Women of the South and the Advancement of the Race, 1895–1925.* Knoxville: University of Tennessee Press, 1989.

Norrell, Robert J. "Caste in Steel: Jim Crow Careers in Birmingham, Alabama." *Journal of American History* 73, no. 3 (December 1986): 669–94.

Northrup, Herbert Roof. *Organized Labor and the Negro.* 2d ed. New York: Harper & Brothers, 1944.

Norton, Mary Beth, and Carol Groneman, eds. *To Toil the Livelong Day: America's Women at Work, 1780–1980.* Ithaca, NY: Cornell University Press, 1987.

Osofsky, Gilbert. *Harlem: The Making of a Ghetto: Negro New York, 1890–1930.* Harper Torchbooks Edition. New York: Harper & Row, 1968.

Ozanne, Robert. "Trends in American Labor History." *Labor History* 21, no. 4 (Fall 1980): 513–22.

Painter, Nell Irvin. *The Narrative of Hosea Hudson: His Life as a Negro Communist in the South.* Cambridge, MA: Harvard University Press, 1979.

———. *The Exodusters: Black Migration to Kansas after Reconstruction.* 1976, Lawrence: University Press of Kansas, 1986.

———. "Remembering Herbert Gutman." *Labor History* 29, no. 3 (Summer 1988): 336–43.

Pfeffer, Paula F. *A. Philip Randolph, Pioneer of the Civil Rights Movement.* Baton Rouge: Louisiana State University Press, 1990.

Phillips, U. B. *American Negro Slavery: A Survey of the Supply, Employment and Control of Negro Labor as Determined by the Plantation Regime.* New York: D. Appleton, 1918.

Piersen, William D. *Black Yankees: The Development of an Afro-American Subculture in Eighteenth Century New England.* Amherst: University of Massachusetts Press, 1988.

Rabateau, Albert J. *Slave Religion: The "Invisible Institution" in the Antebellum South.* New York: Oxford University Press, 1978.

Rachleff, Peter J. *Black Labor in the South: Richmond, Virginia, 1865–1890.* Philadelphia: Temple University Press, 1984.

Rainwater, Lee. *Behind Ghetto Walls: Black Families in a Federal Slum*. Chicago: Aldine Publishing Company, 1970.

Ranson, Roger L., and Richard Sutch. *One Kind of Freedom: The Economic Consequences of Emancipation*. Cambridge: Cambridge University Press, 1977.

Reid, Ira De Augustine. *Negro Membership in American Labor Unions*. New York: National Urban League, Department of Research and Investigations, 1930.

Robinson, Armstead L. "The Difference Freedom Made: The Emancipation of Afro-Americans." In Darlene Clark Hine, ed. *The State of Afro-American History: Past, Present, Future*. Baton Rouge: Louisiana State University Press, 1986, 51–74.

Robinson, Cedric. *Black Marxism: The Making of the Black Radical Tradition*. London: Zed Press, 1983.

Rosengarten, Theodore. *All God's Dangers: The Life of Nate Shaw*. New York: Knopf, 1974.

Saville, Julie. *The Work of Reconstruction: From Slave to Wage Labor in South Carolina, 1860–1870*. New York: Cambridge University Press, 1994.

Schechter, Patricia A. "Free and Slave Labor in the Old South: The Tredegar Ironworkers' Strike of 1847." *Labor History* 35, no. 2 (Spring 1994): 165–86.

Schnittman, Suzanne. "Black Workers in Antebellum Richmond." In Gary M. Fink and Merl E. Reed, eds., *Race, Class, and Community in Southern Labor History*. Tuscaloosa: University of Alabama Press, 1994.

Senechal, Roberta. *The Sociogenesis of a Race Riot: Springfield, Illinois, in 1908*. Urbana: University of Illinois Press, 1990.

Shaw, Stephanie. *"What a Woman Ought to Be and to Do": Black Professional Women during the Jim Crow Era*. Chicago: University of Chicago Press, 1996.

Spear, Allan H. *Black Chicago: The Making of a Negro Ghetto, 1890–1920*. Chicago: University of Chicago Press, 1967.

Spero, Sterling D., and Abram L. Harris. *The Black Worker: The Negro and the Labor Movement*. 1931. New York: Atheneum, 1968.

Stampp, Kenneth M. *The Peculiar Institution: Slavery in the Ante-bellum South*. New York: Vintage Books, 1956.

Starobin, Robert. *Industrial Slavery in the Old South*. New York: Oxford University Press, 1970.

Stein, Judith. "Southern Workers in National Unions: Birmingham Steelworkers, 1936–1951." In Robert Zieger, ed., *Organized Labor in the Twentieth Century South*. Knoxville: University of Tennessee Press, 1991.

———. *The World of Marcus Garvey: Race and Class in Modern Society*. Baton Rouge: Louisiana State University Press, 1986.

Stuckey, Sterling. *Slave Culture: Nationalist Theory and the Foundation of Black America*. New York: Oxford University Press, 1987.

Surface, George T. "The Negro Mine Laborer: Central Appalachian Coal Field." *Annals of the American Academy of Political and Social Sciences* 33 (1909): 114–28.

Swerdlow, Amy, and Hanna Lessinger, eds. *Class, Race, and Sex: The Dynamics of Control*. Boston: G. K. Hall, 1983.

Thomas, Richard Walter. "From Peasant to Proletarian: The Foundation and Organization of the Black Industrial Working Class in Detroit, 1915–1945." Ph.D. dissertation, University of Michigan, 1976.

Trotter, Joe William. *Coal, Class, and Color: Blacks in Southern West Virginia, 1915–1932*. Urbana: University of Illinois Press, 1990.

———. *Black Milwaukee: The Making of an Industrial Proletariat, 1915–1945*. Urbana: University of Illinois Press, 1985.

———. "African Americans in the City: The Industrial Era, 1900–1950." *Journal Urban History* 21, no. 4 (May 1995): 438–57.

———, ed. *The Great Migration in Historical Perspective: New Dimensions of Race, Class, and Gender*. Bloomington: Indiana University Press, 1991.

Tuttle, William M., Jr. "Labor Conflict and Racial Violence: The Black Worker in Chicago, 1894–1919." *Labor History* 10, no. 3 (Summer 1969): 375–407.

———. *Race Riot: Chicago in the Red Summer of 1919*. 1970, New York: Atheneum, 1984.

University of Pennsylvania's Wharton School of Finance. *The Racial Attitudes of American Industry*, Vols. 1–30. Philadelphia: University of Pennsylvania, 1968–1972.

Wade, Richard. *Slavery in the Cities: The South, 1820–1860*. New York: Oxford University Press, 1964.

Walker, Clarence. *Deromanticizing Black History*. Knoxville: University of Tennessee Press, 1992.

Weaver, Robert C. *Negro Labor: A National Problem*. New York: Harcourt, Brace, and World, 1946.

Wesley, Charles H. *Negro Labor in the United States, 1850–1925: A Study in American Economic History*. 1927. New York: Russell and Russell, 1967.

Whatley, Warren. "Black Strikebreaking and the American Labor Movement." *Social Science History* 17 (1993): 528–58.

White, Deborah Gray. *Ar'n't I a Woman?: Female Slaves in the Plantation South*. New York: W. W. Norton, 1985.

White, Shane. *Somewhat More Independent: The End of Slavery in New York City, 1770–1810*. Athens, GA: University of Georgia Press, 1991.

Whitman, T. Stephen. "Industrial Slavery at the Margin: The Maryland Chemical Works." *Journal of Southern History* 59, no. 1. (February 1993): 31–62.

Wilson, Francille R. "The Segregated Scholars: Black Labor Historians, 1895–1950." Ph.D. dissertation, University of Pennsylvania, 1988.

Wood, Peter. *Black Majority: Negroes in Colonial South Carolina from 1670 through the Stono Rebellion*. New York: W. W. Norton, 1974.

Woodman, Harold D. "Economic Reconstruction and the Rise of the New South, 1865–1900." In John Boles and Evelyn Thomas Nolen, eds., *Interpreting Southern History: Historiographical Essays in Honor of Sanford W. Higginbotham*. Baton Rouge: Louisiana State University Press, 1987, 254–307.

Worthman, Paul B. "Black Workers and Labor Unions in Alabama, 1897–1904." *Labor History* 10, no. 3 (Summer 1969): 375–407.

Zieger, Robert, ed. *Organized Labor in the Twentieth Century South*. Knoxville: University of Tennessee Press, 1991.

III

African American Families: Historically Resilient

Aaron Thompson

Throughout history there is ample support for the premise that myths and stereotypes have fostered an overwhelming misunderstanding of the African American family (L. Bennett, 1992; Genovese, 1994; Staples & Mirande, 1989). The black family has become synonymous with instability, disorganization, and deviancy (Zinn & Eitzen, 1990). This is usually attributed to a family structure that purportedly lacks positive male roles that are incidental to and required for the patriarchal system mandated by traditional, white-held views of the family. Modern images of the black family portray these families as lacking black male presence in the home. Moreover, black men are portrayed as deviant, dangerous, and dysfunctional, and black women are categorized as welfare mothers eager to have another child (Gibbs, 1988). This constant barrage of disturbing images inevitably contributes to the public's negative stereotypes of black men, black women, and the black family in general. Some sociologists and family scientists have long tried to explain why the black family is deficient. Others have concluded that the black family has endured tremendous negative societal deterrents and survived, and thus is a resilient family.

Theories postulating the comparative differences between black and white families have all too often asserted a need to "fix" the "deficits" associated with black families to bring them up to the "normalcy" of white families. However, counterarguments conclude that the only way to understand black families is to study them within their individual contexts. This chapter will examine ways African American families have been studied in the past and focus on the more predominate deficit models and strength models that have been used by social scientists. In addition, this chapter will outline specific historical periods and show the resilience of the black family throughout its experiences in America.

THEORETICAL PERSPECTIVES COMMONLY USED TO STUDY BLACK FAMILIES

Historically, many different theoretical perspectives have been used to explain the African American experience. Many of these have focused on the black family and the roles black men play as husbands and/or fathers and on the role black women play as wives and/or mothers in the family unit. It is disconcerting to notice that many of these approaches have focused solely on the structure of the black family and have concluded that the family structure itself fosters a pathological deficit when compared to other family types (e.g., the white nuclear family).

Pathological and dysfunctional views of black families are primarily related to a culturally ethnocentric approach and are most often associated with the work of E. Franklin Frazier (1939) and Daniel P. Moynihan (1965). The contemporary study that best characterizes the deficit perspective is Moynihan's 1965 report "The Negro Family: A Case for National Action" (see Rainwater & Yancey, 1967). This study depicted low-income black families as "a tangle of pathology" because of disproportionately high rates of single-parent families, poverty, unemployment, welfare dependency, and crime. Although some external forces such as racism and economic conditions were acknowledged to have contributed to these "pathologies," the Moynihan report deemphasized their significance and concluded that the internal "matriarchal" structure of black families was "at the center of the tangle of pathology and was mainly responsible for the problems in the Black community" (Staples, 1991).

The "culturally deviant" and the "culturally equivalent" models have been used most when examining the black family. The "culturally deviant" approach holds that black families are different from white families in very negative and potentially destructive ways. The "culturally equivalent" approach assumes that black families are essentially the same as white families with only the effects of social class accounting for any apparent differences (Allen, 1978). Both methods operate on the assumption that America is culturally homogeneous and that there are universal norms for American cultural behavior to which all groups should and must conform. Since African Americans seem not to fit the norms, presumed inadequacies in black people are cited to account for the differences. Similarly, both models place a negative value judgment on black families' deviation from the American norms, and both have as their basis an assumption that the black family is unstable, disorganized, and unable to provide its members with the social and psychological support and development needed to fully assimilate into society (Rubin, 1978). The deficit model is an ideological perspective that attributes the social ills afflicting minority and low-income groups to internal rather than external factors. It is popularly known as "blaming the victim" (Billingsley, 1968).

There are many obvious arguments against using these models when studying black families. Researchers have noted some of these problematic issues that result when these models are used. Rubin's (1978) review of black families studies found the matriarchal theme to be pervasive; more specifically, he revealed that sweeping generalizations were often made about dysfunctional male-female relations based upon very small samples of unrepresentative disadvantaged black individuals or families.

In the appendix to *Black Families in White America*, Billingsley (1968) provides an in-depth critique of the conventional treatment of black families in American social science. In such areas as welfare, Billingsley found that black families were usually examined in a superficial manner.

In summary, deficit models and other conventional models that accept the assumptions of the deficit approach reflect a superficial treatment of black families. In the best-case scenario, many of these conventional models foster research that says black families are not an important unit of focus and thus should be omitted entirely or treated peripherally. In the worst-case scenario, black families are depicted as a unit full of problems caused by internal deficiencies.

COUNTERARGUMENTS TO DEFICIT MODELS

Several models have been developed recently to counterbalance and replace the deficit model for studying black families. These models include the cultural variant model, the cultural relativity model, and comprehensive frameworks (holistic and ecological models), with the latter increasingly used in research regarding the black family.

The "culturally variant" approach assumes that black family life is culturally distinctive as a result of its particular historical and sociocultural context, but it does not consider those distinctions to be necessarily pathological (Allen, 1978).

The "cultural relativity school" begins with the assumption that America is multicultural and concludes that differences are largely accounted for by the variation in cultural backgrounds and experiences of blacks and whites (Hill et al., 1993). Black American culture and family patterns possess a degree of cultural integrity that is neither related to nor modeled on white American norms. Most members of this school trace the origins of these cultural differences back to black Americans' African cultural heritage, and all tend to focus on the "strengths" of black families rather than on their weaknesses. The cultural relativistic view maintains that the black family is a functional entity. This conceptualization is designed to challenge the traditional theories and social policies emanating from the ethnocentric approach.

W.E.B. Du Bois (1898) contended that a proper understanding of blacks in America could not be achieved without systematically assessing the influence of historical, cultural, social, economic, and political forces. Although this was an important and insightful recommendation by a cutting-edge sociologist, many of his recommendations to incorporate a holistic framework in the analysis of black individuals and families have still not been heeded by mainstream social scientists (Hill et al., 1993). In a holistic approach, all factors (external and internal) that affect family functioning are considered in the research process. This approach contends that the social functioning of black families can be better understood if the black family were not looked upon as monolithic, placing priority on balancing the analysis on the basis of the diversity, strengths, and weaknesses of the black family.

Billingsley (1968) developed a conceptual paradigm that characterized black families as a social subsystem mutually interacting with other subsystems in the black community and in the wider (white) society. Black families were depicted as a circle embedded within concentric circles of the two larger systems. According to the systems framework, an adequate understanding of black families requires assessing the separate and combined effects on family functioning of

1. external subsystems in the wider society (i.e., societal forces and institutional policies),

2. external subsystems in the black community (i.e., schools, churches, peers), and

3. internal subsystems in the family (i.e., husband-wife, parent-child [Hill et al., 1993]).

The family ecology approach focuses on human and environmental linkages and attempts to define interrelationships between organisms that exist in a particular environment (Bronfenbrenner, 1979). Family ecology theory assumes that families, regardless of their structure, race, ethnicity, life stage, or social class, take in elements of the environment and gain energy from that environment. Thus they have been able to adapt to adverse conditions in order to survive and grow (Ingoldsby & Smith, 1995:14).

This framework lends itself well to studying black families because it accepts diverse family structures and differing definitions of families; it allows a reciprocal study of the process of how the individual and family relate with the external environment; and it recognizes that the diversity of a particular family may impede or enhance family development and interaction (Ingoldsby & Smith, 1995).

Comprehensive theoretical frameworks, such as the holistic and social ecology approaches, which have been used to counteract the deficit models, have begun to improve the quality of research on black families and have facilitated the development of more relevant, sensitive, and effective public policies and programs for ameliorating the social and economic problems of many black families. Unfortunately, only a small number of social scientists have systematically used these frameworks in their studies (Hill et al., 1993).

HISTORICAL OVERVIEW OF BLACK FAMILIES IN AMERICA

Although it is commonly believed that black in America have lost their African heritage, some theorists believe that African values have been retained and appear or will appear throughout the evolution of the black family in America (Bowen, 1988). Among the West African values that may have influenced African American family development are (1) the precedence of blood ties over all other types of relationships; (2) the extended family's precedence over the nuclear family; (3) the viewing of children as the responsibility of parents and extended family; (4) respect and reverence for family elders; (5) mutual aid among family members; (6) the precedence of family needs over individual needs; (7) cooperation among all family or community members, with the sharing of responsibility for the well-being of others; and (8) the practice of polygamous marriages (paraphrased from Logan, 1996:10).

To what degree West African culture may help explain how black American families work remains unclear. Nevertheless that culture can help us to understand black ethnicity and provide a culturally based stimulus for using that knowledge to strengthen black families. Although black indentured servitude and slavery disrupted black families in America, those institutions did not destroy or devalue the family in the eyes of Africans in this country.

According to Zinn and Eitzen (1990:70), the "stereotype of the Black Family as a deficient form is based on the assumption that slavery destroyed cultural and family life among Blacks, leaving only mothers and children in the home." But there is nothing farther from the truth. As Genovese (1994) notes, family was so important to the slave that one of the dominant motives for slave flight was to find family members. Nash, Jeffrey, Howe, Frederick, Davis, and Winkler (1990) contend that the "most traumatic problem for slaves was the separation of families, a haunting fear rarely absent from slave consciousness." According to the law, slaves could not legally marry but they did certainly pair off (complete with rituals like jumping the broom) and raise children. Owners learned quickly that slaves committed to family relationships were less likely to run away (Genovese, 1974). Though slave families were broken up, many owners would sell unattached slaves first because they were the least stable within the system. Efforts were sometimes made to sell family members to nearby plantations, which were coupled with liberal visitation rights (Boles, 1983). When families were broken up, it was more common to sell children away from their parents than to break up marriages; even then, the greatest attack on the slave family came not from one owner's preference but from the breakup of estates upon an owner's death (Fogel & Engerman, 1974; Genovese, 1974). Derogatory white attitudes toward slaves, which viewed their sale and separation no differently than the sale and separation of beasts in the field, also put considerable stress upon black families (Pinkney, 1993).

Slavery obviously had a great impact upon the black family and its ultimate relationship to society at large, but there are a few facts that need to be established. First, kinship was an important factor in the creation and retention of family integrity among blacks during slavery (Scott & Black, 1994; Zinn & Eitzen, 1990). Citing research conducted by Gutman (1976), Zinn and Eitzen conclude that even though families may have been broken up in their initial transport to America, slaves would ultimately forge kinship ties to other slaves, in blood and fictive kin—unrelated slaves who were honorary family members with all the responsibility that entailed (Boles, 1983) relationships (Scott & Black, 1994). These relationships no doubt enabled slaves to maintain some semblance of the relationships they had while still in Africa.

Another important reality that deserves analysis is that contrary to popular belief, African captives were generally the products "of highly advanced civilizations" (Pinkney, 1993:5). As such, they brought to America a great deal of culture and values. Embedded in the psyche of transplanted Africans was the desire to maintain some of the characteristics that afforded them comfort and stability in their old world. It is therefore not surprising that "language, folk tales, music, social organization, and aesthetic endeavors" survived the captive experience (Pinkney, 1993:6). But other institutions such as the family did not always survive. Obviously, captivity physically separated many families, but this did not dampen the slaves' desires to rekindle familial relationships and ties. Thus the notion of kinship became essential in replacing those familial connections that were so important and vital in Africa.

Even during bondage, slave families showed tremendous resilience. Men and women found ways to maintain some semblance of family life, often with separate quarters on both large and small farms. Perhaps the most interesting aspect of the slave family was the elastic nature of roles necessary to accomplish basic family work. Care of small children, for example, could not be permanently assigned only to parents, as they had no control over their time. Instead, slave family childcare often fell to older children, other relatives, and fictive kin. The roles of the extended family and fictive kin described above have African roots (McDaniel, 1990). Names given to slave children often reflected African naming traditions, particularly with "day names," which were linked to the day the baby was born (Thornton, 1993). The fact that African cultural elements survived slavery at all is a testament to the strength of that culture.

It cannot be argued that slavery destroyed the morals of blacks in this country, or the value that African Americans place on family, but it can be argued that slavery left a legacy that is evident in the lasting attitudes of whites toward blacks. The decision of a country to create slavery on the basis of race created the plethora of myths that would, though grounded initially in economic gain, become the mainstay of racism in this country. Moreover, slavery's greatest impact would be upon the roles black men and women would play after emancipation. Regardless of the misconceptions and myths, the black family would emerge from slavery as a resilient institution.

After slavery, African Americans were forced to count on their blood families and strong kinship networks to combat a society not used to having blacks as free citizens. It was a period when blacks had their first real opportunity, as a racial group in America, to be accepted as American citizens—as humans and not property. However, America's new black citizens were seen as subcitizens and inferior humans when compared to whites. Many argued that this subhumanness was genetic (Logan, 1996), and such assertions remained a vivid part of American life until around 1930, when the revisionist period started. After spurious claims of genetic inferiority were mostly dismissed, sociologists like Frazier (1939) said it was environment that kept blacks at a lower-stratified level when compared to whites. Both theories seemed to argue that black family life was dysfunctional. Frazier (1939) went a step farther in explaining that poor black families were pathologically dysfunctional as a result of the destruction of positive African heritage by slavery. Many researchers after Frazier (e.g., Hill, 1972) started to refute such claims with historical facts of black family life after slavery.

According to Eshleman (1988:185), immediately after emancipation, "the great majority of Black families were couple-headed. Ex-slaves were more likely to reside in couple-headed households and when property holding among ethnic groups was held constant, variations in family composition largely disappeared." This is supported by Zinn and Eitzen (1990), who suggests that large numbers of ex-slaves legalized their marriages at great expense after being set free. This pattern of husband-wife-children persisted well into the 1950s (Scott & Black, 1994).

The end of slavery prompted many blacks to locate relatives sold away as slaves. To assist this process, many black newspapers appeared filled with ads such as the following from the Nashville *Colored Tennessean*:

During the year 1849, Thomas Sample carried away from this city, as his slaves, our daughter, Polly, and son. . . . We will give $100 each for them to any person who will assist them . . . to get to Nashville, or get word to us of their whereabouts. (quoted in Foner, 1988:84)

Former slaves also wanted to live as other Americans lived. They wanted to have a political voice, education for their children, and land of their own. If men had to become wage laborers, they wanted their wives (now legal) to remain at home, as was proper for all nineteenth-century married women. Women were interested in changing their rough, crude slave clothing for the more feminine fashions of the day (which, not surprisingly, brought ridicule from white women). In short, African Americans wanted to live just like European Americans. Land ownership was not to be for most African Americans. By 1880, only 20 percent of African American farmers in the South worked their own land, and when they did own land, their farms tended to be considerably smaller than those owned by white farmers (Boles, 1983). Meanwhile, planters experimented with alternative labor solutions. One Georgia planter brought 100

German immigrants to the South in 1866, with disastrous consequences. Another Mississippi planter enticed some Italian immigrants into farm work in 1885. However, these planters' solution to solve labor shortages never worked (Roark, 1977). If southern farm work was going to be done, African Americans would have to be the ones who did it. A compromise between planter needs and African American dreams came in the form of sharecropping (Royce, 1993). In this system, a contract would be created between a landless laborer and a landowner; the laborer would farm the land and then share the crop at harvest. Typically, if the landowner supplied seed, farm animals, and other materials, the laborer would receive one-third of the sale; if the laborer supplied materials, the split would be equal (Foner, 1988; Roark, 1977). The drawback for the laborer was that he took all the risks. If the landowner supplied materials, this was sometimes done on credit, adding even more risk for the sharecropper, with interest rates occasionally reaching as high as 60 percent (Boles, 1983). This system, within a few decades, practically re-created slavery in the South.

Many former slaves headed to northern cities following the Civil War, often aided by the Freedmen's Bureau. The majority of those who moved were mulattos from the Upper South, many of whom had gained freedom prior to the war. The migration of African Americans certainly did not solve all their problems, however. There was some degree of tension between northern African Americans and the new immigrants, who typically lived in separate neighborhoods and married within their own groups in the nineteenth century. African Americans native to New York went even farther, in 1884 starting a fraternal organization called the Sons of New York, which was not open to southern African American immigrants. They apparently wanted no one to mistake them for the newcomers (Pleck, 1979).

The end of the Civil War clearly brought some civil rights to northern African Americans. Still, the North continued to be home to only 10 percent of the African American population. The occupational opportunities there remained limited. In addition, many newly freed African Americans in the South either feared the cultural change involved in such a move or, more likely, simply could not afford it. In any case, 1880 found the North with a relatively small number of African Americans. That circumstance continued until the early twentieth century when the labor needs of World War I changed northern cities forever.

After slavery, whites created formal and informal laws for the domination of black labor, a labor they once owned. These "Jim Crow" laws were enacted during Reconstruction, and they, as much as anything else, fostered an ideology of blacks as subordinate and whites as superordinate. As Jim Crow laws came into effect, political and economic advantage gained after the Civil War were soon lost. Black men had effectively been placed out of work "not so much by their lack of skills as by fierce racial discrimination" (Genovese, 1994:20). Their only choices were to be sharecroppers or to take other very demeaning jobs. This had a great impact on how the black family would evolve after emancipation. Eshleman (1988:186) describes three patterns of family life that emerged:

First, the majority of Blacks remained on the plantation as tenants of their former owners with little or no wages for their labor. Second, families that had been allowed to establish common residence worked common plots of ground for extra food for the family. Families where the man was an artisan, preacher, or house servant made the transition with the least difficulty. Third, and perhaps most disruptive for family life, in situations where only loose and informal ties held a man and woman together, those ties were severed during the crisis of emancipation. . . . In search of work, many men joined bands of other homeless men who wandered around the countryside.

This forced some females to become the major productive and dependable family element; coupled with the contrasting treatment of female and males slaves, this gave rise to legends of matriarchy (Zinn & Eitzen, 1990:78).

Thus the need for the black man to seek work away from the home when necessary created an image of a "manless" house. Black women were perceived as strong, domineering figures who, for the most part, ran the household. Although it may be true that many black women had to assume such postures in order to survive, it is clear that the black male was generally a very significant figure in the family. Zinn and Eitzen (1990) asserts that children in black families generally had strong male figures, whether blood or fictive in their kinship. These blood and fictive relationships have been a significant part of black family life in the twentieth century. As a result of the economic downturn that affected all families in the 1930s, many black families who were more adversely affected by their already low economic status came together to combat poverty. Much of the matrifocal and fictive communal ties that bound African Americans together throughout these periods was the result of living below poverty lines, and not pathological living (Logan, 1996).

The African American family of the twentieth century started to diversify more than in any other period in American history and continues to do so into the twenty-first century. However across all the diversity, kinship relationships (fictive and blood) continue to be important to survival of black families. Eshleman (1988) concludes that black families are basically more similar to the dominant family forms that exist in the larger society than dissimilar. For blacks and whites, social status is positively related to marital stability, children receive their basic identity and status subscription within the family context, and parents ascribe to the basic achievement and mobility values that exist within the larger society. There are, however, problems. For example, it appears that the incidence of mother-only households among black families has nearly doubled over the past twenty years. Married-couple families have decreased by eighteen percent over the same period. But similar trends are also apparent in white families, albeit to a lesser degree. Although these trends may be alarming, they may be more indicative of the changing status of families than of a dissolution of families. The fact is, patterns of family life are changing. More styles and alternatives to traditional families are now accepted in this country. Often, though, what is deemed acceptable and appropriate for white families is seen as failure in black families. Furthermore, as Pinkney (1993:83) argues, "the organization and behavior patterns of the Black family in the United States result mainly from economic and social conditions that Blacks have encountered." Although some social issues have been addressed, there must be further discussion of the economic status of blacks.

The African American family has changed considerably over the years. Single-parent families have increased because of out-of-wedlock births, death, and divorce (see Lawson & Thompson, 1995). However, black married couples have increased from 3.3 million in 1970 to 3.8 million by 1990 (Massaqui, 1993), although many of these married couples have opted to remain childless (Logan, 1996). The largest group of stable black families are the nonpoor working class (Billingsley, 1992). Turning to children, 35.6 percent live with both parents, 54 percent live with mother only, 3 percent live with father only, and 7.3 percent live with neither parent (usually grandparents) (C. Bennett, 1995).

THE FUTURE OF BLACK FAMILIES

Research suggests that black men may see marriage as a constraint (Anderson, 1989). It has also been argued that mainstream society places a roadblock in the marriage paths of many young blacks (Aborampah, 1989). Research has shown that although the prestige of either partner has no significant influence on marital happiness among black Americans, society teaches that if the husband is not equal or superior to his wife in prestige and/or income, then the marriage will fail (Creighton-Zollar & Williams, 1992). Young black men may tend to move away from marriage in part because of the expectation that their future partner may earn more money and have a more prestigious social position than they. Cazenave (1983:13) calls this situation the "double bind," whereby society tells the young black man that he should expect to take on the traditional prescripts of a man, yet denies him the resources and channels to do so.

Other reasons why young African American men might move away from marriage have been postulated. Anderson (1989) found that young black men expected to lose membership in their peer groups if they were married. These peer groups function as de facto family for many African American young men. They exist to provide, teach, protect, and love. In addition to peer group loss would be a loss of personal freedom (control) in marriage as a result of the perceived strength of the black woman. But when dating occurs with young black couples, each partner demonstrates a strong romantic commitment (similar to that shown by whites), a commitment that goes against societal expectations for black men (Davis & Strube, 1993).

Many African Americans are struggling to balance societal expectations with what they are experiencing as reality. In the United States, there is the expectation that all people of marriageable age will marry an opposite sex partner and remain married until death. This expectation seldom becomes reality for whites and is even less often achieved by blacks (South, 1993). Although marital expectations vary between sexes in the white population, it is speculated that these varying expectations may be even greater in the black population (Lyson, 1986).

Studies have suggested that there are gender differences in expectations of marriage that are unique to the African American population. Much of this uniqueness is grounded in economic inequality, racism, discrimination, sex-ratio imbalance (mainly a result of infant mortality, homicide, incarceration, drug addiction, and AIDS), unemployment, and other structural constraints (Davis & Strube, 1993). For example, Dickson (1993) reports that because of black men's high rate of incarceration, black women are less likely to view them as potential mates. Incarceration, along with homicide, has created an imbalance in the ratio of black females to black males. This imbalance, along with other social constraints, has significantly reduced the percentage of black men perceived to be suitable romantic candidates (Davis & Strube, 1993). Other literature also backs this postulation. Jackson (1978) noted that since 1850 there has been a continuous decline in the number of black males available for marriage. This is true for the traditional marriageable age group, and especially true for the college-educated black female population (Aborampah, 1989; Staples, 1981). This imbalance leads black women to believe that they may have to accept black male partners who have character flaws (Staples, 1981).

In addition to the sex-ratio imbalance, it has been hypothesized that the differential attitudes of black men and women toward family formation are attributable to the limited structural opportunities (e.g., economic and educational opportunities) for black men. Black men's socioeconomic status has a positive effect on marriage prevalence (Fossett & Kiecolt, 1993). As employment and income increase, so does the likelihood of marriage. The increasing rate of joblessness and the declining incomes of young black men directly relate to trends of never marrying, low rates of marriage, and delay in marriage for blacks (Chadiha, 1992). Having enough money to support the wife and family is a measure of a husband-father's worth (Secord & Ghee, 1986), and it gives black males a feeling of fulfilling the "good provider role" (Taylor et al. 1988; Tucker & Taylor, 1987). However, black men have a harder time seeing themselves in the traditional husband-provider and father-provider roles because of racism and discrimination in the paid labor market (Anderson, 1989; South, 1993; Thompson & Lawson, 1994). In turn, black women may see black men as unable to fulfill this traditional role.

The median income for blacks as a whole has lagged behind that of whites and the gap is showing signs of widening, because blacks continue to be unemployed more often than whites (Aborampah, 1989). In 1980, the typical black male worker earned 73 percent of what his white male counterpart earned (Chadiha, 1992). In 1992 the median income for black men was still at 73 percent of that of white men, and black women's median wage was 64 percent to that of white men (U.S. Census Bureau, 1994). Other research also has suggested that black women are socialized to be self-sufficient, independent, hardworking, and resourceful whereas white women are socialized to be emotionally dependent on white males. The former characteristics seem especially true for college-educated black women. As black women increase in education, their pool of suitable black men decreases (Karenga, 1982). Because of this phenomenon, there is a greater chance these black women will focus their attention on materialistic acquirement, develop a self-centered philosophy, and remain single (Aborampah, 1989; Karenga, 1982; Staples, 1981). Binion (1990) in a comparative study of black and white females in their mid-twenties, found that black women reported themselves to be more androgynous and white women reported themselves to be more undifferentiated. Overall, the white and black women who categorized themselves as androgynous or feminine had a more traditional view of women's role in marriage, and women who reported being undifferentiated or masculine had a more liberal view of a wife's role (Binion, 1990). It has been argued that black men and women claim to be more traditional in their gender role views and that sex determines gender role attitudes and beliefs more than race (Binion, 1990). In addition to racial differences in gender roles, there are differences in marital and relationship expectations for black men and black women, when compared to their white counterparts.

Lyson (1986) found that blacks are more likely than whites to feel that a woman's real success comes from motherhood and, at the same time, that women with schoolage children should participate in the paid labor force. It has been found that employed black women have high levels of satisfaction with their family life if they are married and/or parents (Broman, 1991), and that black women do not expect to be stay-at-home wives and to have their husbands support them (Staples, 1994; Staples, 1976). African heritage and American culture have dictated that there be more of an egalitarian partnership in the black family (Beckett & Smith, 1981; Genovese, 1974). Gender identity socialization has also been suggested as being different between blacks and whites (Cazenave, 1983; Lewis, 1975). Other researchers have suggested that there may be less adherence to gender identity and gender role segregation within the black community (Boye-Beaman, Leonard, & Senchak, 1993; Lewis, 1975; Staples, 1978). For example, black women are less likely than white women to perform household work exclusively (Broman, 1991; Farkas, 1976).

It is part of the African American culture to view the black woman as having a strong and independent lifestyle regardless of class, although expectations of their future partners differ based on class (Staples, 1976). In the lower class, black women want their mates to be employed, to treat them with respect, and to be coproviders for the children. Middle-class black women expect financial stability, emotional and sexual satisfaction, and participation by their mates in childrearing (Staples, 1976). In a study of middle-class black men, Cazenave (1983) found that they tended to be more supportive of an overall idea of an egalitarian relationship and of nontraditional roles for women when compared to black men as a whole. Another school of thought suggests that middle-class blacks have adopted middle-class whites lifestyles and value systems. As black males rise up the economic ladder and acquire power, they tend to want a woman who fits the white female stereotype (one who is submissive and dependent), which has not been a stereotype of black women in history.

Throughout the historical periods mentioned in this chapter, none indicates that the black family was a weak structure on the verge of collapsing. If anything, history points out a family full of resilience. No doubt contemporary black families are faced with a high rate of teenage pregnancies, drugs, AIDS, male incarceration, and so on. Still, if history is a guide, the strengths of black families, ranging from African roots of extended kin networks to religious involvement, can still be called upon to offer assistance.

BIBLIOGRAPHY

Aborampah, O. (1989). Black male-female relationships. *Journal of Black Studies*, 19, 320–342.

Allen, W. R. (1978). The search for applicable theories of black family life. *Journal of Marriage and the Family*, 40, 117–129.

Anderson, E. (1989). Sex codes and family life among inner-city youth. *The Annals of the American Academy of Political and Social Science*, 501, 59–78.

Beckett, J. O., & Smith, A. (1981). Work and family roles: Egalitarian marriage in black and white families. *Social Service Review*, 55, 314–326.

Bennett, Claudette E. (1995). *The black population of the United States: March 1994 and 1993*, U.S. Bureau of Census, Current Population Reports, 20–480. Washington, DC: U.S. Government Printing Office,

Bennett, L., Jr. (1992, November). The 10 biggest myths about the black family. *Ebony*, 118, 120, 122, 124.

Billingsley, A. (1968). *Black families in white America*. Englewood Cliffs, NJ: Prentice Hall.

———. (1992). *Climbing Jacob's ladder: The enduring legacy of African American families*. New York: Simon & Schuster.

Binion, V. J. (1990). Psychological androgyny: A black female perspective. *Sex Roles*, 22(7/8), 487–507.

Boles, J. D. (1983). *Black southerners, 1619–1869*. Lexington: University of Kentucky Press.

Bowen, M. (1988). "On the differentiation of self." In M. Bowen, *Family therapy in clinical practice* (2nd ed.), (467–528). Northvale, NJ: Jason Aronson.

Boye-Beaman, J., Leonard, K., & Senchak, M. (1993). Male premarital aggression and gender identity among black and white newlywed couples. *Journal of Marriage and the Family*, 55, 303–313.

Broman, C. (1991). Gender, work-family roles, and psychological well-being of blacks. *Journal of Marriage and the Family*, 53, 509–520.

Bronfenbrenner, U. (1979). *The ecology of human development: Experiments by nature and design*. Cambridge, MA: Harvard University Press.

Cazenave, N. (1983). "A woman's place": The attitudes of middle-class men. *Phylon*, 44(1), 12–32.

Creighton-Zollar, A., & Williams, J. S. (1992). The relative educational attainment and occupational prestige of black spouses and life satisfaction. *Western Journal of Black Studies*, 16, 57–63.

Chadiha, L. A. (1992). Black husbands' economic problems and resiliency during the transition to marriage. *Families and Society*, 73, 542–552.

Davis, L., & Strube, M. J. (1993). An assessment of romantic commitment among black and white dating couples. *Journal of Applied Social Psychology*, 23(3), 212–225.

Dickson, L. (1993). The future of marriage and family in black America. *Journal of Black Studies*, 23, 472–491.

Du Bois, W.E.B. (1898). The study of the Negro problem. *Annals*, 1, 1–23.

Eshleman, J. R. (1988). *The family: An introduction* (5th ed.). Boston: Allyn and Bacon.

Farkas, G. (1976). Education, wage rates, and the division of labor between husband and wife. *Journal of Marriage and the Family*, 38, 473–484.

Fogel, R. W., & Engerman, S. L. (1974). *Time on the cross: The economics of American Negro slavery*. Boston: Little, Brown.

Foner, E. (1988). *Reconstruction: America's unfinished revolution, 1863–1877*. New York: Harper & Row.

Fossett, M., & Kiecolt, J. (1993). Mate availability and family structure among African Americans in U.S. metropolitan areas. *Journal of Marriage and the Family*, 55, 288–302.

Frazier, E. F. (1939). *The Negro family in the United States*. Chicago: University of Chicago Press.

Genovese, E. (1974). *Roll Jordan roll: The world the slaves made*. New York: Pantheon.

———. (1994). "The myth of the absent family." In R. Staples (ed.), *The black family: Essays and studies* (5th ed.) (20–25). Belmont, CA: Wadsworth Publishing.

Gibbs, J. T. (1988). "Young black males in America: Endangered, embittered, and embattled." In J. T. Gibbs, A. F. Brunswick, M. E. Connor, R. Dembo, T. E. Larson, R. J. Reed, & B. Solomon (eds.), *Young, black, and male in America: An endangered species* (1–36). New York: Auburn House.

Gutman, H. G. (1976). *The black family in slavery and freedom: 1750–1925*. New York: Vintage.

Hill, R. B. (1972). *The strengths of black families*. New York: Emerson Hall Publishing.

Hill, R. B., Billingsley, A., Engram, E., Malson, M. R., Rubin, R. H., Stack, C. B., Stewart, J. B., & Teele, J. E. (1993). *Research on the African American family*. Westport, CT: Auburn House.

Ingoldsby, B. B., & Smith, S. (1995). *Families in multicultural perspective*. New York: Guilford Press.

Jackson, J. (1978). "But where are the men." In Robert Staples (ed.), *The black family: Essays and studies*. Belmont, CA: Wadsworth Publishing.

Karenga, M. (1982). "Black male/female relationships." In M. Karenga (ed.), *Introduction to black studies*. Los Angeles: Kawaida.

Lawson, E. J., & Thompson, A. (1995). Black men make sense of marital distress and divorce: An exploratory study. *Family Relations*, 44(2), 211–218.

Lewis, D. (1975). The black family: socialization and sex roles. *Phylon*, 36, 221–237.

Logan, Sadye L. (1996). "A strength perspective on black families: Then and now." In Sadye L. Logan (ed.), *The black family: Strengths, self-help, and positive change*. Colorado: Westview Press.

Lyson, T. (1986). Race and sex differences in sex role attitudes of southern college students. *Psychology of Women Quarterly*, 10, 421–428.

Massaqui, H. (1993). The new black family is determined, dynamic, and diverse: The black family nobody knows. *Ebony*, 47(10), 28–31.

McDaniel, A. (1990). The power of culture: A review of the idea of Africa's influence on family structure in antebellum America. *Journal of Family History*, 15(2), 225–238.

Moynihan, D. P. (1965). *The Negro family: The case for national action.* Washington, DC: U.S. Department of Labor, Office of Planning and Research.

Nash, G. B., Jeffrey, J. R., Howe, J. R., Frederick, P. J., Davis, A. F., & Winkler, A. M. (eds.). (1990). *The American people: Creating a nation and a society* (2nd ed.), (vol. 1). New York: HarperCollins Publishers.

Pinkney, A. (1993). *Black Americans* (4th ed.). Englewood Cliffs, NJ: Prentice Hall.

Pleck, E. H. (1979). *Black migration and poverty: Boston, 1865–1900.* New York: Academic Press.

Rainwater, L., & Yancey, W. (1967). *The Moynihan Report and the Politics of Controversy.* Cambridge, MA: MIT Press.

Roark, J. L. (1977). *Masters without slaves: Southern planters in the Civil War and Reconstruction.* New York: W. W. Norton.

Royce, E. (1993). *The Origins of Southern sharecropping.* Philadelphia: Temple University Press.

Rubin, R. H. (1978). Matriarchal themes in black family literature: Implications for family life education. *The Family Coordinator*, 11(1), 33–41.

Scott, J. W., & Black, A. (1994). "Deep structures of African-American family life: Female and male kin networks." In R. Staples (ed.), *The black family: Essays and studies* (5th ed.), (204–213). Belmont, CA: Wadsworth Publishing.

Secord, P. F., & Ghee, K. (1986). Implications of the black marriage market for marital conflict. *Journal of Family Issues*, 7(1), 45–55.

South, S. (1993, May). Racial and ethnic differences in the desire to marry. *Journal of Marriage and the Family*, 55, 357–370.

Staples, R. (1976). *Introduction to black sociology.* New York: McGraw-Hill.

———. (1978). "The black dating game." In R. Staples (ed.), *The black family: Essays and studies* (2nd ed.). Belmont, CA: Wadsworth Publishing.

———. (1981). *The world of black singles.* Westport, CT: Greenwood Press.

———. (1991). "The sexual revolution and the black middle class." In R. Staples (ed.), *The black family: Essays and studies.* Belmont, CA: Wadsworth Publishing.

———. (1994). "Changes in black family structure: The conflict between family ideology and structural conditions." In R. Staples (ed.), *The black family: Essays and studies* (5th ed.), (11–19). Belmont, CA: Wadsworth Publishing.

Staples, R., & Mirande, A. (1989). "Racial and cultural variations among American families: A decennial review of the literature on minority families." In A. S. Skolnick & J. H. Skolnick (eds.), *Family in transition*, 480–503. Glenview, IL: Scott, Foresman.

Taylor, R. J., et al. (1988). An assessment of the provider role as perceived by black males. *Family Relations*, 27, 426–431.

Thompson, A., & Lawson, E. J. (1994). Divorce and fatherhood: Insights from black men. *Family Perspective*, 28(3), 169–181.

Thornton, John (1993). Central African names and African American naming patterns. *William & Mary Quarterly*, 50(4), 727–742.

Tucker, M. B., & Taylor, R. T. (1987). Demographic correlates of relationship status among black americans. *Journal of Marriage and the Family*, 51, 655–665.

U.S. Census Bureau. (1994). *Statistical abstract of the United States* (National Data Book, 114th ed.). Washington, DC: Author.

U.S. Department of Commerce. (1994, September). *Statistical abstract of the United States*. (National Data Book, 114th ed.). Washington, DC: Author.

Zinn, M. B., & Eitzen, D. S. (1990). *Diversity in families* (2nd ed.). New York: HarperCollins Publishers.

IV

African American Women

Wilma King

For reasons that continue to defy a satisfactory explanation, fewer African women than men were part of the overseas slave trade. Differentials in the gender ratios interfered with family and community formations among Africans in the New World. Reasons for the initial disparities notwithstanding, the gender ratios began to even out during the eighteenth century. By the end of the century North American slaves, unlike those in other New World countries, were sustaining their population through reproduction. Europeans transported less than 1,000,000 Africans into North America before 1808, yet by 1860 the number of slaves had reached 3,953,760. Of that population, 1,756,431 were females of all ages. Concomitant with the increase in the slave population, the number of free persons had escalated to 488,070 by 1860. Of that number, 235,950 were females of all ages.

A century passed before there was any systematic attempt to study or write about these women. The development of women's history since the 1960s introduced new scholarship and concepts into the field. But there were charges of the omission of black women along with questions about the accepted body of traditional knowledge within women's studies. As the field expanded it became clear that class and gender were necessary analytical categories. Evelyn Brooks Higginbotham's cogent writing about the "metalanguage of race" leaves no doubt about whether race ought to be included.

Some historians insist that profession, region, and age are equally significant areas for analysis. If used, this range of categories yields a multiplicity of differences that poses problems for researchers desiring a manageable "common core" of knowledge. Nevertheless, it is essential to incorporate variations. Otherwise, distortions of reality along with omitting the experiences of a great portion of the American population, black women, will prevail. Many scholars recoil at such thoughts and insist upon a holistic approach. As a result, there have been notable advancements in women's history, and the scholarship on black women is burgeoning.

At the outset, scholars complained about the paucity of resources to remove the shadows of invisibility engulfing black women. "Their records lie buried, seldom read, rarely interpreted," writes the well-known historian Gerda Lerner in *Majority Finds Its Past* (1979). In the chapter "Black Women in the United States: A Problem in Historiography and Interpretation," Lerner continued, "Their names and achievements are known to only a few specialists." Even worse, Lerner claimed, "when they do appear in history textbooks at all it is merely as victims, as helpless sufferers of conditions imposed upon them by others." The solution, said Lerner, was to "unearth, compile, and organize the raw materials on which interpretation can be based." The situation was not as dire as it appeared to the uninitiated, for there were numerous sources dating back to the nineteenth century. In fact, Anna Julia Cooper's *Voice from the South* (1892) spoke unabatedly of black women when she proclaimed: "Only the BLACK WOMAN can say 'when and where I enter, in the quiet, undisputed dignity of my womanhood, without violence and without suing or special patronage, then and there the whole Negro race enters with me.' " The recovery of the sources progressed apace, as did the proliferation of scholarship.

Nevertheless, as late as 1989 Evelyn Brooks Higginbotham's "Beyond the Sound of Silence: Afro-Americans Women in History" noted that despite a plethora of publications, the voices of African American women were still "largely unheard." Higginbotham charged that the "scholarship on Afro-Americans and women" reflected the "failure to recognize black women's history" as both an "identifiable field of inquiry in its own right" and as an integral part of African American, American, and women's history. "Afro-American history has failed to address gender issues adequately," writes Higginbotham, "while women's history has similarly failed to address questions of race."

One of the most poignant examples of Higginbotham's complaint was the eminent historian Anne Firor Scott's use of her 1984 address "On Seeing and Not Seeing: A Case of Historical Invisibility" to chide members of the Organization of American Historians (OAH) for ignoring women in their scholarship. Yet, she appeared oblivious to African American women until Tom Holt asked, "Are not black women invisible to you?" Scott admitted negligence and moved beyond it.

To a great extent the first wave of scholars engaged in black women's studies succeeded in exposing the neglect and marginalization of black women. Once heard, many of the same scholars were not content with the simple addition of black women to the historical mix without reconceptualizing the existing theoretical frameworks. It was necessary to "raise new questions, introduce imaginative methodologies, and unearth new and reassess old sources," writes Darlene

Clark Hine. Hine's assessment was in keeping with her 1994 essay "Lifting the Veil, Shattering the Silence: Black Women's History in Slavery and Freedom," which commented on the current state of African American history.

A second wave of historical scholarship was underway and women scholars would play a major role in moving black women from the margin to the center. In so doing it was necessary to scuttle the notion that African American women had not been visible in American history. Among the earliest publications to destroy this concept and to answer questions about the role of black women in America are works by Toni Cade (Bambara), Gerda Lerner, and Angela Davis. Cade's *Black Woman* (1970) features a collection of contemporary writings by authors including Nikki Giovani, Audre Lorde, Abbey Lincoln, and Shirley Williams; Lerner's *Black Women in White America* (1972) is a sourcebook of historical documents spanning the period from 1811 to 1971. As she waited liberation from a California prison, Angela Davis penned "Reflections on the Black Woman's Role in the Community of Slaves" (1971), in which she challenged scholars to include race, sex, and class in their historical analyses. Before the end of the decade Sharon Harley and Rosalyn Terborg-Penn's *Afro-American Woman: Struggles and Images* (1978) appeared. It included essays about black women in the Jacksonian era and the women's movement along with biographical treatments of Charlotte A. Bass and Anna Julia Cooper.

Coupled with these advancements, George P. Rawick edited and Greenwood Press published the Works Progress Administration (WPA) narratives (1972–1978), running into thousands of pages. This testimonial treasure trove illuminates the lives of enslaved women who toiled alongside men and gave birth to children who sickened and died in record numbers. The women's own words suggest that they were not passive victims in significant areas of their own lives and that of their loved ones while in bondage.

The WPA narratives make a more gendered analysis of slavery possible, since far fewer autobiographies were published by ex-slave women than by men because of disparities in literacy rates. Furthermore, women were less likely than men to run away to the North, where someone could, if needed, assist them in writing narratives. The former slave Harriet Jacobs is an exception in that she fled to the North, was literate, and published *Incidents in the Life of a Slave Girl* (1861).

Publication of *The Schomburg Library of Nineteenth-Century Black Women Writers*, under the directions of general editor Henry Louis Gates, Jr., expands the literature with more than twenty volumes. Included in the collection is *Six Women's Slave Narratives* (1988), which contains firsthand accounts of bondage by the American-born Kate Drumgoold, Lucy Delaney, Annie Burton, and Mattie Jackson. Other publications in the *Schomburg Library* are the autobiographical writings of Elizabeth Keckley in *Behind the Scenes* (1988), and Harriet Jacobs's *Incidents in the Life of a Slave Girl*. These accounts provide another dimension of slavery because Keckley and Jacobs were adults when freed from bondage.

The first monograph about enslaved women, *Ar'n't I a Woman? Female Slaves in the Plantation South*, appeared in 1985. The author, Deborah Gray White, argued that self-reliant enslaved women played a central role in their families. In fact, White posits that the mother-child dyad challenged the husband-wife bond. Additionally, she argued that within their private world the women developed and shared a "network." *Ar'n't I a Woman?* fits within the range of studies arguing against the total victimization of bond servants and emerges as one dedicated to rescuing the women from the amorphous mass of slaves.

Since 1985 a number of dissertations, scholarly essays, and autobiographies by and about bondwomen have appeared including Kent Anderson Leslie's *Woman of Color* (1995), which offers a rarely seen perspective of slavery through a biographical study of Amanda America Dickson, a slave-born biracial child who came of age in a wealthy white central Georgia household.

A sharp contrast to Leslie's biography is Melton A. McLaurin's *Celia, a Slave* (1991), which examines the exploitive relationship between the teenaged Celia and her sixty-year-old widowed owner, Robert Newsom. Slaves had no legal or social recourse against sexual abuse. The apparent hopelessness of their situations does not mean that they acquiesced. In fact, during a confrontation between Celia and Newsom, she killed him. Celia's court-appointed attorneys presented a brilliant defense in *Missouri v. Celia* (1855). Based upon an 1845 statute, the lawyers argued that "any woman" could defend herself against sexual abuse. Had the plea been accepted, it could have signaled an end to the sexual exploitation of slaves and the demise of slavery.

The intricacies of sexual exploitation of slaves are explored by Catherine Clinton in "Caught in the Web of the Big House" (1985) and by Thelma Jennings in " 'Us Colored Women Had to Go through a Plenty' " (1991). Further study is needed in this area to add a more nuanced understanding of intimate relationships between slaveowners and slaves. Many of the associations between the two were exploitative because of the differences in status, but this is not entirely true of them all.

In addition to the published primary sources, biographies, and scholarly essays, several anthologies include discussion about enslaved women. *Working toward Freedom* (1994) edited by Larry Hudson, Jr., contains specific chapters about women in bondage such as Cheryl Cody's "Sale and Separation: Four Crises for Enslaved Women in the Ball Plantation, 1764–1854" and Josephine Beoku-Betts's "She Make Funny Flat Cake She Call Saraka: Gullah Women and Food Practices under Slavery." Beoku-Betts's essay, which proposes to "validate the continuance of African-derived food tradition as form of resistance," adds another dimension to the culture of African Americans during slavery.

The agency of black women surfaces in *Discovering the Women in Slavery*, a 1996 publication edited by Patricia Morton. *Discovering the Women* contains fourteen chapters that examines the lives of women, black and white, rich and poor, across time and regions. At the outset, Morton uses a historiographical discussion to contextualize the major issues—paternalism, sexuality, and gender identification—addressed in the volume. Among the essays is Carolyn J. Powell's "In Remembrance of Mira," a vivid account of the treatment and death of an enslaved woman. Marie Jenkins Schwartz's "At Noon, Oh How I Ran" examines the bond between enslaved women and their children, and Margaret M. R. Kellor's work explores antislavery feminism and the construction of black womanhood in the United States.

Making use of a different theoretical construct from *Discovering the Women* is *More than Chattel* (1996), an anthology edited by David Barry Gaspar and Darlene Clark Hine, which focuses entirely on slave women in the Americas. Chapters on bondwomen in Brazil, Antigua, and Saint-Domingue along with Bernard Moitt's study of resistance among enslaved women in the French Caribbean, and Barbara Bush's study of slave resistance in the British Caribbean make this anthology especially versatile.

Other contributions in *More than Chattel* include Brenda Stevenson's "Gender Conventions, Ideals, and Identity among Antebellum Virginia Slave Women," and Robert Olwell's " 'Loose, Idle and Disorderly': Slave Women in the Eighteenth-Century Charleston Marketplace." Based largely upon the testimony of former slaves and manuscripts, Stevenson argues that slave women in Virginia created a "counterimage" that contradicted the popularly accepted notions of the women as degraded, promiscuous, and passive. Similarly, Olwell shows that enslaved women in the Charleston marketplace were anything but passive. Their success in marketing goods allowed them to "escape the smothering metaphors of patriarchy" and to "assert their own property rights." In so doing, the women gained "a degree of autonomy and self-control."

In a backward glance over the recent literature, it is evident that most of the publications focus on the nineteenth century. Among the exceptions are Joan R. Gundersen's "Double Bonds of Race and Sex: Black and White Women in a Colonial Virginia Parish" (1986), reprinted in Hine, King, and Reed, "*We Specialize in the Wholly Impossible*" (1995); Gary B. Mills's "Coincoin: An Eighteenth-Century 'Liberated' Woman" (1976); Jean R. Sonderlund's "Black Women in Colonial Pennsylvania" (1983); and Debra Newman's "Black Women in the Era of the American Revolution in Pennsylvania" (1976), reprinted in Hine, King, and Reed, "*We Specialize in the Wholly Impossible*." It should also be noted that the anthologies occasionally include scholarship based upon eighteenth-century sources. When taken together, they make important contributions to the literature, however, a systematic effort is still necessary to reduce the void in the study of black women in colonial North America across regions.

Despite this observation, the expanded interest in women's history, black and white, caused scholars to raise questions about the interactions between southern black and white woman. Catherine Clinton's *Plantation Mistress* (1982), Suzanne Lebsock's *Free Women of Petersburg* (1985), and Elizabeth Fox-Genovese's *Within the Plantation Household* (1988) address issues related to the interactions between white women, often plantation mistresses in households with twenty or more slaves, and the black women they owned. To be sure, the monographs do not focus on quid pro quo relationships between the women who are sometimes chapters apart, but they do answer many questions about their day-to-day activities.

For firsthand accounts see Frances Anne Kemble's *Journal of a Residence on a Georgian Plantation in 1838–1839* (1984), edited by John Scott, and *A Northern Woman in the Plantation South* (1993), edited by Wilma King. Other published diaries and letters of slaveholding women confirm that color and class, as well as demographics, prevented black and white women from forming communities and enjoying a true sisterhood.

Moving from a different trajectory, Victoria E. Bynum's *Unruly Women* gives attention to less formal interactions between white and black women in nineteenth-century Orange, Granville, and Montgomery Counties, North Carolina. Bynum regards the selected counties as a "microcosm of the various permutations in race, class, and gender in the Old South." Based largely upon archival sources and public records, the author's "unruly" white women are not elite plantation mistresses nor are all the black women slaves. Moreover, *Unruly Women* challenges the "stereotype of the antebellum South as a land populated primarily by slaves and slaveholders."

The stereotype has been so pervasive that it obscures the reality that only 25 percent of the southern white population owned slaves in 1860. The mythical notion also clouds the fact that 261,918 of the 488,070 free blacks lived in the South in 1860. A significant number of that free population owed their liberty to relatives and friends. The historian Judith Schafer's study of wills in antebellum Louisiana reinforces this idea. In other instances, the women purchased their liberty, won emancipations through the courts, and escaped to freedom either by portraying themselves as free or fleeing from bondage.

Persons interested in studying free black women before 1865 may consult many disparate sources across disciplines. Free women left a cornucopia of poems, newspaper commentaries, speeches, books, and manuscripts. This is sometimes difficult to manage, but it is far better than lamenting the dearth of resources. The great variety of materials yield enough data to develop a nuanced understanding of free women across classes and regions. For example, Charlotte Forten's journals offer a glimpse of the life of a middle-class woman while chronicling her school days in New England and work as a teacher in post-1865 South Carolina. By contrast, Eliza Potter's *Hairdresser's Experience in the High Life* (1859) details her work as a hair stylist for wealthy white women.

Potter's book is significant for other reasons. She cleverly uses a double structure to portray an "outsider," herself, "inside" social circles that were ordinarily closed to black women. The hairdresser gained entry because of her profession and won the confidence of wealthy white clients who divulged their deepest secrets to a woman who presented no threat to their economic security or social positions.

General studies by Whittington B. Johnson, "Free African-American Women in Savannah, 1800–1860: Affluence and Autonomy amid Adversity" (1992), and Loren Schweninger, "Property Owning Free African-American Women" (1990), both reprinted in Hine, King, and Reed, *We Specialize in the Wholly Impossible*," show the variety of methods free women used to secure their economic well-being. Johnson's essay limits itself to Savannah, whereas Schweninger's work examines the entire South.

The desire for economic security prompted the freeborn Nancy Prince and Harriet Wilson to pen books that distinguished them as the first African American women to publish a travel account, *A Black Woman's Odyssey* (1850), and Wilson as the first African American woman to publish a novel, *Our Nig* (1859). The autobiographical but fictional *Our Nig* neither elevated Wilson from poverty nor bestowed upon her a national reputation. More than a century later, however, Wilson is recognized as the creator of the black woman's novel. Her craft rejected the domestic and sentimental novel structure, defined black womanhood, and developed a plot that was uniquely her own.

Unlike Wilson's *Our Nig*, Frances Ellen Watkins's *Poems on Miscellaneous Subjects* (1857) was immensely popular at the time of publication. It sold more than 10,000 copies in three years. Three nationally distributed newspapers, including William Lloyd Garrison's *Liberator*, reprinted Watkins's "Eliza Harris," a poem about a fugitive slave mother. This helps to explain why Watkins was one of the nineteenth century's most popular writers.

Wilson's "Two Choices" (1859) was the first short story published by an African American woman. It represents the author's thinking about selecting marital partners and her attitude regarding women dedicating their lives to a career rather than to marriage and family. In a similar vein, Harper's novels— *Minnie's Sacrifice* (1869), *Sowing and Reaping* (1876–1877), and *Trail and Triumph* (1888–1889)—impart social messages that reflect her interest in women's rights, moral reform, and abolition.

Several other free black women chronicled their spiritual lives. Writings by Jarena Lee, Julia A. J. Foote, and Zilpah Elaw are included in *Sisters of the Spirit*, edited by William Andrews. Rebecca Cox Jackson shared a Methodist background with her "sisters of the spirit." These women struggled to live up to their religious convictions, and they fought for entry and acceptance in a profession ordinarily closed to women. Of the spiritual autobiographies, Rebecca Cox Jackson's *Gifts of Power* (1981) is the most expansive. Unlike her contemporaries, Jackson broke away from the church and joined the Shakers. This sect provided the spiritual community Jackson sought along with the feminist theology that coincided with her desire for autonomy and control over her own sexuality. Because of perceived racism within the Shakers, Jackson eventually formed her own religious community. In this sense, she may be compared to Richard Allen, founder of the African Methodist Episcopal Church, in moving away from an organized white religious body to establish a religious community where they and their followers could worship without white interference.

In each of the spiritual autobiographies, the women record their struggles for liberation from confining ideologies, overwhelming paternalism, or suffocating racism. Ironically, Maria W. Stewart, known as America's first black woman political speaker and writer, had similar experiences once she entered the public arena. Her public-speaking career was short lived because of gender conventions against women speaking to mixed audiences. Stewart, who was influenced by David Walker's *Appeal* (1829), spoke eloquently about colonization, self-determination, racial harmony, educational goals, and abolition.

Aside from the primary sources, biographies add texture to the lives of free men and women. Adele Logan Alexander's *Ambiguous Lives* (1991), for example, highlights the lives of several free women in antebellum middle Georgia. The author is particularly adept at historicizing the study and showing how the state statutes influenced the lives of free persons.

In *Sojourner Truth* (1996) Nell Irvin Painter untangles the myths about and realities of Truth's life as a slave and emancipated woman. One facet of Truth's life that is likely to linger without alteration, despite Painter's efforts, is the "Ar'n't I a Woman" speech, which Painter attributes in part to the historical creation of Frances Gage.

A chapter about free black women appears in Suzanne Lebsock's *Free Women of Petersburg* (1984). Lebsock's discussion of free women makes the supposition that they chose not to marry, thereby retaining autonomy and control over their property. The historians Michael P. Johnson and James Roark challenge the thesis and suggest that imbalances in the sex ratio among free persons, economic conditions, married couples living apart, and mortality rates do much to explain why so many women appeared in the census as heads of households. Johnson and Roark also posit that marriage offered protection and support especially to poor free women. The extant evidence across geographical regions shows that women, black and white, married or single, wanted and often demanded autonomy. Further study must be completed before anyone can say, without equivocation, what influenced the circumstances of the women who appeared alone in the census.

Beyond thinking of free women as individuals with self-serving interests, it is important to note that they were often involved in organizations to improve the lives of their contemporaries and to build communities that served as a refuge from oppression. The number of literary and benevolent organizations, some dating back to the eighteenth century, among free women is testimony to their concerns. With meager resources, the women added to their collection of books and magazines. The clubs served as forums for members to receive responses to their creative writings along with learning or practicing leadership skills. In addition to the literary facet, many clubs had a benevolent side whereby members received financial assistance from the treasury during illnesses or bereavements.

Sometimes black women found themselves in positions to institute changes that had wider effects than upon their organizations and themselves. For example, an 1854 Sunday afternoon outing for the New Yorker Elizabeth Jennings precipitated a class action suit against the Third Avenue Railway Company. The transit conductor forcefully ejected the twenty-four-year-old teacher from a public carrier, and she countered with physical and legal protests. Similarly, Sarah Parker Remond filed a civil suit against the management of Boston's Howard Athenaeum in 1853 because of its segregated seating.

Free women also participated in the abolitionist movement and tried to make legal differences in the lives of millions of their contemporaries. Among the most vocal and best-known black women abolitionists are Maria W. Stewart, Frances E. W. Harper, and Mary Ann Shadd. Part II of Jean Fagan Yellin and John C. Van Horne's *Abolitionist Sisterhood* (1994) features several essays about the antislavery activities of black women. Data related to the abolitionism of other women are also included in Shirley Yee's *Black Women Abolitionists* (1992), Dorothy Sterling's *We Are Your Sisters* (1984), and Charlotte Forten's activities recorded in her journals. Their public protests are published in the *Liberator*, the *Christian Recorder*, and the *National Anti-Slavery Standard.*

Because northern states either abolished slavery or made provisions for gradual abolition during the Revolutionary War era, black northerners had more freedom in public protests than their southern contemporaries. This does not mean southern blacks did nothing. Many became fugitives from bondage or assisted others. Their numbers remain unknown and their names unrecognized. Others, including Harriet Tubman, became well known as a result of their feats through the Underground Railroad or by the abolitionists popularizing individual acts, as was the case with the Georgia fugitive Ellen Craft.

Despite the efforts of abolitionists and the untold number of runaways, slavery did not end until the U.S. Congress adopted the Thirteenth Amendment following the Civil War. Although many black women contributed to the war efforts, only Susie King Taylor recorded and published an account of her work within the Union lines. For insight into the conditions under which many black women lived during the war see Victor B. Howard's essay "The Civil War in Kentucky: The Slave Claims His Freedom" (1982) and Leon F. Litwack's *Been in the Storm So Long* (1980).

Once emancipated, former slaves redefined labor and the ownership thereof. In giving meaning to their liberty, many newly freed women withdrew from the fields. Rather than "playing the lady" or being guilty of "female loaferism," as claimed by critics, the women busied themselves caring for their children, going to schools, or working in family-based labor units.

The transition from slavery to freedom was not easy because many ex-slaveholders were unwilling to relinquish claims to former slaves. Several of the chapters in Catherine Clinton's *Half Sisters of History* (1994) probe into the lives of black women in slavery and freedom. Clinton's "Bloody Terrain" hones in on the reconfiguration of conflicts between blacks and whites during Reconstruction. Amid the postwar violence, which included the sexual abuse of freedwomen, Clinton shows the women fighting the challenges to their liberty. "Black women wanted respectability and the public image of virtue," writes Clinton, "first for survival and then as a foundation for their own and their family's prosperity." Both Tera Hunter's *To 'Joy My Freedom: Southern Black Women's Lives and Labors after the Civil War* (1997) and Leslie Schwalm's *Hard Fight for We: Women's Transition from Slavery to Freedom in South Carolina* (1997) make major contributions to this facet of the literature.

Carolyn Ashbaugh's *Lucy Parsons: American Revolutionary* (1976) is a moving account of Parsons's role as a labor activist in the late nineteenth century. Historians tend to ignore Parsons in their discussion of nineteenth-century labor strikes, violence at the Haymarket, and foiled attempts to form lasting labor unions.

In "Negotiating and Transforming the Public Sphere" (1994), Elsa Barkley Brown asserts that women were not always pursuing new authority in the postwar years but were seeking a "lost authority." Brown explores the public discourse to show why "women in the 1880s and 1890s needed to create their own pulpits from which to speak—to restore their voices to the community." Brown notes that African American women did not receive the franchise, but "this does not mean that they were not active in that [political] arena." They attended meetings, listened to debates, and "took the day off from work and went to the polls." As a part of their political worldview, the women believed freedom "would accrue to each of them individually only when it was acquired by all of them collectively."

Attention to the collective interest of all African Americans is evident in the black women's fight against oppression in the late nineteenth and early twentieth centuries. In "Civilization, the Decline of Middle-Class Manliness," reprinted in Hine, King, and Reed, *We Specialize in the Wholly Impossible*," Gail Bederman demonstrates how Ida B. Wells used rhetoric to garner support in the antilynching campaign. Jacqueline Ann Rouse shows that Lugenia Burns Hope was equally diligent in her work to improve the living conditions among blacks in Atlanta. Women developed social consciousness early on, according to Stephanie Shaw's *What a Woman Ought to Be and to Do* (1996). The black women's clubs in the late nineteenth and early twentieth centuries also exemplify consideration for others in their motto "Lifting as We Climb." Few could ever misunderstand their aims.

In November 1989 Anne Firor Scott prefaced her presidential address, "Most Invisible of All: Black Women's Voluntary Associations," at the Southern Historical Association with references to "On Seeing and Not Seeing," the 1984 OAH address. "In the process of lecturing everyone else about the dangers of not seeing what was before one's eyes," said Scott, "I had exemplified the error." She again lectured an august body of scholars saying, "It is time to change this situation."

Of greater importance than public admission of the historical slight, Scott's address, which appeared in *Journal of Southern History*, called attention to the central role of the women's organizations in the formation of black communities. When tracing the growth and significance of the organizations, Scott relied heavily upon the works of African American women, including Hallie Q. Brown, Fannie Barrier Williams, and Mary Church Terrell, along with the contemporary research and writings of Mamie Gavin Fields, Paula Giddings, Rosalyn Terborg-Penn, Darlene Clark Hine, Elsa Barkley Brown, and Jacqueline Rouse. At bottom, the address contained data familiar to many African Americans, but it was now "in the face" of others as well as the lead article in a mainstream publication.

Many discussions of black women's clubs place them within the context of the high tide of racism, summary executions, and libelous attacks upon black women. The clubs predate these late-nineteenth- and early-twentieth-century phenomena, as do the slanderous assaults upon the women's character. Much of the abuse heaped upon black women by whites emanated from the erroneous belief that black women were naturally promiscuous "Jezebels." This is akin to an observation made by Alexander Hamilton. "The contempt," he wrote, "we have been taught to entertain for blacks makes us fancy many things that are founded neither in reason nor in experience." In any case, the popularization of the licentious-Jezebel myth served as a rationalization for the mistreatment of black women.

An equally pervasive and demeaning myth, "Mammy" is a literary creation that received life from writers who romanticized bygone days. Phil Patton, who contributed a story about Mammy to the September 1993 *American Heritage*, acknowledged that the myth was born in the minds of slavery's defenders before the war and "raised in its painful aftermath to become one of the most powerful American icons."

Deborah Gray White devotes considerable time to explaining and debunking the mythical Jezebel and Mammy as well as the "bitchy" twentieth-century Sapphire. Other scholars, including Patricia Morton, author of *Disfigured Images* (1991), and Beverly Guy-Sheftall, author of *"Daughters of Sorrow"* (1984), contribute to our understanding of the negative characterizations of black women through historical writings and the popular media. Morton's examination includes the 1965 Labor Department document "The Negro Family: The Case for National Action," commonly called the (Daniel Patrick) Moynihan Report, which perpetuated the mythical notion that black women, rather than racism, were responsible for the black family's "tangle of pathology." Guy-Sheftall looks at the attitudes about black women held by whites, male and female, and black men between 1880 and 1920.

Black women without regard to class responded to these assaults and defended their names in their own way. For example, some of the women joined the National Association of Colored Women in its counterattack upon the negative stereotypes and images. The struggle continued as evidenced in the gathering of more than two thousand women at Massachusetts Institute of Technology's "Black Women in the Academy: Defending Our Name, 1894–1994" conference.

Black women were very much a part of the demographic transformations that occurred in northeastern and midwestern cities before 1920. In 1991 Darlene

Clark Hine's "Black Migration to the Urban Midwest" pointed to the "egregious void" regarding black women and called for a gender analysis of migration. Hine encouraged examination of noneconomic reasons why women left their birthplaces. How important, she asked, were their desires for autonomy or the pressing need to remove themselves from abuse at the hands of black and white men?

Women occupy important places in the post–World War I migration studies. In *The Promised Land* (1991), Nicholas Lemann traces Ruby Lee Daniels's migration from her Clarksdale, Mississippi, home to Chicago, but her move is only one facet of a larger study. In a similar vein, Irma Watkins-Owens's *Blood Relations* (1996) contains a gendered analysis in her study of ethnic relations in Harlem between 1900 and 1930. The testimony of fifty southern-born women who migrate to California serves as the foundation of Gretchen Lemke-Santangelo's *Abiding Courage* (1996).

The migration of black Americans in the early twentieth century was a major factor in the development of a great literary movement, the Harlem Renaissance. According to Langston Hughes in Hiroko Sato's essay in *The Harlem Renaissance Remembered*, "Jessie Fauset at the *Crisis*, Charles Johnson at *Opportunity*, and Alain Locke in Washington, were the three people who midwifed the so-called New Negro literature into being." Acting as mentors, the three were "kind and critical—but not too critical for the young—they nursed us along until our books were born," wrote Hughes.

Jessie Fauset produced four novels, *There Is Confusion* (1924), *Plum Bun* (1929), *The Chinaberry Tree* (1931), and *Comedy: American Style* (1933), in which race, class, and gender are important issues. The Cornell University Phi Beta Kappan wrote about a facet of American life, middle-class educated African Americans, that garnered little attention from other writers. Fauset did not deviate. Richard Wright considered her among "the prim and decorous ambassadors who went a-begging of servility, curtsying to show that the Negro was not inferior, that he was human, and that he had a life comparable to that of other people." W.E.B. Du Bois and William Stanley Braithwaite were more supportive.

Nella Larsen also wrote about educated, ambitious, well-born African Americans. Critics considered her more successful than Fauset at infusing color identification into her work, especially *Passing* (1929). In the *Negro Novels in America* (1965), Robert Bone asserts that Larsen's treatment of the subject is exceptional.

Unlike Fauset and Larsen, Zora Neale Hurston developed folk characters who spoke an unparalleled dialect. *Their Eyes Were Watching God* (1937) shows Hurston's craft as a writer and skill as an anthropologist in collecting the folk language. Race and color are less important than gender in Hurston's fiction. Janie, the protagonist in *Their Eyes*, like other women in Fauset's novels, is searching for self-fulfillment along with freedom of body and spirit.

Gloria T. Hull gives her full attention to three women writers of the Harlem

Renaissance in *Color, Sex, and Poetry* (1987). She effectively presents Angelina Weld Grimke, Georgia Douglas Johnson, and Alice Dunbar Nelson as writers who continued their creative productivity during the Harlem Renaissance despite sexism and chauvinism among their contemporaries. Beyond the gendered analysis of the historical context in which women writers functioned, Hull's study is valuable, since all too often Harlem Renaissance scholars tend to focus on the novelists.

The wealth of scholarship about the Harlem Renaissance kindles interest in the creative talents of persons in other areas of the country at the time. The literary outpouring of Chicago writers, including Margaret Walker and Gwendolyn Brooks, falls into this group.

The Great Depression and World War II deflected the attention of many African Americans. Economic survival became paramount. There is no comprehensive gender-balanced study of the period, but Jacqueline Jones's *Labor of Love, Labor of Sorrow* (1986) provides general discussion of black women during the Depression, New Deal, and war years. Other useful sources are Dolores E. Janiewski's *Sisterhood Denied* (1985), B. Joyce Ross's "Mary McLeod Bethune and the National Youth Administration," (1975) and Karen Tucker Anderson's "Last Hired, First Fired" (1982). Janiewski's monograph concentrates on race, class, and gender in the Durham, North Carolina, tobacco industry. Ross's 1975 scholarly essay is a case study of power relationships in President Franklin Roosevelt's black cabinet, and it tells much about Mary McLeod Bethune's role in the New Deal. Finally, Anderson adds insight into the work of black women during World War II. Although different in scope, these studies reveal the presence of racism and sexism.

Pauli Murray's *Song in a Weary Throat* (1987), reissued under the highly descriptive title, *The Autobiography of a Black Activist, Feminist, Lawyer, Priest & Poet* (1989) brings together most major historical events of the twentieth century and calls attention to race and gender discrimination. In a dispassionate and selfless manner, Murray provides the historical context for her seventy-year chronicle of an "American pilgrimage." The posthumously published autobiography is arresting when one considers that Murray's accomplishments, including university professorship in Ghana and the United States, touched the lives of so many other women in their quest for freedom from segregated schools, restricted covenants, and second-class citizenship.

When attending an educational conference near Columbus, Mississippi, in 1967, Murray met Fannie Lou Hamer. The conference was memorable, writes Murray, "because a small flurry of excitement developed reminiscent of earlier civil rights struggles." The meeting was also symbolic in that women from different periods of history fought for the same goals and saw some of them come to fruition.

For a myriad of civil rights–era views and participants, see Anne Moody, *Coming of Age in Mississippi* (1968); Sheyann Webb and Rachel West Nelson, *Selma, Lord, Selma* (1980); Joanne Grant, *Ella Baker: Freedom Bound* (1998),

Vicki L. Crawford, Jacqueline Anne Rouse, and Barbara Woods, eds., *Women in the Civil Rights Movement* (1993); Kaye Mills, *This Little Light of Mine* (1993): and especially Jo Ann Gibson Robinson, *The Montgomery Bus Boycott and the Women Who Started It* (1987). See also Elaine Brown, *A Taste of Power* (1992), and Assata Shakur, *Assata: An Autobiography* (1987).

The civil rights movement was not without disquiet for many women, black and white. Ella Baker recognized and complained about organizational and structural patterns in established organizations. As a founder of the Student Nonviolent Coordinating Committee (SNCC), an organization described as "militant in its tactics and egalitarian in its structure," Baker reexamined her position. Joanne Grant's *Ella Baker: Freedom Bound* (1998) is an even-handed treatment of Baker. An unexpected dimension of the biography is Grant's autobiographical commentary based upon her interactions with Baker in the 1960s and as producer of the documentary film *Fundi: The Story of Ella Baker*.

At the 1964 Waveland, Mississippi, conference the circulation of an unsigned commentary about the gender-bound treatment of women within SNCC pointed to dissension. The criticism reflected larger issues. White women "were being relegated to minor responsibilities," writes Paula Giddings, whereas "the influence of Black women was actually increasing." The indiscriminate sexual behavior of some civil rights activists widened the breech between men and women, black and white. The strife was among the factors that rekindled the feminist movement. President John F. Kennedy's establishment of the Presidential Commission on the Status of Women was also a motivating force for the movement. The commission's 1963 report documented sexual discrimination in the workplace. As a corrective measure, Congress passed the 1964 Civil Rights Act, which outlawed discrimination in public places and in employment based on race, sex, religion, and national origin. An Equal Employment Opportunity Commission (EEOC) received and investigated complaints. By 1966, dissatisfaction with the EEOC's failure to actively enforce gender equity under the Civil Rights Act served as the catalyst for founding the National Organization for Women (NOW). Pauli Murray was among the twenty-eight founding members of the predominately white, middle-class organization. Fannie Lou Hamer and Shirley Chisholm were among the well-known African American women affiliated with NOW.

Ideological differences with white women alienated some of the black women who supported NOW. A poignant incident occurred in summer 1970 when tens of thousands of women participated in a national demonstration commemorating the fiftieth anniversary of the Nineteenth Amendment. Reacting to placards protesting the treatment of Angela Davis carried by black women in the New York City demonstration, an alarmed NOW leader approached Frances Beale saying, "Angela Davis has nothing to do with the women's liberation." Beale agreed that the "Hands off Angela Davis" placard was inconsequential to white women's liberation; "but," said Beale, "it has everything to do with the kind of liberation that we're talking about." To be sure, this singular example does not explain all facets of black distrust of the feminists movement, but it points to the differences in perceptions based upon race and class.

Clearly, black women needed to define feminism for themselves. Among the earliest publications to address the issue were Cade's *Black Woman*, bell hooks's *Ain't I a Woman* (1981), Alice Walker's *In Search of Our Mother's Garden* (1983), Barbara Smith's *Home Girls* (1983), and Angela Davis's *Women, Race & Class* (1983). More recently, bell hooks's *Talking Back* (1989) and Patricia Hill Collins's *Black Feminist Thought* (1990) enrich the literature.

Much of the contemporary literature by black women incorporates subjects that may be perceived as feminist issues. Numbers of African American men have charged that writers, including Terry McMillan, Alice Walker, Toni Morrison, and Ntozake Shange, have put gender ahead of race, thereby serving a feminist rather than a black nationalist agenda. The women use their creativity as an affirmation of black womanhood, but male critics see their works as a "programmatic assault on black men." Ann du Cille's "Phallus(ies) of Interpretation" (1993) examines the male-authored criticism of some black women's fiction. The author explains the "collision" between the black writers, male and female, over "truths" as they know it. Moreover, the critics see the writers gravitating away from the "discourse of deference" in presenting the "somebody-done-somebody wrong" plots. As a result, it appears that the women are "doing hatchet jobs" on black men. According to du Cille, the critics "have misread the refusal of a certain kind of male behavior as a rejection of black men." Vitriolic criticism caused at least one writer, Gayl Jones, to alter her writing; however, she "remains committed to exploring relationships between men and women." Ann du Cille sees external influences that interfere with creativity as reminiscent of the oppressive patriarchy found in selected black women's fiction.

It is not surprising that black women view the writings of black women with a different lens. "Literature by Black women writers," writes Patricia Hill Collins, "provides the most comprehensive view of Black women's struggle to form positive self-definition in the face of denigrated images of Black womanhood." Moving beyond the literature, even a cursory reading of Toni Morrison's *Raceing Justice, En-Gendering Power: Essays on Anita Hill, Clarence Thomas, and the Construction of Social Reality* (1992) reveals how scholars outside the creative genres also contribute to defining black womanhood.

As a result of empowerment through the civil and women's rights movements, along with the Civil Rights Act of 1964 and the Voting Rights Act of 1965, black women have become more active than ever before in local, state, and national politics. This is not to suggest that they had no political interests prior to the 1960s. For a historical overview see Rosalyn Terborg-Penn's "Discontented Black Feminists" (1983), reprinted in Hine, King and Reed, *"We Specialize in the Wholly Impossible,"* along with a discussion of Charlotta Bass's 1952 vice-presidential campaign by Gerald R. Gill. For more recent treatment see La Verne McCain Gill's *African American Women in Congress* (1997). Finally, Willa Mae Hemmons's *Black Women in the New World Order* (1996) contains a chapter on black women in the political area. Other chapters examine a plethora of contemporary topics related to health delivery services and the criminal justice system.

In looking over the great mass of publications about African American women, written or edited by men and women, black and white, across disciplines in the past generation, Ann du Cille confessed that she was "pleased, puzzled, and perturbed" by this seeming commercialization of black women's studies. She labels the "politically correct, intellectually popular, and commercially precious" phenomenon "The Occult of True Black Womanhood." Without a doubt, she raises many questions worthy of careful consideration. For example, what does it mean for young black women academics to have their manuscripts refereed by seasoned black women scholars and male—black and white—intellectuals? Even more poignant is the following question raised by du Cille:

What does it mean for the future of black feminist studies that a large portion of the growing body of scholarship on black women is now being written by white feminists and by men whose work frequently achieves greater critical and commercial success than that of the black female scholars who carved out a field in which few "others" were then interested?

Ann du Cille admits ambivalence and animosity over the "new-found enthusiasm" for the field. She could not wish away haunting questions related to "turf," "appropriation," and "cooptation." Her disquiet remained unabated, and she ended her essay with a suggestion of "hope about what yet might be." How and when the historiography of African American women will arrive at that point remains unknown, but it is comforting to know that black women will never again be relegated to "silence" and "invisibility," real or imaginary.

BIBLIOGRAPHY

Alexander, Adele Logan. *Ambiguous Lives: Free Women of Color in Rural Georgia, 1789–1879*. Fayetteville: University of Arkansas Press, 1991.

Anderson, Karen Tucker. "Last Hired, First Fired: Black Women Workers during the World War II." *Journal of American History* 69 (June 1982): 82–97.

Andrews, William L., ed. *Sisters of the Spirit: Three Black Women's Autobiographies of the Nineteenth Century*. Bloomington: Indiana University Press, 1986.

Ashbaugh, Carolyn. *Lucy Parsons: American Revolutionary*. Chicago: Charles H. Kerr, 1976.

Bone, Robert. *Negro Novels in America*. New Haven, CT: Yale University Press, 1965.

Braxton, Joanne M. *Black Women Writing Autobiography: A Tradition within a Tradition*. Philadelphia: Temple University Press, 1989.

Breen, William J. "Black Women and the Great War: Mobilization and Reform in the South." *Journal of Southern History* 44 (1978): 421–40.

Brown, Elaine. *A Taste of Power: A Black Woman's Story*. New York: Pantheon Books, 1992.

Brown, Elsa Barkley. "Negotiating and Transforming the Public Sphere: African American Political Life in the Transition from Slavery to Freedom." *Public Culture* 7 (1994): 107–46.

Bynum, Victoria E. *Unruly Women: The Politics of Social & Sexual Control in the Old South.* Chapel Hill: University of North Carolina Press, 1992.

Cade, Toni. *The Black Woman: An Anthology.* New York: A Mentor Book, 1970.

Campbell, John. "Work, Pregnancy, and Infant Mortality among Southern Slaves." *Journal of Interdisciplinary History* 14 (Spring 1984): 792–812.

Carby, Hazel V. *Reconstructing Womanhood: The Emergence of the Afro-American Woman Novelist.* New York: Oxford University Press, 1987.

Chisholm, Shirley. *Unbought and Unbossed.* Boston: 1970.

Christian, Barbara. *Black Feminist Criticism: Perspectives on Black Women Writers.* New York: Pergamon Press, 1985.

Clinton, Catherine. *Half Sisters of History: Southern Women and the American Past.* Durham, NC: Duke University Press, 1994.

———. "Caught in the Web of the Big House: Women and Slavery." In *The Web of Southern Social Relations: Women, Family and Education,* edited by Walter Fraser, Jr., 19–34. Athens: University of Georgia Press, 1985.

———. *The Plantation Mistress: Woman's World in the Old South.* New York: Pantheon Books, 1982.

Collins, Patricia Hill. *Black Feminist Thought: Knowledge, Consciousness, and the Politics of Empowerment.* New York: Routledge, 1990.

Cooper, Anna Julia. *A Voice from the South.* 1892. New York: Negro Universities Press, 1969.

Crawford, Vicki L., Jacqueline Anne Rouse, and Barbara Woods, eds. *Women in the Civil Rights Movement: Trailblazers & Torchbearers, 1941–1965.* Bloomington: Indiana University Press, 1993.

Davis, Angela. "Reflections on the Black Woman's Role in the Community of Slaves." *Black Scholar* 3 (December 1971): 2–16.

———. *Women, Race & Class.* New York: Vintage Books, 1983.

Dubey, Madhu. *Black Women Novelists and the Nationalist Aesthetic.* Bloomington: Indiana University Press, 1994.

du Cille, Ann. "The Occult of True Black Womanhood: Critical Demeanor and Black Feminist Studies." *Signs* 19 (Spring 1994): 591–629.

———. "Phallus(ies) of Interpretation toward Engendering the Black Critical "I." *Callaloo* 16, no. 3 (1993): 559–73.

Faucet, Jessie Raymond. *The Chinaberry Tree: A Novel of American Life.* New York: Negro Universities Press, 1931.

———. *Comedy: American Style.* College Park, MD: McGrath Publishing Company, 1933.

———. *Plum Bun: A Novel without a Moral.* New York: Frederick Stokes, 1929.

———. *There Is Confusion.* New York: Boni and Liveright, 1924.

Fields, Mamie Gavin. *Lemon Swamp and Other Places: A Carolina Memoir.* New York: Free Press, 1983.

Forbes, Ella. *African American Women during the Civil War.* New York: Garland Publishing, 1998.

Forten, Charlotte. *The Journals of Charlotte Forten.* Edited by Brenda Stevenson. New York: Oxford University Press, 1988.

Foster, Frances Smith, ed. *Minnie's Sacrifice, Sowing and Reaping, Trial and Triumph: Three Rediscovered Novels by Frances E. W. Harper*. Boston: Beacon Press, 1994.

Fox-Genovese, Elizabeth. *Within the Plantation Household: Black and White Women of the Old South*. Chapel Hill: University of North Carolina Press, 1988.

Gaspar, David Barry, and Darlene Clark Hine, eds., *More than Chattel: Black Women and Slavery in the Americas*. Bloomington: Indiana University Press, 1996.

Gates, Henry Louis, Jr., gen. ed. *Six Women's Slave Narratives*. In *The Schomburg Library of Nineteenth-Century Black Women Writers* Series. Introduction by William Andrews. New York: Oxford University Press, 1988.

Gates, Henry Louis, Jr., and Nellie Y. McKay, eds., *The Norton Anthology of African American Literature*. New York: W. W. Norton, 1997.

Giddings, Paula. *When and Where I Enter: The Impact of Black Women on Race and Sex in America*. New York: Bantam Books, 1988.

Gill, Gerald R. " 'Win or Lose—We Win': The 1952 Vice-Presidential Campaign of Charlotta A. Bass." In *The Afro-American Woman: Struggles and Images*, edited by Sharon Harley and Rosalyn Terborg-Penn, 109–118. Port Washington, NY: National University Publications, 1978.

Gill, LaVerne McCain. *African American Women in Congress: Forming and Transforming History*. New Brunswick, NJ: Rutgers University Press, 1997.

Grant, Joanne. *Ella Baker: Freedom Bound*. New York: John Wiley and Sons, 1998.

Green, Venus. "Race and Technology: African American Women in the Bell System, 1945–1980." *Technology and Culture* 36 (April 1995): S101–43.

Gutman, Herbert G. *The Black Family in Slavery and Freedom, 1750–1925*. New York: Vintage Books, 1977.

Guy-Sheftall, Beverly. *"Daughters of Sorrow": Attitudes toward Black Women, 1880–1920*. Brooklyn: Carlson Publishing, 1984.

Harley, Sharon, and Rosalyn Terborg-Penn, eds. *The Afro-American Woman: Struggles and Images*. Fort Washington, NY: National University Publications, 1978.

Hemmons, Willa Mae. *Black Women in the New World Order: Social Justice and the African American Female*. Westport, CT: Praeger, 1996.

Hewitt, John H. "The Search for Elizabeth Jennings, Heroine of a Sunday Afternoon in New York City." *New York History* 71 (October 1990): 387–415.

Higginbotham, Evelyn Brooks. *Righteous Discontent: The Women's Movement in the Baptist Church, 1880–1920*. Cambridge: Harvard University Press, 1993.

———. "African-American Women's History and the Metalanguage of Race." *Signs* 17 (Winter 1992): 251–74.

———. "Beyond the Sound of Silence: Afro-American Women in History." *Gender & History* 1 (Spring 1989): 50–67.

Hine, Darlene Clark. "Black Migration to the Urban Midwest: The Gender Dimension, 1915–1945." In *The Great Migration in Historical Perspective: New Dimensions of Race, Class, & Gender*, edited by Joe Trotter, Jr., 127–46. Bloomington: Indiana University Press, 1991.

———. "Lifting the Veil, Shattering the Silence: Black Women's History in Slavery and Freedom." In *Hine Sight: Black Women and the Re-Construction of American History*, edited by Darlene Clark Hine, 3–26. Brooklyn: Carlton Publishing, 1994.

Hine, Darlene Clark, Elsa Barkley Brown, Tiffany R. L. Patterson, and Lillian S. Wil-

liams, eds. *Black Women in United States History*. 16 vols. Brooklyn: Carlson
   Publishing, 1990.

Hine, Darlene Clark, Elsa Barkley Brown, and Rosalyn Terborg-Penn, eds. *Black Women
   in America: An Historical Encyclopedia*. Brooklyn, NY: Carlson Publishing, 1993.

Hine, Darlene Clark, Wilma King, and Linda Reed, eds. *"We Specialize in the Wholly
   Impossible."* Brooklyn, NY: Carlson Publishing, 1995.

hooks, bell. *Ain't I a Woman: Black Women and Feminism*. Boston, MA: South End
   Press, 1981.

———. *Talking Back: Thinking Feminist–Thinking Black*. Boston: South End Press,
   1989.

Howard, Victor B. "The Civil War in Kentucky: The Slave Claims His Freedom." *Journal of Negro History* 67 (Fall 1982): 245–56.

Hudson, Larry, Jr., ed. *Working Toward Freedom: Slave Society and Domestic Economy
   in the American South*. Rochester, NY: University of Rochester Press, 1994.

Hull, Gloria T. *Color, Sex, and Poetry: Three Women Writers of the Harlem Renaissance*.
   Bloomington: Indiana University Press, 1987.

Hunter, Tera. *To 'Joy My Freedom: Southern Black Women's Lives and Labor's after
   the Civil War*. Cambridge, MA: Harvard University Press, 1997.

Hurston, Zora Neale. *Their Eyes Were Watching God*. Philadelphia: Lippincott, 1937.

Ione, Carole. *Pride of Family: Four Generations of American Women of Color*. New
   York: Avon Books, 1991.

Jackson, Rebecca Cox. *Gifts of Power: The Writings of Rebecca Jackson, Black Vision-
   ary, Shaker Eldress*. Edited by Jean McMahon Humez. Amherst: University of
   Massachusetts Press, 1981.

Janiewski, Dolores E. *Sisterhood Denied: Race, Gender and Class in the New South*.
   Philadelphia: Temple University Press, 1985.

Jennings, Thelma. " 'Us Colored Women Had to Go through a Plenty': Sexual Exploitation of African American Slave Women." *Journal of Women's History* 1 (Winter 1991): 45–74.

Johnson, Michael P., and James L. Roark. "Strategies of Survival: Free Negro Families
   and the Problems of Slavery." *In Joy and in Sorrow: Women, Family, and Marriage in the Victorian South, 1830–1900*, edited by Carol Blesser, 88–102. New
   York: Oxford University Press, 1991.

Johnson, Whittington B. "Free African-American Women in Savannah, 1800–1860: Affluence and Autonomy amid Adversity." *Georgia Historical Quarterly* 76 (Summer 1992): 260–83.

Jones, Jacqueline. *Labor of Love, Labor of Sorrow: Black Women, Work and the Family,
   from Slavery to the Present*. New York: Vintage Books, 1986.

Keckley, Elizabeth. *Behind the Scenes, or Thirty Years a Slave, and Four Years in the
   White House*. New York: Oxford University Press, 1988.

Kemble, Frances Anne. *Journal of a Residence on a Georgian Plantation in 1838–1839*.
   Edited by John A. Scott. Athens: University of Georgia Press, 1984.

King, Wilma, ed. *A Northern Woman in the Plantation South: Letters of Tryphena
   Blanche Holder Fox, 1856–1876*. Columbia: University of South Carolina Press,
   1993.

Lebsock, Suzanne. *The Free Women of Petersburg: Status and Culture in a Southern
   Town, 1784–1860*. New York: W. W. Norton, 1985.

Lemann, Nicholas. *The Promised Land: The Great Black Migration and How It Changed America.* New York: A.A. Knopf, 1991.

Lemke-Santangelo, Gretchen. *Abiding Courage: African American Migrant Women and the East Bay Community.* Chapel Hill: University of North Carolina Press, 1996.

Lerner, Gerda. *The Majority Finds Its Past.* New York: Oxford University Press, 1979.

———. *Black Women in White America: A Documentary History.* New York: Vintage Books, 1973.

Leslie, Kent Anderson. *Woman of Color, Daughter of Privilege: Amanda America Dickson.* Athens: University of Georgia Press, 1995.

Litwack, Leon F. *Been in the Storm So Long: The Aftermath of Slavery.* New York: Vintage Books, 1980.

Loewenberg, Bert James, and Ruth Bogin, eds. *Black Women in Nineteenth-Century American Life: Their Words, Their Thoughts, Their Feelings.* University Park: Pennsylvania State University Press, 1976.

Logan, Onnie Lee. *Motherwit: An Alabama Midwife's Story as Told to Katherine Clark.* New York: A Plum Book, 1991.

McLaurin, Melton A. *Celia: A Slave.* Athens: University of Georgia Press, 1991.

McMillan, Terry. *Waiting to Exhale.* New York: Viking, 1992.

Mills, Gary B. "Coincoin: An Eighteenth-Century 'Liberated' Woman." *Journal of Southern History* 42 (May 1976): 205–22.

Mills, Kaye. *This Little Light of Mine: The Life of Fannie Lou Hamer.* New York: Dutton, 1993.

Moody, Anne. *Coming of Age in Mississippi.* New York: Dial Press, 1968.

Morrison, Toni, ed. *Race-ing Justice En-Gendering Power: Essays on Anita Hill, Clarence Thomas, and the Construction of Social Reality.* New York: Pantheon Books, 1992.

Morton, Patricia, ed. *Discovering the Women in Slavery: Emancipating Perspectives on the American Past.* Athens GA: University of Georgia Press, 1996.

———. *Disfigured Images: The Historical Assault on African American Women.* Westport, CT: Greenwood Press, 1991.

Murray, Pauli. *The Autobiography of a Black Activist, Feminist, Lawyer, Priest & Poet.* Knoxville: University of Tennessee Press, 1989.

Olwell, Robert. " 'Loose, Idle and Disorderly' ": Slave Women in the Eighteenth-Century Charleston Marketplace." In *More Than Chattel: Black Women and Slavery in the Americas*, edited by David Barry Gaspar and Darlene Clark Hine, 97–110. Bloomington: Indiana University Press, 1996.

Painter, Nell Irvin. *Sojourner Truth: A Life, a Symbol.* New York: W. W. Norton, 1996.

Patton, Phil. "Mammy, Her Life and Times." *American Heritage* (September 1993): 78–79.

Payne, Charles. "Ella Baker and Models of Social Change." *Signs* 14 (Summer 1989): 885–900.

Porter, Dorothy Burnett. "Sarah Parker Remond, Abolitionist and Physician." *Journal of Negro History* 20 (July 1935): 287–93.

Potter, Eliza. *A Hairdresser's Experiences in the High Life. The Schomburg Library of Nineteenth-Century Black Women Writers.* 1859. New York: Oxford University Press, 1991.

Prince, Nancy. *A Black Woman's Odyssey through Russia and Jamaica.* New York: Markus Wiener Publishing, 1990.

Rawick, George P., ed. *The American Slave: A Composite Autobiography*. 19 vols. West-
    port, CT: Greenwood Press, 1972.
————. *The American Slave: A Composite Autobiography*. Supplement, Series 1, 12
    vols. Westport, CT: Greenwood Press, 1978.
————. *The American Slave: A Composite Autobiography*. Supplement, Series 2, 10
    vols. Westport, CT: Greenwood Press, 1979.
Robinson, Jo Ann Gibson. *The Montgomery Bus Boycott and the Women Who Started
    It: The Memoir of Jo Gibson Robinson*. Edited by David Garrow. Knoxville:
    University of Tennessee Press, 1987.
Ross, B. Joyce. "Mary McLeod Bethune and the National Youth Administration: A Case
    Study of Power Relationships in the Black Cabinet of Franklin D. Roosevelt."
    Journal of Negro History 60 (January 1975): 1–28.
Rouse, Jacqueline Ann. *Lugenia Burns Hope: Black Southern Reformer*. Athens, GA:
    University of Georgia Press, 1989.
Sato, Hiroko. "Under the Harlem Shadow: A Study of Jessie Fauset and Nella Larsen."
    In *The Harlem Renaissance Remembered: Essays, Edited, with a Memoir by Arna
    Bontemps*, edited by Arna Bontemps. New York: Dodd, Mead, 1972.
Schafer, Judith. " 'Open and Notorious Concubinage': The Emancipation of Slave Mis-
    tresses by Will and the Supreme Courts in Antebellum Louisiana." *Lousiana
    History* 28 (Spring 1987): 165–82.
Schwalm, Leslie. *A Hard Fight for We: Women's Transition from Slavery to Freedom
    in South Carolina*. Urbana: University of Illinois Press, 1997.
Scott, Anne Firor. "Most Invisible of All: Black Women's Voluntary Associations."
    Journal of Southern History 56 (February 1990): 3–22.
Shakur, Assata. *Assata: An Autobiography*. Chicago: Lawrence Hill Books, 1987.
Shaw, Stephanie. *What a Woman Ought to Be and to Do: Black Professional Women
    Workers during the Jim Crow Era*. Chicago: University of Chicago Press, 1996.
Smith, Barbara. *Home Girls: A Black Feminist Anthology*. New York: Kitchen Table
    Women of Color Press, 1983.
Smith, Susan. *Sick and Tired of Being Sick and Tired*. Philadelphia: University of Penn-
    sylvania Press, 1995.
Sonderlund, Jean R. "Black Women in Colonial Pennsylvania." *Pennsylvania Magazine
    of History and Biography* 107 (January 1983): 49–68.
Sterling, Dorothy. *We Are Your Sisters: Black Women in the Nineteenth Century*. New
    York: W. W. Norton, 1984.
Stetson, Erlene, ed. *Black Sister: Poetry by Black American Women, 1746–1980*. Bloo-
    mington: Indiana University Press, 1981.
Stevenson, Brenda. "Distress and Discord in Virginia Slave Families, 1830–1860." In *In
    Joy and in Sorrow: Women, Family, and Marriage in the Victorian South, 1830–
    1900*, edited by Carol Bleser, 103–24. New York: Oxford University Press, 1991.
Stewart, Maria W. *Maria W. Stewart, America's First Black Woman Political Writer:
    Essays and Speeches*. Edited by Marilyn Richardson. Bloomington: Indiana Uni-
    versity Press, 1987.
Taylor, Susie King. *Reminiscences of My Life in Camp with the 33D United States
    Colored Troops Late 1st S.C. Volunteers*. Boston: Published by the author, 1902.
Terborg-Penn, Rosalyn. "Discontented Black Feminists: Prelude and Postscript to the
    Passage of the Nineteenth Amendment." In *Decades of Discontent: The Women's*

Movement, 1920–1940, edited by Lois Scharf and Joan Jenson, 261–78. Westport, CT: Greenwood Press, 1983.

Walker, Alice. *In Search of Our Mother's Garden: Womanist Prose*. San Diego: Harcourt Brace Jovanovich, 1983.

Walker, David. *David Walker's Appeal, in four articles, together with a preamble to the citizens of the world, but in particular, and very expressly to those of the United States of America*. 1829. Edited by Sean Wilentz. New York: Hill and Wang, 1995.

Watkins, Frances. *Poems on Miscellaneous Subjects*. Philadelphia: Merrihew and Thompson, 1857.

Watkins-Owens, Irma. *Blood Relations: Caribbean Immigrants and the Harlem Community, 1900–1930*. Bloomington: Indiana University Press 1996.

Webb, Sheyann, and Rachel West Nelson. *Selma, Lord, Selma: Girlhood Memories of the Civil Rights Movement as told to Frank Sikora*. University: University of Alabama Press, 1980.

Wells Barnett, Ida B. *Crusade for Justice: The Autobiography of Ida B. Wells*. Chicago: University of Chicago Press, 1970.

Wheatley, Phillis. *The Collected Works of Phillis Wheatley: The Schomburg Library of Nineteenth-Century Black Women Writers*. Edited by John C. Shields. New York: Oxford University Press, 1988.

White, Deborah Gray. *Ar'n't I a Woman? Female Slaves in the Plantation South*. New York: W. W. Norton, 1985.

White, E. Frances. "Africa on My Mind: Gender, Counter Discourse and African-American Nationalism." *Journal of Women's History* 2 (Spring 1990): 73–97.

Williams, Patricia. *The Alchemy of Race and Rights: Diary of a Law Professor*. Cambridge MA: Harvard University Press, 1991.

Wilson, Harriet. *Our Nig; or, Sketches from the Life of a Free Black in a Two-Story White House, North. Showing That Slavery's Shadows Fall Even There*. New York: Vintage Books, 1983.

Yee, Shirley. *Black Women Abolitionists: A Study in Activism*. Knoxville: University of Tennessee Press, 1992.

Yellin, Jean Fagan, and John C. Van Horne, eds. *The Abolitionist Sisterhood: Women's Political Culture in Antebellum America*. Ithaca, NY: Cornell University Press, 1994.

V

The African American Educational Experience

Carolyn A. Dorsey

Individuals are generally educated for their intended roles in society. Education, called one of the "essential amenities of human progress," has historically been withheld from African American as a means to keep them under control. Concurrently, blacks have waged a long-standing battle to attain equal education and full socioeconomic mobility.

One of the first scholars to examine the historic African American educational experience was George Washington Williams (1849–1891). William's important 1882 work *The History of the Negro Race in America* included information related to education. His chapter "Negro School Laws, 1619–1860," provides interesting details of activities by state, selected institutions, and educators.

William Edward Burghardt Du Bois (1868–1963), one of the most important and productive scholars of all time, wrote extensively on African American education. In regards to Du Bois's work on education, Herbert Aptheker in his 1973 edited work *The Education of Black People: Ten Critiques, 1906–1960, by W.E.B. Du Bois*, asserted that Du Bois "had no peer . . . on the specific subject of the education of Black people in the United States."

Du Bois's disagreement with Booker T. Washington regarding the efficacy of "liberal arts education" versus "industrial education" is the best-known expression of his attitudes relating to education. This is documented in a number of publications, including Du Bois's 1903 classic, *The Souls of Black Folk* (see chapters "Of Mr. Booker T. Washington and Others" and "Of the Training of Black Men") and Julius Lester's 1971 edited book *The Seventh Son: The Thought and Writings of W.E.B. Du Bois*.

Besides his debate with Booker T. Washington, W.E.B. Du Bois used his important Atlanta University Conference on Negro Problems (1897–1910) to address issues relating to African American education. Publications generated from the 1900 and 1901 conferences, *The College Bred Negro* and *The Negro Common School*, represent path-breaking examinations of their respective subjects. Likewise, Du Bois's magisterial *Black Reconstruction in America: An Essay toward a History of the Part Which Black Folk Played in the Attempt to Reconstruct Democracy in America, 1860–1880* (1935), examined the issue of African American education during this important period. Moreover, *Black Reconstruction*'s bibliography included the graduate theses of several young black scholars, including Rufus E. Clement's "History of Negro Education in North Carolina"; Frank R. Horne's "The Present Status of Negro Education in Certain of the Southern States, Particularly Georgia"; O'Hara R. Lanier's "The History of Negro Education of Florida"; and Richard T. Williams's "A History of Public Education and Charitable Institutions in South Carolina during the Reconstruction Period."

W.E.B. Du Bois's intellectual adversary, Booker T. Washington, likewise produced a number of works relating to African American education (from his own perspective). See in particular, Washington's *My Larger Education* (1911) and "The Educational Outlook in the South," (*Journal of the Proceedings and Addresses of the National Education Association, Session of the Year 1884, at Madison, Wisconsin*).

In the year of Washington's death (1915) and three years after he received the Ph.D., Carter G. Woodson wrote *The Education of the Negro prior to 1861: A History of the Education of the Colored People of the United States from the Beginning of Slavery to the Civil War*. His original goal was to write a book on "the leading facts of the development of Negro education," but after reviewing background materials he decided to limit the study to the antebellum period. Previous studies and writings included only the Special Report of the United States Commissioner of Education of 1871, which contained M. B. Goodwin's "History of the Schools for the Colored Population in the District of Columbia" and a survey of the "Legal Status of the Colored Population in Respect to Schools and Education in the Different States." He found the latter "neither comprehensive nor thorough." Other studies, not identified, Woodson found limited to "localities" or "special phases."

The impact of Woodson's work is suggested by a joint book review of *The Education of the Negro prior to 1861* and R. W. Shufeldt's *America's Greatest Problem: The Negro*, which appeared in the July 18, 1915, issue of the *New York Times*. The reviewer found *America's Greatest Problem: The Negro* so racist that "its violence and prejudice destroy its value." He took exception to such statements as "the full-blooded negro in this country has never contributed a single line to literature worth the printing" and "it is impossible to improve the morals of a people when they have no morals to improve." The reviewer concluded that "the book is so intemperate and unjust that it defeats its own ends."

Conversely, Woodson's *Education of the Negro prior to 1861* was very well received. Such phrases as "a dispassionate monograph, done in the modern scientific spirit," "soundness of his conclusions," "well-authenticated American history," and "thorough and intelligent study, with just enough sympathetic spirit to humanize its array of well-ordered facts" appeared in the review. Moreover, for the reviewer, much that Woodson wrote "controvert Dr. Shufeldt's sweeping negatives."

Woodson continued his interest in the education of blacks. In 1921, he published a small booklet, *Early Negro Education in West Virginia*. In 1933, Woodson's well-known and highly respected *Mis-education of the Negro* appeared. Similar to arguments waged some thirty years later for "relevant" education and an education that does not alienate "black leaders from the indigenous culture of their people," *The Mis-education of the Negro* stated that education should be "determined by the make-up of the Negro himself and by what his environment requires of him." In his view, the "only" question of concern was "were blacks being educated to face the ordeal before them?"

At the time of *The Mis-education of the Negro*'s publication, African American historiography was in the throes of a significant change in orientation. The "racial uplift" theme, promoted by scholars such as Woodson, began to give way to more economic and social interpretations of the black experience. Along with Du Bois's *Black Reconstruction in America*, Horace Mann Bond's *Education of the Negro in the American Social Order* (1934) exemplified this trend.

Even before the publication of *The Education of the Negro in the American Social Order*, Horace Mann Bond had visibly broken with the scholarly tradition personified by Woodson. In their 1986 work *Black History and the Historical Profession, 1915–1980*, August Meier and Elliott Rudwick described Bond's review of Carter G. Woodson's *Mis-education of the Negro* (which appeared in the April 1933 issue of the *Journal of Negro Education*) as a "devastating analysis." Bond wrote that the collection of essays and speeches were "weekly sledge hammer blows," but brought together in a book, "their fatal defect is repetitious contradiction and sensational overstatement." He did not consider the book history. He considered it a "compilation of the rather bitter 'reflections' and 'observations' " of Woodson.

Bond's own book, *The Education of the Negro in the American Social Order*, sought to point out the interrelationships between the American social order and the public schooling of blacks. In it, he noted inherent educational (racial) inequality and warned against viewing the schools as a means to solve social problems. Moreover, his biographer, Wayne J. Urban, in *Black Scholar: Horace Mann Bond, 1904–1972* (1992), points out that Bond's *Education of the Negro in the American Social Order* was the first book to argue that because of migration, greater emphasis should be placed upon the educational problems of urban blacks.

Bond's Ph.D. dissertation, "Social and Economic Influences on the Public Education of Negroes in Alabama, 1865–1930," was completed in 1936 and published as his second book, *Negro Education in Alabama: A Study in Cotton and Steel* in 1939. Urban considers *Negro Education in Alabama* Bond's "greatest contribution" to scholarship and states that the social and economic analysis of educational institutions made Bond's book "distinctive." According to Urban, Bond never became a "complete economic determinist" because as a black he could not relegate discrimination to a minor role. Urban also points out that by the 1960s, "revisionist interpretations such as Bond's had gained the ascendancy." According to him, Bond's contribution to the historiography of education includes anticipating contemporary scholarship, "an admirable historical sophistication," and "interpretive virtuosity"; further, Urban believes Bond's work stands out as one of the "premier" works in the development of black history. Bond also wrote sections on the education of blacks in *The Modern Encyclopedia of Education* and in the *Encyclopedia of Educational Research* (1941), the latter of which, in particular, has an excellent bibliography.

Another highly respected Ph.D. dissertation during this period was Marion M. Thompson Wright's published work *The Education of Negroes in New Jersey* (1940) It provided a historical survey of social factors that influenced the development of educational opportunities for blacks in New Jersey. Chronologically, it began with the introduction of slavery into the state and ended at 1900. Horace Mann Bond's review of *The Education of Negroes in New Jersey*, which appeared in the January 1942 issue of the *Journal of Negro Education*, described it as a "significant contribution" to the history of American culture and to students of social trends and of educational institutions. As in his own work, Wright studied "social and economic cleavages." Noted also were "sectional differentiations . . . in . . . the white population," factors "always and inevitably reflected in the status of Negroes in the public schools." According to J. D. Jerome's review of the book in the October 1941 issue of the *Journal of Negro History*, Wright emphasized the struggle of blacks for the right to be educated. Wright also included in the text a summary of studies dealing with more recent conditions.

Despite this movement toward more positive studies concerning blacks, a year later in 1941, Henry L. Swint published the widely discussed *Northern Teacher in the South, 1862–1870* which was tinged with a pro-southern bias.

Vincent P. Franklin, in an analysis (1978b) of the work of the period, concluded that by the end of the 1930s, there was general agreement among historians of the Afro-American that the "social, political, economic, and educational development of Afro-America must be viewed within the evolving social and economic context of American society in general." By this time, international concern over the shabby treatment of blacks while America ostensibly fought World War II for the Four Freedoms proved embarrassing to the United States. This, and more, resulted in efforts to increase positive interracial contacts.

In the late 1930s Andrew Carnegie, known particularly for his support of Hampton and Tuskegee Institutes, was told by Corporation board member Newton D. Baker that "more knowledge and better organized and interrelated knowledge were essential before the Corporation could intelligently distribute its own funds." This led to the commissioning of Gunnar Myrdal, who started work on *An American Dilemma: The Negro Problem & Modern Democracy* late in 1938. Scholars of the black educational experience who offered criticisms and suggestions early in the study included Du Bois; Thomas Jesse Jones, ed., *Negro Education: A Study of the Private and Higher Schools for Colored People in the United States* (1917); Charles H. Thompson, founder and first editor of the *Journal of Negro Education* (1933); Charles S. Johnson, *The Negro College Graduate* (1938); and Doxey A. Wilkerson, *Special Problems of Negro Education* (1939). The manuscript done for the study was "The Negro in American Education" (1940).

In *An American Dilemma*, "The Negro School" is treated in chapter 41. It concluded by asserting "The American nation will not have peace with its conscience until inequality is stamped out, and the principle of public education is realized universally." Meier and Rudwick discuss how Myrdal, working with a number of outstanding black scholars, "elevated to the level of a scientific theory the strategy that black Americans throughout their history had employed in their struggle for social change: appealing to the democratic value system and making whites sensitive to the contradictions between their ideological protestations and social reality." This combined with New Deal reformism and widespread revulsion to the racialist underpinnings of Nazism, created a general "sense of moral indignation" about racism that led more white scholars to research the history of race relations and the black experience. Again, according to Meier and Rudwick, "preeminence in Afro-American historiography passed from blacks to whites."

In the field of African American education, white Mississippi-born Louis R. Harlan became a leading figure. Harlan, who later became Booker T. Washington's most noteworthy biographer, first achieved prominence for his 1958 book *Separate and Unequal: Public School Campaigns and Racism in the Southern Seaboard States, 1901–1915*. Reviewer Paul Cooke, in the fall 1958 issue of the *Journal of Negro Education*, stated that Harlan wrote "more than a reliably documented exposition of education inequalities." Harlan's book revealed the educational discrimination directed toward both black and white students in rural areas, and discussed the public school movement in the South, as well as the role of the Southern Education Board during the years 1901–1915 (when it did not oppose segregation and weakly opposed outright discrimination). Significantly, Harlan, as did Bond, found that education did not "condition people out of their prejudices and practice of discrimination. The key likely is not simply education but the right kind of education." Harlan's "Desegregation in New Orleans Public Schools during Reconstruction," which appeared in the April 1962 issue of the *American Historical Review*, further enhanced his reputation as an expert on African American educational history.

Despite the increasing number of white scholars who began to specialize in African American educational history after World War II, blacks continued to do important (if not sometimes overlooked) research in this field. James P.

Anderson's 1984 monograph "Toward a History and Bibliography of the Afro-American Doctorate and Professorate in Education, 1896–1980" included an extensive list of Ph.D dissertations completed by black scholars. Among those completed in the immediate post–World War II period were Nehemiah M. Christopher, "The History of Negro Public Education in Texas, 1865–1900" (1949); Lillian G. Dabney, "The History of Schools for Negroes in the District of Columbia, 1807–1947" (1949); George L. Mann, "The Historical Development of Public Education in St. Louis, Missouri for Negroes" (1949); and Prince A. Taylor, "A History of Gammon Theological Seminary" (1949).

During the 1950s, the issue of African American education took center stage with the U.S. Supreme Court's monumental May 17, 1954, decision in the *Brown v. Board of Education* case. Not surprisingly, the Supreme Court's actions generated subsequent examinations of the 1954 *Brown* decision and its implementation. Among the most significant are Richard Kluger, *Simple Justice: The History of "Brown v. Board of Education" and Black America's Struggle for Equality* (1975); and Raymond W. Mack, ed., *Our Children's Burden: Studies of Desegregation in Nine American Communities* (1968); as well as the work of non-historian Carl T. Rowan, *Dream Makers, Dream Breakers: The World of Justice Thurgood Marshall* (1993). More recent studies that have revisited the desegregation struggles of the 1950s and 1960s include Liva Baker's *Second Battle of New Orleans: The Hundred-Year Struggle to Integrate the Schools* (1996); and Davison M. Douglas's *Reading, Writing, and Race: The Desegregation of the Charlotte Schools* (1995).

Despite the significance of later studies surveying the nuances of the *Brown* decision, important contemporary works promoted the notion of educational racial desegregation mandated by the Supreme Court. Such books, clearly "integrationist" in their outlook, included Willard Range, *The Rise and Progress of Negro Colleges in Georgia, 1865–1949* (1951); Elisabeth S. Peck, *Berea's First Century, 1855–1955* (1955); Louis R. Harlan's *Separate and Unequal: Public School Campaigns and Racism in the Southern Seaboard States, 1901–1915* (1958); and Henry Bullock, *A History of Negro Education in the South; from 1619 to the Present* (1970). The latter, according to V. P. Franklin, was especially "explicit" in conveying the pro-integration perspective.

The *Brown* decision affected not only elementary and secondary schools but higher education as well. The widespread desegregation of colleges and universities that took place during the 1950s and 1960s also stimulated scholarly study of previously desegregated institutions of higher learning. Important works focusing upon Kentucky's Berea College include Elisabeth S. Peck's *Berea's First Century* (1955); Paul D. Nelson's 1974 article in the *Journal of Negro History*, "Experiment in Interracial Education at Berea College, 1858–1908," and his 1996 article in *Journal of Blacks in Higher Education*, "The Roller-Coaster Ride of Black Students at Berea College." Several scholars have been interested in Oberlin College. The classic work on this topic is Robert S. Fletcher's 1943 study, *A History of Oberlin College: From Its Foundation through the Civil*

War. Other significant works on this topic are W. E. Bigglestone's 1971 *Journal of Negro History* article, "Oberlin College and the Negro Student, 1865–1940"; Ellen Henle and Marlene Merrill's 1979 article in the *Women's Studies Newsletter*, "Antebellum Black Coeds at Oberlin College"; Ellen Lawson and Marlene Merrill's "The Antebellum 'Talented Thousandth': Black College Students at Oberlin before the Civil War," which appeared in the spring 1983 issue of the *Journal of Negro Education*; and Juanita D. Fletcher's 1974 Ph.D. dissertation, "Against the Consensus: Oberlin College and the Education of American Negroes, 1835–1865."

Other antebellum educational facilities that featured interracial instruction—and have been examined by scholars—were Central College, founded in 1849 in McGrawville, New York, by the American Baptist Free Missionary Society, and the Oneida Institute located in Whitesboro, New York (the latter was not an institution of higher education). New York Central College has been surveyed in Albert H. Wright's *Cornell's Three Precursors: 1. New York Central College* (1960); Kenneth R. Short's 1962 article "New York Central College: A Baptist Experiment in Integrated Higher Education, 1848–61"; Benjamin Quarle's *Black Abolitionists* (1969); and Carleton Mabee's *Black Education in New York State: From Colonial to Modern Times* (1979). An Excellent source on Oneida is Milton C. Sernett's *Abolition's Axe: Beriah Green, Oneida Institute, and the Black Freedom Struggle* (1986).

Interest in blacks on these white campuses during the early years is not limited to students who gained access but includes the experiences of black professors. The first black professors on a white campus, Charles Lewis Reason, William G. Allen, and George Boyer Vashon, worked at Central College. For additional information about these "pioneer" African Americans in higher education, see Carolyn Dorsey's 1990 *Western Journal of Black Studies* article "Black Faculty at White Institutions before 1900." Also consult the following sources that appeared in various issues of the *Journal of Blacks in Higher Education*: Robert Bruce Slater's "Blacks Who First Entered the World of White Higher Education" (Summer 1994); Caldwell Titcomb, "Letter to the Editor: Black Pioneers in American Higher Education" (Autumn 1994); and Carolyn A. Dorsey, "Letter to the editor" (Winter 1994–1995).

The literature concerning black professors on white campuses after the antebellum period, but before the 1960s, includes Rufus B. Atwood, H. S. Smith, and Catherine O. Vaughan, "Negro Teachers in Northern Colleges and Universities in the United States," (1949); Edward A. Jones and Virginia L. Jones, "Negroes on White College Faculties," (1946); James Allen Moss, "Negro Teachers in Predominantly White Colleges," (1958); and Ivan E. Taylor, "Negro Teachers in White Colleges" (1947). William Moore and Lonnie H. Wagstaff's *Black Educators in White Colleges* appeared in 1974.

The civil rights–integrationist paradigm of the 1950s and early 1960s gave way in the mid-1960s to the black power movement. This development, among other things, led to the demand for black studies programs on college campuses.

Moreover, scholars, clearly affected by the growing militancy of African American students on U.S. campuses, changed their focus from racial integration to the development and evolution of institutions in the black community.

According to Ronald E. Butchart's important 1995 essay "Outthinking and Outflanking the Owners of the World: An Historiography of the African American Struggle for Education," the years since the late 1960s have featured "an unparalled richness in the field of African American education history." Moreover, this new research, according to Butchart, "rivaled the best of Du Bois, Bond, and Harlan." Some recently explored topics and themes include slavery as an educative institution; northern black schooling; relationships between white teachers and black students; the response of the black community to educational opportunity; effects of black cultural values on education; and black educational achievement studied empirically, not impressionistically. The history of scientific racism and its "insinuation into the school in the form of intelligence tests and other standardized tests" has also increasingly attracted the attention of scholars.

Two of the leading figures in the recent "renaissance" of African American education history are Vincent P. Franklin and James D. Anderson. In 1978, they coedited *New Perspectives on Black Educational History*. According to the editors, the purpose behind *New Perspectives on Black Educational History* was also to show "how the black ghetto or 'community' was educated and educated itself." Some essays included in the book were a study of the Institute for Colored Youth in Philadelphia by Linda Perkins; June Patton's discussion of how blacks in Augusta, Georgia, struggled to maintain Ware High School; James D. Anderson's studies of Hampton Institute and Fisk University; V. P. Franklin's description of the involvement of black Philadelphia social organizations in educational matters between 1900 and 1930; and Lillian Williams's depiction of the founding and educational programs of the Michigan Avenue YMCA for blacks in Buffalo in 1922–1940.

Significantly, in his editorial commentary, Franklin asserted that his and Lillian Williams's articles were "the first to document the role of community education programs' in the social development of urban black communities." Rounding out this important volume were discussions by Genna Rae McNeil of the "transformation" of Howard University Law School between 1920 and 1935 and by Darlene Clark Hine of changes at Meharry Medical College between 1921 and 1938.

Another example of recent scholarship in the field of African American education history is David N. Plank and Marcia Turner's 1987 article "Changing Patterns in Black School Politics: Atlanta, 1872–1973." This essay, which appeared in the August 1987 issue of the *American Journal of Education*, sought to consciously spotlight the efforts of blacks to secure improved educational opportunity for their children. Plank and Turner maintained that some previous studies in the field tended to show blacks either as beneficiaries of white largess or as helpless victims of white oppression. Works in this genre included Horace Mann Bond's *Education of the Negro in the American Social Order* (1934) and *Negro Education in Alabama* (1939); Louis R. Harlan's *Separate and Unequal* (1958); Henry Bullock's *History of Negro Education* (1970); and Carl V. Harris's "Stability and Change in Discrimination against Black Public Schools: Birmingham, Alabama, 1871–1931" (1985).

In addition, Plank and Turner complained about another body of works that "focused on the evolution of national attitudes and policies" without adequate attention to the "ways in which national policies were shaped and implemented at the local level, especially in the South." J. Harvie Wilkinson's *From Brown to Bakke* (1974); Richard Kluger's *Simple Justice* (1976); Gary Orfield's "Why It Worked in Dixie: Southern School Desegregation and Its Implications for the North" (1981); David L. Kirp's *Just Schools: The Idea of Racial Equality in American Education* (1982); and Jennifer L. Hochschild's *New American Dilemma* (1984) were cited in this category.

In their own work on Atlanta, Plank and Turner demonstrated that among local blacks, school integration was "not an end in itself." The objectives and strategies of black leaders changed with the changes in political circumstances. For example, at one point the goal was integration of the schools; at another, the goal was "to improve the quality of education provided to all children . . . without further regard to race."

The theme of black self-determination, in reference to education, clearly resonates in a number of recent accounts examining historic African American education. Such studies include Raymond Wolter's *New Negro on Campus: Black College Rebellions of the 1920s* (1975); Ronald E. Butchart's *Northern Schools, Southern Blacks, and Reconstruction: Freedmen's Education, 1862– 1875* (1980); Robert C. Morris's *Reading, 'Riting, and Reconstruction: The Education of Freedmen in the South, 1861–1870* (1981); Thomas Webber's *Deep like the Rivers: Education in the Slave Quarter Community, 1831–1865* (1978); Carleton Mabee's *Black Education in New York State: From Colonial to Modern Times* (1979); Jacqueline Jones's *Soldiers of Light and Love: Northern Teachers and Georgia Blacks, 1865–1873* (1980); Donald Spivey's *Schooling for the New Slavery: Black Industrial Education, 1868–1915,* (1978); and James D. Anderson's "The Hampton Model of Normal School Industrial Education, 1868–1900" (1978). Some of the primary issues explored in these works are the historic relationship between white teachers and black students (and black preferences for teachers of their own race), conflict between blacks and whites regarding the aims and goals associated with educating African Americans, and the "mis-education" of blacks following emancipation.

Interestingly, the historiography of African American educational history appears to have gone full circle. Pioneers such as George Washington Williams, W.E.B. Du Bois, and Carter G. Woodson felt compelled to write a "corrective" history that vindicated African Americans against mainstream assertions of inherent black inferiority. Although this paradigm fell into disfavor for more than a generation, since the late 1960s black education historians have resurrected notions of African American self-assertion, agency, and pride.

The eightieth anniversary issue (1996) of the *Journal of Negro History*, entitled "Vindicating the Race: Contributions to African-American Intellectual History," provided further evidence of this trend. This special volume, edited by Vincent P. Franklin and Bettye Collier-Thomas, included several essays of interest to the African American educational historian: June O. Patton's "And the Truth Shall Make You Free"; Richard Robert Wright, Sr.'s "Black Intellectual and Iconoclast, 1877–1897"; Jacqueline Anne Rouse's "Out of the Shadow of Tuskegee: Margaret Murray Washington, Social Activism, and Race Vindication"; Sharon Harley's "Nannie Helen Burroughs: 'The Black Goddess of Liberty' "; Linda M. Perkins's "Lucy Diggs Slowe: Champion of the Self-Determination of African-American Women in Higher Education"; and Elaine M. Smith's "Mary McLeod Bethune's 'Last Will and Testament': A Legacy for Race Vindication."

Clearly, the historiography of Afro-American education is vast. There were distinct and differing educational experiences for blacks both during slavery and afterward. Moreover, the massive twentieth-century migration of African Americans out of the rural South into northern, southern, and western cities appeared partially based on the desires of black parents to provide their children with a good education. Although black parents have expressed ongoing disappointment regarding the way their children are treated in urban school districts, the institution of affirmative action programs to increase black access to higher education has benefited many African Americans.

Perhaps the most controversial contemporary issue related to African American education is the debate regarding Afrocentrism. Significantly, much of this discussion is based upon political, rather than educational, considerations. Gerald Early, in his 1994 essay "Afrocentrism: From Sensationalism to Measured Deliberation," contended that Afrocentrism is not a "new" phenomenon. In fact, it is "probably embedded in earlier forms of black nationalist thought, the black aesthetic of the 1970s, black power of the 1960s, and Pan-Africanism in its various forms since the eighteenth century." He sees it as a result of the longing of blacks for an ideology that binds them as a community and for an alternative to assimilation as well as an alternative to being bound together as a result of a common history of oppression.

Those scholars opposing "centrism" support what they view as the only fair concept, multiculturalism. Although not widely recognized as a proponent of multicuturalism, Molefi Kete Asante, a leader in the Afrocentric movement, says his movement is about "pluralism without hierarchy." Moreover, Asante, in his 1991 *American Scholar* article entitled "Controversy: Multiculturalism: An Exchange," stated that "education must present the totality of the African experience within the context of American society."

The discussion involving Afrocentrism is obviously much more complex than presented here. Yet, despite the various viewpoints, Ed Wiley III's 1991 essay in *Black Issues in Higher Education* entitled "Afrocentrism: Many Things to Many People" plausibly asserts that most people can agree that "Afrocentrism is about education."

The history of the black struggle to gain a meaningful education is a fascinating one, especially when told by those who actually fought for it. Frederick Douglass's famous narrative revealed how he tricked white boys to teach him to read after his mistress, who had taught him the alphabet, stopped teaching Douglass at the behest of her husband. Similarly, Thomas L. Webber, in his 1978 book *Deep like the Rivers: Education in the Slave Quarter Community, 1831–1865*, in his chapter entitled "The Desirability of Learning to Read and Write," reveals the slaves' expressed strong desire to read and write despite punishment. This desire has remained strong throughout the black experience in this country and remains evident as we reassess the impact of school desegregation and busing, as well as prepare to do battle with those who want to destroy educational affirmative action.

BIBLIOGRAPHY

"America's Greatest Problem: The Negro." Review of *America's Greatest Problem* by R. W. Shufeldt; *The Education of the Negro Prior to 1861* by Carter G. Woodson, and *The Negro* by W.E.B. Du Bois. In the *New York Times Book Review*, July 18, 1915.

Anderson, James D. *The Education of Blacks in the South, 1860–1935*. Chapel Hill: University of North Carolina Press, 1988.

———. "The Hampton Model of Normal School Industrial Education, 1868–1900." In *New Perspectives on Black Educational History*, ed. Vincent P. Franklin and James D. Anderson. Boston: G. K. Hall, 1978.

———. "The Hampton Model of Normal School Industrial Education, 1868–1915." In *The Education of Blacks in the South, 1860–1935*, by James D. Anderson. Chapel Hill: University of North Carolina Press, 1988.

Anderson, James D., Warren Chapman, and Larry Parker. "Doctoral Dissertations in Education by Afro-Americans, 1925–1951." In *The Black Education Professorate*. Society of Professors of Education Monograph Series, 1984.

———. "Philanthropic Control over Private Black Higher Education." In *Philanthropy and Cultural Imperialism: The Foundations at Home and Abroad*, ed. Robert F. Arnove. Boston: G. K. Hall, 1980.

———. "Toward a History and Bibliography of the Afro-American Doctorate and Professorate in Education, 1896–1980." In *The Black Education Professorate*. Society of Professors of Education Monograph Series, 1984.

Anderson, Karen. "Brickbats and Roses: Lucy Diggs Slowe, 1883–1937." In *Lone Voyagers: Academic Women in Coeducational Universities, 1870–1937*, ed. Geraldine J. Clifford. New York: Feminist Press at the City University of New York, 1989.

Andrews, Charles C. *The History of the New York African Free-Schools, from Their*

Establishment in 1787, to the Present Time: Embracing a Period of More Than Forty Years. New York: Mahlon Day, 1830.

Aptheker, Herbert, ed. *The Education of Black People: Ten Critiques, 1906–1960, by W.E.B. Du Bois.* Amherst: University of Massachusetts, 1973.

Armstrong, Mary F., and Helen W. Ludlow. *Hampton and Its Students by Two of Its Teachers with Fifty Cabin and Plantation Songs, Arranged by Thomas P. Fenner, in Charge of Musical Department at Hampton.* New York: G. P. Putnam, 1874.

———. *Hampton Institute: Its Work for Two Races 1868–1885.* Hampton, VA: Normal School, 1885.

Asante, Molefi Kete. "Controversy: Multiculturalism: An Exchange." *American Scholar* (Spring 1991): 267–72.

Atwood, Rufus B. "The Origin and Development of the Negro Public College with Especial Reference to the Land-Grant College." *Journal of Negro Education* 3 (Summer 1962): 240–50.

Atwood, Rufus, H. S. Smith, and Catherine O. Vaughan. "Negro Teachers in Northern Colleges and Universities in the United States." *Journal of Negro Education* 18 (Fall 1949): 559–67.

Bacote, Clarence A. *The Story of Atlanta University: A Century of Service, 1865–1965* Atlanta: Atlanta University, 1969.

Baker, Liva. *The Second Battle of New Orleans: The Hundred-Year Struggle to Integrate the Schools.* New York: HarperCollins, 1996.

Ballard, Allen B. *The Education of Black Folk: The Afro-American Struggle for Knowledge in White America.* New York: Harper & Row, 1973.

Barrows, Isabel C. *The First Mohonk Conference on the Negro Question, June 4, 5, 6, 1890.* New York: Negro Universities, 1969.

Bell-Scott, Patricia. "Black Women's Higher Education: Our Legacy." *SAGE: A Scholarly Journal on Black Women* 1 (Spring 1984): 8–11.

Bellamy, Donnie D. "The Education of Blacks in Missouri Prior to 1861." *Journal of Negro History* 59 (April 1974): 143–57.

Berry, Mary Frances. "Twentieth-Century Black Women in Education." *Journal of Negro Education* 51 (Summer 1982): 288–300.

Bigglestone, W. E. "Oberlin College and the Negro Student, 1865–1940." *Journal of Negro History* 56 (July 1971): 198–219.

Billington, Ray Allen, ed. *The Journal of Charlotte L. Forten: A Young Black Woman's Reactions to the White World of the Civil War Era.* New York: W. W. Norton, 1953.

"Black Women's Education." *SAGE: A Scholarly Journal on Black Women* 1 (Spring 1984).

Blackett, R.J.M. "William G. Allen: The Forgotten Professor." *Civil War History* 26 (March 1980): 39–52.

Bond, Horace Mann. "A History of the American Negro Scholar and Doctorate." In *Black American Scholars.* Detroit: Balamp, 1972.

———. *Education for Freedom: A History of Lincoln University, Pennsylvania.* Lincoln University, PA: Lincoln University, 1976.

———. *Negro Education in Alabama: A Study in Cotton and Steel.* New York: Octagon, 1939.

———. "Origin and Development of the Negro Church-Related College." *Journal of Negro Education* 29 (Summer 1960): 217–26.

————. *The Education of the Negro in the American Social Order*. New York: Prentice-Hall, 1934.

————. "Dr. Woodson Goes Wool-Gathering." Review of *The Mis-Education of the Negro* by Carter G. Woodson. In *Journal of Negro Education* 2 (April 1933): 210–13.

————. Review of *The Education of Negroes in New Jersey* by Marion M. Thompson Wright. In *Journal of Negro Education* 11 (January 1942): 64–65.

Brazzell, Johnetta Cross. "Bricks without Straw: Missionary-Sponsored Black Higher Education in the Post-Emancipation Era." *Journal of Higher Education* 63 (January/February 1992) 26–49.

Britts, Maurice W. "Blacks on White College Campuses: 1823–Present." *Negro History Bulletin* 37 (June/July 1974): 269–72.

Bullock, Henry Allen. *A History of Negro Education in the South; from 1619 to the Present*. New York: Praeger, 1970.

Butchart, Ronald E. *Northern Schools, Southern Blacks, and Reconstruction: Freedmen's Education, 1862–1875*. Westport, CT: Greenwood, 1980.

————. "Outthinking and Outflanking the Owners of the World: An Historiography of the African-American Struggle for Education." In *Too Much Schooling, Too Little Education: A Paradox of Black Life in White Societies*, ed. Mwalimu J. Shujaa. Trenton, NJ: Africa World Press, 1995.

Butler, Addie Louise Joyner. *The Distinctive Black College: Talladega, Tuskegee and Morehouse*. Metuchen, NJ: Scarecrow, 1977.

Butler, J. H. "An Historical Account of the John F. Slater Fund and the Anna T. Jeanes Foundation." Ph.D. dissertation, University of California, 1931.

Carter, Ann L. "Black Americans and Education: An Historical Perspective." *Journal of the National Association of Women Deans, Administrators, & Counselors* 43 (Winter 1980): 14–21.

Cash, W. J. *The Mind of the South*. New York: Alfred A. Knopf, 1941.

Citro, Joseph F. "Booker T. Washington's Tuskegee Institute: Black School–Community, 1900–1915." Ed.D. dissertation, University of Rochester, 1973.

Clement, Rufus E. "A History of Negro Education in North Carolina." Ph.D. dissertation, Northwestern University, 1930.

————. "The Historical Development of Higher Education for Negro Americans." *Journal of Negro Education* 35 (Fall 1966): 299–305.

Coleman, J.F.B. *Tuskegee to Voorhees: The Booker T. Washington Idea Projected by Elizabeth Evelyn Wright*. Columbia, SC: R. L. Bryan, 1922.

Coleman, James S., et al. "Equality of Educational Opportunity." Washington, DC: U.S. Government Printing Office, 1966.

Cooke, Paul. Review of *Separate and Unequal: Public School Campaigns and Racism in the Southern Seaboard States, 1901–1915* by Louis R. Harlan. In *Journal of Negro Education* 27 (Fall 1958): 500–501.

Cooper, Anna. *A Voice from the South*. New York: Negro Universities, 1892.

Coppin, Fanny Jackson. *Reminiscences of School Life and Hints on Teaching*. New York: Garland, 1987.

Cremin, Lawrence A. *American Education: The Metropolitan Experience, 1876–1980*. New York: Harper & Row, 1988.

Crouchett, L. "Early Black Studies Movements." *Journal of Black Studies* 2 (December): 189–200.

Culp, D. W., ed. *Twentieth Century Negro Literature or a Cyclopedia of Thought on the Vital Topics Relating to the American Negro.* Naperville, IL: J. L. Nichols, 1902.

Curry, Jabez L. M. *A Brief Sketch of George Peabody, and a History of the Peabody Education Fund through Thirty Years.* New York: Negro Universities, 1969.

———. "Difficulties, Complications and Limitations Connected with the Education of the Negro." In *Social History of American Education*, vol. 2., ed. Rena Vassar. Chicago: Rand McNally, 1965.

Curti, Merle. *The Social Ideas of American Educators.* Totowa, NJ: Littlefield, Adams, 1966.

Dabney, Charles W. *Universal Education in the South*, 2 vols. Chapel Hill: University of North Carolina Press, 1936.

Dabney, Lillian G. *The History of Schools for Negroes in the District of Columbia, 1807–1947.* Washington, DC: Catholic University Press, 1949.

DeBoer, Clara M. *His Truth Is Marching On: African Americans Who Taught the Freedmen for the American Missionary Association, 1861–1877.* New York: Garland, 1994.

Denton, Virginia Lantz. *Booker T. Washington and the Adult Education Movement.* Gainesville: University Press of Florida, 1993.

Dollard, John. *Caste and Class in a Southern Town.* New Haven, CT: Yale University, 1937.

Dorsey, Carolyn A. "Black Faculty at White Institutions before 1900." *Western Journal of Black Studies* 14 (1990): 1–8.

———. Blacks and Higher Education: Reconstruction or Restoration." *Western Journal of Black Studies* (1 June 1977): 70–75.

———. "Despite Poor Health: Olivia Davidson Washington's Story." *SAGE* 2 (Fall 1985): 69–72.

———. "Letter to the Editor." *Journal of Blacks in Higher Education*, no. 6 (Winter 1994–1995): 7.

———. "The Pre-Hampton Years of Olivia A. Davidson." *Hampton Review* (Fall 1988).

Douglas, Davison M. *Reading, Writing, and Race: The Desegregation of the Charlotte Schools.* Chapel Hill: University of North Carolina, 1995.

Douglass, Frederick. *Life and Times of Frederick Douglass, written by himself; his early life as a slave, his escape from bondage, and his complete history.* 1892. New York: Macmillan, 1962.

Du Bois, W.E.B. "A Negro Student at Harvard at the End of the 19th Century." *Massachusetts Review* 1 (May 1960): 439–58.

———. *Black Reconstruction in America: An Essay toward a History of the Part Which Black Folk Played in the Attempt to Reconstruct Democracy in America, 1860–1880.* Cleveland: Meridian Books, 1969.

———. "Education and Work." In *The Education of Black People: Ten Critiques, 1906–1960, by W.E.B. Du Bois*, ed. Herbert Aptheker. Amherst: University of Massachusetts Press, 1973.

———, ed. "The College Bred Negro." *Report of a Social Study Made under the Direction of Atlanta University; Together with the Proceedings of the Fifth Conference for the Study of the Negro Problems.* Atlanta, GA: Atlanta University, 1900.

———, ed. "The Negro Common School." *Report of a Social Study Made under the Direction of Atlanta University; Together with the Proceedings of the Sixth Con-*

ference for the Study of the Negro Problems. Atlanta, GA: Atlanta University, 1901.

———. *The Souls of Black Folk.* Chicago: McClurg Publishers, 1903.

Early, Gerald. "Afrocentrism: From Sensationalism to Measured Deliberation." *Journal of Blacks in Higher Education,* no. 5 (Autumn 1994): 86–87.

Enck, Henry S. "The Burden Borne: Northern White Philanthropy and Southern Black Industrial Education, 1900–1915." Ph.D. dissertation, University of Chicago, 1970.

———. "Tuskegee Institute and Northern White Philanthropy: A Case Study in Fund Raising, 1900–1915." *Journal of Negro History* 65 (Fall 1980): 336–348.

Engs, Robert F. "They Gave Them Schools . . . but Why Only Schools?" Review of *Northern Schools, Southern Blacks and Reconstruction: Freedmen's Education, 1862–1875* by Ronald E. Butchart and *Reading, 'Riting, and Reconstruction: The Education of Freedmen in the South, 1861–1870* by Robert C. Morris. In *History of Education Quarterly* 24 (Winter 1884): 619–25.

Evans, Art, and Annette M. Evans. "Black Educators before and after 1960." *Phylon: The Atlanta University Review of Race and Culture* 63 (1982): 254–61.

Faragher, John M., and Florence Howe, eds. *Women and Higher Education in American History: Essays from the Mount Holyoke College Sesquicentennial Symposia.* New York: W. W. Norton, 1988.

Fleming, Walter L. *Documentary History of Reconstruction,* 2 vols. Cleveland, OH: Arthur H. Clark, 1907.

Fletcher, Juanita D. "Against the Consensus: Oberlin College and the Education of American Negroes, 1835–1865." Ph.D. dissertation, American University, 1974.

Fletcher, Robert S. "The Students—The Oppressed Race." In *A History of Oberlin College: From Its Foundation through the Civil War,* vol. 2. Oberlin: Oberlin College, 1943.

Foner, Eric. *A Short History of Reconstruction, 1863–1877.* New York: Harper and Row, 1990.

Fosdick, Raymond B. *Adventure in Giving: The Story of the General Education Board.* New York: Harper and Row, 1962.

Franklin, John Hope. *George Washington Williams: A Biography.* Chicago: University of Chicago Press, 1987.

———. "Jim Crow Goes to School: The Genesis of Legal Separation in Southern Schools." *South Atlantic Quarterly* 58 (Spring 1959): 225–35.

———. "On the Evolution of Scholarship in Afro-American History." In *The State of Afro-American History: Past, Present, and Future,* ed. Darlene Clark Hine. Baton Rouge: Louisiana State University Press, 1986.

Franklin, Vincent P., and James D. Anderson, eds. *New Perspectives on Black Educational History.* Boston: G. K. Hall, 1978a.

———. "Introductory Essay: Changing Historical Perspectives on Afro-American Life and Education." In *New Perspectives on Black Educational History.* Boston: G. K. Hall, 1978b.

———. Review of *Reading, Writing, and Race: The Desegregation of the Charlotte Schools.* In *American Historical Review* (February 1997): 219–20.

Franklin, Vincent P., and Bettye Collier-Thomas, eds. "Vindicating the Race: Contributions to African American Intellectual History." *Journal of Negro History* 81 (1996): 1–144.

Frederickson, George M. *The Black Image in the White Mind: The Debate on Afro-American Character and Destiny, 1877–1914.* New York: Harper and Row, 1971.

"Fulfilling the Letter and Spirit of the Law: Desegregation of the Nation's Public Schools." Report of the U.S. Commission on Civil Rights, August 1976.

Gabel, Leona C. *From Slavery to the Sorbonne and Beyond: The Life and Writings of Anna J. Cooper.* Northampton, MA: Department of History of Smith College, 1982.

Gallagher, Buell. *American Caste and the Negro College.* New York: Columbia University Press, 1938.

Goodenow, Ronald K., and Arthur O. White, eds. *Education and the Rise of the New South.* Boston: G. K. Hall, 1981.

Griffith, Helen. *Dauntless in Mississippi: The Life of Sarah A. Dickey, 1838–1904.* South Hadley, MA: Dinosaur, 1996.

Guy-Sheftall, Beverly. "Black Women and Higher Education: Spelman and Bennett Colleges Revisited." *Journal of Negro Education* 51 (Summer 1982): 278–83.

Guzman, Jessie P. "Twenty Years of Court Decisions Affecting Higher Education in the South, 1938–1958." *Journal of Educational Sociology* 32 (February 1959): 247–53.

Haley, James T., comp. *Afro-American Encyclopaedia, or the Thoughts, Doings, and Sayings of the Race.* Nashville: Haley and Florida, 1896.

Hanchett, Catherine M. "Charles Lewis Reason, 1818–1893: The Nation's First Black Professor." Paper delivered at the Unitarian-Universalist Church, Cortland, New York, January 19, 1986.

———. "George Boyer Vashon, 1824–1878: Black Educator, Poet, Fighter for Equal Rights." Part 1 and Part 2, *Western Pennsylvania Historical Magazine* 68 (July 1985): 206–9; and (October 1985): 333–49.

Hare, Nathan. "The Battle for Black Studies." *Trends in Afro-American Studies.* Washington, DC: *Journal of Afro-American Issues,* 1975.

Harlan, Louis R. *Booker T. Washington: The Making of a Black Leader, 1856–1901.* New York: Oxford, 1972.

———. *Booker T. Washington: The Wizard of Tuskegee, 1901–1915.* New York: Oxford, 1983.

———. "Desegregation in New Orleans Public Schools during Reconstruction." *American Historical Review* 67 (April 1962).

———. *Separate and Unequal: Public School Campaigns and Racism in the Southern Seaboard States, 1901–1915.* Chapel Hill: University of North Carolina, 1958.

Harris, Carl V. "Stability and Change in Discrimination against Black Public Schools: Birmingham, Alabama, 1871–1931." *Journal of Southern History* 51 (August 1985): 375–416.

Harris, Robert L., Jr. "Coming of Age: The Transformation of Afro-American Historiography." *Journal of Negro History* 67 (Summer 1982): 107–21.

Harris, William H. "Trends and Needs in Afro-American Historiography." In *The State of Afro-American History: Past, Present, and Future,* ed. Darlene Clark Hine. Baton Rouge: Louisiana State University Press, 1986.

Hartvik, Allen. "Catherine Ferguson, Black Founder of a Sunday-School." *Negro History Bulletin* 35 (December 1972): 176–77.

Hawkins, Hugh. "Edward Jones: First American Negro College Graduate?" *School and Society* (November 4, 1961): 375–76.

Heningburg, Alphonse. "The Relation of Tuskegee Institute to Education in the Lower South." *Journal of Educational Sociology* 7 (November 1933): 157–62.

Henle, Ellen, and Marlene Merrill. "Antebellum Black Coeds at Oberlin College." *Women's Studies Newsletter* 7 (Spring 1979): 6–11.

Higginbotham, Evelyn Brooks. "The Female Talented Tenth." In *Righteous Discontent: The Women's Movement in the Black Baptist Church, 1880–1920*. Cambridge: Harvard University, 1993.

Hilliard, David Moss. *The Development of Public Education in Memphis, Tennessee, 1848–1945*. Chicago: University of Chicago Press, 1946.

Hine, Darlene Clark, ed. *The State of Afro-American History: Past, Present, and Future*. Baton Rouge: Louisiana State University Press, 1986.

"History of the Five School Cases." *The Crisis* 86 (June/July 1979): 189–94.

Holmes, Dwight O. W. *The Evolution of the Negro College*. New York: Teachers College, 1934.

"How Black Studies Happened." *Yale Alumni Magazine* (May 1969): 22–27.

Huggins, Nathan I. *Afro-American Studies*. New York: Ford Foundation, Office of Reports, 1985.

Hundley, Mary Gibson. *The Dunbar Story: 1870–1955*. New York: Vantage, 1965.

Hunter, Gregory. "Howard University: 'Capstone of Negro Education' during World War II." *Journal of Negro History* 79 (Winter 1994): 54–70.

Hutchinson, Louise D. *Anna J. Cooper: A Voice from the South*. Washington, DC: Smithsonian, 1982.

Ihle, Elizabeth L., ed. *Black Women in Higher Education: An Anthology of Essays, Studies, and Documents*. New York: Garland, 1992.

"The Impact of Black Women in Education." *Journal of Negro Education Yearbook* 51 (summer 1982): 173–367.

Jackson, Luther Porter. "The Educational Activities of the Freedman's Bureau and Freedmen's Aid Societies in South Carolina, 1862–1872." MA thesis, Columbia University, 1922.

Jackson, McArthur. "A Historical Study of the Founding and Development of Tuskegee Institute." Ed.D. dissertation, University of North Carolina at Greensboro, 1983.

Jencks, Christopher, and David Riesman. "Negroes and Their Colleges." In *The Academic Revolution*. Chicago: University of Chicago Press, 1977.

———. "The American Negro College." *Harvard Educational Review* 37 (Winter 1967): 3–60.

Jerome, J. D. Review of *The Education of Negroes in New Jersey* by Marion M. Thompson Wright. In *Journal of Negro History* 26 (October 1941): 527–29.

Johnson, Charles S. *The Negro College Graduate*. Chapel Hill: University of North Carolina, 1938.

Jones, Edward A. *A Candle in the Dark: A History of Morehouse College*. Valley Forge, PA: Judson Press, 1967.

Jones, Edward A., and Virginia L. Jones. "Negroes on White College Faculties." *Negro College Quarterly* 4 (December 1946): 184–238.

Jones, Jacqueline. *Soldiers of Light and Love: Northern Teachers and Georgia Blacks, 1865–1873*. Chapel Hill: University of North Carolina Press, 1980.

———. "Women Who Were More than Men: Sex and Status in Freedmen's Teaching." *History of Education Quarterly* 19 (Spring 1979): 47–59.

Jones, Thomas Jesse. *Negro Education: A Study of the Private and Higher Schools for*

Colored People in the United States, 2 vols. Washington, D.C.: U.S. Government Printing Office, 1917.

Joyce, William L. "Education of Negroes in Ante-bellum America: A Guide to an Exhibition in the William L. Clements Library." Ann Arbor: University of Michigan, 1969.

Kelleher, Daniel T. "The Case of Lloyd Lionel Gaines: The Demise of the Separate but Equal Doctrine." *Journal of Negro History* 56 (October 1971): 262–71.

Kelley, Don Quinn. "The Political Economy of Booker T. Washington: A Bibliographic Essay." *Journal of Negro Education* 46 (Fall 1977): 403–18.

Kilson, Martin. "Realism in Afro-American Studies." In *Black Studies: Myths & Realities*, with an introduction by Bayard Rustin. New York: A. Philip Randolph Educational Fund, 1969.

Kluger, Richard. *Simple Justice: The History of "Brown v. Board of Education" and Black America's Struggle for Equality*. New York: Alfred A. Knopf, 1975.

Knight, Edgar W. *Public Education in the South*. Boston: Ginn and Co., 1922.

Kozol, Jonathan. *Death at an Early Age: The Destruction of the Hearts and Minds of Negro Children in the Boston Public Schools*. Boston: Houghton Mifflin, 1967.

Lawson, Ellen. *The Three Sarahs: Documents of Antebellum Black College Women*. New York: Edwin Mellen, 1984.

———, and Marlene Merrill. "The Antebellum 'Talented Thousandth': Black College Students at Oberlin before the Civil War." *Journal of Negro Education* 52 (Spring 1983): 142–155.

Leavell, Ullin W. *Philanthropy in Negro Education*. Nashville: George Peabody College for Teachers, 1930.

Leloudis, James L. *Schooling the New South: Pedagogy, Self, and Society in North Carolina, 1880–1920*. Chapel Hill: University of North Carolina, 1996.

Lester, Julius, ed. *The Seventh Son: The Thought and Writings of W.E.B. Du Bois*. New York: Random House, 1971.

Lewis, David L. *W.E.B. Du Bois: Biography of a Race, 1868–1919*. New York: Henry Holt, 1993.

Link, William A. Review of *Schooling the New South: Pedagogy, Self, and Society in North Carolina, 1880–1920* by James L. Leloudis. In *American Historical Review* (June 1997): 906–907.

Little, Monroe H. "Shall This Be All? Historians and Afro-American Education." Review of *New Perspectives on Black Educational History,* ed. by Vincent P. Franklin and James D. Anderson; *Subordination or Liberation? The Development and Conflicting Theories of Black Education in Nineteenth Century Alabama* by Robert Sherer; and *The New Negro on Compus: Black College Rebellions of the 1920s* by Raymond Wolters. In *Harvard Educational Review* 50 (August 1980): 415–421.

Litwack, Leon F. "Education: Separate and Unequal." In *North of Slavery: The Negro in the Free States, 1790–1860*. Chicago: University of Chicago Press, 1967.

Logan, Rayford W. "Educational Segregation in the North." *Journal of Negro Education* 2 (January 1933): 65–67.

———. "The Evolution of Private Colleges for Negroes." *Journal of Negro Education* 27 (Summer 1958): 213–220.

————. *Howard University: The First Hundred Years, 1867–1977.* New York: New York University Press, 1969.

Ludlow, Helen W. *Twenty-Two Years' Work of the Hampton Normal and Agricultural Institute at Hampton, Virginia: Records of Negro and Indian Graduates and Ex-Students.* Hampton, VA: Normal School, 1893.

Mabee, Carleton. *Black Education in New York State: From Colonial to Modern Times.* Syracuse, NY: Syracuse University, 1979.

Mack, Raymond W., ed. *Our Children's Burden: Studies of Desegregation in Nine American Communities.* New York: Vintage, 1968.

Mangum, Claude J. "The Education of Women at Hampton Institute, 1868–1878." Paper presented at annual meeting of the Association for the Study of Afro-American Life and History, October 1985.

Margo, Robert A. Review of *The Second Battle of New Orleans: The Hundred-Year Struggle to Integrate the Schools* by Liva Baker. In *American Historical Review* (October 1997): 249–50.

McGinnis, Frederick A. *A History and an Interpretation of Wilberforce University.* Wilberforce, OH: Wilberforce University Press, 1941.

McPherson, James M. *The Abolitionist Legacy: From Reconstruction to the NAACP.* Princeton, NJ: Princeton University, 1975.

————. *The Negro's Civil War.* New York: Pantheon Books, 1965.

————. "The New Puritanism: Values and Goals of Freedmen's Education in America." In *The University in Society*, 2 vols., ed. Laurence Stone. Princeton, NJ: Princeton University, 1974.

————. *The Struggle for Equality: Abolitionists and the Negro in the Civil War and Reconstruction.* Princeton, NJ: Princeton University, 1964.

————. "White Liberals and Black Power in Negro Education, 1865–1915." *American Historical Review* 75 (June 1970): 1357–79.

Meece, Leonard E. *Negro Education in Kentucky: A Comparative Study of White and Negro Education on the Elementary and Secondary School Levels.* Lexington: University of Kentucky, 1938.

Meier, August. *Negro Thought in America, 1880–1915: Racial Ideologies in the Age of Booker T. Washington.* Ann Arbor, MI: Ann Arbor Paperbacks, 1966.

————. "The Beginning of Industrial Education in Negro Schools." *Midwest Journal* 7 (Spring, Fall 1955): 21–44, 241–66.

————, and Elliott Rudwick. *Black History and the Historical Profession, 1915–1980.* Urbana: University of Illinois Press, 1986.

Mills, Nicolaus, ed. *The Great School Bus Controversy.* New York: Teachers College/Columbia University Press, 1973.

Monroe, Walter S., ed. *Encyclopedia of Educational Research.* New York: Macmillan, 1941.

Moore, William, and Lonnie H. Wagstaff. *Black Educators in White Colleges.* San Francisco: Jossey-Bass, 1974.

Morgan, Harry. *Historical Perspectives on the Education of Black Children.* Westport, CT: Praeger, 1995.

Morris, Robert C. *Reading, 'Riting, and Reconstruction: The Education of Freedmen in the South, 1861–1870.* Chicago: University of Chicago Press, 1981.

Moss, James Allen. "Negro Teachers in Predominantly White Colleges." *Journal of Negro Education* 27 (Fall 1958): 451–62.

Moton, Robert R. "Hampton Institute's Relation to Tuskegee." In *Tuskegee and Its People*, ed. Booker T. Washington. New York: D. Appleton, 1906.

———. "The Scope and Aim of Tuskegee Institute." *Journal of Educational Sociology* 7 (November 1933): 151–56.

Myrdal, Gunnar. *An American Dilemma: The Negro Problem & Modern Democracy*, 2 vols. New York: Harper & Row, 1944.

Nelson, Paul D. "Experiment in Interracial Education at Berea College, 1858–1908." *Journal of Negro History* 59 (January 1974): 13–27.

———. "The Roller-Coaster Ride of Black Students at Berea College." *Journal of Blacks in Higher Education*, no. 13 (Winter 1996): 62–64.

Noble, Jeanne L. "The Higher Education of Black Women in the Twentieth Century." In *Women and Higher Education in American History*, ed. John Mack Faragher and Florence Howe. New York: W. W. Norton, 1988.

———. *The Negro Women's College Education*. New York: Teachers College, Columbia University Press, 1956.

Noble, Stuart G. *Forty Years of the Public Schools in Mississippi with Special Reference to the Education of the Negro*. New York: Teachers College/Columbia University Press, 1918.

O'Connor, Ellen. *Myrtilla Miner: A Memoir*. Miami: Mnemosyne, 1969.

Park, Robert E. Review of *The Education of the Negro Prior to 1861* by Carter G. Woodson. In *American Journal of Sociology* 21 (July 1915): 119–20.

Peabody, Francis G. *Education for Life: The Story of Hampton Institute*. Garden City, NY: Doubleday, Page, 1919.

Pearson, Ralph L. "Reflections on Black Colleges: The Historical Perspectives of Charles S. Johnson." *History of Education Quarterly* 23 (Spring 1983): 55–68.

Peck, Elisabeth S. "A Century of Interrace Education." In *Berea's First Century, 1855–1955*. Lexington: University of Kentucky, 1955.

Perkins, Linda M. "Essay Reviews: Black Education, for What Purpose?" Review of *Black Education in New York State: From Colonial to Modern Times* by Carleton Mabee and *Soldiers of Light and Love: Northern Teachers and Georgia Blacks, 1865–1873* by Jacqueline Jones. In *Harvard Educational Review* 52 (May 1982): 203–7.

———. *Fanny Jackson Coppin and the Institute for Colored Youth, 1837–1902*. New York: Garland, 1987.

———. "Heed Life's Demands: The Educational Philosophy of Fanny Jackson Coppin." *Journal of Negro Education* 51 (Summer 1982): 181–190.

———. "The Black Female Missionary Educator during and after the Civil War." *Black Women's Educational Policy and Research Network Newsletter* 1 (March/April 1982): 6–9.

———. "The Education of Black Women in the Nineteenth Century." In *Women and Higher Education in American History: Essays from the Mount Holyoke College Sesquicentennial Symposia*, ed. John Mack Faragher and Florence Howe. New York: W. W. Norton, 1988.

———. "The History of Blacks in Teaching: Growth and Decline within the Profession." In *American Teachers: Histories of a Profession at Work*, ed. Donald Warren. New York: Macmillan, 1989.

———. "The Impact of the 'Cult of True Womanhood' on the Education of Black Women." *Journal of Social Issues* 39 (1983): 17–28.

Plank, David N., and Marcia Turner. "Changing Patterns in Black School Politics: At-
    lanta, 1872–1973." *American Journal of Education* 95 (August 1987): 584–608.

Preston, Vaughn W. *Schools for All: The Blacks and Public Education in the South,
    1865–1877.* Lexington: University Press of Kentucky, 1974.

Quarles, Benjamin. *Black Abolitionists.* New York: Oxford University Press, 1969.

———. "The Good Fight: From Plessy to Brown." *The Crisis* 86 (June/July 1979):
    215–17.

Range, Willard. *The Rise and Progress of Negro Colleges in Georgia, 1865–1949.* Ath-
    ens: University of Georgia Press, 1951.

Read, Florence. *The Story of Spelman College.* Princeton, NJ: Princeton University Press,
    1961.

———. "The Place of the Women's College in the Pattern of Negro Education." *Op-
    portunity: Journal of Negro Life* 15 (September 1937): 267–70.

Rector, Theresa A. "Black Nuns as Educators." *Journal of Negro Education* 51 (Summer
    1982): 238–53.

Reddick, Lawrence D. "A New Interpretation for Negro History." *Journal of Negro
    History* 22 (January 1937): 17–28.

Richardson, Joe M. *A History of Fisk University.* Alabama: University of Alabama, 1980.

Roche, Richard. *Catholic Colleges and the Negro Student.* Washington, D.C.: Catholic
    University of America, 1948.

Rose, Willie Lee. *Rehearsal for Reconstruction: The Port Royal Experiment.* Indianap-
    olis: Bobbs-Merrill, 1964.

Rowan, Carl T. *Dream Makers, Dream Breakers: The World of Justice Thurgood Mar-
    shall.* Boston: Little, Brown, 1993.

Rudwick, Elliott M. "W.E.B. Du Bois and the Atlanta University Studies on the Negro."
    Journal of Negro Education 26 (Fall 1957): 466–76.

Sawyer, Robert M. "The Gaines Case: Its Background and Influence on the University
    of Missouri and Lincoln University, 1936–1950." Ph.D. dissertation, University
    of Missouri–Columbia, 1966.

Scott, Patricia Bell. "Schoolin' 'Respectable' Ladies of Color: Issues in the History of
    Black Women's Higher Education." *Journal of the National Association for
    Women Deans, Administrators, & Counselors* 43 (Winter 1980): 22–28.

Sernett, Milton C. *Abolition's Axe: Beriah Green, Oneida Institute, and the Black Free-
    dom Struggle.* New York: Syracuse University, 1986.

Sherer, Robert G. *Subordination or Liberation? The Development and Conflicting The-
    ories of Black Education in Nineteenth Century Alabama.* Alabama: University
    of Alabama, 1977.

Short, Kenneth R. "New York Central College: A Baptist Experiment in Integrated
    Higher Education, 1848–61." *Foundations* (July 1962): 250–56.

Shujaa, Mwalimu J., ed. *Too Much Schooling, Too Little Education: A Paradox of Black
    Life in White Societies.* Trenton, NJ: Africa World Press, 1995.

Slater, Robert Bruce. "The Blacks Who First Entered the World of White Higher Edu-
    cation." *Journal of Blacks in Higher Education*, no. 4 (Summer 1994): 47–56.

Slowe, Lucy. "Higher Education of Negro Women." *Journal of Negro Education* 2 (July
    1933): 352–58.

———. "The Colored Girl Enters College: What Shall She Expect?" *Opportunity: Jour-
    nal of Negro Life* 15 (September 1937): 276–79.

Smith, Robert C. *They Closed Their Schools: Prince Edward County, Virginia, 1951–1964.* Chapel Hill: University of North Carolina, 1968.

Society of Professors of Education. *The Black Education Professorate,* ed. by Ayers Bagley. Minnesota: College of Education, University of Minnesota, 1984.

Sollors, Werner, Caldwell Titcomb, and Thomas A. Underwood, eds. *Blacks at Harvard: A Documentary History of African-American Experience at Harvard and Radcliffe.* New York: New York University, 1993.

Spivey, Donald. *Schooling for the New Slavery: Black Industrial Education, 1868–1915.* Westport, CT: Greenwood, 1978.

St. Clair, Sadie. "Myrtilla Miner: Pioneer in the Teacher Education of Negroes." *Journal of Negro History* 34 (1949): 30–45.

Stokes, Anson Phelps. *Tuskegee Institute: The First Fifty Years, Founder's Day Historical Address, April 14, 1931.* Tuskegee: Institute Press, 1931.

Stone, Chuck. "The Psychology of Whiteness vs. the Politics of Blackness: An Educational Power Struggle." *Educational Researcher* 1 (January 1972): 4–6, 16.

Strane, Susan. *A Whole-Souled Woman: Prudence Crandall and the Education of Black Women.* New York: W. W. Norton, 1990.

Summerville, James. *Educating Black Doctors: A History of Meharry Medical College.* Alabama: University of Alabama, 1983.

Swint, Henry Lee. *The Northern Teacher in the South, 1862–1870.* 1941. New York: Octagon, 1967.

Talbot, Alfred K., Jr. "The Virginia Teachers Association: Establishment and Background." *Negro History Bulletin* 45 (January, February, March 1982): 8–10.

Taylor, Alrutheus A. "Historians of the Reconstruction." *Journal of Negro History* 23 (January 1938): 16–34.

Taylor, Ivan E. "Negro Teachers in White Colleges." *School and Society* 65 (May 24, 1947): 369–72.

Terrell, Mary Church. "I Enter Oberlin College." In *A Colored Woman in a White World.* Washington, D.C.: National Association of Colored Women's Clubs, 1968.

Thorpe, Earl E. *Black Historians: A Critique.* New York: William Morrow, 1971.

Titcomb, Caldwell. "Letter to the Editor: Black Pioneers in American Higher Education." *Journal of Blacks in Higher Education,* no. 5 (Autumn 1994): 4–5.

Urban, Wayne J. *Black Scholar: Horace Mann Bond, 1904–1972.* Athens: University of Georgia Press, 1992.

Vaughan, William P. *Schools for All: The Blacks and Public Education in the South, 1865–1877.* Lexington: University Press of Kentucky, 1974.

Washington, Booker T. *My Larger Education: Being Chapters from My Experience.* Garden City, NY: Doubleday, Page, 1911.

———. "The Educational Outlook in the South." In National Education Association, *Journal of Proceedings and Addresses: Session of the Year 1884, at Madison, WI.* Boston: J. E. Farwell, 1885.

———, ed. *Tuskegee and Its People: Their Ideals and Achievements.* New York: D. Appleton, 1906.

Webber, Thomas L. *Deep like the Rivers: Education in the Slave Quarter Community, 1831–1865.* New York: W. W. Norton, 1978.

Weeks, Stephen B. *History of Public School Education in Alabama.* Washington, DC: U.S. Bureau of Education, 1915.

Weinberg, Meyer. *A Chance to Learn: The History of Race and Education in the United States*. Cambridge: Cambridge University Press, 1977.

Wesley, Charles H. Review of *The Northern Teacher in the South, 1862–1870*, by Henry Lee Swint. In *Journal of Negro Education* 11 (January 1942): 67–70.

West, Earle H. *The Black American and Education*. Columbus, OH: Charles E. Merrill, 1972.

West, Emory J. "Harvard's First Black Graduates: 1865–1890." *Harvard Bulletin* 74 (May 1972): 24–28.

Wharton, Vernon Lane. *The Negro in Mississippi, 1865–1890*. Chapel Hill: University of North Carolina, 1947.

Wiley, Ed, III. "Afrocentrism: Many Things to Many People." *Black Issues in Higher Education* 8 (October 1991): 1, 20–21.

Wilkerson, Doxey A. *Special Problems of Negro Education*. 1939. Westport, CT: Greenwood, 1970.

Williams, George W. *History of the Negro Race in America from 1619–1880*, 2 vols. New York: G.P. Putnam's, 1882.

Wilson, Reginald. "GI Bill Expands Access for African Americans." *Educational Record* (Fall 1994): 32–39.

———. "Good Thing a Bell Curve Didn't Block the GI Bill." *Black Issues in Higher Education* 11 (January 26, 1995): 42–43.

Wolters, Raymond. *The New Negro on Campus: Black College Rebellions of the 1920s*. Princeton, NJ: Princeton University, 1975.

———. "It's All Right If It's Not White: Recent Books on the History of Black Education." Review of *Deep like the Rivers: Education in the Slave Quarter Community, 1831–1865* by Thomas L. Webber and *Schooling for the New Slavery: Black Industrial Education, 1868–1915* by Donald Spivey. In *History of Education Quarterly* 20 (Summer 1980): 197–205.

———. "The Puritan Ethic and Black Education." Review of *The Abolitionist Legacy: From Reconstruction to the NAACP* by James M. McPherson. In *History of Education Quarterly* 17 (Spring 1977): 63–74.

Woodson, Carter G. *The Mis-education of the Negro*. 1933. Washington, DC: Associated Publishers, 1969.

———. *The Education of the Negro prior to 1861*. Salem, NH: Ayer Company, Publishers, 1986.

Wormley, S. Smith. "Myrtilla Miner." *Journal of Negro History* 5 (1920): 448–57.

Wright, Albert H. *Cornell's Three Precursors: 1. New York Central College*. Ithaca, NY: New York State College of Agriculture, 1960.

Wright, C. T. "The Development of Education for Blacks in Georgia, 1865–1900." Ph.D. dissertation, Boston University, 1977.

Wright, Marion M. Thompson. *The Education of Negroes in New Jersey*. New York: Columbia University, Teachers College, 1940.

Wright, Stephen J. "The Negro College in America." *Harvard Educational Review* 30 (Summer 1960): 280–97.

Wright, Stephen J., Benjamin Mays, Hugh M. Gloster, and Albert W. Dent. "The American Negro College: Four Responses and a Reply." *Harvard Educational Review* 37 (Summer 1967): 451–68.

VI

The African American Literary Tradition

Clenora Hudson-Weems

AMERICAN SLAVERY AND ANTI-SLAVERY (1619–1865)

From the very beginning, with the landing of the first slave ship in Jamestown, Virginia, African Americans have been expressing their reactions to their abject conditions in many ways. Most of these responses have been preserved in what is referred to today as the African American literary tradition.

Although transplanted Africans were purposely kept illiterate, illiteracy is not synonymous with ignorance. Enslaved blacks brought with them a vibrant oral tradition that reflected African culture and languages. They verbally transmitted traditional customs, values, and history to their offspring and each other. In fact, the only black literature that survived the early period of enslavement was of the oral tradition, which vividly and collectively expressed a cadre of black emotions, ranging from extreme fear to acquiescence, to anger, to confusion, to hope, to defiance, and to celebration.

The earliest types of the African oral tradition were the work songs and field hollers, which blacks used to communicate to each other while working in the fields. There was also the folktale, with stories expressing African American values, explaining the unexplainable, and identifying acceptable and unaccept-able behavior. Exemplifying this category are "How Buck Won His Freedom," "The Knee-High Man Tries to Get Sizeable," and "People Who Could Fly."

Although there are debates regarding the origins of the oral tradition, which includes also proverbs, cries, and shouts, religious (spirituals) and secular (work) songs, according to Richard Barksdale and Kenneth Kinnamon in *Black Writers of America: A Comprehensive Anthology* (1972), all these oral traditions have their origins in an African folk tradition. Folklorists most noted for collecting and expounding on the origins of the folktale in particular include Richard Dorson *(American Negro Folktales* and *African Folklore)* and Julius Lester *(Black Folktales).* To be sure, oral literature issued forth the earliest call for the deliverance of blacks from abject servitude. In profound ways, such as double meanings in old Negro spirituals like "Go Down, Moses" and "Swing Low, Sweet Chariot," ostensibly addressing only religious needs of blacks, these issuing forth of freedom quests invaded American slavery, collectively enabling blacks to forge a plan for escape.

Signaling the beginning of the African American written literary tradition was the slave narrative of the early eighteenth century. Expressing an insatiable desire for the same human needs (liberty, fraternity, and equality) expressed by many white writers and thinkers of the period, the slave narrative was a genre that presented the physical and psychological conditions of servitude. Forerunner of this literary form is Olaudah Equiano, a spokesperson for the equality of all people, carrying out the mission for blacks in particular during the critical Revolutionary War era. His slave narrative, *The Interesting Narrative of the Life of Olaudah Equiano, or Gustavus Vassa, the African* (1789), carries us through a voyage from African freedom to American slavery in which he topsy-turveys and refutes the stereotypes of Africa as a heathen land and its people as uncivilized. This reversed movement motif was appropriate for the first slave narrative, whose protagonist himself experienced such regression from having been kidnapped from his native land and relegated to servitude. According to Wilfred D. Samuel's introduction to the 1988 two-volume Bicentennial Edition of Equiano's slave narrative, earlier Equiano critics, including Paul Edwards, see Equiano's slave narrative as black book authors' "most remarkable [account] of the 18th century." His narrative technique was later transposed to a slavery to freedom motif by African American slave narrators whose experience started out differently. An example of these narrators and orators include Briton Hammon in his *Narrative of the Uncommon Sufferings, and Surprising Deliverance of Briton Hammon* (1760), the first published writing by an African American. This first attempt at African American autobiography displays many affinities to later examples of the genre, such as Frederick Douglass's *Narrative of the Life of Frederick Douglass, an American Slave, Written by Himself* (1845) and Gilbert Osofsky's collection of slave narratives, *Puttin' on Ole Massa* (1969), which includes a discussion of the slave narrative tradition. Equiano makes clear the quest for learning and the difficulty involved in acquiring it in his *Interesting Narrative*, wherein he sets up the trope of the talking book. Observing his master and others moving their lips and reading aloud when examining a book, he surmised that they were "talking" to the book, which was demystified the moment Equiano became literate. His telling of early childhood slave experiences and adolescence evolved, shifting from a naive, childlike persona to that of an experienced, disenchanted adult, therein constituting the primary commitment of the entire genre of the slave narrative or autobiography.

Vernon Loggins further discusses the slave narrative in *The Negro Author: His Development in America to 1900* (1931), in which he claims that Equiano's narrative renders the "spirit and vitality and the angle of vision responsible for the most effective prose writing by Black Americans." In *Great Slave Narratives* (1969) Arna Bontemps refers to it as "the first truly notable book in the genre." And William L. Andrews's *To Tell a Free Story: The First Century of Afro-American Autobiography, 1760–1865* (1986) offers the most cumulative assessment of the African American slave narrative as an autobiographical form.

The eighteenth century also brought forth one of the most intellectually skilled and well-versed figures of all times, Benjamin Banneker, who like Equiano, voiced his position on the need for the equality for all, including African Americans. In his "Letter to Thomas Jefferson," Banneker confronts the issue of contradictions and hypocrisy in a national leader who claims to be a proponent of equality. This century also witness its first African American poets—Jupiter Hammon, Lucy Terry, Phillis Wheatley, and Ann Plato—most of whom demonstrated in their verses a strong religious appeal in their quest for freedom. For example, Hammon's opening line, "Salvation comes by Christ alone," in "An Evening Thought: Salvation by Christ and Penitential Cries," and Wheatley's closing heroic couplet, "Remember, Christians, Negroes, black as Cain. May be refin'd, and join th' angelic train," in "On Being Brought from Africa to America" both appeal strongly to Christianity. Sterling Stuckey apprises us in his *Slave Culture* that "fortunate for the slave, the retention of important features of the African culture heritage provided a means by which the new reality could be interpreted and spiritual needs at least partially met." Black poststructuralist critic Houston Baker offers both a chronological overview of black literature and an informative discussion of social and historical trends, critical standards and their effects on black artists beginning with Phillis Wheatley up to LeRoi Jones (Imamu Amiri Baraka) in his anthology *Black Literature in America* (1971).

Stimulating the drive toward literary production during the embryonic stage of the African American literary tradition was the conviction of such figures as Wheatley. She, among others, believed that success in a variety of literary genres would refute conclusions by whites like Thomas Jefferson, who claimed that the absence of true literature by blacks justified their enslavement. Hence, black poets composed lyrics, hymns, odes, short epics, pastorals, elegies, and pastoral elegies. Wheatley, whose life, work, and example virtually dominated African American literary history until the mid-nineteenth century, wrote the most in these genres, although she was not the first black to write or publish. Lucy Terry's "Bars Fight" (written in 1746; published until 1855) represents the first recognized writing in English by an African American. Of a different style, she, according to the head notes on the poet in Patricia Liggins Hill's *Call and Response: The Riverside Anthology of the African American Literary Tradition* (1997), offers "the first symbolic portrayal portending race relations in the United States for the next two centuries: a battle between Native-Americans and

Euro-Americans as witnessed and recorded by an African-American" in "Bars Fight." Terry joined in with other protest voices of the times and together they did their share in moving us on the abolitionist movement, which dominated the first half of the nineteenth century.

Jupiter Hammon's "An Evening Thought: Salvation by Christ, with Penitential Cries," composed in common hymn stanza, the first poem published by an African American, appeared in December 1760. It contains two arresting, subversive moments: Calling Jesus "thy captive Slave," Hammon suggests that the central and most acceptable focus of the Christian son of God is Hammon himself and his fellow African American rather than white oppressors. The phrase "To set the Sinner free," especially when read within the context of "thy captive Slave," constructs a subversive "freeing" of Hammon and his fellow slaves. Literary critic Sondra O'Neale, in *Jupiter Hammon and the Biblical Beginnings of African-American Literature* (1993), and others have recently called attention to the anti-slavery subtext within "A Dialogue, Entitled, The Kind Master and Dutiful Servant" (1783). Other key studies of these authors include Benjamin Brawley's *Early Negro American Writers* (1935), Richard Walser's *Black Poet* (1966), Saunders Reddings's *To Make a Poet Black* (1939), and Shirley Graham's *Story of Phillis Wheatley* (1949).

African American literature during the first sixty years of the nineteenth century is best characterized as a call for resistance against slavery. This era witnessed considerable abolitionist and black nationalist activities, including fugitive slave narratives, pamphlets, poetry, and published sermons and speeches. Among the more significant works were David Walker's *Appeal* (1829), *The Confessions of Nat Turner* (1831), Henry Highland Garnet's "An Address to the Slaves of the United States" (1843), *The Narrative of Frederick Douglass* (1845), Sojourner Truth's "And Aren't I a Woman?" (1852), Frederick Douglass's "Independence Day Speech" (1852), Martin R. Delany's *Condition, Elevation, and Destiny of the Colored People of the United States* (1852), Francis Ellen Watkins Harper's *Poems on Miscellaneous Subjects* (1854), and Harriet Jacobs's *Incidents in the Life of a Slave Girl* (1861).

The antebellum period also featured important milestones in the development of African American literature. William Wells Brown's *Escape, or Leap to Freedom* (1858) represented the first play published by an African American. Similarly, Brown's *Clotel*, published in England in 1853, has the distinction of being the first novel published in English by someone of African descent. Harriet E. Wilson's *Our Nig; or, Sketches from the Life of a Free Black* (1859), represented the first novel published in the United States by an African American.

THE CIVIL WAR (1861–1865)

Many writers continued to write on the peculiar institution of slavery prior to its abolishment, such as William Wells Brown and his *Negro in the American Rebellion: His Heroism and His Fidelity* (1867) and George Washington Williams and his *History of the Negro Troops in the War of the Rebellion, 1861–1865*. Most notable, however, was Elizabeth Keckley, known for her autobiography, *Behind the Scenes* (1868), in which she depicts the interior lives of the Lincoln family and Washington during the Civil War years.

POST-CIVIL WAR, RECONSTRUCTION, AND REACTION (1865–1920)

The Reconstruction era was marked by significant transitions in black literature. Some of the writers, whose careers began before emancipation, remained active, such as Harper, who published new poetry and four novels, including her celebrated novel *Iola Leroy* (1892), and Brown, who produced a post-emancipation edition of *Clotel* (1867). Douglass wrote the final versions of his autobiography, *Life and Times of Frederick Douglass (1881–1892)*. With the end of slavery came new forces in black writing, with the rapid progression of education in black communities, thereby creating a growing middle class with strong literary interests.

Rebecca C. Barton's *Witnesses for Freedom: Negro Americans in Autobiography* (1948) provides an examination of the review of themes and perspectives in selected black autobiographies with sociological summaries of the struggles, goals, and achievements of writers, such as Booker T. Washington's *Up from Slavery* (1901). Black women writers, such as Anna Julia Cooper, Frances Ellen Watkins Harper, Josephine D. Henderson Heard, Lucy A. Delaney, and Angelina Weld Grimke, wrote ex-slave narratives, novels, essays, poetry, and drama. Ida B. Wells, a journalist and essayist, crusaded against lynchings in newspaper articles and pamphlets such as "Southern Horrors: Lynch Law in All Its Phases" (1892). James Weldon Johnson, author of *The Autobiography of an Ex-coloured Man* (1912), published novels and sermons in verse of the black tradition, such as "Creation" and "Go Down, Death." This literature, however, was often ignored by white literary critics.

African American literature written between 1865 and 1920 reflects the disappointments, fears, and frustrations produced by America's failure to fulfill its promises of freedom and equality after the Civil War. Yet, the literature of the Reconstruction era manifested middle-class roots in its major characteristics. Dickson D. Bruce, Jr., in *Black American Writing from the Nadir: The Evolution of a Literary Tradition, 1877–1915* (1989), maintains that through the 1890s, black writers participated in a genteel, sentimental tradition that dominated American middle-class culture. This integrationist-oriented literature emphasized their similarities to other educated Americans and protested their exclusion from the American mainstream. Many writers like James H. W. Howard in his novel *Bond and Free* (1886) built on the tradition of the "tragic mulatto," the cultured, virtuous young man or woman who grows up as white, and whose subsequent confrontation with racial barriers confirms the arbitrariness and injustice of racial lines.

Their Victorian conservatism should not be interpreted as African Americans' absolute rejection of their identity. Encouraged by such figures as Alexander Crummell, most made racial pride a dominant motif. They took special interest in black history, details of which they often incorporated into their works. This interest was supported by one of the more ambitious projects in African American letters from the period, that of George Washington Williams, who published one of the first scholarly histories of African Americans. One was a two-volume *History of the Negro Race in America from 1619 to 1880* (1883), the other, *History of the Negro Troops in the War of the Rebellion, 1861–1865* (1888). In Williams's histories and elsewhere, racial pride was central, if expressed less in terms of any distinctive African American characteristics than in terms of African American accomplishments measured within the framework of the larger society.

Outside the middle class, pre-emancipation oral traditions, with roots in slave culture, had retained their vigor after freedom. The popular trickster tales, celebrating the power of wit in the face of oppression, remained current, as did the spirituals, with their profound understanding of suffering and freedom. Reflecting the abiding force of racism and discrimination, as well as the growing independence of such institutions as the church, these traditions had even come to play a more vital role in folk society in the Reconstruction era, helping to center identity and community ties.

Despite a reliance on stereotypes, popular entertainments, including minstrelsy, used genuine black folk materials and, though performed by whites in blackface as well as by blacks, helped to diffuse those materials. Joel Williamson in *The Crucible of Race: Black-White Relations in the American South since Emancipation* (1984) states that the emergence of a white "plantation tradition" literature, while equally dominated by stereotypes romanticizing the slave society of the Old South, did the same. White Georgia journalist Joel Chandler Harris, through his stories of the obsequious "Uncle Remus," gave traditional African American trickster tales a national audience. Williamson also reveals that Hampton Institute's *Southern Workman*, though a white-edited periodical, became a treasure trove of traditional materials contributed by members of the Black student body, particularly tales, folk beliefs, and songs. In Richmond, Virginia, African American preacher John Jasper achieved celebrity status with his much-preached sermon "De Sun Do Move," providing a popular view of traditional folk religion to white as well as African American audiences.

African American writers, who hoped to explore the literary possibilities of oral traditions, attempted to build on this interest, appealing to an audience that had already shown its receptiveness. Many also wanted to rescue folk society from the stereotypes that minstrel versions and such plantation writers as Harris employed in their renditions of the African American tradition. Such efforts led directly to the success of the first African American writers to achieve a genuine national audience, Charles Waddell Chestnutt and Paul Laurence Dunbar.

Chestnutt's works written in the folk tradition appeared first. Written in the black "dialect," his "Uncle Julius" stories appeared in such popular journals as the *Atlantic* as early as 1889. Building on the trickster figure, Chestnutt recontextualized the white plantation tradition by deromanticizing the southern setting, dramatizing its violence and exploitation, with Uncle Julius, unlike Harris's Uncle Remus, leaving no doubt about the stories' aggressive possibilities.

Dunbar, however, had the greater impact, chiefly through his "dialect poetry," which was written in the putative voice of the slaves and ex-slaves of the South. He wrote out of the plantation and minstrel traditions and was most noted for his dialect poetry, evoking pathos and pity in his presentation of a humorous and sympathetic view of African American life. Although his popularity was based upon this style of writing, which epitomizes the very plight of black people as victimized accommodationists, he also wrote some of the most effective non-dialect poetry expressing the plight of black people in poems like "Sympathy," "We Wear the Mask," and "The Poet," the last one dramatically answering to his dilemma of forced accommodation: "But ah, the world, it turned to praise/A jingle in a broken tongue." When *Lyrics of Lowly Life* (1896), his first major volume, appeared, endorsed by the dean of American letters, William Dean Howells, Dunbar attracted national attention, becoming, perhaps, the most popular poet, white or black, in America. Many began to write in dialect poetry, including James Edwin Campbell and James D. Corrothers. By the end of the century, virtually every African American writer had tried the form.

Neither Dunbar and Chestnutt nor their contemporaries broke entirely from the older plantation tradition. Most, with the possible exception of Campbell, used a dialect based as much on literary models as on folk speech rooted in popular writing and the oral tradition. Together they defined possibilities for a folk-based literature that few of their predecessors had thought possible.

At the same time, worsening conditions also brought a growing sense of the dilemma of being African American in a racist society, the dilemma of formulating an identity, as earlier writers had, in American terms. Here, too, Dunbar and Chestnutt were pioneers, departing from dialect to reorient genteel themes and traditional modes of protest to confront the changing times. Dunbar, who was never entirely comfortable with his success in dialect, expressed his frustration in his novel *The Uncalled* (1898). Chestnutt, in stories published as early as the late 1880s and appearing most prominently in a collection entitled *The Wife of His Youth and Other Stories of the Color Line* (1900), used the older motif of racial mixture and the "tragic mulatto" to delineate, pessimistically, relationships between racial structures and questions of identity and moral choice. In his *Conjure Woman* (1900), and *The Marrow of Tradition* (1901), he depicted more complex characters to counter the literary counterpart of the black-faced minstrel.

Since Dunbar's death, his reputation has passed through various stages—from hero to accommodationist villain, to human. What previous scholars have not noted, and what John Keeling argues convincingly in "Paul Dunbar and the

Mask of Dialect," is the presence of several layers of protest contained within even the "happiest" of Dunbar poems. Keeling's argument indicates the extent to which scholars are rehabilitating Dunbar's reputation in light of new understanding about the context, which must be considered in any assessment of both Dunbar and the dialect poetry movement. Dickson Bruce's *Black American Writing from the Nadir* makes the point that the 1890s saw the rise of a particularly virulent strain of racism and oppression in America, a tendency that necessitated the use of subtle means of protest in the African American community.

The dilemmas Dunbar and Chestnutt identified were to receive increasing attention among black writers as the Reconstruction era drew to a close, especially as an understanding of those dilemmas was given theoretical shape by W.E.B Du Bois in "The Strivings of the Negro People" (1897). There, Du Bois described the "double-consciousness" of the African American, a problem of being simultaneously American and black. Du Bois proposed to resolve the problem through the encouragement of distinctive African genius, pointing toward a distinctive African American culture and literature as well. According to Lawrence Levine's *Black Culture and Black Consciousness*, literary attempts to realize Du Bois's vision did not appear until after 1900, although the growing concern about "duality" rendered a profound legacy from Reconstruction to the present.

The two most visible political and literary figures during this period were Booker T. Washington and W.E.B Du Bois. The former, approximately ten years the latter's senior, had emerged from the immediate Nadir era, which was characterized by extreme fear and insecurity, an era that witnessed the emergence of an accomodationist mentality. Although dialect was not his mode of writing, Washington, too, was considered an accommodationist. His autobiography, *Up from Slavery* (1900), in which his well-known "Cast down your buckets where you are" conciliatory "Atlanta Exposition Address" appears would outline his prescription for industrial education and black subservience as an entry level to self-help, which would dominate his political persuasion and activity up to his death. In that address to a white plantation audience, Washington's anti–Du Boisean position called for survival and progress via accommodation and compromise, advocating that "there is as much dignity in tilling a field as in writing a poem. It is at the bottom of life we must begin, and not at the top." Du Bois challenged him in chapter 3 of *The Souls of Black Folk* (1903), in which he prophetically announced the central theme of the new century: "The problem of the twentieth century is the problem of the color line." Moreover, he expounded further on the phenomenon of "double consciousness" and called for a "better and truer" self, which required investigations of European, African, and specifically American traditions. Casting his assertive approach against Washington, Du Bois emphasized the responsibility of the "talented tenth" of black professionals to the less-privileged members of their communities. Although Du Bois later repudiated the elitism of this position and embraced Marxism, the ideas of "double consciousness" and the "talented tenth" exerted a major influence on African American life prior to and during the Harlem Renaissance.

Du Bois, William Monroe Trotter, and other blacks of their persuasion organized the Niagara movement in 1905 and with white liberals, the National Association for the Advancement of Colored People (NAACP) in 1909, which was concerned primarily with legally combating racism and mob violence. Du Bois founded and became the editor of its publishing organ, *The Crisis* magazine. In those publications, he would formulate the later posture of the Black Aesthetics and the Black Art's Movement of the 1960s as not "l'art pour l'art" but, rather, art for people's sake, by contending that "while we [*The Crisis*] believe in Negro art, we do not believe in art simply for art's sake." Shortly after the establishment of the NAACP, the National Urban League was formed. Also Dr. Carter G. Woodson, the father of black historiography, organized the Association for the Study of Negro Life and History in 1915, which would document the contributions of blacks, thus creating black pride with the realization of the significant contributions of blacks.

Inspired by Anna Julia Cooper, noted southern woman activist who insisted on the importance of women's contributions to "uplifting the race," and by Ida B. Wells-Barnett, anti-lynching crusader who focused attention on lynching while editing the Memphis *Free Speech*, women working in the club movement combined Du Bois's analytical sophistication with community-based activism. Writers affiliated with the clubs contributed frequently to church publications and journals, including *Colored American Magazine* (1900), *The Crisis* (1910), *Opportunity* (1923) and *The Messenger* (1917). Pauline E. Hopkins, besides her editorship of *Colored American Magazine*, provided a woman's perspective on double consciousness in her 1900 novel *Contending Forces*. This work shares numerous thematic concerns with Paul Laurence Dunbar's *Sport of the Gods* (1902), Charles Waddell Chestnutt's *House behind the Cedars* (1900), and James Weldon Johnson's *Autobiography of an Ex-coloured Man* (1912).

HARLEM RENAISSANCE (1920–1930)

Beginning with the years just preceding World War I up to the subsequent Great Migration of blacks from the South to the North in search of jobs and a better life, leadership in the black community radically shifted from Washington to Du Bois and Marcus Garvey. During this time, we witnessed the most prolific period for African American literary activity, the Harlem Renaissance, with the spirit of the "New Negro" forcing the black middle class to reevaluate their relationship to the black masses. The Harlem Renaissance, a term credited to black philosopher and writer Alain Locke, was a celebration of African American culture at a time in America's history when the restraints of the Victorian age were succumbing to the bold Roaring Twenties. It demonstrated a sense of cultural heritage and racial pride, which Patricia Liggins Hill calls in *Call and Response* "a rebirth of artistic forms, . . . a rebirth of the abolitionist spirit of self-definition." It was the first opportunity blacks had to give birth to and celebrate the uniqueness of their culture. It was a cultural and intellectual movement or awakening of the black intelligentsia, during which time an interest in black publications was at an all-time high. Young, educated blacks migrated to New York City and particularly to Harlem to establish themselves in the literary scene. It was the Mecca for what Du Bois called the talented tenth. Whereas some conservative black critics believed that black literature should "uplift" the race, by showing blacks in a positive light, younger, more radical blacks believed that a "realistic" view of black life had to be presented.

Many young black writers came into prominence during the Harlem Renaissance, the prime ones being Claude McKay, the master sonneteer; Jean Toomer, author of the experimental lyrical novel *Cane*; Countee Cullen, ambivalent Romantic poet; Nella Larsen, author of the celebrated *Quicksand*; and Langston Hughes, the most prolific writer of the period. Others recognized for their poetry and fiction include James Weldon Johnson, author of the national black anthem "Lift Every Voice and Sing"; poetess Anne Spencer; Zora Neale Hurston, folklorist and author of the celebrated novel *Their Eyes Were Watching God*; poetess Helen Johnson; Dorothy West, author of 1995 novel *The Wedding*; Sterling Brown, poet and critic who, in the words of Richard Barksdale in *Black Writers of America: A Comprehensive Anthology*, wrote with "hard-hitting emphasis on social protest"; and Rudolf Fisher. Du Bois continued his work by producing books and essays on the position of blacks in this country and on the necessary steps they needed to take to achieve equality.

Also called the "New Negro movement," the Harlem Renaissance was the first cultural movement to attain widespread recognition in and outside the black communities. According to David Levering Lewis in *When Harlem Was in Vogue* (1981), this movement attracted poets, dramatists, fiction writers, painters, musicians, and intellectuals with its promise of an atmosphere in which black artists could interact with each other and with their white contemporaries. Defined by the "Harlem" issue of *Survey Graphic* magazine (March 1925, edited by Locke and reprinted in expanded form as *The New Negro*), the Harlem Renaissance drew energy from activity surrounding the drama of the Great Migration and the excitement and limited opportunities experienced by oppressed rural southerners now on the urban scene. Moreover, there was the response of disillusioned black soldiers, returning home from World War I, only to experience discrimination and second-class citizenship in housing and job opportunities. Violence, too, fueled the rich literary period, epitomized by major race riots, such as the bloody "Red Summer" during 1919 when blacks were being slaughtered in urban America. McKay's "If We Must Die" was a response to such atrocities. All these forces and the new possibilities for dissenting voices created by the death of Washington inspired the revolutionary writings. Inspiration and energy also came from literary centers in Boston, Washington, the Midwest and West, the Caribbean, and Philadelphia, where Jessie Fauset's career began before she moved to New York to serve as editor of *The Crisis*.

Most Harlem Renaissance writers had direct contact with white patrons and modernist artists, many of whom had been inspired by African and African American visual and musical traditions. Although the financial support provided by Carl Van Vechten, author of the controversial novel *Nigger Heaven* (1926), and Charlotte Osgood Mason, who supported Hughes and Hurston, helped writers find time for their work, white patronage remains a controversial topic, as indicated in George Kent's *Blackness and the Adventure of Western Culture* (1972). Many black intellectuals of the period condemned most white participants for their stereotypical views of blacks, and the interracial politics of the period received a scathing denunciation in Wallace Thurman's *Infants of the Spring* (1932), the dystopian double to the romantic image advanced in McKay's *Home to Harlem* (1928).

Abby Arthur Johnson and Ronald Maberry Johnson, in *Propaganda and Aesthetics: The Literary Politics of Afro-American Magazines in the Twentieth Century* (1979), assert that in addition to meeting at social events hosted by Van Vechten and black heiress A'Lelia Walker, Harlem Renaissance writers published their works in *The Crisis, The Opportunity*, and the short-lived periodicals *Harlem* and *Fire!!* (both edited by Thurman), as well as in anthologies such as Cullen's *Caroling Dust* (1927), Richardson's *Plays and Pageants of Negro Life* (1930), and Johnson's *Book of American Negro Poetry* (1922; expanded 1931). Tony Martin's *Literary Garveyism: Garvey, Black Arts, and the Harlem Renaissance* (1983) suggests that although it has attracted less recognition, Garvey's *Negro World* newspaper played a unique role in black literature. The most widely circulated black periodical of the time, *Negro World* sponsored literary contests and published hundreds of poets and fiction writers from throughout the diaspora while advancing the Pan-Africanist agenda of Garvey's Universal Negro Improvement Association.

According to Sterling Brown's *Negro in American Fiction* (1937), the Harlem Renaissance introduced issues, both thematically and aesthetically, that dominated African American literary consciousness throughout the century. Locke in "The New Negro," Hughes in "The Negro Artist and the Racial Mountain," and Johnson in his preface to *The Book of American Negro Poetry* define concerns such as the relationship between African American expression and the American mainstream, the significance of oral and folk traditions, and the impact of modern urban society on literary forms. Similarly, Marita Bonner's essay "On Being Young—a Woman—and Colored" (*The Crisis*, 1925) and Elise Johnson McDougald's "The Task of Negro Womanhood" (*The New Negro*, 1925) connect the pioneering work of Wells-Barnett and Cooper with that of later black women activists. Anticipating later debates over Afrocentricity, Helene Johnson's "Bottled" and Cullen's "Heritage" raise the question Cullen posed in "What Is Africa to Me?" Like McKay, who expressed his militancy in his sonnets," Cullen used highly conventional formal structures to articulate his tormented double consciousness. Clenora Hudson-Weems's "Claude McKay: Black Protest in Western Traditional Form" (*WJBS*, 1992) interprets the pitting of antithetical form and content against each other as an effective form of masking. Conversely, both Hughes and Hurston explored the literary possibilities of the blues, jazz, sermons, and folktales in experimental forms paralleling those of their white modernist associates. Exploring the ambiguities of its author's position on the margins of both white and black worlds, Robert Bone's *Negro Novel in America* (1965), points to the fact that Toomer's multigenre epic *Cane* (1923) initiates a black modernist tradition that includes Hurston's *Moses: Man of the Mountain* (1939), Hughes's *Montage of a Dream Deferred* (1951), Ralph Ellison's *Invisible Man* (1952), and Melvin B. Tolson's *Harlem Gallery* (1965).

The tension between the minstrel tradition, masking, and open expression, personified by the great black actor Bert Williams's compulsory blackface routines, haunted black playwrights throughout the first half of the century. Brown's *Negro Poetry and Drama* (1937) elaborated upon this phenomenon. Despite Paul Robeson's emergence as a prominent black actor who eschewed stereotypical roles during the 1920s, before the Federal Theatre Project in the 1930s, black playwrights were forced to choose between the lucrative Broadway revues that paid well but catered to white stereotypes, and "little theatres" such as Cleveland's Karamu House, Washington's Krigwa Players, and Harlem's Lafayette Theatre. Although their audiences could not support playwrights financially, these theatres provided authors such as May Miller, Willis Richardson, and Georgia Douglas Johnson with opportunities to focus on significant social problems and explore the theatrical possibilities of folk materials. The most vital forms of black performance, however, developed on the Theatre Owners Booking Association circuit, where comedians like Pigmeat Markham and blues singers like Ma Rainey manipulated minstrel conventions while tapping into the West African–based folk traditions explored at length in Hurston's *Mules and Men* (1935). The lyrics of Rainey, Ida Cox, and Bessie Smith frequently addressed women and lesbian themes with a frankness that would have been impossible for writers such as Larsen, Marita Bonner, Fauset, and Alice Moore Dunbar-Nelson (1875–1935), wife of Paul Lawrence Dunbar, all of whom were forced to negotiate the genteel literary convention.

In the final analysis, the Harlem Renaissance writers, according to Nathaniel Irvin Huggins in *Harlem Renaissance* (1971), reflected both the "uplifting" theme of the conservative black critics and the "realistic" artist movement of the younger, more radical black critics. Each succeeded in showing blacks and the world that their culture was both "beautiful" and a worthy literary topic, themes that would reemerge during the civil rights, black power, Black Panther and black arts movements of the searing 1960s and early 1970s.

SOCIAL CHANGES (EARLY 1930 TO 1950)

The Great Depression began with the stock market crash in 1929. In 1932 President Franklin D. Roosevelt was elected, promising the country a New Deal, one being the Federal Writer's Project under the supervision of the Works Progress administration. Established black writers, such as Hughes, Hurston, and Arna Bontemps, who participated in the Project, and others like Walter White, social critic and lynching investigator, Eric Walrond, avant-garde writer, Gwendolyn Bennett, poetess and painter, Thurman, fiction writer and critic, and Helene Johnson, race conscious poetess, were able to earn a living with their writing. New black literary voices emerged as well, including Richard Wright, Robert Hayden, and Frank Yerby. In the 1940s, black writers continued to address the plight of their people, with celebrated black modernists and urban realists Wright and Chester B. Himes portraying blacks as victims of American racism in *Native Son* and *If He Hollows Let Him Go*, respectively. Also emerging on the scene were poet Frank Marshall Davis, Ann Petry, author of *The Street*, and Margaret Walker, who won the Yale Poetry Prize for her 1942 collection of poetry, *For My People*. Hence, the dominant theme of the last half of this era was characterized by racial unrest and organized protest.

Wright was considered the major writer during the late 1930s and the 1940s. *Native Son* (1940), in which he protested the growing violence of northern urban ghetto life for blacks, was the most popular novel published by a black writer. Hence, almost every black writer of the 1940s was automatically assigned to the "School of Wright." Unfortunately, this negatively affected the reception of Petry, Bontemps, Himes, and especially Sterling Brown, who was valued more for his protest poems than for his pioneering literary histories or sophisticated modernist lyrics such as "Ma Rainey." Most crucially, Wright's dominance contributed to the invisibility of women writers such as Hurston and Dorothy West, who only initially shared his leftist politics when she edited the leftist journal *Challenge*. Hurston's *Their Eyes Were Watching God* (1937), published during the grim Depression years, is now recognized as an African American classic, though the author was initially greeted by critics with apathy or hostility because they viewed her as apolitical. The book went out of print until its rediscovery by literary descendants June Jordan and Alice Walker.

The 1930s forged links between black writers and white contemporaries such as Theodore Dreiser, Carl Sandburg, and Michael Gold, who as literary editor of the communist newspaper the *Daily Worker* played a major role in shaping a leftist response to Wright, Hughes, McKay, and William Attaway. Leftist publications, such as *New Masses, Challenge*, and *Anvil*, published black writers interested in Marxist approaches to the economic and political problems of the Great Depression. Wright, Ellison, Shirley Graham (who later married Du Bois), Theodore Ward, and Walker were among black writers who joined white contemporaries such as Nelson Algren and Saul Bellow in working for the Federal Theatre or Writer's Project of the Works Progress Administration.

Recognizing the gradual shift of cultural activity away from New York, the idea of a black "Chicago Renaissance" (not to be confused with the earlier white-dominated Chicago Renaissance) provides what many critics find the most satisfactory approach to the culturally diverse production of the period and its impact on later developments. *New Challenge* (1937) played a similar role in this new movement to that of the "New Negro" issue of *Survey Graphic* in the Renaissance. The touchstone of the issue was Wright's "Blueprint for Negro Writing," which highlights the tension between the period's leftist and folk-nationalist tendencies. Literary institutions of the period pursued various approaches to these tensions with the left attempting to appropriate the literary folk form for propagandistic purposes. Several black writers explored proletarian aesthetics in the communist-sponsored John Reed Clubs. Walker participated in the South Side Writers group, as did many other South Side poets, including Davis, Margaret Esse Danner, and Brooks, who later won the Pulitzer Prize for poetry for her collection *Annie Allen*. They developed their poetry in workshops such as that sponsored by white socialite Inez Cunningham Stark at the South Side Community Center.

Many blacks saw the end of World War II as a sign that they could assimilate into the dominant culture. For example, black literary critics believed that the black writers should merge into the mainstream of American literature, thereby denying that the African American experience in this country had any influence on their work. However, poets such as Naomi Long Madgett, Walker, and Brooks continued to write poetry that reflected their knowledge of the African American community. Those fighting for integration into mainstream literature were doing so in much the same way the fight for integration was being manifested in the political arena, such as the 1954 *Brown v. Board of Education* Supreme Court case.

Wright, who insisted upon the credibility of protest literature, fled the country for Paris because of his impatience with the legal system to grant blacks their civil rights. Yerby and Willard Motley completely abandoned anything black in their novels, including characters and themes. Both were awarded commercial success with their focus on white life instead of black life. Ellison, who won the National Book Award for *Invisible Man* (1952), had earlier defended a black aesthetics position that art and politics are inseparable, only to change his position in his 1964 article "The Art of Fiction." John Oliver Killens whose first novel *Youngblood* (1954) in its title connotes a new spirit, and Paule Marshall were writers during this era who did not give up the struggle. Playwrights, too, though few in number, were ever vigilant on the question of race, like Alice Childress and her one-act play *Florence*, and Lorraine Hansberry and her award-winning play *A Raisin in the Sun*.

Nevertheless, by the 1940s, most blacks writers assumed a pronouncedly integrationist posture, a Lockean posture of mainstreaming, evidenced by pivotal essays by integrationist critics and writers, including Saunders Redding's "American Negro Literature" (1949) and James Baldwin's, "Everybody's Protest Novel" (1949). Baldwin's position changed during the latter part of his life, as reflected in many of his novels and in his dramatization of the Till murder case, *Blues for Mr. Charlie*. Other writers include Hugh Gloster in "Race and the Negro Writer" (1950), Arthur P. Davis in "Integration and Race Literature" (1956), and Sterling Brown in Rayford Logan et al.'s *The New Negro Thirty*

Years Afterward (1955), who paradoxically wrote very black conscious poetry like "Strong Men," were upholding the trend of so-called universal literature. But again staunch black aesthetics critics, like Nick Aaron Ford (1904–1984) in "A Blueprint for Negro Authors" (1950) and Ann Petry in "The Novel as Social Criticism" (1950 in Patricia Hill's *Call and Response*) held firm to their beliefs in the validity of racial themes in black art. Moreover, because of the demise of McCarthyism and the change in the global political climate, the conservative integrationist posture was short lived. Evident was the onset of the modern civil rights movement of the 1950s and 1960s, ignited by the August 28, 1955, brutal lynching of the fourteen-year-old black Chicago youth Emmett Louis "Bobo" Till in Money, Mississippi, followed by the refusal of Rosa Parks to relinquish her bus seat to a white man in Montgomery, Alabama, three months later on December 1, 1955. The year-long 1956 Montgomery bus boycott ensued. According to Hudson-Weems in *Emmett Till: The Sacrificial Lamb of the Civil Rights Movement* (1994), Till's lynching was the true catalyst of the civil rights movement, setting the stage for the bus boycott. Many writers responded to this atrocity, such as Brooks in "The Last Quatrain in the Ballad of Emmett Till." The chief concern of the black artist became not only black liberation at home but also global black liberation.

Especially affecting black writers was the emergence of free and independent African countries. Poets, like other literary writers, embraced the global black liberation struggle, as reflected in the poetry of Melvin Tolson and his "Libretto for the Republic of Liberia" and by Robert Hayden in "Middle Passage" and "Yardbird." Other poets, like Dudley Randall, Owen Dodson, Margaret Esse Danner, Walker, Brooks, and Naomi Long Madget presented their views on race issues of the time. Needless to say, the fiction writers, the literary critics, and the poets had emerged on the scene where two distinct opposing literary positions would force their hands to a commitment. They would have to choose to concentrate their literary energy in one of two camps—the integrationist aesthetics or the black aesthetics, the latter being the dominate posture for the next era, the decade of the 1960s.

Wright continued to dominate as a national and international literary figure throughout the 1950s, publishing three novels—*The Outsider* (1953), *Savage Holiday* (1954), and *The Long Dream* (1958)—and four works of nonfiction— *Black Power* (1954), *The Color Curtain* (1956), *Pagan Spain* (1956), and *White Man, Listen!* (1957). *Eight Men, Lawd Today*, and *American Hunger* appeared posthumously. His mentoring of and breaks with Ellison and Baldwin are often described in critical histories of the period, for their disagreements about the relationship between art and ideology in black writings, debates that continue to shape ideas about the function of non-white literatures.

In 1952 Ellison's *Invisible Man* established that black writers could write social protest literature with stylistic and philosophical complexity. His collection of essays, *Shadow and Act (1964)*, and *Going to the Territory* (1987) have contributed substantially to the world of ideas.

Baldwin was a versatile writer who frequently inspired controversy because of his own homosexuality, the place of homosexuality, the place of homosexual relationships in some of his work, and his unwillingness to adopt easy political positions. The author of major works of fiction, including *Go Tell It on the Mountain* (1953), *Giovanni's Room* (1956), *Another Country* (1962), and several plays, including *Blues for Mister Charlie* (1964), he was an especially brilliant essayist. His reputation may rest ultimately on his achievement of collections such as *Notes of a Native Son* (1955), *Nobody Knows My Name: More Notes on a Native Son* (1961), *The Fire Next Time* (1963), and *The Devil Finds Work* (1976). Baldwin's first novel, *Go Tell It on the Mountain*, further stressed black writers' abilities to present a uniquely black viewpoint and universal concern for personal identity. These works and those by black writers such as dramatist Alice Childress showed that works by African Americans did not have to fit within literary mainstream to qualify as fine literature.

Traditionally studies of African American literary production identify Wright, Ellison, and Baldwin as the dominant authors of the period from the early 1950s through the mid-1960s, but recent critiques of canon formation have made it impossible to ignore the significance of a wider range of influential writers of the period. Ann Petry, for example, ranks among the most versatile of African American writers. *The Street* (1946) addresses the plight of a black mother struggling against race, gender, and class oppression in Harlem during the 1940s. Her second and third novels—*Country Place* (1947) and *The Narrows* (1953)— interrogate with extraordinary subtlety the notion of community in the context of small New England villages. Additionally, Petry has published many short stories as well as several books based on black history and folklore for children and adolescent readers.

BLACK NATIONALISM, BLACK AESTHETICS, AND THE BLACK ARTS MOVEMENT (1960s)

The 1960s was a decade of richness, an era that shifted from the integrationist posture to a position of black cultural nationalism. Motivated by the resurgence of Pan-Africanism, the writers of the 1960s demanded a new black aesthetics, later defined by Addison Gayle, Jr., in his edited book *The Black Aesthetic* (1971), which took the position of conscious disassociation on the part of black people from European style and ideology. Descriptively called the era of Black Nationalism, Black Aesthetics, and the Black Arts Movement, it was an era of definition and affirmation, a period when blacks created their own paradigms and their own criteria for their own distinct art.

"Black Is Beautiful" and "Black Power" were the slogans of the era. For the first time since the Harlem Renaissance, a movement emphasizing the beauty and uniqueness of African American culture was underway. African Americans began to openly celebrate and incorporate into their lives the songs, stories, and customs of their African ancestors.

In response to the emergent nationalist movement of the mid- to late 1960s arose its cultural or aesthetic counterpart, the black arts movement, and the concept of black aesthetics developed. Hoyt Fuller defined it well: The "black aesthetics [is] a system of isolating and evaluating the artistic works of black people which reflect the special character and imperatives of black experience." In *Black Fire* (1968), a classic black nationalist anthology of the time coedited by Larry Neal and Imamu Amiri Baraka, Neal declared that the "artist and the political activist are one." Continuing the tradition of the twenties and thirties, black art is seen as a political weapon.

Many of the urban ghettos erupted into riots in the mid-1960s, during which time black poetry became a political weapon. Poets like Imamu Amiri Baraka, Larry Neal, Don L. Lee (Haki Madhubuti), Sonia Sanchez, Etheridge Knight, Kristin Hunter, Conrad Kent Rivers, Nikki Giovanni, A. B. Spellman, Mari Evans, June Jordan, Dudley Randall, Lucille Clifton, and Gwendolyn Brooks used their poetry, not to speak for themselves as individuals, but to speak in a dramatic voice for all African Americans. The black power movement also made an impact on African American novels, such as Margaret Walker's *Jubilee* (1966) and William Melvin Kelley's *dem* (1967), satirizing "dem white folks." Powerful autobiographies and biographies appeared, including *The Autobiography of Malcolm X* (1964), by Malcolm X and Alex Haley; *Soul on Ice* (1968), by Eldridge Cleaver; and *I Know Why the Caged Bird Sings* (1970), by Maya Angelou. Playwrights dramatized the new awareness on the stage in works such as Adrienne Kennedy's *Funnyhouse of a Negro* (1963), Baraka's *Dutchman* (1964), Douglas Turner Ward's *Day of Absence* (1965), Charles Gordon's *No Place to Be Somebody* (1967), and Alice Childress's *Wine in the Wilderness* (1969). Short stories by Paule Marshall and Ernest Gaines and books by Julius Lester expressed the feeling of black pride.

In 1968 Baraka (earlier called LeRoi Jones) and Larry Neal published *Black Fire: An Anthology of Afro-American Writing*. In the forward, the editors claimed that a new day had arrived for black art. This anthology served as the birth of the black arts movement. Neal explained that this movement was opposed to any concept that separated black artists from their community, that African American art was directly related to the quest for African American self-determination. Many African American writers and critics embraced the ideas of the black arts movement. Other more conservative African American critics argued against it. Either way, the black arts movement focused attention on African American literature, and more independent African American and white publishers began to seek out and publish literature by black writers. The increased availability of African American literature allowed the number of readers, both African American and white, to grow.

The superb black oratorical tradition as exemplified by Douglass, Truth, Washington, Du Bois, and Garvey was revitalized in the 1960s. There were civil rights orations by Martin Luther King, Jr., such as his famous "I Have a Dream" speech delivered at the 1963 March on Washington, the major civil rights protest in the United States. There were black nationalist speeches by Malcolm X that swept the nation. There were "Black Power" slogans and writings by Stokely Carmichael demanding economic as well as social and political parity.

The prime mover of the black arts movement, Baraka, along with his contemporary Neal, set out to define the criteria for black art. They held that black art must be written to and about black people in the language of the masses. It must serve a threefold function: It must entertain, as all art must do; it must educate black people about their predicament in America; and it must arouse black people to political action. Baraka's landmark poem "Black Art" clearly defined black art as concrete and functional.

These new poets, along with new black arts dramatists like Ed Bullins and Tom Dent, critics like Stephen Henderson and Mercer Cook (*Militant Black Writers*), and black nationalists like Maulana Karenga, joined Franz Fanon (*The Wretched of the Earth*) and black psychologist, Nathan Hare. Other black critics include Clarence Major, Hoyt Fuller, Carolyn Fowler, and Sarah Webster Fabio. In an effort to consolidate black economic and cultural power, the black arts movement gave rise to a range of journals such as *Negro Digest* (later called *Black World*), *The Journal of Black Poetry, Black Expression, Black Orpheus: A Journal of African and Afro-American Literature, Black Review, Black Scholar, College Language Association Journal*, and *Phylon*, thereby giving black conscious writers new avenues for getting their works published without the infringement of mainstream mandates in style and content. Moreover, black presses came forth, such as *Broadside Press, Jihad Press, Free Black Press, Black Dialogue Press*, and *Third World Press*. Indeed, the black arts movement influenced cultural production in a variety of media: music, theatre, art, dance, and literature.

CONTEMPORARY ERA (1970 TO PRESENT)

In the early and mid-1970s, the civil rights protest movement began losing strength as attention shifted from gaining equal rights for African Americans as a whole to the quest for individual rights. Blacks had made some economic and political gains through the civil rights and black power movements, but unemployment, poverty, and discrimination still plagued African Americans across the United States. The literary text of African American writers in the middle and late 1970s reflected the shift in national focus. Writers like Nikki Giovanni and Haki Madhubuti moved from writing only black power poetry to writing poetry about political and economic conditions of people of color throughout the world. Ishmael Reed's novels *Mumbo Jumbo* (1972) and *Flight to Canada* (1976) satirized America's culture. One theme running throughout these works is still prominent in African American literature in the 1980s and 1990s: It is important for African Americans to know their history. August Wilson's dramas

Fences (1987), which won a Pulitzer Prize, and *Piano Lesson* (1990), along with Charles Johnson's National Book Award winner *Middle Passage* (1990), illustrate the power of historical knowledge.

Although the early 1970s continued the spirit of the 1960s, new interests divided the focus. There was an evolving interest in black women writers in the early 1970s that continues today, following the intrusion of the white women's movement in the midst of the civil rights and black power movements of the 1960s. During this time, a host of black women writers found publishers among mainstream publishing houses as well as a wide reception of their works as demonstrated by the numerous awards granted to them. Toni Morrison was one of the first and most prolific and highly respected black women writers during the early part of the era, earning her numerous awards, including both the Pulitzer Prize and the Nobel Prize for literature, the first African American woman to receive the prize. Her first novel, *The Bluest Eye*, was published in 1970, followed by *Sula* (1974), *Song of Solomon* (1977), *Tar Baby* (1981), *Dreaming Emmett* (1985), *Beloved* (1987), *Jazz* (1992), *Playing in the Dark: Whiteness and the Literary Imagination* (1992), and her edited book *Race-ing Justice, En-Gendering Power: Essays on Anita Hill, Clarence Thomas, and the Construction of Social Reality* (1992). Alice Walker, too, had her share of publications and awards. In 1970, her first novel, *The Third Life of Grange Copeland* appeared, followed by *In Love and Trouble: Stories of Black Women* (1973), *Meridian* (1976), and numerous collections of essays and poetry. Her later novel *The Color Purple* (1982) was made into a controversial movie, followed by the publication of two more novels, *Temple of My Familiar* (1989) and *Possessing the Secret of Joy* (1992). Later, novelist Terry McMillan authored four popular novels, *Mama* (1987), *Disappearing Acts* (1989), *Waiting to Exhale* (1992), and *How Stella Got Her Groove Back* (1996), the last two novels giving Walker competition in the movie industry for the film versions. She also edited an anthology entitled *Breaking Ice: An Anthology of Contemporary African-American Fiction* (1990). Other black writers of the era include Maya Angelou, author of the autobiographical novel *I Know Why the Caged Bird Sings* (1970) and the first African American and first woman to read her poetry at a U.S. presidential inauguration; Toni Cade Bambara and her celebrated novel *The Salt Eaters* (1980); Gloria Naylor and her novels *The Women of Brewster Place* (1982), *Linden Hills* (1985), *Mama Day* (1988), *Bailey's Cafe* (1992), and *The Men of Brewster Place* (1998); and Gayl Jones, whose most well-known works are the novels *Corregidora* (1975) and *Eva's Man* (1976). Other creative women writers of the era include Shirley Anne Williams, critic, poet, and novelist; Ntozake Shange, author of the award-winning play *for colored girls who have considered suicide when the rainbow is enuf (1977)*; Jamaica Kincaid, West Indian–born author of the controversial semi-autobiographical novel *The Autobiography of My Mother* (1996); and Rita Dove, the first African American and first woman to be named poet laureate of the United States and Pulitzer Prize–winning poet for her *Thomas and Beulah* volume (1986).

There is also the much-debated question regarding the role of black women within the constructs of the modern feminist movement. Women in all genres have attempted to address this issue in many ways, presenting their position on the subject in their works. Barbara Smith, and bell hooks became the leading advocates for black feminism. Although contending that gender, race, and class were being simultaneously addressed, most of their energy went to gender issues as a priority. Moreover, much of their emphasis on gender reflects their complaints about their exclusion from the feminist arena, as in the case of hooks in her *Feminist Theory: From Margin to Center* (1984), who complains about the racist exclusion of black women and their writings from feminist criticism. In addition, Smith, in "Toward a Black Feminist Criticism," addresses the problem of exclusion that she and other black lesbians experience within the feminist arena. Needless to say, although the most frequently accepted label for black women in academe has been that of black feminist, most women outside and some inside academe have found the terminology problematic, since any and all brands of feminism see female empowerment as their collective priority. Alice Walker attempted to offer a solution to this dilemma with her label womanist. Unfortunately, her term and definition of womanist in the introduction to her collection of essays *In Search of Our Mother's Gardens: Womanist Prose* (1983) as "a black feminist or feminist of color. . . . Womanist is to feminist as purple to lavender" was insufficient. Clenora Hudson-Weems, who named and refined a new terminology and paradigm relative to the true role of Africana women within the constructs of today's women movement, introduced Africana womanism in her *Africana Womanism: Reclaiming Ourselves* (1993). This concept, which earlier in the mid-1980s she called black womanism, was designed for all women of Africana descent. It addresses the particular needs and desires relative to Africana women's unique lives revolving around their worldview and thus is distinct from all other female-based theories because it prioritizes the triple plight—race, class, and gender—of Africana women. According to *Call and Response*, "Hudson-Weems has launched a new critical discourse in the Black Women's Literary Movement," which, unlike feminism or black feminism, is family-centered rather than female-centered and is concerned first and foremost with race empowerment rather than female empowerment. Other black women writes focusing with race, class, and gender issues in their works include race conscious lesbian poets and essayists, June Jordan and Audrey Lorde, and Angela Davis in *Women, Race, and Class* (1983).

Besides the rise of black women's literature, the recent appearance of new black structuralist and deconstructionist critics, such as Robert Stepto in his coauthored book with Dexter Fisher, *Afro-American Literature: The Reconstruction of Instruction* (1979), Houston Baker, Jr., in his *Journey Back: Issues in Black Literature and Criticism* (1980) and *Blues Ideology and Afro-American Literature and Criticism* (1984), and Henry Louis "Skip" Gates in his *Black Literature and Literary Theory* (1984) and *The Signifying Monkey: A Theory of African-American Literary Criticism* (1988), represents an important paradigm shift in African American literature. Yet, literary critic Richard K. Barksdale in his essay "Critical Theory and Problems of Canonicity in African American Literature," which appeared in his swan song essay collection *Praisesong of Survival* (1992), lamented the growing fascination with "French-based theories of textual criticism . . . [emphasizing] ignoring history and personal experience." Such was and is the case with these new black structuralist and deconstructionist critics, who approach black texts by applying white theory, thereby awarding them power, high visibility, and credibility in academe. Be that as it may, however, successfully countering this Eurocentric bias is Molefe Asante, author of *The Afrocentric Ideal* (1987), in which he both named and refined an African-centered paradigm, Afrocentricity. He, along with other Afrocentric scholars, served as a reminder to all that Africa must be placed at the center of all analyses related to people of African descent in much the same way that Europe is placed at the center of all other analyses. Some black aesthetics critics, like Haki Madhubuti in his *Claiming Earth: Race, Rage, Rape, Redemption* (1994), have attempted to identify, critique, and analyze the strategy of black Eurocentric scholars, but none has been more successful than general editor Patricia Liggins Hill in the recent definitive black aesthetics anthology *Call and Response: The Riverside Anthology of the African American Literary Tradition* (1997), who has set the record straight about the continuing struggle of black aesthetics literature and critics.

Other male writers of the era include the following: Albert Murray, Henry Dumas, William Melvin Kelley, Michael Harper, Al Young, Quincy Troupe, James McPherson, Askia Muhammad Toure, John Edgar Wideman, Yusef Komunyakaa, and Reginald McKnight.

Indeed, the explosion of African American writing since the 1970s has made it increasingly difficult to generalize about major themes and styles characteristic of the contemporary period. However, some of the most significant trajectories include the rise of African American women writing, the reclamation of history, the resurgence of autobiography, the rise of black gay literature and lesbian literature, incursions into popular literary forms, and postmodernist experimentations.

As we move into a next millennium, African American writers such as J. California Cooper, Angela Jackson, Tina McElroy Ansa, Walter Mosely, Bebe Moore Campbell, and Paula Childress White have established themselves in the black literary tradition. As the works of these and other black writers show, African American literature continues to build on the foundation established in the eighteenth century: the structures of oral tradition and the quest for freedom and equality. This foundation has supported African Americans as they moved from the chains of slavery through war and peace, to poverty and prosperity. African American literature has recorded the defeats and the triumphs, the fears and the dreams. Its strength lies in its ability to present the truth—the good, the bad, and the ugly. To be sure, African American literature gives voice to the eternal spirit of African Americans and the legacy of black life.

BIBLIOGRAPHY

Anthologies

Barksdale, Richard K., and Kenneth Kinnamon. *Black Writers of America: A Comprehensive Anthology*. New York: Macmillan Company, 1972.

Bontemps, Arna, ed. *American Negro Poetry*. New York: Hill and Wang, 1963.

Bullins, Ed, ed. *New Plays from the Black Theatre*. New York: Bantam Books, 1969.

Davis, Arthur P., and Saunders Redding, eds. *Cavalcade: Negro American Writing from 1760 to the Present*. Boston: Houghton Mifflin, 1971.

Ford, Nick Aaron, ed. *Black Insights: Significant Literature by Afro-Americans, 1760 to the Present*. Waltham, MA: Ginn, 1971.

Hill, Patricia Liggins, general editor. *Call and Response: The Riverside Anthology of the African American Literary Tradition*. Boston: Houghton Mifflin, 1997.

Huggins, Nathan Irvin. *Harlem Renaissance*. New York: Oxford University Press, 1971.

Johnson, James Weldon, ed. *The Book of American Negro Poetry*, revised ed. New York: Harcourt, Brace and Co., 1931.

Jones, LeRoi, and Larry Neal, eds. *Black Fire: An Anthology of Afro-American Writing*. New York: Morrow, 1968.

Richardson, Willis. *Plays and Pageants from the Life of Negro Life*. Associated Publishers, 1930.

Troupe, Quincy, ed. *Watts Poets: A Book of New Poetry and Essay*. Los Angeles: House of Respect, 1968.

Turner, Darwin T., ed. *Black American Literature: Essays, Poetry, Fiction, Drama*. Columbus, OH: Charles E. Merrill, 1969.

Criticism

Andrews, Williams L. *To Tell a Free Story: The First Century of Afro-American Autobiography, 1760–1865*. Urbana: University of Illinois Press, 1986.

Asante, Molefi K. *The Afrocentric Ideal*. Philadelphia: Temple University Press, 1987.

Baker, Houston A., Jr. *Black Literature in America*. New York: McGraw-Hill, 1971.

Barksdale, Richard K. *Praisesong of Survival*. Urbana: University of Illinois Press, 1992.

Barton, Rebecca C. *Witnesses for Freedom: Negro Americans in Autobiography*. New York: Harper, 1948.

Bone, Robert A. *The Negro Novel in America*. New Haven, CT: Yale University Press, 1965.

Bontemps, Arna. *Great Slave Narratives*. Boston: Beacon Press, 1969.

Brawley, Benjamin. *Early Negro American Writers*. Plainview, NY: Books for Libraries Press, 1935.

———. *The Negro in Literature and Art*. New York: Duffield and Company, 1930.

Braxton, Joanne. *Black Women Writing Autobiography: A Tradition within a Tradition*. Philadelphia: Temple University Press, 1989.

Brown, Sterling. *The Negro in American Fiction*. Port Washington, NY: Kennikat Press, 1937.

Bruce, Dickson D., Jr. *Black American Writing from the Nadir: The Evolution of a Lit-*

erary Tradition, 1877–1915. Baton Rouge: Louisiana State University Press, 1989.

Christian, Barbara. *Black Feminist Criticism: Perspectives on Black Women Writers*. New York: Pergamon, 1985.

Cook, Mercer, and Stephen Henderson. *The Militant Black Writers in Africa and the United States*. Madison: University of Wisconsin Press, 1969.

Davis, Angela. *Women, Race and Class*. New York: Vintage, 1983.

Du Bois, W.E.B. *The Souls of Black Folk*. Greenwich, CT: Fawcett, 1961.

Ellison, Ralph. *Shadow and Act*. New York: Random House, 1964.

Ford, Nick Aaron. *The Contemporary Negro Novel: A Study in Race Relations*. Boston: Meader Publishing, 1936.

Gates, Henry Louis. *The Signifying Monkey: A Theory of African-American Literary Criticism*. New York: Oxford University Press, 1988.

Gayle, Addison, Jr., ed. *The Black Aesthetic*. New York: Doubleday, 1971.

Giddings, Paule. *When and Where I Enter: The Impact of Black Women on Race and Sex in America*. New York: Bantam, 1984.

Graham, Shirley Du Bois. *The Story of Phillis Wheatley*. New York: J. Messner, 1949.

hooks, bell. *Feminist Theory: From Margin to Center*. Boston: Southend, 1984.

Howard, H. W. *Bond and Free: A True Tale of Slave Times*. College Park, MD: McGrath Publishing, 1969.

Hudson-Weems, Clenora. *Africana Womanism: Reclaiming Ourselves*. Troy, MI: Bedford, 1993.

———. *Emmett Till: The Sacrificial Lamb of the Civil Rights Movement*. Troy, MI: Bedford, 1994.

Johnson, Abby Arthur, and Ronald Maberry Johnson. *Propaganda and Aesthetics: The Literary Politics of Afro-American Magazines in the Twentieth Century*. Amherst: University of Massachusetts Press, 1979.

Jones, LeRoi, and Larry Neal, eds. *Black Fire*. New York: William Morrow, 1968.

Kent, George. *Blackness and the Adventure of Western Culture*. Chicago: Third World Press, 1972.

Levine, Lawrence W. *Black Culture and Black Consciousness: Afro-American Folk Thought from Slavery to Freedom*. New York: Oxford University Press, 1977.

Lewis, David Levering. *When Harlem Was in Vogue*. New York: Knopf, 1981.

Locke, Alain, ed. *The New Negro: An Interpretation*. New York: Alfred and Charles Boni, 1925.

Logan, Rayford W., et al., eds. *The New Negro Thirty Years Afterward*. Washington, DC: Howard University Press, 1955.

Loggins, Vernon. *The Negro Author: His Development in America to 1900*. New York: Columbia University Press, 1931.

Martin, Tony. *Literary Garveyism: Garvey, Black Arts, and the Harlem Renaissance*. Dover, MA: Majority Press, 1983.

Mbalia, Doreatha Drummond. *Toni Morrison's Developing Class Consciousness*. Selinsgrove, PA: Susquehanna University Press, 1991.

———. *John Wideman: Reclaiming the African Personality*. Selinsgrove, PA: Susquehanna University Press, 1995.

Mitchell, Loften. *Black Drama: The Story of the American Negro in the Theater*. New York: Hawthorn, 1967.

Mootry, Maria, ed. *Gwendolyn Brooks: A Life Distilled.* Champaign: University of Illinois Press, 1987.

O'Neal, Sondra. *Jupiter Hammon and the Biblical Beginnings of African-American Literature.* Lanham, MD: Scarecrow Press, 1993.

Osofsky, Gilbert, ed. *Puttin' on Ole Massa.* New York: Harper and Row, 1969.

Redding, J. Saunders. *To Make a Poet Black.* Chapel Hill: University of North Carolina Press, 1939.

Samuels, Wilfred D., and Clenora Hudson-Weems. *Toni Morrison.* Boston: Prentice-Hall/Twayne, 1990.

Walser, Richard. *The Black Poet.* New York: Philosophical Library, 1966.

Williams, George Washington. *History of the Negro Race in America from 1619–1880.* New York: G. P. Putnam, 1883.

———. *History of the Negro Troops in the War of the Rebellion, 1861–1865.* 1888. New York: Kraus Reprint, 1969.

Williamson, Joel. *The Crucible of Race: Black-White Relations in the American South since Emancipation.* New York: Oxford University Press, 1984.

Folk Tradition

Dance, Daryl C., ed. *Shuckin' and Jivin': Folklore from Contemporary Black Americans.* Bloomington: Indiana University Press, 1978.

Dorson, Richard M., *African Folklore.* New York: Doubleday, 1972.

———. *American Negro Folktales.* New York: Fawcett, 1967.

Lester, Julius. *Black Folktales.* New York: Grove Press, 1969.

Selected Works of Selected Novelists, Poets, and Playwrights

Angelou, Maya. *I Know Why the Caged Bird Sings.* New York: Random House, 1970.

———. *Just Give Me a Cool Drink of Water 'For I Die.* New York: Random House, 1971.

———. *All God's Children Need Traveling Shoes.* New York: Random House, 1986.

Baldwin, James. *Go Tell It on the Mountain.* New York: Knopf, 1953.

———. *Notes of a Native Son.* Boston: Beacon Press, 1955.

———. *Giovanni's Room.* New York: Dial, 1956.

———. *Nobody Knows My Name: More Notes of a Native Son.* New York: Dial, 1961.

———. *Another Country.* New York: Dial, 1962.

———. *The Fire Next Time.* New York: Dial, 1963.

———. *Blues for Mister Charlie.* New York: Dial, 1964.

———. *Going to Meet the Man.* New York: Dial, 1965.

———. *The Amen Corner.* New York: Dial, 1968.

———. *If Beale Street Could Talk.* New York: Dial, 1974.

———. *Just above My Head.* New York: Dial, 1979.

———. *The Price of the Ticket: Collected Nonfiction, 1948–1985.* New York: St. Martin/Marek, 1985.

Bambara, Toni Cade. *Tales and Stories for Black Folks.* New York: Doubleday, 1971.

———. *The Salt Eaters.* New York: Random House, 1980.

Baraka, Imamu Amiri (LeRoi Jones). *Preface to a Twenty Volume Suicide Note.* New York: Totem Press and Corinth Books, 1961.

————. *Black Magic: Sabotage: Target Study: Black Art: Collected Poetry, 1961–1967.* Indianapolis: Bobbs-Merrill, 1969.

————. *It's Nation Time.* Chicago: Third World Press, 1970.

Brooks, Gwendolyn. *A Street in Bronzeville.* New York: Harper, 1945.

————. *Annie Allen.* New York: Harper, 1949.

————. *The Bean Eaters.* New York: Harper, 1960.

————. *Riot.* Detroit: Broadside Press, 1969.

Brown, Sterling. *Southern Road.* New York: Harcourt, 1932.

Brown, William Wells. *The Escape, Or a Leap to Freedom: A Drama in Five Acts.* Boston: R. F. Walcutt, 1858. Reprinted in 1969.

Bullins, Ed. *Five Plays by Ed Bullins.* Indianapolis: Bobbs-Merrill, 1969.

————. *The Theme Is Blackness: "The Corner" and Other Plays.* New York: William Morrow, 1972.

Campbell, James Edwin. *Echoes from the Cabin and Elsewhere.* Chicago: Donahue and Henneberry, 1895.

Chestnut, Charles W. *The Conjure Woman.* New York: Houghton, Mifflin, 1900.

————. *The Wife of His Youth and Other Stories of the Color Line.* New York: Houghton, Mifflin, 1900.

————. *The House behind the Cedars.* New York: Houghton, Mifflin, 1900.

————. *The Marrow of Tradition.* New York: Houghton, Mifflin, 1901.

Childress, Alice. *Wedding Band: A Love/Hate Story in Black and White.* New York: Samuel French, 1973.

Corrothers, James D. *In Spite of the Handicap.* New York: George H. Doran, 1916.

Cullen, Countee. *Color.* New York: Harper, 1925.

————. *The Black Christ and Other Poems.* New York: Harper, 1929.

————. *On These I Stand: An Anthology of the Best Poems of Countee Cullen, Selected by Himself and Including Six New Poems Never Before Published.* New York: Harper, 1947.

Dove, Rita. *The Yellow House on the Corner: Poems.* Pittsburgh: Carnegie-Mellon University Press, 1980.

————. *Thomas and Buelah.* Pittsburgh: Carnegie-Mellon University Press, 1986.

Du Bois, W.E.B. *Darkwater: Voices from within the Veil.* New York: Harcourt, Brace, and Howe, 1920. Reprinted in 1969.

Dunbar, Paul Laurence. *Oak and Ivy.* Dayton, OH: United Brethren Publishing House, 1893.

————. *Lyrics of Lowly Life.* New York: Dodd, Mead, 1896. Reprinted in 1968.

————. *Lyrics of the Hearthside.* New York: Dodd, Mead, 1899. Reprinted in 1970, 1972.

————. *The Sport of the Gods.* New York: Dodd, Mead, 1902.

————. *Lyrics of Sunshine and Shadow.* New York: Dodd, Mead, 1905. Reprinted in 1970, 1972.

————. *The Complete Poems of Paul Laurence Dunbar.* New York: Dodd, Mead, 1913.

Elder III, Lonne. *Ceremonies in Dark Old Men.* New York: Farrar, Straus, and Giroux, 1969.

Ellison, Ralph. *Invisible Man.* New York: Random House, 1952.

————. *Shadow and Act.* New York: Random House, 1964.

————. *Going to the Territory*. New York: Random House, 1986.

Equiano, Olaudah. *The Interesting Narrative of the Life of Olaudah Equiano, or Gustavus Vassa*. London: Self-published, 1789.

Evans, Mari. *I Am a Black Woman*. New York: Morrow, 1970.

Gaines, Ernest J. *The Autobiography of Miss Jane Pittman*. New York: Dial Press, 1971.

————. *Bloodline*. New York: W. W. Norton, 1976.

————. *A Gathering of Old Men*. New York: Vintage, 1983.

Giovanni, Nikki. *Black Feeling, Black Talk, Black Judgement*. New York: Morrow, 1970.

————. *My House*. New York: Morrow, 1972.

————. *Ego-Tripping and Other Poems for Young People*. New York: Lawrence Hill, 1973.

————. *The Women and the Men*. New York: Morrow, 1975.

Gordone, Charles. *No Place to Be Somebody: A Black Black Comedy in Three Acts*. Indianapolis: Bobbs-Merrill, 1969.

Hammon, Jupiter. *An Evening Thought: Salvation by Christ, with Penitential Cries*. Long Island, NY: Self-published, 1760.

Hansberry, Lorraine. *A Raisin in the Sun*. New York: Random House, 1959.

Harper, Frances Ellen Watkins. *Poems on Miscellaneous Subjects*. Boston: J. B. Yerrington and Son, 1854. Reprinted in 1974.

————. *Sketches of Southern Life*. Philadelphia: Merrihew and Son, 1872.

————. *Iola LeRoy or Shadows Uplifted*. Philadelphia: Garrigues Bros., 1893.

Hayden, Robert. *Heart Shape in the Dust*. Detroit: Falcon Press, 1940.

————. *Selected Poems*. New York: October House, 1966.

————. *Angle of Ascent: New and Selected Poems*. New York: Liveright, 1975.

Howard, James H. W. *Bond and Free*. Harrisburg, PA: E. K. Meyers, printer, 1886.

Hughes, Langston. *The Weary Blues*. New York: Knopf, 1926.

————. *The Negro Mother and Other Dramatic Recitations*. New York: Golden Stair Press, 1932.

————. *Shakespeare in Harlem*. New York: Knopf, 1942.

————. *Montage of a Dream Deferred*. New York: Henry Holt, 1951.

————. *The Langston Hughes Reader*. New York: George Braziller, 1958.

————. *Ask Your Mama: 12 Moods for Jazz*. New York: Knopf, 1961.

————. *The Panther and the Lash: Poems of Our Times*. New York: Knopf, 1967.

Hurston, Zora Neale. *Jonah's Wine Gourd*. Philadelphia: Lippencott, 1934.

————. *Mules and Men*. Philadelphia: Lippincott, 1935.

————. *Their Eyes Were Watching God*. Philadelphia: Lippencott, 1937.

————. *Moses: Man of the Mountain*. Philadelphia: Lippencott, 1939.

————. *Seraph on the Suwanee*. New York: Scribners, 1948.

Joans, Ted. *All of Ted Joans and No More: Poems and Collages*. New York: Excelsior-Press, 1961.

————. *Black Pow-Wow: Jazz Poems*. New York: Hill and Wang, 1969.

————. *A Black Manifesto in Jazz Poetry and Prose*. London: Calder and Boyars, 1971.

Johnson, Charles. *Middle Passage*. New York: Macmillan, 1990.

Johnson, James Weldon. *Fifty Years and Other Poems*. Boston: Cornhill, 1917.

————. *God's Trombones: Seven Negro Sermons in Verse*. New York: Viking, 1927.

Killens, John Oliver. *Youngblood*. New York: Dial, 1954.

————. *And Then We Heard the Thunder*. New York: Knopf, 1963.

————. *Sippi*. New York: Simon and Schuster, 1967.

Knight, Etheridge. *Poems from Prison*. Detroit: Broadside Press, 1968.

Larsen, Nella. *Quicksand*. New York: A. A. Knopf, 1928. Reprinted, 1969, 1971.

———. *Passing*. New York: A. A. Knopf, 1929. Reprinted, 1969, 1971.

McKay, Claude. *Harlem Shadows*. New York: Harcourt, Brace, 1922.

———. *Home to Harlem*. New York: Harper and Brothers, 1928.

———. *Banana Bottom*. New York: Harper and Row, 1933.

———. *Harlem Glory: A Fragment of Aframerican Life*. Chicago: Charles H. Kerr, 1990, published posthumously.

McMillan, Terry. *Mama*. Boston: Houghton, 1987.

———. *Disappearing Acts*. New York: Viking Press, 1989.

———. *Waiting to Exhale*. New York: Viking Press, 1992.

Madgett, Naomi Long. *Exits and Entrances*. Detroit: Lotus Press, 1978.

———. *Octavia and Other Poems*. Chicago: Third World Press, 1988.

Madhubuti, Haki R. (Don L. Lee). *Think Black*. Detroit: Broadside Press, 1967.

———. *Black Pride*. Detroit: Broadside Press, 1968.

———. *Don't Cry, Scream*. Detroit: Broadside Press, 1969.

———. *We Walk the Way of the New World*. Detroit: Broadside Press, 1970.

Marshall, Paule. *Brown Girl, Brownstones*. New York: Random House, 1959.

———. *Soul Clap Hands and Sing*. New York: Atheneum, 1961.

———. *The Chosen Place, the Timeless People*. New York: Harcourt, 1969.

———. *Praisesong for the Widow*. New York: Putnam's Sons, 1983.

———. *Daughters*. New York: A Plume Book, 1991.

Milner, Ron. *What the Wine-Sellers Buy*. New York: Samuel French, 1974.

Morrison, Toni. *The Bluest Eye*. New York: Holt, Rinehart and Winston, 1970.

———. *Sula*. New York: Knopf, 1974.

———. *Song of Solomon*. New York: Knopf, 1977.

———. *Tar Baby*. New York: Knopf, 1981.

———. *Beloved*. New York: Knopf, 1987.

———. *Jazz*. New York: Knopf, 1992.

———. *Paradise*. New York: Knopf, 1998.

Naylor, Gloria. *The Women of Brewster Place: A Novel in Seven Stories*. New York: Viking Press, 1982.

———. *Linden Hills*. New York: Ticknor and Fields, 1985.

———. *Mama Day*. New York: Ticknor and Fields, 1988.

———. *Bailey's Café*. New York: Vintage Books, 1993.

Neal, Larry. *Black Boogaloo (Notes on Black Liberation)*. San Francisco: Journal of Black Poetry Press, 1969.

———. *Hoodoo Hollerin' Bebop Ghosts*. Washington, DC: Howard University Press, 1974.

Petry, Ann. *The Street*. Boston: Houghton, 1946.

———. *The Narrows*. Boston: Houghton, 1953. Reprinted in 1988.

Randall, Dudley. *More to Remember: Poems of Four Decades*. Chicago: Third World Press, 1971.

Redmond, Eugene. *River of Bones and Flesh and Blood*. East St. Louis, IL: Black River Writers, 1971.

———. *Songs from an Afro/Phone: New Poems*. East St. Louis, IL: Black River Writers, 1972.

Reed, Ishmael. *The Free-Lance Pallbearers.* Garden City, NY: Doubleday, 1967.

———. *Conjure: Selected Poems, 1963–1970.* Amherst: University of Massachusetts Press, 1972.

———. *Mumbo Jumbo.* Garden City, NY: Doubleday, 1972.

———. *Flight to Canada.* New York: Random House, 1976.

———. *Reckless Eyeballing.* New York: St. Martin's Press, 1986.

Rogers, Carolyn. *Paper Soul.* Chicago: Third World Press, 1968.

Sanchez, Sonia. *We a Badddd People.* Detroit: Broadside Press, 1970.

———. *It's A New Day (Poems for Young Brothas and Sistuhs).* Detroit: Broadside Press, 1971.

———. *A Blues Book for Black Magical Women.* Detroit: Broadside Press, 1974.

———. *Homegirls and Handgrenades: A Collection of Poetry and Prose.* New York: Thunder Mouth Press, 1984.

Shange, Ntozake. *for colored girls who have considered suicide when the rainbow is enuf: choreopoem.* New York: Macmillan Publishing, 1977.

Thurman, Wallace. *The Blacker the Berry: A Novel of Negro Life.* New York: Macaulay, 1929. Reprinted in 1969.

———. *Infants of the Spring.* New York: Macaulay, 1932.

Toomer, Jean. *Cane.* New York: Boni and Liveright, 1923.

Walker, Alice. *Meridian.* New York: Harcourt Brace Jovanovich, 1976.

———. *The Color Purple.* New York: Harcourt Brace Jovanovich, 1982.

———. *In Search of Our Mothers' Gardens: Womanist Prose.* San Diego: Harcourt Brace Jovanovich, 1983.

———. *The Temple of My Familiar.* San Diego: Harcourt Brace Jovanovich, 1989.

———. *Possessing the Secret of Joy.* New York: Harcourt Brace Jovanovich, 1992.

Walker, Margaret. *For My People.* New Haven, CT: Yale University Press, 1942.

———. *Jubilee.* Boston: Houghton, 1966.

———. *Prophets for a New Day.* Detroit: Broadside Press, 1970.

———. *This Is My Country: New and Collected Poems.* Athens, GA: University of Georgia Press, 1988.

Washington, Booker T. *Up from Slavery.* New York: Doubleday, 1901.

Wheatley, Phyllis. *Poems on Various Subjects, Religious and Moral.* London: A. Bell, Bookseller, 1773.

———. *Liberty and Peace, a Poem.* Boston: Warden and Russell, 1784.

Wideman, John Edgar. *The Lynchers.* New York: Henry Holt and Company, 1973.

———. *Hiding Place.* New York: Vintage, 1981.

———. *Brothers and Keepers.* New York: Penguin, 1984.

———. *Philadelphia Fire.* New York: Henry Holt and Company, 1990.

Wright, Richard. *Uncle Tom's Children: Four Novellas.* New York: Harper, 1938.

———. *Native Son.* New York: Harper, 1940.

———. *Black Boy: A Record of Childhood and Youth.* New York: Harper, 1945.

———. *The Outsider.* New York: Harper, 1953.

———. *Savage Holiday.* New York: Avon, 1954.

———. *White Man, Listen!* Garden City, NY: Doubleday, 1957.

VII

The African American Musical Experience: There's a Story in the Song

John A. Taylor

It has been said that one can better understand the history of a people by exploring the events and movements that have shaped their collective lives, and by studying their artistic expressions—music, dance, visual arts, literature, drama, dance, and other genre. This is a cogent observation relevant particularly in piecing together or researching the history and culture of African Americans, a people whose rich heritage is linked to a motherland where creative and artistic expression is central to everyday living. In this context, historians and musicologists not only recognize the prominence of musical activity in all aspects of life in the African village but also have come to realize that this cultural pattern is prominent in the African American experience.

The oral tradition of documenting historical events served well as the basis of preserving and perpetuating the culture of Africa. This important phenomenon continued to be practiced by those Africans who were brought to America and by their offspring born in this new world. Although most of the Africans came to the new land as slaves stripped of their material possessions and often separated from their families and tribes, there was no way to deny them their memories and the abilities upon which many of their skills, understandings, and talents were based. Therefore, even in a new environment where their cultural remnants and output were not necessarily understood outside their own group, no one could ignore the distinctiveness of their musical expressions and the uniqueness even in their adaptation to a new way of living.

The African American musical experience is a phenomenon that is rich in tradition, seasoned in adaptation, and fresh in reflections of life as it is encountered in a constantly changing world. Considering the early omissions, misrepresentations, and oversights that have occurred, recounting and documenting the authentic history of the African American experience is a challenge that research scholars have recognized and are making gallant efforts to overcome. Theoretically, uncovering and interpreting facts in a society that utilizes the literate tradition of historical preservation should be easier to achieve than gaining such knowledge in a society where the oral tradition—word of mouth transferal—prevails. The point being made here is that accurate documentation of the African American musical experience, of necessity and at best, requires reference to both oral and written accounts.

It can be argued that the practice of the African oral tradition in the New World had both merits and limitations. On the one hand, a people were bound together by a common cultural heritage preserved in an oral tradition of which they could not be stripped. On the other hand, the preservation of this common cultural heritage was subject to annihilation if the conditions essential to the continued flourishing of an oral tradition were not maintained. A dichotomy then existed between competing historical traditions—oral expression and written accounts. In an oral culture musical expression is valued for its spontaneity and relevance to the occasion. Little attention is given to documenting or notating the actual sensory attributes and characteristics essential to written notation of the performance. Under these conditions, describing and analyzing social and artistic phenomena in literary parlance do not come easy, nor are many attempts made to do so.

It is no secret that the conditions under which Africans were brought to the new land were not ideal and the prevailing mood was not one of friendly deliverance. On the contrary, the value associated with slaves most often was expressed in terms of proprietary benefits. These facts notwithstanding, African Americans performed in roles of servitude but continued to perform musically in the traditions that were their custom. Some of them also turned to European musical practices when learning opportunities in this area were permitted. Such experiences contributed to acculturation processes and practices.

The writings of those who observed the earliest of the African Americans' musical events and expressions are presented in a descriptive manner and primarily from recall. Frequently the writers cited the perceived "oddities" of musical expression and performance (different from European practices) rather than called attention to features that were unique in character and indigenous to a people. Therefore the folk music—work songs, play songs, blues, spirituals, and other forms—received relatively little attention and the character of these musical types was preserved primarily through the oral tradition. Recognizing on any significant scale the aesthetics found in such expressions was to come later. At about the same time, other writers cautiously recognized the skills and talents of those African Americans who, when given the opportunity, experienced success as performers and teachers in the European tradition. In doing so these writers often described the African American musicians in comparison to persons of European origin rather than recognized them for their own abilities.

The African American musical experience may be likened to a cultural mosaic that parallels the history of the people it reflects. In the New World this history by all accounts began in 1619, when Africans were brought to a land later to become known as America. Their arrival marked the beginnings of an extended period of slavery and struggle for survival. These people used music in functional, creative, and expressive forms to help them facilitate work activities, communicate thoughts and plans, retain historical memory, and survive the stress and demands of the times. Such struggles were continued for nearly two-and-one-half centuries and until, with the ending of the Civil War in the 1860s, there came a declaration of freedom for an enslaved people. The forty years that followed were a period of adjustment to a new status of existence. Many of these oppressed people found themselves free and not free at the same time. They were required to carve out new roles in society, and most of them found it challenging. The federal government as well as certain benevolent societies and other groups made efforts to assist African Americans during this period of transition. As a result of these efforts, some special educational institutions were established for the freed people and, to the extent that resources could support, many of them took advantage of the opportunities to learn and to develop their creative talents.

By the turn of the twentieth century the number of skilled musicians and other professionals among African Americans had increased significantly. Within the group of musicians were those who had acquired enhanced performance skills and a musical education in the European tradition. More of them took center stage and presented a broadened musical image reflecting both the people's music and music in the European tradition. Even as this transformation was occurring, the folk-derived music of African Americans, while receiving more attention, was tempered with skepticism as mainstream society was yet to understand the nature and value of the musical expressions emanating from this people's culture.

Around the turn of the last century a mood of nationalism was to emerge in America similar to that experienced in other countries around the world. People generally felt good about their nation's achievements and took pride in exhibiting the offspring of their respective cultures. The United States, in this context, was perceived to be stable and reserved as a nation because it had, on the one hand, been successful in emulating many of the practices and traditions common to the European culture. On the other hand, its African American population was thought by some to have introduced musical practices and traditions that were, based on their African derivatives, unique and significant in the shaping of an American culture with unique features.

Through expositions, festivals, concert tours, and other public performances during the early 1900s, the character of African American music became more familiar to an expanding audience. The mood of nationalism was to be continued even as the rumblings of World War I occurred. Within the African American community, pride in black identity and consciousness became prominently reflected in the 1920s with the emergence of the Harlem Renaissance, a period encouraging and celebrating the creativity and ingenuity exhibited by African American artists in all genre of artistic expression. The transitional grid was continued as an agrarian society gave ground to an industrial society and later inventions like the wire recorder and radio became technological means of preserving musical expression.

The 1940s brought with it new musical forms and an insurgence of blues, jazz, and gospel music expression. These folk-derived forms gained acceptance within the country and received admiration beyond America's boundaries. The potency of the music was such that it began to cross cultural boundaries and establish strains of influence not previously recognized.

Another era of American consciousness evolved in the 1960s. African Americans again rose up in protest against the racial repression still imposed on them and found themselves joined by a large number of sympathizers and others resistant to the Vietnam War and other social issues. The call for racial justice was strong and forceful, and the response was a new level of consciousness about race and historical perspective. People began to denounce more boldly the destructive outcomes of prejudice, bias, and social deprivation that Americans had allowed to exist within their society and called for greater learning and healing. A concerted effort was made to produce and inform people about the values of the African American experience and its manifestations, and education in formal settings became one of the strategic processes through which the message was delivered. More scholars turned their attention to raising levels of awareness and understanding about African Americans and other minorities by rediscovering and documenting past accomplishments, achievements, and contributions, as well as by calling attention to new creations. Their efforts have led to an increase in the number of reference materials and instructional aids now available for educational and other purposes.

Looking at the writings that have been produced about the African American musical experience, there is unevenness in both quality and quantity. There has not been consistency in production, and literary and research efforts conducted in more recent years have been undertaken to fill in historical gaps and to clarify perspectives.

The challenge of placing the African American musical experience into a literary and historical context is somewhat daunting. Similar to the African tradition of making music central to village life, the African American has used music as a means of depicting and commenting on sociological, economic, political, religious, philosophical, creative, and other developments. These expressions present a history of the African American in a musical context because the story is in the song.

The early accounts of African American music history were preserved primarily in an oral and descriptive context. It was only later that scholars made efforts to sketch in musical notation the sound events that occurred or were to take place. The very nature of spontaneous creation presented a challenge, but the advent of sound recordings and the increasing prevalence of composed and notated music made accurate documentation possible.

An increasing number of scholars have committed themselves to making the substance of the African American musical experience more readily understood by the masses. Such activity is leading to a growing appreciation of artistic expression and to a better understanding of the people whom it represents. Increased efforts have been made to document the African American musical experience as it occurred and as it unfolds in the present. In addition to the proliferation of ideas and creations in keeping with the current times, there too have been rediscoveries of heretofore unknown creations and re-creations or new interpretations of existing works. New information is being presented about bygone occurrences, and reiterations of standard works not only preserve but also lead to transformations of ideas previously presented. Scholars are seeking to establish perspectives previously ignored, to uncover extant works, to bridge gaps between events and eras, and to ensure that music emanating from the African American experience never again does go through neglect.

THE AFRICAN AMERICAN MUSICAL LANDSCAPE: COLORS OF SOUND (1619–1999)

Several works provide comprehensive overviews of the African American musical experience. The authors looked back at the various uses of music in African society, described performance practices, and identified carryovers found in African American music. They also highlighted historical movements in America in an African American musical context. Such writings are represented in the works of Eileen Southern in *The Music of Black Americans* (1971, 1983, and 1997); Samuel Floyd in *The Power of Black Music* (1995); James Haskins in *Black Music in America: A History through Its People* (1993), Hildred Roach in *Black American Music: Past and Present* (1992); Tilford Brooks in *America's Black Musical Heritage* (1984), and John Storm Roberts in *Black Music in Two Worlds* (1972). Within the periods they cover, these works explore the full gamut of African American musical expression.

AFRICAN MUSICAL PRACTICES: THE GROUND BASS (BEFORE 1619)

Musical practices in Africa were central to the existence of early African American musical expression and creativity. For every occasion and function there was musical activity to accompany them. In essence, African music and musical practices served as the ground bass or the basis upon which African American music expressions were built. Accounts of African musical performance are included in the book *The Interesting Narrative of the Life of Olaudah Equiano, or Gustavus Vassa, the African. Written by Himself* (1789). Recognizing the source, this is a unique contribution. Other writings about music and musical practices in Africa are found in works such as Bruno Nettl's *Music in Primitive Culture* (1956); A. M. Jones's *Studies in African Music* (1959), Nketia's *African Music in Ghana* (1963), Francis Beby's *African Music: A People's Art* (1975), Fred Warren's *Music of Africa: An Introduction* (1970), and Alan Merriam's *African Music in Perspective* (1982). More recent writings include John Gray's *African Music: A Bibliographical Guide to the Traditional, Popular, Art, and Liturgical Musics of Sub-Saharan Africa* (1991); and DjeDje's *African Musicology: Current Trends*, Vols. 1 and 2 (1989 and 1992). Samuel Floyd, Jr., in *The Power of Black Music* (1995), cited earlier, advances the theory that the power and aesthetics that characterize black music owe their origin to the early musical practices found in African everyday life and culture. He links the history, music, myths, and rituals of Africa to the genres of African American musical expression that have evolved over time.

AFRICAN SOUNDS IN AMERICAN MUSIC: CHARACTERISTICS AND PRACTICES (1619–1865)

For approximately the first 250 years of their existence on what became known as American soil, African Americans lived as an enslaved people. In this setting music was vital to their survival because it was used for both functional and social purposes. Their musical expressions reflected the rhythms, melodies, timbres, call-and-response patterns, and dance patterns found in their motherland. The power of their musical exhortations served to unify and create a sense of community. Musical performance was used as a means of synchronizing and increasing work activities, venting anxieties and stress, enhancing worship services, communicating feelings and plans of escape, serving as the impetus of dance activities, and accompanying many other events. Work songs, play songs, worship songs, ritual songs, rowing songs, social songs, spirituals, and other musical expressions were just some of the song types that resulted. As many slaves were a transient people, their musical expressions were spread from location to location, and because the music reflected the oral tradition, there were multiple variations of songs.

The character and usage of such music were often described in the diaries and recollections of the controlling class. Nicholas Cresswell's *Journal of Nicholas Cresswell* (1924) is one of the early works that contain comments on black musicians and dancers in the United States. Dena Epstein's *Sinful Tunes and Spirituals* (1977) provides a summary of all extant writings, primarily descriptive, about the music of Africans and African Americans from the time of their arrival in the English colonies up until the 1820s. Allen, Ware, and Garrison produced an anthology in 1867, *Slave Songs of the United States* (1867 and 1995), which described the nature of the music and included notation of songs heard and collected in several regions of the country. This work served as a frame of reference for years to come as few attempts at preservation of music primarily of this type had been made. Other writers who later were to focus on the music of this period include Miles Mark Fisher in *Negro Slave Songs in the United States* (1968), Howard Washington Odum in *Negro Workaday Songs* (1969), and J. R. Lovell in *Black Song: The Forge and the Flame: The Story of How the Afro-American Spiritual Was Hammered Out* (1972).

A NEW LEITMOTIF: OH FREEDOM (1865–1919)

With the ending of the Civil War in 1865, African Americans were declared to be a free people. This new status brought with it new opportunities: the establishment of learning centers, the growth of churches, freedom to move geographically, opportunities to build secure and stable family units, new though limited employment opportunities, and opportunities to participate in political processes. Accompanying these opportunities were new and expanded musical expressions reflective of the changing times. In the schools and churches that were established, music played a significant role.

Old folk music forms were enhanced and new song types evolved. Both sacred and secular expressions flourished. Spirituals and jubilee songs were performed in conjunction with European-derived religious song styles. The blues evolved in the southern United States as a form of personal expression. Ragtime music was created as a counterpart to the European classics, and the musical cells, which were to develop into jazz also, had their origin during this period. African American music clubs sprang up with a focus primarily on the performance of European classical music. Minstrelsy, initially a form of musical ridicule and imitation of African American musicians, continued to flourish as African Americans adapted the genre to their own expressions and helped pave the way for vaudeville and the Broadway show that was yet to come.

From the lyrics of the songs and the character of the instrumental music, one can learn much about the culture of the changing times. Storytelling remained central to the lyrics even as new metaphors and double entendres evolved. The blues was one of the new song forms to emerge, and individual expression was at the heart of its existence. Beginning in rural communities, it spread to urban areas and became an entertainment music with a life all its own.

Many blues have been written and written about. William C. Handy's *Father of the Blues: An Autobiography* (1955) is a significant work because it focuses on the life of the person who first placed the blues in notated musical form. But the blues owe so much of its existence to spontaneous storytelling, and the performers have been many. The nature, character, and content of the blues have been analyzed by several writers. Samuel Charters contributed two major works, *The Country Blues* (1959) and *The Legacy of the Blues* (1977). In the second book, Charters describes the social perspective, which served as the backdrop for the origin and development of the blues. In acknowledging the African American origin of the blues, he also calls attention to the lyrics and suggests that they express social class as well as racial concerns. Other writers on the blues include Charles Keil in *Urban Blues* (1966), Eric Sackheim in *The Blues Line: A Collection of Blues Lyrics* (1969), Alan Lomax in *The Land Where the Blues Began* (1973), Paul Oliver in *Savannah Syncopators: African Retentions in the Blues* (1970) and *Blues Fell This Morning* (1960 and 1990). Oliver, in the second work, made extensive use of interviews and analytical transcriptions of thousands of blues recordings to document the relationship existing between musical lyrics and social events.

Harold Courlander in *Negro Folk Music* (1963 and 1993) discusses and describes a broad range of musical types—anthems, spirituals, cries, calls, hollers, work songs, dances, play and party songs, ballads, minstrel songs, instruments, and other aspects of musical expression. Courlander maintained that Negro folk music represented the largest body of genuine folk music existing in America. Antonin Dvořák, a Czechoslovakian composer prominent at the turn of the twentieth century, had made a similar observation earlier during his evaluation of artistic expression emanating from America as a relatively young nation.

Hans Nathan's *Dan Emmett and the Rise of Early Negro Minstrelsy* (1962) chronicles a challenging period in the life of the African American as an entertainer. However, ridicule and admiration apparently made strange bedfellows, and the outcome that emerged tended to have positive overtones. Works such as Edward Hipsher's *American Opera and Its Composers: A Complete History of Serious American Opera, with a Summary of the Lighter Forms Which Led up to Its Birth* (1934), Henry Sampson's *Black in Blackface: A Source Book on Early Black Musical Shows* (1980), and Thomas Riis's *Just before Jazz: Black Musical Theater in New York, 1890 to 1915* (1989) collectively chronicle the evolution of theatrical performance into an art form of sophistication and finesse.

James Trotter's *Music and Some Highly Musical People* (1878) is one of the earliest works to give attention to black musicians on the concert stage. His accounts documented the high quality of their performances and the receptivity they experienced as professionals. Maude Cuney Hare in *Negro Musicians and Their Music* (1936) is another example of an early writer who called attention to the musical skills and talents of African Americans in nineteenth-century America who performed the European classics.

In his book *The Jubilee Singers and Their Campaign for Twenty Thousand Dollars* (1974), Gustavus Pike described how the Fisk Jubilee Singers used their singing talents to raise funds to help build a school. Such an activity was representative of a practice common to several of the black colleges that came into being after the Civil War. Groups like the Fisk Jubilee Singers helped refine the Negro spirituals and made them more accessible and accepting to the general public. These choral expressions formed a pathway for solo artists who took to the concert stage and made the world aware of the musical gifts, and the talents and skills, existing among African American people.

Ann Simpson in her book *Hard Trials: The Life and Music of Harry Burleigh* (1990) described the experiences and contributions of one musician who, at the turn of the last century and in spite of his formal music education, was challenged in his efforts to present Negro spirituals and folk songs as art songs worthy of presentation on the concert stage. His story was just one of many. It took years for mainstream America to recognize and accept the fact that the African American musician could be a consummate performer whose musical talents were not limited to those of entertainer status. Nevertheless, it was in the latter role that the African American was more likely to find employment.

The turn of the twentieth century marked a new era. Secular music gained even more prominence as ragtime, blues, and jazz took a stronger hold in American society. Susan Curtis in *Dancing to a Black Man's Tune: A Life of Scott Joplin* (1994) recounted the life of Joplin, the "king of ragtime," and examined the social milieu out of which he and his music came. Using two historical events to frame the duration of Joplin's life—the ratification of the Fourteenth Amendment to the Constitution (1868) and America's entrance into World War I (1917)—Curtis implied that Joplin's life and music reflect the times of a changing America. Reconstruction, the emergence of the industrial era, a reassessment of human values, and the search for cultural identity by immigrants and descendants of former slaves were among the social issues of the day. Other writers about ragtime include Rudi Blesh and Harriet Janis in *They All Played Ragtime: The True Story of an American Music* (1959), William Schafer and Johannes Riedel in *The Art of Ragtime: Form and Meaning of an Original Black American Art* (1973), and Edward Berlin in *King of Ragtime: Scott and Joplin and His Era* (1994). *The Collected Works of Scott Joplin* (1971) is accessible for reprint because the works represent some of the earliest musical manuscripts preserved and reproduced for purchase. Many in America found the sounds of ragtime fresh to their ears; some found them to be attractive to their musical tastes. In either case, the compositions were another reflection of the changing times.

A SHOW OF PRIDE: NEW THEMES, NEW SOUNDS (1920–1940)

The 1920s gave rise to new expressions. The Jazz Age and the Harlem Renaissance developed as parallel themes and movements. Storytelling took on new forms as poets challenged the public with their writings. Painters depicted life as they saw it. Dancers sent messages through emotive gestures. Musicians created new sound palettes reflecting the other arts, the rhythms of work and play, and the tensions in society.

Building on its precursors—piano ragtime, instrumental rags, blues, brass bands repertoire, and other musical types—jazz became recognized as an improvised art form during the closing years of World War I. The range of stories about jazz's origin is wide, and following its birth, its sound makers followed the paths of those who migrated to points north and elsewhere seeking a better life. In works like Henry Osgood's *So This Is Jazz* (1926), Hughes Panassié's *Hot Jazz: The Guide to Swing Music* (1936), Alan Lomax's *Mister Jelly Roll;*

The Fortunes of Jelly Roll Morton, New Orleans Creole and "Inventor of Jazz" (1973), Rudi Blesh's *Shining Trumpets: A History of Jazz* (1958), Thomas Hennessey's *From Jazz to Swing: African-American Jazz Musicians and Their Music, 1890–1935* (1994), and Richard Hadlock's *Jazz Masters of the 20s* (1988), we learn about the jazz pioneers, their sounds, and the times in which they lived.

Gunther Schuller's *Early Jazz: Its Roots and Musical Development* (1968) is recognized as one of the most definitive works to provide both an historical and a theoretical approach to the study of early jazz. Its scope of analytical detail and musical examples makes it stand out as one of the most authoritative reference sources on the topic.

Works such as Benjamin G. Brawley's *The Negro Genius: A New Appraisal of the Achievement of the American Negro in Literature and the Fine Arts* (1937), Margaret Just Butcher's *Negro in American Culture* (1956), and Nathan Huggins's *Voices from the Harlem Renaissance* (1976) focus on the broad range of African American artistic expression but also give just due to the music that evolved during the period. More recently, in *Black Music in the Harlem Renaissance: A Collection of Essays* (1990), Samuel Floyd and Marsha Reisser called on ten contemporary scholars to look back at the period and share their perspectives on a bygone era of splendor.

LIFT EVERY VOICE: UNLIMITED EXPRESSIONS TO ALL (1940–)

By 1940, the fervor of the blues, jazz, and gospel music expression had begun to intensify, and the number of musicians pursuing formalized study grew even as the country was soon to be engaged in World War II. Experimentation with electrically powered instruments led to new musical timbres, and the development of new sound technologies also contributed to greater consumer access. Levels of musicianship were elevated to an all-time high, and the skills of jazz musicians were to gain the respect of consumers comparable to that traditionally given only to the classical musician.

Works like Leonard Feather's *Inside Bebop* (1949), Stanley Dance's *Jazz Era: The Forties* (1962), Joe Goldberg's *Jazz Masters of the Fifties* (1966), Gene Fernett's *Swing Out: Great Negro Dance Bands* (1970), George Simon's *Big Bands* (1967), and Sally Placksin's *American Women in Jazz: 1900 to the Present* (1982) all focused on the musicians who helped make jazz an American art form of distinctive proportions. Mark Gridley, in *Jazz Styles: History & Analysis* (1997), focuses on the major artists and the techniques that they use in their creative expressions.

Today, America's musical palette is comprised of several types of artistic expression that owe their origin to the African American experience. Spirituals, blues, ragtime, jazz, tin pan alley songs, gospel, rhythm 'n' blues, soul music, and rap are among the most obvious examples. However, there also is that realm of concert music often referred to as classical music where African American musicians (composers and performers) also have excelled. During the 1960s when racial consciousness took on new meaning, efforts to substantiate the contributions of African Americans, cultural and otherwise, went unrivaled. Researchers and musical scholars in significant numbers began to uncover and rediscover events gone by, to arrange performances of seldom heard compositions and new works, to document contributions made but long ignored, and to create opportunities for new learning and creativity.

Increased research and scholarship have led to growth in the number of reference materials and artifacts available for study, performance, and general consumer access. Since the 1960s movement of new awareness and consciousness, publications of all types have emerged. The perspective of African American musicians active in classical music is defined in works such as Lindsay Patterson's *The Negro in Music and Art* (1970), Raoul Abdul's *Blacks in Classical Music: A Personal History* (1977), Willis Patterson's *Anthology of Art Songs by Black American Composers* (1977), David Baker, Lida Belt, and Herman Hudson's *Black Composer Speaks* (1978), and Glenn Barbour's *Afro-American Classical Music: A New Awareness* (1985). Reference works such as Dominique-René De Lerma's *Bibliography of Black Music* (1981–1984), John Gray's *Blacks in Classical Music: A Bibliographic Guide to Composers, Performers, and Ensembles* (1988), Eileen Southern's *Biographical Dictionary of Afro-American and African Musicians* (1983), and Patricia Turner's *Dictionary of Afro-American Performers: 78 RPM and Cylinder Recordings of Opera, Choral Music, and Songs, c. 1900–1949* (1990) are comprised of citations that document the existence and contributions of African American musicians over the vast expanse of their presence in America.

Themes of social consciousness and cultural perspectives have been presented and preserved in works such as Imam Amiri Baraka's (LeRoi Jones) *Blues People: Negro Music in White America* (1963), Frank Kofsky's *Black Nationalism and the Revolution in Music* (1970), Lawrence Levine's *Black Culture and Black Consciousness: Afro-American Thought from Slavery to Freedom* (1970), John Sinclair's *Music & Politics* (1971), and Bill Moody's *Jazz Exiles* (1993). In *The William Grant Still Reader: Essays on African American Music* (1992), Jon Spencer presented a compilation of selected writings in which Still, the composer, expressed his varying views on societal issues as he observed and experienced them. Often referred to as the "Dean of Afro-American Composers," Still knew what it was like to have one's musical voice muted because of bias and other social inhibitors, on the one hand, and then to experience creative success, on the other.

Sentiments about social unrest and protest often were expressed in musical performance through both individual and group singing. The chanted rhythms contributed to the orderly movement of the people, and the lyrics expressed their innermost feelings. Works such as E. Fowke's *Songs of Work and Protest* (1973), Guy Carawan's *Sing for Freedom: The Story of the Civil Rights*

Movement through Its Songs (1990), Reebee Garofalo's *Rockin' the Boat: Mass Music and Mass Movements* (1992), and Kerran Sanger's *"When the Spirit Says Sing": The Role of Freedom Songs in the Civil Rights Movement* (1995) address the protest movement, speaking about ideas and musical events in both secular and sacred contexts.

The centrality of music to the African American religious experience is emphasized in such works as Wyatt Tee Walker's *Somebody's Calling My Name: Black Sacred Music and Social Change* (1979), Milton Sernett's *Afro-American Religious History: A Documentary Witness* (1985), Jon Spencer's *Black Hymnody: A Hymnological History of the African American Church* (1992), and Kip Lornell's *Happy in the Service of the Lord: African-American Sacred Vocal Harmony Quartets in Memphis* (1995). The significance of the early Negro spiritual as a precursor of other religious forms is underscored in these writings.

Gospel music, a music of praise and celebration, owes its origin to both sacred expression and secular expression. Because of it musical vibrancy and its intense emotional appeal, it too has become an area of special musical focus. Robert Anderson and Gail North's *Gospel Music Encyclopedia* (1979), Anthony Heilbut's *Gospel Sound: Good News and Bad Times* (1985), Bernice Reagon's *We'll Understand It Better By and By* (1992), Michael Harris's *Rise of Gospel Blues: The Story of Thomas A. Dorsey in the Urban Church* (1992), Andrew Wilson-Dickson's *Story of Christian Music: From Gregorian Chant to Black Gospel* (1992), and Alan Young's *Woke Me up This Morning: Black Gospel Singers and the Gospel Life* (1997) all tell versions of the musical good news story.

The blues as a musical form took on new twists while sustaining its basic shape. More rhythmic drive and harmonic content are added to the blues, and their potency flavors other musical expressions. The resulting intensity of emotion is described as being "soulful" in its impact. Writers such as Phyl Garland in *The Sound of Soul* (1969), Michael Haralambos in *Soul Music: The Birth of A Sound in Black America* (1974), Peter Guralnick in *Sweet Soul Music: Rhythm and Blues and the Southern Dream of Freedom* (1986) discussed this new phenomenon and the musicians who contributed to it.

The 1980s brought with it the music of hip-hop and a mostly verbal form known as rap. These more contemporary forms have received significant literary attention. Arnold Shaw connected several musical forms together in his *Black Popular Music in America: From the Spirituals, Minstrels, and Ragtime to Soul, Disco, and Hip-Hop* (1982). Writers such as Lawrence Stanley in *Rap: The Lyrics* (1992), Tricia Rose in *Black Noise: Rap Music and Black Culture in Contemporary America* (1994), Adam Sexton in *Rap on Rap: Straight-up Talk on Hip-Hop Culture* (1995), Ronin Ro in *Gansta: Merchandizing the Rhymes of Violence* (1996), and Steven Stancell in *Rap Whoz Who* (1996) have called attention to the originators of this rhythmically chanted verbal expression that comments on social, sexual, racial, and political issues reflective of the turmoil that often is found in today's urban America.

CODA: MUSIC YET TO COME

The story of African Americans is told in their song. Themes and variations abound as do the events that have shaped their lives. From work songs to joyous dance, from contemplation to aspiration, from struggle to triumph, for the sake of beauty and the call to duty, the music of African Americans chronicles and symbolizes life, liberty, and the pursuit of happiness. The twenty-first century will mark a new era in history and the musical sounds that emanate from the African American experience will continue to be vibrant, fresh, and reflective of the times as the story is in their song.

BIBLIOGRAPHY

Abdul, Raoul. *Blacks in Classical Music: A Personal History.* New York: Dodd and Mead, 1977.

Allen, William Francis, Charles Pickard Ware, and Lucy McKin Garrison. *Slave Songs of the United States.* Mineola, NY: Dover Publications, 1995 (a reprint of the work originally published by A. Simpson and Co., New York, 1867).

Anderson, Robert, and Gail North. *Gospel Music Encyclopedia.* New York: Sterling Publishing Company, 1979.

Austin, William. *Susanna, Jeanie, and the Old Folks at Home: The Songs of Stephen C. Foster from His Time to Ours.* New York: Macmillan Publishing, 1975.

Baker, David N. *New Perspectives on Jazz.* Washington, DC: Smithsonian Institution Press, 1986.

Baker, David N., Lida Belt, and Herman Hudson. *The Black Composer Speaks.* Metuchen, NJ: Scarecrow Press, 1978.

Baraka, Imamu Amiri. *Black Music.* New York: W. Morrow, 1971.

———. *Blues People: Negro Music in White America.* New York: W. Morrow, 1963.

Baraka, Imamu Amiri (LeRoi Jones), and Amina Baraka. *The Music: Reflections on Jazz and Blues.* New York: William Morrow and Company, 1987.

Barbour, Glenn. *Afro-American Classical Music: A New Awareness.* Atlanta: C. Noland Publishing, 1985.

Beby, Francis. *African Music: A People's Art.* New York: Lawrence Hill and Co., 1975.

Berlin, Edward A. *King of Ragtime: Scott Joplin and His Era.* New York: Oxford University Press, 1994.

Bernhardt, Clyde E. B. *I Remember: Eighty Years of Black Entertainment, Big Bands and the Blues.* Philadelphia: University of Pennsylvania Press, 1986.

Berry, Jason. *Up from the Cradle of Jazz: New Orleans Music since World War II.* Athens, GA: University of Georgia Press, 1986.

Blesh, Rudi. *Shining Trumpets: A History of Jazz.* New York: Knopf, 1958.

Blesh, Rudi, and Harriet Janis. *They All Played Ragtime: The True Story of an American Music.* 1959. 4th ed. New York: Oak Publications, 1971.

Brawley, Benjamin G. *The Negro Genius: A New Appraisal of the Achievement of the American Negro in Literature and the Fine Arts.* New York: Dodd Mead and Company, 1937.

Broadcast Music, Inc. *Five Decades of Rhythm and Blues*. New York: Broadcast Music, 1969.

Brooks, Tilford. *America's Black Musical Heritage*. Englewood Cliffs, NJ: Prentice Hall, 1984.

Brown, Scott, and Bob Hilbert. *James P. Johnson: A Case of Mistaken Identity*. Metuchen, NJ: Scarecrow Press and the Institute of Jazz Studies, 1982.

Buerkle, Jack Vincent. *Bourbon Street Black: The New Orleans Black Jazzman*. New York: Oxford University Press, 1973.

Bushell, Garvin. *Jazz from the Beginning*. Ann Arbor: University of Michigan Press, 1988.

Butcher, Margaret Just. *The Negro in American Culture*. 1st ed. New York: Alfred A. Knopf, 1956.

Carawan, Guy, and Candie Carawan. *Sing for Freedom: The Story of the Civil Rights Movement through Its Songs*. Bethlehem, PA: Sing Out Corp., 1990.

Carner, Gary. *Jazz Performers: An Annotated Bibliography of Biographical Materials*. Westport, CT: Greenwood Press, 1990.

———. *The Miles Davis Companion*. New York: Schirmer Books, 1996.

Carter, Madison H. *An Annotated Catalog of Composers of African Ancestry*. New York: Vantage Press, 1986.

Carter, William. *Preservation Hall*. New York: W. W. Norton, 1991.

Carver, Gary. *Jazz Performers: An Annotated Bibliography of Biographical Materials*. Westport, CT: Greenwood Press, 1990.

Charters, Samuel. *The Country Blues*. New York: Rinehart, 1959.

———. *The Legacy of the Blues*. New York: Da Capo Press, 1977.

Charters, Samuel, and Leonard Kunstadt. *Jazz: A History of the New York Scene*. Garden City, NY: Doubleday, 1962.

Chase, Gilbert. *America's Music from the Pilgrims to the Present (1955)*. 3rd rev. ed. New York: McGraw-Hill, 1987.

Chilton, John. *Who's Who in Jazz*. London: Macmillan, 1985.

Cobbins, Otho B., ed. *History of the Church of Christ (Holiness) U.S.A., 1895–1965*. New York: Vantage Press, 1966.

Collier, James Lincoln. *Ellington*. New York: Oxford University Press, 1987.

Cone, James H. *The Spirituals and the Blues*. Maryknoll, NY: Orbis Books, 1972 and 1991.

Conway, Cecelia. *African Banjo Echoes in Appalachia: A Study of Folk Traditions*. Knoxville: University of Tennessee Press, 1995.

Courlander, Harold. *Negro Folk Music, U.S.A.* New York: Dover Publications, 1993 (first published by Columbia University Press, New York, 1963).

Cresswell, Nicholas. *The Journal of Nicholas Cresswell*. New York: Dial Press, 1924.

Curtis, Susan. *Dancing to a Black Man's Tune: A Life of Scott Joplin*. Columbia: University of Missouri Press, 1994.

Dance, Stanley, ed. *Jazz Era: The Forties*. London: Jazz Book Club, 1962.

———. *The World of Duke Ellington*. New York: C. Scribner's Sons, 1970.

Davis, Francis. *Outcats: Jass Composers, Instrumentalists and Singers*. New York: Oxford University Press, 1990.

Deffaa, Chip. *Blue Rhythms: (Six Lives in Rhythm and Blues)*. Urbana: University of Illinois Press, 1996.

———. *Voices of the Jazz Age*. Urbana: University of Illinois Press, 1990.

De Lerma, Dominique-René. *Bibliography of Black Music*. Westport, CT: Greenwood Press, Vol. 1, *Reference Materials*, 1981; Vol. 2, *Afro-American Idioms*, 1981; Vol. 3, *Geographical Studies*, 1982; and Vol. 4, *Theory, Education and Related Studies*, 1984.

De Lerma, Dominique-René, and Marsha J. Reisser. *Black Music and Musicians in the New Grove Dictionary of American Music and the New Harvard Dictionary of Music*. Chicago: Center for Black Music Research, 1989.

DjeDje, Jacqueline Cogdell, and William G. Carter. *African Musicology: Current Trends*. Vol. 1 and 2, Los Angeles: African Studies Center and African Arts Magazine, and Crossroads Press/African Studies Association, 1989 and 1992, respectively.

DjeDje, Jacqueline Cogdell, and Eddie S. Meadows. *California Soul: Music of African Americans in the West*. Berkeley: University of California Press, 1998.

Du Bois, William E. B. *The Souls of Black Folk* (1903). Millwood, NY: Kraus-Thompson Organization, 1973.

Ellington, Edward Kennedy "Duke." *Music Is My Mistress*. Garden City, NY: Doubleday, 1973.

Epstein, Dena. *Sinful Tunes and Spirituals*. Urbana: University of Illinois Press, 1977.

Equiano, Olaudah. *The Interesting Narrative of the Life of Olaudah Equiano, or Gustavus Vassa, the African. Written by Himself* 1789. New York: W. Durrell, 1971.

Feather, Leonard G. *The Encyclopedia of Jazz in the Seventies*. New York: Horizon Press, 1976.

———. *The Encyclopedia of Jazz in the Sixties*. New York: Horizon Press, 1966.

———. *Inside Bebop*. New York: J. J. Robbins, 1949.

Fernett, Gene. *Swing Out: Great Negro Dance Bands*. Midland, MI: Pendell, 1970.

Fisher, Miles Mark. *Negro Slave Songs in the United States*. Ithaca, NY: Russell and Russell, 1968.

Fitterling, Thomas. *Thelonious Monk: His Life and Music*. Berkeley, CA: Berkeley Hills Books, 1997.

Fletcher, Tom. *The Tom Fletcher Story: 100 Years of the Negro in Show Business*. New York: Burdge, 1954.

Floyd, Samuel A., Jr. *The Power of Black Music*. New York: Oxford University Press, 1995.

Floyd, Samuel A., and Marsha J. Reisser. *Black Music Biography: An Annotated Bibliography*. White Plains, NY: Kraus International Publications, 1987.

———. *Black Music in the Harlem Renaissance: A Collection of Essays*. Westport, CT: Greenwood Press, 1990.

———. *Black Music in the United States: An Annotated Bibliography of Selected Reference and Research Materials*. Millwood, NY: Kraus International Publications, 1983.

Fowke, E. *Songs of Work and Protest*. Mineola, NY: Dover Publications, 1973.

Garland, Phyl. *The Sound of Soul*. Chicago: Regnery, 1969.

Garner, Gary. *The Miles Davis Companion*. New York: Schirmer Books, 1996.

Garofalo, Reebee. *Rockin' the Boat: Mass Music and Mass Movements*. Boston: South End Press, 1992.

George, Luvenia A. *Teaching the Music of Six Different Cultures*. Danbury, CT: World Music Press, 1987.

Gitler, Ira. *Jazz Masters of the Forties*. New York: Macmillan, 1966.

Goldberg, Joe. *Jazz Masters of the Fifties*. New York: Macmillan, 1966.

Gray, John. *African Music: A Bibliographical Guide to the Traditional, Popular, Art, and Liturgical Musics of Sub-Saharan African.* Westport, CT: Greenwood Press, 1991.

———. *Blacks in Classical Music: A Bibliographic Guide to Composers, Performers, and Ensembles.* Westport, CT: Greenwood Press, 1988.

Green, Jeffrey P. *Edmund Thornton Jenkins: The Life and Times of an American Black Composer.* Westport, CT: Greenwood Press, 1982.

Green, Mildred Denby. *Black Women Composers: A Genesis.* Boston: Twayne Publishers, 1980.

Gridley, Mark. *Jazz Styles: History & Analysis.* 6th ed. Upper Saddle River, NJ: Prentice Hall, 1997.

Guralnick, Peter. *Sweet Soul Music: Rhythm and Blues and the Southern Dream of Freedom.* New York: Harper and Row, 1986.

Haas, Robert Bartlett. *William Grant Still and the Fusion of Cultures in American Music.* Los Angeles: Black Sparrow Press, 1975.

Hadlock, Richard. *Jazz Masters of the 20s.* New York: Da Capo Press, 1988.

Ham, Debra Newman, ed. *The African-American Mosaic: A Library of Congress Guide for the Study of Black History and Culture.* Washington, DC: Library of Congress, 1993.

Handy, D. Antoinette. *Black Conductors.* Metuchen, NJ: Scarecrow Press, 1995.

———. *Black Women in American Bands and Orchestras.* Metuchen, NJ: Scarecrow Press, 1981.

Handy, William C. *Father of the Blues: An Autobiography.* New York: Macmillan, 1955.

Haralambos, Michael. *Soul Music: The Birth of A Sound in Black America.* New York: Da Capo Press, 1974.

Hare, Maud Cuney. *Negro Musicians and Their Music.* Washington, DC: Associated Publishers, 1936; New York: Da Capo Press, 1974.

Harris, Michael W. *The Rise of Gospel Blues: The Story of Thomas A. Dorsey in the Urban Church.* New York: Oxford University Press, 1992.

Harris, Sheldon. *Who's Who: A Biographical Dictionary of Blues Singers.* New Rochelle, NY: Arlington House, 1979.

Harrison, Daphne Duval. *Black Pearls: Blues Queens of the 1920s.* New Brunswick, NJ: Rutgers University Press, 1988.

Haskins, James. *Black Music in America: A History through Its People.* New York: Harper Trophy, 1993.

Hatch, James V. *Black Images on the American Stage: A Bibliography of Plays and Musicals, 1770–1970.* New York: DRS Publications, 1979.

Havelock, Nelson. *Bring the Noise: A Guide to Rap Music and Hip-Hop Culture.* New York: Harmony Books, 1991.

Hefele, Bernhard. *Jazz-Bibliography: International Literature on Jazz, Blues, Spirituals, Gospel and Ragtime Music.* Munich: K. G. Saur, 1981.

Heilbut, Anthony. *The Gospel Sound: Good News and Bad Times.* New York: Harper and Row, Limelight Editions, 1985.

Heintze, James R. *Early American Music: A Research and Information Guide.* New York: Garland Publishing, 1990.

Hennessey, Thomas J. *From Jazz to Swing: African-American Jazz Musicians and Their Music, 1890–1935.* Detroit: Wayne State University Press, 1994.

Hipsher, Edward Ellsworth. *American Opera and Its Composers: A Complete History of*

Serious American Opera, with a Summary of the Lighter Forms Which Led up to Its Birth. 1927. Expanded ed. Philadelphia: Theodore Presser, 1934.

Hodeir, André. *Toward Jazz*. New York: Grove Press, 1962.

Holly, Ellistine Perkins. *Biographies of Black Composers and Songwriters*. Dubuque, IA: Wm. C. Brown Publishers, 1990.

Horn, David. *The Literature of American Music in Books and Folk Music Collections: A Fully Annotated Bibliography*. Metuchen, NJ: Scarecrow Press, 1977.

Horne, Aaron. *Brass Music of Black Composers: A Bibliography*. Westport, CT: Greenwood Press, 1996.

————. *Keyboard Music of Black Composers: A Bibliography*. Westport, CT: Greenwood Press, 1992.

————. *String Music of Black Composers: A Bibliography*. Westport, CT: Greenwood Press, 1991.

————. *Woodwind Music of Black Composers: A Bibliography*. Westport, CT: Greenwood Press, 1991.

Horricks, Raymond. *Count Basie and His Orchestra, Its Music and Its Musicians*. Westport, CT: Negro Universities Press, 1971.

Huggins, Nathan Irvin. *Voices from the Harlem Renaissance*. New York: Oxford University Press, 1976.

Hughes, Langston, and Milton Meltzer. *Black Magic: A Pictorial History of the Negro in American Entertainment*. Englewood Cliffs, NJ: Prentice-Hall, 1967.

Jackson, Bruce. *Wake up Dead Man: Afro-American Worksongs from Texas Prisons*. Cambridge: Harvard University Press, 1972.

Jackson, Irene. *Afro-American Religious Music: A Bibliography and a Catalogue of Gospel Music*. Westport, CT: Greenwood Press, 1979.

Johnson, James Weldon, and J. Rosamond Johnson. *The Book of American Negro Spirituals*. New York: Viking Press, 1954.

Jones, A. M. *Studies in African Music*: London: Oxford University Press, 1959.

Jones, K. Maurice. *The Story of Rap Music*. Brookfield, CT: Millbrook Press, 1994.

Jones, Max, and John Chilton. *LOUIS: The Louis Armstrong Story*. New York: Da Capo Press, 1988.

Joplin, Scott. *The Collected Works of Scott Joplin*. Ed. Vera Broadsky Lawrence. 2 vols. New York: New York Public Library, 1971.

Katz, Bernard, ed. *The Social Implications of Early Negro Music in the United States: With over 150 of the Songs, Many of Them with Their Music*. New York: Arno Press, 1969.

Keil, Charles. *Urban Blues*. Chicago: University of Chicago Press, 1966.

Kofsky, Frank. *Black Nationalism and the Revolution in Music*. New York: Pathfinder Press, 1970.

Krehbiel, Henry Edward. *Afro-American Folk Songs*. New York: Frederick Ungar Publishing Co., 1971.

Laubrich, Arnold. *Art Tatum: A Guide to His Recorded Music*. Metuchen, NJ: Scarecrow Press and the Institute of Jazz Studies, Rutgers University, 1982.

Lees, Gene. *Oscar Peterson: The Will to Swing*. Rocklin, CA: Prima Publishing and Communications, 1990.

Levine, Lawrence. *Black Culture and Black Consciousness: Afro-American Thought from Slavery to Freedom*. New York: Oxford University Press, 1977.

Locke, Alain LeRoy. *The Negro and His Music*. New York: Arno Press, 1969.

Lomax, Alan. *The Folk Songs of North America*. Garden City, NY: Doubleday and Company, 1975.

———. *The Land Where the Blues Began*. New York: Pantheon Books, 1973.

———. *Mister Jelly Roll: The Fortunes of Jelly Roll Morton, New Orleans Creole and "Inventor of Jazz."* 2nd ed. Berkeley: University of California Press, 1973.

Lornell, Kip. *Happy in the Service of the Lord: African-American Sacred Vocal Harmony Quartets in Memphis*. Knoxville: University of Tennessee Press, 1995.

Lovell, J. R. *Black Song: The Forge and the Flame: The Story of How the Afro-American Spiritual Was Hammered Out*. 1972. Reprint. New York: Paragon House, 1986.

Lyons, Len. *The Great Jazz Pianist*. New York: William Morrow and Company, 1983.

Machlin, Paul S. *Stride, The Music of Fats Waller*. Boston: Twayne Publishers, 1985.

Mapp, Edward. *Directory of Blacks in the Performing Arts*. Metuchen, NJ: Scarecrow Press, 1978.

McIntyre, Paul. *Black Pentecostal Music in Windsor*. Ottawa: National Museums of Canada, 1976.

McKee, Margaret. *Beale Black & Blue: Life and Music on Black America's Main Street*. Baton Rouge: Louisiana State University Press, 1982.

Meadows, Eddie S. *Jazz Research and Performance Materials: A Select Annotated Bibliography*. 2nd ed. New York: Garland Publishing, 1995.

Meeker, David. *Jazz in the Movies*. New Rochelle, NY: Arlington House, 1977.

Megill, Donald D., and Richard S. Demory. *Introduction to Jazz History*. Englewood Cliffs, NJ: Prentice-Hall, 1984.

Merriam, Alan P. *African Music in Perspective*. New York: Garland Publishing, 1982.

Mongan, Norman. *The History of the Guitar in Jazz*. New York: Oak Publication; distributed by Music Sales Corp., 1983.

Moody, Bill. *The Jazz Exiles*. Reno: University of Nevada Press, 1993.

Moore, Carman. *Somebody's Angel Child: The Story of Bessie Smith*. New York: Browell, 1969.

Morath, Max, comp. *100 Ragtime Classics*. Denver: Donn Print Co., 1963.

Nathan, Hans. *Dan Emmett and the Rise of Early Negro Minstrelsy*. Norman: University of Oklahoma Press, 1962.

Nettl, Bruno. *Music in Primitive Culture*. Cambridge: Harvard University Press, 1956.

Nketia, Joseph H. Kwabena. *African Music in Ghana*. Evanston, IL: Northwestern University Press, 1963.

Obrecht, Jas. *Jazz Guitar (The Men Who Made the Music)*. San Francisco: Miller Freeman, 1993.

Odum, Howard Washington. *Negro Workaday Songs*. (1926). Westport, CT: Greenwood Press, 1969.

Odum, Howard, and Guy Johnson. *The Negro and His Songs*. Westport, CT: Negro Universities Press, 1968.

Oliver, Paul. *Blues Fell This Morning* (1960). New York: Cambridge University Press, 1990.

———. *Savannah Syncopators: African Retentions in the Blues*. New York: Stein and Day, 1970.

Osgood, Henry Osborne. *So This Is Jazz*. Boston: Little, Brown, 1926.

Panassié, Hugues. *Hot Jazz: The Guide to Swing Music*. New York: M. Withmark, 1936.

———. *Louis Armstrong*. New York: C. Scribner's Sons, 1971.

Patterson, Lindsay. *The Negro in Music and Art*. New York: United Publishers Co., 1970.

Patterson, Willis C., comp. *Anthology of Art Songs by Black American Composers*. New York: Edward B. Marks Corporation, 1977.

Peretti, Burton W. *The Creation of Jazz: Music, Race, and Culture in Urban America*. Urbana: University of Illinois Press, 1992.

Peterson, Bernard L., Jr. *A Century of Musicals in Black and White: An Encyclopedia of Musical Stage Works by, about, or Involving African Americans*. Westport, CT: Greenwood Press, 1993.

Pike, Gustave D. *The Jubilee Singers and Their Campaign for Twenty Thousand Dollars*. Boston: Lee, Shepard and Dillingham, 1873. First AMS Press, edition published in 1974.

Placksin, Sally. *American Women in Jazz: 1900 to the Present*. New York: Seaview Books, 1982.

Porter, Lewis. *John Coltrane: His Life and Music*. Ann Arbor: University of Michigan Press, 1998.

Porter, Lewis, and Michael Ullman. *Jazz: From Its Origins to the Present*. Englewood Cliffs, NJ: Prentice-Hall, 1993.

Ramsey, Frederic. *Been Here and Gone*. New Brunswick, NJ: Rutgers University Press, 1960.

Rattenbury, Ken. *Duke Ellington: Jazz Composer*. London: Yale University Press, 1990.

Reagon, Bernice Johnson. *We'll Understand It Better By and By*. Washington, DC: Smithsonian Institution Press, 1992.

Reisner, Robert George. *Bird: The Legend of Charlie Parker*. New York: Citadel Press, 1992.

Riis, Thomas L. *Just before Jazz: Black Musical Theater in New York, 1890 to 1915*. Washington, DC: Smithsonian Institution Press, 1989.

Roach, Hildred. *Black American Music: Past and Present*. Malabar, FL: Krieger Publishing Company, 1992.

Roberts, John Storm. *Black Music in Two Worlds*. New York: Praeger, 1972.

Ronin, Ro. *Gansta: Merchandizing the Rhymes of Violence*. New York: St. Martin's Press, 1996.

Rose, Adam. *Eubie Blake*. New York: Schirmer Books, 1979.

Rose, Tricia. *Black Noise: Rap Music and Black Culture in Contemporary America*. Hanover, NH: University Press of New England, 1994.

Rosenthal, David. *Hard Bop: Jazz and Black Music, 1955–1965*. New York: Oxford University Press, 1992.

Rublowsky, John. *Black Music in America*. New York: Basic Books, 1971.

Russell, Ross. *The High Life and Hard Times of Charlie Parker*. New York: Charterhouse, 1973.

———. *Jazz Style in Kansas City and the Southwest*. Berkeley: University of California Press, 1971.

Sackheim, Eric. *The Blues Line: A Collection of Blues Lyrics*. New York: Grossman, 1969.

Sampson, Henry. *Blacks in Blackface: A Source Book on Early Black Musical Shows*. Metuchen, NJ: Scarecrow Press, 1980.

Samuels, William Everett. *Union and the Black Musician*. Lanham, MD: University Press of America, 1984.

Sanger, Kerran. *"When the Spirit Says Sing": The Role of Freedom Songs in the Civil Rights Movement*. New York: Garland Publishing, 1995.

Schafer, William J. *Brass Bands & New Orleans Jazz*. Baton Rouge: Louisiana State University Press, 1977.

Schafer, William, and Johannes Riedel. *The Art of Ragtime: Form and Meaning of an Original Black American Art*. Baton Rouge: Louisiana State University Press, 1973.

Schuller, Gunther. *Early Jazz: Its Roots and Musical Development*. New York. Oxford University Press, 1968 (paperback version, 1986).

Sears, Ann. *"Keyboard Music by Nineteenth-Century Afro-American Composers." Feel the Spirit: Studies in Nineteenth-Century Afro-American Music*. Ed. by George R. Keck and Sherrill V. Martin. Westport, CT: Greenwood Press, 1988.

Sernett, Milton C., ed. *Afro-American Religious History: A Documentary Witness*. Durham, NC: Duke University Press, 1985.

Sexton, Adam. *Rap on Rap: Straight-up Talk on Hip-Hop Culture*. New York: Dell Publishing, 1995.

Shaw, Arnold. *Black Popular Music in America: From the Spirituals, Minstrels, and Ragtime to Soul, Disco, and Hip-Hop*. New York: Schirmer Books, 1982.

Sheridan, Chris, comp. *Count Basie: A Bio-Discography*. Westport, CT: Greenwood Press, 1986.

Silvester, Peter J. *A Left Hand like God: A History of Boogie-Woogie Piano*. New York: Da Capo Press, 1988.

Simon, George T. *The Big Bands*. 4th ed. New York: Schirmer Books, 1981.

Simpson, Anne Key. *Follow Me: The Life and Music of R. Nathaniel Dett*. Metuchen, NJ: Scarecrow Press, 1993.

————. *Hard Trials: The Life and Music of Harry Burleigh*. Metuchen, NJ: Scarecrow Press, 1990.

Sims, Janet. *Marian Anderson: An Annotated Bibliography and Discography*. Westport, CT: Greenwood Press, 1981.

Sinclair, John. *Music & Politics*. New York: World Publishing Company, 1971.

Skowronski, JoAnn. *Black Music in America: A Bibliography*. Metuchen, NJ: Scarecrow Press, 1981.

Smith, Eric Ledell. *Black in Opera: An Encyclopedia of People and Companies, 1873–1993*, Jefferson, NC: McFarland, 1995.

Smith, Jessie Carney. *Images of Blacks in American Culture: A Reference Guide to Information Sources*. Westport, CT: Greenwood Press, 1998.

Smith, Willie. *Music on My Mind: The Memoirs of an American Pianist*. Garden City, NY: Doubleday, 1964.

Southern, Eileen. *Biographical Dictionary of Afro-American and African Musicians*. Westport, CT: Greenwood Press, 1983.

————. *The Music of Black Americans: A History*. 3rd. ed. New York: W. W. Norton, 1997.

————, ed. *Readings in Black American Music*. New York: W. W. Norton, 1971.

Southern, Eileen, and Josephine Wright. *African-American Traditions in Song, Sermon, Tale and Dance, 1600s–1920: An Annotated Bibliography of Literature, Collections, and Artworks*. Westport, CT: Greenwood Press, 1990.

Spellman, A. B. *Black Music: Four Lives in the Bebop Business*. New York: Schocken Books, 1970.

Spencer, Jon Michael. *Black Hymnody: A Hymnological History of the African American Church*. Knoxville: University of Tennessee Press, 1992.

———. *Re-Searching Black Music*. Knoxville: University of Tennessee Press, 1996.

———. *The R. Nathaniel Dett Reader: Essays on Black Sacred Music*. Durham, NC: Duke University Press, 1991.

———. *Sacred Symphony: The Chanted Sermon of the Black Music Preacher*. Westport, CT: Greenwood Press, 1987.

———. *The William Grant Still Reader: Essays on African American Music*. Vol. 6, no 2. Durham, NC: Duke University Press, Fall 1992.

Stancell, Steven. *Rap Whoz Who (Rap: The World of Rap Music)*. New York: Schirmer Books, 1996.

Stanley, Lawrence, ed. *Rap: The Lyrics*. New York: Penguin Books, 1992.

Stewart-Baxter, Derrick. *Ma Rainey and the Classic Blues Singers*. New York: Stein and Day, 1970.

Still, Judith Ann, ed. *William Grant Still and the Fusion of Cultures in American Music*. 2nd ed. Flagstaff, AZ: Master-Player Library, 1995.

Still, Judith Anne, Michael J. Dabrishus, and Carolyn L. Quinn. *William Grant Still: A Bio-Bibliography*. Westport, CT: Greenwood Press, 1996.

Talalay, Kathryn. *Composition in Black and White: The Life of Philippa Schuyler*. New York: Oxford University Press, 1995.

Taylor, Billy. *Jazz Piano*. Dubuque, IA: Wm. C. Brown Company, 1982.

Thomas, Henry V. S. *What Do You Know about Blacks in Classical Music*. Baltimore: Gateway Press, 1989.

Thomas, J. C. *Chasin' the Trane: The Music and Mystique of John Coltrane*. New York: Doubleday, 1975.

Tirro, Frank. *Jazz: A History*. New York: W. W. Norton, 1977.

Toop, David. *The Rap Attack*. Boston: South End Press, 1984.

Trotter, James. *Music and Some Highly Musical People; with Sketches of the Lives of Remarkable Musicians of the Colored Race: With Portraits, and an Appendix Containing Copies of Music Composed by Colored Men* (1978). Reprint. New York: Johnson Publishing, 1968.

Tucker, Mark. *Duke Ellington Reader*. New York: Oxford University Press, 1993.

———. *Ellington: The Early Years*. Urbana: University of Illinois Press, 1954.

Turnbull, Walter, and Howard Manly. *Lift Every Voice: Expecting the Most and Getting the Best from All of God's Children*. New York: Hyperion, 1995.

Turner, Patricia. *Dictionary of Afro-American Performers; 78 RPM and Cylinder Recordings of Opera, Choral Music, and Songs, c. 1900–1949*. New York: Garland Publishing, 1990.

Ulanov, Barry. *A History of Jazz in America*. New York: Viking Press, 1952.

Unterbrinck, Mary. *Jazz Women at the Keyboard*. Jefferson, NC: McFarland, 1983.

Walker, Evelyn Davidson. *Choral Music by African-American Composers*. 2nd ed. New York: Scarecrow Press, 1996.

Walker, Wyatt Tee. *Somebody's Calling My Name: Black Sacred Music and Social Change*. Valley Forge, PA: Judson Press, 1979.

Walker-Hill, Helen. *Piano Music by Black Women Composers: A Catalog of Solo and Ensemble Works*. Westport, CT: Greenwood Press, 1992.

Walton, Ortiz. *Music: Black, White and Blue*. New York: Morrow, 1972.

Warren, Fred, with Lee Warren. *The Music of Africa: An Introduction*. Englewood Cliffs, NJ: Prentice-Hall, 1970.

Whitburn, Joel. *Top Rhythm & Blues Records, 1949–1971*. Menomonee Falls, WI: Record Research, 1973.

White, Evelyn Davidson. *Choral Music by African-American Composers*. 2nd ed. New York: Scarecrow Press, 1992.

White, William Carter. *A History of Military Music in America*. New York: Exposition Press, 1944.

Williams, Martin. *Jazz Masters of New Orleans*. New York: Macmillan, 1967.

———. *Jazz Masters in Transition, 1957–69*. New York: Macmillan, 1970.

Wilson-Dickson, Andrew. *The Story of Christian Music: From Gregorian Chant to Black Gospel*. Oxford: Lion Publishing, 1992.

Woideck, Carl. *Charlie Parker: His Music and Life*. Ann Arbor: University of Michigan Press, 1996.

Woll, Allen. *Black Musical Theatre: From Coontown to Dreamgirls*. Baton Rouge: Louisiana State University Press, 1989.

Woodson, Carter G. *The History of the Negro Church*. 1921: Reprint. Washington, DC: Associated Publishers, 1972.

Work, John W. *American Negro Songs*. New York: Howell, Soskis and Co., 1940.

Young, Alan. *Woke Me up This Morning: Black Gospel Singers and the Gospel Life*. Jackson: University Press of Mississippi, 1997.

VIII

African American Intellectual and Political Thought

Robert L. Harris, Jr.

African American intellectual and political thought concerns the ideas that black people in the United States have developed and the actions that they have taken based on those ideas. It involves an examination of ideology, of political consciousness and programmatic thinking. Intellectual and political thought is a part of African American culture, part of the pattern of beliefs, symbols, myths, and behaviors, but it is not the whole of it. Although we may speak in general of the African American mind, worldview, and cosmology, there is and has been great variation in the thinking and activities of African Americans based on class, color, region, gender, and status. Earl E. Thorpe's *The Mind of the Negro: An Intellectual History of Afro-Americans* is still the most comprehensive study of black thought in the United States. He suggests that the central theme of black thought has been the quest for freedom and equality. In their quest for freedom and equality, African Americans have challenged the United States in its definition and practice of humanity, citizenship, and democracy.

Leonard I. Sweet in *Black Images of America, 1784–1870* explains that black leaders shared a providential understanding of history similar to that of their white counterparts who saw America as having a special role in the progress of humankind. Black leaders during the late eighteenth and most of the nineteenth century believed that African Americans were critical to the realization of America's promise. They maintained that divine providence placed black people in the United States to test the country's commitment to its ideals of freedom, justice, and equality. As such, African Americans were a chosen people, part of a divine plan to redeem America and to resurrect African civilization. This ideology is further examined by S. P. Fullinwider in *The Mind and Mood of*

Black America: 20th Century Thought. Lawrence W. Levine in *Black Culture and Black Consciousness: Afro-American Folk Thought from Slavery to Freedom* affirms that one of the most persistent images in slave songs is that of a chosen people.

The question of identity has been central to African American thought and action. In *The Souls of Black Folk*, W.E.B. Du Bois observed that the history of African Americans has been the tension between being "An American, A Negro; two souls, two thoughts, two unreconciled strivings; two warring ideals in one dark body." This twoness has been at the heart of African American thinking in the way that Afro-Americans have perceived themselves and in their relation to the broader society. In part, this has been a problem because the broader society has held African Americans at bay. African Americans have been a part of, but simultaneously apart from, the dominant society. This schism has influenced the way in which African Americans individually and collectively have identified themselves and have sought freedom and equality. Sterling Stuckey in *Slave Culture: Nationalist Theory and the Foundations of Black America* asserts that the controversy over whether to use the designation African, colored, Afro-American, Negro, black, or African American reveals important ideological and organizational trends among African Americans. In *Race, Class, Nationality and Color: The African American Search for Identity*, Bettye Collier-Thomas and James Turner argue that intragroup color discrimination and race designation have been central to the black experience but overlooked by scholars. Skin color has affected the ability to advance socially, politically, and economically within both black and white America.

To address issues of identity and the place of African Americans in American society, black leaders have generally adopted integrationist (freedom, civil rights, racial equality) or nationalist (group solidarity, self-help, separatism) strategies. Harold Cruse in *The Crisis of the Negro Intellectual* claims that the pendulum has always swung between these poles without a synthesis of the two. Lerone Bennett, Jr.'s insightful essay "Beyond Either/Or: A Philosophy of Liberation" in *The Challenge of Blackness* perceptively defines the terms *integration* and *separation* and concludes that the issue is one of liberation. The either/or dichotomy confuses means and ends. Most ordinary or "drylongso" African Americans as brilliantly revealed in John Langston Gwaltney's *Drylongso: A Self-Portrait of Black America* possess a sense of nationhood rooted in their solidarity of opposition to racial oppression, in their self-dignity, and in their desire to live their lives and raise their families like other citizens of the United States. Ironically, the upwardly mobile black middle class today expresses greater anger and alienation than the underclass as reported by Ellis Cose in *The Rage of a Privileged Class* and Jennifer L. Hochschild in *Facing up to the American Dream: Race, Class, and the Soul of the Nation*. Charles T. Banner-Haley in *The Fruits of Integration: Black Middle-Class Ideology and Culture, 1960–1990* argues that the results of integration have been sweet and bitter as African Americans grapple with new concerns about racial identity.

One of the first issues to arise in African American intellectual and political thought was whether to emigrate abroad or to remain in the United States. Floyd J. Miller, in *The Search for a Black Nationality, Black Emigration and Colonization, 1787–1863*, examines the impulse among African Americans to leave the United States beginning in the 1780s, especially for Africa, to escape slavery and racial oppression and to take Western culture and religion to their benighted brethren in Africa. Paul Cuffe, a black sea captain and shipowner, transported thirty-eight emigrants to Sierra Leone in 1815 with the idea of establishing legitimate trade, rescuing Africans from their "backwardness," and elevating the African continent to reflect positively on the status of black people in America and around the world. Biographies by Thomas D. Lamont, *Rise to Be a People: A Biography of Paul Cuffe*, and Sheldon H. Harris, *Paul Cuffe: Black America and the African Return*, tell Cuffe's story. Given the success of Cuffe's voyage, many slaveholders in particular saw colonization as a way to rid the United States of its free black population. Whereas emigration refers to black initiatives, colonization was primarily white initiated. Philip J. Staudenraus in *The African Colonization Movement, 1816–1865* traces the rise of the American Colonization Society that founded the colony of Liberia and transported African Americans to that settlement. Approximately 13,000 African Americans were settled in Liberia between 1835 and 1860. During that same period, about 20 percent of free African Americans left the United States, with 13,000 emigrating to Haiti and 60,000 fleeing to Canada. Elizabeth Rauh Bethel explores emigration in the context of black visions of freedom and development of historical consciousness in *The Roots of African-American Identity: Memory and History in Free Antebellum Communities*.

With the rise of the American Antislavery Society in 1833, African American enthusiasm for emigration waned. African Americans generally supported immediate, uncompensated emancipation and opposed colonization. William Lloyd Garrison and the abolitionists now advocated those same principles. Benjamin Quarles in *Black Abolitionists* explains how African Americans were "pioneers in protest" and abolition's "different drummer." They were both a symbol of the struggle to end slavery and to achieve racial equality and a participant in the battle. Quarles was one of the early historians to demonstrate that African Americans were not mere pawns but forerunners in the struggle for freedom. This theme is advanced by Robert C. Dick in *Black Protest: Issues and Tactics* and by Jane H. and William H. Pease in *They Who Would Be Free: Black's Search for Freedom, 1830–1861*.

August Meier and Elliott Rudwick in John H. Bracey, Jr., et al., eds., *Black Nationalism in America*, suggest that nationalist sentiment tends to emerge and to become most pronounced when African Americans' status has declined or when they have experienced a letdown following a period of heightened expectations. They identify four periods: the 1790s to 1820s, the 1840s to 1850s, the 1880s to 1920s, and the mid-1960s as times of pronounced black nationalism. After the American Revolution and the abolition of slavery in the North, it appeared that the status of African Americans would improve, but slavery was solidified in the South after invention of the cotton gin in 1793. There was an interlude with the rise of the abolitionist movement in the 1830s, but expectations waned during the 1840s and 1850s as the abolitionist movement split into moral suasionists and political activists, the South tightened the noose of slavery after Nat Turner's 1831 slave rebellion, Congress passed the Fugitive Slave Law of 1850, and the Supreme Court ruled in the 1857 *Dred Scott* decision that black men had no rights as citizens of the United States. The hopes of Reconstruction were dashed by Supreme Court rulings that curtailed enforcement of the Fourteenth and Fifteenth Amendments and the Civil Rights Act of 1875, the rise of white terrorist violence, segregation, and disenfranchisement, highlighted by the 1896 *Plessy v. Ferguson* Supreme Court decision that condoned the idea of separate but equal. The civil rights movement of the late 1950s and early 1960s was followed by white resistance and flight from urban centers, urban rebellions, and a growing gulf between black and white America. John Bracey demurs from his coeditors and sees a more consistent thread of black nationalism coursing throughout African American history.

Bracey and his colleagues define black nationalism as a body of social thought, attitudes, and actions ranging from basic expressions of ethnocentrism and racial solidarity to the more sophisticated ideologies of Pan-Africanism. Most scholars trace black nationalism to the 1840s and 1850s. Wilson J. Moses characterizes the 1850s to the 1920s as the "golden age of the black nationalism." In *The Golden Age of Black Nationalism, 1850–1925*, Moses contends that the ideology of black nationalism during this period was conservative in that it concentrated on the idea of the "civilizing mission" or uplifting black people on the African continent and throughout the world. For Moses, the fundamental element of black nationalism is the concept of racial unity that makes it close to the idea of Pan-Africanism. Sterling Stuckey in *The Ideological Origins of Black Nationalism* defines black nationalism as the idea that African Americans should rely primarily on themselves in economic, political, religious, and intellectual areas of life to secure liberation from racial oppression. Fundamentally, as Rodney Carlisle has written in *The Roots of Black Nationalism*, the ideology has involved group solidarity, self-definition, and self-determination. Tunde Adeleke in *UnAfrican Americans: Nineteenth-Century Black Nationalists and the Civilizing Mission* has examined black nationalism from an African perspective and has suggested that there has been a contradiction between African American nationalism and African interests and nationalism. Because of their socialization in the West, even black nationalists have asserted a "superiority" over Africa.

Nationalists such as Martin R. Delany and even "integrationists" such as Frederick Douglass concluded that African Americans constituted a "nation within a nation." The dominant society has proscribed African Americans externally, but African Americans have shaped their own society internally. In *The Mind of Frederick Douglass*, Waldo E. Martin, Jr., suggests that for Douglass the concept of a "nation within a nation" meant racial unity for emancipation and elevation. For Delany, as examined in Victor Ullman's *Martin R. Delany: The Beginnings of Black Nationalism*, the idea resulted from African Americans' being excluded from the government that controlled their destiny and indicated the need for African Americans to emigrate to a place where they could determine their own future. Although free black leaders debated the ideology of black nationalism, especially the merits of emigration, enslaved African Americans, in particular, forged a common culture in religion, music, dance, and folklore that enabled them to resist racial oppression and degradation. Ira Berlin's *Many Thousands Gone: The First Two Centuries of Slavery in North America*, John W. Blassingame's *The Slave Community; Plantation Life in the Antebellum South*, Margaret Washington Creel's *A Peculiar People: Slave Religion and Community-Culture among the Gullahs*, Eugene D. Genovese's *Roll, Jordan, Roll: The World the Slaves Made*, Herbert G. Gutman's *The Black Family in Slavery and Freedom, 1750–1925*, Charles W. Joyner's *Down by the Riverside: A South Carolina Slave Community*, Leslie H. Owens's *This Species of Property: Slave Life and Culture in the Old South*, George P. Rawick's *From Sundown to Sunup: The Making of the Black Community*, and Brenda Stevenson's *Life in Black and White: Family and Community in the Slave South* tell the story of slave resistance and cultural development.

African American intellectual and political thought during the Civil War and Reconstruction turned to acquiring citizenship and to exercising the same rights and privileges as other citizens of the United States. About 20 percent of the black male population over the age of fifteen served in the Union Army to end slavery and to preserve the Union. During the days following the Civil War, African Americans held meetings throughout the South to protest denial of their rights as free men and women and to petition the federal government for the right to vote. Eric Foner, in *Reconstruction: America's Unfinished Revolution, 1863–1877*, extends the work of W.E.B. Du Bois, in *Black Reconstruction in America, 1860–1880* that examined African Americans' role in rebuilding the South after the war. Du Bois revised the racist depictions of Reconstruction that characterized the era as an imposition of inept and corrupt black domination on the South that required redemption of the region and removal of African Americans from politics.

Elsa Barkley Brown, in "Negotiating and Transforming the Public Sphere: African American Political Life in the Transition from Slavery to Freedom," explains that African Americans saw freedom as a collective struggle with men, women, and children participating in meetings held after the Civil War. They all joined in voice votes or in rising from their seats. Black women participated in the political process through parades, rallies, mass meetings, and conventions, although only black men would secure the vote through the Fifteenth Amendment. But their vote was seen more as a family than an individual vote. Black legislators fought more for public than for social equality. They pushed for equal access to restaurants, bars, theatres, hotels, railway and street cars, ship accommodations, and places of amusement. They did not attack segregation in education, prisons, cemeteries, and asylums. Rosalyn Terborg-Penn in *African American Women and the Struggle for the Vote, 1850–1920*, demonstrates the problems that black women confronted in gaining the vote, especially in relation to the women's suffrage movement.

Eric Foner's *Freedom's Lawmakers: A Directory of Black Officeholders during Reconstruction* indicates that most of the first black legislators were born free or acquired their freedom before the Civil War. Persons within this group focused more on civil and political rights. Conversely, those black lawmakers who gained their freedom during and after the war prioritized land redistribution. Both groups supported education. Thomas Holt in *Black over White: Negro Political Leadership in South Carolina during Reconstruction* examines these internal divisions in a state where African Americans were a majority of the population and held more political offices than in any other southern state but still never dominated political life during Reconstruction.

After the Civil War, African Americans, especially in the South, developed the religious, economic, and social infrastructure for their "nation within a nation." The black church, an invisible institution during slavery, became visible and expanded throughout the South as African Americans withdrew from white churches where they were not welcome. Clarence G. Walker, *A Rock in a Weary Land: The African Methodist Episcopal Church during the Civil War and Reconstruction*, James M. Washington, *Frustrated Fellowship: The Black Baptist Quest for Social Power*, and William E. Montgomery, *Under Their Own Vine and Fig Tree: The African American Church in the South, 1865–1900*, explore the growth of black church denominations. African Americans interpreted the Gospel differently from white Christians. Whereas white southerners in the main had used the Bible to justify slavery, African Americans stressed the fatherhood of God and the brotherhood of humankind. Not only did they interpret the Gospel differently, but they transmitted the word of God in a distinctive manner. Orality was the way that African Americans learned their religion, its stories and songs. White churches were generally reflective, whereas black churches of necessity were expressive. Most African Americans could not read and learned hymns by lining the words in which the preacher sang a verse and the congregation repeated it. Given that preachers transmitted religious lessons orally, there was much interaction between minister and congregation, with call and response. African American churches became communal institutions, where black people not only worshiped but also organized mutual aid and benevolent societies, literary clubs, social groups, and bands. The churches were centers for fairs, suppers, concerts, and picnics. They were havens for African Americans in a hostile environment.

Although the church helped to sustain African Americans during slavery with the idea that all men and women were equal in the sight of God, black religion began to turn otherworldly with the downfall of Reconstruction and dashed hopes for racial equality. Although he argued that African Americans' idea of

God has been primarily compensatory and otherworldly, Benjamin E. Mays in *The Negro's God as Reflected in His Literature* also noted that the most important finding in his study was that the African Americans' idea of God is related to their social condition. Gayraud S. Wilmore in *Black Religion and Black Radicalism: An Interpretation of the Religious History of African Americans* suggests that during the Jim Crow era, black churches became more like orthodox white Christian churches in not opposing the status quo.

In the aftermath of Reconstruction, observes August Meier in *Negro Thought in America, 1880–1915: Racial Ideologies in the Age of Booker T. Washington*, there was growing prejudice against African Americans throughout the country. Consequently, notions of black racial solidarity, self-help, and economic development took precedence over politics, agitation, and integration. Large numbers of African Americans sought refuge in the West in what became known as the Kansas Exodus, when more than fifteen thousand black people from Mississippi, Louisiana, Texas, Tennessee, and Arkansas migrated to Kansas in search of better opportunities and freedom from racial violence. During the late 1870s, as Nell I. Painter explains in *Exodusters: Black Migration to Kansas after Reconstruction*, African Americans in the South wrote more frequently to the American Colonization Society about emigrating to Liberia. Initially, they sought information about the Liberian Exodus Joint-Stock Steamship Company that was organized in Charleston, South Carolina, in 1877, sold shares of stock, purchased a ship the *Azor*, and sailed for Liberia with 206 emigrants in April 1878. Because of financial difficulty, the ship did not undertake another voyage. Given the expense involved in emigrating to Liberia and establishing settlements, attention turned to Kansas. Robert G. Athearn's *In Search of Canaan: Black Migration to Kansas, 1879–80* explores the hardships that migrants encountered in reaching Kansas.

In 1890, T. Thomas Fortune, editor of the *Indianapolis Freeman*, presided over a meeting in Chicago of 135 delegates from twenty-three states to found the National Afro-American League to secure the rights of African Americans guaranteed by the U.S. Constitution. Fortune, according to his biographer, Emma Lou Thornbrough in *T. Thomas Fortune: Militant Journalist*, saw African Americans as principally Americans and opposed emigration to Africa. He criticized Bishop Henry McNeal Turner and Edward Wilmot Blyden for their support of emigration. Edwin S. Redkey, in *Black Exodus: Black Nationalist and Back-to-Africa Movements, 1890–1910*, surveys emigrationist thought and activity during the late nineteenth and early twentieth centuries. Contrary to Booker T. Washington, who would soon exert control over the National Afro-American League that became the National Afro-American Council in 1898, Fortune advocated black migration from the South to other parts of the country where African Americans might be able to exercise rights of citizenship.

Although racial solidarity, self-help, and economic development marked black thought during the Jim Crow era, the accommodationist philosophy of Booker T. Washington did not overshadow black protest. Washington's public stance was one of working within the system, while privately he sought to prevent disenfranchisement. Washington's duality is clearly revealed in Louis R. Harlan's two-volume study, *Booker T. Washington: The Making of a Black Leader, 1856–1901* and *Booker T. Washington: The Wizard of Tuskegee, 1901–1915*.

William Monroe Trotter, as described by Stephen R. Fox in *The Guardian of Boston: William Monroe Trotter*, was perhaps Booker T. Washington's most severe critic and opponent. Trotter, editor of the Boston *Guardian*, believed that African Americans should not compromise their civil and political rights even temporarily for racial harmony in the South. Trotter vigorously opposed Washington in his newspaper and at public meetings and influenced W. E. B. Du Bois to take on Washington. Du Bois did not initially oppose Washington. He wrote to Washington after the Atlanta Exposition Address in 1895 that the speech might be a step toward resolving the race problem in the South. It was not until 1903 in *The Souls of Black Folk* that W. E. B. Du Bois openly criticized Washington in his essay "Of Mr. Booker T. Washington and Others," for causing great harm to African Americans with his policy of conciliation and accommodation.

In 1905, Du Bois, Trotter, and twenty-seven other black men formed the Niagara movement to let white America know that African Americans were not satisfied with their condition and that they would agitate for their rights. Although the Niagara movement established branches in some seventeen states, it never had more than about 500 members and was plagued by financial problems. Its greatest achievement was in laying the groundwork for the National Association for the Advancement of Colored People (NAACP) that was organized in 1909 in the aftermath of the Springfield, Illinois, race riot of 1908, in which African Americans were murdered and driven from their homes in the city where Abraham Lincoln was buried. Charles Flint Kellogg, *NAACP: A History of the National Association for the Advancement of Colored People*, tells how the NAACP revived the spirit of the abolitionist movement and sought to define the citizenship rights of African Americans into law through the legislative and judicial system. Harold Cruse in *Plural but Equal: A Critical Study of Blacks and Minorities and America's Plural Society* examines what he describes as the major failure of the NAACP in adopting a policy of non-economic liberalism that focused on civil rights with an expectation that dismantling segregation would gain African Americans access to American society and parity with other citizens. The National Urban League organized in 1910, as studied by Nancy J. Weiss, *The National Urban League, 1910–1940*, and Jesse T. Moore, *A Search for Equality: The National Urban League, 1910–1961*, focused its attention on the adjustment of black migrants to the city, health, education, housing, and employment.

At the beginning of the twentieth century, African Americans sought to shed the image of the plantation "darkey" and the urban "dandy" that had been popularized by minstrelsy. Alain Locke, in *The New Negro: An Interpretation*, observed in the introduction to this anthology that "the mind of the Negro seems suddenly to have slipped from under the tyranny of social imitation and implied inferiority." The New Negro sought to share fully in American society, but based on race values. Langston Hughes, the Harlem Renaissance poet and writer, put it best in his famous essay "The Negro Artist and the Racial Mountain" when he wrote: "We younger Negro artists who create now intend to express our individual dark-skinned selves without fear or shame. If white people are pleased we are glad. If they are not, it doesn't matter. We know we are beautiful. And ugly too. The tom-tom cries and the tom-tom laughs. If colored people are pleased we are glad. If they are not, their displeasure doesn't matter either. We build our temples for tomorrow, strong as we know how, and we stand on top of the mountain, free within ourselves." The New Negro was race conscious, assertive, proud, interested in the past, aspiring to middle-class status, and creating an artistic expression of separate group life while aiming for integration into American society.

The New Negro movement spawned an artistic and cultural revival known as the Harlem Renaissance, as well as the largest mass-based movement ever among African Americans, the Garvey movement. Nathan I. Huggins, *The Harlem Renaissance*, David L. Lewis, *When Harlem Was in Vogue*, George Hutchinson, *The Harlem Renaissance in Black and White*, and Cary Wintz, *Black Culture and the Harlem Renaissance*, reveal the development and content of African American artistic and cultural revival during the 1920s.

Marcus Garvey's Universal Negro Improvement Association (U.N.I.A.) and African Communities League, organized in Jamaica in 1914, had 725 branches throughout the United States and claimed a membership worldwide of 6 million as described in Tony Martin's *Race First: The Ideological and Organizational Struggles of Marcus Garvey and the Universal Negro Improvement Association*. One of the major influences on Garvey was Booker T. Washington. Garvey came to the United States in 1916 to find out more about Washington and the Tuskegee Institute. He remained in the United States and saw his organization enjoy tremendous growth after the "Red Summer" of 1919 when some twenty-five race riots took place in the aftermath of World War I with growing competition in urban areas for jobs, housing, and recreation. Garvey advocated race pride, self-help, racial solidarity, economic self-sufficiency, and African redemption from colonial domination. Recent scholarship on Garvey and the U.N.I.A. such as John Henrik Clarke, ed. *Marcus Garvey and the Vision of Africa*, Robert A. Hill, ed., *The Marcus Garvey and Universal Negro Improvement Association Papers*, and Rupert Lewis, *Marcus Garvey: Anti-colonial Champion*, revise previous work that depicted the U.N.I.A. as a hopelessly romantic back-to-Africa movement.

Both Marcus Garvey and W. E. B. Du Bois advanced the idea of Pan-Africanism, although still tinged by the concept of civilizing mission. Whether applied in the United States or Africa, racial uplift ideology as defined by Kevin K. Gaines in *Uplifting the Race: Black Leadership, Politics, and Culture in the Twentieth Century* involved the black elites' use primarily of class distinctions to indicate advancement for the race. Whether expressed in Du Bois's idea of the talented tenth or in nationalist and Pan-Africanist formulations, the project of racial uplift has generally involved a process of reclamation and restoration. The term *Pan-Africanism*, according to Tony Martin in *The Pan-African Connection*, was first popularized by Henry Sylvester Williams of Trinidad, who organized a Pan-African Conference in London in 1900. Du Bois later spearheaded the Pan-African Congresses of 1919 in Paris; 1921 in London, Brussels, and Paris; and 1923 in London; and 1927 in New York, both sponsored by the National Association of Colored Women. The basic premise of Pan-Africanism was the need for black people in the United States, the Caribbean, and Africa to join their struggles for mutual benefit. The Fifth Pan-African Congress in 1945 held in Manchester, England, began to recognize the goal of African leadership for independence from colonial rule. An independent Africa would positively influence the condition and status of people of African ancestry in the Caribbean and the United States. Winston James's *Holding Aloft the Banner of Ethiopia: Caribbean Radicalism in Early Twentieth Century America* explores the Caribbean influence on socialist and Pan-Africanist movements in the United States.

As James O. Young has written in *Black Writers of the Thirties*, black intellectual and political thought during the Great Depression split along lines of race men and radicals. Race men such as W.E.B. Du Bois, Kelly Miller, Carter G. Woodson, and James Weldon Johnson adhered to the old ideas of racial solidarity and self-help to weather the economic storms of the Depression. The radicals, generally younger social scientists, such as Ralph J. Bunche, E. Franklin Frazier, Abram Harris, and leftists like A. Philip Randolph looked to alliances with working-class whites, especially in the labor movement, to improve the circumstances of African Americans. In 1936, 800 delegates representing 585 organizations met in Chicago to form the National Negro Congress, which fought for New Deal benefits for African Americans, better housing, and improved employment opportunities. The National Negro Congress, with A. Philip Randolph as its president, helped to organize black workers in the steel industry and the nascent Congress of Industrial Organizations (CIO). As the Communist Party gained greater influence within the National Negro Congress, A. Philip Randolph in 1940 resigned as president. The Communist Party during the Depression, as described by Mark Solomon in *The Cry Was Unity: Communists and African Americans, 1917–1936*, made an effort to organize African Americans as the most oppressed class in American society. The Communists were the one group of white Americans advocating racial equality, but their ties to the Soviet Union broke apart the united front that they sought to forge in the United States. After the Soviet Union concluded a nonaggression pact with Nazi Germany, the Communists declared that the war in Europe was of little concern to African Americans. Later, when A. Philip Randolph, as examined in Herbert Garfinkel's *When Negroes March: The March on Washington Movement in the Organizational Politics for FEPC*, organized the March on Washington movement, he excluded whites from membership for fear of communist infiltration and a repeat of his experience with the National Negro Congress.

After World War II, African American intellectual and political thought turned to the struggle for civil rights. African Americans had been determined during the war to wage a "Double V" campaign for freedom at home and abroad. The civil rights movement coincided with decolonization struggles in Africa, Asia, and the Caribbean. Many African American leaders saw their status in the United States as similar to that of colonized people abroad. As African nations in particular became independent, African Americans grew impatient for civil rights progress in the United States. Martin Luther King, Jr., who attended independence ceremonies for Ghana in 1957, wrote in his famous "Letter from Birmingham Jail" on April 16, 1963, that "the nations of Asia and Africa are moving with jet-like speed toward the goal of political independence, and we still creep at horse and buggy pace toward the gaining of a cup of coffee at a lunch counter." Although Martin Luther King, Jr., saw the capacity of the United States for socioeconomic change and the inclusion of African Americans into American society, Malcolm X doubted the capacity for self-change without pressure from abroad. James H. Cone in *Martin & Malcolm & America: A Dream or a Nightmare* probes this juxtaposition and their differing assessments of American society.

In Steven F. Lawson and Charles M. Payne, *Debating the Civil Rights Movement, 1945–1968*, Payne points to new interpretations of the civil rights struggle that examine the role of everyday people rather than the familiar leaders and reveals the complexity of the black community, its class, gender, ideological, regional, and political differences. He suggests that segregation has not been an accurate term to describe what the civil rights movement confronted. It was more an issue of white supremacy, not just the separation of the races but the dominance of one over the other in which segregation was but one instrument of white supremacy. The goal of most African Americans was, therefore, not integration but the realization of American democracy in which equality became a reality rather than a promise.

Vincent Harding in *Hope and History: Why We Must Share the Story of the Movement* questions use of the very term "civil rights movement" as too narrow to describe the black-led and -inspired revolution that challenged the white supremacist and anti-democratic roots of this nation and that reverberated around the globe in Europe, Asia, and South Africa. "We Shall Overcome" has become an international anthem of freedom.

With the achievement of civil rights legislation in 1964 and 1965, the civil rights era came to a close. In the post–civil rights era, many African Americans turned to black power and black consciousness, although a significant segment of the black population still adhered to the old civil rights legacy. It was not so much a matter of integration or separation but the manner in which African Americans should perceive and define themselves in a situation of racial hostility where whites fled central cities and sought to isolate themselves from African

Americans. Black power, according to Stokely Carmichael and Charles Hamilton in *Black Power: The Politics of Liberation in America*, was necessary for African Americans to come together in an effort to enter the broader society. Similar to the New Negro movement at the beginning of the century, the black consciousness movement focused on racial pride, self-definition, and self-determination.

William L. Van Deburg, in *New Day in Babylon: The Black Power Movement in American Culture, 1965–1975*, explores the influence of black power and black pride on American society. There were two wings of the black power movement—cultural nationalists and revolutionary nationalists. Both groups believed that African Americans had the right to self-definition and self-determination and in that sense were nationalists. They also adhered to the goal of liberation from racial oppression but sought different means. The Black Panther Party, organized by Huey P. Newton and Bobby Seale in Oakland, California, drew inspiration from Malcolm X on the principle of self-defense but identified capitalism as the major problem confronting African Americans. In Marxist terms, the Black Panther Party saw capitalism as the base on which the superstructure of racism rested. Destroy the base and the superstructure would fall. The Black Panther Party as examined by Hugh Pearson in *The Shadow of the Panther: Huey Newton and the Price of Black Power in America* became caught up in its own internal contradictions, especially Huey Newton's drug addiction, as well as attacks from the outside. The FBI targeted the Black Panther Party in COINTELPRO, the bureau's counterintelligence program against the Communist Party, as the most dangerous internal threat to American security. Ward Churchill and Jim Vander Hall describe the FBI effort to destroy the Black Panther Party in *Agents of Repression: The FBI's Secret Wars against the Black Panther Party and the American Indian Movement*.

It is ironic that the Black Panthers considered themselves heirs to Malcolm X, given the religious orthodoxy of the Nation of Islam. Elijah Muhammad, whom Malcolm X considered his spiritual father, taught that African Americans were descendants of the original man, that they were God's chosen people, and that they would be rescued from the imminent destruction of the earth, which they would later inherit. The Nation of Islam under Elijah Muhammad and Louis Farrakhan as studied by Mattias Gardell, *In the Name of Elijah Muhammad: Louis Farrakhan and the Nation of Islam*, has primarily been non-engaged with American society, which it considers doomed to destruction anyway.

Although not fully disengaged from American society, the cultural nationalists focused their attention more on the reclamation of black people from the despair of racial inferiority than on the reformation or restructuring of American society. Maulana Karenga in *Kwanzaa: A Celebration of Family, Community, and Culture* has suggested that the views and values of African Americans must change to a more positive image of self and future possibility before African Americans can contemplate the improvement of humanity. A strain of African American thought that persists to this day is the special role of African Americans in rescuing humanity, especially in the United States. Jesse Jackson's organization Operation PUSH was initially People United to *Save* (later changed to *Serve*) Humanity.

The black studies movement grew out of the black consciousness and black power era. Black studies has a deep lineage in this country going back to the early twentieth century Atlanta University studies of W.E.B. Du Bois, in which he set out to examine significant themes about black life in ten-year cycles. Black studies, however, became institutionalized primarily on white college campuses during the late 1960s as large numbers of black students entered predominantly white schools for the first time and challenged the omissions, myths, and distortions of black life and culture that prevailed in the white academy. Black studies scholarship opened new ways of looking at black life and culture by concentrating on the voice and agency of African Americans that had been neglected and ignored in the past. Abdul Alkalimat's *Paradigms in Black Studies: Intellectual History, Cultural Meaning and Political Ideology* surveys the ideas animating black studies.

Afrocentricity is one of the ideas that sprang from the black studies movement. It is a complex idea with proponents who define it as using black people as a starting point, wherever located, for studying them from the inside out rather than from the outside in, to those who promote an African-centered approach that stresses the commonality of African-descended people wherever located. Molefi Asante in *Afrocentricity* and in *The Afrocentric Idea* suggests that all African-descended people possess a common cosmology, history, and destiny.

Because black people have been held at bay from the dominant society in the United States, African American intellectual and political thought has been primarily oppositional—against slavery, discrimination, segregation, racism, and white supremacy. At times radical, sometimes militant, often moderate, and generally liberal, African American intellectual and political thought has rarely been conservative. African Americans have basically sought to change rather than to preserve the status quo. Nevertheless, Peter Eisenstadt in *Black Conservatism: Essays in Intellectual and Political History* indicates that conservative ideas have influenced black intellectual and political thought since the late eighteenth century. As this essay has attempted to demonstrate, African American intellectual and political thought has been complex and even conservative in a few instances. Black conservatism has generally been pro-capital, moralistic, and conciliatory. Both integrationists and nationalists have embraced conservative ideas. In fact, conservatism as faith in individual achievement without group solidarity or government intervention has produced a small but vocal chorus with the success of the civil rights movement.

The growth of a large black middle class and the prominence of African Americans, particularly in sports and entertainment, have given the illusion of progress. This is not to deny that African Americans have made incredible progress since the 1960s, but still a quarter of the black population remains mired in poverty. African American intellectual and political thought is probably more divided today than in the past. The battle lines are not as clearly drawn as when racial denigration, segregation, and colonial oppression were the issues. Most African Americans have opted for social and political incorporation into American society. In 1963, when *Ebony* magazine first published its list of the 100 most influential African Americans, 27 members on the list held elected and appointed government office. By 1971, when *Ebony* revived the list, there were 37 government officeholders. In 1978, there were 45 government officeholders, 46 in 1988, and 70 by 1997. The number of government officeholders had grown so large that the magazine revised its listing as the "100+ Most Influential Black Americans and Organization Leaders." Forty members of the 1997 list were members of Congress, 14 were mayors of major cities, 8 held cabinet or executive appointments, and 8 were federal or state judges.

As Katherine Tate has suggested in *From Protest to Politics: The New Black Voters in American Elections*, black voters since 1965 have gained greater confidence in the importance of their vote. They believe that their votes make a difference and that the election of black officeholders has a positive effect on their lives. Black officeholders have largely replaced traditional protest leaders as spokespersons for black communities. Civil rights is not as much of a concern today as unemployment, poverty, police brutality, housing, crime, and education. At the beginning of the twenty-first century, however, the quest for freedom and equality remains the central theme of African American intellectual and political thought.

BIBLIOGRAPHY

Adeleke, Tunde. *UnAfrican Americans: Nineteenth-Century Black Nationalists and the Civilizing Mission*. Lexington: University Press of Kentucky, 1998.

Alkalimat, Abdul, ed. *Paradigms in Black Studies: Intellectual History, Cultural Meaning and Political Ideology*. Chicago: Twenty-first Century Books, 1990.

Anderson, James D. *The Education of Blacks in the South, 1860–1935*. Chapel Hill: University of North Carolina Press, 1988.

Aptheker, Herbert. *American Negro Slave Revolts*. New York: Columbia University Press, 1944.

Asante, Molefi. *The Afrocentric Idea*. Philadelphia: Temple University Press, 1998.

———. *Afrocentricity*. Trenton, NJ: Africa World Press, 1988.

Athearn, Robert G. *In Search of Canaan: Black Migration to Kansas, 1879–80*. Lawrence: Regents Press of Kansas, 1978.

Banner-Haley, Charles T. *The Fruits of Integration: Black Middle Class Ideology and Culture, 1960–1990*. Jackson: University Press of Mississippi, 1994.

Bennett, Lerone, Jr. *The Challenge of Blackness*. Chicago: Johnson Publishing, 1972.

Berlin, Ira. *Many Thousands Gone: The First Two Centuries of Slavery in North America*. Cambridge: Harvard University Press, 1998.

Bethel, Elizabeth R. *The Roots of African-American Identity: Memory and History in Free Antebellum Communities*. New York: St. Martin's Press, 1997.

Bittle, William E., and Gilbert Geis. *The Longest Way Home: Chief Alfred C. Sam's Back-to-Africa Movement*. Detroit: Wayne State University Press, 1964.

Blackett, Richard J. M. *Building an Antislavery Wall: Black Americans in the Atlantic Abolitionist Movement, 1830–1860*. Baton Rouge: Louisiana State University Press, 1983.

Blassingame, John W., ed. *The Frederick Douglass Papers*. 5 vols. New Haven, CT: Yale University Press, 1979–92.

————. *The Slave Community: Plantation Life in the Antebellum South*. rev. ed. New York: Oxford University Press, 1979.

————, ed. *Slave Testimony: Two Centuries of Letters, Speeches, Interviews, and Autobiographies*. Baton Rouge: Louisiana State University Press, 1977.

Bracey, John H., Jr., et al., eds. *Black Nationalism in America*. New York: Bobbs-Merrill, 1970.

Branch, Taylor. *Parting the Waters: America in the King Years, 1954–1963*, New York: Simon and Schuster, 1988.

————. *Pillar of Fire: America in the King Years, 1963–65*. New York: Simon and Schuster, 1998.

Brotz, Howard, ed. *Negro Social and Political Thought, 1850–1920: Representative Texts*. New York: Basic Books, 1966.

Brown, Elaine. *A Taste of Power: A Black Woman's Story*. New York: Doubleday, 1994.

Brown, Elsa Barkley. "Negotiating and Transforming the Public Sphere: African American Political Life in the Transition from Slavery to Freedom." *Public Culture* 7, no. 1 (Fall 1994): 107–46.

Burkett, Randall K. *Garveyism as a Religious Movement: The Institutionalization of a Black Civil Religion*. Metuchen, NJ: Scarecrow Press, 1978.

Bush, Roderick D. *We Are Not What We Seem: Black Nationalism and Class Struggle in the American Century*. New York: New York University Press, 1999.

Carlisle, Rodney. *The Roots of Black Nationalism*. Port Washington, NY: Kennikat Press, 1975.

Carmichael, Stokely, and Charles Hamilton. *Black Power: The Politics of Liberation in America*. New York: Vintage Books, 1967.

Carroll, Joseph C. *Slave Insurrections in the United States, 1800–1865*. Westport, CT: Greenwood Press, 1968 (1938).

Carson, Clayborne. *In Struggle: SNCC and the Black Awakening of the 1960s*. Cambridge, MA: Harvard University Press, 1981.

Cheek, William F. *Black Resistance before the Civil War*. Beverly Hills, CA: Glencoe Press, 1970.

Churchill, Ward, and Jim Vander Hall. *Agents of Repression: The FBI's Secret Wars against the Black Panther Party and the American Indian Movement*. Boston: South End Press, 1988.

Clarke, John Henrik, ed. *Marcus Garvey and the Vision of Africa*. New York: Random House, 1974.

Clay, William L. *Just Permanent Interests: Black Americans in Congress, 1870–1991*. New York: Amistad Press, 1992.

Clegg, Claude Andrew. *An Original Man: The Life and Times of Elijah Muhammad*. New York: St. Martin's Press, 1997.

Collier-Thomas, Bettye, and James Turner. *Race, Class, Nationality and Color: The*

African American Search for Identity. Philadelphia: Temple University Center for African American History and Culture Occasional Papers Series no. 1, 1992.

Colton, Elizabeth O. *The Jackson Phenomenon: The Man, the Power, the Message.* New York: Doubleday, 1989.

Cone, James H. *Martin & Malcolm & America: A Dream or a Nightmare.* Maryknoll, NY: Orbis Books, 1991.

Cose, Ellis. *The Rage of a Privileged Class.* New York: HarperCollins, 1993.

Creel, Margaret Washington. *A Peculiar People: Slave Religion and Community-Culture among the Gullahs.* New York: New York University Press, 1988.

Cruse, Harold. *The Crisis of the Negro Intellectual.* New York: William Morow, 1967.

———. *Plural but Equal: A Critical Study of Blacks and Minorities and America's Plural Society.* New York: William Morrow, 1987.

DeCaro, Louis A. *Malcolm and the Cross: The Nation of Islam, Malcolm X, and Christianity.* New York: New York University Press, 1998.

Dick, Robert C. *Black Protest: Issues and Tactics.* Westport, CT: Greenwood Press, 1974.

Duberman, Martin B. *Paul Robeson.* New York: Knopf, 1988.

Du Bois, W. E. B. *Black Reconstruction in America, 1860–1880.* New York: Russell and Russell, 1935.

———. *The Souls of Black Folk.* New York: Penguin Books, 1989 (1903).

Egerton, Douglas R. *Gabriel's Rebellion: The Virginia Slave Conspiracies of 1800 and 1802.* Chapel Hill: University of North Carolina Press, 1993.

Eisenstadt, Peter, ed. *Black Conservatism: Essays in Intellectual and Political History.* New York: Garland, 1999.

Esedebe, P. Olisanwuche. *Pan-Africanism: The Idea and Movement, 1776–1991.* 2nd ed. Washington, D.C.: Howard University Press, 1994.

Foner, Eric. *Freedom's Lawmakers: A Directory of Black Officeholders during Reconstruction.* New York: Oxford University Press, 1993.

———. *Reconstruction: America's Unfinished Revolution, 1863–1877.* New York: Harper and Row, 1988.

Ford, Nick Aaron. *Black Studies: Threat or Challenge?* Port Washington, NY: Kennikat Press, 1973.

Forman, James. *The Making of Black Revolutionaries.* New York: Macmillan, 1972.

Fox, Stephen R. *The Guardian of Boston: William Monroe Trotter.* New York: Athenaeum, 1970.

Frady, Marshall. *Jesse: The Life and Pilgrimage of Jesse Jackson.* New York: Random House, 1996.

Franklin, John Hope. *Race and History: Selected Essays, 1938–1988.* Baton Rouge: Louisiana State University Press, 1989.

Franklin, V. P. *Black Self-Determination: A Cultural History of the Faith of the Fathers.* Westport, CT: Lawrence Hill, 1984.

Fredrickson, George M. *Black Liberation: A Comparative History of Black Ideologies in the United States and South Africa.* New York: Oxford University Press, 1995.

Fullinwider, S. P. *The Mind and Mood of Black America: 20th Century Thought.* Homewood, IL: Dorsey Press, 1969.

Gaines, Kevin K. *Uplifting the Race: Black Leadership, Politics, and Culture in the Twentieth Century.* Chapel Hill: University of North Carolina Press, 1996.

Gardell, Mattias. *In the Name of Elijah Muhammad: Louis Farrakhan and the Nation of Islam*. Durham, NC: Duke University Press, 1996.

Garfinkel, Herbert. *When Negroes March: The March on Washington Movement in the Organizational Politics for FEPC*. Glencoe, IL: Free Press, 1959.

Garrow, David J. *Bearing the Cross: Martin Luther King, Jr., and the Southern Christian Leadership Conference*. New York: William Morrow, 1986.

Geiss, Imanuel. *The Pan-African Movement*. London: Methuen and Co., 1974.

Genovese, Eugene D. *From Rebellion to Revolution: Afro-American Slave Revolts in the Making of the Modern World*. Baton Rouge: Louisiana State University Press, 1979.

————. *Roll, Jordan, Roll: The World the Slaves Made*. New York: Pantheon Books, 1974.

Goggins, Jacqueline. *Carter G. Woodson: A Life in Black History*. Baton Rouge: Louisiana State University Press, 1993.

Grant, Joanne. *Ella Baker: Freedom Bound*. New York: Wiley, 1998.

Greenberg, Kenneth S., ed. *The Confessions of Nat Turner and Related Documents*. Boston: Bedford Books, 1996.

Griffith, Cyril E. *The African Dream: Martin R. Delany and the Emergence of Pan-African Thought*. University Park: Pennsylvania State University Press, 1975.

Gutman, Herbert G. *The Black Family in Slavery and Freedom, 1750–1925*. New York: Pantheon Books, 1976.

Gwaltney, John Langston. *Drylongso: A Self-Portrait of Black America*. New York: Random House, 1980.

Halasz, Nicholas. *The Rattling Chains: Slave Unrest and Revolt in the Antebellum South*. New York: McKay, 1966.

Harding, Vincent. *Hope and History: Why We Must Share the Story of the Movement*. Maryknoll, NY: Orbis Books, 1990.

Harlan, Louis R. *Booker T. Washington: The Making of a Black Leader, 1856–1901*. New York: Oxford University Press, 1972.

————. *Booker T. Washington: The Wizard of Tuskegee, 1901–1915*. New York: Oxford University Press, 1983.

————. *The Booker T. Washington Papers*. 14 vols. Urbana: University of Illinois Press, 1972–89.

Harris, Jr., Robert L., Darlene Clark Hine, and Nellie McKay. *Three Essays: Black Studies in the United States*. New York: Ford Foundation, 1990.

Harris, Sheldon H. *Paul Cuffe: Black America and the African Return*. New York: Simon and Schuster, 1972.

Harris, William H. *Keeping the Faith: A. Philip Randolph, Milton P. Webster, and the Brotherhood of Sleeping Car Porters, 1925–37*. Urbana: University of Illinois Press, 1977.

Haywood, Harry. *Negro Liberation*. Chicago: Liberator Press, 1976.

Henry, Charles P. *Ralph Bunche: Model Negro or American Other?* New York: New York University Press, 1999.

Hill, Robert A., ed. *The Marcus Garvey and Universal Negro Improvement Association Papers*. 9 vols. Berkeley: University of California Press, 1983–95.

Hine, Darlene Clark, and Katherine Thompson. *A Shining Thread of Hope: The History of Black Women in America*. New York: Broadway Books, 1998.

Hinks, Peter P. *To Awaken My Afflicted Brethren: David Walker and the Problem of*

Antebellum Slave Resistance. University Park: Pennsylvania State University Press, 1997.

Hochschild, Jennifer L. *Facing up to the American Dream: Race, Class, and the Soul of the Nation.* Princeton, NJ: Princeton University Press, 1995.

Holt, Thomas C. *Black over White: Negro Political Leadership in South Carolina during Reconstruction.* Urbana: University of Illinois Press, 1977.

Horne, Gerald. *Black Liberation/Red Scare: Ben Davis and the Communist Party.* Newark, DE: University of Delaware Press, 1994.

Huggins, Nathan I. *Harlem Renaissance.* New York: Oxford University Press, 1971.

Hughes, Langston. "The Negro Artist and the Racial Mountain." *Nation* (June 23, 1926): 692–94.

Hutchinson, Earl Ofari. *Blacks and Reds: Race and Class in Conflict, 1919–1990.* East Lansing: Michigan State University Press, 1995.

Hutchinson, George. *The Harlem Renaissance in Black and White.* Cambridge,: MA Harvard University Press, 1995.

James, C.L.R. *A History of Pan-African Revolt.* Washington, DC: Drum and Spear Press, 1969.

James, Joy. *Transcending the Talented Tenth: Black Leaders and American Intellectuals.* New York: Routledge, 1997.

James, Winston. *Holding Aloft the Banner of Ethiopia: Caribbean Radicalism in Early Twentieth Century America.* London: Verso, 1998.

Janken, Kenneth R. *Rayford W. Logan and the Dilemma of the African-American Intellectual.* Amherst: University of Massachusetts Press, 1993.

Joyner, Charles W. *Down by the Riverside: A South Carolina Slave Community.* Urbana: University of Illinois Press, 1984.

Karenga, Maulana. *An Introduction to Black Studies.* Los Angeles: University of Sankore Press, 1993.

———. *Kwanzaa: A Celebration of Family. Community and Culture.* Los Angeles: University of Sankore Press, 1998.

Kelley, Robin D. G. *Hammer and Hoe: Alabama Communists during the Great Depression.* Chapel Hill: University of North Carolina Press, 1990.

———. *Race Rebels: Culture, Politics, and the Black Working Class.* New York: Free Press, 1994.

Kellogg, Charles Flint. *NAACP: A History of the National Association for the Advancement of Colored People.* Baltimore: Johns Hopkins University Press, 1967.

Keppel, Ben. *The Work of Democracy: Ralph Bunche, Kenneth B. Clark, Lorraine Hansberry, and the Cultural Politics of Race.* Cambridge, MA: Harvard University Press, 1995.

Kinshasa, Kwando M. *Emigration vs. Assimilation: The Debate in the African American Press, 1827–1861.* Jefferson, NC: McFarland, 1988.

Lamont, Thomas D. *Rise to Be a People: A Biography of Paul Cuffe* Urbana: University of Illinois Press, 1986.

Lawson, Steven F. *Running for Freedom: Civil Rights and Black Politics in America since 1941.* New York: McGraw-Hill, 1991.

Lawson, Steven F., and Charles M. Payne. *Debating the Civil Rights Movement, 1945–1968.* Lanham, MD: Rowman and Littlefield, 1998.

Legum, Colin. *Pan-Africanism: A Short Political Guide.* New York: Praeger, 1965.

Levine, Lawrence W. *Black Culture and Black Consciousness: Afro-American Folk Thought from Slavery to Freedom.* New York: Oxford University Press, 1977.

Levy, Eugene. *James Weldon Johnson; Black Leader, Black Voice.* Chicago: University of Chicago Press, 1973.

Lewis, David L. *W. E. B. Du Bois: Biography of a Race, 1868–1919.* New York: Henry Holt, 1993.

———. *When Harlem Was in Vogue.* New York: Knopf, 1981.

Lewis, Rupert. *Marcus Garvey: Anti-colonial Champion.* Trenton, NJ: Africa World Press, 1988.

Lincoln, C. Eric. *The Black Muslims in America.* Trenton, NJ: Africa World Press, 1994.

Litwack, Leon F. *Been in the Storm So Long: The Aftermath of Slavery.* New York: Knopf, 1979.

———. *Trouble in Mind: Black Southerners in the Age of Jim Crow.* New York: Knopf, 1998.

Locke, Alain, ed. *The New Negro: An Interpretation.* 1925. New York: Atheneum, 1983.

Lofton, John. *Denmark Vesey's Revolt: The Slave Plot That Lit a Fuse to Fort Sumter.* Kent, OH: Kent State University Press, 1983.

Lowery, Charles D., and John F. Marszalek. *Encyclopedia of African-American Civil Rights: From Emancipation to the Present.* Westport, CT: Greenwood Press, 1992.

Madhubuti, Haki, and Maulana Karenga, eds. *Million Man March, Day of Absence: A Commemorative Anthology.* Chicago: Third World Press, 1996.

Magida, Arthur J. *Prophet of Rage: A Life of Louis Farrakhan and His Nation.* New York: Basic Books, 1996.

Malcolm X, with the assistance of Alex Haley. *The Autobiography of Malcolm X.* 1965. New York: Ballantine Books, 1973.

Marable, Manning. *Black American Politics: From the Washington Marches to Jesse Jackson.* London: Verso, 1985.

———. *Black Leadership.* New York: Columbia University Press, 1998.

———. *W. E. B. Du Bois: Black Radical Democrat.* Boston: Twayne, 1986.

Marsh, Clifton E. *From Black Muslims to Muslims: The Transition from Separatism to Islam 1930–1980.* Metuchen, NJ: Scarecrow Press, 1984.

Martin, Tony. *Literary Garveyism: Garvey, Black Arts, and the Harlem Renaissance.* Dover, MA: Majority Press, 1983.

———. *The Pan-African Connection: From Slavery to Garvey and Beyond.* Dover, MA: Majority Press, 1983.

———. *Race First: The Ideological and Organizational Struggles of Marcus Garvey and the Universal Negro Improvement Association.* Dover, MA: Majority Press, 1986.

Martin, Waldo E., Jr. *The Mind of Frederick Douglass.* Chapel Hill: University of North Carolina Press, 1984.

Mays, Benjamin E. *The Negro's God as Reflected in His Literature.* Boston: Chapman and Grimes, 1938.

McAdoo, Bill. *Pre–Civil War Black Nationalism.* New York: David Walker Press, 1983.

Meier, August. *Negro Thought in America, 1880–1915; Racial Ideologies in the Age of Booker T. Washington.* Ann Arbor: University of Michigan Press, 1963.

Meier, August, and Elliott Rudwick. *Black History and the Historical Profession, 1915–1980.* Urbana: University of Illinois Press, 1986.

——. *CORE: A Study in the Civil Rights Movement, 1942–1968*. New York: Oxford University Press, 1973.

Miller, Floyd J. *The Search for a Black Nationality: Black Emigration and Colonization, 1787–1863*. Urbana: University of Illinois Press, 1975.

Montgomery, William E. *Under Their Own Vine and Fig Tree: The African American Church in the South, 1865–1900*. Baton Rouge: Louisiana State University Press, 1993.

Moore, Jesse T. *A Search for Equality: The National Urban League, 1910–1961*. University Park: Pennsylvania State University Press, 1981.

Morris, Aldon. *The Origins of the Civil Rights Movement: Black Communities Organizing for Change*. New York: Free Press, 1984.

Moses, Wilson J. *Alexander Crummell: A Study of Civilization and Discontent*. New York: Oxford University Press, 1989.

——. *The Golden Age of Black Nationalism, 1850–1925*. Hamden, CT: Archon Books, 1978.

——, ed. *Classical Black Nationalism: From the American Revolution to Marcus Garvey*. New York: New York University Press, 1996.

Naison, Mark. *Communists in Harlem during the Depression*. Urbana: University of Illinois Press, 1983.

Oates, Stephen B. *The Fires of Jubilee: Nat Turner's Fierce Rebellion*. New York: Harper and Row, 1975.

Owens, Leslie H. *This Species of Property: Slave Life and Culture in the Old South*. New York: Oxford University Press, 1976.

Padmore, George. *Pan-Africanism or Communism*. Garden City, NY: Doubleday, 1971.

Painter, Nell I. *Exodusters: Black Migration to Kansas after Reconstruction*. New York: Knopf, 1977.

——. *The Narrative of Hosea Hudson: His Life as a Negro Communist in the South*. Cambridge, MA: Harvard University Press, 1979.

Payne, Charles M. *I've Got the Light of Freedom: The Organizing Tradition and the Mississippi Freedom Struggle*. Berkeley: University of California Press, 1995.

Pearson, Edward A., ed. *Designs against Charleston: The Trial Record of the Denmark Vesey Slave Conspiracy of 1822*. Chapel Hill: University of North Carolina Press, 1999.

Pearson, Hugh. *The Shadow of the Panther: Huey Newton and the Price of Black Power in America*. Reading, MA: Addison-Wesley, 1994.

Pease, Jane H., and William H. Pease. *They Who Would Be Free: Blacks' Search for Freedom 1830–1861*. New York: Atheneum, 1974.

Pinkney, Alphonso. *Red, Black, and Green: Black Nationalism in the United States*. New York: Cambridge University Press, 1976.

Plummer, Brenda Gayle. *Rising Wind: Black Americans and U.S. Foreign Affairs, 1935–1960*. Chapel Hill: University of North Carolina Press, 1996.

Quarles, Benjamin. *Black Abolitionists*. New York: Oxford University Press, 1969.

——. *Black Mosaic: Essays in Afro-American History and Historiography*. Amherst: University of Massachusetts Press, 1988.

Rawick, George P. *From Sundown to Sunup: The Making of the Black Community*. Westport, CT: Greenwood Press, 1972.

Redkey, Edwin S. *Black Exodus: Black Nationalist and Back-to-Africa Movements, 1890–1910*. New Haven, CT: Yale University Press, 1969.

Reed, Adolph L., Jr. *W. E. B. Du Bois and American Political Thought: Fabianism and the Color Line.* New York: Oxford University Press, 1997.

Reynolds, Barbara. *Jesse Jackson: America's David.* Washington, DC: JFJ Associates, 1985.

Ripley, C. Peter, ed. *Witness for Freedom: African American Voices on Race, Slavery, and Emancipation.* Chapel Hill: University of North Carolina Press, 1993.

Ripley, C. Peter, et al., eds. *The Black Abolitionist Papers,* 5 vols. Chapel Hill: University of North Carolina Press, 1985–92.

Robeson, Paul. *Here I Stand.* New York: Othello Associates, 1958.

Robinson, Cedric. *Black Marxism: The Making of a Black Radical Tradition.* London: Zed, 1983.

Robnett, Belinda. *How Long? How Long?: African American Women in the Struggle for Civil Rights.* New York: Oxford University Press, 1997.

Seale, Bobby. *Seize the Time: The Story of the Black Panther Party and Huey P. Newton.* New York: Random House, 1970.

Singh, Robert. *The Farrakhan Phenomenon: Race, Reaction, and the Paranoid Style in American Politics.* Washington, DC: Georgetown University Press, 1997.

Smith, Robert C. *We Have No Leaders: African Americans in the Post–Civil Rights Era.* Albany: State University of New York Press, 1996.

Smith, Samuel Denny. *The Negro in Congress, 1870–1901.* Port Washington, NY: Kennikat Press, 1966.

Solomon, Mark. *The Cry Was Unity: Communists and African Americans, 1917–36.* Jackson: University Press of Mississippi, 1998.

Staudenraus, Philip J. *The African Colonization Movement, 1816–1865.* New York: Columbia University Press, 1961.

Stein, Judith. *The World of Marcus Garvey: Race and Class in Modern Society.* Baton Rouge: Louisiana State University Press, 1986.

Stevenson, Brenda. *Life in Black and White: Family and Community in the Slave South.* New York: Oxford University Press, 1996.

Strickland, Arvarh, ed. *Working with Carter G. Woodson, the Father of Black History: A Diary, 1928–1930, by Lorenzo J. Greene.* Baton Rouge: Louisiana State University Press, 1989.

Stuckey, Sterling, ed. *The Ideological Origins of Black Nationalism* Boston: Beacon Press, 1972.

———. *Slave Culture: Nationalist Theory and the Foundations of Black America.* New York: Oxford University Press, 1987.

Swain, Carol M. *Black Faces, Black Interests: The Representation of African Americans in Congress.* Cambridge: Harvard University Press, 1993.

Sweet, Leonard I. *Black Images of America, 1784–1870.* New York: W. W. Norton, 1976.

Tate, Katherine. *From Protest to Politics: The New Black Voters in American Elections.* Cambridge, MA: Harvard University Press, 1993.

Terborg-Penn, Rosalyn. *African American Women in the Struggle for the Vote, 1850–1920.* Bloomington: Indiana University Press, 1998.

Thomas, Lamont D. *Rise to Be a People: A Biography of Paul Cuffe.* Urbana: University of Illinois Press, 1986.

Thornbrough, Emma Lou. *T. Thomas Fortune: Militant Journalist.* Chicago: University of Chicago Press, 1972.

Thorpe, Earl E. *Black Historians: A Critique*. New York: William Morrow & Co., 1971.

———. *The Mind of the Negro: An Intellectual History of Afro-Americans*. Baton Rouge, LA: Ortlieb Press, 1961.

Toll, William. *The Resurgence of Race: Black Social Theory from Reconstruction to the Pan-African Conference*. Philadelphia: Temple University Press, 1979.

Tragle, Henry I. *Nat Turner's Slave Revolt, 1831*. New York: Grossman, 1972.

T'Shaka, Oba. *The Political Legacy of Malcolm X*. Chicago: Third World Press, 1983.

Ullman, Victor. *Martin R. Delany: The Beginnings of Black Nationalism*. Boston: Beacon Press, 1971.

Van Deburg, William L., ed. *Modern Black Nationalism: From Marcus Garvey to Louis Farrakhan*. New York: New York University Press, 1997.

———. *New Day in Babylon: The Black Power Movement in American Culture, 1965–1975*. Chicago: University of Chicago Press, 1992.

Van Eschen, Penny M. *Race against Empire: Black Americans and Anticolonialism, 1937–1957*. Ithaca, NY: Cornell University Press, 1997.

Vincent, Theodore. *Black Power and the Garvey Movement*. Oakland: Nzinga Publishing House, 1988.

Walker, Clarence E. *A Rock in a Weary Land: The African Methodist Episcopal Church during the Civil War and Reconstruction*. Baton Rouge: Louisiana State University Press, 1982.

Walters, Ronald W. *Pan-Africanism in the African Diaspora: An Analysis of Modern Afrocentric Political Movements*. Detroit: Wayne State University Press, 1993.

Washington, Booker T. *Up from Slavery*. 1901. New York: Oxford University Press, 1995.

Washington, James M. *Frustrated Fellowship: The Black Baptist Quest for Social Power*. Macon: Mercer, 1986.

Watson, Steven. *The Harlem Renaissance: Hub of African-American Culture*. New York: Pantheon Books, 1995.

Weisbrot, Robert. *Freedom Bound: A History of America's Civil Rights Movement*. New York: W. W. Norton, 1990.

Weiss, Nancy J. *Farewell to the Party of Lincoln: Black Politics in the Age of FDR*. Princeton, NJ: Princeton University Press, 1983.

———. *The National Urban League, 1910–1940*. New York: Oxford University Press, 1974.

White, John. *Black Leadership in America: From Booker T. Washington to Jesse Jackson*. New York: Longman, 1990.

Wilmore, Gayraud S. *Black Religion and Black Radicalism: An Interpretation of the Religious History of African Americans*. Maryknoll, NY: Orbis Books, 1998.

Wilson, James Q. *Negro Politics: The Search for Leadership*. New York: Octagon Books, 1980.

Wintz, Cary D., ed. *African American Political Thought, 1890–1930: Washington, Du Bois, Garvey, and Randolph*. Armonk, NY: M. E. Sharpe, 1996.

———. *Black Culture and the Harlem Renaissance*. Houston: Rice University Press, 1988.

Wolfenstein, E. Victor. *The Victims of Democracy: Malcolm X and Black Revolution*. New York: Guilford Press, 1993.

Woodson, Carter G., ed. *The Mind of the Negro as Reflected in Letters, Written during the Crisis, 1800–1860*. 1926. New York: Russell and Russell, 1969.

Young, James O. *Black Writers of the Thirties*. Baton Rouge: Louisiana State University Press, 1973.

Zinn, Howard. *SNCC: The New Abolitionists*. 2nd ed. Boston: Beacon Press, 1979.

IX

The African American Political Experience

Sharon D. Wright and Minion K. C. Morrison

The political experience of African Americans may easily be dated from the first half of the seventeenth century when Africans began to be enslaved in large numbers in the United States. Almost immediately public policy decisions were enunciated about how to handle the enslaved population. With some variations from territory to territory, formal structures and processes were developed for use of African labor, often based on slave practices seen in Latin America and the Caribbean. The documentation provided in this chapter tracks the political processes and activities that determined the status of African Americans and shows how African Americans responded to these from the earliest days of the organized and identifiable European community in North America.

For much of early U.S. history, African Americans were not routinely part of the formal political process. They were objects whose status in the community was defined as "other than citizens" by constitutional provision. Milton Morris, *The Politics of Black America* (1975), describes these constitutional provisions denying African Americans equal participation in a political community whose very basis was equality. Leon Higginbotham, *In the Matter of Color, Race and the Legal Process* (1980), has also done a critical political history of this early period; and Winthrop Jordan, *White over Black: American Attitudes toward the Negro, 1550–1812* (1977), shows the attitudes and ideas that undergirded these policies.

The outsider status systematically assigned to African Americans bred in them a persistent quest for human rights. This was given efficacy by the ideology of democracy, whose ideals of equality, life, liberty, and the pursuit of happiness animated blacks as much as others. Moreover, the ideals were seen as especially appropriate for the situation of African Americans, whose status was clearly limited by enslavement, the Constitution, and publicly sanctioned discrimination. Witness some of the earliest documentable political acts and tracts by indigenous political spokespersons lobbying legislatures. See Lamont Thomas, *Rise to Be a People: A Biography of Paul Cuffe* (1986), and David Walker, *David Walker's Appeal* (1829). These early black political spokespersons were consumed by a desire for formal structures and processes through which they could effectuate equal status, matching the philosophy and values associated with U.S. citizenship and participation.

We know very little about organized political activity in the contemporary sense during the slave period. What we know we have learned largely from political historians; disciplinary political scientists rarely do this work. We do know that as Vincent Harding, *There Is a River: The Black Struggle for Freedom in America* (1983), has said, "subterranean acts of individual defiance, resistance, creative rebellion, sabotage, and flight" occurred. These essentially political acts were used by the enslaved to enhance their role and status as human beings and citizens. Margaret Walker, *Jubilee* (1966), provides a striking fictional rendering of these acts. Then there were organized political revolts, many like those of Nat Turner and Gabriel Prosser in Virginia, and Denmark Vesey in South Carolina documented in Herbert Aptheker, *American Negro Slave Revolts* (1943).

One of the most sustained and successful subterranean but highly organized system for securing political freedom was the Underground Railroad. Harriett Tubman spirited many blacks from South to North in this system. See Wilbur Siebert, *The Underground Railroad from Slavery to Freedom* (1968).

At the same time that violent and subterranean acts were occurring, a parallel campaign of petitioning and lobbying was occurring among free blacks, often within the context of traditional political structures. There were those like Paul Cuffe and Richard Allen, *inter alia*. Documentary evidence is available in several collections. See Leslie Fishel, Jr., and Benjamin Quarles, eds., *The Black American: A Brief Documentary History* (1967); and John Bracey et al., eds., *Black Nationalism in America* (1970).

Moreover, an abolitionist campaign was mounting. Whites opposed to enslavement and some of the formerly enslaved were beginning an essentially protest campaign against the institution of slavery. William Lloyd Garrison, who published *The Liberator* newspaper, was as prominent as any white in this group. Several studies detail his activities and that of other abolitionists. See Eileen Kraditor, *Means and Ends in American Abolitionism: Garrison and His Critics on Strategy and Tactics, 1834–1850* (1969) also see Benjamin Quarles, *The Black Abolitionists* (1969), who details the work of blacks.

The emerging political community among blacks also included runaway slaves who presented descriptions of their experiences in slavery, offered orations, and created propaganda outlets in the interest of freeing others. Many of them became public speakers in bureaus making oration significant in the development in the African American community. The most prominent of these were Frederick Douglass, Harriet Tubman, and Sojourner Truth. Frederick Douglass among this group issued several major documents and analyses of his own describing his experiences during enslavement, his view of abolition, and a vision for political activity by African Americans. See Philip Foner, ed., *The Life and Writings of Frederick Douglass*, four volumes (1950); and Benjamin Quarles, *Frederick Douglass* (1968). Meanwhile, Dorothy Sterling, *Freedom Train: The Story of Harriet Tubman* (1954), remains the standard work of biography on Tubman's life. Nell Painter, *Sojourner Truth: Life, a Symbol* (1996) provides a recent critical biography of the period's other central black woman.

Perhaps the most important characterization that can be made of this period of politics in the context of enslavement is what Vincent Harding has called the constancy of resistance by a people who were marginal in the truest sense of the word and were deemed outsiders to the routine American political process. The activities of a political nature during this time were therefore largely carried on internal to the black community and beyond the reaches of formal U.S. government structures. The aims, however, were always to have an impact upon those structures and to seek to acquire a formal and routine means of participation therein. Many of the spokespersons in the period made quite radical statements, yet the beliefs and models they offered were entirely in the context of the democratic ideology. This certainly was largely also indicative of the abolition campaign.

POLITICS IN THE CONTEXT OF SECTIONAL DIVISION: PRE–CIVIL WAR AND BEYOND

The emergence of a concept of national community also crystallized in the period of around 1800–1840, though the antecedents appeared much earlier. During this time many blacks began to offer programs designed for the furtherance of African American social and political life as an independent community, albeit not always antithetical to the American political system or its democratic foundations. David Walker's *Appeal* was probably the most prominent of these exhortations. Others were Martin R. Delaney's *Blake* (1859) and Henry Highland Garnet's "An Address to the Slaves of the United States" (1843).

Other leaders articulated the concept of nationalism in back-to-Africa movements. Mary Frances Berry and John W. Blassingame's *Long Memory: The Black Experience in America* (1982) gave an analysis of the complexity of the views of African Americans, many of whom were opposed to the notion. However, some prominent spokespeople—Paul Cuffe and James Forten among them—supported colonization. Whites and African Americans were thinking about Africa as a place for the relocation of the enslaved population, though often for quite different reasons. Whites largely saw colonization as a means of ridding the American Republic of the terrible presence, whereas African Americans were more concerned about Africa as a means of attaining independence, being imbued with the continent as homeland symbol. Philip Staudenraus's *African Colonization Movement, 1816–1865* (1961) and Floyd John Miller's *Search for a Black Nationality: Black Colonization and Emigration, 1787–1863* (1975) represent important studies of this phenomenon. Tom Shick's *Behold the Promised Land* (1980) studies the experiences of those blacks who migrated to Liberia.

Farther along in the history of African Americans as the contention over enslavement began to draw a wedge between the North and South there emerged other significant anti-slavery campaigns. In 1859 John Brown, a white man, organized a military raid against slavery at Harper's Ferry. The best-known study of Brown is W. E. B. Du Bois, *John Brown* (1962). Okon Uya's *From Slavery to Public Service: Robert Smalls, 1839–1915* (1971) examines Robert Smalls's commandeering of slave ships off the coast of South Carolina during the Civil War.

Hanes Walton is the authority on independent black political activity leading up to the Civil War and beyond. His *Negro in Third Party Politics* (1969) is especially important. Other useful depictions of this period—which highlight the Negro convention movement—are found in such general history texts as John Hope Franklin and Alfred A. Moss, Jr., *From Slavery to Freedom* (1994); Lerone Bennett, *Before the Mayflower* (1984); and August Meier and Elliott Rudwick, *From Plantation to Ghetto* (1966).

At the eve of the Civil War, African American leaders became more engaged by presidential politics. The emergence of the Republican Party as the anti-slave party and the prominence of Abraham Lincoln as the party's standard bearer quickly attracted the attention of African Americans. By the election of 1860, African Americans conveyed a clear preference for the Republican Party. William Douglas's *Mr. Lincoln and the Negroes: The Long Road to Equality* (1963); Benjamin Quarles's *Lincoln and the Negro* (1962); and Hanes Walton's *Black Politics* (1972) provide important examinations of black political inclinations during this period. Moreover, Benjamin Quarles in *The Negro in the Civil War* (1953) provides even more details about the activities of blacks during this crucial period in American history.

RECONSTRUCTION

The war was fought, the South vanquished, and a reconstruction program was put into place by Abraham Lincoln. Among the sources that examine the nuances of newfound black freedom are John Hope Franklin, *The Emancipation Proclamation* (1963); La Wanda Cox, *Lincoln and Black Freedom: A Study in Presidential Leadership* (1981); and George Bentley, *A History of the Freedmen's Bureau* (1955).

This ushered in the first great period of legal formal participation by African Americans in the American political structure. Throughout the South, as the shackles of enslavement were thrown off, blacks began to run for electoral office and to assume positions within the organized political structure. The most comprehensive study of the period is W.E.B. Du Bois's *Black Reconstruction* (1969). Another work that described this process in state-by-state detail is Lerone Bennett's *Black Power U.S.A.: The Human Side of Reconstruction, 1867–1877* (1967). Perhaps the best-known analysis of the period by a participant at the time is John R. Lynch, *The Facts of Reconstruction* (1913, reissued with a very long introduction and new editing by William Harris in 1970).

There are many state studies describing the reconstruction process: Thomas Holt, *Black over White: Negro Political Leadership in South Carolina during Reconstruction* (1979); Joe Richardson, *The Negro and Reconstruction of Florida* (1965); and John W. Blassingame, *Black New Orleans, 1860–1880* (1973), among others. There are also collections of the writings and speeches of blacks elected to the U.S. Congress. Annjeannette McFarlin's *Black Congressional Reconstruction Orators and Their Orations, 1869–1879* (1976) and Howard N. Rabinowitz's edited volume *Southern Black Leaders of the Reconstruction Era* (1982) are examples of such collections. Moreover, excellent contemporary analyses may be found in the general surveys of African American politics, most notably in those by Hanes Walton, Lucius Barker, and Jesse McCorry, Jr.

The war and the reconstruction apparatus also laid the groundwork for national discussion of African Americans as members of the political community. The U.S. Congress began to have great impact on both the discussion and faith of these new electors during Reconstruction. Radicals were in the ascendancy in the Congress and argued strenuously for the full participation of African Americans. The Thirteenth, Fourteenth, and Fifteenth Amendments gave blacks the right to vote, citizenship, and protection of the Constitution in the exercise of these political rights. John Hope Franklin described the political activities during the period in his *Reconstruction after the Civil War* (1961), and Bernard Schwartz collected a substantial amount of material on the most complex and controversial of the amendments passed during the period in *The Fourteenth Amendment* (1970). William Gillette's *Right to Vote: Politics and the Passage of the Fifteenth Amendment* (1965) is a study of voting rights.

THE JIM CROW ERA

At the end of the Reconstruction years, federal troops were withdrawn from the South and the Democratic Party again dominated the region's political scene. The 1896 *Plessy v. Ferguson* decision created the "separate but equal" principle, which legally required the separation of blacks and whites in all aspects of American life. "Jim Crow" would thereafter be used as a nickname for racial segregation. During the era of Jim Crow, states implemented restrictions to legally segregate blacks and whites and to create an environment of white supremacy. C. Vann Woodward's *Origins of the New South, 1877–1913* (1951) and the four editions of *The Strange Career of Jim Crow* (1955, 1966, 1974, 1976) are two classic texts that examine the political and social dimensions of the Jim Crow period.

Many other scholars have examined racial segregation in the South. These include Peter A. Carmichael, in *The South and Segregation* (1965); David R. Goldfield, in *Black, White and Southern: Race Relations and Southern Culture, 1940s to the Present* (1990); and James W. Vander Zanden, in *Race Relations in Transition: The Segregation Crisis in the South* (1965). Scholars examined white supremacist ideologies in texts such as Idus A. Newby's *Jim Crow's Defense: Anti-Negro Thought in America, 1900–1930* (1965) and *The Development of Segregationist Thought* (1968), Claude H. Nolen's *Negro's Image in the South: The Anatomy of White Supremacy* (1967), and Forrest G. Wood's *Black Scare: The Racist Response to Emancipation and Reconstruction* (1968).

Several racist groups formed during the Jim Crow era to disfranchise and intimidate blacks. The Ku Klux Klan (KKK) has probably been the most notorious of these groups. There are a number of scholarly studies of this organization, including David M. Chalmer's *Hooded Americanism: The First Century of the KKK, 1865–1965* (1965), Kenneth T. Jackson's *KKK in the City, 1915–1930* (1967), and Allen N. Trelease's *White Terror: The KKK Conspiracy and Southern Reconstruction* (1979). William H. Fisher's *Invisible Empire: A Bibliography of the KKK, 1865–1965* (1980) and Lenwood G. Davis's *KKK: A Bibliography* (1984) provide summaries of articles and texts on the Klan.

According to Ida B. Wells-Barnett in *On Lynchings: Southern Horrors, a Red Record, Mob Rule in New Orleans* (1892, 1895, 1900), whites used lynchings as the "new Negro crime" to terrorize blacks during the era of Jim Crow. James H. Chadbourn's *Lynching and the Law* (1933), James E. Cutler's *Lynch Law: An Investigation into the History of Lynching in the U.S.* (1905), and Arthur F. Raper's *Tragedy of Lynching* (1933) are historical accounts of lynchings in the United States. Robert L. Zangrando in "The NAACP and a Federal Anti-lynching Bill, 1930–1940" (1965) and *The NAACP Crusade against Lynching, 1909–1950* (1980) examined the efforts of the National Association for the Advancement of Colored People's (NAACP) to influence the passage of a federal anti-lynching law.

THE GREAT MIGRATION

From the turn of the century to the 1940s, large numbers of black southerners moved to large cities in the North. While civil rights and other empowerment organizations fought discrimination, disfranchisement, and violence, other groups aided black migrants as they made the transition to an urban environment. Brailsford R. Brazeal in *The Brotherhood of Sleeping Car Porters: Its Origin and Development* (1946) discussed the formation of the Brotherhood, which served mostly as a labor union for black porters who were excluded from white unions. Guichard Parris in *Blacks in the City: A History of the National*

Urban League (1971), Arvarh E. Strickland in *History of the Chicago Urban League* (1966), and Nancy J. Weiss in *The National Urban League, 1910–1945* (1974) analyzed the League, which helped black migrants find employment and housing.

The NAACP continues to be one of the nation's most prominent civil rights organizations. It was founded during the migration years, and texts such as Langston Hughes's *Fight for Freedom: The Story of the NAACP* (1962), Mary O. White's *How the NAACP Began* (1914), and Barbara J. Ross's *J. E. Springarn and the Rise of the NAACP, 1911–1939* (1972) have discussed its origin and development. Minnie Finch in *The NAACP: Its Fight for Justice* (1981) and Mary O. White in *The Walls Came Tumbling Down* (1969) examined the NAACP's legal battles. Clement E. Vose in *Caucasians Only: The Supreme Court, the NAACP and the Restrictive Covenant Cases* (1959) discussed the organization's efforts against racial discrimination in housing, and Mark V. Tushnet in *The NAACP's Legal Strategy against Segregated Education, 1925–1950* (1987) examined the legal strategies that led to landmark cases in the field of education.

Black political and economic development in the North was hindered by housing, job, and wage discrimination. Ralph J. Bunche in "The Negro in the Political Life of the U.S." (1941) and *The Political Status of the Negro in the Age of F.D.R.* (1973) analyzed black political development during the Franklin D. Roosevelt administrations. In 1941, A. Philip Randolph, founder of the Brotherhood of Sleeping Car Porters, threatened a mass march on Washington to address job discrimination in the defense industries. The march never took place because President Roosevelt issued an executive order prohibiting employment discrimination in the defense industries and established the Fair Employment Practice Committee (F.E.P.C.). Herbert Garfinkel in *When Negroes March: The March on Washington Movement in the Organizational Politics for F.E.P.C.* (1950) and Louis Ruchames in *Race, Jobs and Politics: The Story of the F.E.P.C.* (1953) discussed the events that led to the formation of the F.E.P.C.

In some cities, political machines hampered the elections and success of black politicians and predominantly black regimes during the migration years. Hanes Walton in *Black Politics: A Theoretical and Structural Analysis* (1972) pointed out that blacks were usually "of," not "in," political machines. Machine bosses often allowed black community leaders to mobilize black voters in support of the machine's candidates, but they were not appointed to high-level posts within the organization. Classic studies that examine the relationship between political machines and black voters include Harold F. Gosnell's *Machine Politics: Chicago Style* (1937), David M. Tucker's *Memphis since Crump: Bossism, Blacks and Civic Reformers, 1948–1968* (1980), Milton Rakove's *Don't Make No Waves, Don't Back No Losers* (1975), William L. Riordan's *Plunkitt of Tammany Hall* (1905, 1963), and James Q. Wilson's *Negro Politics: The Search for Leadership* (1960, 1965). Despite the machine's dominance, black congressmen Oscar DePriest and William Dawson of Illinois and Adam Clayton Powell of

New York were elected during the migration years. In 1960, James Q. Wilson contrasted the styles of congressmen Adam Clayton Powell and William Dawson in "Two Negro Politicians: An Interpretation" (1960).

In some cities, machine rule continues. The most significant studies on contemporary machine politics in these cities include William J. Grimshaw's *Bitter Fruit: Black Politics and the Chicago Machine, 1931–1991* (1992), Michael B. Preston's "Black Politics in the Post-Daley Era" (1982), and Raymond E. Wolfinger's "Why Machines Have Not Withered Away and Other Revisionist Thoughts" (1972).

CIVIL RIGHTS INSURGENCY

In the post–World War II era, scholars have examined the role of the presidency, U.S. Supreme Court, and Congress, or the "politics of civil rights." President Harry S. Truman and the Democratic Party emphasized a pro–civil rights platform in the 1948 elections, but they did not pursue an active agenda after Truman's election. According to Robert Frederick Burk in *The Eisenhower Administration and Black Civil Rights* (1984), Dwight D. Eisenhower believed in gradualism on civil rights issues. In addition, Pat Watters and Reese Cleghorn in *Climbing Jacob's Ladder: The Arrival of Negroes in Southern Politics* (1967), Carl M. Bauer in *JFK and the Second Reconstruction* (1971), and Harry Golden in *Mr. Kennedy and the Negroes* (1964) pointed out that John F. Kennedy's civil rights record was not as impressive as it could have been. Hugh Davis Graham in *Civil Rights and the Presidency: Race and Gender in American Politics, 1960–1972* (1992), James Sundquist in *Politics and Policy: The Eisenhower, Kennedy and Johnson Years* (1968), and Allen Wolk in *The Presidency and Black Civil Rights: Eisenhower to Nixon* (1971) provided a general history and comparison of each president's civil rights record.

The political developments of the Jim Crow and Great Migration years resulted in the successful lawsuits and protests that occurred during the mid–1950s and 1960s. Bernard Sternsher's edited text *The Negro in Depression and War: Prelude to Revolution, 1930–1945* (1969) and Raymond Wolters's *Negroes and the Great Depression: The Problem of Economic Recovery* (1970) discussed the frustrations blacks faced during these years. Henry Hampton, Steve Fayer, and Sarah Flynn's *Voices of Freedom: An Oral History of the Civil Rights Movement from the 1950s through the 1980s* (1990), Juan Williams's *Eyes on the Prize: America's Civil Right's Years, 1954–1965* (1987), Aldon Morris's *Origins of the Civil Rights Movement* (1984), and David J. Garrow's edited text *We Shall Overcome: The Civil Rights Movement in the U.S. in the 1950s and 1960s* (1989) described the protests and mobilization strategies during the height of the movement. Also, Manning Marable's *Race, Reform, and Rebellion: The Second Reconstruction in Black America, 1945–1982* (1984) detailed activities during the movement that has been called the "second Reconstruction." Arthur I. Waskow in *From Race Riots to Sit-Ins, 1919 and the 1960s: A Study in the*

Connections between Conflict and Violence (1966) compared the 1919 riots to the sit-in movement of the 1960s.

The U.S. Supreme Court under Chief Justice Earl Warren played a significant role during the civil rights movement. Alexander Bickel, *Politics and the Warren Court* (1965) and Robert J. Harris, *The Quest for Equality: The Constitution, Congress and the Supreme Court* (1960) examined reactions to many of the Supreme Court's civil rights decisions. *Brown v. Board of Education of Topeka, Kansas* was one of the Warren Court's best-known cases. Information on *Brown I* (1954) and *Brown II* (1955) can be found in Richard Kluger's *Simple Justice: The History of Brown v. Board of Education and Black America's Struggle for Equality* (1976). Scholars have examined the progress or lack thereof after the 1954 *Brown* decision in Albert P. Blaustein and Clarence Ferguson, Jr.'s *Desegregation and the Law: The Meaning and Effect of the School Segregation Cases* (1962), Michael V. Namorato's *Have We Overcome?: Race Relations since Brown* (1979), Raymond W. Mack's *Our Children's Burden: Studies of Desegregation in Nine American Communities* (1968), and Benjamin Muse's *Ten Years of Prelude: The Story of Integration since the Supreme Court's 1954 Decision* (1964).

Before Congress ratified the Voting Rights Act of 1965, African Americans could not vote in the majority of southern states because of gerrymanders, literacy tests, poll taxes, and white primaries. States created districts in a way to exclude black voters, as Robert J. Norrell points out in *Reaping the Whirlwind: The Civil Rights Movement in Tuskegee* (1985). The U.S. Supreme Court prohibited racial gerrymandering in the 1948 case *Gomillion v. Lightfoot*. Frederic D. Ogden in *The Poll Tax in the South* (1958) provides a comprehensive examination of the poll tax. The winners of white primaries were almost assured of winning subsequent general elections in the South. Because black citizens could not vote in primary elections, they had little say over who won office. In *The Rise and Fall of the White Primary in Texas* (1979), Darlene Clark Hine examined the end of the white primary in the 1944 U.S. Supreme Court case *Smith v. Allwright*.

As a result of the *Baker v. Carr, Reynolds v. Sims*, and *Wesberry v. Sanders* decisions, states had to reapportion congressional and legislative districts according to the principle of "one person, one vote." In later decades, reappointment led to increased black representation. Gordon Baker in *The Reapportionment Revolution: Representation, Political Power and the Supreme Court* (1966), Harlan Hahn in *Urban-Rural Conflict: The Politics of Change* (1971), and Malcolm Jewell, ed., in *The Politics of Reapportionment* (1962) examined the factors that led to the 1962 case. Lani Guinier in *The Tyranny of the Majority* (1994), Timothy O'Rourke in *The Impact of Reapportionment* (1980), and E. E. Schattsneider in "Urbanization and Reapportionment" (1962) analyzed the overall impact of reapportionment in urban areas.

After the Voting Rights Act of 1965, black citizens gained the right to vote but desired the right to elect representation. Steven F. Lawson's *Black Ballots:*

Voting Rights in the South, 1944–1969 (1976) and *Running for Freedom: Black Politics and Civil Rights since 1941* (1991) and Frank R. Parker's *Black Votes Count* (1990) analyzed suffrage discrimination both before and after passage of the Act. Also, David Garrow's *Protest at Selma: Martin Luther King and the Voting Rights Act of 1965* (1978) examined the marches in Selma, Alabama, and others that led to its enactment. To measure the impact of the Voting Rights Act on black political participation, see Chandler Davidson and Bernard Grofman, eds., *Quiet Revolution in the South: The Impact of the Voting Rights Act, 1965–1990* (1994), and Harold W. Stanley, *Voter Mobilization and the Politics of Race: The South and Universal Suffrage, 1952–1984* (1987).

Despite the act's implementation, Derrick Bell in *Race, Racism and the Law* (1973) pointed out that states created other restrictions such as at-large elections, majority vote requirements, and racial gerrymanders that diluted the black vote and prevented the election of black officials. Chandler Davidson, ed., and others in *Minority Vote Dilution* (1984) and Bernard Grofman, Lisa Handley, and Richard G. Niemi in *Minority Representation and the Quest for Voting Equality* (1992) also discuss these and other impediments.

Because of the belief that when attempting to vote and run for office African Americans faced more obstacles in the South than in the North many studies have analyzed black political campaigns in this region. V. O. Key's *Southern Politics in State and Nation* (1949) remains one of the most significant studies of southern politics to date. Other important writings on black politics in the South include: Jack Bass and Walter DeVries's *Transformation of Southern Politics: Social Change and Political Consequence since 1945* (1995); Charles V. Hamilton's *Minority Politics in Black Belt Alabama* (1960); Lawrence J. Hanks's *Struggle for Black Political Empowerment in Three Georgia Countries* (1987); Harry Holloway's *Politics of the Southern Negro: From Exclusion to Big City Organization* (1969); Laurence Moreland, Robert P. Steed, and Tod A. Baker's *Blacks in Southern Politics* (1987); and Minion K. C. Morrison's *Black Political Mobilization* (1987).

POST–CIVIL RIGHTS ELECTORAL POLITICS

During the latter half of the 1960s, a shift occurred from nonviolent, direct action civil rights protests to the search for black power. August Meier's edited text *Black Protest Thought in the 20th Century* (1971) is a general examination of black protest ideologies. Eldridge Cleaver in *Soul on Ice* (1968), Stokely Carmichael in *Stokely Speaks* (1971), Benjamin Muse in *The American Negro Revolution: From Nonviolence to Black Power, 1963–1967* (1968), Bayard Rustin in "From Protest to Politics: The Future of the Civil Rights Movement" (1965), and Bobby Seale in *Seize the Time: The Story of the Black Panther Party and Huey P. Newton* (1970) discussed the fact that many communities focused on electing black representation during the late 1960s and early 1970s as well as on protests as a way to gain black power.

According to Dr. Martin Luther King, Jr., in *Where Do We Go from Here: Chaos or Community* (1967), race riots occurred in cities during the mid- and late 1960s after black citizens grew impatient with nonviolent protests. James Button's *Black Violence: Political Impact of the 1960s Riots* (1978), Allen D. Grimshaw's *Racial Violence in the U.S.* (1969), and Joe R. Feagin and Harlan Hahn's *Ghetto Revolts* (1973) examined the causes of racial tension and whether these riots meant that blacks would thereafter use violence as a way to protest injustices.

In *Protest Is Not Enough* (1984), Rufus Browning, Dale Rogers Marshall, and David H. Tabb also found that African Americans and other minority groups placed less emphasis on protest and more on electoral politics during the late 1960s and early 1970s. Rod Bush examined the "from protest to politics" theme in four cities in *The New Black Vote: Politics and Power in Four American Cities* (1984). Primarily during the first (post–Civil War) and second (mid-1950s to mid-1960s) Reconstruction eras, citizens used direct action protests as a way to both gain and protect their civil and suffrage rights. After many of the barriers were removed, they focused on electoral politics and black power during the late 1960s and early 1970s. Adolph Reed Jr.'s edited text *Race, Politics and Culture: Critical Essays on the Radicals of the 1960s* (1986) examined the search for black political power in the 1960s.

During the era of the "new black politics," black citizens assumed that black politicians would be more concerned about their community's interests. In 1967, Carl Stokes of Cleveland and Richard Hatcher of Gary became the first black mayors of major American cities. William E. Nelson and Philip J. Meranto in *Electing Black Mayors* (1977) analyzed their victories and the implications for black mayoral candidates in other cities. Jeffrey K. Hadden, Louis Massoti, and Victor Thiesson's "Making of Negro Mayors," 1967 (1968) was one of the first articles on the elections of black mayors. Articles such as Charles S. Bullock III's "Racial Crossover Voting and the Election of Black Officials" (1984), Richard Murray and Arnold Vedlitz's "Racial Voting Patterns in the South: An Analysis of Mayoral Elections from 1960 to 1977 in Five Cities" (1978), and Thomas F. Pettigrew's "Black Mayoralty Campaigns" (1976) found that the first black mayors and other officeholders were elected in either largely or predominantly black cities with racially polarized electorates who usually voted along racial lines and seldom cast crossover votes.

According to Doug McAdams in *Political Process and the Development of Black Insurgency* (1982), most of the candidates used insurgency as their dominant strategy. In *Dilemmas of Black Politics: Issues of Leadership and Strategy* (1993), Georgia Persons defined this term as "challenges to the prevailing political order, embrace of a social reform agenda and utilization of a pattern of racial appeals to mobilize a primary support groups of Black voters." Black mayoral contenders focused heavily on neighborhood mobilization while seeking as many white votes as possible. As a result, they usually received the majority of black votes and a small percentage of white crossover support (20 percent or less) in racially polarized elections. The majority of black candidates in predominantly black cities continue to use the insurgent strategy.

In cities with large Asian and Latino populations, black candidates formed biracial coalitions with other minorities and with progressive white voters. Raphael J. Sonenshein's *Politics in Black and White: Race and Power in Los Angeles* (1993) used Los Angeles as a case study and is one of the most comprehensive texts on biracial coalitions. In this study, Sonenshein examined whether these coalitions ended after Mayor Tom Bradley's retirement and the subsequent defeat of Asian American mayoral candidate Michael Woo in 1993.

Stokely Carmichael and Charles V. Hamilton in *Black Power: The Politics of Liberation in America* (1967) and Peter K. Eisinger in *Patterns of Interracial Politics: Conflict and Cooperation in the City* (1976) gave the elements for successful biracial coalition formation. Parties must have similar goals and interests, be willing to cooperate in order to achieve them, believe that they can benefit from the coalition, and have their own independent power base. However, Paula D. McClain and Joseph Stewart pointed out in *Can We All Get Along?: Racial and Ethnic Minorities in American Politics* (1995) that biracial coalitions are usually short lived. Other studies of biracial coalitions include Bryan O. Jackson and Michael B. Preston's *Ethnic and Racial Politics in California* (1991), Paula D. McClain and Albert Karnig's "Black and Hispanic Socioeconomic and Political Competition" (1990), and Wilbur C. Rich's *Politics of Minority Coalitions: Race, Ethnicity, and Shared Uncertainties* (1996).

In subsequent years, some black candidates used the political strategy of deracialization to win elections in predominantly white cities. Charles V. Hamilton defined a deracialized campaign as one that placed little emphasis on racial issues in favor of those issues of concern to all voters. According to John M. McCormick and Charles E. Jones in "The Conceptualization of Deracialization" (1993) and Huey L. Perry, ed., in *Race, Politics, and Governance in the United States* (1996), deracialization strategy has three major components: projecting a "nonthreatening" image, avoiding overt racial appeals when mobilizing the electorate, and ignoring racial issues. Huey L. Perry's edited text, *Race, Politics and Governance in the United States* (1996), includes three chapters on deracialization in statewide politics: Alvin J. Schexnider's "Analyzing the Wilder Administration through the Construct of Deracialization Politics," Charles L. Prysby's "1990 U.S. Senate Election in North Carolina," and Roger K. Oden's "Election of Carol Moseley-Braun in the U.S. Senate Race in Illinois."

POSTMODERN RACIAL POLITICS

As a result of successful campaign strategies and biracial coalitions, the numbers of black candidates increased dramatically after the 1960s. In the early 1970s, the Joint Center for Political Studies was founded to conduct research and provide information on the political behavior of black elected officials. In addition to publishing the *National Roster of Black Elected Officials* annually, other Center publications have included *Black Crime: A Police View* (1977), *Black State Legislators: A Survey and Analysis of Black Leadership in State Capitals* (1992), *Municipal Budgeting: A Primer for Elected Officials* (1977), *New Federalism and Community Development: A Preliminary Evaluation of the Housing and Community Development Act of 1974* (1974), *Tom Bradley's Campaigns for Governor: The Dilemmas of Race and Political Strategies* (1988), and *Urban Governance and Minorities* (1975). Other studies such as James S. Jackson and Patricia Gurin's *National Survey of Black Americans, 1979–1990* (1987), Jackson, Gurin and Shirley Hatchett's *1984 National Black Election Study* (1989) and Robert C. Smith and Richard Seltzer's *Race, Class and Culture: A Study in Afro-American Mass Opinion* (1992) analyzed the political beliefs and electoral behavior of the black electorate.

During the era of postmodern racial politics, black communities continued to elect representation, but they also sought political incorporation. Browning, Marshall, and Tabb in the first and second editions of *Racial Politics in American Cities* (1990, 1997) defined this term as "an equal or leading role in a dominant coalition that is strongly committed to minority interests." Adolph Reed's essay "The Black Urban Regime: Structural Origins and Constraints" (1988) and a number of other studies have found that black citizens have not always benefited from majority black governing coalitions. In order to gain political incorporation, black communities are now concentrating on "empowerment activism." James B. Jennings in *The Politics of Black Empowerment: The Transformation of Black Activism in Urban America* (1993) defined it as a new kind of black political activism in which black voters and politicians sought economic and political power rather than simply trying to win offices.

Clarence Stone in *Regime Politics: Governing Atlanta, 1946–1988* (1989) defined an urban regime as "the informal arrangements that surround and complement the formal workings of governmental authority." Paul Friesema in "Black Control of Central Cities: The Hollow Prize" (1969) found that black urban regimes have inherited a "hollow prize" in many predominantly black cities. Although most of the elected officials are African American, cities suffer from white flight, decreased governmental aid, declining tax bases, and high crime, poverty, and unemployment rates.

Mack H. Jones in "Black Mayoral Leadership in Atlanta: A Comment" (1990) and Claude W. Barnes, Jr., in "Black Mecca Reconsidered: An Analysis of Atlanta's Post–Civil Rights Political Economy" (1994) found that despite Atlanta's reputation as a black mecca and international hub for Fortune 500 companies and cultural attractions, black political management of its urban regime has been a "hollow prize." Peter K. Eisinger in *The Politics of Displacement: Racial and Ethnic Transition in Three American Cities* (1980) found that conditions worsened rather than improved for the underclass in many cities with majority black regimes. Wilbur C. Rich's text *Coleman Young and Detroit Politics* (1989) detailed former mayor Coleman Young's administrations and found that conditions for the black underclass worsened in that city as well. However,

Huey L. Perry's essay "The Evolution and Impact of Biracial Coalitions and Black Mayors in Birmingham and New Orleans" in Browning, Marshall, and Tabb's *Racial Politics in American Cities* (1990) found that the black middle-class benefited from black governance in Birmingham and New Orleans in terms of appointments and employment opportunities.

Despite increased black representation, the role of blacks in Congress and state legislatures is a topic that has not received adequate study. Samuel D. Smith in *The Negro in Congress* (1940) represented the classic study of black congressmen before the formation of the Congressional Black Caucus (CBC) in the late 1960s. Important studies relating to the CBC include David Bositis's *Congressional Black Caucus in the 103rd Congress* (1994), Maurine Christopher's *America's Black Congressmen* (1971), Bruce Ragsdale and Joel Treese's *Black Americans in Congress* (1990), and Carol Swain's *Black Faces, Black Interests: The Representation of African Americans in Congress* (1993), among others. Former or current members of Congress have also been the subject of biographies that detailed their political careers, such as William L. Clay's *Just Permanent Interests: Black Americans in Congress, 1870–1991* (1992), Gray Franks's *Searching for the Promised Land: An African American's Optimistic Odyssey* (1996), Charles V. Hamilton's *Adam Clayton Powell, Jr.: The Political Biography of an American Dilemma* (1991), Wil Haygood's *King of the Cats: The Life and Times of Adam Clayton Powell Jr.* (1993), and Kweisi Mfume's *No Free Ride: From the Mean Streets to the Mainstream* (1996).

Articles and texts on blacks in state legislatures have analyzed the agendas of black state legislative caucuses and obstacles to their success. They include David M. Bositis's *Black State Legislators: A Survey and Analysis of Black Leadership in State Capitals* (1992), Albert J. Nelson's *Emerging Influentials in State Legislatures: Women, Blacks, and Hispanics* (1991), and Hanes Walton, Jr.'s *Invisible Politics: Black Political Behavior* (1985).

Since Jesse Jackson's 1984 and 1988 presidential campaigns, the role of black voters in presidential elections has been an increased topic of interest. Ronald W. Walters's *Black Presidential Politics in America: A Strategic Approach* (1988) have examined black presidential campaign participation in general. See also Michael Dawson, *Behind the Mule: Race and Class in African American Politics* (1994). In terms of the Jackson campaigns, Katherine L. Tate in *From Protest to Politics: The New Black Voters in American Elections* (1993) and Mfanya Donald Tryman's "Jesse Jackson's Campaigns for the Presidency: A Comparison for the 1984 and 1988 Democratic Primaries" in Perry's *Race, Politics and Governance in the U.S.* (1995) found that they led to an increase in black voter turnout. Lucius Barker wrote two books on the 1984 campaign strategy: *Our Time Has Come* (1989) and, with Ronald W. Walters *Jesse Jackson's 1984 Presidential Campaign* (1989). Lorenzo Morris's edited text *The Social and Political Implications of the 1984 Jesse Jackson Presidential Campaign* (1990) analyzed the social and political implications of the 1984 campaign. Also see Adolph Reed, Jr.'s *The Jesse Jackson Phenomenon: The Crisis of Purpose in Afro-American Politics* (1986).

After the Jackson presidential campaigns, an increased number of black citizens believed that they should abandon the Democratic and Republican Parties to focus on an independent party in order to win elective office. Hanes Walton, Jr.'s texts *Black Political Parties* (1972) and *The Negro in Third Party Politics* (1969) provided historical perspective to this phenomenon. William Pleasant analyzed the political activism of Minister Louis Farrakhan, Dr. Lenora B. Fulani, and Rev. Al Sharpton in *Independent Black Leadership in America* (1990). Dr. Fulani, a 1988 and 1992 independent presidential candidate, also discussed this topic in her autobiography, *The Making of a Fringe Candidate, 1992* (1992).

The experiences of black women in politics has been the focus of more studies in recent years. Autobiographies and biographies have examined the role of black women during the civil rights and black power movements such as Daisy Bates's *Long Shadow of Little Rock* (1962), Elaine Brown's *Taste of Power* (1992), Shirley Chisholm's *Unbought and Unbossed* (1970), Angela Davis's *Angela Davis: An Autobiography* (1974), David J. Garrow's *Montgomery Bus Boycott and the Women Who Started It: The Memoir of Jo Ann Gibson Robinson* (1987), Kay Mills's *This Little Light of Mine: The Life of Fannie Lou Hamer* (1993), Barbara Jordan and Shelby Hearon's *Barbara Jordan: A Self Portrait* (1979), and Anne Moody's *Coming of Age in Mississippi* (1968).

Other essays and texts examined the role of black women in politics generally. These include Jewell L. Prestage's "Political Behavior of American Black Women: An Overview" (1980) and Eddie N. Williams's "Black Women in Politics and Government" (1982). Hanes Walton, Jr.'s edited text *Black Politics and Black Political Behavior: A Linkage Analysis* (1994) includes four chapters on black women's electoral experiences: Saundra C. Ardrey's "Political Behavior of Black Woman: Contextual, Structural, and Psychological Factors," Sheila F. Harmon-Martin's "Black Women in Politics: A Research Note," Hanes Walton and Johnny Campbell's "First Black Female Gubernatorial Candidate in Georgia: State Representative Mildred Glover," and Walton's "Black Female Presidential Candidates: Bass, Mitchell, Chisholm, Wright, Reid, David, and Fulani."

In 1989, Virginia's L. Douglas Wilder became the nation's first elected black governor. The following articles and books have examined the Wilder victory: Matthew Holden, Jr.'s "Rewards of Daring and the Ambiguity of Power: Perspectives on the Wilder Election of 1989" (1990) and Dwayne Yancey's *When Hell Froze Over: The Untold Story of Doug Wilder* (1988).

Since the Wilder victory, other black candidates have unsuccessfully sought statewide political seats. Thus, scholars are beginning to examine the obstacles black candidates face when seeking these offices. Marilyn Davis and Alex Willingham analyzed Andrew Young's unsuccessful gubernatorial bid in Georgia in "Andrew Young and the Georgia State Elections of 1990" (1993). Thomas F. Pettigrew in *Tom Bradley's Campaigns for Governor: The Dilemmas of Race and Political Strategies* (1988) examined former Los Angeles mayor Tom Bradley's unsuccessful gubernatorial bids in California. Zaphon Wilson looked at the issue of race in the 1990 North Carolina U.S. Senate race in "Gantt versus Helms: Deracialization Confronts Southern Traditionalism" (1993).

This chapter has provided an overview of the major themes and works on the African American political experience. It can clearly be seen that initially, blacks were totally excluded from the formal political process. In later years, they faced discriminatory measures that disfranchised them and inhibited their ability to elect representation. Eventually, black citizens became important formal political actors electing officials for their identifiable communities and/or influencing elections in the general electorate. Thus during various periods in their political development, African Americans have gone from being "outsiders" to becoming important actors in the local, state, and national political arena.

BIBLIOGRAPHY

Aptheker, Herbert. *American Negro Slave Revolts.* New York: International Publishers, 1943.

Bailey, Jr., Harry A., ed. *Negro Politics in America.* Columbus, OH.: Charles E. Merrill Publishing Company, 1967.

Baker, Gordon. *The Reapportionment Revolution: Representation, Political Power and the Supreme Court.* New York: Random House, 1966.

Barker, Lucius J. *Our Time Has Come.* Urbana and Chicago, IL: University of Illinois Press, 1989.

Barker, Lucius, and Mack Jones. *African Americans and the American Political System.* 3rd ed. Englewood Cliffs, NJ: Prentice-Hall, 1994.

Barker, Lucius J., and Ronald W. Walters, eds. *Jesse Jackson's 1984 Presidential Campaign.* Urbana and Chicago: University of Illinois Press, 1989.

Barnes, Claude W., Jr. "Black Mecca Reconsidered: An Analysis of Atlanta's Post–Civil Rights Political Economy." In *African Americans and the New Policy Consensus: Retreat of the Liberal State*, edited by Marilyn E. Lashley and Melanie Njeri Jackson. Westport, CT: Greenwood Press, 1994.

Barnett, Marguerite Ross. "A Theoretical Perspective on American Racial Public Policy." In *Public Policy for the Black Community*, edited by Marguerite Ross Barnett and James A. Hefner. New York: Alfred Publishing Company, 1976.

Barnett, Marguerite Ross, and James A. Hefner, eds. *Public Policy for the Black Community.* New York: Alfred Publishing Company, 1976.

Bass, Jack, and Walter De Vries. *The Transformation of Southern Politics: Social Change and Political Consequence since 1945.* Athens; University of Georgia Press, 1995.

Bates, Daisy. *The Long Shadow of Little Rock.* New York: David McKay, 1962.

Bauer, Carl M. *JFK and the Second Reconstruction.* New York: Columbia University Press, 1971.

Beard, Charles. *An Economic Interpretation of the Constitution.* New York: McMillan, 1913.

Bell, Derrick. *Race, Racism and the Law*. Boston: Little, Brown, 1973.

Bennett, Lerone. *Black Power U.S.A.: The Human Side of Reconstruction, 1867–1877*. Chicago: Johnson Publishers, 1967.

———. *Before the Mayflower: A History of Black America*. New York: Penguin, 1984.

Bentley, George. *A History of the Freedmen's Bureau*. Philadelphia: University of Pennsylvania, 1955.

Berman, William Carl. *The Politics of Civil Rights in the Truman Administration*. Columbus: Ohio State University Press, 1970.

Berry, Mary Frances, and John W. Blassingame. *Long Memory: The Black Experience in America*. New York: Oxford, 1982.

Bickel, Alexander. *Politics and the Warren Court*. New York: Harper and Row, 1965.

Black, Earl, and Merle Black. *Politics and Society in the South*. Cambridge: Harvard University Press, 1987.

Blassingame, John W. *Black New Orleans, 1860–1880*. Chicago: University of Chicago Press, 1973.

Blauner, Herbert. "Internal Colonialism and Ghetto Revolt." In *Racial Conflict*, edited by Gary Marx. Boston: Little, Brown, 1971.

Blaustein, Albert P., and Clarence Ferguson, Jr. *Desegregation and the Law: The Meaning and Effect of the School Segregation Cases*. New Brunswick, NJ: Rutgers University Press, 1962.

Bositis, David M. *Black State Legislators: A Survey and Analysis of Black Leadership in State Capitals*. Washington, DC: Joint Center for Political and Economic Studies, 1992.

———. *The Congressional Black Caucus in the 103rd Congress*. Washington, DC: Joint Center for Political and Economic Studies, 1994.

Bracey, John, August Meier, and Elliot Rudwick, eds. *Black Nationalism in America*. Indianapolis: Bobbs-Merrill, 1970.

Brazeal, Brailsford R. *The Brotherhood of Sleeping Car Porters: Its Origin and Development*. New York: Harper and Brothers, 1946.

Brown, Elaine. *A Taste of Power: A Black Woman's Story*. New York: Bantam Books, 1992.

Browning, Rufus, Dale Rogers Marshall, and David H. Tabb. *Protest Is Not Enough*. Berkeley: University of California Press, 1984.

———, ed. *Racial Politics in American Cities*. New York: Longman, 1990, 1997.

Bryce, Herrington. *Black Crime: A Police View*. Washington, DC: Joint Center for Political Studies, 1977.

———. *Urban Governance and Minorities*. Washington, DC: Joint Center for Political Studies, 1975.

Bullock III, Charles S. "Racial Crossover Voting and the Election of Black Officials." *Journal of Politics* 46 (February 1984): 238–51.

Bunche, Ralph J. "The Negro in the Political Life of the U.S." *Journal of Negro Education* 10 (July 1941): 567–84.

———. *The Political Status of the Negro in the Age of F.D.R.* Chicago: University of Chicago Press, 1973.

Burgess, M. Elaine. *Negro Leadership in a Southern City*. Chapel Hill: University of North Carolina Press, 1960.

Burk, Robert Frederick. *The Eisenhower Administration and Black Civil Rights*. Knoxville: University of Tennessee Press, 1984.

Burkhead, Jesse, and Paul Bungewatt. *Municipal Budgeting: A Primer for Elected Officials*. Washington, DC: Joint Center for Political Studies, 1977.

Bush, Rod, ed. *The New Black Vote: Politics and Power in Four American Cities*. San Francisco: Synthesis Publications, 1984.

Button, James. *Black Violence: Political Impact of the 1960s Riots*. Princeton, NJ: Princeton University Press, 1978.

Carmichael, Peter A. *The South and Segregation*. Washington, DC: Public Affairs Press, 1965.

Carmichael, Stokely. *Stokely Speaks*. New York: Vintage, 1971.

Carmichael, Stokely, and Charles V. Hamilton. *Black Power: The Politics of Liberation in America*. New York: Random House, 1967.

Chadbourn, James H. *Lynching and the Law*. Chapel Hill: University of North Carolina Press, 1933.

Chalmers, David M. *Hooded Americanism: The First Century of the KKK, 1865–1965*. Garden City, NY: Doubleday, 1965.

Chisholm, Shirley. *Unbought and Unbossed*. Boston: Houghton Mifflin, 1970.

Christopher, Maurine. *America's Black Congressmen*. New York: Crowell, 1971.

Clay, William L. *Just Permanent Interests: Black Americans in Congress, 1870–1991*. New York: Amistad Press, 1992.

Cleaver, Eldridge. *Soul on Ice*. New York: McGraw-Hill, 1968.

Cox, La Wanda. *Lincoln and Black Freedom: A Study in Presidential Leadership*. Columbia: University of South Carolina Press, 1981.

Cronon, E. David. *Marcus Garvey and the Universal Negro Improvement Association*. 2nd ed. Madison: University of Wisconsin Press, 1981.

Crummell, Alexander. *Africa and America: Addresses and Discourses*. New York: Arno, 1969.

Cutler, James E. *Lynch Law: An Investigation into the History of Lynching in the U.S.*. New York: Longmans, Green and Company, 1905.

Dahl, Robert. *Who Governs*. New Haven, CT: Yale University Press, 1961.

Davidson, Chandler, ed. *Minority Vote Dilution*. Washington, DC: Howard University Press, 1984.

Davidson, Chandler, and Bernard Grofman, eds. *Quiet Revolution in the South: The Impact of the Voting Rights Act, 1965–1990*. Princeton, NJ: Princeton University Press, 1994.

Davis, Angela. *Angela Davis: An Autobiography*. New York: Random House, 1974.

Davis, Lenwood G. *The KKK: A Bibliography*. Westport, CT: Greenwood Press, 1984.

Davis, Marilyn, and Alex Willingham. "Andrew Young and the Georgia State Elections of 1990." In *Dilemmas of Black Politics: Issues of Leadership and Strategy*, edited by Georgia Persons. New York: HarperCollins-College Publishers, 1993, 176–93.

Dawson, Michael C. *Behind the Mule: Race and Class in African American Politics*. Princeton, NJ: Princeton University Press, 1994.

Delaney, Martin R. *Blake: Or the Huts of America*. 1859. Boston: Beacon, 1970.

Douglas, William. *Mr. Lincoln and the Negroes: The Long Road to Equality*. New York, 1963.

Douglass, Frederick. *The Life and Times of Frederick Douglass*. New York: Crowell-Collier, 1967.

Du Bois, William Edward Burghardt. *The Souls of Black Folk*. 1903. Greenwich, CT: Fawcett, 1961.

———. *John Brown*. New York: International, 1962.

———. *Dusk of Dawn: An Essay toward an Autobiography of a Race Concept*. New York: Schocken, 1968.

———. *Black Reconstruction*. Cleveland: Meridian, 1969.

Eisinger, Peter K. "Black Mayors and the Politics of Racial Economic Advancement." In *Readings in Urban Politics: Past, Present and Future*, edited by Harlan Hahn and Charles H. Levine. New York: Longman, 1980, 249–60.

———. *Patterns of Interracial Politics: Conflict and Cooperation in the City*. New York: Academic Press, 1976.

———. *The Politics of Displacement: Racial and Ethnic Transition in Three American Cities*. New York: Academic Press, 1980.

Feagin, Joe R., and Harlan Hahn, *Ghetto Revolts*. New York: Macmillan, 1973.

Finch, Minnie. *The NAACP, Its Fight for Justice*. Metuchen, NJ: Scarecrow Press, 1981.

Fishel, Leslie, Jr., and Benjamin Quarles, eds. *The Black American: A Brief Documentary History*. Glenview, IL: Scott, Foresman, 1967.

Fisher, William H. *Invisible Empire: A Bibliography of the KKK*. Metuchen, NY: Scarecrow Press, 1980.

Foner, Philip, ed. *The Life and Writings of Frederick Douglass*. 4 vols. New York: International, 1950.

Franklin, John Hope. *Reconstruction after the Civil War*. Chicago: University of Chicago Press, 1961.

———. *The Emancipation Proclamation*. Garden City, NY: Doubleday, 1963.

Franklin, John Hope, and August Meier, eds. *Black Leaders of the Twentieth Century*. Urbana: University of Illinois Press, 1982.

Franklin, John Hope, and Alfred Moss, Jr. *From Slavery to Freedom: A History of African Americans*. 7th ed. New York: McGraw-Hill, 1994.

Franks, Gary. *Searching for the Promised Land: An African American's Optimistic Odyssey*. New York: Regan Books, 1996.

Friesema, H. Paul. "Black Control of Central Cities: The Hollow Prize." *American Institute of Planners Journal* 35 (March 1969): 75–79.

Fulani, Lenora B. *The Making of a Fringe Candidate, 1992*. New York: Castillo International, 1992.

Garfinkel, Herbert. *When Negroes March: The March on Washington Movement in the Organizational Politics for F.E.P.C.* Glencoe, IL: Free Press, 1959.

Garrow, David. *Bearing the Cross: Martin Luther King, Jr., and the Southern Christian Leadership Conference*. New York: William Morrow, 1986.

———, ed. *The Montgomery Bus Boycott and the Women Who Started It: The Memoir of Jo Ann Gibson Robinson*. Knoxville: University of Tennessee Press, 1987.

———. *Protest at Selma: Martin Luther King and the Voting Rights Act of 1965*. New Haven, CT: Yale University Press, 1978.

———, ed. *We Shall Overcome: The Civil Rights Movement in the U.S. in the 1950s and 1960s*. Brooklyn, NY: Carlson Publishing, 1989.

Garnet, Henry Highland. "An Address to the Slaves of the United States." 1843. In John Bracey et al., eds. *Black Nationalism in America*. Indianapolis: Bobbs-Merrill, 1970.

Gillette, William. *The Right to Vote: Politics and the Passage of the Fifteenth Amendment*. Baltimore: Johns Hopkins University Press, 1965.

Githens, Marianne, and Jewell L. Prestage, eds. *A Portrait of Marginality: The Political Behavior of the American Woman.* New York: David McKay, 1977.

Golden, Harry. *Mr. Kennedy and the Negroes.* Cleveland, OH: World Publishing Company, 1964.

Goldfield, David R. *Black, White and Southern: Race Relations and Southern Culture, 1940s to the Present.* Baton Rouge: Louisiana State University Press, 1990.

Gosnell, Harold F. *Machine Politics: Chicago Style.* Chicago: University of Chicago Press, 1937.

———. *Negro Politicians: The Lives of Negro Politicians in Chicago.* 1935. Chicago: University of Chicago Press, 1967.

Graham, Hugh Davis. *Civil Rights and the Presidency: Race and Gender in American Politics, 1960–1972.* New York: Oxford University Press, 1992.

Greenberg, Edward, Neal Milner, and David J. Olson, eds. *Black Politics: The Inevitability of Conflict.* New York: Holt, Rinehart and Winston, 1971.

Grimshaw, Allen D. *Racial Violence in the U.S.* Chicago: Aldine Publishing Company, 1969.

Grimshaw, William J. *Bitter Fruit: Black Politics and the Chicago Machine, 1931–1991.* Chicago: University of Chicago Press, 1992.

Grofman, Bernard, Lisa Handley, and Richard G. Niemi. *Minority Representation and the Quest for Voting Equality.* Cambridge: Cambridge University Press, 1992.

Guinier, Lani. *The Tyranny of the Majority: Fundamental Fairness and Representative Democracy.* New York: Free Press, 1994.

Hadden, Jeffrey K., Louis Masotti, and Victor Thiesson. "The Making of Negro Mayors, 1967." *Transaction* (January–February 1968): 21–30.

Hahn, Harlan. *Urban-Rural Conflict: The Politics of Change.* Berkeley: University of California Press, 1971.

Hamilton, Charles V. *Adam Clayton Powell, Jr.: The Political Biography of an American Dilemma.* New York: Atheneum, 1991.

———. "Deracialization." *First World* 1 (1977): 3–5.

———. *Minority Politics in Black Belt Alabama.* New Brunswick, NJ: Rutgers University Press, 1960.

———, ed. *The Black Experience in American Politics.* New York: Capricorn, 1973.

Hampton, Henry, Steve Fayer, and Sarah Flynn. *Voices of Freedom: An Oral History of the Civil Rights Movement from the 1950s through the 1980s.* New York: Bantam Books, 1990.

Hanks, Lawrence J. *The Struggle for Black Political Empowerment in Three Georgia Counties.* Knoxville: University of Tennessee Press, 1987.

Harding, Vincent. *There Is a River: The Black Struggle for Freedom in America.* New York: Vintage, 1983.

Harlan, Louis R. *Booker T. Washington: The Making of a Black Leader, 1856–1901.* New York: Oxford, 1972.

Harris, Robert J. *The Quest for Equality: The Constitution, Congress and the Supreme Court.* Baton Rouge: Louisiana State University Press, 1960.

Haygood, Wil. *King of the Cats: The Life and Times of Adam Clayton Powell Jr.* New York: Houghton Mifflin, 1993.

Henderson, Lenneal, ed. *Black Political Life in the United States.* San Francisco: Chandler, 1972.

Higginbotham, A. Leon. *In the Matter of Color, Race and the Legal Process: The Colonial Period.* New York: Oxford, 1980.

Higham, John, ed. *Ethnic Leadership in America.* Baltimore: Johns Hopkins University Press, 1978.

Hine, Darlene Clark. *The Rise and Fall of the White Primary in Texas.* Millwood, NY: KTO Press, 1979.

Holden, Matthew, Jr. *The Politics of the Black Nation.* New York: Chandler, 1973.

———. *The White Man's Burden.* New York: Chandler, 1973.

———. "The Rewards of Daring and the Ambiguity of Power: Perspectives on the Wilder Election of 1989." In *The State of Black America*, edited by Janet Dewart. New York: National Urban League, 1990.

Holloway, Harry. *The Politics of the Southern Negro: From Exclusion to Big City Organization.* New York: Random House, 1969.

Holt, Thomas. *Black over White: Negro Political Leadership in South Carolina during Reconstruction.* Urbana: University of Illinois Press, 1979.

Huggins, Nathan. "Afro-Americans." In *Ethnic Leadership in America*, edited by John Higham. Baltimore: Johns Hopkins University Press, 1978.

Hughes, Langston. *Fight for Freedom: The Story of the NAACP.* New York: Norton, 1962.

Hunter, Floyd. *Community Power Structure.* Chapel Hill: University of North Carolina Press, 1953.

Jackson, Byran O., and Michael B. Preston. *Ethnic and Racial Politics in California.* Berkeley, CA: Institute for Governmental Studies, 1991.

Jackson, James S., and Patricia Gurin. *The National Survey of Black Americans, 1979–1990.* Ann Arbor, MI: Inter-university Consortium for Political and Social Research, 1987.

Jackson, James S., Patricia Gurin, and Shirley Hatchett. *The 1984 National Black Election Study.* Ann Arbor, MI: Inter-university Consortium for Political and Social Research, 1989.

Jackson, Kenneth T. *The KKK in the City, 1915–1930.* New York: Oxford University Press, 1967.

Jacques-Garvey, Amy. *The Philosophy and Opinions of Marcus Garvey.* New York: Atheneum, 1969.

Jennings, James B. *The Politics of Black Empowerment: The Transformation of Black Activism in Urban America.* Detroit, MI: Wayne State University Press, 1993.

Jewell, Malcolm, ed. *The Politics of Reapportionment.* New York: Atherton Press, 1962.

Jones, Charles E. "Testing a Legislative Strategy: The Congressional Black Caucus's Action-Alert Communications Network." *Legislative Studies Quarterly* (November 1987): 521–37.

Jones, Mack H. "Black Mayoral Leadership in Atlanta: A Comment." In *Black Electoral Politics*, edited by Lucius Barker. New Brunswick, NJ: Transaction Publishers, 1990, 138–44.

———. "Black Political Empowerment in Atlanta: Myth and Reality." *Annals of the American Academy of Political and Social Sciences* 439 (September 1978): 90–117.

———. "A Frame of Reference for Black Politics." In *Black Political Life in the United States*, edited by Lenneal Henderson. San Francisco: Chandler, 1972, 7–20.

Jordan, Barbara, and Shelby Hearon. *Barbara Jordan: A Self Portrait.* Garden City, NY: Doubleday and Company, 1979.

Jordan, Winthrop. *White over Black: American Attitudes toward the Negro, 1550–1812.* New York: Norton, 1977.

Key, V. O. *Southern Politics in State and Nation.* New York: Knopf, 1949.

King, Martin Luther. *Stride toward Freedom: The Montgomery Story.* New York: Harper, 1958.

———. *Where Do We Go from Here: Chaos or Community.* New York: Harper and Row, 1967.

———. *Why We Can't Wait.* New York: New American Library, 1964.

Kraditor, Eileen. *Means and Ends in American Abolitionism: Garrison and His Critics on Strategy and Tactics, 1834–1850.* New York: Pantheon, 1969.

Kluger, Richard. *Simple Justice: The History of Brown v. Board of Education and Black America's Struggle for Equality.* New York: Knopf, 1976.

Ladd, Everett Carll. *Negro Political Leadership in the South.* Ithaca, NY: Cornell University Press, 1966.

Lawson, Steven F. *Black Ballots: Voting Rights in the South, 1944–1969.* New York: Columbia University Press, 1976.

———. *Running for Freedom: Black Politics and Civil Rights since 1941.* Philadelphia: Temple University Press, 1991.

Lewinson, Paul. *Race, Class and Party: A History of Negro Suffrage and White Politics in the South.* New York: Grosset and Dunlap, 1965.

Lynch, John R. *The Facts of Reconstruction.* Edited by William Harris. Indianapolis: Bobbs Merrill, 1970.

McAdam, Doug. *Political Process and the Development of Black Insurgency.* Chicago, IL: University of Chicago Press, 1982.

McClain, Paula D., and Albert Karnig. "Black and Hispanic Socioeconomic and Political Competition." *American Political Science Review* 84 (June 1990): 535–45.

McClain, Paula D., Albert Karnig, and Joseph Stewart, Jr. *Can We All Get Along?: Racial and Ethnic Minorities in American Politics.* Boulder, CO: Westview Press, 1995.

McCormick, John M., II, and Charles E. Jones. "The Conceptualization of Deracialization." In *Dilemmas of Black Politics: Issues of Leadership and Strategy*, edited by Georgia A. Persons. New York: HarperCollins College Publishers, 1993, 76–77.

McFarlin, Annjeannette. *Black Congressional Reconstruction Orators and Their Orations, 1869–1879.* Metuchen, NJ: Scarecrow Press, 1976.

McKitrick, Eric. *Andrew Johnson and Reconstruction.* Chicago: University of Chicago Press, 1960.

Mack, Raymond W., ed. *Our Children's Burden: Studies of Desegregation in Nine American Communities.* New York: Random House, 1968.

Marable, Manning. *Race, Reform, and Rebellion: The Second Reconstruction in Black America, 1945–1982.* Jackson, MS: University Press of Mississippi, 1984.

Marx, Gary, ed. *Racial Conflict.* Boston: Little, Brown, 1971.

Matthews, Donald, and James Prothro. *Negroes and the New Southern Politics.* New York: Harcourt, Brace and World, 1966.

Meier, August, ed. *Black Protest Thought in the 20th Century.* 2nd ed. Indianapolis: Bobbs-Merrill, 1971.

Meier, August, and Elliott Rudwick. *From Plantation to Ghetto*. New York: Hill and Wang, 1966.

Mfume, Kweisi. *No Free Ride: From the Mean Streets to the Mainstream*. New York: One World, 1996.

Miller, Floyd John. *The Search for a Black Nationality: Black Colonization and Emigration, 1787–1863*. Urbana: University of Illinois Press, 1975.

Mills, Kay. *This Little Light of Mine: The Life of Fannie Lou Hamer*. New York: Dutton, 1993.

Moody, Anne. *Coming of Age in Mississippi*. New York: Dial Press, 1968.

Moreland, Laurence W., Robert P. Steed, and Tod A. Baker. *Blacks in Southern Politics*. New York: Praeger Publishers, 1987.

Morris, Aldon. *The Origins of the Civil Rights Movement*. New York: Free Press, 1984.

Morris, Lorenzo, ed. *The Social and Political Implications of the 1984 Jesse Jackson Presidential Campaign*. New York: Praeger Publishers, 1990.

Morris, Milton D. *The Politics of Black America*. New York: Harper and Row, 1975.

———. *New Federalism and Community Development: A Preliminary Evaluation of the Housing and Community Development Act of 1974*. Washington, DC: Joint Center for Political Studies, 1974.

Morrison, Minion K. C. *Black Political Mobilization*. Albany: State University of New York Press, 1987.

Murray, Richard, and Arnold Vedlitz. "Racial Voting Patterns in the South: An Analysis of Major Elections from 1960 to 1977 in Five Cities." *Annals of the American Academy of Political and Social Sciences* (Spring 1978): 29–39.

Muse, Benjamin. *Ten Years of Prelude: The Story of Integration since the Supreme Court's 1954 Decision*. New York: Viking, 1964.

———. *The American Negro Revolution: From Nonviolence to Black Power, 1963–1967*. Bloomington: Indiana University Press, 1968.

Myrdal, Gunnar. *An American Dilemma*. New York: McGraw-Hill, 1944.

Namorato, Michael V., ed. *Have We Overcome?: Race Relations since Brown*. Jackson: University of Mississippi Press, 1979.

Nelson, Albert J. *Emerging Influentials in State Legislatures: Women, Blacks, and Hispanics*. New York: Praeger Publishers, 1991.

Nelson, William E., Jr., and Philip J. Meranto. *Electing Black Mayors*. Columbus: Ohio State University Press, 1977.

Newby, Idus A. *Jim Crow's Defense: Anti-Negro Thought in America, 1900–1930*. Baton Rouge, LA: Louisiana State University Press, 1965.

———, ed. *The Development of Segregationist Thought*. Homewood, IL: Dorsey Press, 1968.

Nolen, Claude H. *The Negro's Image in the South: The Anatomy of White Supremacy*. Lexington, KY: University Press of Kentucky, 1967.

Norrell, Robert J. *Reaping the Whirlwind: The Civil Rights Movement in Tuskegee*. New York: Vintage, 1985.

Ogden, Frederic D. *The Poll Tax in the South*. Tuscaloosa, AL: University of Alabama Press, 1958.

O'Rourke, Timothy. *The Impact of Reapportionment*. New Brunswick, NJ: Transaction Books, 1980.

Painter, Nell. *Sojourner Truth: Life, a Symbol*. New York: Norton, 1996.

Parenti, Michael. *Power and the Powerless*. New York: St Martin's Press, 1978.

Parker, Frank R. *Black Votes Count*. Chapel Hill: University of North Carolina Press, 1990.

Parris, Guichard. *Blacks in the City: A History of the National Urban League*. Boston: Little, Brown, 1971.

Perry, Huey L., ed. *Race, Politics, and Governance in the United States*. Gainesville: University of Florida Press, 1996.

Persons, Georgia, ed. *Dilemmas of Black Politics: Issues of Leadership and Strategy*. New York: HarperCollins, 1993.

Pettigrew, Thomas F. "Black Mayoralty Campaigns." In *Urban Governance and Minorities*, edited by Herrington Bryce. New York: Praeger, 1976, 14–29.

———. *Tom Bradley's Campaigns for Governor: The Dilemmas of Race and Political Strategies*. Washington, DC: Joint Center for Political Studies, 1988.

Pinderhughes, Dianne. *Race and Ethnicity in Chicago Politics*. Urbana: University of Illinois Press, 1987.

Pleasant, William. *Independent Black Leadership in America*. New York: Castillo International, 1990.

Poinsett, Alex. *Black Power, Gary Style: The Making of Mayor Richard G. Hatcher*. Chicago: Johnson Publishing, 1970.

Prestage, Jewell L. "Political Behavior of American Black Woman: An Overview." In *The Black Woman*, edited by L. R. Rose. Beverly Hills, CA: Sage Publications, 1980.

Preston, Michael B. "Black Politics in the Post-Daley Era." In *After Daley*, edited by Samuel K. Gove and Louis H. Masotti. Urbana: University of Illinois Press, 1982, 88–117.

Quarles, Benjamin. *The Negro in the Civil War* New York: Russell and Russell, 1953.

———. *Lincoln and the Negro*. New York: Oxford, 1962.

———. *Frederick Douglass*. New York: Atheneum, 1968.

———. *The Black Abolitionists*. New York: Oxford, 1969.

Rabinowitz, Howard N., ed. *Southern Black Leaders of the Reconstruction Era*. Urbana: University of Illinois Press, 1982.

Ragsdale, Bruce, and Joel Treese. *Black Americans in Congress*. Washington, DC: Office of the Historian, U.S. House of Representatives, 1990.

Rakove, Milton. *Don't Make No Waves, Don't Back No Losers*. Bloomington, IN: Indiana University Press, 1975.

Raper, Arthur F. *The Tragedy of Lynching*. Chapel Hill: University of North Carolina Press, 1933.

Reed, Jr., Adolph, ed. *Race, Politics and Culture: Critical Essays on the Radicals of the 1960s*. Westport, CT: Greenwood, 1986.

———. "The Black Urban Regime: Structural Origins and Constraints." In *Power, Community and the City: Comparative Urban and Community Research*, vol. 1, edited by Michael Peter Smith. New Brunswick, NJ: Transaction Books, 1988.

———. *The Jesse Jackson Phenomenon: The Crisis of Purpose in Afro-American Politics*. New Haven, CT: Yale University Press, 1986.

Rich, Wilbur C. *Coleman Young and Detroit Politics*. Detroit: Wayne State University Press, 1989.

———, ed. *The Politics of Minority Coalitions: Race, Ethnicity, and Shared Uncertainties*. Westport, CT: Praeger, 1996.

Richardson, Joe. *The Negro and Reconstruction of Florida*. Tallahassee: University of Florida Press, 1965.

Riordan, William L. *Plunkitt of Tammany Hall*. New York: E. P. Dutton, 1905, 1963.

Ross, Barbara J. *J. E. Springarn and the Rise of the NAACP, 1911–1939*. New York: Atheneum, 1972.

Ross-Barnett, Marguerite. "The Congressional Black Caucus." In *The New Black Politics: The Search for Political Power*, edited by Michael B. Preston, Lenneal Henderson, Jr., and Paul Puryear. 1st ed. New York: Longman, 1982.

Ruchames, Louis. *Race, Jobs and Politics: The Story of the F.E.P.C.* New York: Columbia University Press, 1953.

Rustin, Bayard. "From Protest to Politics: The Future of the Civil Rights Movement."*Commentary* 39 (February 1965): 25–31.

Schattschneider, E. E. "Urbanization and Reapportionment." *Yale Law Journal*. 72 (November 1962): 7–12.

Schwartz, Bernard. *The Fourteenth Amendment*. New York: New York University Press, 1970.

Seale, Bobby. *Seize the Time: The Story of the Black Panther Party and Huey P. Newton*. New York: Random House, 1970.

Shick, Tom. *Behold the Promised Land: A History of Afro-American Settler Society in Nineteenth Century Liberia*. Baltimore: Johns Hopkins University Press, 1980.

Siebert, Wilbur. *The Underground Railroad from Slavery to Freedom*. New York: Arno, 1968.

Sitkoff, Howard. *A New Deal for Blacks*. New York: Oxford University Press, 1978.

———. "Harry Truman and the Election of 1948: The Coming of Age of Civil Rights in American Politics." *Journal of Southern History* 37 (November 1971).

Smith, Kenneth L., and Ira G. Zepp, Jr. *Search for the Beloved Community*. Valley Forge, PA: Judson Press, 1974.

Smith, Robert C., and Richard Seltzer. *Race, Class and Culture: A Study in Afro-American Mass Opinion*. Albany: State University of New York Press, 1992.

Smith, Samuel D. *The Negro in Congress*. Chapel Hill: University of North Carolina Press, 1940.

Sonenshein, Raphael J. *Politics in Black and White: Race and Power in Los Angeles*. Princeton, NJ: Princeton University Press, 1993.

Stanley, Harold W. *Voter Mobilization and the Politics of Race: The South and Universal Suffrage, 1952–1984*. New York: Praeger, 1987.

Staudenraus, Philip. *The African Colonization Movement, 1816–1865*. New York: Columbia University Press, 1961.

Sterling, Dorothy. *Freedom Train: The Story of Harriet Tubman*. New York: Doubleday, 1954.

Sternsher, Bernard, ed. *The Negro in Depression and War: Prelude to Revolution, 1930–1945*. Chicago: Quadrangle Books, 1969.

Stone, Clarence. *Regime Politics Governing Atlanta: 1946–1988*. Lawrence: University of Kansas Press, 1989.

Strickland, Arvarh E. *History of the Chicago Urban League*. Urbana: University of Illinois Press, 1966.

Sundquist, James. *Politics and Policy: The Eisenhower, Kennedy and Johnson Years*. Washington, DC: Brookings Institution, 1968.

Swain, Carol. *Black Faces, Black Interests: The Representation of African Americans in Congress.* Cambridge, MA: Harvard University Press, 1993.

Tate, Katherine L. *From Protest to Politics: The New Black Voters in American Elections.* Cambridge, MA: Harvard University Press, 1993.

Thomas, Lamont. *Rise to Be a People: A Biography of Paul Cuffe.* Urbana: University of Illinois Press, 1986.

Thompson, Daniel. *The Negro Leadership Class.* Englewood, NJ: Prentice-Hall, 1963.

Trelease, Allen N. *White Terror: The KKK Conspiracy and Southern Reconstruction.* Westport, CT: Greenwood Press, 1979.

Truman, David B. *The Government Process.* New York: Alfred Knopf, 1951.

Tucker, David M. *Memphis since Crump: Bossism, Blacks and Civic Reformers, 1948–1968.* Knoxville: University of Tennessee Press, 1980.

Tushnet, Mark V. *The NAACP's Legal Strategy against Segregated Education, 1925–1950.* Chapel Hill; University of North Carolina Press, 1987.

Uya, Okon. *From Slavery to Public Service: Robert Smalls, 1839–1915.* New York: Oxford, 1971.

Vander Zanden, James W. *Race Relations in Transition: The Segregation Crisis in the South.* New York: Random House, 1965.

Vose, Clement E. *Caucasians Only: The Supreme Court, the NAACP and the Restrictive Covenant Cases.* Berkeley: University of California Press, 1959.

Walker, David. *David Walker's Appeal.* 1829. New York: Arno, 1969.

Walker, Margaret. *Jubilee.* Boston: Houghton Mifflin, 1966.

Walters, Ronald W. *Black Presidential Politics in America: A Strategic Approach.* Albany: State University of New York Press, 1988.

Walton, Hanes, Jr. *Black Political Parties.* New York: Free Press, 1972.

———. *Black Politics: A Theoretical and Structural Analysis.* Philadelphia: J. B. Lippincott, 1972.

———. *Invisible Politics: Black Political Behavior.* Albany: State University of New York Press, 1985.

———. *The Negro in Third Party Politics.* Philadelphia: Doriance, 1969.

Waskow, Arthur I. *From Race Riots to Sit-Ins, 1919 and the 1960s: A Study in the Connections between Conflict and Violence.* Garden City, NY: Doubleday, 1966.

Watters, Pat, and Reese Cleghorn. *Climbing Jacob's Ladder: The Arrival of Negroes in Southern Politics.* New York: Harcourt, Brace and World, 1967.

Weiss, Nancy J. *Farewell to the Party of Lincoln: Black Politics in the Age of FDR.* Princeton, NJ: Princeton University Press, 1983.

———. *The National Urban League, 1910–1945.* New York: Oxford, 1974.

Wells-Barnett, Ida B. *On Lynchings: Southern Horrors, a Red Record, Mob Rule in New Orleans.* 1892. New York: Arno Press, 1969.

White, Mary O. *How the NAACP Began.* New York: NAACP, 1914.

———. *The Walls Came Tumbling Down.* New York: Arno Press, 1969.

Williams, Eddie N. "Black Women in Politics and Government." In *Contributions of Black Women to America.* Vol. 2, edited by M. W. Davis. Columbia, SC: Kenday Press, 1982.

Williams, Juan. *Eyes on the Prize: America's Civil Right's Years, 1954–1965.* New York: Penguin Books, 1987.

Wilson, James Q. *Negro Politics: The Search for Leadership.* New York: Free Press, 1960.

————. "Two Negro Politicians: An Interpretation." *Midwest Journal of Political Science* 4 (November 1960): 349–69.

Wilson, Zaphon. "Gantt versus Helms: Deracialization Confronts Southern Traditionalism." In *Dilemmas of Black Politics: Issues of Leadership and Strategy*, edited by Georgia Persons. New York: HarperCollins College Publishers, 1993, 176–93.

Wolfinger, Raymond E. "Why Machines Have Not Withered Away and Other Revisionist Thoughts." *Journal of Politics* 34, no. 2 (May 1972): 365–98.

Wolk, Allen. *The Presidency and Black Civil Rights: Eisenhower to Nixon*. Rutherford, NJ: Fairleigh Dickinson University Press, 1971.

Wolters, Raymond. *Negroes and the Great Depression: The Problem of Economic Recovery*. Westport, CT: Greenwood, 1970.

Wood, Forrest G. *Black Scare: The Racist Response to Emancipation and Reconstruction*. Berkeley: University of California Press, 1968.

Woodward, C. Vann. *Origins of the New South, 1877–1913*. Baton Rouge: Louisiana State University Press, 1951.

————. *The Strange Career of Jim Crow*. New York: Oxford University Press, 1955, 1957, 1966, 1974.

Yancey, Dwayne. *When Hell Froze Over: The Untold Story of Doug Wilder*. Roanoke, VA: Taylor Publishing, 1988.

Zangrando, Robert L. "The NAACP and a Federal Anti-lynching Bill, 1930–1940." *Journal of Negro History* 50 (April 1965): 106–17.

————. *The NAACP Crusade against Lynching, 1990–1950*. Philadelphia: Temple University Press, 1980.

X

The African American Press

Julius E. Thompson

The black press in the United States began in New York City in 1827, when Samuel E. Cornish and John B. Russwurm established *Freedom's Journal* as an organ for African Americans. Since that time, thousands of black publications have been created in this country to address the various social, political, economic, and cultural issues of the day. Although the black commercial newspaper has been the dominant black press medium in the past, it has always received competition from black religious newspapers, newsletters, and magazines; and in recent years from black interests in radio, film, and television. A central theme dominates the work of the black press in American history, namely, the struggle for African American freedom, equality, and advancement in this nation. Black newspaper publishers and editors have led the drive to promote black freedom while also addressing black viewpoints and perspectives on other issues at home and abroad. In fact, black publishers, editors, and reporters have been major agents for social reforms and change in American life.

The common efforts of the black media in America helped to bring about the defeat of slavery, segregation, mass lynching, widespread discrimination, and other forms of oppression against blacks and other citizens of this country over the last 170 years. The black press has also been a leader in the struggle to reform society by compelling the general public and the U.S. government to deal with such continuing problems as racism, classism, imperialism, peace issues, sexism, and economic injustice.

The struggle has not been an easy one. Black journalists have paid dearly for their contributions in promoting the black perspective for the world. The costs can be measured in terms of economic hardships, social isolation, and in some cases an early death. Nevertheless, many black men and women have met the challenges of their historical times and have left to American society a rich tradition of struggle and of knowledge, and understanding of the black experience in American life.

Scholars have estimated that black Americans produced at least 1,240 newspapers in the nineteenth century, and at least 1,500 in the twentieth century. The over 2,700 black newspapers produced since 1827 can basically be classified as commercial, religious, fraternal, and organizational organs. The noted African American scholar Charles H. Wesley wrote in his 1968 book, *The Quest for Equality: From Civil War to Civil Rights*, that the black press has been especially significant in black history because it has served as a unifying force and helped to promote the influence and power of black Americans. Indeed, only the black church and black music, which offers readers an appreciation for the soul of black people, can match the impact of the black press (and black literature) on black history, with their focus on aiding and interpreting the heart and meaning of black life and thought in America.

Yet, a paradox and a dilemma emerges for black publishers and editors in that while their greatest challenge comes in getting the black viewpoint published and distributed to the world, they must also sell their product if they wish to stay in business for long. This dichotomy has historically produced great stress in the lives of black publishers and editors. How does a newspaper remain truly free when its economic survival often depends upon advertising revenue generated outside the black community? This issue has faced the black press across generations. It is complicated by the harsh economic realities of black America. As black economist Lloyd Hogan has assessed in his 1984 book *Principles of Black Political Economy*, the problem is one whereby blacks have historically suffered economic discrimination in the nation. Such a situation has greatly affected the development of black institutions.

The black press must also contend with a black population base where one-third of the citizens live in or near poverty conditions. Furthermore, the number, income, and profits of most black businesses in America are very small. Hogan notes that in 1969, not more than 3,000 black businesses in the United States had at least ten employees hired full time. The 3,000 major black companies contributed only $250 million to the U.S. economy. According to Theodore Cross, author of *The Black Power Imperative* (1987), by 1984 only 17,760 employees worked for the largest black business enterprise in this country, and only 9,000 black families held wealth in excess of a half million dollars. Meanwhile, the U.S. Census Bureau in 1987 listed the total black population of the United States at just under 30 million people.

It has been under these severe economic conditions, in addition to political and social pressures, in which twentieth-century black press organs have attempted to stay in business. Their labor history is a very difficult story. As late as 1973, America's 250 black newspapers employed only 2,500 people. Less than 10 percent of this number owned their printing presses, and most were weeklies. Yet, the over 200 active black newspapers in the contemporary world were successful in producing and distributing 1 million newspapers in 1937, 2 million in 1947, and 4 million in 1973. The struggle to keep the black newspaper afloat has involved great sacrifices and dedication to the cause of publishing made by black publishers, editors, reporters, and the staffs of black press organizations in this nation.

During the era of slavery (1619–1865), black journalists were especially committed to using the newspaper as an anti-slavery instrument while pressing for equal rights and an end to discrimination against free blacks, who numbered 488,000 in 1860 (about 10 percent of the black population in the United States). In 1827 blacks in New York City produced the first black newspaper, *Freedom's Journal* (1827–1829), edited by John B. Russwurm and Samuel E. Cornish. Between 1827 and 1865, African Americans produced thirty-eight newspapers in this country. Other early major antebellum black newspapers are *Rights of All* (1829), edited in New York City by Samuel Cornish; the *Colored American* (1837–1841), published by Samuel Cornish, Philip Bell, and Charles B. Ray in New York City; the *National Reformer* (1838–1839), at Philadelphia, Pennsylvania, by William J. Whipper; the *Mirror of Liberty* (1838–1840), edited by David Ruggles at New York City; the *Mystery* (1843–1847), edited by Martin R. Delaney, in Pittsburgh, Pennsylvania; *the Ram's Horn* (1846–1848), edited in New York City by Van Rensselaer and Frederick Douglass; three papers by Frederick Douglass, the *North Star* (1847–1851), *Frederick Douglass' Paper* (1851–1859), and *Douglass' Monthly* (1859–1860), all published in Rochester, New York; the *Mirror of the Times* (1855), established at San Francisco by Mifflin W. Gibbs; the *Christian Recorder*, edited in Philadelphia by Bishop Jabez Campbell from 1856 to 1865; and, among others, the *Weekly Anglo-African* (1859–1860), edited in New York City by Thomas Hamilton.

This rich history is explored in a number of significant studies on the period, including Frankie Hutton, *The Early Black Press in America, 1827 to 1860* (1993); Lionel C. Barrow, Jr., "Our Own Cause: Freedom's Journal and the Beginnings of the Black Press," *Journalism History* (1977–78); Bernell E. Tripp, *Origins of the Black Press: New York, 1827–1847* (1992); Carter R. Bryan, *Negro Journalism in America before Emancipation* (1969); Donald M. Jacobs, ed., *Antebellum Black Newspapers* (1978). Other scholars who supplement the above treatments on this period are John Hope Franklin and Alfred A. Moss, Jr., *From Slavery to Freedom: A History of African Americans* (1994); Benjamin Quarles, *Black Abolitionists* (1969) and *Frederick Douglass* (1976); and Roland E. Wolseley, *The Black Press, U.S.A.* (1990).

Scholars have long had great difficulty in locating copies of the historic black press in America. Studies that have helped to alleviate this problem are Vilma Raskin Potter, *A Reference Guide to Afro-American Publications and Editors, 1827–1946* (1993); Carl Senna, *The Black Press and the Struggle for Civil Rights* (1993); a Ph.D. dissertation by Armistead Scott, "A Register and History of Negro Newspapers in the United States, 1827–1950" (1950); and Penelope I. Bullock, *The Afro-American Periodical Press, 1838–1909* (1977).

The dominant theme in the black press during the antebellum period was liberation. African Americans used the press as one means by which they could address their concerns to the world. Since the majority of U.S. blacks at that time were enslaved in the South and border states, black newspaper publishers, editors, and reporters sought to use the press to demand black freedom and an improvement in their lives in the North. A minority of blacks argued that free African Americans should seek liberty elsewhere by migrating from the United States and seeking new homes in either Africa, the Caribbean region, or Central or South America. Studies that address these concerns are Kwando M. Kinshasa, *Emigration vs. Assimilation: The Debate in the African American Press, 1827–1961* (1988); Vincent Harding, *There Is a River: The Black Struggle for Freedom in America* (1981); Martin E. Dann, *The Black Press, 1827–1890: The Quest for National Identity* (1971); Frederick Douglass, *Narrative of the Life of Frederick Douglass, an American Slave, Written by Himself* (1845); and David Walker, *Walker's Appeal in Four Articles; Together with a Preamble to the Coloured Citizens of the World* (1830).

Contemporary scholars note the chief importance of black abolitionists to the cause of African American freedom in the nineteenth century. Among the persons in this group are journalists and writers such as Martin R. Delaney, Frederick Douglass, Frances E. W. Harper, and Henry Highland Garnet. Biographies that examine and analyze these figures include Frank A. Rollin's *Life and Public Services of Martin R. Delaney* (1969), William S. McFeely's *Frederick Douglass* (1991), Melba Joyce Boyd's *Discarded Legacy: Politics and Poetics in the Life of Frances E. W. Harper, 1825–1911* (1994), and Joel Schor's *Henry Highland Garnet: A Voice of Black Radicalism in the Nineteenth Century* (1977).

In the late nineteenth century, black Americans established a tremendous number of new newspapers. By 1899, at least 117 African American papers were actively reaching the black community. Major voices of the black press during this period were the *New Era*, established in 1870, in Washington, D.C.; the Savannah (Ga.) *Tribune*, created in 1885; the Philadelphia (Pa.) *Tribune* (1884); the Washington (D.C.) *Bee*, founded by William Calvin Chase in 1879; the Indianapolis (Ind.) *World* (1883); the *A.M.E. Church Review* (active since 1841), edited by Rev. L. J. Coppin during Reconstruction; the *Star of Zion* (1867), Charlotte, N.C., a paper of the African Methodist Episcopal Church; the Cleveland (Ohio) *Gazette* (1883); the *Afro-American* (1892), founded in Baltimore, Md., by Carl Murphy; the *New York Age* (1887), edited by T. Thomas Fortune; and Ida B. Wells, one of the significant editors of *Free Speech and Headlight* (1889–1891), circulated in Memphis, Tennessee.

Black newspapers during Reconstruction and afterward—what scholars have called the "Nadir" and the "Age of Lynching"—were faced with a host of key challenges. Most were weekly newspapers with small staffs and budgets that generated limited distribution. Although the black press had helped to achieve the eradication of slavery in 1865, the search for freedom continued. The hardships facing black Americans during the late nineteenth century forced the black press to continue its early emphasis on ending discrimination against African Americans in this nation.

The first pioneering study to be published on the black press came in 1891, when I. Garland Penn wrote *The Afro-American Press and Its Editors*. Penn's work effectively documented the black press as an institution in late-nineteenth-century black life. In recent years, a group of American scholars have combined their efforts to produce two very important collections of essays on this and later periods in the history of the black press. In 1983, historian Henry Lewis Suggs edited *The Black Press in the South, 1865–1979*, with essays contributed to this volume by Allen Woodrow Jones on Alabama; Calvin Smith on Arkansas; Jerrell H. Shofner on Florida; Alton Hornsby, Jr., on Georgia; Thomas J. Davis on Louisiana; Julius E. Thompson on Mississippi; George Everett Slavens on Missouri; Henry Lewis Suggs and Bernadine Moses Duncan on North Carolina; Theodore "Ted" Hemmingway on South Carolina; Samuel Shannon on Tennessee; James Smallwood on Texas; and Henry Lewis Suggs on Virginia. The book was the first major scholarly overview ever written on the black press in America. Suggs also edited *The Black Press in the Middle West, 1865–1985* (1996). Eleven essays appeared in this book, treating the history of the black press in Illinois, by Juliet E. K. Walker; Indiana, by Darrel E. Bigham; Iowa, by Allen W. Jones; Kansas, by Dorothy V. Smith; Michigan, by Julius E. Thompson; Minnesota and South Dakota, by Henry Lewis Suggs; Nebraska, by D. G. Paz; Ohio, by Felecia G. Jones Ross; Oklahoma, by Nudie Eugene Williams; and Wisconsin, by Genevieve G. McBride. Like *The Black Press in the South*, this volume represents a major scholarly achievement of modern research on the American black press.

Other students of the black press who have captured the complex nature of the institution during the late nineteenth century include Arnold H. Taylor, *Travail and Triumph: Black Life and Culture in the South since the Civil War* (1977); Julius E. Thompson, *The Black Press in Mississippi, 1865–1985* (1993); a Ph.D. dissertation by Warren Brown, "Social change and the Negro Press, Social Change, 1860–1880" (1941); and Louis R. Harlan, *Booker T. Washington: The Wizard of Tuskegee, 1901–1915* (1983).

Biographies on leading figures associated with the late-nineteenth-century African American press have also helped to shape the purpose and meaning of the black press over historical time. Key works in this regard include William J. Simmons's *Men of Mark* (1887), which highlights a number of black press editors; Ida B. Wells's autobiography, *Crusade for Justice*, edited by her daughter, Alfreda M. Duster (1970); Emma Lou Thornbrough's *T. Thomas Fortune: Militant Journalist* (1972); Rea McCain, Aris A. Mallas, Jr., and Margaret K. Hedden, *Forty Years in Politics: The Story of Ben Pelham* (1958), publisher of the first black newspaper in Detroit, the *Plaindealer*; and Darlene Clark Hine, ed., *Black Women in America: An Historical Encyclopedia* (1993), which denotes the achievements of several key black women journalists of this period.

The primary goals of the black press between 1866 and 1899 were to strengthen the basic institutions of the black community, including the family, the school, the church, and labor. African American newspapers also advocated black pride, leadership development, anti-imperialism, anti-lynching, and an end to extreme white racism as reflected in the establishment of the Jim Crow system in the South after 1890.

In the early decades of the twentieth century the black press experienced growth; however, after World War II, a decline took place. From a high of 1,500 active newspapers in the 1920s, only 175 remained active by 1950. The development of the African American press between 1900 and 1950 was influenced by a variety of factors: increase in the black population, which reached 15,042,286 in 1950; the migration of blacks to American cities not only in the South but in the North and West as well; black business development; activities of the civil rights movement and other organizational developments among blacks and their allies; an expanding literacy rate among blacks (83.7 percent by 1930); an increase in the number of black nationalist organizations, such as Marcus Garvey's Universal Negro Improvement Association; and worldwide developments, such as World Wars I and II and the anti-colonial struggles in Africa, Asia, and other parts of the world.

The important black newspapers of this period were the Boston *Guardian* (1901), edited by Monroe Trotter; the *Chicago Defender* (1905), created by Robert S. Abbott, who was succeeded by his nephew, John H. Sengstacke, Sr.; the Pittsburgh *Courier* (1910), edited by Robert Lee Vann; the Baltimore *Afro-American* (1892), edited by John H. Murphy III; and the Atlanta (Ga.) *Daily World* (1928), edited by W. A. Scott and C. A. Scott. The black press's range of influence is revealed in its circulation figures. For example, by 1917 the *Chicago Defender* produced more than 250,000 weekly copies, and by 1947 the *Courier*'s circulation stood at 350,000 weekly issues.

A number of studies in the early twentieth century offered critical perspectives on the black press. Frederick G. Detweiler's 1922 monograph *The Negro Press in the United States* was among the leaders in the field to document the achievements and problems that faced the black press in America. Also in 1922, George Gore, Jr., wrote *Negro Journalism: An Essay on the History and Present Condition of the Negro Press*. In 1948, Vishnu Oak published *The Negro Newspaper*, which continued this scholarly analysis of the black press. Other studies that helped to document the black press by name, location, founders and editors, price, and circulation and distribution were Monroe Work's edited work, *Negro Year Book* (1912, 1918–19, 1922, 1947); Warren Brown's *Check List of Negro Newspapers in the United States, 1827–1946* (1946); Dorothy DeLoris Boone's Ph.D. dissertation, "A Historical Review and a Bibliography of Selected Negro Magazines, 1910–1969" (1970); Lawrence D. Hogan, *A Black National News*

Service: The Associated Negro Press and Claude Barnett, 1919–1945 (1984); Armistead Scott Pride, "The Names of Negro Newspapers," *American Speech* (1954); and Jessie Parkhurst Guzman, ed., *The Negro Year Book, 1941–1946* (1947).

Another significant body of published work has examined specialized components of the black press. Key works in this group of scholarship include P. L. Prattis, "Racial Segregation and Negro Journalism," *Phylon* (1947); Tony Martin, *Race First: The Ideological and Organizational Struggles of Marcus Garvey and the Universal Negro Improvement Association* (1976); Theodore Kornweibel, Jr., *No Crystal Stair: Black Life and the Messenger, 1917–1928* (1975); John D. Stevens, "The Black Press Looks at 1920's Journalism," *Journalism History* (1980); George James Flemming, *"The Negro Press: A Research Memorandum"* (1940); Rayford W. Logan, ed., *The Attitude of the Southern White Press toward Negro Suffrage* (1940); Lee Finkle, *Forum for Protest: The Black Press during World War II* (1975); and John D. Stevens, *From the Black of the Fox Hole: Black Correspondents in World War II* (1973).

Biographies on early-twentieth-century black press leaders abound. Among the major published works are Andrew Buni's *Robert L. Vann of the Pittsburgh Courier: Politics and Black Journalism* (1974); Stephen R. Fox's *The Guardian of Boston: William Monroe Trotter* (1970); Roi Ottley, *The Lonely Warrior: The Life and Times of Robert S. Abbott* (1955); Arnold Rampersad, *The Life of Langston Hughes, Volume 1:1902–1941: I, Too, Sing America* (1986) and *Volume II: 1941–1967: I Dream a World* (1988); Henry Lewis Suggs, *P. B. Young, Newspaperman: Race, Politics, and Journalism in the New South, 1910–62* (1988); Julius E. Thompson, *Percy Greene and the Jackson Advocate: The Life and Times of a Radical Conservative Black Newspaperman, 1897–1977* (1994); and Roy Wilkins, with Tom Mathews, *Standing Fast: The Autobiography of Roy Wilkins* (1982).

The early twentieth century also represented a major period in the development of the African American magazine. Scholars credit the *Colored American Magazine* (1900), edited by Walter W. Wallace, as the first significant organ in this class of black publications. Hundreds of African American magazines have appeared in the twentieth century, but like most black newspapers, they have had short existences as publications. Other important early black magazines include the *Moon Illustrated Weekly*, established by William E. B. Du Bois at Memphis, Tennessee, in 1906; followed in 1907 by *Horizon*, a monthly organ. Du Bois's greatest service as an editor was his work with *The Crisis* (1910–1934), the official organ of the NAACP. In 1920, Du Bois created a children's magazine entitled the *Brownies' Book*, which survived until 1922. In 1940, while teaching at Atlanta University, he helped to create *Phylon*, a scholarly and literary magazine. Other black individuals and organizations also produced major magazines between 1900 and 1950. To this list must be added *Opportunity: Journal of Negro Life* (1923–1949), edited by Charles S. Johnson, which was the official publication of the National Urban League; *Black Man* (1933), just one of many organs published by Marcus Garvey and the Universal Negro Improvement Association; *The Messenger* (1917), edited by A. Philip Randolph and Chandler Owen; the *Journal of Negro History* (1915), edited by Carter G. Woodson; *Abbott's Monthly* (1919), by Robert S. Abbott; the *Negro Quarterly* (1942), edited in New York City by Ralph Ellison; and *Negro Digest* (1942), founded by John H. Johnson in Chicago, Illinois. At the beginning of World War II, African Americans produced at least 120 active magazines.

A related, but equally important, theme associated with the black magazine has been the efforts of blacks to create black-owned book-publishing companies in the United States since the nineteenth century. Important studies that have told the histories and struggles of the black magazine and publishing companies are Charles S. Johnson, "The Rise of the Negro Magazine," *Journal of Negro History* (1928); Abby Johnson and Ronald M. Johnson, *Propaganda and Aesthetics: The Literary Politics of Afro-American Magazines in the Twentieth Century* (1979); Lorenzo Greene, *Selling Black History for Carter G. Woodson: A Diary, 1930–1933*, edited by Arvarh E. Strickland (1996); Jacqueline Goggin, *Carter G. Woodson: A Life in Black History* (1993); Donald Franklin Joyce, *Gatekeepers of Black Culture: Black-Owned Book Publishing in the United States, 1817–1981* (1983); Junette A. Pinkney, "Independent Black Publishing," *American Visions* (1989); and Julius E. Thompson, *Dudley Randall, Broadside Press, and the Black Arts Movement in Detroit, 1960–1995* (1998).

In the contemporary world, 1951–1998, the black press has continued its ageless quest for survival and service to the African American community. Over 200 black newspapers and a similar number of magazines have been active during this period. Nevertheless, a large number of black press organs have ceased publication during these years. The economics of publishing have been especially harsh on black publications. However, the rich history of the black press has continued to unfold during this period because of the commitment of many individuals and black organizations to the media interests of black Americans. The black press was profoundly affected during this period by the modern civil rights movement, the black arts movement, and the black power movement. A large number of new black publications were created to support and advance black political, social, economic, and cultural interests through the above movements. Black magazines have been especially active. The most active have been John H. Johnson's *Ebony* (1945), *Jet* (1951), and *Black World* (earlier known as *Negro Digest*, (1942); *Black Scholar* (1969); *College Language Association Journal* (1957); *Freedomways* (1961); *Negro History Bulletin* (1937); *Encore* (1972); *Callaloo* (1976); *First World* (1977); *Journal of Black Studies* (1970); *Essence* (1970); *Obsidian: Black Literature in Review* (1975); *Sepia* (1952); and *Western Journal of Black Studies* (1976). Major new independent black publishers have included Dudley F. Randall, who created Broadside Press in Detroit in 1965 to promote black poetry and literature; Haki R. Madhubuti, creator of

Chicago's Third World Press (1967); and Naomi Long Madgett, creator of Detroit's Lotus Press in 1972. Their companies have featured, among other things, the works of black poets.

Modern scholars have continued to document the presence of black newspapers, periodicals, and other media interests among African Americans. Noteworthy works include *Black List: The Concise Reference Guide to Publications* (1970) and *Broadcasting Media of Black America, Africa and the Caribbean* (1970); George H. Hill's *Black Media in America: A Resource Guide* (1984); *National Black Business Directory* (1970); *National Newspaper Publishers Association Black Press Information Handbook* (1985); *Black Press Periodical Directory* (1974); *Black Resource Guide* (1982); Armistead S. Pride's *Black Press: A Bibliography* (1968); *The Ebony Handbook* (1966); Ben Johnson and Mary Ballard Johnson, *Who's What and Where: A Directory of America's Black Journalists* (1985); Henry LaBrie, *The Black Newspaper in America: A Guide* (1970); Barbara K. Henritze, *Bibliographic Checklist of African American Newspapers* (1995); Library of Congress, *Negro Newspapers on Microfilm: A Selected List* (1953); Armistead S. Pride and Clint C. Wilson II, *A History of the Black Press* (1997); and Charles A. Simmons, *The African American Press: A History of News Coverage during National Crises, with Special Reference to Four Black Newspapers, 1827–1965* (1998).

Black biographies, the organs of black organizations, the work of black women journalists, and special studies on the modern black press are captured in such works as Harold Cruse, *The Crisis of the Negro Intellectual* (1967); DeWayne Wickham, ed., *Thinking Black: Some of the Nation's Best Black Columnists Speak Their Minds* (1996); Jessie Carney Smith, *Notable Black American Women* (1992); Gloria T. Hull, Patricia Bell Scott, and Barbara Woods, eds., *But Some of Us Are Brave: Black Women's Studies* (1982); William Gardner Smith, *Return to Black America* (1970); Dudley Randall, *Broadside Memories: Poets I Have Known* (1975); C. Eric Lincoln, *The Black Muslims in America* (1961, 1994); and John H. Johnson, with Lerone Bennett, Jr., *Succeeding against the Odds: The Autobiography of a Great American Businessman* (1989).

Studies that reflect on black interests in the mass media, including television and radio, are Vaughnchille Molden's *Telecommunications and Black Americans: A Survey of Ownership, Participation and Control* (1975); J. Fred MacDonald, *Black and White T.V.: Afro-Americans in Television since 1948* (1983); Anthony W. Johnson, ed., *Black Families and the Medium of Television* (1982); John Gray, compiler, *Blacks in Film and Television: A Pan-African Bibliography of Films, Filmmakers, and Performers* (1990); Jannette L. Dates and William Barlow, eds., *Split Image: African Americans in the Mass Media* (1990).

Several contemporary studies highlight the continuing special challenges facing the black press in the late twentieth century. At the forefront of these works are Maxwell R. Brooks, *The Negro Press Re-examined* (1959); J. William Snorgrass, "Freedom of the Press and Black Publications," *Western Journal of Black Studies* (1980); James S. Tinney and Justine J. Rector, eds., *Issues and Trends in Afro-American Journalism* (1980); Clint C. Wilson II, *Black Journalists in Paradox: Historical Perspectives and Current Dilemmas* (1991); and Carl Senna, *The Black Press and the Struggle for Civil Rights* (1993).

Many scholars in the twentieth century have argued that too many black press organs have focused valuable news space on sensational topics such as crime, entertainment, and sports. Others have called for a more radical press. Over time, most of the black press has generally fallen somewhere in the middle of these concerns. The fight for survival has been a major theme in the history of the black press in America. Black press organs have also had to address a host of issues facing the black community in this nation while building and maintaining a readership. These challenges from the past remain vibrant concerns for the black press today.

BIBLIOGRAPHY

Barger, Harold. "Political Content of Black Newspapers: Chicago and Nation, 1969–1970." Ph.D. dissertation, Northwestern University, 1971.

Barrow, Lionel C., Jr. "Our Own Cause: Freedom's Journal and the Beginnings of the Black Press." *Journalism History* 4, no. 4 (Winter 1977–78): 118–22.

Black List: The Concise Reference Guide to Publications and Broadcasting Media of Black America, Africa and the Caribbean. New York: Panther House, 1970.

The Black Press Periodical Directory, 1974. New York: Amalgamated Publishers, 1975.

Black Resource Guide. Washington, DC: Black Resource Guide, 1982.

Boone, Dorothy DeLoris. "A Historical Review and a Bibliography of Selected Negro Magazines, 1910–1969." Ph.D. dissertation, University of Michigan, 1970.

Boyd, Melba Joyce. *Discarded Legacy: Politics and Poetics in the Life of Frances E. W. Harper, 1825–1911.* Detroit: Wayne State University Press, 1994.

Brooks, Maxwell R. *The Negro Press Re-examined.* Boston: Christopher, 1959.

Brown, Warren. "Social Change and the Negro Press, 1860–1880." Ph.D. dissertation, New School for Social Research, 1941.

Brown, Warren, comp. *Check List of Negro Newspapers in the United States, 1827–1946.* Jefferson City, MO: School of Journalism, Lincoln University, 1946.

Bryan, Carter R. *Negro Journalism in America before Emancipation.* Lexington; Association for Education in Journalism, University of Kentucky, Monograph 12, September 1969.

Bullock, Penelope I. *The Afro-American Press, 1838–1909.* Baton Rouge: Louisiana State University Press, 1977.

Buni, Andrew. *Robert L. Vann of the Pittsburgh Courier: Politics and Black Journalism.* Pittsburgh: University of Pittsburgh Press, 1974.

Cross, Theodore. *The Black Power Imperative: Racial Inequality and the Politics of Nonviolence.* New York: Faulkner Books, 1987.

Cruse, Harold. *The Crisis of the Negro Intellectual.* New York: William Morrow, 1967.

Dann, Martin E. *The Black Press, 1827–1890: The Quest for National Identity.* New York: G. P. Putnam's Sons, 1971.

Dates, Jannette L., and William Barlow, eds. *Split Image: African Americans in the Mass Media.* Washington, DC: Howard University Press, 1990.

Detweiler, Frederick G. *The Negro Press in the United States.* Chicago: University of Chicago Press, 1922.

Douglass, Frederick. *Narrative of the Life of Frederick Douglass, an American Slave, Written by Himself.* 1845. Garden City, NY: Doubleday, 1963.

The Ebony Handbook, 1966. Chicago: Johnson Publishing Co., 1966.

Finkle, Lee. *Forum for Protest: The Black Press during World War II.* Cranbury, NJ: Associated University Presses, 1975.

Fleming, George James. "The Negro Press: A Research Memorandum." New York: Carnegie-Myrdal Study/Schomburg Collection, New York Public Library, 1940.

Fox, Stephen R. *The Guardian of Boston: William Monroe Trotter.* New York: Atheneum Press, 1970.

Franklin, John Hope, and Alfred A. Moss, Jr. *From Slavery to Freedom: A History of African Americans.* New York: Knopf, 1994.

Goggin, Jacqueline. *Carter G. Woodson: A Life in Black History.* Baton Rouge: Louisiana State University Press, 1993.

Gore, George, Jr. *Negro Journalism: An Essay on the History and Present Condition of the Negro Press.* Grencastle, IN: DePauw University, 1922.

Gorham, Thelma T. "The Negro Press: Past, Present & Future." *U.S. Negro World* 9 (1969–70): 1–21.

Gray, John, comp. *Blacks in Film and Television: A Pan-African Bibliography of Films, Filmmakers, and Performers.* New York: Greenwood Press, 1990.

Greene, Lorenzo. *Selling Black History for Carter G. Woodson: A Diary, 1930–1933.* Ed. by Arvarh E. Strickland. Columbia: University of Missouri Press, 1996.

Guzman, Jessie Parkhurst, ed. *Negro Year Book, 1941–1946.* Tuskegee, AL: Tuskegee Institute, 1947.

Harding, Vincent. *There Is a River: The Black Struggle for Freedom in America.* New York: Harcourt Brace Jovanovich, 1981.

Harlan, Louis R. *Booker T. Washington: The Wizard of Tuskegee, 1901–1915.* New York: Oxford University Press, 1983.

Hecht, Michael L., Mary Jane Collier, and Sidney A. Bibeau. *African American Communication: Ethnic Identity and Cultural Interpretation.* Newbury Park, CA: Sage Publications, 1993.

Henritze, Barbara K. *Bibliographic Checklist of African American Newspapers.* Baltimore, MD: Genealogical Publishing Co., 1995.

Hill, George H. *Black Media in America: A Resource Guide.* Boston: G. K. Hall and Co., 1984.

Hill, George H., and Sylvia Saverson Hill. *Blacks on Television: A Selectively Annotated Bibliography.* Metuchen, NJ: Scarecrow Press, 1985.

Hine, Darlene Clark, ed. *Black Women in America: An Historical Encyclopedia.* New York: Carlson, 1993.

Hogan, Lawrence D. *A Black National News Service: The Associated Negro Press and Claude Barnett, 1919–1945.* Rutherford, NJ: Fairleigh Dickinson University Press, 1984.

Hogan, Lloyd. *Principles of Black Political Economy.* Boston: Routledge and Kegan Paul, 1984.

Holleb, Doris B. *Colleges and the Urban Poor: The Role of Public Higher Education in Community Service.* Lexington, MA: Lexington Books, 1972.

Holtz, Herman. *Marketing with Seminars and Newsletters.* Westport, CT: Quorum Books, 1986.

Hudson, Howard Penn. *Publishing Newsletters.* New York: Charles Scribner's Sons, 1982.

Hull, Gloria T., Patricia Bell Scott, and Barbara Woods, eds. *But Some of Us Are Brave: Black Women's Studies.* Old Westbury, NY: Feminist Press, 1982.

Hutton, Frankie. *The Early Black Press in America, 1827 to 1860.* Westport, CT: Greenwood Press, 1993.

Jacobs, Donald M., ed. *Antebellum Black Newspapers.* Westport, CT: Greenwood Press, 1978.

Johnson, Abby, and Ronald M. Johnson. *Propaganda and Aesthetics: The Literary Politics of Afro-American Magazines in the Twentieth Century.* Amherst: University of Massachusetts Press, 1979.

Johnson, Anthony W., ed. *Black Families and the Medium of Television.* Ann Arbor: Bush Program in Child Development, University of Michigan, 1982.

Johnson, Ben, and Mary Ballard Johnson. *Who's What and Where: A Directory of America's Black Journalists.* Detroit: Who's What and Where, 1985.

Johnson, Charles S. "The Rise of the Negro Magazine." *Journal of Negro History* 13, no. 1 (January 1928): 7–21.

Johnson, John H., with Lerone Bennett, Jr. *Succeeding against the Odds: The Autobiography of a Great American Businessman.* New York: Amistad Press, 1989.

Joyce, Donald Franklin. *Gatekeepers of Black Culture: Black-Owned Book Publishing in the United States, 1817–1981.* Westport, CT: Greenwood Press, 1983.

———. *Black Book Publishers in the United States: A Historical Directory of the Presses, 1817–1990.* Westport, CT: Greenwood Press, 1991.

Kinshasa, Kwando M. *Emigration vs. Assimilation: The Debate in the African American Press, 1827–1861.* Jefferson, NC: McFarland Press, 1988.

Kobre, Sidney, and Reva H. *A Gallery of Black Journalists Who Advanced Their Race.* Hamilton, VA: United Brothers and Sisters Communication Systems, 1993.

Kornweibel, Theodore, Jr. *No Crystal Stair: Black Life and the Messenger, 1917–1928.* Westport, CT: Greenwood Press, 1975.

LaBrie, Henry. *The Black Newspaper in America: A Guide.* Iowa City: Institute For Communication Studies, University of Iowa, 1970.

———. *A Survey of Black Newspapers in America.* Kennebunkport, ME: Mercer House, 1979.

Library of Congress. *Negro Newspapers on Microfilm: A Selected List.* Washington, DC: Library of Congress, 1953.

Lincoln, C. Eric. *The Black Muslims in America.* Boston: Beacon Press, 1961; reprint ed., Grand Rapids, MI: William B. Eerdmans Publishing Co.; and Trenton, NJ: Africa World Press, 1994.

Logan, Rayford W., ed. *The Attitude of the Southern White Press toward Negro Suffrage.* Washington, DC: Foundation Publishers, 1940.

Low, W. Augustus, and Virgil A. Clift, eds. *Encyclopedia of Black America.* New York: McGraw-Hill, 1981.

Lyle, Jack, ed. *The Black American and the Press.* Los Angeles: L. Ward Ritchie Press, 1968.

MacDonald, J. Fred. *Blacks and White T.V.: Afro-Americans in Television since 1948.* Chicago: Nelson-Hall, 1983.

Martin, Tony. *Race First: The Ideological and Organizational Struggles of Marcus Garvey and the Universal Negro Improvement Association.* Westport, CT: Greenwood Press, 1976.

McCain, Rea, Aris A. Mallas, Jr., and Margaret K. Hedden, *Forty Years in Politics: The Story of Ben Pelham.* Detroit: Wayne State University Press, 1958.

McFeely, William S. *Frederick Douglass.* New York: W. W. Norton, 1991.

Molden, Vaughnchille. *Telecommunications and Black Americans: A Survey of Ownership, Participation and Control.* St. Louis, MO: Center for Development Technology and Program in Technology and Human Affairs, Washington University, 1975.

National Black Business Directory, 1971. Minneapolis, MN: National Buy-Black Campaign, National Minority Business Directories, 1970.

National Newspaper Publishers Association. *Dedication of the Black Archives and Gallery of Distinguished Newspaper Publishers on the Occasion of the Sesquicentenary of the Founding of the Black Press in the United States.* Washington, DC: Howard University, 1977.

———. *Black Press Information Handbook.* Washington, DC: National Newspaper Publishers Association, 1985.

Oak, Vishnu. *The Negro Newspaper.* Westport, CT: Negro Universities Press, 1948.

Ottley, Roi. *The Lonely Warrior: The Life and Times of Robert S. Abbott.* Chicago: Regnery, 1955.

Penn, I. Garland. *The Afro-American Press and Its Editors.* Springfield, MA: Willey, 1891; reprint ed., New York: Arno Press and the New York Times, 1969.

Pinkney, Alphonso. *The Myth of Black Progress.* New York: Cambridge University Press, 1984.

Pinkney, Junete A. "Independent Black Publishing." *American Visions* (April 1989): 50–54.

Ploski, Harry, and James Williamson. *The Negro Almanac, A Reference Work on the Afro-American.* New York: John Wiley and Sons, 1983.

———, eds. *Reference Library of Black America.* New York: John Wiley and Sons, 1990.

Pohlmann, Marcus D. *Black Politics in Conservative America.* New York: Longman, 1990.

Potter, Vilma Raskin. *A Reference Guide to Afro-American Publications and Editors, 1827–1946.* Ames: Iowa State University Press, 1993.

Prattis, P. L. "Racial Segregation and Negro Journalism." *Phylon* 8, no. 4 (Fourth Quarter, 1947): 305–14.

Pride, Armistead Scott. "A Register and History of Negro Newspapers in the United States, 1827–1950." Ph.D. dissertation, Northwestern University, 1950.

———. "The Names of Negro Newspapers." *American Speech* 29, no. 2 (May 1954): 114–18.

———. *The Black Press: A Bibliography.* Jefferson City, MO: Department of Journalism, Lincoln University, 1968.

Pride, Armistead S., and Clint C. Wilson II. *A History of the Black Press.* Washington, DC: Howard University Press, 1997.

Quarles, Benjamin. *Black Abolitionists.* New York: Oxford University Press, 1969.

———. *Frederick Douglass.* New York: Oxford University Press, 1976.

Rampersad, Arnold. *The Life of Langston Hughes. Volume 1: 1902–1941: I, Too, Sing America*. New York: Oxford University Press, 1986.

———. *Volume II: 1941–1967: I Dream a World*. New York: Oxford University Press, 1988.

Randall, Dudley. *Broadside Memories: Poets I Have Known*. Detroit: Broadside Press, 1975.

Redmond, Eugene. "Stridency and the Sword: Literary and Cultural Emphasis in Afro-American Magazines." In Elliott Anderson and Mary Kinzie, eds., *The Little Magazine in America: A Modern Documentary History*. Yonkers, NY: Pushcart Press, 1978.

Rollin, Frank A. *Life and Public Services of Martin R. Delaney*. New York: Arno Press, 1969.

Sawyer, Frank B., and Ruth Castor, eds. *U.S. Negro World, 1966: Directory of United States Negro Newspapers, Magazines and Periodicals*. Ann Arbor, MI: University Microfilms, 1970.

Schor, Joel. *Henry Highland Garnet: A Voice of Black Radicalism in the Nineteenth Century*. Westport, CT: Greenwood Press, 1977.

Senna, Carl. *The Black Press and the Struggle for Civil Rights*. New York: African-American Experience—Franklin Watts, 1993.

Simmons, Charles A. *The African American Press: A History of News Coverage during National Crises, with Special Reference to Four Black Newspapers, 1827–1965*. Jefferson, NC: McFarland Press, 1997.

Simmons, William J. *Men of Mark*. Chicago: George M. Rewell and Co., 1887; reprint ed., New York: Arno Press and the *New York Times*, 1968.

Smith, Jessie Carney. *Notable Black American Women*. Detroit: Gale Research, 1992.

Smith, William Gardner. *Return to Black America*. Englewood Cliffs, NJ: Prentice-Hall, 1970.

Snorgrass, J. William. "Freedom of the Press and Black Publications." *Western Journal of Black Studies* 4, no 3 (Fall 1980): 172–78.

Sorin, Sullivan. *Freedom's Journal: A History of the Black Press in New York State*. New York: New York Public Library, 1986.

Stevens, John D. *From the Back of the Foxhole: Black Correspondents in World War II*. Lexington: Department of Journalism, University of Kentucky, Association for Education in Journalism, 1973.

———. "The Black Press Looks at 1920's Journalism." *Journalism History* 7, nos. 3–4 (Autumn–Winter 1980): 109–113.

Suggs, Henry L., ed. *The Black Press in the South, 1865–1979*. Westport, CT: Greenwood Press, 1983.

———. *P. B. Young Newspaperman: Race, Politics, and Journalism in the New South, 1910–62*. Charlottesville: University Press of Virginia, 1988.

———, ed. *The Black Press in the Middle West, 1865–1985*. Westport, CT: Greenwood Press, 1996.

Taylor, Arnold H. *Travail and Triumph: Black Life and Culture in the South since the Civil War*. Westport, CT: Greenwood Press, 1977.

Thiong'o, wa Ngugi. *Decolonizing the Mind: The Politics of Language in African Literature*. London: Currey, 1986.

Thompson, Julius E. *Dudley Randall, Broadside Press, and the Black Arts Movement in Detroit, 1960–1995*. Jefferson, NC: McFarland Press, 1998.

————. *The Black Press in Mississippi, 1865–1985: A Directory*. West Cornwall, CT: Locust Hill Press, 1993.

————. *The Black Press in Mississippi, 1865–1985*. Gainesville, FL: University Press of Florida, 1993.

————. *Percy Greene and the Jackson Advocate: The Life and Times of a Radical Conservative Black Newspaperman, 1897–1977*. Jefferson, NC: McFarland Press, 1994.

Thornbrough, Emma Lou. *T. Thomas Fortune: Militant Journalist*. Chicago: University of Chicago Press, 1972.

Tinney, James S., and Justine J. Rector, eds. *Issues and Trends in Afro-American Journalism*. Washington, DC: University Press of America, 1980.

Tripp, Bernell E. *Origins of the Black Press: New York, 1827–1847*. Northport, AL: Vision Press, 1992.

Walker, David. *Walker's Appeal in Four Articles; Together with a Preamble to the Coloured Citizens of the World*. Boston, 1830.

Walker, Wyatt Tee. *Somebody's Calling My Name: Black Sacred Music and Social Change*. Valley Forge, PA: Judson Press, 1979.

Washburn, Patrick S. *A Question of Sedition: The Federal Government's Investigation of the Black Press during World War II*. New York: Oxford University Press, 1986.

Wells, Ida B. *Crusade for Justice*. Edited by Alfreda M. Duster. Chicago: University of Chicago Press, 1970.

Wesley, Charles H. *The Quest for Equality: From Civil War to Civil Rights*. Washington, DC: Association for the Study of Negro Life and History, 1968.

Wickham, De Wayne, ed. *Thinking Black: Some of the Nation's Best Black Columnists Speak Their Minds*. New York: Crown Publishers, 1996.

Wilkins, Roy, with Tom Mathews. *Standing Fast: The Autobiography of Roy Wilkins*. New York: Viking Press, 1982.

Williams, Gilbert Anthony. *The Christian Recorder, Newspaper of the African Methodist Episcopal Church: History of a Forum for Ideas, 1854–1902*. Jefferson, NC: McFarland Press, 1996.

Wilson, Clint C., II. *Black Journalists in Paradox: Historical Perspectives and Current Dilemmas*. New York: Greenwood Press, 1991.

Wolseley, Roland E. *The Black Press, U.S.A.* Ames: Iowa State University Press, 1990.

Work, Monroe. *Negro Year Book*. Tuskegee AL: Negro Year Book Publishing Co., 1912, 1918–19, 1922, 1947.

XI

African Americans in the Military of the United States

John F. Marszalek and Horace D. Nash

The writing on the role of blacks in the armed forces of the United States has mirrored the study of African American history in general. White historians, reflecting the dominant society's attitudes, long ignored the black presence, mentioning African Americans only in passing and then as negatively as possible. A few African American historians wrote books or articles contesting this omission, discussing not merely a black presence in American wars but also black loyalty and courage. These comments were patronizingly ignored, the historians' black skins or liberal outlook negating any possibility of white society's acceptance of their findings. Though these pioneer historians accomplished significant work, black faces remained absent from mainstream American historiography.

The major change in this pattern of omission in the history books as well as in society as a whole resulted from the civil rights movement of the 1960s. Educational and intellectual institutions came to recognize the depth of their anti-black discrimination and scrambled to make amends. As a result, historians, both black and white, began looking at American history in a new light. The search was on for black faces—more correctly, for black heroes—to take their places alongside the white heroes long enshrined in the history books. Since wars created heroes, the black role in the American military became a particularly logical place for white society to try to make amends. The obvious fact of discrimination in the military was expertly documented in a variety of books and articles. Not surprisingly, the neglected work of the pioneer historians was also reprinted.

In many ways, this insistence that blacks had participated in all American wars and that they had been heroes despite the tremendous discrimination against them still controls the historiography of the topic. In recent times, however, as African American history has no longer had to justify its existence, the study of blacks in the military has expanded beyond victims and heroes. Recent work has dealt with more sophisticated topics of race relations, such as the impact on communities of the presence of black soldiers and the community's surprisingly complicated response to the black soldiers in their midst. A multitude of other questions are also being asked: Was there a regional difference to the American attitude toward African American soldiers? What was the relationship between white and black soldiers and between officers of different races? What role did black members of the armed forces play in the larger black community? And, most significantly, what impact has the presence of black men (and now black women) in the military had in reflecting the black status in American society as a whole. In short, historians are viewing the question of African Americans in the military from a wider perspective than ever before. Clearly, however, the process is only in its earliest stages.

This chapter and the bibliography that accompanies it can cover only a limited and selective sampling of the works published in this field. *Blacks in the American Armed Forces, 1776–1983: A Bibliography* (1985), by Lenwood G. Davis and George Hall, comps., lists 2,386 books, articles, and dissertations, but this book is already out of date. The *America: History and Life* database and the book review sections of the *Journal of American History* and of other journals include the latest articles and monographs on the topic. A more specialized source is Roger Dale Hardaway's *A Narrative Bibliography of the African-American Frontier: Blacks in the Rocky Mountain West, 1535–1912* (1995).

Basic information on blacks in the military appears in all the traditional overviews of African American history such as John Hope Franklin and Alfred A. Moss, Jr., *From Slavery to Freedom*, 7th ed. (1994). There are also, however, several books that are helpful in-depth surveys and contain useful bibliographies. Jack D. Foner's *Blacks and the Military in American History: A New Perspective* (1974) is the first synthesis of the historiographical renaissance created by the civil rights years, whereas Bernard C. Nalty, *Strength for the Fight: A History of Black Americans in the Military* (1986) is a more recent study and considered the standard book on the topic. John F. Marszalek's 1973 article "The Black Man in Military History" is a brief analysis that discusses how, throughout American history, the need for black soldiers overcame white society's fear of them. Marszalek points out that blacks saw participation in military service as providing the promise of a better postwar life.

Helpful to those doing research on this topic are the several published document collections. Still the most complete is Morris J. MacGregor, Jr., and Bernard C. Nalty's edited work: *Blacks in the United States Armed Forces: Basic Documents*, 13 vols. (1977). Available in five reels of microfilm from the National Archives is Elon A. Woodward's 1888 compilation of *The Negro in the Military Service of the United States, 1639–1886*. Ira Berlin, Joseph P. Reidy, and Leslie S. Rowland's edited work *The Black Military Experience*

(1982) is part of the multivolume *A Documentary History of Emancipation, 1861–1867* and provides sources for the study of the role of African Americans in the Civil War military.

Black people arrived with the European conquerors and settlers; thus blacks had the opportunity to appear early in this hemisphere's military history. During the North American colonial period, they fought with whites in wars against the Native Americans and in those between European colonial empires. Black participation depended on the need for their services, which need manifested itself frequently. As soon as white society felt confident in its own ability to defend itself without black help, however, whites immediately excluded blacks. Since slavery was growing at the same time that these colonial and anti–Native American wars were taking place, white fear of armed blacks was intense. Could their loyalty be trusted, or would they turn on their white masters and fight with the French, Spanish, or English or the Native Americans?

Important early studies of blacks in the colonial period are Lorenzo J. Greene's *Negro in Colonial New England* (1942) and his article "The Negro in the Armed Forces of the United States, 1619–1783" (1951). Benjamin Quarles's "Colonial Militia and Negro Manpower" (1959) is another valuable journal account. A more recent study is Peter Voelz's *Slave and Soldier: The Military Impact of Blacks in the Colonial Americas* (1993). In this published dissertation, Voelz analyzes the role of blacks in the military throughout the New World. He concludes that whenever there was a shortage of white fighters, colonial governments were quick to utilize blacks in the military against an external enemy or an internal slave rebellion. Kenneth Porter, in *The Negro on the American Frontier* (1971), discusses how, in 1740, blacks, Native Americans, and Spaniards cooperated against an English invasion of Spanish Florida; and Jane Lander's 1993 article "Black-Indian Interaction in Spanish Florida" provides an analysis of one of the successful Native American–black alliances with the Spanish against invaders from the north.

The role of African Americans in the American Revolution was an early focus of historians' attention. William C. Nell made the first serious attempt to write this history in *Colored Patriots of the American Revolution* (1855), but also important is a recently republished nineteenth-century book by Leila Amos Pendleton, *A Narrative of the Negro. Missing Pages in American History: Revealing the Services of Negroes in the Early Wars in the United States of America, 1641–1815*, ed. by Laura E. Wilkes (1996). Benjamin Quarles's *Negro in the American Revolution* (1961), however, had the first real impact on the historical profession's view of the African American role in the conflict. Quarles argued that both the British and the Americans used blacks in the military whenever needed, though at first both feared arming either slaves or free blacks. When the British governor of Virginia, Lord Dunmore, promised freedom to any slaves who left their masters and joined the British side, the Americans reversed themselves and reluctantly accepted black support. By war's end, over 5,000 blacks served in the American land and sea forces. On the British side, there was a so-called Lord Dunmore's Ethiopian Regiment. Historian George Fenwick Jones discusses the black tie to German mercenary troops in his 1982 article "The Black Hessians: Negroes Recruited by the Hessians in South Carolina and Other Colonies."

Once the American Revolution ended, northern states gradually abolished slavery. Thereafter, the post-Revolutionary American land forces primarily consisted of state and local militias, from which blacks were almost uniformly excluded. The navy also became smaller, but blacks still remained a part of this service. Rayford W. Logan's 1951 article "The Negro in the Quasi War, 1798–1800" discusses African Americans' role in this minor conflict with France. In 1807, when the British ship *Leopard* stopped the American frigate *Chesapeake* off the Virginia coast looking for deserters, the captain impressed four sailors, three of whom were black.

During the War of 1812, blacks played an important part in Oliver Hazard Perry's victory on Lake Erie and helped to man ocean-going vessels and privateers. Blacks, such as the free men of color who fought with Andrew Jackson at New Orleans, also fought on land. William C. Nell discussed War of 1812 African American soldiers and sailors in his *Services of Colored Americans in the Wars of 1776 and 1812* (1851), as did Joseph T. Wilson in *The Black Phalanx* (1887). Ira Dye's 1973 article "Seafarers of 1813: A Profile" indicates that in some instances American ships were fully manned by blacks, with the exception of the captain. Gerard T. Altoff's *Amongst My Best Men: African-Americans and the War of 1812* (1996) discusses blacks on land and sea, and Martha S. Putney's *Black Sailors: Afro-American Merchant Seamen and Whalemen prior to the Civil War* (1987) argues that blacks were integral parts of the navy, merchant marine, and whaling industry from the nation's birth. W. Jeffrey Bolster's *Black Jacks: African American Seamen in the Age of Sail* (1997) presents important information on black merchantmen and black naval personnel from 1740 to 1865. Harold D. Langley's *Social Reform in the United States Navy, 1798–1862* (1967) includes a discussion of black sailors after the War of 1812, and Roland C. McConnell's *Negro Troops of Antebellum Louisiana: A History of the Battalion of Free Men of Color* (1968) describes the unit that fought with Jackson and shows how it was pushed aside in the years after the battle.

During the two Seminole wars in the post–War of 1812 period, blacks played an important role; in fact, they were one of the major causes for the fighting. Until Kenneth W. Porter's articles in the early 1940s, historians saw these wars primarily as an American attempt to force the Seminoles from Florida. Porter argued that the initial 1816 and 1818 American invasions of Florida resulted from the desire to break up runaway slave settlements considered a threat to the American frontier and slavery. Such Indian and black settlements had existed since the eighteenth century, but they were not viewed as particularly dangerous until the nineteenth century. Fortunately, Porter's essays have been consolidated in his *Negro on the American Frontier* (1971).

Reflecting Porter's influence, William Loren Katz's 1977 article "Black and Indian Cooperation and Resistance to Slavery" asserts that during the Second Seminole War, American military authorities concluded that blacks dominated Seminole councils. Cheryl Race Boyett supports this position in her 1996 master's thesis "The Seminole-Black Alliance during the Second Seminole War, 1835–1842." Phillip Thomas Tucker describes one such leader in his 1992 article "John Horse: Forgotten African-American Leader of the Second Seminole War." Kenneth W. Porter's *Black Seminoles*, which was edited by Alcione M. Amos and Thomas P. Senter (1996), discusses in detail these African American Seminoles and their leader, John Horse, and describes their movement to the West, where they fought as border guards for the Mexican government and as cavalry guides in the post–Civil War Indian wars. They won Medals of Honor, but the army disbanded their unit anyway.

Whereas other wars have experienced increased interest, the literature on black participation in the Mexican War is slight because the black role in this war was so minimal. Robert E. May's 1987 article "Invisible Men: Blacks and the U.S. Army in the Mexican War" demonstrates that though few blacks fought in the war, they served in a variety of roles, sometimes even as soldiers. A few slaves with the American army, noting Mexico's laws against slavery, fled to enemy lines to gain their freedom.

The black role in the Civil War has been the focus of a variety of studies dating from the nineteenth century. This topic has also shared in the increased interest resulting from the 125th anniversary of the conflict. Joseph Wilson's *Black Phalanx* (1887) and George Washington Williams's *History of the Negro Troops in the War of the Rebellion, 1861–1865* (1888) are the earliest major black accounts of African American service in the war. Thomas Wentworth Higginson, a white Union officer in an all-black unit, argued in his frequently republished memoirs, *Army Life in a Black Regiment* (1870), that because African Americans were fighting for their own freedom, they were better soldiers than their white counterparts.

As he did later for the American Revolution, Benjamin Quarles in *The Negro in the Civil War* (1953) wrote the first comprehensive scholarly treatment of blacks in the Civil War. Dudley Cornish's *The Sable Arm: Negro Troops in the Union Army, 1861–1865* (1956) is a pioneer study of the black soldier in combat. *Thomas Morris Chester, Black Civil War Correspondent: His Dispatches from the Virginia Front*, edited by R.J.M. Blackett (1989), is a collection of newspaper articles from the white *Philadelphia Press* highlighting the contributions of black soldiers in the Union army's final push on Richmond.

James M. McPherson's *Struggle for Equality: Abolitionists and the Negro in the Civil War and Reconstruction* (1964) discusses the key relationship of these two groups in advancing the conflict's emancipation agenda. McPherson's book *The Negro's Civil War* (1965) is a collection of documents presenting the black perspective on the war. Mary Frances Berry, in *Military Necessity and Civil Rights Policy* (1977), argues that military manpower needs provided a dominant reason for including blacks in the Union's Civil War military effort and that the black soldier's excellent performance helped bring about emancipation and the civil rights laws of the Reconstruction years.

Two recent books have had a significant influence on Civil War historiography. Joseph T. Glatthaar's *Forged in Battle: The Civil War Alliance of Black Soldiers and White Officers* (1990) is now the standard account of African Americans in the war. He argues that during the conflict a bond developed between the black soldiers and their white officers, but this relationship disappeared quickly when the war ended. Within a short time, even Union veterans dismissed the wartime contributions of the United States Colored Troops. More controversial is Ervin L. Jordan, Jr.'s *Black Confederates and Afro-Yankees in Civil War Virginia* (1995), which argues that a small number of blacks fought for the Confederacy and that large numbers played an important role in other aspects of the Confederate war effort. Some amateur historians and enthusiasts have manufactured claims that numerous blacks fought to preserve the Confederacy, thus allegedly proving that slavery did not cause the Civil War; but Jordan makes no such assertion. Edwin S. Redkey, editor of *A Grand Army of Black Men: Letters from African-American Soldiers in the Union Army, 1861–1865* (1992), reveals the feelings of Union soldiers in letters home and to friends. James G. Hollandsworth's *Louisiana Native Guard: The Black Military Experience during the Civil War* (1995) is an in-depth account of one unit. The most famous all-black unit was the 54th Massachusetts. The movie *Glory*, one of the best motion pictures ever made on a military topic, movingly portrays the 54th's contribution to the Union victory.

A recurring topic in the historiography of blacks in the Civil War is the discussion of whether the Fort Pillow incident of April 12, 1864, was a slaughter of black troops after Confederate general Nathan Bedford Forrest had secured their surrender. As early as 1958, Albert Castel's article "The Fort Pillow Massacre: A Fresh Examination of the Evidence" presented proof to demonstrate the existence of a massacre, and in recent years John Cimprich and Robert C. Mainfort, Jr.'s "Fort Pillow Revisited: New Evidence about an Old Controversy" (1982) and "The Fort Pillow Massacre: A Statistical Note" (1989), as well as Richard L. Fuchs's *Unerring Fire: The Massacre at Fort Pillow* (1994), provided further proof to buttress this indisputable point. Kenneth Bancroft Moore's 1995 article "Fort Pillow, Forrest, and the United States Colored Troops in 1864" points out that in subsequent actions against Forrest, United States Colored Troops fought fiercely, concerned that they not suffer the same fate as their comrades at Fort Pillow.

Several articles deal with additional maltreatment of black soldiers. Mike Fisher's "First Kansas Colored: Massacre at Poison Spring" (1979) and "Remember Poison Spring" (1980), as well as Anne J. Bailey's "Was There a Massacre at Poison Spring?" (1990), conclude that statistical data as well as eyewitness accounts show conclusively that Samuel Bell Maxey's Confederate troops massacred black soldiers at this skirmish. Gregory J. Urwin's " 'We Cannot Treat Negroes. . . . as Prisoners of Wars' " (1996) analyzes the Poison Spring incident as well as other atrocities in Arkansas.

Studies of African Americans in the Civil War naturally go beyond the battlefield. Paul E. Steiner's *Medical History of a Civil War Regiment* (1977) analyzes the harsh impact of disease on the 65th United States Colored Infantry Regiment. Susie King Taylor's *Black Woman's Civil War Memoirs: Reminiscences of My Life in Camp with the 33rd U.S. Colored Troops, Late 1st South Carolina Volunteers*, edited by Patricia W. Romero (1988) details the life of a slave woman who worked as a laundress, teamster, teacher, and nurse in a black regiment. Jeffrey D. Wert's 1979 article "Camp William Penn and the Black Soldier" discusses the positive white community–black soldier relationship of eleven black regiments in training outside of Philadelphia. Edwin S. Redkey's "Black Chaplains in the Union Army" (1987) studies fourteen of these chaplains, arguing that there were so few of them that most black soldiers never saw one, and that these chaplains were so non-threatening that they made the concept of black officers somewhat more palatable to whites.

Although the research concerning black service during the Civil War concentrates on black soldiers, there are a few studies of African Americans in the Union navy. Herbert Aptheker's 1947 article "The Negro in the Union Navy" is a thorough study that shows that African Americans constituted about 25 percent of all naval personnel and provided significant service. David L. Valuska's *African American in the Union Navy, 1861–1865* (1993) is a published doctoral dissertation and provides up-to-date research on the important black naval role. Oden Edet Uya's *From Slavery to Public Service: Robert Smalls, 1839–1915* (1971) and Edward A. Miller, Jr.'s *Gullah Statesman: Robert Smalls from Slavery to Congress, 1839–1915* (1995) are accounts of the slave pilot and later black congressman who became a national sensation when he ran the Confederate ship *Planter* out of Charleston harbor for surrender to the Union blockade.

A controversial aspect of Reconstruction, which followed the Civil War, was the existence of blacks serving in southern state militias. Otis Singletary's *Negro Militia and Reconstruction* (1957) remains an important study on this topic. Although Leon Litwack's *Been in the Storm So Long* (1979) is not a military study, it does present good insight into the overall impact black soldiers made on black and white southerners during this period. All the general studies of Reconstruction contain discussion and analyses of the black soldier, including the now standard book by Eric Foner *Reconstruction: America's Unfinished Revolution, 1863–1877* (1988).

From Reconstruction to the turn of the twentieth century, as C. Vann Woodward has shown in his *Strange Career of Jim Crow* (1974), the nation grappled with the proper place for the newly freed slaves, finally settling, through custom and law, on segregation. This practice was dramatically evident in the important debate on the African American role in the postwar military. The navy systematically eliminated black sailors, and in 1869 Congress passed an army reorganization law that, among other changes, consolidated the black 38th, 39th, 40th, and 41st Infantry Regiments into two units, the 24th and the 25th. Meanwhile, the black 9th and 10th Cavalry Regiments remained intact.

The history of black participation in the military during the period from Reconstruction to the post–World War I years, therefore, is largely the story of these four units. Since they spent almost all their time in the West, their history has primarily focused on the impact they had on this region. Influenced by new social history, historians of the black military experience during these years have examined not simply military operations but also camp and community life, as well as the social, economic, and political aspects of the African American military experience.

The literature for this period has continued to grow in volume and depth. William H. Leckie in his 1967 book *The Buffalo Soldiers: A Narrative of the Negro Cavalry in the West* described the role of the 9th and 10th Cavalry Regiments in the settlement of the West and how such units provided blacks with an honorable place in an American society that otherwise shunned them. Arlen Fowler's *Black Infantry in the West 1869–1891* (1971) narrates the activities of the 24th and 25th Infantry Regiments, citing their interaction with white society and the hostility they often faced. In his 1970 doctoral dissertation, "The Black Regulars: Negro Soldiers in the United States Army, 1866–1891," Tom Phillips provides a comprehensive study of his subject. Jack D. Foner's *United States Soldier between Two Wars: Army Life and Reforms, 1865–1898* (1970) points out that life for both white and black soldiers on the frontier was difficult, but it was worse for blacks because of the discrimination they faced. In addition to harsher court-martial sentences and other unfair treatment, for example, only one company of late-nineteenth-century black regulars ever served east of the Mississippi, near a large population area. John M. Carroll's *Black Military Experience in the American West* (1971) is a collection of earlier historical accounts on this topic; William Loren Katz's *The Black West* (1971), W. Sherman Savage's *Blacks in the West* (1976), Edward M. Coffman's *Old Army: A Portrait of the American Army in Peacetime 1784–1898* (1986), and Frank N. Schubert's *Black Valor: Buffalo Soldiers and the Medal of Honor, 1870–1898* (1997) all contain important information on this topic.

L. D. Reddick's 1949 article "The Negro Policy of the United States Army, 1775–1945" states that this period, despite its difficulties, was the "golden day," the time when black soldiers received the greatest number of military honors. A good insight into the significant role of the important black chaplains is Alan K. Lamm's 1995 dissertation, "Buffalo Soldier Chaplains: A Case Study of the Five Black United States Army Chaplains, 1884–1901."

It was also during these years that blacks first became cadets at West Point, attempting to overcome the long-standing prejudice against black officers. Except for the black chaplains who held officer rank but were non-threatening because of their non-command status, the only regular army black officers during the late-nineteenth-century period were West Point graduates Henry O. Flipper, John H. Alexander, and Charles Young. All suffered severe discrimination during their West Point and later army careers. Flipper wrote the remembrances of his life in *The Colored Cadet at West Point* (1878), and Charles M. Robinson III's *Court-Martial of Lieutenant Henry Flipper* (1994) and Barry C. Johnson's *Flipper's Dismissal: The Ruin of Lt. Henry O. Flipper, U.S.A., First Colored Graduate of West Point* (1972) present the most thorough accounts of his unfair dismissal from the army in 1881. Willard B. Gatewood's 1982 article "John Hanks Alexander of Arkansas: Second Black Graduate of West Point" is the best account of this West Pointer who had a heart attack and died soon after he went on active duty. For the story of Charles Young, who served in the army until the eve of World War I and then was summarily retired to prevent his commanding white soldiers, there is Abraham Chew's *A Biography of Colonel Charles Young* (1923) and Nancy G. Heinl's 1977 article "Colonel Charles Young: Pointman." Thorough short sketches of these individuals and a host of other major black figures may be found in the *Dictionary of Negro Biography* (1983), edited by Rayford W. Logan and Michael R. Winston; and *On the Trail of the Buffalo Soldier: Biographies of African-Americans in the U.S. Army, 1866–1917* (1995), compiled and edited by Frank N. Schubert.

Over twenty other individuals applied to West Point, and a number who never graduated attended the institution for varying lengths of time. William P. Vaughn's 1971 article "West Point and the First Negro Cadet" discusses the experiences of James Webster Smith. He was the Academy's first black cadet and battled mightily and unsuccessfully against the prejudice and the ostracism he encountered in his failed effort to graduate. John F. Marszalek's *Court-Martial: A Black Man in America* (1972) examines the experiences of Johnson Chesnut Whittaker, who was separated from the Academy after a sensational court case. A 1994 made-for-television motion picture, *Assault at West Point*, and a paperback edition of the 1972 book, under the new title, resulted in President William Jefferson Clinton's, during a 1995 White House ceremony, righting the century-old wrong and awarding Whittaker a posthumous army commission. For a study of an even smaller number of African Americans, black naval cadets, the first one of whom did not graduate until 1949, there is R. L. Field's 1973 article "The Black Midshipman at the U.S. Naval Academy."

The 1890s saw the advent of both full-blown Jim Crowism in American life and the Spanish-American War, each of which influenced the role of blacks in the military. The Supreme Court decision in *Plessy v. Ferguson* (1896) established segregation as the law of the land. The Spanish-American War included among its American fighting force the regular black regiments and the several black national guard units. One of the contemporary accounts is Miles V. Lynk's *Black Troopers, or The Daring Heroism of the Negro Soldier in the Spanish American War* (1899). Marvin E. Fletcher's *Black Soldier and Officer in the United States Army, 1891–1917* (1974) discusses how the existing discrimination created the situation that led to the black nadir during World War I. Willard B. Gatewood, Jr.'s *Black Americans and the White Man's Burden,*

1898–1903 (1975) and *"Smoked Yankees" and the Struggle for Empire: Letters from Negro Soldiers, 1898–1902* (1971) demonstrate that blacks had mixed reactions to fighting other people of color in the imperialistic battles of this period but did so because they believed it was their patriotic duty. Further, they hoped that such loyalty would lessen white prejudice against them. Blacks were badly mistreated in an army allegedly bringing democracy and freedom to benighted peoples around the world. Especially hurtful was Rough Rider Theodore Roosevelt's unfounded criticism of black troops as cowards. The difficult times blacks suffered in the National Guard during this war is later described in Charles Johnson, Jr.'s *African American Soldiers in the National Guard: Recruitment and Deployment during Peacetime and War* (1992).

With the Spanish-American War and the Philippine insurrection over, the army returned to peacetime status. Black troops were sent to the nation's newly acquired possessions or once more returned to the West, the areas far from population centers. The Mexican Revolution brought black troops to the Mexican border in Arizona and New Mexico. When authorities sent a punitive expedition into Mexico against Pancho Villa for his 1916 attack on Columbus, New Mexico, the 10th Cavalry Regiment and the 24th Infantry participated in the operation. Clarence C. Clendenen's *Blood on the Border: The United States Army and the Mexican Irregulars* (1969) and Bruce Johnson's 1964 dissertation, "The Punitive Expedition: A Military, Diplomatic, and Political History of Pershing's Chase after Pancho Villa, 1916–1917," both provide thorough accounts of the black troops involved.

Recent historical study concerning blacks in the military is shedding increased light on the interaction between black soldiers and white civilians in the West. Many of the works previously cited discuss these matters, and there are numerous specialized works besides. Leading the way is Frank N. Schubert's 1971 article "Black Soldiers on the White Frontier: Some Factors Influencing Race Relations." In this study of Wyoming from 1885 to 1912, Schubert argues that the varying conditions of frontier life played an important role in shaping white racial attitudes toward black soldiers. Urban versus rural areas, location near Indian reservations, and the need for security, all helped shape the degree of racial prejudice. Consequently, black soldiers' experiences with white society in Wyoming varied, and, Schubert argues, the same generalization could be made for the entire West. He called for studies of other locations in the region to test his hypothesis. In 1992 he published such an investigation himself entitled *Buffalo Soldiers, Braves, and the Brass: The Story of Fort Robinson, Nebraska*.

Other historians have also risen to the challenge, and their studies have refined Schubert's views. Monroe L. Billington, in *New Mexico's Buffalo Soldiers, 1866–1900* (1991) while discussing the major role black troopers played in the territory, suggested that factors such as sports and cultural events may have lessened the existing white civilian prejudice. Black and white soldiers, when garrisoned in the same area, lived a segregated existence but with little overt animosity. Michael J. Clark's 1979 dissertation, "A History of the Twenty-fourth

United States Infantry Regiment in Utah, 1896–1900," discusses the attempt of black soldiers and their families to improve the quality of their lives by creating their own communities while at the same time interacting with civilian blacks and even whites. Such activities and the economic benefits to the white community resulting from the presence of the black soldiers mitigated the existing racism. Horace D. Nash in his 1996 dissertation, "Town and Sword: Black Soldiers in Columbus, New Mexico, in the Early Twentieth Century," finds that in that town, despite deeply ingrained racial prejudice, local attitudes toward black soldiers were less discriminatory than they were in many other areas of the nation. Though Columbus citizens would have preferred white soldiers, they worried about losing the garrison and kept their attitudes to themselves. The absence of preexisting forms of black-white relations, recreational interaction, economic benefits of the military presence, a mixture of individuals originally from various geographic locations, all combined to prevent hard-core racism from dominating the community.

Garna L. Christian, in a series of articles and in *Black Soldiers in Jim Crow Texas, 1899–1917* (1995), builds on earlier research and advances the thesis that black resentment toward the increasing racism of the Jim Crow era (1899–1917) helped fuel eight racial clashes. Christian argues that blacks simply refused to endure further abuse and fought back against the growing discrimination and violence they faced. Rising expectations fueled in the Spanish-American War came face to face with rising racism, and the result was conflict. The most famous was the Brownsville affair in Texas. Ann J. Lane's *Brownsville Affair: National Crisis and Black Reaction* (1971) and John D. Weaver's *Brownsville Raid* (1970/1992) provided detailed descriptions of the event when, after white civilians in the Texas town accosted black soldiers, an unidentified group of men shot up a three-block area near the army fort. No soldier admitted involvement in the shooting, but after an investigation tinged with prejudice, President Theodore Roosevelt ordered, without any trial, the dishonorable discharge of the entire suspected unit, some 167 soldiers. In the early 1970s, the Secretary of the Army changed all the discharges to honorable.

Robert V. Haynes's *Night of Violence: The Houston Riot of 1917* (1976) details this terrible event. In the early months of World War I the Houston police beat a soldier of the 24th Infantry Regiment. A number of his angry colleagues took to the streets in retaliation and were subsequently court-martialed; several were later executed. Once again, white racism and black refusal to accept blatant discrimination fueled the bloodshed.

When the United States entered World War I in 1917, racism, discrimination, and bad feelings existed between whites and blacks in the military. Blacks, despite previous discouragement, once more hoped that courageous participation in the World War would temper such anti-black feelings and result in a better life for all African Americans afterward. White society, however, continued to regard the idea of black soldiers as threatening.

An important early account of the black combat role is *Scott's Official History of the American Negro in the World War* by Emmett J. Scott (1919). Charles H. Williams's *Negro Soldiers in World War I: The Human Side* (1970) is the report of Williams's eighteen-month investigation of the conditions black soldiers faced in both the United States and France. Addie W. Hunton and Katherine M. Johnson's *Two Colored Women with the American Expeditionary Forces* (1920) is a discussion of the role of black women. Edward M. Coffman's *War to End Wars: The American Military Experience in World War I* (1968) contains an excellent overview of the black wartime experience, including an account of the all-black 92nd Division.

Arthur E. Barbeau and Florette Henri's *Unknown Soldiers: Black American Troops in World War I* (1974) is now the standard account. The authors demonstrate that discrimination, army racial stereotyping, and the consequent attempt to use black men only as laborers and not as front-line soldiers reflected white society's view of black soldiers. Believing that blacks were inferior fighting men, white society and military officials leapt at any opportunity to buttress their racism. When some units in the all-black 92nd Division performed poorly in France, the result provided new justification for white racism. Barbeau and Henri argue, in response, that inadequate training, outdated equipment, and lack of confidence shown by white officers in their black subordinates caused the poor performances.

Gerald W. Patton in *War and Race: The Black Officer in the American Military, 1915–1941* (1981) studies the black officer during World War I and the years before World War II. The federal government established a training camp for black officers at Fort Des Moines, Iowa, as a result of black community pressure, but it maintained its policy of not allowing black officers to command whites. Black officers were not even allowed to command at the higher echelons of all-black units. Patton finds, however, that despite enormous discrimination, black officers performed well as a group. Their performance made no difference. After the war, racism in the military resulted in the reduction of the historic black infantry and cavalry regiments to service functions. In the navy, blacks served only as mess men and stevedores and not as front-line sailors.

When in 1941 the Japanese attack on Pearl Harbor caused the United States to enter World War II, the black presence in the U.S. military was limited to a few national guard units and menial service in the regular armed forces. Yet, during the war almost a million blacks served in the military, some 500,000 of them deployed overseas. Theirs was, yet again, not an easy existence. Walter White's *Rising Wind* (1945) is an important race relations study written by the former executive director of the National Association for the Advancement of Colored People who visited the military in Europe and saw firsthand the conditions blacks suffered. John D. Silvera's *Negro in World War II* (1947) contains excellent photographs. The standard account of the black role in the war is Ulysses Lee's *Employment of Negro Troops* (1966), which is a part of the U.S. Army official history series. Lee points out that had it not been for Pearl Harbor and the sense of urgency after the attack, blacks would have been destined to remain in supply and service units. Instead, the nation's need paved the way for black participation in all branches of the armed forces. Segregation remained, however, with the first combat integration since the American Revolution coming only during the 1944 Battle of the Bulge when the need for riflemen resulted in a sprinkling of black infantrymen in otherwise all-white units. Histories of the most famous black unit in the war are Charles E. Francis's *Tuskegee Airmen: The Story of the Negro in the U.S. Air Force* (1955) and Robert J. Jakeman's *Divided Skies: Establishing Segregated Flight Training at Tuskegee, Alabama 1934–1942* (1992). A more general study is Stanley Sandler, *Segregated Skies: Black Combat Squadrons of World War II* (1992); and, though the 1995 Home Box Office Incorporated film *The Tuskegee Airmen* contains a few errors, it tells its important story well.

A number of other important books on the role of blacks appeared during the celebration of the fiftieth anniversary of World War II. Marvin E. Fletcher's *America's First Black General: Benjamin O. Davis, Sr., 1880–1970* (1989) describes how determined the army was to keep General Davis from assuming command over whites. Benjamin O. Davis, Jr.'s *Benjamin O. Davis: American* (1991) is the memoir of the son of the nation's first black general, the first twentieth-century graduate of West Point, and the founding leader of the Tuskegee Airmen.

Another memoir, this one demonstrating that black women played a role in the war, is Charity Adams Earley's *One Woman's Army: A Black Officer Remembers the WAC* (1989). Brenda L. Moore's *To Serve My Country, to Serve My Race: The Story of the Only African American WACs Stationed Overseas during World War II* (1996) is a broader account of the struggles of black women in the 6888th Postal Directory Battalion. Martha S. Putney's *When the Nation Was in Need: Blacks in the Women's Army Corps during World War II* (1992) is another account of the segregation of black women in the military.

Since the 1980s, a number of works have appeared treating different aspects of the African American military experience during World War II. Phillip McGuire's *Taps for a Jim Crow Army: Letters from Black Soldiers in World War II* (1983) provides a good insight into what black soldiers were thinking and saying. Graham Smith's *When Jim Crow Met John Bull: Black American Soldiers in World War II Britain* (1987) discusses the confusing position for black soldiers in a segregated army coming into contact with the more tolerant attitudes of a foreign nation. *Remaking Dixie : The Impact of World War II on the American South* (1997), edited by Neil R. McMillen, is a collection of stimulating essays. Phillip McGuire's *He, Too, Spoke for Democracy: Judge Hastie, World War II, and the Black Soldier* (1988) discusses the role an African American judge played in trying to ease prejudice against soldiers of his race. Robert Franklin Jefferson's 1995 dissertation, "Making the Men of the 93rd: African-American Servicemen in the Years of the Great Depression and the Second World War, 1935–1947," analyzes the uncertain relationship among the federal government, black soldiers, and black civilians. Laurence P. Scott and William

M. Womack, Sr., in *Double V: The Civil Rights Struggle of the Tuskegee Airmen* (1994), Lee Finkle in "The Conservative Aims of the Militant Rhetoric: Black Protest during World War II" (1973), and Charles W. Eagles in "Two 'Double V's: Jonathan Daniels, FDR, and Race Relations during World War II" (1982) discuss various aspects of the attempted black victory both in war and against domestic discrimination.

In 1949, despite strong opposition from civilian and congressional segregationists and military leaders at the highest echelon, President Harry Truman promulgated an executive order integrating the armed forces. Charles C. Moskos, Jr., in *The American Enlisted Man* (1970) studies the results of this decision and concludes that once integration became standard, the fighting ability of blacks and whites was similar. Also providing information on World War II and its tie to the civil rights revolution of the 1960s is Neil A. Wynn's *Afro-American and the Second World War* (1976). Richard M. Dalfiume's *Desegregation of the U.S. Armed Forces: Fighting on Two Fronts, 1939–1953* (1969) carries the story from before World War II to the end of the Korean War. Perhaps the best account of the integration of the military services is Morris J. MacGregor, Jr.'s *Integration of the Armed Forces, 1940–1965* (1981), which explores the changes in the armed forces' policy toward blacks. Studies of individual services include Dennis Denmark Nelson's *Integration of the Negro into the United States Navy, 1776–1947* (1948), Alan L. Gropman's *Air Force Integrates, 1945–1964* (1978), and Henry I. Shaw, Jr., and Ralph W. Donnelly's *Blacks in the Marine Corps* (1975).

Despite the president's order, the army was essentially segregated when the Korean War began, though largely desegregated during the conflict. Troops in Europe remained racially separated until the mid-1950s. Charles M. Bussey's *Firefight at Yechon: Courage and Racism in the Korean War* (1991) and Lyle Rishell's *With a Black Platoon in Combat: A Year in Korea* (1993) amply demonstrate the continuance of this discrimination. Selika Marianne Ducksworth, in her 1994 dissertation, "What Hour of the Night: Black Enlisted Men's Experiences and the Desegregation of the Army during the Korean War, 1950–1951," shows the important role the black soldier played despite the prejudice he faced.

In 1996, these problems surfaced again when the U.S. Army Center of Military History completed its nine-year study of the performance in the Korean War of the army's last all-black unit. This study, published as William T. Bowers, William M. Hammond, and George L. MacGarrigle's *Black Soldier, White Army: The 24th Infantry Regiment in Korea* (1996), concluded that poor training, unreliable equipment, and white commanders' racism caused the unit's failure in combat. This monograph took the blame off the black soldiers placed there by earlier studies, but it continued the long-believed story that blacks in this unit abandoned their positions under fire. Both white and black veterans have protested this conclusion, and Secretary of the Army Togo West, himself an African American, ordered a review. One black West Point graduate who fought next to the 24th believed that it was no better or worse than any other unit and even attempted unsuccessful court action to try to prevent the publication of what he considers a slanderous book.

The Vietnam War was the first truly integrated war in American history. Although problems did not disappear, they were different from those black servicemen had previously experienced. In earlier wars, blacks were kept out of the army and combat roles, but during this unpopular war, they were heavily drafted and served in large numbers as combat infantry men. Like their white counterparts, they were alternately enthusiastic and cynical about the war and their part in it. In the May 1967 issue of *Time* magazine, the article "Democracy in the Foxhole" reported that for the first time in history, blacks were fully integrated in combat and held significant leadership positions. The following year *Ebony* released a special August issue entitled "The Black Soldier." Vietnam, an article said, gave blacks in the military a visibility that their forefathers had never had; and ironically, the most totalitarian segment of American society, the military, seemed to be providing blacks with the most freedom and opportunity they had ever experienced in the nation's history. Racial distinctions were not evident in combat, the article concluded, but they continued to exist in the rear echelons. That a white news magazine and a black news magazine agreed about the improvement of race relations in the U.S. military was a historic event, whether or not the optimism was justified.

In the years since the end of the Vietnam War, numerous books and articles have discussed the war's meaning. One of the most significant books concerning the black role is Wallace Terry's edited work *Blood: An Oral History of the Vietnam War by Black Veterans* (1984). This excellent collection of interviews with black military personnel portrays their highs and lows. Public Broadcasting System's program *Frontline* aired a documentary based on this book entitled "Bloods in the Nam," which was a 1986 Blue Ribbon Winner of the American Film and Video Festival. James Edward Westheider's 1993 dissertation, " 'My Fear Is for You:' African Americans, Racism, and the Vietnam War," is also helpful, as is Stanley Goff and Robert Sanders's *Brothers: Black Soldiers in the Nam* (1982).

Since the U.S. disengagement from Vietnam, the African American presence in the military has increased substantially. Charles C. Moskos, a prominent military sociologist, wrote a 1986 article, "Success Story: Blacks in the Military," detailing the enormous progress that has been achieved. Of 2.1 million people in the armed forces in 1985, 400,000 were African American, approximately 19 percent. This percentage is significant because the black population as a whole was then only about 12 percent of the nation's total. One in ten army officers was black in 1986, and there were numerous black generals, so many, in fact, that promotion of a black to a top leadership position in any of the services no longer merited comment. Even more significant, according to Moskos, "a visitor to a military installation will witness a degree and a quality of racial integration that are rarely encountered elsewhere." Racial harmony was hardly perfect in the military, and African Americans were the first to realize it, Moskos points out; but blacks were generally content with their status and proud of their achievements. General Colin Powell demonstrates this attitude in his autobiography, *My American Journey* (1995), and James R. McGovern's *Black Eagle: General Daniel "Chappie" James, Jr.* (1985) documents the sucessess of the nation's first black four-star general.

Charles C. Moskos and John Sibley Butler's *All That We Can Be* (1996) calls for society to copy the lessons the military has used to improve race relations. The authors argue that whites in the army possess racial attitudes that are more liberal than those of white civilians, whereas blacks in the army are more conservative than black civilians. The result, they say, is an "Afro-Anglo" culture of "shared experiences and genuinely equal opportunity." The authors conclude that there are real "lessons" the military has learned for better race relations. These include being "ruthless against discrimination," realizing that blacks and whites view race relations and opportunities in different ways, and doing everything possible to prepare disadvantaged people to compete with those who are more privileged, what Moskos and Butler call "supply side" affirmative action. The authors point out that the military services were on the verge of disintegration over racial problems in the 1970s, but they worked hard to find answers and created the favorable climate of the 1980s and 1990s. American society, as a whole, the authors believe, should take notice and act accordingly.

That the military continues to have to battle to maintain the progress that has been achieved is obvious from the articles that appeared in popular and specialized journals and magazines in the 1990s. A sampling of their titles express their themes: "Threat of Gulf War Re-ignites Concern over Disproportionate Representation of Blacks in Military" (1990); Kara B. Richards and Gary L. Bowen, "Military Downsizing and Its Potential Implications for Hispanic, Black, and White Soldiers" (1993); Daniel Voll, "A Few Good Nazis [White Supremacist Problems at Fort Bragg]" (1996); and Jane McHugh, "NAACP Claims Racism in Army Sex Scandal Investigations" (1997).

Overall, the situation for African Americans in the military of the United States in the 1990s is encouraging. Like any human institution, the military will never solve all its problems, but its attempt to eradicate official discrimination is impressive. In 1996 President Clinton awarded posthumous Medals of Honor to several black heroes of World War II previously denied the award. When he presented a medal to the last living hero, the ceremony was fraught with symbolism. The wrongs of past history are being righted as much as they can be righted, and the works of generations of historians in pointing them out are being vindicated. Elliott V. Converse III et al., *The Exclusion of Black Soldiers for the Medal of Honor in World Wars* (1996) is the publication of the army study that presented the information on which the president made his decision to grant the awards.

Historians have a great deal of work still to do concerning the black role in the American military. There is no longer debate over whether there were black heroes, and the existence of past institutional discrimination is obvious. Historians, having established a solid historical record of blacks in the military and seeing that this record is influencing society, have the opportunity now to move on to newer approaches and more complicated issues of race relations. Building on the success of those who came before them, today's historians can work in the confidence that their discoveries will be given attention and will have an influence. The future looks promising for African American military historiography.

BIBLIOGRAPHY

Books

Altoff, Gerard T. *Amongst My Best Men: African-Americans and the War of 1812*. Put-in-Bay, OH: Perry Group, 1996.

Barbeau, Arthur E., and Florette Henri. *The Unknown Soldiers: Black American Troops in World War I*. Philadelphia: Temple University Press, 1974.

Berlin, Ira, Joseph P. Reidy, and Leslie S. Rowland, eds. *A Documentary History of Emancipation, 1861–1867. The Black Military Experience, Series II*. Cambridge: Cambridge University Press, 1982.

Berry, Mary Frances. *Military Necessity and Civil Rights Policy: Black Citizenship and the Constitution, 1861–1868*. Port Washington, NY: National University Publications, 1977.

Billington, Monroe L. *New Mexico's Buffalo Soldiers, 1866–1900*. Niwot: University Press of Colorado, 1991.

Blackett, R.J.M., ed. *Thomas Morris Chester, Black Civil War Correspondent: His Dispatches from the Virginia Front*. Baton Rouge: Louisiana State University Press, 1989. Reprint. Da Capo Press Paperback, 1991.

Bolster, W. Jeffrey. *Black Jacks: African American Seamen in the Age of Sail*. Cambridge, MA: Harvard University Press, 1997.

Bowers, William T., William M. Hammond, and George L. MacGarrigle. *Black Soldier, White Army: The 24th Infantry Regiment in Korea*. Washington, DC: Center of Military History, United States Army, 1996.

Bussey, Charles M. *Firefight at Yechon: Courage and Racism in the Korean War*. Washington, DC: Brassey's, 1991.

Carroll, John M., ed. *The Black Military Experience in the American West*. New York: Liveright, 1971.

Chew, Abraham. *A Biography of Colonel Charles Young*. Washington, DC: n.p., 1923.

Christian, Garna L. *Black Soldiers in Jim Crow Texas, 1899–1917*. College Station: Texas A&M University Press, 1995.

Clendenen, Clarence C. *Blood on the Border: The United States Army and the Mexican Irregulars*. London: Macmillan, Collier-Macmillan, 1969.

Coffman, Edward M. *The War to End All Wars: The American Military Experience in World War I*. New York: Oxford University Press, 1968.

———. *The Old Army: A Portrait of the American Army in Peacetime, 1784–1898*. New York: Oxford University Press, 1986.

Converse, Elliott V., III, Daniel K. Gibran, John A. Cash, Robert K. Griffith, Jr., and

Richard H. Kohn. *The Exclusion of Black Soldiers from the Medal of Honor in World War II: The Study Commissioned by the United States Army to Investigate Racial Bias in the Awarding of the Nation's Highest Military Decoration.* Jefferson, NC: McFarland and Company, 1996.

Cornish, Dudley T. *The Sable Arm: Black Troops in the Union Army, 1861–1865.* 1956. Reprint. Lawrence: University Press of Kansas, 1987.

Dalfiume Richard M. *Desegregation of the U.S. Armed Forces: Fighting on Two Fronts, 1939–1953.* Columbia: University of Missouri Press, 1969.

Davis, Benjamin O., Jr. *Benjamin O. Davis Jr., American: An Autobiography.* Washington, DC: Smithsonian Institution Press, 1991.

Davis, Lenwood G., and George Hill, comps. *Blacks in the American Armed Forces, 1776–1983: A Bibliography.* Westport, CT: Greenwood Press, 1985.

Earley, Charity Adams. *One's Woman's Army: A Black Officer Remembers the WAC.* College Station: Texas A&M University Press, 1989.

Fletcher, Marvin E. *The Black Soldier and Officer in the United States Army, 1891–1917.* Columbia: University of Missouri Press, 1974.

———. *America's First Black General: Benjamin O. Davis, Sr., 1880–1970.* Lawrence: University Press of Kansas, 1989.

Flipper, Henry O. *The Colored Cadet at West Point.* New York: Homer Lee and Company, 1878. Reprint. Salem, NH: Ayer Company Publishing, 1986.

Foner, Eric. *Reconstruction: America's Unfinished Revolution, 1863–1877.* New York: Harper and Row Publishers, 1988.

Foner, Jack D. *The United States Soldier between Two Wars: Army Life and Reforms, 1865–1898.* New York: Humanities Press, 1970.

———. *Blacks and the Military in American History: A New Perspective.* New York: Praeger Publishers, 1974.

Fowler, Arlen L. *The Black Infantry in the West, 1869–1891.* Westport, CT: Greenwood Press, 1971.

Francis, Charles E. *The Tuskegee Airmen: The Story of the Negro in the U.S. Air Force.* 1955. Rev. ed. Boston: Branden Publishing Company, 1993.

Franklin, John Hope, and Alfred A. Moss, Jr. *From Slavery to Freedom: A History of Negro Americans.* 7th ed. New York: Alfred A. Knopf, 1994.

Fuchs, Richard L. *An Unerring Fire: The Massacre at Fort Pillow.* Rutherford, NJ: Fairleigh Dickinson University Press; London: Associated University Presses, 1994.

Gatewood, Willard B. *Black Americans and the White Man's Burden, 1898–1903.* Urbana: University of Illinois Press, 1975.

———. *"Smoked Yankees" and the Struggle for Empire: Letters from Negro Soldiers, 1898–1902.* Urbana: University of Illinois Press, 1971. Reprint. Fayetteville: University of Arkansas Press, 1987.

Glatthaar, Joseph T. *Forged in Battle: The Civil War Alliance of Black Soldiers and White Officers.* New York: Free Press, 1990.

Goff, Stanley, and Robert Sanders. *Brothers: Black Soldiers in the Nam.* Novato, CA: Presidio Press, 1982.

Greene, Lorenzo J. *The Negro in Colonial New England.* 1942. Reprint. New York: Atheneum, 1969.

Gropman, Alan L. *The Air Force Integrates, 1945–1964.* Washington, DC: Office of Air Force History U.S. Air Force, 1978.

Hardaway, Roger D. *A Narrative Bibliography of the African-American Frontier: Blacks in the Rocky Mountain West, 1535–1912*. Lewiston, NY: Edwin Mellen Press, 1995.

Haynes, Robert V. *A Night of Violence: The Houston Riot of 1917*. Baton Rouge: Louisiana State University Press, 1976.

Higginson, Thomas Wentworth. *Army Life in a Black Regiment*. 1870. Reprint. New York: W. W. Norton, 1984.

Hollandsworth, James G. *The Louisiana Native Guard: The Black Military Experience during the Civil War*. Baton Rouge: Louisiana State University Press, 1995.

Hunton, Addie W., and Katherine Johnson. *Two Colored Women with the American Expeditionary Forces*. Brooklyn, NY: Brooklyn Eagle Press, 1920. Reprint. New York: G. K. Hall, 1997.

Jakeman, Robert J. *The Divided Skies: Establishing Segregated Flight Training at Tuskegee, Alabama, 1934–1942*. Tuscaloosa: University of Alabama Press, 1992.

Johnson, Barry C. *Flipper's Dismissal: The Ruin of Lt. Henry O. Flipper, U.S.A., First Coloured Graduate of West Point*. London: Privately printed, 1972.

Johnson, Charles, Jr. *African American Soldiers in the National Guard: Recruitment and Deployment during Peacetime and War*. Westport, CT: Greenwood, 1992.

Jordan, Ervin L., Jr. *Black Confederates and Afro-Yankees in Civil War Virginia*. Charlottesville: University Press of Virginia, 1995.

Katz, William Loren. *The Black West*. New York: Doubleday and Company, 1971. Reprint. 3rd ed. Seattle, WA: Open Hand Publishing Company, 1987.

Lane, Anne J. *The Brownsville Affair: National Crisis and Black Reaction*. Port Washington, NY: National University, 1971.

Langley, Harold D. *Social Reform in the United States Navy, 1798–1862*. Urbana: University of Illinois Press, 1967.

Leckie, William H. *The Buffalo Soldiers: A Narrative of the Negro Cavalry in the West*. Norman: University of Oklahoma, 1967.

Lee, Ulysses. *The Employment of Negro Troops*. Washington, DC: Office of the Chief of Military History, United States Army, 1966.

Litwack, Leon. *Been in the Storm So Long*. New York: Alfred A. Knopf, 1979.

Logan, Rayford W., and Michael R. Winston, eds. *Dictionary of Negro Biography*. New York: W. W. Norton, 1983.

Lynk, Miles V. *The Black Troopers, or The Daring Heroism of the Negro Soldier in the Spanish American War*. 1899. Reprint. New York: AMS, 1971.

McConnell, Roland C. *Negro Troops of Antebellum Louisiana: A History of the Battalion of Free Men of Color*. Baton Rouge: Louisiana State University Press, 1968.

McGovern, James R. *Black Eagle: General Daniel "Chappie" James, Jr*. University: University Press of Alabama, 1985.

MacGregor, Morris J., Jr. *Integration of the Armed Forces, 1940–1965*. Washington, DC, Center of Military History, United States Army, 1981, Reprint. 1985.

MacGregor, Morris J., Jr., and Bernard C. Nalty, eds. *Blacks in the United States Armed Forces: Basic Documents*. 13 vols. Wilmington, DE: Scholarly Resources, 1977.

McGuire, Phillip. *He, Too, Spoke for Democracy: Judge Hastie, World War II, and the Black Soldier*. Westport, CT: Greenwood Press, 1988.

———, ed. *Taps for a Jim Crow Army: Letters from Black Soldiers in World War II*. Santa Barbara, CA: ABC-Clio, 1983.

McMillen, Neil R., ed. *Remaking Dixie: The Impact of World War II on the American South*. Jackson: University Press of Mississippi, 1997.

McPherson, James M. *The Negro's Civil War: How American's Felt and Acted during the War for the Union*. New York: Pantheon Books, 1965. Reprint. Urbana: University of Illinois Press, Illini Books, 1982.

———. *The Struggle for Equality: Abolitionist and the Negro in the Civil War and Reconstruction*. 1964. 2nd ed. Princeton, NJ.: Princeton University Press, Princeton Paperbacks, 1995.

Marszalek, John F. *Assault at West Point: The Court-Martial of Johnson Whittaker*. Originally published as *Court-Martial: A Black Man in America*. New York: Charles Scribner's Sons, 1972; New York: Collier Books, 1994.

Miller, Edwin A., Jr. *Gullah Statesman Robert Smalls from Slavery to Congress, 1839–1915*. Columbia: University of South Carolina Press, 1995.

Moore, Brenda L. *To Serve My Country, to Serve My Race: The Story of the Only African American WACs Stationed Overseas during World War II*. New York: New York University Press, 1996.

Moskos, Charles C., Jr. *The American Enlisted Man: The Rank and File in Today's Military*. New York: Russell Sage Foundation, 1970.

Moskos, Charles C., and John Sibley Butler. *All That We Can Be: Black Leadership and Racial Integration the Army Way*. New York: Basic Books, 1996.

Nalty, Bernard C. *Strength for the Fight: A History of Black Americans in the Military*. New York: Free Press, 1986.

Nell, William C. *Services of Colored Americans in the Wars of 1776 and 1812*. Boston: Prentiss and Sawyer, 1851. Reprint. New York: AMS Press, 1976.

———. *Colored Patriots of the American Revolution*. Boston: Robert F. Wallcut, 1855. Reprint. Salem, NH: Ayer Company, Publishers, 1986.

Nelson, Dennis Denmark. *The Integration of the Negro into the United States Navy, 1776–1947, with a Brief Historical Introduction*. Washington, DC: Department of the Navy, 1948. Reprint. New York: Farrar, Straus, and Young, 1951.

Patton, Gerald W. *War and Race: The Black Officer in the American Military, 1915–1941*. Westport, CT: Greenwood Press, 1981.

Pendleton, Leila Amos. *A Narrative of the Negro. Missing Pages in American History: Revealing the Services of Negroes in the Early Wars in the United States of America, 1641–1815*. Ed. by Laura E. Wilkes. Washington, DC: Press of R. L. Pendleton, 1919. Reprint. New York: G. K. Hall, 1996.

Porter, Kenneth W. *The Negro on the American Frontier*. New York: Arno Press and the *New York Time*, 1971.

———. *The Black Seminoles*. Edited by Alcione M. Amos and Thomas P. Senter. Gainesville: University Press of Florida, 1996.

Powell, Colin. *My American Journey*. New York: Random House, 1995.

Putney, Martha S. *Black Sailors: Afro-American Merchant Seamen and Whalemen prior to the Civil War*. Westport, CT: Greenwood Press, 1987.

———. *When the Nation Was in Need: Blacks in the Women's Army Corps during World War II*. Metuchen, NJ: Scarecrow Press, 1992.

Quarles, Benjamin. *The Negro in the American Revolution*. Chapel Hill: University of North Carolina Press, 1961.

———. *The Negro in the Civil War*. Boston: Little, Brown and Company, 1953. Reprint. New York: Da Capo Press, Paperback ed. 1988.

Redkey, Edwin, S., ed. *A Grand Army of Black Men: Letters from African-American Soldiers in the Union Army, 1861–1865*. Cambridge: Cambridge University Press, 1992.

Rishell, Lyle. *With a Black Platoon in Combat: A Year in Korea*. College Station: Texas A&M University Press, 1993.

Robinson, Charles M., III. *The Court-Martial of Lieutenant Henry Flipper*. El Paso: Texas Western Press, 1994.

Sandler, Stanley. *Segregated Skies: Black Combat Squadrons of World War II*. Washington, DC: Smithsonian Institution, 1992.

Savage, W. Sherman. *Black in the West*. Westport, CT: Greenwood Publishing Company, 1976.

Schubert, Frank N. *Buffalo Soldiers, Braves, and the Brass: The Story of Fort Robinson, Nebraska*. Shippensburg, PA: White Main Publishing, 1992.

———. *Black Valor: Buffalo Soldiers and the Medal of Honor, 1870–1898*. Wilmington, DE: Scholarly Resources, 1997.

———, comp. and ed. *On the Trail of the Buffalo Soldier: Biographies of African-Americans in the U.S. Army, 1866–1917*. Wilmington, DE: Scholarly Resources, 1995.

Scott, Emmett J. *Scott's Official History of the American Negro in the World War*. N.p., 1919. Reprint. New York: Arno Press and the *New York Times*, 1969.

Scott, Lawrence P., and William M. Womack, Sr. *Double V: The Civil Rights Struggle of the Tuskegee Airmen*. East Lansing: Michigan State University Press, 1994.

Shaw, Henry I., Jr., and Ralph W. Donnelly. *Blacks in the Marine Corps*. Washington, DC: History and Museums Division, Headquarters, U.S. Marine Corps, 1975.

Silvera, John D., comp. *The Negro in World War II*. 1947. Reprint. New York: Arno Press and the *New York Times*, 1969.

Singletary, Otis. *Negro Militia and Reconstruction*. Austin: University of Texas Press, 1957.

Smith, Graham. *When Jim Crow Met John Bull: Black American Soldiers in World War II Britain*. London: I.B. Tauris and Company, 1987.

Steiner, Paul E. *Medical History of a Civil War Regiment: Disease in the Sixty-fifth United States Colored Infantry*. Clayton, MO: Institute of Civil War Studies, 1977.

Taylor, Susie King. *A Black Woman's Civil War Memoirs: Reminiscences of My Life in Camp with the 33rd U.S. Colored Troops, Late 1st South Carolina Volunteers*. Boston: S. K. Taylor, 1902. Reprint. Edited by Patricia W. Romero. New York: Markus Wiener Publishing, 1988.

Terry, Wallace. *Bloods: An Oral History of the Vietnam War by Black Veterans*. New York: Random House, 1984.

Uya, Oden Edet. *From Slavery to Public Service: Robert Smalls, 1839–1915*. New York: Oxford University Press, 1971.

Valuska, David L. *The African American in the Union Navy, 1861–1865*. New York: Garland Publishing, 1993.

Voelz, Peter M. *Slave and Soldier: The Military Impact of Blacks in the Colonial Americas*. New York: Garland Publishing, 1993.

Weaver, John D. *The Brownsville Raid*. New York: W. W. Norton and Company, 1970. Reprint. College Station: Texas A&M University Press, 1992.

White, Walter. *A Rising Wind*. Garden City, NY: Doubleday, Doran, and Company, 1945.

Williams, Charles H. *Negro Soldiers in World War I: The Human Side. Formerly titled Sidelights on Negro Soldiers.* Boston: n.p., 1923. Reprint. New York: AMS Press, 1970.

Williams, George Washington. *A History of the Negro Troops in the War of the Rebellion, 1861–1865.* New York: Harper and Brothers, 1888. Reprint. New York: Negro Universities Press, 1969.

Wilson, Joseph T. *The Black Phalanx: African American Soldiers in the War of Independence, the War of 1812, and the Civil War.* Hartford, CT: American Publishing Company, 1887. Reprint. New York: Da Capo Press Paperback, 1994.

Woodward, C. Vann. *The Strange Career of Jim Crow.* 3rd ed. New York: Oxford University Press, 1974.

Woodward, Elon A., comp. *The Negro in the Military Service of the United States, 1639–1886.* Washington, DC: National Archives, 1888; Washington, DC: National Archives and Record Service, 1973. Microfilm, Microcopy no. M858.

Wynn, Neil A. *The Afro-American and the Second World War.* New York: Holmes and Meier, 1976.

Articles

Aptheker, Herbert. "The Negro in the Union Navy." *Journal of Negro History* 32 (April 1947): 169–200.

Bailey, Anne J. "Was There a Massacre at Poison Spring?" *Military History of the Southwest* 20 (Fall 1990): 157–80.

"The Black Soldier." *Ebony* 23, no. 10 (August 1968).

Castel, Albert. "The Fort Pillow Massacre: A Fresh Examination of the Evidence." *Civil War History* 4 (March 1958): 37–50.

Cimprich, John, and Robert C. Mainfort, Jr. "Fort Pillow Revisited: New Evidence about an Old Controversy." *Civil War History* 28 (December 1982): 293–306.

———. "The Fort Pillow Massacre: A Statistical Note." *Journal of American History* 76 (December 1989): 830–37.

"Democracy in a Foxhole." *Time* 89, no. 21 (May 26, 1967): 15–19.

Dye, Ira. "Seafarers of 1813: A Profile." *Prologue: The Journal of the National Archives* 5 (Spring 1973): 1–13.

Eagles, Charles W. "Two 'Double V's': Jonathan Daniels, FDR, and Race Relations during World War II." *North Carolina Historical Review* 59 (July 1982): 252–70.

Field, R. L. "The Black Midshipman at the U.S. Naval Academy." *U.S. Naval Institute Proceedings* 99 (April 1973): 28–36.

Finkle, Lee. "The Conservative Aims of Militant Rhetoric: Black Protest during World War II." *Journal of American History* 60 (December 1973): 692–713.

Fisher, Mike. "The First Kansas Colored: Massacre at Poison Spring." *Kansas History* 2 (Summer 1979): 121–28.

———. "Remember Poison Spring." *Missouri Historical Review* 74 (April 1980): 323–42.

Gatewood, Willard B. "John Hanks Alexander of Arkansas: Second Black Graduate of West Point." *Arkansas Historical Quarterly* 41 (Summer 1982): 103–28.

Greene, Lorenzo. "The Negro in the Armed Forces of the United States, 1619–1783." *Negro History Bulletin* 14 (March 1951): 123–27, 138.

Heinl, Nancy G. "Colonel Charles Young: Pointman." *Crisis* 84 (May 1977): 173–79.

Jones, George Fenwick. "The Black Hessians: Negroes Recruited by the Hessians in South Carolina and Other Colonies." *South Carolina Historical Magazine* 83 (October 1982): 287–302.

Katz, William Loren. "Black and Indian Cooperation and Resistance to Slavery." *Freedomways* 17 (3rd Quarter, 1977): 164–74.

Landers, Jane. "Black-Indian Interaction in Spanish Florida." *Colonial Latin American Historical Review* 29 (Spring 1993): 141–62.

Logan, Rayford, W. "The Negro in the Quasi War, 1798–1800." *Negro History Bulletin* 14 (March 1951): 131–32.

McHugh, Jane. "NAACP Claims Racism in Army Sex Scandal Investigations/Group Asks Why Accusers Are Overwhelmingly White; Accused, Black." *Army Times* (March 10, 1997).

Marszalek, John F. "The Black Man in Military History." *Negro History Bulletin* 36 (October 1973): 122–25.

May, Robert E. "Invisible Men: Blacks and the U.S. Army in the Mexican War." *Historian* 49 (August 1987): 463–77.

Moore, Kenneth Bancroft. "Fort Pillow, Forrest, and the United States Colored Troops in 1864." *Tennessee Historical Quarterly* 54 (Summer 1995): 112–23.

Moskos, Charles C. "Success Story: Blacks in the Military." *Atlantic Monthly* 257 (May 1986): 64–72.

Phillips, Thomas D. "The Black Regulars." In *The West of the American People*, edited by Allen G. Bogue, Thomas D. Phillips, and James E. Wright, 138–43. Itasca, IL: F. E. Peacock Publishers, 1970.

Quarles, Benjamin. "The Colonial Militia and Negro Manpower." *Mississippi Valley Historical Review* 45 (March 1959): 643–52.

Reddick, L. D. "The Negro Policy of the United States Army, 1775–1945." *Journal of Negro History* 34 (January 1949): 9–29.

Redkey, Edwin S. "Black Chaplains in the Union Army." *Civil War History* 33 (December 1987): 331–50.

Richards, Kara B., and Gary L. Bowen. "Military Downsizing and Its Potential Implications for Hispanic, Black, and White Soldiers." *Journal of Primary Prevention* 14 (Fall 1993): 73.

Schubert, Frank N. "Black Soldiers on the White Frontier: Some Factors Influencing Race Relations." *Phylon* 33 (Winter 1971): 410–15.

"Threat of Gulf War Re-ignites Concern over Disproportionate Representation of Blacks in Military." *Black Issues in Higher Education* 7 (December 20, 1990): 16.

Tucker, Philip Thomas. "John Horse: Forgotten African-American Leader of the Second Seminole War." *Journal of Negro History* 77, no. 2 (1992): 74–83.

Urwin, Gregory J. " 'We Cannot Treat Negroes . . . as Prisoners of War': Racial Atrocities and Reprisals in Civil War Arkansas." *Civil War History* 42 (September 1996): 193–210.

Vaughn, William P. "West Point and the First Negro Cadet." *Military Affairs* 35 (October 1971): 100–102.

Voll, Daniel. "A Few Good Nazis [White Supremacist Problems at Fort Bragg]." *Esquire* 125 (April 1, 1996): 102–12.

Wert, Jeffrey D. "Camp William Penn and the Black Soldier." *Pennsylvania History* 46, no. 4 (1979): 335–46.

Dissertations and Theses

Boyett, Cheryl Race. "The Seminole-Black Alliance during the Second Seminole War, 1835–1842." M.A. thesis, California State University, Dominguez Hills, 1996.

Clark, Michael James Tinsley. "A History of the Twenty-fourth United States Infantry Regiment in Utah, 1896–1900." Ph.D. dissertation, University of Utah, 1979.

Ducksworth, Selika Marianne. "What Hour of the Night: Black Enlisted Men's Experiences and the Desegregation of the Army during the Korean War, 1950–1951." Ph.D. dissertation, Ohio State University, 1994.

Jefferson, Robert Franklin, "Making the Men of the 93rd: African-American Servicemen in the Years of the Great Depression and the Second World War, 1935–1947." Ph.D. dissertation, University of Michigan, 1995.

Johnson, Robert Bruce. "The Punitive Expedition: A Military, Diplomatic, and Political History of Pershing's Chase after Pancho Villa, 1916–1917." Ph.D. dissertation, University of Southern California, 1964.

Lamm, Alan K. "Buffalo Soldier Chaplains: A Case Study of the Five Black United States Army Chaplains, 1884–1901." Ph.D. dissertation, University of South Carolina, 1995.

Nash, Horace D. "Town and Sword: Black Soldiers in Columbus, New Mexico, in the Early Twentieth Century." Ph.D. dissertation, Mississippi State University, 1996.

Phillips, Tom D. "The Black Regulars: Negro Soldiers in the United States Army, 1866–1891." Ph.D. dissertation, University of Wisconsin, 1970.

Westheider, James Edward. " 'My Fear Is for You': African Americans, Racism, and the Vietnam War." Ph.D. dissertation, University of Cincinnati, 1993.

Video Recordings and Film

Assault at West Point: The Court Martial of Johnson Whittaker. Film. Showtime Networks, Capital Cities/ABC Video Production, 1994.

"*The Bloods of Nam*." V-568–1. *Frontline*, television series, 1989.

Glory. Film. Tri-Star Pictures, 1990.

The Tuskegee Airman. Film. Home Box Office, A Time Warner Entertainment Company, 1995.

XII

The African American Athletic Experience

David K. Wiggins

African Americans have been participants in sport at various levels of competition and in a number of different settings since at least the early nineteenth century. The first person to trace this participation was Edwin B. Henderson, the well-known physical educator and civil rights activist from Washington, D.C. At the request of Carter G. Woodson, the "Father of Negro History," Henderson wrote the frequently cited *Negro in Sports* (1939, 1949). Several years later he authored, along with the editors of *Sport* magazine, *The Black Athlete: Emergence and Arrival* (1968).

Henderson's books were general histories and patterned after the Woodson model in that they were meant to inspire and prove the worth of African Americans through the chronicling of individual successes in a society marked by racial discrimination and inequality. Many of the subsequent general histories, while sometimes varying in format and organization from Henderson's works, also chart the triumphs of African American athletes in celebratory terms to instill a sense of pride and furnish examples of achievement in the black community. Included among this group are Andrew S. "Doc" Young's *Negro Firsts in Sports* (1963); Arna Bontemps's *Famous Negro Athletes* (1964); Jack Olsen's *Black Athlete: A Shameful Story* (1968); Jack Orr's *Black Athlete: His Story in American History* (1969); Wally Jones and Jim Washington's *Black Champions Challenge American Sports* (1972); Ocania Chalk's *Pioneers of Black Sport: The Early Days of the Black Professional Athlete in Baseball, Basketball, Boxing, and Football* (1975); Art and Edna Rust's *Art Rust's Illustrated History of the Black Athlete* (1985); and Arthur Ashe, Jr.'s *Hard Road to Glory: A History of the African American Athlete* (1978).

Complementing the general histories are a number of historical surveys and sociology texts on American sport that include information on African American athletes. Some of the best work of this type are William J. Baker, *Sports in the Western World* (1988); Allen Guttmann, *A Whole New Ball Game: An Interpretation of American Sports* (1988); John A. Lucas and Ronald A. Smith, *Saga of American Sport* (1978); Benjamin G. Rader, *American Sports: From the Age of Folk Games to the Age of Spectators* (1983); Randy Roberts and James Olson, *Winning Is the Only Thing: Sports in America since 1945* (1989); Elliott J. Gorn and Warren Goldstein, *A Brief History of American Sports* (1993); Harry Edwards, *Sociology of Sport* (1973); Jay J. Coakley, *Sport in Society: Issues and Controversies* (1994); Wilbert M. Leonard II, *A Sociological Perspective of Sport* (1993); and D. Stanley Eitzen and George H. Sage, *Sociology of North American Sport* (1993).

Standing apart from the historical surveys and sociology texts are a number of more critical review essays, anthologies, and bibliographical works that provide overviews of African American participation in sport. The most thorough and thought-provoking review essay is Jeffrey T. Sammons's " 'Race' and Sport: A Critical, Historical Examination," *Journal of Sport History* (1994). Other important works of this genre are David K. Wiggins, "From Plantation to Playing Field: Historical Writings on the Black Athlete in American Sport," *Research Quarterly for Exercise and Sport* (1986); Manning Marable, "Black Athletes in White Men's Games, 1880–1920," *Maryland Historian* (1973); and Barry D. McPherson, "Minority Group Involvement in Sport: The Black Athlete," *Exercise and Sport Science Reviews* (1974). The best of the anthologies on African American participation in sport are David K. Wiggins, *Glory Bound: Black Athletes in a White America* (1997); Gerald Early, *Tuxedo Junction: Essays on American Culture* (1989) and *The Culture of Bruising: Essays on Prizefighting, Literature, and Modern American Culture* (1994). Influential bibliographic works include Lenwood G. Davis and Belinda Daniels, comps., *Black Athletes in the United States: A Bibliography of Books, Articles, Autobiographies, and Biographies on Professional Black Athletes, 1800–1981* (1983); Lenwood G. Davis, *Joe Louis: A Bibliography of Articles, Books, Pamphlets, Records, and Archival Material* (1983); David L. Porter, ed., *African-American Sports Greats: A Biographical Dictionary* (1995); Bruce L. Bennett, "Bibliography on the Negro in Sports," *Journal of Health, Physical Education, and Recreation* (1970); "Supplemental Selected Annotated Bibliography on the Negro in Sports," *Journal of Health, Physical Education, and Recreation* (1970); and Grant Henry, "A Bibliography concerning Negroes in Physical Education, Athletics, and Related Fields," *Journal of Health, Physical Education, and Recreation* (1973).

The involvement of African Americans in sport prior to the Civil War was limited and sporadic at best. Slaves on both farms and large southern plantations were sometimes able to transcend their horrible conditions and realize periods of leisure time as well as find opportunities to participate in recreation and sport.

Free blacks nourished a vibrant community life, including involvement in various sporting activities. A very select number of African American athletes during this period found success at the highest levels of sport, most notably Tom Molineaux, who fought twice for the heavyweight championship of the world. Not unexpectedly, the scholarship on pre–Civil War topics is as limited and sporadic as the level of participation by African American athletes themselves. There are, however, a few studies that provide information on African Americans and sport prior to emancipation. In "The Play of Slave Children in the Plantation Communities of the Old South, 1820–1860," *Journal of Sport History* (1980), and "Sport and Popular Pastimes: The Shadow of the Slavequarter," *Canadian Journal of History of Sport and Physical Education* (1980), David K. Wiggins furnishes insights into the leisure patterns and recreational activities of slaves. Additional information on this topic can be found in Wilma King, *Stolen Childhood: Slave Youth in Nineteenth-Century America* (1995), and Bernard Mergen, *Play and Playthings: A Reference Guide* (1982). The fighting career of Tom Molineaux, and sometimes that of his mentor Bill Richmond, is analyzed in Michael H. Goodman, "The Moor vs. Black Diamond," *Virginia Cavalcade* (1980); Carl B. Cone, "The Molineaux-Cribb Fight, 1810: Wuz Tom Molineaux Robbed?" *Journal of Sport History* (1982); Paul Magriel, "Tom Molineaux," *Phylon* (1951); Dennis Brailsford, *Bareknuckles: A Social History of Prize-fighting* (1988); and Elliott J. Gorn, *The Manly Art: Bare-Knuckle Prize Fighting in America* (1994).

In the latter half of the nineteenth century a number of elite African American athletes distinguished themselves in predominantly white organized sport at the highest levels of competition. Although much more research needs to be completed on these individuals, a number of important studies provide insights into the interconnection between African American athletes, white athletes, and this country's sport establishment during this time period. Jack W. Berryman's "Early Black Leadership in Collegiate Football: Massachusetts as a Pioneer," *Historical Journal of Massachusetts* (1981), analyzes the involvement of African American football players at Amherst and other predominantly white institutions in the state of Massachusetts. He concludes that a large number of African American football players, like William H. Lewis and Matthew Bullock, were able to compete at predominantly white colleges in Massachusetts because of that state's more liberalized racial attitudes. David K. Wiggins takes a close look at the careers of Isaac Murphy, the great jockey from Kentucky, and the outstanding Australian boxer Peter Jackson in Wiggins's "Isaac Murphy: Black Hero in Nineteenth-Century American Sport, 1861–1896," *Canadian Journal of History of Sport and Physical Education* (1979), and "Peter Jackson and the Elusive Heavyweight Championship: A Black Athlete's Struggle against the Late Nineteenth-Century Color-Line," *Journal of Sport History* (1985). Wiggins makes clear that Murphy and Jackson, though from different socioeconomic backgrounds and participants in different sports, both suffered the pangs of racial discrimination in a society steadily moving toward legalized segregation. Andrew Ritchie's *Major Taylor: The Extraordinary Career of a Champion Bicycle Racer* (1988) is a detailed and highly interesting account of the black bicyclist who found athletic success in both this country and foreign climes. While there is much to praise in the book, perhaps Ritchie's greatest contribution is his analysis of Taylor's experiences and racing career in Europe. David W. Zang's *Fleet Walker's Divided Heart: The Life of Baseball's First Black Major Leaguer* (1995) is the latest and one of the best accounts of an African American athlete in the late nineteenth century. Utilizing census records, newspaper accounts, and a number of other primary sources, Zang crafts the complicated story of a man of "mixed blood" who became not only major league baseball's first black player but also an owner of an opera house and a member of the back-to-Africa movement.

Most African American athletes would be eliminated from predominantly white organized sport by the turn of the century. With the notable exceptions of professional boxing and selected participation in predominantly white college sport and Olympic competition, African Americans were forced to organize their own teams and leagues as a result of Jim Crow laws and hardening racial policies. The most famous and most written about of these separate sporting organizations were the black baseball teams and leagues that sprang up in various parts of the country. Michael E. Lomax's "Black Entrepreneurship in the National Pastime: The Rise of Semiprofessional Baseball in Black Chicago 1890–1915," *Journal of Sport History* (1998) is an important study of baseball in Chicago's black community. Robert W. Peterson's classic study *Only the Ball Was White* (1970) has withstood the test of time and provides detailed information on the players and teams in black baseball. One of the significant contributions of Peterson's work was his reliance on heretofore little-used black newspapers. John Holway's *Voices from the Great Negro Baseball Leagues* (1975), and *Blackball Stars: Negro League Pioneers* (1988) and Stephen Banker's *Black Diamonds: An Oral History of Negro League Baseball* (1989) provide some interesting firsthand accounts of those who participated in black baseball. Both Donn Rogosin's *Invisible Men: Life in Baseball's Negro Leagues* (1987) and Mark Ribowsky's *Complete History of the Negro Leagues, 1884 to 1955* (1995) are fashioned from the Peterson mold in that they are secondary accounts that provide broad overviews of black baseball. Phil Dixon and Patrick J. Hannigan's *Negro Baseball Leagues: A Photographic Essay* (1992) and Bruce Chadwick's *When the Game Was Black and White: The Illustrated History of Baseball's Negro Leagues* (1992) are beautiful coffee table books that furnish not only terrific photographs but important analyses of black baseball. Neil Lanctot's *Fair Dealing and Clean Playing: The Hilldale Club and the Development of Black Professional Baseball, 1910–1932* (1994) is a relatively little known but valuable study of baseball, the economy, and black entrepreneurship. Janet Bruce's *Kansas City Monarchs: Champions of Black Baseball* (1985) is a thoughtful and detailed case study of one of black baseball's most famous teams. William Brashler's *Josh Gibson: A Life in the Negro Leagues* (1978);

Mark Ribowsky's *Power and the Darkness: The Life of Josh Gibson in the Shadows of the Game* (1996) and *Don't Look Back: Satchel Paige in the Shadows of Baseball* (1994) are biographies of two of the best and most colorful players in black baseball. Finally, Rob Ruck's *Sandlot Seasons: Sport in Black Pittsburgh* (1987) is a highly innovative and interpretative study that examines various black sporting organizations in Pittsburgh, including the highly successful Pittsburgh Crawfords and Homestead Grays. Perhaps Ruck's greatest contribution is his discussion of Cum Posey and Gus Greenlee, two of the several great black entrepreneurs of sport still waiting for their biographers.

Far fewer scholarly studies have been completed on other professional sports in the African American community. Like the sport history field in general, football and basketball in the black community have received relatively little coverage from academicians and other writers. There are some exceptions, however. Rob Ruck's "Soaring above the Sandlots: The Garfield Eagles," *Pennsylvania Heritage* (1982), an essay that is included in his *Sandlot Seasons*, is a rare look at an all-black football team. The essay is particularly good in illustrating how the Garfield Eagles contributed to a sense of racial pride and helped to bring Pittsburgh's black community together to share in the excitement of sport. The two most famous black basketball teams, the Harlem Globetrotters and the New York Renaissance Five, are given space in Robert W. Peterson's *Cages to Jump Shots: Pro Basketball's Early Years* (1990) and Nelson George's *Elevating the Game: Black Men and Basketball* (1992). Both authors place the Rens and Globetrotters within the context of African American culture and adequately assess the roles played by Robert Douglas and Abe Saperstein, the founders and organizers of the two clubs. Gerald R. Gems's "Blocked Shot: The Development of Basketball in the African American Community of Chicago," *Journal of Sport History* (1995), is an astute analysis of the growth of basketball in Chicago's black community.

Studies on amateur sport in the African American community are not any more plentiful than those completed on professional football and basketball. Information on interscholastic athletics is almost nonexistent except for the limited data provided in Nelson George's work and the general surveys on black sport. The works dealing with sport and historically black colleges are somewhat more promising. Limited but worthwhile information on this topic can be found in such standard institutional histories as Clarence A. Bacote's *Story of Atlanta University: A Century of Service, 1865–1965* (1969), Benjamin Brawley's *History of Morehouse College* (1917); Rayford Logan's *Howard University, The First Hundred Years, 1867–1967* (1969); Joe Richardson's *History of Fisk University, 1865–1946* (1980); and George Woolfolk's *Prairie View: A Study in Public Conscience, 1878–1946* (1962). Three works intended for general readers that furnish information on various aspects of sport at historically black colleges are O. K. Davis's *Gambling's Gridiron Glory: Eddie Robinson and the Tigers Success Story* (1983); Michael Hurd's *Black College Football 1892–1992: One Hundred Years of History, Education, and Pride* (1992); and Ted Chambers,

The History of Athletics and Physical Education at Howard University (1986). One view of African American women athletics and historically black colleges is provided in Gwendolyn Captain's "Enter Ladies and Gentlemen of Color: Gender, Sport, and the Ideal of African American Manhood and Womanhood during the Late Nineteenth and Early Twentieth Centuries," *Journal of Sport History* (1991). The best work on sport and historically black colleges is Patrick B. Miller's " 'To Bring the Race Along Rapidly': Sport, Student Culture, and Educational Mission at Historically Black Colleges during the Interwar Years," *History of Education Quarterly* (1995). Utilizing an impressive blend of secondary and primary sources emanating from the black community, Miller astutely analyzes the debates waged over the role of sport in historically black colleges in the context of the assimilation and racial uplift promoted by middle-class African Americans.

The elite African American athletes who participated in predominantly white organized sport during the first half of the twentieth century garnered far more scholarly attention than separate black sporting organizations. Perhaps because of the more readily available source material and fascination with interracial athletic contests, academicians have devoted an inordinate amount of time to African American athletes who triumphed in predominantly white organized sport at the national and international levels of competition. Few athletes have fascinated scholars more than Jack Johnson, the great heavyweight champion who caused much controversy by refusing to acquiesce to the norms of the dominant culture and insisted on living life on his own terms. William H. Wiggins places Johnson within the context of hero types in African American folklore with his path-breaking article "Jack Johnson as Bad Nigger: The Folklore of His Life," *Black Scholar* (1971). Wiggins also provides another interesting look at Johnson in his study "Boxing's Sambo Twins: Racial Stereotypes in Jack Johnson and Joe Louis Newspaper Cartoons, 1908 to 1938," *Journal of Sport History* (1988). This study, which was one of four articles included in a special issue on the "Black Athlete in American Sport," offers a wonderful analysis, not just of Johnson but of the interconnection between sport, race, and popular culture. Al-Tony Gilmore's *Bad Nigger: The National Impact of Jack Johnson* (1975) is a public reaction study that owes much to the earlier work of Wiggins. Randy Roberts, *Papa Jack: Jack Johnson and the Era of White Hopes* (1983) is the best full-scale biography of Johnson. Utilizing heretofore unused court documents from the National Archives and taking a far more critical approach to Johnson's autobiography, Roberts weaves a fascinating story of Johnson's ring triumphs, personal life, and various struggles against the U.S. government.

Far less controversial than Johnson were Jesse Owens and Joe Louis, two of the most renowned African American athletes in history. Owens, who achieved fame first at East Technical High in Cleveland, then later at Ohio State University, and finally at the 1936 Berlin Olympics, has received relatively little attention from academicians. Although his athletic exploits were truly extraor-

dinary and accomplished under the most extraordinary circumstances, Owens
has never captured the imagination of scholars. Fortunately, the one scholarly
biography of Owens is an extremely well-researched and superbly written study
that furnishes much insight into the great Olympian's life and career. William
J. Baker, in *Jesse Owens: An American Life* (1986), recounts Owens's life from
his earliest days in Alabama up through his four gold medal–winning performances in Berlin and later years as a public speaker and goodwill ambassador.
Using Owens's autobiographies written with Paul Neimark, a host of personal
interviews, and a variety of additional primary sources, Baker shatters several
myths surrounding Owens's life and describes the philosophical differences between the famous Olympic hero and the younger breed of African American
athletes of the late 1960s and early 1970s who were espousing a belief in black
power and disrupting the sacred institution of sport.

Whereas Owens has not received the attention from scholars that one might
expect, Joe Louis has been the focus of several scholarly articles and books.
Academicians have been enthralled by Louis, a man who achieved heroic status
in the African American community through his great triumphs in the ring
against both black and white fighters. Anthony O. Edmonds provides an interesting look at the symbolism inherent in Louis's second fight with Max Schmel-
ing in his "Second Louis-Schmeling Fight: Sport, Symbol, and Culture," *Journal
of Popular Culture* (1973). Edmonds offers a much broader interpretation of
Louis as cultural symbol in his *Joe Louis* (1973). This work, which depends
heavily on Alexander J. Young's unpublished 1968 doctoral dissertation, "Joe
Louis, Symbol," depicts the various responses to Louis as a boxer, African
American, and cultural symbol. Jeffrey T. Sammons furnishes an insightful anal-
ysis of the southern response to Louis in his "Boxing as a Reflection of Society:
The Southern Reaction to Joe Louis," *Journal of Popular Culture* (1983).
Sammons adds even more information on Louis and other black boxers, includ-
ing Muhammad Ali, in his well-known study *Beyond the Ring: The Role of
Boxing in American Society* (1988). Al-Tony Gilmore's "The Myth, Legend and
Folklore of Joe Louis: The Impression of Sport on Society," *South Atlantic
Quarterly* (1983), and Dominic J. Capeci, Jr., and Martha Wilkerson's "Multifarious Hero: Joe Louis, American Society and Race Relations during World
Crisis, 1935–1945," *Journal of Sport History* (1983), are two highly interpretative essays that emphasize Louis's role as a black boxer in racially torn American society. Chris Mead's *Champion: Joe Louis, Black Hero in White America*
(1985) is perhaps the best and most thorough biography of Louis. The book,
which began as a Yale senior thesis, examines Louis's life and career in great
detail and with much passion. In addition to the above works, more information
on Louis can be found in such books as Gerald Astor's *And a Credit to His
Race: The Hard Life and Times of Joseph Louis Barrow* (1974); Joe Louis
Barrow, Jr., and Barbara Munder's *Joe Louis: 50 Years an American Hero*
(1988) and Richard Bak's *Joe Louis: The Great Black Hope* (1996).

The experiences of African Americans who competed in predominantly white college sport between the two world wars has received increasing coverage from historians. Through the use of NAACP documents, black and white newspapers, presidential papers, and a host of other primary sources, scholars have chronicled the triumphs and the incidents of racial discrimination encountered by the select number of African American athletes who participated in college sport at such well-known institutions as Ohio State, Michigan, Harvard, Syracuse, and the University of California at Los Angeles (UCLA). The earliest study on this topic was John Behee's *Hail to the Victors! Black Athletes at the University of Michigan* (1974). Behee provides an insightful examination of Willis Ward, DeHart Hubbard, Cazzie Russell, and the other outstanding African American athletes who brought fame to the famous Big Ten institution. David K. Wiggins's "Prized Performers but Frequently Overlooked Students: The Involvement of Black Athletes in Intercollegiate Sports on Predominantly White University Campuses, 1890–1972," *Research Quarterly for Exercise and Sport* (1991), furnishes a general overview of black athletic participation on predominantly white university campuses. Patrick B. Miller's "Harvard and the Color Line: The Case of Lucien Alexis" (1991) relates the story of a Harvard lacrosse player who was denied the opportunity to compete against the U.S. Naval Academy on account of his color. Donald Spivey and Tom Jones's "Intercollegiate Athletic Servitude: A Case Study of the Black Illinois Student Athletes, 1931–1967," *Social Science Quarterly* (1975), examines the role of African American athletes at the University of Illinois over a period of thirty-five years. Spivey's "End Jim Crow in Sports: The Protest at New York University, 1940–1941," *Journal of Sport History* (1988), is an interpretative case study of the protest lodged on behalf of New York University's Leonard Bates, who was denied the opportunity to compete against southern institutions because of their unspoken "gentlemen's agreements." John M. Carroll's *Fritz Pollard: Pioneer in Racial Advancement* (1992) is a good biography of the famous black running back from Brown University.

The elimination of the color line in predominantly white organized sport took place at an uneven rate depending on the particular sport and level of competition. A number of scholars have charted this process in professional sport with great skill and passion. Not surprisingly, the reintegration of major league baseball, because of its enormous popularity and characterization as America's national pastime and most democratic of all sports, has garnered the most attention from academicians. David K. Wiggins traces the nearly twelve-year campaign waged by sportswriter Wendell Smith and the black *Pittsburgh Courier-Journal* against organized baseball's exclusionary policies in his "Wendell Smith, the *Pittsburgh Courier-Journal*, and the Campaign to Include Blacks in Organized Baseball, 1933–1945," *Journal of Sport History* (1983). Ronald A. Smith provides an interpretation of the differing philosophies of Jackie Robinson and Paul Robeson, including the latter's part in the struggle to erase the color line in baseball, in "The Paul Robeson–Jackie Robinson Saga and a Political Collision," *Journal of Sport History* (1979). William Simons furnishes an insightful interpretation of how the press perceived the shattering of the color line in baseball in "Jackie Robinson and the American Mind: Journalistic Perceptions of the Reintegration of Baseball," *Journal of Sport History* (1985). In " 'I Never Want to Take Another Trip like This One': Jackie Robinson's Journey to Integrate Baseball," *Journal of Sport History* (1997), Chris Lamb describes the hardships experienced by Robinson during his first spring training. Arnold Rampersad furnishes an intimate look at the life and career of Robinson in his *Jackie Robinson: A Biography* (1997). Jules Tygiel provides the definitive study on Jackie Robinson, the integration process, and the role of African American ballplayers in the 1950s in his well-known book *Baseball's Great Experiment: Jackie Robinson and His Legacy* (1983). The less-publicized story of Larry Doby and the integration of the American League is told quite well in Joseph T. Moore's *Pride against Prejudice: The Biography of Larry Doby* (1988). Finally, Jack E. Davis furnishes an interesting look at the elimination of segregation at southern spring training sites in "Baseball's Reluctant Challenge: Desegregating Major League Spring Training Sites, 1961–1964," *Journal of Sport History* (1992).

The shattering of the color line in other professional sports has received far less coverage. By and large, scholars have not been as interested in uncovering the facts and recounting the integration process in football, basketball, and other sports. There are, however, notable exceptions to this general trend. Gerald R. Gems adroitly recounts the reintegration of professional football in his little-known study "Shooting Stars: The Rise and Fall of Blacks in Professional Football," *Professional Football Research Association Annual Bulletin* (1988). Well written and full of important information, Gems's study makes clear that the reintegration of professional football was very complex and the result of various political maneuvers. Thomas G. Smith's case study "Civil Rights on the Gridiron: The Kennedy Administration and the Desegregation of the Washington Redskins," *Journal of Sport History* (1987), and his more broadly based "Outside the Pale: The Exclusion of Blacks from the National Football League, 1934–1946," *Journal of Sport History* (1988), details the reintegration of professional football in an interesting fashion. Studies on the integration of professional basketball are even less plentiful than those on football, but information on this topic can be found in Nelson George's *Elevating the Game: Black Men and Basketball* (1992) and Charles Salzberg's *From Set Shot to Slam Dunk: The Glory Days of Basketball in the Words of Those Who Played It* (1987). Information on the integration of professional golf can be found in historical surveys.

The elimination of the color line in intercollegiate sport has been of great interest to some historians. Primarily, that interest has revolved around the integration of southern institutions and conferences. An early scholarly study on this topic is by John Paul and his colleagues, "The Arrival and Ascendence of Black Athletes in the Southeastern Conference, 1966–1980," *Phylon* (1984). The authors provide rich detail concerning the process of integration in one of the most famous yet rigidly segregated conferences in the country. Richard Pennington's *Breaking the Ice: The Racial Integration of Southwest Conference*

Football (1987) is an informative, if not overly interpretative, work on the integration of the gridiron sport in the old Southwest Conference. Ronald E. Marcello's "The Integration of Intercollegiate Athletics in Texas: North Texas State College as a Test Case, 1956," *Journal of Sport History* (1987), is a solid case study of integration at one southern institution. Marked by its use of oral interviews, the study is largely concerned with the effects that integration of the North Texas athletics program had on the school's overall racial climate. Charles H. Martin has contributed greatly to the literature dealing with the integration of college sport in the South, most notably in his "Jim Crow in the Gymnasium: The Integration of College Basketball in the American South," *International Journal of the History of Sport* (1993); "Racial Change and Big-Time College Football in Georgia: The Age of Segregation, 1892–1957," *Georgia Historical Quarterly* (1996); and "Integrating New Year's Day: The Racial Politics of College Bowl Games in the American South," *Journal of Sport History* (1997). The three essays, all solidly written and characterized by thorough research, make clear that the integration process in southern college sport took place rather slowly and was fraught with much tension and controversy.

African American athletes were involved in the black power movement and the larger civil rights struggle of the late 1960s and early 1970s. Although not always politically savvy and sometimes reluctant to speak out on controversial issues for fear that they would be jeopardizing their careers, African American athletes increasingly voiced their complaints about the racism existing in sport and the larger society. No African American athlete came to symbolize the struggle for equality more than Muhammad Ali, the great heavyweight champion who inspired members of his race and a large portion of the dominant culture through his boxing exploits, membership in the Nation of Islam, and refusal to enter military service. Gerald Early's *Muhammad Ali Reader* (1998) is a wonderful collection of writings about the great heavyweight champion. Included in the collection are the writings of such people as Leroi Jones, Jackie Robinson, Norman Mailer, Joyce Carol Oates, and George Plimpton. Thomas Hauser, author of the well-known *Black Lights: Inside the World of Professional Boxing* (1986), is also author of a nicely written book on Ali entitled *Muhammad Ali: His Life and Times* (1991). Based on interviews with many of Ali's closest friends and associates, the work is required reading for anyone interested in the life and career of the great heavyweight champion. Perhaps the most important work on Ali, however, is Elliot J. Gorn's *Muhammad Ali: The People's Champ* (1995). A collection of seven essays originally given as presentations at a special conference at Miami University in Ohio, the book is primarily concerned with Ali as a cultural symbol and what he meant to Americans—both black and white, boxing aficionados and non-fans alike—during one of the most tumultuous periods in this nation's history. Additional information on Ali can be found in such important works as Jeffrey T. Sammons's *Beyond the Ring: The Role of Boxing in American Society* (1988); Jose Torres's *Sting Like a Bee: The Muhammad Ali Story* (1971); and Ali A. Mazuri's "Boxer Muhammad Ali and

Soldier Idi Amin as International Political Symbols: The Bioeconomics of Sports and War," *Comparative Studies in Society and History* (1977).

African American athletes exerted their greatest influence on the civil rights movement on predominantly white college campuses and in Olympic competition. Influenced by the examples set by Ali, Bill Russell, Jimmy Brown, and others, young African American athletes staged protests and revolts at white institutions and during both the 1968 and 1972 Olympic Games in an effort to disclose the racial discrimination in sport and American society. David K. Wiggins examines the black athletic revolts on several predominantly white college campuses in "The Year of Awakening: Black Athletes, Racial Unrest, and the Civil Rights Movement of 1968," *International Journal of the History of Sport* (1992), and "The Future of College Athletics Is at Stake: Black Athletes and Racial Turmoil on Three Predominantly White University Campuses, 1968–1972," *Journal of Sport History* (1988). Adolph Grundman explores the origins of black athletic involvement in the civil rights struggle in "Image of Intercollegiate Sports and the Civil Rights Movement: A Historian's View," *Arena Review* (1979). Donald Spivey analyzes African American involvement in various Olympic protests in "Black Consciousness and Olympic Protest Movements, 1964–1980," in Donald Spivey, ed., *Sport in America: New Historical Perspectives* (1985). Harry Edwards offers a largely firsthand account of the black athletic protests in *The Revolt of the Black Athlete* (1970). Two books that provide important insights into African American athletes and the black power movement are Richard Lapchick's *Broken Promises: Racism in American Sports* (1984) and William Van Deburg's *New Day in Babylon: The Black Power Movement and American Culture, 1965–1975* (1992).

African American women athletes had little involvement in the protests lodged on predominantly white college campuses and in Olympic competition. Although no less race conscious than their male counterparts, African American women athletes were generally not consulted by those who led the protests nor asked to join any of the staged revolts. Their lack of involvement in the civil rights struggle, however, did not diminish their past athletic accomplishments or deny their increasing presence in highly organized sport. African American women athletes have garnered many victories and realized great triumphs in a variety of sports at various levels of competition. Although slow to analyze these victories and triumphs, scholars have recently begun to provide important information on African American women athletes through more sophisticated and thorough research studies. Patricia Vertinsky and Gwendolyn Captain explore the historical construction of racist and sexualized myths surrounding African American female athletes in their insightful essay "More Myth than History: American Culture and Representations of the Black Female Athletic Ability," *Journal of Sport History* (1998). Susan Birrell provides an interesting sociological analysis of African American women and sport in her "Women of Color, Critical Autobiography, and Sport," in Michael A. Messner and Donald F. Sabo, eds., *Sport, Men, and the Gender Order: Critical Feminist Perspectives* (1990).

Linda Williams takes a look at the black press and African American women athletes in her "Sportswomen in Black and White: Sports History from an Afro-American Perspective," in Pamela J. Creeden, ed., *Women Media and Sport: Challenging Gender Values* (1994). Cindy Himes Gissendanner furnishes interpretative essays on sport and African American women athletes in her "African American Women and Competitive Sport, 1920–1960," in Susan Birrell and Cheryl Cole, eds., *Women, Sport, and Culture* (1993), and her "African American Women Olympians: The Impact of Race, Gender, and Class Ideologies, 1932–1968," *Research Quarterly for Exercise and Sport* (1996). Susan Cahn furnishes, perhaps, the most complete and thought-provoking analysis of African American women athletes in her well-known book *Coming on Strong: Gender and Sexuality in Twentieth-Century Women's Sport* (1994). Through the use of oral interviews and a variety of other primary and secondary sources, Cahn discusses the status of African American women athletes in the black community and the influence of both race and gender on their sport participation. Yvonne Smith's "Women of Color in Society and Sport," *Quest* (1992); Michael D. Davis's *Black American Women in Olympic Track and Field: A Complete Illustrated Reference* (1992); Ellen Gerber and others, *The American Woman in Sport* (1974); Tina Sloan-Green and others, *Black Women in Sport* (1981); and Alfred Dennis Mathewson's "Black Women, Gender Equity and the Function at the Junction," *Marquette Sports Law Journal* (1996) (an article appearing in a special issue entitled "Symposium on Race and Sports") are other works on African American women athletes that are worth consulting.

The last several years have seen an overrepresentation of African American athletes in certain sports and underrepresentation in others. African American athletes have also been overrepresented at certain playing positions within sport and underrepresented at others. It is apparent, moreover, that although the more blatant forms of racial discrimination have been eliminated from sport, African Americans continue to suffer racial slights and have limited access to coaching, managerial, and administrative positions within both college sport and professional sport.

The above issues have been explored through a number of important qualitative and quantitative studies. John Loy and Joseph McElvoque's "Racial Segregation in American Sport," *International Review of Sport Sociology* (1970); Donald Ball's "Ascription and Position: A Comparative Analysis of 'Stacking' in Professional Football," *Canadian Review of Sociology and Anthropology* (1973); Greg Jones and others, "A Log-linear Analysis of Stacking in College Football,"*Social Science Quarterly* (1987); Wilbert M. Leonard's, "Stacking in College Basketball: A Neglected Analysis," *Sociology of Sport Journal* (1987); and Mark Lavoie's "Economic Hypothesis of Positional Segregation: Some Further Comments," *Sociology of Sport Journal* (1989), are sociological studies dealing with "stacking" in sport (the overrepresentation of African Americans in certain playing positions). Gerald Skully's "Economic Discrimination in Professional Sports," *Law and Contemporary Problems* (1973); Wilbert M. Leonard's "Salaries and Race/Ethnicity in Major League Baseball: The Pitching Component," *Sociology of Sport Journal* (1989); and Robert Jiobu's "Racial Inequality in a Public Arena: The Case of Professional Baseball," *Social Forces* (1988), are studies that explore race-based economic discrimination in sport. Timothy Davis's "Myth of the Superspade: The Persistence of Racism in College Athletics," *Fordham Urban Law Journal* (1995); "African American Student-Athletes: Marginalizing the NCAA Regulated Structure," *Marquette Sports Law Journal* (1996); and Robert Sellers's "Black Student-Athletes: Reaping the Benefits or Recovering from the Exploitation," in Dana D. Brooks and Ronald C. Althouse, eds., *Racism in College Athletics: The African American Athlete's Experience* (1993), are works examining the experiences of African American athletes in contemporary college sport. Dana D. Brooks and Ronald C. Althouse, "Racial Imbalance in Coaching and Managerial Positions," in Dana D. Brooks and Ronald C. Althouse, eds., *Racism in College Athletics: The African American Athlete's Experience* (1993) discuss the status of black coaches in American sport.

Some of the most interesting studies are those concerned with the relationship between race, social structure, and sport orientation as well as the question of racial differences and sport performance. Richard Majors's "Cool Pose: Black Masculinity and Sports," in Michael A. Messner and Donald F. Sabo eds., *Sport, Men, and the Gender Order: Critical Feminist Perspectives* (1990), argues that the "expressive lifestyle behaviors" (or what he terms Cool Pose) articulated by African American athletes have allowed them to realize, among other things, a sense of dignity, to gain recognition and prestige, and to exercise some control in a society marked by racial oppression and discrimination. Majors correctly points out, however, that the "Cool Pose" adopted by African American athletes can be "self-defeating" because it often takes away from a devotion to those pursuits that would challenge male hierarchies and white domination. Michael Eric Dyson's "Be like Mike? Michael Jordan and the Pedagogy of Desire," in Michael Eric Dyson, *Reflecting Black: African American Cultural Criticism* (1993), argues that Michael Jordan is a cultural hero who exemplifies the best in athletic skill and performance, expresses elements of style unique to African American culture, and is a product of market forces characteristic of a capitalistic society. Dyson notes that Jordan's approach to basketball reflects the "will to spontaneity," "stylization of the performed self," and "edifying deception" so central to African American cultural expression. James LeFlore's "Athleticism among American Blacks," in Robert M. Pankin, ed., *Social Approaches to Sport* (1982), claims that African American athletes, like other members of their racial group, interpret their social system through a specific and generalized pool of information. Therefore, they tend to gravitate toward those sports in which the larger society expects them to participate while avoiding those sports that foster disapproval from the white majority. William S. Rudman's "Sport Mystique in Black Culture," *Sociology of Sport Journal* (1986); Richard Lapchick's *Five Minutes to Midnight: Race and Sport in the 1990's* (1991); and Larry E. Jordan's

"Black Markets and Future Superstars: An Instrumental Approach to Opportunity in Sport Forms," *Journal of Black Studies* (1981), are other studies that examine various aspects of race, social structure, and sport participation patterns.

A topic that has caught the interest of academicians is the question of alleged black athletic superiority. Scholars from a variety of disciplines have written about the debate that centers on African American athletes and their supposedly innate physiological gifts. David K. Wiggins provides a historical examination of the subject in his "Great Speed but Little Stamina: The Historical Debate over Black Athletic Superiority," *Journal of Sport History* (1989). Through an examination of important secondary materials, Wiggins traces the debate from the latter half of the nineteenth century to the present day, bringing to light the views of such noteworthy individuals as Montague Cobb, Edwin B. Henderson, and Harry Edwards. Laurel R. Davis examines the topic in "The Articulation of Difference: White Preoccupation with the Question of Racially Linked Genetic Differences among Athletes," *Sociology of Sport Journal* (1990). Well written and cogently analyzed, Davis's study delineates the reasons for the dominant culture's obsession with drawing links between supposedly innate physical gifts and black athletic performance. Patrick B. Miller furnishes an especially thorough and highly interpretive analysis of the topic in his "Anatomy of Scientific Racism: Racialist Responses to Black Athletic Achievement," *Journal of Sport History* (1998). No scholar interested in the subject can afford to overlook this essay. Finally, John Hoberman examines the topic in his *Darwin's Athletes: How Sport Has Damaged Black America and Preserved the Myth of Race* (1997). A work that has drawn much interest from academicians and lay public alike, Hoberman's book provides insights into the debate over black athletic superiority and a valuable introduction to the literature on medicine and biological differences.

In sum, the scholarly literature on African American athletes has increased in number and improved in quality over the last several decades. Academicians from various disciplinary perspectives, many of them taking their initial cues from Edwin B. Henderson, have examined the involvement of African Americans in sport, both behind segregated walls and in integrated athletic contests at different levels of competition. Although much study remains to be done on this topic, it has been broadened significantly by painstaking research and analysis. In the process, we have realized a greater understanding of both race and American society.

BIBLIOGRAPHY

Allen, Maury. *Jackie Robinson: A Life Remembered*. New York: Franklin Watts, 1987.
Ashe, Arthur, Jr. *A Hard Road to Glory: A History of the African American Athlete*. 3 vols. New York: Ballantine, 1976.
Astor, Gerald. *And a Credit to His Race: The Hard Life and Times of Joseph Louis Barrow*. New York: Saturday Review Press, 1974.

Azevedo, Mario, and Jeffrey T. Sammons. "Contributions in Science, Business Film, and Sports." In Mario Azevedo, ed., *Africana Studies: A Survey of Africa and the African Diaspora*. Durham, NC: Carolina Academic Press, 1993, 353–60.

Bacote, Clarence A. *The Story of Atlanta University: A Century of Service, 1865–1965*. Atlanta: Atlanta University Press, 1969.

Bak, Richard. *Joe Louis: The Great Black Hope*. New York: Taylor, 1996.

Baker, William J. *Jesse Owens: An American Life*. New York: Free Press, 1986.

———. *Sports in the Western World*. Urbana: University of Illinois Press, 1988.

Ball, Donald. "Ascription and Position: A Comparative Analysis of 'Stacking' in Professional Football." *Canadian Review of Sociology and Anthropology* 10 (May 1973): 97–113.

Banker, Stephen. *Black Diamonds: An Oral History of Negro League Baseball*. Princeton, NJ: Visual Education Corporation, 1989.

Bankes, James. *The Pittsburgh Crawfords: The Lives and Times of Black Baseball's Most Exciting Team!* Dubuque, IA: Wm. C. Brown Publishers, 1991.

Barrow, Joe Louis, Jr., and Barbara Munder. *Joe Louis: 50 Years an American Hero*. New York: McGraw-Hill, 1988.

Behee, John. *Hail to the Victors! Black Athletes at the University of Michigan*. Ann Arbor, MI: Swink-Tuttle Press, 1974.

Bennett, Bruce L. "Supplemental Selected Annotated Bibliography on the Negro in Sports." *Journal of Health, Physical Education, and Recreation* 41 (September 1970): 71.

———. "Bibliography on the Negro in Sports." *Journal of Health, Physical Education, and Recreation* 41 (September 1970): 77–78.

Berryman, Jack W. "Early Black Leadership in Collegiate Football: Massachusetts as a Pioneer." *Historical Journal of Massachusetts* 9 (June 1981): 17–28.

Birrell, Susan. "Women of Color, Critical Autobiography, and Sport." In Michael A. Messner and Donald F. Sabo, eds., *Sport, Men, and the Gender Order: Critical Feminist Perspectives*. Champaign, IL: Human Kinetics, 1990, 185–99.

Birrell, Susan, and Cheryl Cole, eds. *Women, Sport, and Culture*. Champaign, IL: Human Kinetics, 1993.

Bontemps, Arna. *Famous Negro Athletes*. New York: Dodd, Mead, 1964.

Brailsford, Dennis. *Bareknuckles: A Social History of Prizefighting*. Cambridge, MA: Lutterworth Press, 1988.

Brashler, William. *Josh Gibson: A Life in the Negro Leagues*. New York: Harper and Row, 1978.

Brawley, Benjamin. *History of Morehouse College*. Atlanta: Morehouse College, 1917.

Brooks, Dana D., and Ronald C. Althouse, eds. *Racism in College Athletics: The African American Athlete's Experience*. Morgantown, WV: Fitness Information Technology, 1993.

———. "Racial Imbalance in Coaching and Managerial Positions." In Dana D. Brooks and Ronald C. Althouse, eds., *Racism in College Athletics: The African American Athlete's Experience*. Morgantown, WV: Fitness Information Technology, 1993, 101–42.

Broome, Richard. "The Australian Reaction to Jack Johnson, Black Pugilist, 1907–09." In Richard Cashman and Michael McKerman, eds., *Sports in History: The Making of Modern Sporting History*. St. Lucia, Australia: University of Queensland Press, 1979, 343–63.

Brown, Roscoe C., Jr. "A Commentary on Racial Myths and the Black Athlete." In Daniel M. Landers, ed., *Social Problems in Athletics*. Urbana: University of Illinois Press, 1976, 168–73.

Bruce, Janet. *The Kansas City Monarchs: Champions of Black Baseball*. Lawrence: University Press of Kansas, 1985.

Cahn, Susan. *Coming on Strong: Gender and Sexuality in Twentieth-Century Women's Sport*. New York: Free Press, 1994.

Capeci, Dominic J., Jr., and Martha Wilkerson, "Multifarious Hero: Joe Louis, American Society, and Race Relations during World Crisis, 1935–1945." *Journal of Sport History* 10 (Winter 1983): 5–25.

Captain, Gwendolyn. "Enter Ladies and Gentlemen of Color: Gender, Sport, and the Ideal of African American Manhood and Womanhood during the Late Nineteenth and Early Twentieth Centuries." *Journal of Sport History* 18 (Spring 1991): 81–102.

Carroll, John M. *Fritz Pollard: Pioneer in Racial Advancement*. Urbana: University of Illinois Press, 1992.

Cashmore, Ernest. *Black Sportsmen*. London: Routledge and Kegan Paul, 1982.

Chadwick, Bruce. *When the Game Was Black and White: The Illustrated History of Baseball's Negro Leagues*. New York: Abberville Press, 1992.

Chalk, Ocania. *Pioneers of Black Sport: The Early Days of the Black Professional Athlete in Baseball, Basketball, Boxing, and Football*. New York: Dodd, Mead, 1975.

Chambers, Ted. *The History of Athletics and Physical Education at Howard University*. Washington, DC: Vantage, 1986.

Coakley, Jay J. *Sport in Society: Issues and Controversies*. 5th ed. St. Louis: Times Mirror/Mosby, 1994.

Cone, Carl B. "The Molineaux-Cribb Fight, 1810: Wuz Tom Molineaux Robbed?" *Journal of Sport History* 9 (Winter 1982): 83–91.

Creeden, Pamela J., ed. *Women, Media and Sport: Challenging Gender Values*. Thousand Oaks, CA: Sage, 1994.

Davis, Jack E. "Baseball's Reluctant Challenge: Desegregating Major League Spring Training Sites, 1961–1964." *Journal of Sport History* 19 (Summer 1992): 144–62.

Davis, John P. "The Negro in American Sports." In John P. Davis, ed., *The American Negro Reference Book*. Englewood Cliffs, NJ: Prentice-Hall, 1966, 775–825.

Davis, Laurel R. "The Articulation of Difference: White Preoccupation with the Question of Racially Linked Genetic Differences among Athletes." *Sociology of Sport Journal* 7 (1990): 179–87.

Davis, Lenwood G. *Joe Louis: A Bibliography of Articles, Books, Pamphlets, Records, and Archival Material*. Westport, CT: Greenwood Press, 1983.

Davis, Lenwood G., and Belinda Daniels, comps. *Black Athletes in the United States: A Bibliography of Books, Articles, Autobiographies, and Biographies on Professional Black Athletes, 1800–1981*. Westport, CT: Greenwood Press, 1983.

Davis, Michael D. *Black American Women in Olympic Track and Field: A Complete Illustrated Reference*. Jefferson, NC: McFarland, 1992.

Davis, O. K. *Grambling's Gridiron Glory: Eddie Robinson and the Tigers Success Story*. Rustin, LA: M&M Printing, 1983.

Davis, Timothy. "African American Student-Athletes: Marginalizing the NCAA Regulatory Structure." *Marquette Sports Law Journal* 6 (Spring 1996): 199–227.

———. "The Myth of the Superspade: The Persistence of Racism in College Athletics." *Fordham Urban Law Journal* 22 (November 3, 1995): 615–98.

Dixon, Phil, and Patrick J. Hannigan. *The Negro Baseball Leagues: A Photographic Essay.* Matotuck, NY: Ameon, 1992.

Dyson, Michael Eric. "Be like Mike? Michael Jordan and the Pedagogy of Desire." In Michael Eric Dyson, *Reflecting Black: African American Cultural Criticism.* Minneapolis: University of Minnesota Press, 1993, 64–75.

Early, Gerald. *The Muhammad Ali Reader.* New York: Ecco Press, 1998.

———. *The Culture of Bruising: Essays on Prizefighting, Literature, and Modern American Culture.* New York: Ecco Press, 1994.

———. *Tuxedo Junction: Essays on American Culture.* New York: Ecco Press, 1989.

Edmonds, Anthony O. "Second Louis-Schmeling Fight: Sport, Symbol, and Culture." *Journal of Popular Culture* 7 (Summer 1973): 42–50.

———. *Joe Louis.* Grand Rapids, MI: William B. Eerdmans, 1973.

Edwards, Harry. *The Revolt of the Black Athlete.* New York: Free Press, 1970.

———. *Sociology of Sport.* Homewood, IL: Dorsey Press, 1973.

Eisen, George, and David K. Wiggins, eds. *Ethnicity and Sport in North American History and Culture.* Westport, CT: Praeger, 1995.

Eitzen, D. Stanley, and George H. Sage. *Sociology of North American Sport.* Dubuque, IA: Brown and Benchmark, 1993.

Farr, Finis. *Black Champion: The Life and Times of Jack Johnson.* London: Macmillan and Company, 1964.

Fleischer, Nat. *Black Dynamite: The Story of the Negro in the Prize Ring from 1782 to 1938.* New York: Ring Magazine, 1947.

Fletcher, Marvin E. "The Black Soldier Athlete in the United States Army, 1890–1916." *Canadian Journal of History of Sport and Physical Education* 3 (December 1971): 16–26.

Gems, Gerald R. "Shooting Stars: The Rise and Fall of Blacks in Professional Football." *Professional Football Research Association Annual Bulletin* (1988): 1–16.

———. "Blocked Shot: The Development of Basketball in the African American Community of Chicago." *Journal of Sport History* 22 (Summer 1995): 135–48.

George, Nelson. *Elevating the Game: Black Men and Basketball.* New York: HarperCollins, 1992.

Gerber, Ellen, et al. *The American Woman in Sport.* Reading, MA: Addison-Wesley, 1974.

Gilmore, Al-Tony. *Bad Nigger: The National Impact of Jack Johnson.* New York: Kennikat, 1975.

———. "The Myth, Legend and Folklore of Joe Louis: The Impressions of Sport on Society." *South Atlantic Quarterly* 82 (Summer 1983): 256–68.

Gissendanner, Cindy Himes. "African American Women Olympians: The Impact of Race, Gender, and Class Ideologies, 1932–1968." *Research Quarterly for Exercise and Sport* 67 (June 1996): 172–82.

———. "African American Women and Competitive Sport, 1920–1960." In Susan Birrell and Cheryl Cole, eds., *Women, Sport and Culture.* Champaign, IL: Human Kinetics, 1993, 81–92.

Goodman, Michael H. "The Moor vs. Black Diamond." *Virginia Cavalcade* 29 (Spring 1980): 164–73.

Gorn, Elliot J., ed. *Muhammad Ali: The People's Champ.* Urbana: University of Illinois Press, 1995.

———. *The Manly Art: Bare-Knuckle Prize Fighting in America.* Ithaca, NY: Cornell University Press, 1994.

Gorn, Elliott J., and Warren Goldstein. *A Brief History of American Sports.* New York: Hill and Wang, 1993.

Grundman, Adolph. "Image of Intercollegiate Sports and the Civil Rights Movement: A Historian's View." *Arena Review* 3 (October 1979): 17–24.

Guttmann, Allen. *A Whole New Ball Game: An Interpretation of American Sports.* Chapel Hill: University of North Carolina Press, 1988.

Hauser, Thomas. *Muhammad Ali: His Life and Times.* New York: Simon and Schuster, 1991.

———. *The Black Lights: Inside the World of Professional Boxing.* New York: McGraw-Hill, 1986.

Henderson, Edwin B. *The Black Athlete: Emergence and Arrival.* Cornwall Heights, PA: Pennsylvania Publishers, 1968.

———. *The Negro in Sports.* Washington, DC: Associated Publishers, 1939, 1949.

———. "Physical Education and Athletics among Negroes." In Bruce L. Bennett, ed., *Proceedings of the Big Ten Symposium on the History of Physical Education and Sport.* Chicago: Athletic Institute, 1972, 67–83.

Henry, Grant. "A Bibliography concerning Negroes in Physical Education, Athletics, and Related Fields." *Journal of Health Physical Education, and Recreation* 44 (May 1973): 65–70.

Hoberman, John. *Darwin's Athletes: How Sport Has Damaged Black America and Preserved the Myth of Race.* Boston: Houghton Mifflin, 1997.

Holway, John. *Blackball Stars: Negro League Pioneers.* Westport, CT: Meckler, 1988.

———. *Voices from the Great Negro Baseball Leagues.* New York: Dodd, Mead, 1975.

Hoose, Philip M. *Necessities: Racial Barriers in American Sports.* New York: Random House, 1989.

Hurd, Michael. *Black College Football, 1892–1992: One Hundred Years of History, Education, and Pride.* Virginia Beach, VA: Donnin and Co. Pub., 1998.

Jable, J. Thomas. "Sport in Philadelphia's African American Community, 1865–1900." In George Eisen and David K. Wiggins, eds., *Ethnicity and Sport in North American History and Culture.* Westport, CT: Greenwood Press, 1994, 157–76.

Jarvie, Grant, ed. *Sport, Racism and Ethnicity.* London: Falmer Press, 1991.

Jiobu, Robert. "Racial Inequality in a Public Arena: The Case of Professional Baseball." *Social Forces* 67 (1988): 524–34.

Jones, Greg, et al. "A Log-linear Analysis of Stacking in College Football." *Social Science Quarterly* (March 1987): 70–83.

Jones, Wally, and Jim Washington. *Black Champions Challenge American Sports.* New York: David McKay, 1972.

Jones, William H. *Recreation and Amusement among Negroes in Washington.* Westport, CT: Negro Universities Press, 1970.

Jordan, Larry E. "Black Markets and Future Superstars: An Instrumental Approach to Opportunity in Sport Forms." *Journal of Black Studies* 11 (March 1981): 289–306.

Kahn, Lawrence M. "Discrimination in Professional Sports: A Survey of the Literature." *Industrial and Labor Relations Review* 44 (April 1991): 395–418.

King, Wilma. *Stolen Childhood: Slave Youth in Nineteenth-Century America.* Blooming-
    ton: Indiana University Press, 1995.

Lamb, Chris. "I Never Want to Take Another Trip like This One: Jackie Robinson's
    Journey to Integrate Baseball." *Journal of Sport History* 24 (Summer 1997):
    177–91.

Lanctot, Neil. *Fair Dealing and Clean Playing: The Hilldale Club and the Development
    of Black Professional Baseball, 1910–1932.* Jefferson, NC: McFarland, 1994.

Lapchick, Richard. *The Politics of Race and International Sport: The Case of South
    Africa.* Westport, CT: Greenwood Press, 1975.

———. *Broken Promises: Racism in American Sports.* New York: St. Martin's Press,
    1984.

———. *Five Minutes to Midnight: Race and Sport in the 1990's.* Lanham, MD: Madison
    Books, 1991.

Lavoie, Mark. "The Economic Hypothesis of Positional Segregation: Some Further Com-
    ments." *Sociology of Sport Journal* 6 (1989): 163–66.

Lawson, Hal A. "Physical Education and Sport in the Black Community: The Hidden
    Perspective." *Journal of Negro Education* 48 (Spring 1979): 187–95.

Lee, George L. *Interesting Athletes: Black American Sports Heroes.* New York: Ballan-
    tine, 1976.

Le Flore, James. "Athleticism among American Blacks." In Robert M. Pankin, ed., *Social
    Approaches to Sport.* Toronto: Associated University Presses, 1982, 104–21.

Leonard, Wilbert M., II. *A Sociological Perspective of Sport.* New York: MacMillan,
    1993.

———. "Stacking in College Basketball: A Neglected Analysis." *Sociology of Sport
    Journal* 4(1987): 403–9.

———. "Salaries and Race/Ethnicity in Major League Baseball: The Pitching Compo-
    nent." *Sociology of Sport Journal* 6 (1989): 152–62.

Logan, Rayford. *Howard University: The First Hundred Years, 1867–1967.* New York:
    New York University Press, 1969.

Lomax, Michael E. "Black Entrepreneurship in the National Pastime: The Rise of Semi-
    professional Baseball in Black Chicago, 1890–1915." *Journal of Sport History*
    25 (Spring 1998): 43–64.

Lowenfish, Lee. "Sport, Race, and the Baseball Business: The Jackie Robinson Story
    Revisited." *Arena Review* 2 (Spring 1978): 2–16.

Loy, John, and Joseph McElvoque. "Racial Segregation in American Sport." *Interna-
    tional Review of Sport Sociology* 5 (1970): 5–23.

Lucas, John A., and Ronald A. Smith. *Saga of American Sport.* Philadelphia: Lea and
    Febiger, 1978.

MacDonald, William W. "The Black Athlete in American Sports." In William J. Baker
    and John M. Carroll, eds., *Sports in Modern America.* St. Louis: River City
    Publishers, 1981, 88–98.

Magriel, Paul. "Tom Molineaux." *Phylon* 12 (December 1951): 329–36.

Majors, Richard. "Cool Pose: Black Masculinity and Sports." In Michael A. Messner
    and Donald F. Sabo, eds., *Sport, Men, and the Gender Order: Critical Feminist
    Perspectives.* Champaign, IL: Human Kinetics, 1990, 109–14.

Marable, Manning. "Black Athletes in White Men's Games, 1880–1920." *Maryland His-
    torian* 4 (Fall 1973): 143–49.

Marcello, Ronald E. "The Integration of Intercollegiate Athletics in Texas: North Texas State College as a Test Case, 1956." *Journal of Sport History* 14 (Winter 1987): 286–316.

Martin, Charles H. "Jim Crow in the Gymnasium: The Integration of College Basketball in the American South." *International Journal of the History of Sport* 10 (April 1993): 68–86.

———. "Racial Change and Big-Time College Football in Georgia: The Age of Segregation, 1892–1957." *Georgia Historical Quarterly* 80 (1996): 532–62.

———. "Integrating New Year's Day: The Racial Politics of College Bowl Games in the American South." *Journal of Sport History* 24 (Fall 1997): 358–77.

Mathewson, Alfred Dennis. "Black Women, Gender Equity and the Function at the Junction." *Marquette Sports Law Journal* 6 (Spring 1996): 239–66.

Mazuri, Ali A. "Boxer Muhammad Ali and Soldier Idi Amin as International Political Symbols: The Bioeconomics of Sports and War." *Comparative Studies in Society and History* 19 (April 1977): 189–215.

McKinney, G. B. "Negro Professional Baseball Players in the Upper South in the Gilded Age." *Journal of Sport History* 3 (Winter 1976): 273–80.

McPherson, Barry D. "Minority Group Involvement in Sport: The Black Athlete." *Exercise and Sport Science Reviews* 2 (1974): 71–101.

Mead, Chris. *Champion: Joe Louis, Black Hero in White America*. New York: Scribner's, 1985.

Mergen, Bernard. *Play and Playthings: A Reference Guide*. Westport, CT: Greenwood Press, 1982.

Messner, Michael A., and Donald F. Sabo, eds. *Sport, Men, and the Gender Order: Critical Feminist Perspectives*. Champaign, IL: Human Kinetics, 1990.

Miller, Patrick B. "The Anatomy of Scientific Racism: Racialist Responses to Black Athletic Achievement." *Journal of Sport History* 25 (Spring 1998): 119–51.

———. "Harvard and the Color Line: The Case of Lucien Alexis." In Ronald Story, ed., *Sports in Massachusetts: Historical Essays*. Westfield, MA: Institute for Massachusetts Studies, 1991, 137–58.

———. " 'To Bring the Race Along Rapidly': Sport, Student Culture, and Educational Mission at Historically Black Colleges during the Interwar Years." *History of Education Quarterly* 35 (Summer 1995): 111–33.

Moore, Joseph T. *Pride against Prejudice: The Biography of Larry Doby*. Westport, CT: Greenwood Press, 1988.

Olsen, Jack. *The Black Athlete: A Shameful Story*. New York: Time-Life Books, 1968.

Orr, Jack. *The Black Athlete: His Story in American History*. New York: Lion Books, 1969.

Paul, Joan, et al. "The Arrival and Ascendence of Black Athletes in the Southeastern Conference, 1966–1980." *Phylon* 45 (December 1984): 284–97.

Pennington, Richard. *Breaking the Ice: The Racial Integration of Southwest Conference Football*. Jefferson, NC: McFarland, 1987.

Peterson, Robert W. *Only the Ball Was White*. Englewood Cliffs, NJ: Prentice-Hall, 1970.

———. *Cages to Jump Shots: Pro Basketball's Early Years*. New York: Oxford University Press, 1990.

Porter, David L., ed. *African American Sports Greats: A Biographical Dictionary*. Westport, CT: Greenwood Press, 1995.

Rader, Benjamin G. *American Sports: From the Age of Folk Games to the Age of Spectators*. Englewood Cliffs, NJ: Prentice-Hall, 1983.

Rampersad, Arnold. *Jackie Robinson: A Biography*. New York: Alfred A. Knopf, 1997.

Reisler, Jim. *Black Writers/Black Baseball: An Anthology of Articles from Black Sportswriters Who Covered the Negro Leagues*. Jefferson, NC: McFarland, 1994.

Ribowsky, Mark. *The Power and the Darkness: The Life of Josh Gibson in the Shadows of the Game*. New York: Simon and Schuster, 1996.

———. *A Complete History of the Negro Leagues, 1884 to 1955*. New York: Birch Lane Press, 1995.

———. *Don't Look Back: Satchel Paige in the Shadows of Baseball*. New York: Simon and Schuster, 1994.

Richardson, Joe. *A History of Fisk University, 1865–1946*. University: University of Alabama Press, 1980.

Ritchie, Andrew. *Major Taylor: The Extraordinary Career of a Champion Bicycle Racer*. San Francisco: Bicycle Books, 1988.

Roberts, Randy. "Heavyweight Champion Jack Johnson: His Omaha Image, a Public Reaction Study." *Nebraska History* 57 (Summer 1976): 226–41.

———. "Galveston's Jack Johnson: Flourishing in the Dark." *Southwestern Historical Quarterly* 82 (July 1983): 37–56.

———. *Papa Jack: Jack Johnson and the Era of White Hopes*. New York: Free Press, 1983.

Roberts, Randy, and James Olson. *Winning Is the Only Thing: Sports in America since 1945*. Baltimore: Johns Hopkins University Press, 1989.

Rogosin, Donn. *Invisible Men: Life in Baseball's Negro Leagues*. New York: Athenaeum, 1987.

Ruck, Rob. *Sandlot Seasons: Sport in Black Pittsburgh*. Urbana: University of Illinois Press, 1987.

———. "Soaring above the Sandlots: The Garfield Eagles." *Pennsylvania Heritage* 8 (Summer 1982): 13–18.

Rudman, William S. "The Sport Mystique in Black Culture." *Sociology of Sport Journal* 3 (1986): 305–19.

Rust, Art, and Edna Rust. *Art Rust's Illustrated History of the Black Athlete*. Garden City, NY: Doubleday, 1985.

Salzberg, Charles. *From Set Shot to Slam Dunk: The Glory Days of Basketball in the Words of Those Who Played It*. New York: E. P. Dutton, 1987.

Sammons, Jeffrey T. "Boxing as a Reflection of Society: The Southern Reaction to Joe Louis." *Journal of Popular Culture* 16 (Spring 1983): 23–33.

———. *Beyond the Ring: The Role of Boxing in American Society*. Urbana: University of Illinois Press, 1988.

———. " 'Race' and Sport: A Critical Historical Examination." *Journal of Sport History* 21 (Fall 1994): 203–98.

Sellers, Robert. "Black Student-Athletes: Reaping the Benefits or Recovering from the Exploitation." In Dana D. Brooks and Ronald C. Althouse, eds., *Racism in College Athletics: The African American Athlete's Experience*. Morgantown, WV: Fitness Information Technology, 1993, 143–74.

Shropshire, Kenneth L. *In Black and White: Race and Sports in America*. New York: New York University Press, 1996.

Simons, William. "Jackie Robinson and the American Mind: Journalistic Perceptions of the Reintegration of Baseball." *Journal of Sport History* 12 (Spring 1985): 39–64.

Skully, Gerald. "Economic Discrimination in Professional Sports." *Law and Contemporary Problems* 39 (Winter–Spring 1973): 67–84.

———. "Merit Ol' Boy Networks and the Black-Bottomed Pyramid." *Hastings Law Journal* 47 (January 1996): 455–72.

Sloan-Green, Tina, et al. *Black Women in Sport*. Reston, VA: AAHPERD, 1981.

Smith, Ronald A. "The Paul Robeson–Jackie Robinson Saga and a Political Collision." *Journal of Sport History* 6 (Summer 1979): 5–27.

Smith, Thomas G. "Outside the Pale: The Exclusion of Blacks from the National Football League, 1934–1946." *Journal of Sport History* 15 (Winter 1988): 255–81.

———. "Civil Rights on the Gridiron: The Kennedy Administration and the Desegregation of the Washington Redskins." *Journal of Sport History* 14 (Summer 1987): 189–208.

Smith, Yvonne. "Women of Color in Society and Sport." *Quest* 44 (Summer 1992): 228–50.

Spivey, Donald. "Black Consciousness and Olympic Protest Movements, 1964–1980." In Donald Spivey, ed. *Sport in America: New Historical Perspectives*. Westport, CT: Greenwood Press, 1985, 239–59.

———. "End Jim Crow in Sports: The Protest at New York University, 1940–1941." *Journal of Sport History* 15 (Winter 1988): 282–303.

———. "Sport, Protest, and Consciousness: The Black Athlete in Big-Time Intercollegiate Sports, 1941–1968." *Phylon* 44 (June 1983): 116–25.

Spivey, Donald, and Tom Jones. "Intercollegiate Athletic Servitude: A Case Study of the Black Illinois Student Athletes, 1931–1967." *Social Science Quarterly* 55 (March 1975): 939–47.

Thompson, Richard. *Race and Sport*. London: Oxford University Press, 1964.

Torres, Jose. *Sting like a Bee: The Muhammad Ali Story*. New York: Abelard-Schuman, 1971.

Tygiel, Jules. *Baseball's Great Experiment: Jackie Robinson and His Legacy*. New York: Oxford University Press, 1983.

Van Deburg, William. *A New Day in Babylon: The Black Power Movement and American Culture, 1965–1975*. Chicago: University of Chicago Press, 1992.

Vertinsky, Patricia, and Gwendolyn Captain. "More Myth than History: American Culture and Representations of the Black Female's Athletic Ability." *Journal of Sport History* 25 (Fall 1998): 532–61.

Watkins, Ralph. "Recreation, Leisure and Charity in the Afro-American Community of Buffalo, New York: 1920–1925." *Afro-Americans in New York Life and History* 6 (July 1982): 7–15.

Weaver, Bill L. "The Black Press and the Assault on Professional Baseball's Color Line, October 1945–April 1947." *Phylon* 40 (Winter 1979): 303–17.

Wiggins, David K. "Great Speed but Little Stamina: The Historical Debate over Black Athletic Superiority." *Journal of Sport History* 16 (Summer 1989): 158–85.

———. "Critical Events Affecting Racism in Athletics." In Dana D. Brooks and Ronald C. Althouse, eds., *Racism in College Athletics: The African American Athlete's Experience*. Morgantown, WV: Fitness Information Technology, 1993, 23–49.

———. *Glory Bound: Black Athletes in a White America*. Syracuse, NY: University Press, 1997.

———. "The Play of Slave Children in the Plantation Communities of the Old South, 1820–1860." *Journal of Sport History* 7 (Summer 1980): 21–39.

———. "Sport and Popular Pastimes: The Shadow of the Slavequarter." *Canadian Journal of History of Sport and Physical Education* 11 (May 1980): 61–88.

———. "Issac Murphy: Black Hero in Nineteenth-Century American Sport, 1861–1896." *Canadian Journal of History of Sport and Physical Education* 10 (May 1979): 15–32.

———. "Prized Performers, but Frequently Overlooked Students: The Involvement of Black Athletes in Intercollegiate Sports on Predominantly White University Campuses, 1890–1972." *Research Quarterly for Exercise and Sport* 62 (June 1991): 164–77.

———. "Wendell Smith, the *Pittsburgh Courier-Journal* and the Campaign to Include Blacks in Organized Baseball, 1933–1945." *Journal of Sport History* 10 (Summer 1983): 5–29.

———. "The Future of College Athletics Is at Stake: Black Athletes and Racial Turmoil on Three Predominantly White University Campuses, 1968–1972." *Journal of Sport History* 15 (Winter 1988): 304–33.

———. "The Year of Awakening: Black Athletes, Racial Unrest, and the Civil Rights Movement of 1968." *International Journal of the History of Sport* 9 (August 1992): 188–208.

———. "From Plantation to Playing Field: Historical Writings on the Black Athlete in American Sport." *Research Quarterly for Exercise and Sport* 57 (June 1986): 101–16.

Wiggins, William H. "Boxing's Sambo Twins: Racial Stereotypes in Jack Johnson and Joe Louis Newspaper Cartoons, 1908 to 1938." *Journal of Sport History* 15 (Winter 1988): 242–54.

———. "Jack Johnson as Bad Nigger: The Folklore of His Life." *Black Scholar* 2 (January 1971): 4–19.

Williams, Linda. "Sportswomen in Black and White: Sports History from an Afro-American Perspective." In Pamela J. Creeden, ed., *Women, Media and Sport: Challenging Gender Values.* Thousand Oaks, CA: Sage, 1994, 45–66.

Woolfolk, George. *Prairie View: A Study in Public Conscience, 1878–1946.* New York: Pageant Press, 1962.

Young, Alexander, Jr. 'The Boston Tarbaby." *Nova Scotia Historical Quarterly* 4 (September 1974): 277–93.

———. "Joe Louis, Symbol." Ph.D. dissertation, University of Maryland, 1968.

Young, Andrew S. "Doc." *Great Negro Baseball Stars and How They Made the Major Leagues.* New York: A. S. Barnes, 1953.

———. *Negro Firsts in Sports.* Chicago: Johnson Publishing, 1963.

Zang, David W. *Fleet Walker's Divided Heart: The Life of Baseball's First Black Major Leaguer.* Lincoln: University of Nebraska Press, 1995.

Zuckerman, Jerome, et al. "The Black Athlete in Post-bellum 19th Century." *Physical Educator* 29 (October 1972): 142–46.

XIII

Constructing an Historiography of African American Business

Juliet E. K. Walker

INTRODUCTION

The agency of blacks in forging their own economic liberation through entrepreneurship and business enterprise has been generally ignored in the historical literature. Yet, there does exist in the record of the black historical experience a coherent body of published scholarly works that illuminate the extent to which blacks, even during the age of slavery, both slave and free, participated in the business community of preindustrial America. The most successful, a comparative few, achieved substantial wealth. Even after slavery, there were always black entrepreneurs who through their business activities achieved economic success. With each subsequent generation, these men and women were not unique in their entrepreneurial activities but, rather, representative of a long tradition of black business participation from slavery to freedom.

Indeed, a persistent theme in the African American experience has been the self-help search for profits, and accumulation beyond subsistence, that propelled blacks to improve their dismal, dispiriting, and bleak material lives. Within this context, this chapter provides a two-part historiographical discussion that reviews the literature that distinguishes the study of African American business activities. First comes a chronological overview of the scholarly literature that provided a foundation for what is emerging as a separate and distinct field in African American history. There is also an introduction of the scholars whose seminal works distinguish the study of black business history. The second part provides an historiographical literature review of studies in black business history, categorized by historical periods and topics ranging from early African commerce to the post–civil rights era.

PART I: EMERGENCE OF AFRICAN AMERICAN BUSINESS HISTORY

In many respects the study of black business history begins with the work of William E. B. Du Bois in his Atlanta University Series publications, particularly *The Negro in Business* (1898), *The Negro Artisan* (1902), and his *Economic Cooperation among Negro Americans* (1907). Yet, whereas most scholars of the African American historical experience are cognizant of Du Bois's studies in black business in the Atlanta University Publication series, Booker T. Washington's *Negro in Business* (1907) has generally been ignored as a source of information on black business activities at the turn of the last century. Likewise, few scholars have examined the *Negro Year Book*, edited by Monroe N. Work, who headed the Division of Records and Research at Tuskegee Normal and Industrial Institute. By 1916, four editions had been published. Each contained a brief chapter entitled "Negro in Business."

Even more telling, from the 1920s to the 1940s, only three works provided a specific examination of the black business experience: J. H. Harmon, Jr., Arnett G. Lindsay, and Carter G. Woodson's *Negro as a Businessman* (1929) and two studies that focused on black financial institutions, Abram L. Harris's *Negro as Capitalist: A Study of Banking and Business among American Negroes* (1936) and M. S. Stuart's *Economic Detour: A History of Insurance in the Lives of American Negroes* (1940). Moreover, subsequent scholars failed to expand on these early examinations of the African American business experience. Even St. Clair Drake and Horace Cayton in their classic study *Black Metropolis: A Study of Negro Life in a Northern City* (1945) provided only a two-chapter assessment of Chicago's black business community in the 1930s and early 1940s.

Interestingly too, the Drake-Cayton study was published a year after Gunnar Myrdal's monumental work *An American Dilemma: The Negro Problem and Modern Democracy* (1944). Significantly, Myrdal limited his assessments of black business to only 15 out of 1,483 pages of information on black life in America. An additional five pages in the Myrdal study provided a review of the informal economic activities of blacks in subsections entitled the "numbers game" and "underworld" activities. Indeed, it was not until nearly a half century after Du Bois's 1898 study, *The Negro in Business*, that the first attempt was made to move the scholarly study of black business activities beyond that of assessing only black financial institutions, considered by some as the only "real" businesses in the black community. In 1947 mathematician Joseph Pierce's study *Negro Business and Business Education* was published. In African American business historiography, Pierce's study represents the first comprehensive systematic analysis of the broad scope of black business activities.

The study, undertaken as a collaborative effort under the joint auspices of Atlanta University and the National Urban League, was funded by the General Education Board. The research took place in 1944, and the findings were based on surveys made of 3,866 black businesses located in twelve cities, all in the South except for St. Louis and Cincinnati. Black businesses in those cities were categorized into 99 lines of enterprise, and information was obtained on several aspects of black business activity, location of the enterprises, motivation of the owners, types of ownership, capital outlays, recordkeeping, employees, business management methods and activities, and problems of business operations. Historical forces such as World War II were also considered—loss of personnel because of the war for example, competition from war industries that paid higher wages, as well as difficulties in getting supplies. Information was also provided on insurance companies, banks and lending institutions, and consumer cooperatives.

Two years later, Vishnu V. Oak's *Negro's Adventure in General Business* (1949) was published. Comprehensive in several ways, Oak's brief work is especially important. Specifically, Oak provides information on various nontraditional black businesses established in the first five decades of the twentieth century. One chapter is entitled "Other Case Histories of Successful Business Ventures." Also in an appendix, "Various Kinds of Businesses Corporations Started during the Negro Business Boom," brief paragraphs provide information on thirty-nine black businesses established in the first three decades of the twentieth century.

By the 1950s, perhaps as a reflection of the absence of a substantial body of scholarship on black business, as well as the negative image of black businesspeople in the minds of black intellectuals, E. Franklin Frazier's negative assessment of black business in his classic *Black Bourgeoisie: The Rise of a New Middle Class* (1957) generated widespread discussion among the nation's public intellectuals. Before *Black Bourgeoisie*, other scholars had questioned the viability and usefulness of black business. For instance, by the 1930s, Du Bois, who in 1898 had urged black consumers to support black businesses, had embraced consumer cooperatives and urged black alliances with the white working class. Also Abram Harris in his 1936 *The Negro as Capitalist* denounced black businesspeople in their promotion of a separate economy as black capitalist exploiters of the wage-earning black masses. Yet, in his chapter "Negro Business: A Social Myth," Frazier went even farther, insisting that the problem with black business resulted from "the simple but fundamental sociological fact that the Negro lacks a business tradition or the experience of people who, over generations, have engaged in buying and selling."

Also in his discussion of the "Myth of Negro Business," Frazier emphasized that another principal factor that limited the success of black business in America was the failure of black consumers to support coethnics in their enterprises.

Finally, Frazier emphasized that his "Myth of Negro Business" also underscored a historical reality, namely, that black business, with its negligible profits, was a limited source of funding for the development of a business infrastructure that would enable African Americans to achieve racial economic parity. This thesis received later support from Nathan Glazier and Daniel Patrick Moynihan. In *Beyond the Melting Pot* (1963), they asserted that the devastating effects of slavery prevented blacks from developing viable business enterprises. As a result, they claimed, freedom found blacks not only without experience in succeeding in a money exchange economy but also lacking the most basic skills in financial planning, business organization, and management. Acknowledging racism as a factor that impeded black business advancement, they emphasized, however, that not only was there an absence of "clannishness" among blacks in support of their businesses but, most important, they claimed, there was also the "failure of Negroes to develop a pattern of saving."

By the 1960s, the critical issue in the black experience was the achievement of civil and political rights. Ironically, as Robert E. Weems, Jr., emphasizes in his article "Out of the Shadows: Business Enterprise and African American Historiography," the marginalization of community-based black enterprise during the civil rights era was one of three factors responsible for the underrepresentation of black business activity in African American historiography throughout the twentieth century. Yet, while the post–civil rights era saw an expansion in black business activity as well as an expansion in the study of African American history, few monographs with a specific focus on black business activities were published. Even then, these studies continued the tradition of the 1930s in their focus on black financial institutions, whereas the biographies focused on antebellum black entrepreneurs.

Nevertheless, by the 1990s, a small core of historians had emerged whose research focused specifically on black business activities. Among these scholars were Walter Weare, Alexa Benson Henderson, Robert E. Weems, Jr., Kenneth Hamilton, Robert C. Kenzer, and Juliet E. K. Walker. In addition, historians Edwin A. Davis and William R. Hogan; Gary B. Mills, Loren Schweninger, Michael P. Johnson, and James L. Roark; and John N. Ingham made significant contributions to black business history.

Moreover, by 1999, as an introduction to the study of African American business history, three important sources were available. The John N. Ingham and Lynne B. Feldman study *African-American Business Leaders: A Biographical Dictionary* (1994) is significantly important. Encyclopedic in format, this massive volume provides scholarly biographical sketches of 123 leading black entrepreneurs. Most of the entrepreneurs included in the volume had established businesses that spanned the period from 1880 to World War II; several black business leaders in both antebellum America and the post–civil rights era are also included. With few studies available on black entrepreneurs in the periodical literature and with even fewer full-length biographies published on America's black entrepreneurs, the Ingham-Feldman study is invaluable, especially, too, for its extensive bibliographic information. An impressive listing of primary and secondary sources is provided for each subject, in addition to the location of archival holdings in those instances when personal papers or company records are available.

Still, it was not until 1998 with Juliet E. K. Walker's *History of Black Business in America: Capitalism, Race, Entrepreneurship* that the first and only comprehensive history of black business was published. This award-winning book examines black business from its origin in the commercial culture of West Africa to the mid-1990s. Each of the chapters, extensively documented through primary and secondary sources, provides the basis for the conceptual, interpretive, and chronological framework needed for the study of black business history.

In addition, the *Encyclopedia of African American Business History* (1999), edited by Juliet E. K. Walker, provides specific entries on black business people, black businesses, and topics and issues important to black business activities. The entries underscore the expansion of scholarship in the study of black business, the diversity of black business activities, and the increasingly interdisciplinary study of black business history.

In addition, the study of black business has been enhanced by the contributions of other scholars, particularly sociologists John Sibley Butler and Robert L. Boyd, who have written extensively on black business history topics. Several economists have also made significant contributions, especially David Whitten for the antebellum period and Timothy Bates and Thomas D. Boston for black business activity since the 1960s.

For twenty-first-century historians, the work of these scholars in sociology and economics will comprise an important body of primary sources in the study of late-twentieth-century black business history. Even now, historians are making use of their research, underscoring the increasing interdisciplinary study of black business history, as seen in Robert Weems's recent work *Desegregating the Dollar: African American Consumerism in the Twentieth Century* (1998). An important study that analyzes black spending patterns since World War I, Weems emphasizes that mass market courting of black consumer by white corporations in the post–civil rights era has contributed significantly to the destruction of black-owned businesses. Increasing awareness of the importance of study of black business history, as well as recognition of the neglect of such study, was demonstrated in 1998 by the Association for the Study of African American Life and History (ASALH), which had as its theme that year "Black Business: The Path towards Economic Empowerment." Under the editor-in chief, Larry Martin, and guest editor Juliet E. K. Walker, the ASALH published a series of articles on black business history, including essays on specific topics important to the black business experience.

PART II: BIBLIOGRAPHY OF BLACK BUSINESS

African Commercial Background

The African American business tradition had its origin in the commercial culture that existed in precolonial West and West Central Africa during the transatlantic slave trade era. Several studies in African history remain unsurpassed in detailing business activities of Africans as producers, traders, brokers, and merchants as well as their corporate forms of trade organizations, including S. F. Nadel, *A Black Byzantium* (1942); Kwame Yeboa Daaku, *Trade and Politics on the Gold Coast: 1600–1720* (1970); Patrick Manning, *Slavery, Colonialism and Economic Growth in Dahomey* (1982); and Ray A. Kea, *Settlements, Trade, and Politics in the Seventeenth-Century Gold Coast* (1982). Lars Sundstrom's study, in *The Exchange Economy of Pre-colonial Tropical Africa* (1974), is especially important for an understanding of taxation and the exchange media that existed during the slave trade era. Also see the articles in Claude Meillassoux, ed., *The Development of Indigenous Trade and Markets in West Africa* (1971). Also, Juliet E. K. Walker's "Trade and Markets in Precolonial West and West Central Africa: The Cultural Foundations of the African American Business Tradition" (1997) is important for information on the African cooperative work ethic, production/land, craft and merchant guilds, and women's production and trade activities.

These studies detail the extent to which Africans brought to the Americas came from a cross-section of the African occupational population. Women's economic activities are included in these studies, but also see Margaret Jean Hay and Sharon Stritcher, eds., *African Women South of the Sahara* (1984). Most familiar to African Americanists is the Olaudah Equiano autobiography, which details how African merchants abetted the transatlantic slave trade. Ultimately, historians who study the commercial culture of the transatlantic slave trade should include a critical reading of primary sources such as William Bosman, *A New and Accurate Description of Guinea* (1704). Studies such as Joseph E. Holloway, ed., *Africanisms in American Culture* (1991), and Gwendolyn Midlo Hall, *Africans in Colonial Louisiana: The Development of Afro-Creole Culture in the Eighteenth Century* (1992), explore the linkage between African cultural influences and self-help activities developed by blacks in colonial America.

Slave Business Activities

Although most of the literature focuses on the English colonies, historians are increasingly expanding their studies to include the activities of blacks in the early Spanish and French territories of Spain and Louisiana. Roderick A. McDonald's *Economy and Material Culture of Slaves: Goods and Chattels on the Sugar Plantations of Jamaica and Louisiana* (1993) is an excellent study on the internal plantation economies of two slave societies. Also, Daniel H. Usner's *Indians, Settlers, & Slaves in a Frontier Exchange Economy* (1992) details how slaves also operated a flourishing underground economy as hustlers and "fence men," which at times was inclusive of the independent slave economy as well as the underground enterprises of maroons, fugitive slaves who lived hidden in isolated settlements in the slave South.

Specialists in American history, influenced by studies on French and Spanish slavery in the Caribbean, are increasingly focusing upon the "informal slave economy" on the North American mainland. Philip D. Morgan's 1982 article "Work and Culture: The Task System and the World of Lowcountry Blacks, 1700–1880" represents one of the pioneering works in this area. Also see Morgan's 1998 book *Slave Counterpoint: Black Culture in the Eighteenth Century Chesapeake and Low Country* and William M. Dusinberre's *Them Dark Days: Slavery in the American Rice Swamps* (1996). Two other studies that illuminate independent slave economic activities in greater detail are Betty Woods's *Women's Work, Men's Work: The Informal Slave Economies of Lowcountry Georgia* (1995) and Larry E. Hudson's *To Have and to Hold: Slave Work and Family Life in Antebellum South Carolina* (1997), especially the chapters "For Better, for Worse: The Slaves' World of Work" and "For Richer, for Poorer: The Family as an Economic Unit."

Whereas plantation slaves' profits from their independent production were generally limited, independent slave-initiated enterprise was much more extensive than the historical record has acknowledged, particularly in terms of property owned and money earned by slaves. See Philip D. Morgan, "The Ownership of Property by Slaves in the Mid-nineteenth Century Low Country" (1983), and Lawrence T. McDonnell, "Money Knows No Master: Market Relations and the American Slave Community" (1998). Also see Larry E. Hudson, Jr., ed., *Working toward Freedom: Slave Society and Domestic Economy in the American South* (1995).

Also, several edited studies provide a collection of articles that examine independent slave economic activities and the informal slave economy. Two edited studies by Ira Berlin and Philip D. Morgan also include articles on these activities in the Caribbean: In Berlin and Morgan's *Slaves' Economy: Independent Production by Slaves in the Americas* (1991), see John T. Schlotterbeck, "The Internal Economy of Slavery in Rural Piedmont Virginia." In their *Cultivation and Culture: Labor and the Shaping of Slave Life in the Americas* (1993), see John Campbell's "As 'A Kind of Freeman'?: Slaves' Market—Related Activities in the South Carolina Up County, 1800–1860," Roderick A. McDonald's "Independent Economic Production by Slaves on Antebellum Louisiana Sugar Plantations," and Joseph R. Reidy's "Obligations and Right: Patterns of Labor, Subsistence, and Exchange in the Cotton Belt of Georgia, 1790–1860."

Few plantation slaves, however, were able to secure their freedom with monies earned from their independent economic activities compared to self-hired slaves, most of whom were skilled craftsmen and women, and some urban and town slaves who developed enterprises. See the two essays "Freemen, Servants, and Slaves: Artisans and the Craft Structure of Revolutionary Baltimore Town" and "Slave Artisans in Richmond, Virginia, 1780–1810" in Howard B. Rock, Paul A. Gilje, and Robert Asher, eds., *American Artisans: Crafting Social Identity, 1750–1850* (1995). Also see James E. Newton and Ronald L. Lewis, eds., *The Other Slaves: Mechanics, Artisans and Craftsmen* (1978).

Those self-hired slaves who made unusual amounts of money were "slave entrepreneurs," a term I introduced in my 1983 article "Pioneer Slave Entrepreneurship—Patterns, Processes, and Perspectives: The Case of the Slave Free Frank on the Kentucky Pennyroyal, 1795–1819" (1983). Slave autobiographies such as Lunsford Lane, *The Narrative of Lunsford Lane, Formerly of Raleigh, N.C.* (1842), also provide information on slave entrepreneurship. A self-hired slave who manufactured cigars, Lane had branch offices in several North Carolina towns.

Invariably, articles that provide information on self-hired slaves focus on those who were manumitted. Early studies that examined this practice include John Hope Franklin, "Slaves Virtually Free in Ante-bellum North Carolina" (1943); Summer E. Matison, "Manumission by Purchase" (1948); Richard B. Morris, "The Measure of Bondage in the Slave States" (1954); Clement Eaton, "Slave-Hiring in the Upper South: A Step toward Freedom" (1960). See in addition the 1973 dissertation "Self-Hire among Slaves, 1820–1860: Institutional Variation or Aberration?" by Edna Chappell McKenzie. Slaves also participated in the economy as intrapreneurs, or managers of their owner's firms, even supervising whites and negotiating their own freedom. See D. Berkeley, Jr., "Christopher McPherson, Free Person of Color" (1969).

Some slave managers set up business on the side. See John Hebron Moore, "Simon Gray, Riverman: A Slave Who Was Almost Free" (1962). The largest number of slave managers were the plantation drivers, many of whom did the work of an overseer but without the title, as indicated in *Without Consent or Contract: The Rise and Fall of American Slavery* by Robert William Fogel, who notes the shift from white managers to slave managers. Although their numbers declined after 1840, he states, "even in 1860 slaves were probably still the chief non-ownership managers on about half of all large plantations" (1989, 44). The most notable was Benjamin Montgomery, who managed the plantation of the brother of Jefferson Davis while running his store on the plantation and serving as the Davis Bend postmaster.

These studies on the independent economic activities of slaves and the internal economy they established in the exchange and sale of goods underscore the degree to which there existed among the slaves a strong propensity to improve their material lives. As they participated in the formal economy, slaves who hired their own time had a chance to purchase their freedom. The significance of these studies is that they provide additional information in answering the question, "Did slaves accept the system created by their masters?"

Ultimately, the source that reveals the extensiveness of independent slave economic activities are slave laws. As I suggest in *The History of Black Business in America*, there were as many laws in force to suppress the independent slave economy as there were laws in force to suppress slave resistance activities. The Black Codes that developed in the immediate post–civil war period to suppress the economic activities of freedmen not only reflect attempts to place freedom in a state approximating slavery but also demonstrate white fear that now free, slaves would achieve even more success in their independent economic activities.

Free Black Business Activities

Lorenzo J. Greene's *Negro in Colonial New England, 1620–1776* (1942) was the first study to illuminate the early business activities of some of the first Africans in America. Subsequent studies of blacks in the North—William D. Piersen's *Black Yankees: The Development of an Afro-American Subculture in Eighteenth-Century New England* (1988), Gary B. Nash's *Forging Freedom: The Formation of Philadelphia's Black Community, 1720–1840* (1988), James Oliver Horton's *Free People of Color: Inside the African American Community* (1993), James Oliver Horton and Lois E. Horton's *In Hope of Liberty: Culture, Community and Protest among Northern Free Blacks, 1700–1860* (1997), and Julie Winch, *Philadelphia's Black Elite: Activism, Accommodation, and the Struggle for Autonomy, 1787–1844* (1998)—though expanding the topical framework provided by Greene, have not generally broadened his discussion of black business activities.

Still, some historians, such as Robert E. Perdue, *Black Laborers and Black Professionals in Early America, 1750–1830* (1975), and Whittington B. Johnson, *The Promising Years, 1750–1830: The Emergence of Black Labor and Business* (1993), have considered the economic life of blacks beyond that of slave laborers. Johnson's *Black Savannah, 1788–1864* (1996) includes a chapter, "Affluence and Autonomy," that discusses black businesspeople and the development of their enterprises. Also, a recent study by Conrad E. Wright and Katheryn P. Viens, *Entrepreneurs: The Boston Business Community, 1700–1850* (1997), includes an article by Lois E. Horton and James Oliver Horton, "Power and Social Responsibility: Entrepreneurs and the Black Community in Antebellum Boston."

One of the first monographs to examine free black business activities in the South was T. H. Breen and Stephen Innes's *"Myne Owne Ground": Race and Freedom on Virginia's Eastern Shore, 1640–1676* (1980), which reviewed the economic activities of Anthony Johnson. One of the first Africans in English colonial America, Anthony Johnson acquired not only his freedom in the mid-1600s but also property rights in both land and indentured servants while developing a successful agribusiness. Important articles that discuss property and slave ownership by blacks are James H. Brewer's "Negro Property Owners in

Seventeenth-Century Virginia" (1955) and Philip J. Schwarz's "Emancipators, Protectors, and Anomalies: Free Black Slaveowners in Virginia" (1987).

Still unsurpassed in its examination of blacks who owned slaves is Larry Koger's *Black Slaveowners: Free Black Slave Masters in South Carolina, 1790–1860* (1985), which provides information on the diversity of black businesspeople who owned slaves. Free black artisans represented the largest occupational groups of black slaveholders. The most extensive study of black property ownership is Loren Schweninger's carefully researched and detailed study *Black Property Owners in the South, 1790–1915* (1990), which provides information on real and slave property owned by blacks.

Assessments of the business activities and property ownership of blacks in the North and South before the Civil War are found in two general historical studies of blacks before the Civil War: Ira Berlin, *Slaves without Masters: The Free Negro in the Antebellum South* (1974), and Leonard P. Curry, *The Free Black in Urban America, 1800–1850: The Shadow of the Dream* (1981). Juliet E. K. Walker's 1986 article "Racism, Slavery, and Free Enterprise: Black Entrepreneurship in the United States before the Civil War" was the first to use the R. G. Dunn and Company credit reports to document the business enterprises and wealth holding of black businesspeople.

In the post–Revolutionary War era and the early national period, the two leading black entrepreneurs were Paul Cuffe and James Forten. Although several books have been published on Cuffe, including the Lamont D. Thomas book *Paul Cuffe: Black Entrepreneur and Pan-Africanist* (1988), and although the Forten family has been the subject of my many studies in which mention is made of Forten's business as sailmaker, a biography has not been undertaken. There is, however, the recent article by Julie Winch, " 'You Know I AM a Man of Business': James Forten and the Factor of Race in Philadelphia's Antebellum Business Community" (1997). Another prominent antebellum business family (catering and hair care enterprises) has been studied by Dorothy Burnett Porter, "The Remonds of Salem, Massachusetts: A Nineteenth Century Family Revisited" (1985), but as with the Fortens, the emphasis is on their antislavery activities.

Indeed, only four biographies of black businesspeople of the antebellum period have been published: Edwin A. Davis and William R. Hogan, *The Barber of Natchez* (1954; repr., 1969); David O. Whitten, *Andrew Durnford: A Black Sugar Cane Planter in Antebellum Louisiana* (1981; repr., 1995); Juliet E. K. Walker, *Free Frank: A Black Pioneer on the Antebellum Frontier* (1983; repr., 1995); and, Michael P. Johnson and James L. Roark, *Black Masters: A Free Family of Color in the Old South* (1984). Also, Gary B. Mills, *The Forgotten People of Color: Cane River's Creoles of Color* (1977), provides extensive biographical information on the Metoyer family, whose wealth was established by the matriarch Coincoin, Marie Theresa Metoyer.

The nation's frontiers during the age of slavery provided opportunities for free blacks to develop various enterprises, especially in the territories controlled by the Spanish and French. Whereas Louisiana under French and Spanish colonial control has been the subject of detailed study, increasingly historians are providing information on blacks in Florida under the Spanish. See particularly the work done by Jane G. Landers: "Gracia Real de Santa Teresa de Mose: A Free Black Town in Spanish Colonial Florida" (1991) and "Acquisition and Loss on a Spanish Frontier: The Free Black Homesteaders of Florida" (1996). Also see Kimberly S. Hanger, "Patronage, Property and Persistence: The Emergence of a Free Black Elite in Spanish New Orleans" (1996). Blacks were also in Illinois while it was French territory. See Thomas A. Meehan, "Jean Baptiste Point Du Sable, the First Chicagoan" (1963), who discusses the extensive trading post established by Haitian immigrant Du Sable on the Chicago River in the 1770s. Also see William Patrick O'Brien, "Hiram Young: Pioneering Black Wagonmaker for the Santa Fe Trade" (1993).

Ironically, the wealthiest black in antebellum America, William Leidesdorff, remains on the periphery of African American history, since in his business activities he passed as white, even becoming San Francisco's first city treasurer. He died intestate in 1848, leaving an estate valued at $1.5 million. See Robert S. Cowan, "The Leidesdorff-Folsom Estate: A Forgotten Chapter in the Romantic History of Early San Francisco" (1928), and William S. Savage, "The Influence of William Alexander Leidesdorff on the History of California" (1953). There was even some success by blacks in Hawaii before substantial American influence. See Marc Scruggs, "Anthony D. Allen: A Prosperous American of African Descent in Early 19th Century Hawaii" (1992).

There is extensive literature on the organizational activities of free blacks during slavery, but only Juliet E. K. Walker's 1997 article "Promoting Black Entrepreneurship and Business Enterprise in Antebellum America: The National Negro Convention, 1830–1860" has examined the business promotional activities of an antebellum black organization. Moreover, although the literature on free blacks during the age of slavery is extensive, only limited assessments have been made of the almost 3,000 businesses owned by free blacks in 1860. Only as more local and state studies are conducted will historians be able to proceed with an extensive systematic analysis of free black business during the age of slavery.

Women's Business Activities

Black women's self-employment activities began during the colonial era. These activities were first documented in Lorenzo J. Greene's *Negro in Colonial New England, 1620–1776* (1942). Subsequent historical studies of the region have restated the details. In addition, see Jean R. Soderland's, "Black Women in Colonial Pennsylvania" (1983) and Kimberly Hanger's " 'Almost All Have Callings': Free Blacks at Work in Spanish New Orleans" (1994). Besides Lorenzo Greene, who also documented the early acquisition of real estate by black women, also consult Judith A. Gilbert, "Esther and Her Sisters: Free Women of Color as Property Owners in Colonial St. Louis, 1765–1803" (1996). In addition to owning land, black women in the South held slaves, a situation that continued until the end of the Civil War. Whereas most plantation-owning slave women inherited these agribusinesses from slave masters, invariably the father of their children, others inherited these plantations from their free black husbands and fathers. In Gary B. Mills, "Coincoin: An Eighteenth-Century 'Liberated' Woman" (1976), information is provided on a former slave who established one of the largest black family slave-owning dynasties in the South.

The most intensive assessment of black women property owners can be found in Loren Schweninger's "Property Owning Free African-American Women in the South, 1800–1870" (1990). Virginia Meacham Gould, in *Chained to the Rock of Adversity* (1998), presents the life of Ann Johnson, the wife and later widow of the successful black barber William Johnson. Mrs. Johnson, a former slave, managed her late husband's slave plantation from the time of his death in 1851 through Reconstruction.

A desire to improve the material condition of their families represented the primary motivating force that propelled black women to develop self-help economic activities. The slave woman hoped to secure the freedom of her children with savings from economic activities. For many, the dream was deferred from generation to generation of successive slave mothers, particularly for the plantation slave woman. These slave entrepreneurs relied primarily upon the production of foodstuffs, important component of the internal slave economy and of surrounding urban markets. The network of female slave production extended to the urban domestic slave, who purchased goods from the market women for their masters. This network is important in underscoring the degree to which internal slave economic activities provided goods for the formal economy. See Robert Olwell's " 'Loose, Idle and Disorderly': Slave Women in the Eighteenth Century Charleston Marketplace" (1996) for his discussion of slave women as hagglers.

Urban slavery, however, also provided more opportunities for slave women to hire their own time. Savings enabled some to establish enterprises comparable in kind but seldom to the degree to that of free black women who established dressmaking, catering, health care, hair care, and boarding house enterprises. Studies that provide information on these activities include Suzanne Lebsock's "Free Women of Color" (1985) and Sharon Dean's *Elizabeth Potter: A Hairdresser's Experience in High Life* (1991), an extraordinary autobiography of a traveling black woman hairdresser. Also see Dorothy Sterling, *We Are Your Sisters: Black Women in the Nineteenth Century* (1984), who includes a section on the business activities of antebellum free black women, including the Remond sisters, who were hairdressers and also wig manufacturers with an extensive mail order business. Information on blacks in dressmaking can be found in

Elizabeth Keckley, *Behind the Scenes, or, Thirty Years a Slave, and Four Years in the White House* (1868), and Wendy Gamber, *The Female Economy: The Millinery and Dressmaking Trades, 1860–1930* (1997).

From the end of the Civil War to the civil rights era, black women expanded their economic activities, including boarding house ownership, with the most famous being that of Mary Ellen Pleasant, the subject of Lynn M. Hudson's dissertation. There was also an increase in the number of black women who owned hotels located in major business districts of black communities. Discussions of these antebellum inns and hotels are found in studies of blacks in New Orleans and Charleston, with advertisements in antebellum newspapers. Also in the twentieth century, many hotels in black business communities were run by women in both the North and the South. See Sunnie Wilson and John Cohassey, *Toast of the Town: The Life and Times of Sunnie Wilson* (1998), the autobiography of a black woman hotel owner in Detroit.

Most black businesswoman continued in establishing personal service and retail establishments; other successful black women entrepreneurs established hair care manufacturing enterprises. The Jim Crow era with its protected markets led to the emergence of the black beauty shops and provided a niche for more black women to be self-employed. Sociologist Robert L. Boyd's "Great Migration to the North and the Rise of Ethnic Niches for African American Women in Beauty Culture and Hairdressing, 1910–1920" (1996) enumerates the women who participated in these enterprises. Ironically, despite the prominence of Madame C. J. Walker, Annie Turnbo-Malone (Poro), and Sarah Spencer Washington (Apex), there are no scholarly biographical studies of these leading black women hair care product manufactures who had sales in millions of dollars. The relatively little attention given to the careers of Walker, Turnbo-Malone, and Spencer clearly illustrates how much work needs to be done in reconstructing black women's business history.

African American Financial Institutions

The study of black financial institutions, especially black insurance companies has generated the most interest from historians, primarily since these are the only enterprises where company records are available. See James Browning, "The Beginnings of Insurance Enterprise among Negroes" (1937). The origin of black financial institutions began during slavery with the formation of mutual aid societies that provided sickness, unemployment, and burial benefits to members who paid monthly dues (premiums). See Robert L. Harris, Jr., "Early "Black Benevolent Societies, 1780–1830 (1979) and "Charleston's Free Afro-American Elite: The Brown Fellowship Society and Humane Brotherhood" (1981), Craig Steven Wilder, "The Rise and Influence of the New York African Society for Mutual Relief, 1808–1865" (1998) detail these origins. Also see C. S. Spencer, "Black Benefit Societies in Nineteenth Century Alabama" (1985), for information on these organizations after slavery.

After the Civil War came a proliferation of black fraternal orders, several of which had originated before the Civil War. See W.E.B. Du Bois, *Economic Cooperation among Negroes* (1907) and *Some Efforts for Social Betterment among Negro Americans* (1909). Both studies provide examples of the institutional community efforts undertaken by benefit societies and fraternal orders founded from the late eighteenth century to the early twentieth century. Also see Edward Nelson Palmer's "Negro Secret Societies" (1944) and William Muraskin's *Middle Class Blacks in a White Society: Prince Hall Masonry in America* (1975).

Throughout the nineteenth century most fraternal orders and benefit societies offered burial benefits. As membership increased, these organizations professionalized by establishing insurance companies. Some expanded their financial services by establishing insurance companies and then banks. The model was the True Reformers, which established a bank in 1888. The fraternal order also set up department stores and acquired extensive real estate holdings. See David Fahey's *Black Lodge in White America: "True Reformer" Browne [William Washington] and His Economic Strategy* (1994). Also, Elsa Barkley Brown's "Womanist Consciousness: Maggie Lena Walker and the Independent Order of St. Luke" (1989) provides information on how this process was genderized with Maggie Lena Walker, who became the first American woman to found a bank. Also see Angel Kwolek-Folland, "The African American Financial Industries: Issues of Class, Race and Gender in the Early 20th Century" (1994).

Early assessments of black insurance companies have included Carter G. Woodson, "Insurance Business among Negroes" (1929) and Merah S. Stuart's *Economic Detour: A History of Insurance in the Lives of American Negroes* (1940), which provided the first systematic study of black insurance companies. Stuart's research established the extent to which black insurance companies were the bedrock of black financial institutions and it also documented the limited holdings of these companies compared to those of the white insurance industry. Two monographs provide information on the history of the nation's largest black insurer, North Carolina Mutual: one, by company president William J. Kennedy, *North Carolina Mutual Story: A Symbol of Progress, 1898–1970* (1970); the other, by historian Walter Weare, *Black Business in the New South: A Social History of the North Carolina Mutual Life Insurance Company* (1973; repr. 1994). Also see Weare's "Charles Clinton Spaulding: Middle-Class Leadership in the Age of Segregation" (1982). The history of the Atlanta Life Insurance Company, the second largest African American insurance company, has been compiled by Alexa Benson Henderson in her 1990 book *Atlanta Life Insurance Company: Guardian of Black Economic Dignity*. Also see Henderson's "Alonzo F. Herndon and Black Insurance in Atlanta" (1977).

The first book-length study of a black northern financial institution was economist Robert C. Puth's *Supreme Life: The History of a Negro Life Insurance Company* (1976), which examined a Chicago-based company. Also see Puth's "From Enforced Segregation to Integration: Market Factors in the Development of a Negro Insurance Company" (1973). Robert E. Weems, Jr., in *Black Business in the Black Metropolis: The Chicago Metropolitan Assurance Company, 1925–1985* (1996), provides a pathbreaking discussion of how a Chicago-based firm evolved from a burial society into a legal reserve insurance company. Also see Weems's "Robert A. Cole and the Metropolitan Funeral System Association: A Profile of a Civic-Minded African-American Businessman" (1993).

Significantly, the study of black banks, 134 of which were founded between 1888 to 1933, has not captured the interest of historians as it has of economists such as Abram L. Harris in his *Negro as Capitalist: A Study of Banking and Business among Negroes* (1936). The first chapter in the Harris book provides an overview of black business activity before the Civil War, but the focus of his study is on black banking activity until 1934. Harris also provides a vehement denunciation of the financial inadequacies of black "separate economies." For a more recent study, see Lila Ammons, "The Evolution of Black-Owned Banks in the United States between the 1880s and 1990s" (1996). Several insurance companies such as North Carolina Mutual also established banks; other banks were founded by blacks who achieved success in other areas of enterprise. For the South, see Alexa B. Henderson, "Herman E. Perry and Black Enterprise in Atlanta, 1908–1925" (1987), who established an insurance company and a bank among his many enterprises, including real estate speculation and construction. Also see Arnett G. Lindsay, "The Negro in Banking" (1929), for information on the founders of the two largest black banks before the Depression, Jesse Binga, a successful real estate speculator, and Anthony Overton, a leading manufacturer of black hair products. By 1920, these two Chicago banks were the largest in the nation, holding two-thirds of all black bank deposits. Also see Carl R. Osthaus, "The Rise and Fall of Jesse Binga, Black Financier" (1973). Information on Chicago's early black banking history is also found in Madrue Chavers-Wright, *The Guarantee: P. W. Chavers, Banker, Entrepreneur, Philanthropist in Chicago's Black Belt of the Twenties* (1985). In 1934, there were only six black banks. With the civil rights era came an expansion in their numbers and then a decline. Studies of black banking history since the 1960s have been written primarily by economists.

Doubtless, the most exciting business venture undertaken by a black financial organization in the post–civil rights era is detailed in the autobiographical account edited by Sheila T. Gregory, *Legacy of Dreams: The Life and Contributions of Dr. William Venoid Banks* (1999). Dr. Banks provides an example of how black fraternal orders in the post–civil rights era used their vast resources to expand black businesses beyond financial institutions. Through working with the Colored Masons and in building the International Free and Accepted Masons, Banks established Detroit's WGRP Radio and also the first black-owned and operated television station in the United States.

Historians however, have continued their assessments of black insurance companies. In the late twentieth century, the prognosis was not encouraging. See Robert Weems, "A Crumbling Legacy: The Decline of African American Insurance Companies in Contemporary America" (1994). Andrew F. Brimmer, "The Dilemma of Black Banking: Lending Risks vs. Community Service" (1992), looks at the black banking industry from the civil rights era. Founded to provide personal loans as well as venture and development capital to black businesses, high-risks loans resulted in a high rate of loan defaults. Brimmer uses Freedom Bank as one example of the black banking dilemma.

Civil War to Civil Rights

Because 90 percent of the black population lived in the South after the Civil War, that region has been the primary focus of study on black business. Indeed, most of the business successes of black entrepreneurs were in the South. See Loren Schweninger's *Black Property Owners* for his "A Profile of Prosperous Blacks," which provides a list of names and occupations of blacks from 1870 to 1915 with wealth ranging from $20,000 to over $100,000. Annie R. Hornsby's "Accumulation of Wealth by Black Georgians, 1890–1915" (1989) provides important information on black investment activity in real estate, as opposed to business enterprises. The social and community activities of these wealthy blacks are discussed in Willard B. Gatewood's *Aristocrats of Color: The Black Elite, 1880–1920* (1990), which details the social activities that distinguished the lives of wealthy blacks during the period. John N. Ingham's "African-American Business Leaders in the South, 1810–1945: Business Success, Community Leadership and Racial Protest" (1993) is also worth consulting.

Studies that focus specifically on the business activities of blacks in the post–Civil War period are relatively new in black business history. Robert C. Kenzer's "Black Business Community in Post Civil War Virginia" (1993), "Black Businessmen in Post–Civil War Tennessee" (1994), and *Enterprising Southerners: Black Economic Success in North Carolina, 1865–1915* (1997) epitomize this trend. One earlier study that provided specific insights on black business was Frenise A. Logan's "Economic Status of the Town Negro in Post-Reconstruction North Carolina" (1958).

Few studies of black business in the post–Civil War era provide an examination of the operations of a single black business. Bettye C. Thomas, "A Nineteenth Century Black Operated Shipyard, 1866–1884: Reflections upon Its Inception and Ownership" (1994); John V. Jezierski "Photographing the Lumber Book: The Goodridge Brothers of Saginaw, Michigan, 1863–1922" (1980); Dannehl M. Twomey, "Into the Mainstream: Early Black Photography in Houston" (1987), Gilles Vandal, "Black Utopia in Early Reconstruction New Orleans: The People's Bakery as a Case-Study" (1997); and Ed Cashin, "Pilgrim's Progress: The First Forty Years of a Minority Business, 1898–1938" (1993), reflect the extent of this historiography. Moreover, in the age of industrialization, many black inventors made significant contributions, but few were able to secure venture capital to establish factories to manufacture their inventions. Thus, African

American innovators eventually assigned their patents to others who capitalized on their inventions. See Sidney Kaplan, "Jan Earnst Matzeliger and the Making of the Shoe" (1955), and Rayvon Fouche, "The Exploitation of an African-American Inventor on the Fringe: Granville T. Woods and the Process of Invention" (1997).

Between the end of Reconstruction and World War, I, 120 all-black towns were founded in the United States. Business activities that developed in black towns during this period are discussed in Kenneth Hamilton's *Black Towns and Profit: Promotion and Development in the Trans-Appalachian West* (1991). Town promotion and town boosterism were economic activities that could prove profitable. Also, black towns provided opportunities for black businesspeople to succeed without confronting white competition. Yet, all attempts in black town founding did not succeed, as Joseph V. Hickey indicates in " 'Pap' Singleton's Dunlap Colony: Relief Agencies and the Failure of a Black Settlement in Eastern Kansas" (1993). Most of the all-black towns were located in the South, especially Oklahoma. See Linda C. Gray, "Taft: Town on the Black Frontier" (1988). Also see Paul Lehman's article on an Oklahoma black family, "The Edwards Family and Black Entrepreneurial Success" (1986–87). Although few whites lived in black towns, they were often involved, primarily owning the land where blacks established their towns. See Claire O'Brien, " 'With One Mighty Pull': Interracial Town Boosting in Nicodemus, Kansas" (1996). The only study that looks at a post–Civil War era black town in the North is Sundiata Keita Cha-Jua's *America's First Black Town: Brooklyn, Illinois, 1830–1915* (2000).

The success of black towns in the South depended primarily on a productive hinterland that could support town businesses. Several articles provide information on black business in rural areas. See Peggy G. Hargis, "Beyond the Marginality Thesis: The Acquisition and Loss of Land by African Americans in Georgia, 1880–1930" (1998), and Valerie Grim, "African American Landlords in the Rural South, 1870–1950: A Profile" (1998) and "The Politics of Inclusion: Black Farmers and the Quest for Agribusiness Participation, 1945–1990s" (1995). Also see William P. O'Hare's "Black Business Ownership in the Rural South" (1990), which found that black business ownership was lower in the 1980s for blacks in rural areas (8.8 per 1,000 people) than the national average (12.5 per 1,000 people).

Also, statewide economic conditions were more important than human capital factors as a factor in determining business success rates. At the turn of the century, for example, Mound Bayou, Mississippi, was the most successful black town because of its location in perhaps the most productive cotton lands in the state. Also, the town gained national recognition because Booker T. Washington promoted it as an example of black economic success. See Janet Sharp Hermann's *Pursuit of a Dream* (1981) for a detailed discussion of Mound Bayou and its founders, Benjamin and Isaiah Montgomery.

Several studies underscore the extent to which black businesspeople supported Washington's belief that profits could be generated by black businesspeople as they developed enterprises in a separate economy. See Michael Andres Fitzpatrick, " 'A Great Agitation for Business': Black Economic Development in Shaw" (1990–91), which notes that businesses that developed in Washington, D.C., black Shaw community from 1890 to 1920 reflected blacks' zealous responses in support of a separate black economy in response to Jim Crow racism. Also see Herbert L. Clark's "James Carroll Napier: National Negro Leader" (1990). Successful in law, banking, and real estate, also president of the National Negro Business League (1915–19) and a Republican, Napier is described by Clark as an accomodationist in the tradition of Booker T. Washington. Also see Howard Pitney David, "Calvin Chase's Washington Bee and Black Middle-Class Ideology, 1882–1900" (1986); Edward R. Crowther, "Charles Octavius Boothe: An Alabama Apostle of 'Uplift' " (1993); and Donald J. Calista, "Booker T. Washington: Another Look" (1964).

Notwithstanding, there were black businesspeople who did not always acquiesce to Booker T. Washington's leadership or ideology. See Maceo C. Dailey's "Booker T. Washington and the Afro-American Realty Company" (1978). Also see Mark R. Schneider, "The *Colored American* and *Alexander's*: Boston's Pro–Civil Rights Bookerites" (1995), on two black publications financed by Booker T. Washington that supported his promotion of a separate black economy but rejected his accomodationist philosophy, especially after the 1906 Brownsville, Texas, riot. Washington's business philosophy has had both critics and supporters. The central issue debated was whether the promotion of a separate black economy would uplift the entire black community or increase the wealth of a few black capitalists. See David M. Tucker, "Black Pride and Negro Business in the 1920's: George Washington Lee of Memphis" (1969), and Darryl M. Trimiew and Michael Greene in "How We Got Over: The Moral Teachings of the African-American Church on Business Ethics" (1997).

Several studies have reviewed Washington's business ideology, which he hoped to promote through the organization he founded in 1900. See Louis R. Harlan's *Booker T. Washington: The Making of a Black Leader, 1856–1901* (1972) and *Booker T. Washington: The Wizard of Tuskegee 1901–1915* (1983). Also see August Meier, *Negro Thought in America, 1880–1915: Race Ideologies in the Age of Booker T. Washington* (1963); Donald J. Calista, "Booker T. Washington: Another Look" (1964); and Don Quinn Kelley, "The Political Economy of Booker T. Washington: A Bibliographic Essay" (1977). More recently, Walter Friedman has explored the Washington-based promotion of black business activity in his "African American Gospel of Success" (1999). William E. B. Du Bois was initially a strong proponent of black business activity. At the 1898 Atlanta University Conference on Business he even proposed an organization of black businesspeople. Differences in how blacks should respond to the loss of civil and political rights prompted Du Bois's chapter "Of Mr. Booker T. Washington and Others" in his 1903 *Souls of Black Folk.*

Du Bois's research on blacks in Philadelphia, which resulted in his seminal sociological work *The Philadelphia Negro* (1899), also influenced his thinking about blacks' economic situation, especially his chapters on "The Occupation of Negroes" and "The Negro Criminal." In the same state, Laurence Glasco's "Taking Care of Business: The Black Entrepreneurial Elite in Turn-of-the-Century Pittsburgh" (1995/96) provides an alternative perspective. Also see Joe W. Trotter, "African Americans in the City: The Industrial Era, 1900–1950" (1995), and Margaret Levenstein, "African American Entrepreneurship: The View from the 1910 Census" (1995).

The expansion of the urban black business community began during the Great Migration of the World War I era. Historians have focused primarily on the broader internal and external forces that created the black urban "ghetto." Sociologists, using their own methodologies, have provided specific information on the business activities that developed in black business districts. The work of Robert Boyd is especially important, including his "Demographic Change and Entrepreneurial Occupations: African Americans in Northern Cities" (1996), "Protected Markets and African American Professionals in Northern Cities during the Great Migration" (1997), and "The Great Migration to the North and the Rise of Ethnic Niches for African American Women in Beauty Culture and Hairdressing, 1910–1920" (1996).

In the South, the success of black business communities, based upon the location of black enterprises in racially distinct geographical spaces described as "entrepreneurial enclaves," has been examined with the context of "Black Wall Streets." See John Sibley Butler, *Entrepreneurship and Self-Help among Black Americans* (1991), for his discussion of the profitable business districts in Tulsa, Oklahoma, and Durham, North Carolina. Assessments of black businesses in other southern cities from the early 1900s to midcentury are provided in Robert J. Alexander's "Negro Business in Atlanta, 1894–1950" (1951), William J. Brophy's "Black Business Development in Texas Cities, 1900–1950" (1981), and Cary D. Wintz's "Black Business in Houston, 1910–1930" (1992).

Black Entrepreneurs and Black Enterprise

Whereas no company histories of leading black businesses in the twentieth century have been published, several biographies and autobiographies exist. Without competition, black funeral enterprises were the one industry that maintained its numbers and profits during the Depression. See Michael A. Plater, *African American Entrepreneurship in Richmond, 1890–1940: The Story of R. C. Scott* (1996), for an examination of the funeral industry in the black community's economy. See Bobby L. Lovett's *Black Man's Dream, the First 100 Years: Richard Henry Boyd and the National Baptist Publishing Board* (1993), an account of one of the most successful black businesses in the early twentieth century that continues today. Also, for the publishing industry see Roi Ottley's *Lonely Warrior: The Life and Times of Robert S. Abbott* (1955); Abbott had achieved millions of dollars in street sales nationally from his *Chicago Defender*, which revolutionized black newspaper publishing with its emphasis on sensationalism in reporting the news. Also see Juliet E. K. Walker, "The Promised Land: The *Chicago Defender* and the Black Press in Illinois, 1862–1970" (1996). By the mid-1930s, the *Defender* had lost its edge as the leading national black newspaper. See Andrew Buni, *Robert L. Vann of the Pittsburgh Courier: Politics and Black Journalism* (1974).

As previously indicated, state and local studies provide information on black business activities. For example, black business activity in Oklahoma is discussed by Paul Lehman in "The Edwards Family and Black Entrepreneurial Success" (1986–87). Edwards established several profitable businesses in Oklahoma City, beginning with a junkyard in the 1920s and then moving on to construction. Family profits were reinvested in the black community, including founding a hospital that provided training for black doctors and nurses. For another Oklahoma business success see Jonathan D. Greenberg's *Staking a Claim: Jake Simmons and the Making of an African American Oil Dynasty* (1990). In Birmingham, Alabama, the multimillion-dollar enterprises of Arthur G. Gaston, honored by *Black Enterprise* as the "Entrepreneur of the Century," included insurance, banking, and construction. See Arthur G. Gaston's 1968 autobiography, *Green Power: The Successful War of A. G. Gaston.*

Historians of the African American business experience in the twenty-first century will owe a debt of gratitude to Earl G. Graves's *Black Enterprise.* Since its inception in 1970 the magazine has chronicled every aspect of black business activity in the post–civil rights era, with featured articles on leading and new successful enterprises and their entrepreneurs. Its publisher has even shared the secrets of his success in a 1997 autobiography, *How to Succeed in Business without Being White.* Also, since 1973, *Black Enterprise* has published a list of the leading black businesses in the United States. See Derek Dingle's *Black Enterprise Titans of the B.E. 100s: Black CEOs Who Redefined and Conquered American Business* (1999), a review of the business success of twelve giants in the post–civil rights era of black business activity.

The enterprises of John H. Johnson, the publisher of *Ebony* and *Jet* magazines, merit special attention. Johnson, who established Johnson Publishing Company in 1942, acquired ownership in Supreme Liberty Life. He also manufactures Fashion Fair cosmetics. Moreover, Johnson publishes *Ebony South Africa.* With Lerone Bennett, Jr., Johnson wrote his 1989 autobiography, *Succeeding against the Odds: The Inspiring Autobiography of One of America's Wealthiest Entrepreneurs.*

The black entrepreneur whose business had the distinction of breaking into a "crossover" market was Berry Gordy, who founded Motown Records. Berry Gordy recounts his success (at one time the leading black business before it was sold) in his book, *To Be Loved: The Music, the Magic, the Memories of Motown, an Autobiography* (1994). Gerald Early's *One Nation under a Groove: Motown and American Culture* (1995) provides another important account of Gordy and Motown's success.

The only black business in the twentieth century that achieved sales in the billions was Reginald Lewis's TLC Beatrice International. For details regarding this milestone, see Reginald Lewis and Blair S. Walker's *"Why Should White Guys Have All the Fun?": How Reginald Lewis Created a Billion-Dollar Business Empire* (1994).

Paradoxically the civil rights movement had a boomerang effect on black-owned business activities. With racial barriers pushed aside, instead of black enterprises profiting from black protest, white corporate America reaped the benefits of a desegregated consumer society, as Robert E. Weems, Jr., shows in his *Desegregating the Dollar* (1998). Also see Weems's "African American Consumer Boycotts during the Civil Rights Era" (1995) and "The Revolution Will Be Marketed: American Corporations and African American Consumers during the 1960s" (1994).

Post–Civil Rights Era

Studies that examine black business activities in the post–civil rights era have been written primarily by sociologists and economists. See John Handy, *An Analysis of Black Business Enterprises* (1989); Shelley Green and Paul Pryde, *Black Entrepreneurship in America* (1989); and Kilolo Kijakazi, *African American Economic Development and Small Business Ownership* (1997). Also see Robert L. Boyd, "A Contextual Analysis of Black Self-Employment in Large Metropolitan Areas, 1970–1980" (1991).

The promotion of minority-owned business under President Richard Nixon is attracting increased attention by scholars. See Robert Yancy, *Federal Government Policy and Black Business* (1974), and Dean Kotlowski, "Black Power—Nixon Style: The Nixon Administration and Minority Business Enterprise" (1998). Also see Wayne J. Villemez and John J. Beggs, "Black Capitalism and Black Inequality: Some Sociological Considerations" (1984).

Yet, federal assistance to minority businesses has generated controversy. See George E. Curry, *The Affirmative Action Debate* (1996). As a result of several recent Supreme Court decisions, studies are increasingly providing assessments and analysis on the retrenchment of affirmative action policies by the federal government. See Thomas D. Boston's *Meeting the Croson Standard: A Research Guide for Policy Makers* (1993) and his *Affirmative Action and Black Entrepreneurship* (1999). Also see Margaret Simms, ed., *Economic Perspectives on Affirmative Action* (1995), and Avon W. Drake and Robert D. Holsworth, *Affirmative Action and the Stalled Quest for Black Progress* (1996). Also, for a collection of court cases, laws, and various federal policies see Gabriel J. Chin and Paul Finkelman, eds., *Affirmative Action and the Constitution* (1998). Moreover, Harvard law professor Christopher F. Edley offers his perspective in *Not All Black and White: Affirmative Action, Race and American Values* (1996).

Another major area of concern in late-twentieth-century black business history is increased competition from other minority and immigrant enterprises. For comparative assessments of African American businesspeople with others, see

Kenneth L. Wilson and Martin W. Allen, "Ethnic Enclaves: A Comparison of the Cuban and Black Economies in Miami" (1982); Robert L. Boyd, "Black and Asian Self-Employment in Large Metropolitan Areas: A Comparative Analysis," *Social Problems* (1990); Frank A. Fratoe, "Social Capital of Black Business Owners" (1988); Gavin M. Chen and John A. Cole, "The Myths, Facts, and Theories of Ethnic Small-Scale Enterprise Financing" (1988); Timothy M. Bates, "The Changing Nature of Minority Business: An Analysis of Asian, Non-minority, and Black-Owned Businesses" (1989); and Robert W. Fairlie, *Ethnic and Racial Entrepreneurship: A Study of Historical and Contemporary Differences* (1996).

Although black business activity has expanded as a result of government programs, racial iniquities continued. See Joe Feagin and Nikitah Imani in their study "Racial Barriers to African American Entrepreneurship: An Exploratory Survey" (1994), which examines the various forms of racial discrimination black contractors experience in the American construction industry. Also, see Gwendolyn Powell Todd, *Innovation and Growth in an African American Owned Business* (1996), an incisive study of the business history of an African American–owned professional firm, founded in the post–civil rights era, with a multiethnic staff of engineers and architects. The study provides a methodological model for historians interested in pursuing research on active black business firms.

Despite the difficulties encountered by blacks in business, several studies are optimistic that there is hope for success. See Robert L. Wallace, *Black Wealth through Black Entrepreneurship* (1993). Also, see the two how-to-books by George C. Fraser: *Success Runs in Our Race: The Complete Guide to Effective Networking in the African-American Community* (1994) and *Race for Success: The Ten Best Business Opportunities for Blacks in America* (1998). For a discussion of the post–civil rights era in black business from the perspective of a historian, see the following chapters in Juliet E. K. Walker's *History of Black Business in America*: "The Federal Government and Black Business, 1950s–1990s," "Rise of Black Corporate America, 1940s–1990s," and "Blacks and White Corporate America."

CONCLUSION

A reconstruction of the black business experience is important, then, for several reasons. First, it defeats assessments of contemporary policy analysts who insist that the comparative poor business performance of blacks stems from the absence of an entrepreneurial and business culture. Also, inclusion of the business activities of African Americans expands interpretive assessments of the black experience, particularly during the age of slavery. Yet, considering that blacks have a historic tradition of economic self-help, the question remains: Why do inequalities persist in the economic life of African Americans?

BIBLIOGRAPHY

Alexander, Robert J. "Negro Business in Atlanta, 1894–1950." *Southern Economic Journal* 17 (April 1951): 452.

Ammons, Lila. "The Evolution of Black-Owned Banks in the United States between the 1880s and 1990s." *Journal of Black Studies* 26 (March 1996): 467–89.

Ballard, Donna. *Doing It for Ourselves: Success Stories of African American Women in Business.* New York: Berkley Books, 1997.

Barrows, David Prescott. *Barbers and Blacks.* New York: Century, 1927.

Bates, Timothy M. *Banking on Black Enterprise: The Potential of Emerging Firms for Revitalizing Urban Economies.* Washington, DC: Joint Center for Political and Economic Studies, 1993.

———. "The Changing Nature of Minority Business: An Analysis of Asian, Non-minority, and Black-Owned Businesses." *Review of Black Political Economy* 18 (1989): 25–42.

Berkeley, D., Jr., "Christopher McPherson, Free Person of Color." *Virginia Magazine of History and Biography* 77, no. 2 (April 1969): 181.

Berlin, Ira, and *Slaves without Masters: The Free Negro in the Antebellum South.* New York: Pantheon, 1974.

Berlin, Ira. and Phillip D. Morgan, eds. *Cultivation and Culture: Labor and the Shaping of Slave Life in the Americas.* Charlottesville: University Press of Virginia, 1993.

———. *The Slaves' Economy: Independent Production by Slaves in the Americas.* London: Frank Cass, 1991.

Bisher, Catherine W. "Black Builders in Antebellum North Carolina." *North Carolina Historical Review* 61 (October 1984): 423–58.

Bosman, William. *A New and Accurate Description of Guinea: Divided into the Gold, the Slave, and the Ivory Coasts.* 1704; reprint, London: Frank Cass and Company, 1967.

Boston, Thomas D. *Affirmative Action and Black Entrepreneurship.* New York: Routledge, 1999.

———. *Meeting the Croson Standard: A Research Guide for Policy Makers.* Washington, DC: Joint Center for Political and Economic Studies, 1993.

Boyd, Robert L. "Black and Asian Self-Employment in Large Metropolitan Areas: A Comparative Analysis." *Social Problems* 37, no. 2 (1990): 258–74.

———. "A Contextual Analysis of Black Self-Employment in Large Metropolitan Areas, 1970–1980." *Social Forces* 70, 2 (December 1991): 409–29.

———. "Demographic Change and Entrepreneurial Occupations: African Americans in Northern Cities." *American Journal of Economics and Sociology* 55 (April 1996): 129–43.

———. "The Great Migration to the North and the Rise of Ethnic Niches for African American Women in Beauty Culture and Hairdressing, 1910–1920." *Sociological Focus* 20, no. 1 (February 1996): 33–45.

———. "Protected Markets and African American Professionals in Northern Cities during the Great Migration." *Sociological Spectrum* 17 (1997): 91–101.

Breen, T. H., and Stephen Innes. *"Myne Owne Ground": Race and Freedom on Virginia's Eastern Shore, 1640–1676.* New York: Oxford University Press, 1980.

Brewer, James H. "Negro Property Owners in Seventeenth-Century Virginia." *William and Mary Quarterly* 12 (October 1955): 576–77.

Brimmer, Andrew F. "The Dilemma of Black Banking: Lending Risks vs. Community Service." *Review of Black Political Economy* 20, no. 3 (1992): 5–29.

———. "The Negro in the American Economy." In John P. Davis, ed., *The American Negro Reference Book*. Englewood Cliffs, NJ: Prentice Hall, 1966.

Brophy, William J. "Black Business Development in Texas Cities, 1900–1950." *Red River Valley Historical Review* 6, no. 2 (1981): 42–55.

Brown, Elsa Barkley. "Womanist Consciousness: Maggie Lena Walker and the Independent Order of St. Luke." *Signs: Journal of Women in Culture and Society* 14, no. 3 (1989): 610–32.

Browning, James. "The Beginnings of Insurance Enterprise among Negroes." *Journal of Negro History* 22 (1937): 417–32.

Bundles, A'Lelia Perry. *Madam C. J. Walker*. New York: Chelsea House, 1991.

Buni, Andrew. *Robert L. Vann of the Pittsburgh Courier: Politics and Black Journalism*. Pittsburgh: University of Pittsburgh Press, 1974.

Butler, John Sibley. *Entrepreneurship and Self-Help among Black Americans*. Albany: State University of New York Press, 1991.

Cabot, Thomas D. "A Short History of Cabot Corporation." *Daedalus* 125, no. 2 (1996): 113–36.

Calista, Donald J. "Booker T. Washington: Another Look." *Journal of Negro History* 49, no. 4 (1964): 240–55.

Campbell, John. "As 'A Kind of Freeman'?: Slaves' Market—Related Activities in the South Carolina Up County, 1800–1860." In Ira Berlin and Philip D. Morgan, eds., *Cultivation and Culture: Labor and the Shaping of Slave Life in the Americas*. Charlottesville: University Press of Virginia, 1993.

Cashin, Ed. "Pilgrim's Progress: The First Forty Years of a Minority Business, 1898–1938." *Richmond County History* 24, no. 1 (1993): 30–54.

Cashin, Joan E. "Black Families in the Old Northwest." *Journal of the Early Republic* 15 (Fall 1995): 449–75.

Chavers-Wright, Madrue. *The Guarantee: P. W. Chavers, Banker, Entrepreneur, Philanthropist in Chicago's Black Belt of the Twenties*. New York: Wright Armstead Associates, 1985.

Cha-Jua, Sundiata Keita. *America's First Black Town: Brooklyn, Illinois, 1830–1915*. Urbana: University of Illinois Press, 2000.

Chen, Gavin M., and John A. Cole. "The Myths, Facts, and Theories of Ethnic Small-Scale Enterprise Financing." *Review of Black Political Economy* 16, no. 4 (1988): 111–23.

Chin, Gabriel J., and Paul Finkelman, eds. *Affirmative Action and the Constitution*. 3 vols. New York: Garland, 1998.

Clark, Herbert L. "James Carroll Napier: National Negro Leader." *Tennessee Historical Quarterly* 49, no. 4 (1990): 243–52.

Cowan, Robert S. "The Leidesdorff-Folsom Estate: A Forgotten Chapter in the Romantic History of Early San Francisco." *Quarterly of the California Historical Society* 7 (June 1928): 106–11.

Crowther, Edward R. "Charles Octavius Boothe: An Alabama Apostle of 'Uplift.' " *Journal of Negro History* 78, no. 2 (Spring 1993): 110–16.

Curry, George E. *The Affirmative Action Debate*. Reading, MA: Addison Wesley, 1996.

Curry, Leonard P. *The Free Black in Urban America, 1800–1850: The Shadow of the Dream.* Chicago: University of Chicago Press, 1981.

Daaku, Kwame Yeboa. *Trade and Politics on the Gold Coast: 1600–1720.* London: Oxford University Press, 1970.

Dailey, Maceo C. "Booker T. Washington and the Afro-American Realty Company." *Review of Black Political Economy* 8 (Winter 1978): 182–201.

Darity, William A., Jr., and Rhonda M. Williams. "Peddlers Forever: Culture, Competition, and Discrimination." *American Economic Review* 75, no. 2 (1985): 256–61.

David, Howard Pitney. "Calvin Chase's Washington Bee and Black Middle-Class Ideology, 1882–1900." *Journalism Quarterly* 63, no. 1 (1986): 89–97.

Davis, Edwin A., and William R. Hogan. *The Barber of Natchez.* Port Washington, NY: Kennikat Press, 1969.

Dean, Sharon, ed. *Elizabeth Potter: A Hairdresser's Experience in High Life.* 1858. New York: Oxford University Press, 1991.

Delany, Martin R. *The Condition, Elevation, Emigration and Destiny of the Colored People of the United States.* Philadelphia, 1852; report, New York: Arno Press, 1968.

Dingle, Derek. *Black Enterprise Titans of the B.E. 100s: Black CEOs Who Redefined and Conquered American Business.* New York: John Wiley and Sons, 1999.

Drake, St. Clair, and Horace Cayton. *Black Metropolis: A Study of Negro Life in a Northern City.* Chicago: University of Chicago Press, 1945.

Drake, W. Avon, and Robert D. Holsworth. *Affirmative Action and the Stalled Quest for Black Progress.* Urbana: University of Illinois Press, 1996.

Du Bois, William E. B. *Economic Cooperation among Negro Americans.* Atlanta: Atlanta University Press, 1907.

———. *The Negro Artisan.* Atlanta: Atlanta University Press, 1902.

———. *The Negro in Business.* Atlanta: Atlanta University Press. 1898.

———. *The Philadelphia Negro.* Philadelphia: University of Pennsylvania Press, 1899.

———. *Some Efforts for Social Betterment among Negro Americans.* Atlanta: Atlanta University Press, 1909.

———. *Souls of Black Folk.* Chicago: A. C. McClurg, 1903.

Dusinberre, William M. *Them Dark Days: Slavery in the American Rice Swamps.* New York: Oxford University Press, 1996.

Early, Gerald. *One Nation under a Groove: Motown and American Culture.* Hopewell, NJ: Ecco Press, 1995.

Eaton, Clement. "Slave-Hiring in the Upper South: A Step toward Freedom." *Mississippi Valley Historical Review* 46 (1960): 663–78.

Edley, Christopher F. *Not All Black and White: Affirmative Action, Race and American Values.* New York: Hill and Wang, 1996.

Edmondson, Vickie Cox, and Archie B. Carroll. "Giving Back: An Examination of the Philanthropic Motivations, Orientations and Activities of Large Black-Owned Businesses." *Journal of Business Ethics* 19, no. 2 (April 1999): 171–79.

Edwards, Paul, ed. *The Interesting Narrative of the Life of Olaudah Equiano, or Gustavus Vasa, the African.* Orig 2 vols., 1798. New York: Praeger, 1967.

Fahey, David M. *The Black Lodge in White America: "True Reformer" Browne [William Washington] and His Economic Strategy.* Dayton, OH: Wright State University Press, 1994.

Fairlie, Robert W. *Ethnic and Racial Entrepreneurship: A Study of Historical and Contemporary Differences*. New York: Garland, 1996.

Feagin, Joe, and Nikitah Imani. "Racial Barriers to African American Entrepreneurship: An Exploratory Survey." *Social Problems* 41, no. 4 (1994): 562–84.

Fitzpatrick, Michael Andres. " 'A Great Agitation for Business': Black Economic Development in Shaw [1890–1920]." *Washington History* 2, no. 2 (1990–91): 48–73.

Fogel, Robert William. *Without Consent or Contract: The Rise and Fall of American Slavery*. New York: Norton, 1989.

Fouche, Rayvon. "The Exploitation of an African-American Inventor on the Fringe: Granville T. Woods and the Process of Invention." *Western Journal of Black Studies* 21 (Fall 1997): 190–98.

Frady, Marshall. *Jesse Jackson: A Biography*. New York: Random House, 1996.

Franklin, John Hope. "Slaves Virtually Free in Ante-bellum North Carolina." *Journal of Negro History* 28 (1943): 284–310.

———, and Alfred Moss. *From Slavery to Freedom: A History of African Americans*. 7th ed. New York: McGraw-Hill, 1994.

Fraser, George C. *Race for Success: The Ten Best Business Opportunities for Blacks in America*. New York: W. Morrow and Company, 1998.

———. *Success Runs in Our Race: The Complete Guide to Effective Networking in the African American Community*. New York: W. Morrow and Company, 1994.

Fratoe, Frank A. "Social Capital of Black Business Owners." *Review of Black Political Economy* 16, no. 4 (1988): 33–50.

Frazier, E. Franklin. *Black Bourgeoisie: The Rise of a New Middle Class*. New York: Macmillan Publishing, 1957.

Friedman, Walter. "The African American Gospel of Success." In Peter Eisenstadt, ed. *Black Conservatism: An Historical Overview*. New York: Garland Publishing, 1999.

Gamber, Wendy. *The Female Economy: The Millinery and Dressmaking Trades, 1860–1930*. Urbana: University of Illinois Press, 1997.

Gaston, Arthur G. *Green Power: The Successful War of A. G. Gaston*. Birmingham: Southern University Press, 1968.

Gatewood, Willard, ed. *Free Man of Color: The Autobiography of Willis Augustus Hodges*. Knoxville: University of Tennessee Press, 1982.

Gatewood, Willard B. *Aristocrats of Color: The Black Elite, 1880–1920*. Bloomington: Indiana University Press, 1990.

Gilbert, Judith A. "Esther and Her Sisters: Free Women of Color as Property Owners in Colonial St. Louis, 1765–1803." *Gateway Heritage* 17, no. 1 (1996): 14–23.

Gilje, Paul, and Howard B. Rock. " 'Sweep O! Sweep O': African-American Chimney Sweeps and Citizenship in the New Nation." *William and Mary Quarterly* 51, no. 3 (1994): 507–38.

Glasco, Laurence. "Taking Care of Business: The Black Entrepreneurial Elite in Turn-of-the Century Pittsburgh." *Pittsburgh History* 78 (Winter 1995/96): 177–82.

Glazer, Nathan, and Daniel Patrick Moynihan. *Beyond the Melting Pot*. Cambridge: Massachusetts Institutes Press, 1963.

Gliozzo, Charles A. "John Jones: A Study of a Black Chicagoan." *Illinois Historical Journal* 80, no. 3 (1987): 177–88.

Gordy, Berry. *To Be Loved: The Music, the Magic, the Memories of Motown, an Auto-biography*. New York: Warner Books, 1994.

Gould, Virginia Meacham. *Chained to the Rock of Adversity*. Athens: University of Georgia Press, 1998.

Graves, Earl G. *How to Succeed in Business without Being White*. New York: Harper-Business, 1997.

Gray, Linda C. "Taft: Town on the Black Frontier." *Chronicles of Oklahoma* 66, no. 4 (1988): 430–47.

Green, Shelley, and Paul Pryde. *Black Entrepreneurship in America*. New Brunswick, NJ: Transaction Publisher, 1989.

Greenberg, Jonathan D. *Staking a Claim: Jake Simmons and the Making of an African American Oil Dynasty*. New York: Atheneum, 1990.

Greene, Lorenzo J. *The Negro in Colonial New England, 1620–1776*. 1942. Port Washington, NY: Kennikat Press, 1966.

Gregory, Sheila T., ed. *A Legacy of Dreams: The Life and Contributions of Dr. William Venoid Banks*. Lanham, MD: University Press of America, 1999.

Grim, Valerie. "African American Landlords in the Rural South, 1870–1950: A Profile." *Agricultural History* 72 (Spring 1998): 399–416.

———. "The Politics of Inclusion: Black Farmers and the Quest for Agribusiness Participation, 1945–1990s." *Agricultural History* 69, no. 2 (1995): 257–71.

Hall, Gwendolyn Midlo. *Africans in Colonial Louisiana: The Development of Afro-Creole Culture in the Eighteenth Century*. Baton Rouge: Louisiana State University Press, 1992.

Haller, Mark. "Policy Gambling, Entertainment, and the Emergence of Black Politics: Chicago from 1900–1940." *Journal of Social History* 24 (Summer 1991): 719–39.

Hamilton, Kenneth. *Black Towns and Profit: Promotion and Development in the Trans-Appalachian West*. Urbana: University of Illinois Press, 1991.

———. ed. *Records of the National Negro Business League* [microfilm]. Bethesda, MD: University Publications of America, 1994.

Handy, John. *An Analysis of Black Business Enterprises*. New York: Garland Publishing, 1989.

Hanger, Kimberly S. "Patronage, Property and Persistence: The Emergence of a Free Black Elite in Spanish New Orleans." In Jane G. Landers, ed., *Against the Odds: Free Blacks in the Slave Societies of the Americas*. Portland, OR: Frank Cass, 1996.

———. " 'Almost All Have Callings': Free Blacks at Work in Spanish New Orleans." *Colonial Latin American Historical Review* 3, no. 2 (1994): 141–64.

Hargis, Peggy G. "Beyond the Marginality Thesis: The Acquisition and Loss of Land by African Americans in Georgia, 1880–1930." *Agricultural History* 72 (Spring 1998): 241–62.

Harlan, Louis R. *Booker T. Washington: The Making of a Black Leader, 1856–1901*. New York: Oxford University Press, 1972.

———. *Booker T. Washington: The Wizard of Tuskegee, 1901–1915*. New York: Oxford University Press, 1983.

Harmon, J. H., Jr., Arnett G. Lindsay, and Carter G. Woodson. *The Negro as a Businessman*. 1929; reprint, College Park, MD: McGrath Publishing Company, 1969.

Harris, Abram L. *The Negro as Capitalist: A Study of Banking and Business among*

Negroes. Washington, DC: American Academy of Political and Social Science, 1936; reprint, College Park, MD: McGrath Publishing Company, 1963.

Harris, Robert L., Jr. "Charleston's Free Afro-American Elite: The Brown Fellowship Society and Humane Brotherhood." *South Carolina Historical Magazine* 82 (1981): 289–310.

————. "Early Black Benevolent Societies, 1780–1830." *Massachusetts Review* 20 (Autumn 1979): 603–28.

Hay, Margaret Jean, and Sharon Stritcher, eds. *African Women South of the Sahara.* London: Longman Group, 1984.

Henderson, Alexa Benson. "Alonzo F. Herndon and Black Insurance in Atlanta." *Atlanta Historical Bulletin* 21 (Spring 1977): 34–47.

————. *Atlanta Life Insurance Company: Guardian of Black Economic Dignity.* Tuscaloosa: University of Alabama Press, 1990.

————. "Herman E. Perry and Black Enterprise in Atlanta, 1908–1925." *Business History Review* 61, no. 2 (1987): 216–42.

Hermann, Janet Sharp. *The Pursuit of a Dream.* New York: Oxford University Press, 1981.

Hewitt, John H. "Mr. Downing and His Oyster House: The Life and Works of an African American Entrepreneur." *New York History*, 74, no. 3 (1993): 228–52.

Hickey, Joseph V. " 'Pap' Singleton's Dunlap Colony: Relief Agencies and the Failure of a Black Settlement in Eastern Kansas." *Great Plains Quarterly* 11, no. 1 (1993): 23–36.

Higbee, Mark David. "W. E. B. DuBois, F. B. Ransom, the Madam Walker Company, and Black Business Leadership in the 1930s." *Indiana Magazine of History* 89, no. 2 (1993): 102–24.

Holloway, Joseph E., ed. *Africanisms in American Culture.* Bloomington: Indiana University Press, 1991.

Hornsby, Annie R. "The Accumulation of Wealth by Black Georgians, 1890–1915." *Journal of Negro History* 74 (1989): 11–30.

Horton, James Oliver. *Free People of Color: Inside the African American Community.* Washington, DC: Smithsonian Institution Press, 1993.

————, and Lois E. Horton. *In Hope of Liberty: Culture, Community and Protest among Northern Free Blacks, 1700–1860.* New York: Oxford University Press, 1997.

Horton, Lois F., and James Oliver Horton. "Power and Social Responsibility: Entrepreneurs and the Black Community in Antebellum Boston." In Conrad Edick Wright and Katheryn P. Viens, eds., *The Boston Business Community, 1700–1850.* Boston: Northeastern University Press, 1997.

Howard-Pitney, David. "Calvin Chase's Washington Bee and Black Middle Class Ideology, 1882–1900." *Journalism Quarterly* 63, no. 1 (1986): 89–97.

Hudson, Larry E. *To Have and to Hold: Slave Work and Family Life in Antebellum South Carolina.* Athens: University of Georgia Press, 1997.

Hudson, Larry E., Jr., ed. *Working toward Freedom: Slave Society and Domestic Economy in the American South.* Rochester, NY: University of Rochester Press, 1995.

Hudson, Lynn M. "When 'Mammy' Becomes a Millionaire: Mary Ellen Pleasant, an African American Entrepreneur." Ph.D. dissertation, Indiana University, 1996.

Ingham, John N. "African-American Business Leaders in the South, 1810–1945: Business Success, Community Leadership and Racial Protest." *Business and Economic History* 22, no. 1 (Fall 1993): 262–72.

————, and Lynne B. Feldman. *African American Business Leaders: A Biographical Dictionary.* Westport, CT: Greenwood Press, 1994.

Jackson, Luther Porter. *Free Negro Labor and Property Holding in Virginia, 1830–1860.* New York: D. Appleton-Century Company, 1942.

Jezierski, John V. "Photographing the Lumber Book: The Goodridge Brothers of Saginaw, Michigan, 1863–1922." *Michigan History* 64, no. 6 (1980): 28–33.

Johnson, John H., with Lerone Bennett, Jr. *Succeeding against the Odds: The Inspiring Autobiography of One of America's Wealthiest Entrepreneurs.* New York: Warner Books, 1989.

Johnson, Michael P., and James L. Roark. *Black Masters: A Free Family of Color in the Old South.* New York: W. W. Norton, 1984.

Johnson, Whittington B. *The Promising Years, 1750–1830: The Emergence of Black Labor and Business.* New York: Garland Publishers, 1993.

————. *Black Savannah, 1788–1864.* Fayetteville: University of Arkansas Press, 1996.

Jones, Yvonne V. "Street Peddlers as Entrepreneurs: Economic Adaptation to an Urban Area." *Urban Anthropology* 17 (1988): 143–70.

Kaplan, Sidney. "Jan Earnst Matzeliger and the Making of the Shoe." *Journal of Negro History* 40, no. 1 (January 1955): 8–33.

Kea, Ray A. *Settlements, Trade, and Polities in the Seventeenth-Century Gold Coast.* Baltimore: Johns Hopkins University Press, 1982.

Keckley, Elizabeth. *Behind the Scenes, or, Thirty Years a Slave, and Four Years in the White House.* 1868; reprint, New York: Oxford University Press, 1988.

Kelley, Don Quinn. "The Political Economy of Booker T. Washington: A Bibliographic Essay." *Journal of Negro Education* 45, no. 4 (Fall 1977): 403–18.

Kennedy, William J. *The North Carolina Mutual Story: A Symbol of Progress, 1898–1970.* Durham, NC: North Carolina Mutual Life Insurance Company, 1970.

Kenzer, Robert C. *Enterprising Southerners: Black Economic Success in North Carolina, 1865–1915.* Charlottesville: University Press of Virginia, 1997.

————. "The Black Business Community in Post Civil War Virginia." *Southern Studies* 4 (Fall 1993): 229–52.

————. "Black Businessmen in Post–Civil War Tennessee." *Journal of East Tennessee History* 66 (1994): 59–80.

Kern-Foxworth, Marilyn. *Aunt Jemima, Uncle Ben, and Rastus: Blacks in Advertising Yesterday, Today, and Tomorrow.* Westport, CT: Greenwood Press, 1994.

Kijakazi, Kilolo. *African American Economic Development and Small Business Ownership.* New York: Garland Publishing, 1997.

Koger, Larry. *Black Slaveowners: Free Black Slave Masters in South Carolina, 1790–1860.* Jefferson, NC: McFarland & Company, 1985.

Kotkin, Joel. *Tribes: How Race, Religion and Identity Determine Success in the New Global Economy.* New York: Random House, 1993.

Kotlowski, Dean. "Black Power—Nixon Style: The Nixon Administration and Minority Business Enterprise." *Business History Review* 72, no. 3 (1998): 409–45.

Kwolek-Folland, Angel. *Incorporating Women: A History of Women and Business in the United States.* New York: Macmillan Library Reference, 1998.

————. "The African American Financial Industries: Issues of Class, Race and Gender in the Early 20th Century." *Business and Economic History* 23, no. 2 (Winter 1994): 85–107.

Lachance, Paul. "The Limits of Privilege: Where Free Persons of Colour Stood in the

Hierarchy of Wealth in Antebellum New Orleans." In Jane G. Landers, ed., *Against the Odds: Free Blacks in the Slave Societies of the Americas*. Portland, OR: Frank Cass, 1996.

Landers, Jane G. "Acquisition and Loss on a Spanish Frontier: The Free Black Homesteaders of Florida." In Jane G. Landers, ed., *Against the Odds: Free Blacks in the Slave Societies of the Americas*. Portland, OR: Frank Cass, 1996.

———. "Gracia Real de Santa Teresa de Mose: A Free Black Town in Spanish Colonial Florida." *Escribano* 28 (1991): 81–112.

Lane, Lunsford. *The Narrative of Lunsford Lane, Formerly of Raleigh, N.C.* Boston, 1842.

Latifah, Queen, with Karen Hunter. *Ladies First: Revelations from a Strong Woman*. New York: William Morrow, 1999.

Lebsock, Suzanne. "Free Women of Color." In *The Free Women of Petersburg: Status and Culture in a Southern Town, 1784–1860*. New York: W. W. Norton, 1985.

Lehman, Paul. "The Edwards Family and Black Entrepreneurial Success." *Chronicles of Oklahoma* 64, no. 4 (1986–87): 88–97.

Levenstein, Margaret. "African American Entrepreneurship: The View from the 1910 Census." *Business and Economic History* 25, no. 1 (Fall 1995): 106–23.

Lewis, Reginald F., and Blair S. Walker. *"Why Should White Guys Have All the Fun?": How Reginald Lewis Created a Billion-Dollar Business Empire*. New York: John Wiley and Sons, 1994.

Lindsay, Arnett G. "The Negro in Banking." *Journal of Negro History* 14 (April 1929): 156–201.

Logan, Frenise A. "The Economic Status of the Town Negro in Post-Reconstruction North Carolina." *North Carolina Historical Review* 35 (October 1958): 448–460.

Lomax, Michael E. "Black Entrepreneurship in the National Pastime: The Rise of Semiprofessional Baseball in Chicago, 1890–1915." *Journal of Sports History* 25 (Spring 1998): 43–64.

Lovett, Bobby L. *A Black Man's Dream, the First 100 Years: Richard Henry Boyd and the National Baptist Publishing Board*. Jacksonville, FL: Mega Corp., 1993.

Manning, M. M. *Slave in a Box: The Strange Career of Aunt Jemima*. Lanham, MD: University Press of America, 1998.

Manning, Patrick. *Slavery, Colonialism and Economic Growth in Dahomey*. Cambridge: Cambridge University Press, 1982.

Martin, Tony. *Race First: The Ideological and Organization Struggles of Marcus Garvey and the Universal Negro Improvement Association*. Westport, CT: Greenwood Press, 1976.

Mathewson, Alfred Dennis. "Major League Baseball's Monopoly Power and the Negro Leagues." *American Business Law Journal* 35 (Winter 1998): 291–318.

Matison, Summer E. "Manumission by Purchase." *Journal of Negro History* 33 (1948): 146–67.

Matthews, John M. "Black Newspapermen and the Black Community in Georgia, 1880–1930." *Georgia Historical Quarterly* 68, no. 3 (1984): 356–81.

McDonald, Roderick A. "Independent Economic Production by Slaves on Antebellum Louisiana Sugar Plantations." In Ira Berlin and Philip D. Morgan, eds., *Cultivation and Culture: Labor and the Shaping of Slave Life in the Americas*. Charlottesville: University Press of Virginia, 1993.

———. *The Economy and Material Culture of Slaves: Goods and Chattels on the Sugar*

Plantations of Jamaica and Louisiana. Baton Rouge: Louisiana State University Press, 1993.

McDonnell, Lawrence T. "Money Knows No Master: Market Relations and the American Slave Community." In Winifred B. Moore et al., *Developing Dixie: Modernization in a Traditional Society.* Westport, CT: Greenwood, 1988.

McKenzie, Edna Chappell. "Self-Hire among Slaves, 1820–1860: Institutional Variation or Aberration?" Ph.D. dissertation, University of Pittsburgh, 1973.

Meehan, Thomas A. "Jean Baptiste Point Du Sable, the First Chicagoan." *Journal of the Illinois State Historical Society* 56 (Autumn 1963): 439–53.

Meier, August. *Negro Thought in America, 1880–1915: Race Ideologies in the Age of Booker T. Washington.* Ann Arbor: University of Michigan, 1963.

Meillassoux, Claude, ed. *The Development of Indigenous Trade and Markets in West Africa.* London: Oxford University Press, 1971.

Mills, Gary B. "Coincoin: An Eighteenth-Century 'Liberated Woman.'" *Journal of Southern History* 42 (May1976): 205–222.

———. *The Forgotten People: Cane River's Creoles of Color.* Baton Rouge: Louisiana State University Press, 1977.

Minton, Henry M. "Early History of Negroes in Business in Philadelphia." In R. R. Wright, ed., *The Philadelphia Colored Business Directory.* Philadelphia, 1913.

Moore, John Hebron. "Simon Gray, Riverman: A Slave Who Was Almost Free." *Mississippi Valley Historical Review* 49 (December 1962): 472–84.

Morgan, Philip D. "The Ownership of Property by Slaves in the Mid-nineteenth Century Low Country." *Journal of Southern History* 49 (August 1983): 399–420.

———. *Slave Counterpoint: Black Culture in the Eighteen Century Chesapeake and Low Country.* Chapel Hill: University of North Carolina Press, 1998.

———. "Work and Culture: The Task System and the World of Lowcountry Blacks, 1700–1880." *William and Mary Quarterly* 39 (1982): 563–99.

Morris, Richard B. "The Measure of Bondage in the Slave States." *Mississippi Valley Historical Review* 41 (1954): 219–40.

Muraskin, William. *Middle Class Blacks in a White Society: Prince Hall Masonry in America.* Berkeley: University of California Press, 1975.

Myrdal, Gunnar. *An American Dilemma: The Negro Problem and Modern Democracy.* New York: Harper and Brothers Publishers, 1944.

Nadel, S. F. *A Black Byzantium.* London: Oxford University Press, 1942.

Nash, Gary B. *Forging Freedom: The Formation of Philadelphia's Black Community, 1720–1840.* Cambridge, MA: Harvard University Press, 1988.

Newton, James E., and Ronald L. Lewis, eds. *The Other Slaves: Mechanics, Artisans and Craftsmen.* Boston: G. K. Hall and Company, 1978.

Oak, Vishnu V. *The Negro's Adventure in General Business.* Yellow Springs, OH: Antioch Press, 1949.

O'Brien, Claire. "'With One Mighty Pull': Interracial Town Boosting in Nicodemus, Kansas." *Great Plains Quarterly* 16 (Spring 1996): 117–30.

O'Brien, William Patrick. "Hiram Young: Pioneering Black Wagonmaker for the Santa Fe Trade." *Gateway Heritage* 14, no. 1 (1993): 56–67.

O'Hare, William P. "Black Business Ownership in the Rural South." *Review of Black Political Economy* 18, no. 3 (1990): 93–104.

Oliver, Melvin, and Thomas M. Shapiro. *Black Wealth, White Wealth: A New Perspective on Racial Inequality.* New York: Routledge, 1995.

Olwell, Robert. "Becoming Free: Manumission and the Genesis of a Free Black Community in South Carolina." In Jane G. Landers, ed., *Against the Odds: Free Blacks in the Slave Societies of the Americas*. Portland, OR: Frank Cass, 1996.

———. " 'Loose, Idle and Disorderly': Slave Women in the Eighteenth Century Charleston Marketplace." In David Barry Gaspar and Darlene Clark Hine, eds., *More than Chattel: Black Women and Slavery in the Americas*. Bloomington: Indiana University Press, 1996.

Osthaus, Carl R. "The Rise and Fall of Jesse Binga, Black Financier." *Journal of Negro History* 58, no. 1 (1973): 39–60.

Ottley, Roi. *The Lonely Warrior: The Life and Times of Robert S. Abbott*. Chicago: Henry Regnery Co., 1955.

Overmyer, James. *Queen of the Negro Leagues: Effa Manley and the Newark Eagles*. Lanham, MD: Scarecrow Press, 1998.

Palmer, Edward Nelson. "Negro Secret Societies." *Social Forces* 23, no. 2 (December 1944): 207–12.

Papanek, John L., ed. "The Power of Enterprise." In *African Americans: Voices of Triumph, Leadership*. Richmond, VA: Time Life Books, 1994.

Perdue, Robert E. *Black Laborers and Black Professionals in Early America, 1750–1830*. New York: Vantage Press, 1975.

Phillips, Christopher. "The Roots of Quasi-Freedom: Manumission and Term Slavery in Early National Baltimore." *Southern Studies* 4 (Spring 1993): 39–66.

Pierce, Joseph A. *Negro Business and Business Education*. New York: Harper and Brothers Publishers, 1947.

Piersen, William D. *Black Yankees: The Development of an Afro-American Subculture in Eighteenth-Century New England*. Amherst: University of Massachusetts Press, 1988.

Plater, Michael A. *African American Entrepreneurship in Richmond, 1890–1940: The Story of R. C. Scott*. New York: Garland Publishing, 1996.

Porter, Dorothy Burnett. "The Remonds of Salem, Massachusetts: A Nineteenth Century Family Revisited." *Proceedings of the American Antiquarian Society* 95, no. 2 (1985): 259–95.

Puth, Robert C. "From Enforced Segregation to Integration: Market Factors in the Development of a Negro Insurance Company." In Louis B. Cain and Paul J. Uselding, eds., *Business Enterprise and Economic Change*. Kent, OH: Kent State University Press, 1973, 295–98.

———. *Supreme Life: The History of a Negro Life Insurance Company*. New York: Arno Press, 1976.

———. "Supreme Life: The History of a Negro Life Insurance Company." *Business History Review* 43 (Spring 1969): 1–21.

Putney, Martha S. "New York City Directory Listing of Occupations of Blacks in the 1840s and 1850s and Black-Owned Businesses in the 1840s: An Analysis." *Journal of the Afro-American Historical and Genealogical Society* 9, no. 2 (1988): 58–63.

Reed, Adolph L. *The Jesse Jackson Phenomenon: The Crisis of Purpose in Afro-American Politics*. New Haven, CT: Yale University Press, 1986.

Reed, Harry. *Platform for Change: The Foundations of the Northern Free Black Community, 1775–1865*. East Lansing: Michigan State University Press, 1994.

Reidy, Joseph P. "Obligations and Right: Patterns of Labor, Subsistence, and Exchange in the Cotton Belt of Georgia, 1790–1860." In Ira Berlin and Philip D. Morgan, eds., *Cultivation and Culture: Labor and the Shaping of Slave Life in the Americas*. Charlottesville: University Press of Virginia, 1993.

Reinders, Robert. "The Free Negro in the New Orleans Economy, 1850–1860." *Louisiana History* 6 (1965): 273–85.

Rich-McCoy, Lois. *Millionairess: Self Made Women of America*. New York: Harper and Row, 1978.

Richardson, Joe M. "Albert W. Dent: A Black New Orleans Hospital and University Administrator." *Louisiana History* 37, no. 3 (1996): 309–23.

Rock, Howard B., Paul A. Gilje, and Robert Asher, eds. *American Artisans: Crafting Social Identity, 1750–1850*. Baltimore: Johns Hopkins University Press, 1995.

Rooks, Noliwe M. *Hair Raising: Beauty, Culture, and African American Women*. New Brunswick, NJ: Rutgers University Press, 1996.

Savage, William S. "The Influence of William Alexander Leidesdorff on the History of California." *Journal of Negro History* 38 (July 1953): 322–32.

Schatzberg, Rufus, and Robert J. Kelley. *African American Organized Crime: A Social History*. New Brunswick, NJ: Rutgers University Press, 1996.

Schlotterbeck, John T. "The Internal Economy of Slavery in Rural Piedmont Virginia." In Ira Berlin and Philip D. Morgan, eds., *The Slaves' Economy: Independent Production by Slaves in the Americas*. London: Frank Cass, 1991.

Schneider, Mark R. "The *Colored American* and *Alexander's*: Boston's Pro–Civil Rights Bookerites." *Journal of Negro History* 80 (1995): 157–69.

Schwalm, Leslie A. *A Hard Fight for We: Women's Transition from Slavery to Freedom in South Carolina*. Urbana: University of Illinois Press, 1997.

Schwarz, Philip J. "Emancipators, Protectors, and Anomalies: Free Black Slaveholders in Virginia." *Virginia Magazine of History and Biography* 95 (1987): 317–38.

Schweniger, Loren. "Black-Owned Businesses in the South, 1790–1880." *Business History Review* 63 (Spring 1989): 22–60.

Schweninger, Loren. *Black Property Owners in the South, 1790–1915*. Urbana: University of Illinois Press, 1990.

———. "Property Owning Free African-American Women in the South, 1800–1870." *Journal of Women's History* 3, no. 1 (Winter 1990): 13–44.

———. "Slave Independence and Enterprise in South Carolina, 1780–1865." *South Carolina Historical Magazine* 93 (1992): 101–25.

———. "The Underside of Slavery: The Internal Economy, Self-Hire, and Quasi-freedom." *Slavery and Abolition* 12 (September 1991): 1–22.

———, ed. *From Tennessee Slave to St. Louis Entrepreneur: The Autobiography of James Thomas*. Columbia; University of Missouri Press, 1984.

Scruggs, Marc, "Anthony D. Allen: A Prosperous American of African Descent in Early 19th Century Hawaii." *Hawaiian Journal of History* 26 (1992): 55–93.

Shields, Cydney, and Leslie C. Shields. *Work, Sister, Work: How Black Women Can Get Ahead in Today's Business Environment*. New York: Simon and Schuster, 1994.

Silverman, Robert Mark. "The Effects of Racism and Racial Discrimination on Minority Business Development: The Case of Black Manufacturers in Chicago's Ethnic Beauty Aids Industry." *Journal of Social History* 31, no. 3 (1998): 571–97.

Simms, Margaret, ed. *Economic Perspectives on Affirmative Action*. Washington, DC: Joint Center for Political and Economic Studies, 1995.

Slevin, Kathleen F., and C. Ray Wingrove. *From Stumbling Blocks to Stepping Stones:*

The Life Experiences of Fifty Professional African Women. New York: New York University Press, 1998.

Smith, A. Wade, and Joan V. Moore. "East-West Differences in Black Economic Development." *Journal of Black Studies* 16, no. 2 (1985): 131–54.

Soderland, Jean R. "Black Women in Colonial Pennsylvania." *Pennsylvania Magazine of History and Biography* 197, no. 1 (1983): 49–68.

Spencer, C. S. "Black Benefit Societies in Nineteenth Century Alabama." *Phylon* 46 (September 1985): 45–58.

Stack, Carol B. *All Our Kin: Strategies for Survival in a Black Community*. New York: Harper and Row, 1974.

Sterling, Dorothy. *We Are Your Sisters: Black Women in the Nineteenth Century*. New York: W. W. Norton, 1984.

Stuart, M. S. *An Economic Detour: A History of Insurance in the Lives of American Negroes*. New York: Wendell Malliett and Company, 1940.

Sundstrom, Lars. *The Exchange Economy of Pre-colonial Tropical Africa* [published as *The Trade of Guinea* (Sweden, 1963)]; reprint, London: C. Hurst and Company, 1974.

Thomas, Bettye C. "A Nineteenth Century Black Operated Shipyard, 1866–1884: Reflections upon Its Inception and Ownership." *Journal of Negro History* 59 (1994): 1–12.

Thomas, Lamont D. *Paul Cuffe: Black Entrepreneur and Pan-Africanist*. Urbana: University of Illinois Press, 1988.

Thornbrough, Emma Lou. "American Negro Newspapers, 1880–1914." *Business History Review* 40, no. 4 (Winter 1966): 467–90.

Todd, Gwendolyn Powell. *Innovation and Growth in an African American Owned Business*. New York: Garland Publishing, 1996.

Trimiew, Darryl M., and Michael Greene. "How We Got Over: The Moral Teachings of the African-American Church on Business Ethics." *Business Ethics Quarterly* 7 (March 1997): 133–47.

Trotter, Joe W. "African Americans in the City: The Industrial Era, 1900–1950." *Journal of Urban History* 21 (May 1995): 438–457.

Tucker, David M. "Black Pride and Negro Business in the 1920's: George Washington Lee of Memphis." *Business History Review* 43, no. 4 (Winter 1969): 435–51.

Twomey, Dannehl M. "Into the Mainstream: Early Black Photography in Houston." *Houston Review* 9, 1 no. (1987): 39–48.

Usner, Daniel H. *Indians, Settlers, & Slaves in a Frontier Exchange Economy*. Chapel Hill: University of North Carolina Press, 1992.

Vandal, Gilles. "Black Utopia in Early Reconstruction New Orleans: The People's Bakery as a Case-Study." *Louisiana History* 38 (Fall 1997): 437–52.

Venkatesh, Sudhir Alladi. "Gender and Outlaw Capitalism: A Historical Account of the Black Sisters United 'Girl Gang' " *Signs* 34 (Spring 1998): 683–709.

Villemez, Wayne J., and John J. Beggs. "Black Capitalism and Black Inequality: Some Sociological Considerations." *Social Forces* 63, no. 1 (1984): 117–44.

Walker, Juliet E. K. *African-American Business and Entrepreneurship: Critical Historiographical and Bibliographical Assessments in the Economic and Cultural Life of Blacks and Capitalism*. Westport, CT: Greenwood Publishing Group, forthcoming.

————. "Black Entrepreneurship: An Historical Inquiry." *Business and Economic History* 12 (1983): 37–55.

Walker, Juliet E. K. *Encyclopedia of African American Business History*. Westport, CT: Greenwood Press, 1999.

————. *Free Frank: A Black Pioneer on the Antebellum Frontier*. Lexington: University Press of Kentucky, 1983; reprint, 1995.

————. *The History of Black Business in America: Capitalism, Race, Entrepreneurship*. New York/London: MacMillan/Prentice Hall International, 1998.

————. "Pioneer Slave Entrepreneurship—Patterns, Processes, and Perspectives: The Case of the Slave Free Frank on the Kentucky Pennyroyal, 1795–1819." *Journal of Negro History* 68 (Summer 1983): 289–308.

————. "Prejudices, Profits, Privileges: Commentaries on 'Captive Capitalists' Antebellum Black Entrepreneurs." *Essays in Economic and Business History* 8 (1990): 399–422.

————. "The Promised Land: The *Chicago Defender* and the Black Press in Illinois, 1862–1970." In Henry Lewis Suggs, ed., *The Black Press in the Middle West, 1865–1985*. Westport, CT: Greenwood Press, 1996.

————. "Promoting Black Entrepreneurship and Business Enterprise in Antebellum America: The National Negro Convention, 1830–1860." In Thomas D. Boston, ed., *A Different Vision: Race and Public Policy*. New York: Routledge, 1997.

————. "Racism, Slavery, and Free Enterprise: Black Entrepreneurship in the United States before the Civil War." *Business History Review* 60 (Autumn 1986): 343–82.

————. "The Rise of the New Black Entrepreneur, 1939–2000." In Robert L. Harris and Rosalyn-Terborg Penn, eds., *The Columbia Guide to African American History since 1939*. New York: Columbia University Press, forthcoming 2001.

————. "Trade and Markets in Precolonial West and West Central Africa: The Cultural Foundations of the African American Business Tradition." In Thomas D. Boston, ed., *A Different Vision: Race and Public Policy*. New York: Routledge, 1997.

————. "Whither Liberty, Equality, or Legality? Slavery, Race, Property and the 1787 American Constitution." *New York Law School Journal of Human Rights* 6, Part 2 (Spring 1989): 299–352.

————, ed., in Larry Martin, editor in chief. *African Americans in Business: The Path towards Empowerment: Essays on Black Entrepreneurship from the African Background to the Present*. Washington, DC: Associated Publishers, 1998.

Wallace, Robert L. *Black Wealth through Black Entrepreneurship*. Edgewood, MD: Duncan and Duncan, 1993.

Washington, Booker T. *The Negro in Business*. Boston: Hertel, Jenkins and Co., 1907.

Watts, Jill. *God, Harlem, USA: The Father Divine Story*. Berkeley: University of California Press, 1992.

Weare, Walter B. *Black Business in the New South: A Social History of the North Carolina Mutual Life Insurance Company*. Urbana: University of Illinois Press, 1973.

————. "Charles Clinton Spaulding: Middle-Class Leadership in the Age of Segregation." In John Hope Franklin and August Meier, eds., *Black Leaders of the Twentieth Century*. Urbana: University of Illinois Press, 1982.

Weems, Robert E., Jr. "African American Consumer Boycotts during the Civil Rights Era." *Western Journal of Black Studies* 19 (Spring 1995): 72–79.

————. *Black Business in the Black Metropolis: The Chicago Metropolitan Assurance Company, 1925–1985.* Bloomington: Indiana University Press, 1996.

————. "A Crumbling Legacy: The Decline of African American Insurance Companies in Contemporary America." *Review of Black Political Economy* 23 (Fall 1994): 25–37.

————. *Desegregating the Dollar: African American Consumerism in the Twentieth Century.* New York: New York University Press, 1998.

————. "Out of the Shadows: Business Enterprise and African American Historiography," *Business and Economic History* 26 (Fall 1997): 200–212.

————. "The Revolution Will Be Marketed: American Corporations and African American Consumers during the 1960s." *Radical History Review* 23 (Fall 1994): 25–37.

————. "Robert A. Cole and the Metropolitan Funeral System Association: A Profile of a Civic-Minded African American Businessman." *Journal of Negro History* 78 (Winter 1993): 1–15.

Wesley, Charles H. *Negro Labor in the United States, 1850–1925: A Study in American Economic History.* New York: Russell and Russell, 1927.

Whitman, Stephen T. *The Price of Freedom: Slavery and Manumission in Baltimore and Early National Maryland.* Lexington: University Press of Kentucky, 1997.

Whitten, David O. "A Black Entrepreneur in Antebellum Louisiana." *Business History Review* 45, no. 2 (1971): 201–19.

————. *Andrew Durnford: A Black Sugar Planter in Antebellum Louisiana.* Natchitoches, LA: Northwestern State University Press, 1981; reprint, New Brunswick, NJ: Transaction Publishers, 1995.

Wier, Sadye H., and John F. Marszalek. *A Black Businessman in White Mississippi, 1886–1974.* Jackson: University Press of Mississippi, 1977.

Wilder, Craig Steven. "The Rise and Influence of the New York African Society for Mutual Relief, 1808–1865." *Afro-Americans in New York Life and History* 22 (July 1998): 7–18

Wilson, Kenneth L., and Martin W. Allen. "Ethnic Enclaves: A Comparison of the Cuban and Black Economies in Miami." *American Journal of Sociology* 88, no. 1 (1982): 135–60.

Wilson, Sunnie, and John Cohassey. *Toast of the Town: The Life and Times of Sunnie Wilson.* Detroit: Wayne State University Press, 1998.

Winch, Julie, ed. *The Colored Aristocracy of St. Louis by Cyprian Clamorgan.* 1858; reprint, Columbia: University of Missouri Press, 1999.

————. *Philadelphia's Black Elite: Activism, Accommodation, and the Struggle for Autonomy, 1787–1844.* Philadelphia: Temple University Press, 1998.

————. " 'You Know I AM a Man of Business': James Forten and the Factor of Race in Philadelphia's Antebellum Business Community." *Business and Economic History* 26 (Fall 1997): 213–28.

Wintz, Cary D. "Black Business in Houston, 1910–1930." *Essays in Economic and Business History* 10 (1992): 29–40.

Wolcott, Victoria W. "The Culture of the Informal Economy: Numbers Runners in Inter-war Black Detroit." *Radical History Review* 69 (Fall 1997): 46–75.

————. "Mediums, Messages, and Lucky Numbers: African-American Female Spiritualists and Numbers Runners in Inter-war Detroit." In Patricia Yeager, ed., *The Geography of Identity.* Ann Arbor: University of Michigan Press, 1996.

Woods, Betty. *Women's Work, Men's Work: The Informal Slave Economies of Low-country Georgia.* Athens: University of Georgia Press, 1995.

Woodson, Carter G. "Insurance Business among Negroes." *Journal of Negro History* 14 (April 1929): 202–226.

———. "The Negroes of Cincinnati prior to the Civil War." *Journal of Negro History* 1 (January 1916): 20–23.

Woodward, Michael D. *Black Entrepreneurs in America: Stories of Struggle and Success.* New Brunswick, NJ: Rutgers University Press, 1997.

Work, Monroe, N., ed. *Negro Year Book and Annual Encyclopedia of the Negro*, vols. 1–5. Tuskegee, AL: Negro Year Book Company, 1912, 1913, 1916, 1918.

Wright, Conrad E., and Katheryn P. Viens, eds. *Entrepreneurs: The Boston Business Community, 1700–1850.* Boston: Northeastern University Press, 1997.

Wright, Richard Robert. *Eighty Seven Years behind the Black Curtain: An Autobiography.* Philadelphia: Rare Book Company, 1965.

Yancy, Robert. *Federal Government Policy and Black Business.* Cambridge, MA: Ballinger Press, 1974.

XIV

Sexuality and Race

Stanley O. Gaines, Jr.

Perhaps no stereotype about African Americans has persisted as tenaciously within the United States as has the stereotype of black hypersexuality. From the time of slavery onward, European American culture has perpetuated the myth that African Americans—both male and female—are animalistic, libidinous beings. Given that African American slaves typically were regarded and treated by European American masters as cattle, perhaps it is not surprising that many European Americans engaged in after-the-fact rationalizations of the physical and psychological brutalities visited upon African Americans largely by caricaturing slaves as oversexed. Long after the demise of slavery, however, successive generations of European Americans in all regions of the country continued to invoke the stereotype of black hypersexuality as a part of the attempt to justify segregation and discrimination.

Before the Civil War, and particularly during the years after the slave trade was officially abolished by Congress, many white masters exercised enormous control over African American slaves' sexuality. Not only did white masters routinely select specific African American men and women to "breed" with each other; but since an individual's race was assigned on the basis of the mother's racial designation, many European American slaveowners "sired" slave offspring themselves by mating with African American female slaves. Conversely, European American men were often ruthless in their attempts to keep white southern belles out of the clutches of ostensibly bestial African American male slaves. After the Civil War, former Confederate soldiers met secretly to form the Ku Klux Klan, with the prevention of the "defilement" of white women by black men as one of its primary goals. One former Confederate sympathizer,

D. W. Griffith, romanticized the Klan's terrorist acts against African American men in his film *Birth of a Nation*.

By the dawn of the twentieth century, many European American social scientists in emerging disciplines such as sociology and psychology had begun to incorporate the stereotype of black hypersexuality into their writings on race, ethnicity, and culture. Fueled to a large extent by the eugenics movement that first swept Europe and subsequently reached the shores of the United States, some of the most influential early sociologists and psychologists reified popular European American misconceptions about African Americans' sexuality into their own pseudoscientific works. Certain social scientists believed it was their patriotic duty to promote social programs such as mass sterilization of African American women in order to curb the growth of the African American population.

By the beginning of the civil rights era, sociological and psychological books dealing with black sexuality increasingly called the legitimacy of the stereotype of black hypersexuality into question. With the advent of the black power movement and the emergence of black studies programs and departments throughout the United States, social scientists en masse began to free themselves from the yoke of stereotyping that had plagued much, if not most, of the literature on race, ethnicity, and sexuality. By the 1990s, a growing body of scholarship on African American sexuality suggested that African Americans were not "hypersexual" at all, compared to their European American counterparts. Ironically, much of this recent scholarship indicates that in certain respects, the sexual practices of many African Americans tend to be rather conservative compared to the sexual practices of many European Americans.

During the pre-slavery colonial era, many blacks and whites who shared a common fate as indentured servants developed romantic relationships and sometimes married, as the "color line" described by W.E.B. Du Bois in *The Souls of Black Folk* (1903/1969) had not yet been drawn by American society. As Lerone Bennett, Jr., noted in *Before the Mayflower: A History of Black America* (1993), skin pigmentation was simply not strongly associated with social class or social identity during the colonial era. Furthermore, in *Black Majority: Negroes in Colonial South Carolina from 1670 through the Steno Rebellion*, Peter H. Wood (1975) offered an account of a white Englishman who, upon visiting colonial South Carolina, was surprised by the ease with which blacks and whites intermingled.

Some post–World War II writers have depicted black-white romantic relationships of the colonial era as the trysts of the lowest common denominator of American society. For example, in *Black Tide* (1963), Julius A. Pierce contended that only those European American indentured servants who were morally unfit would consent to sexual relations with African American indentured servants of the opposite gender. Other writers have sought to downplay the extent to which blacks and whites (e.g., see Herbert G. Gutman, *The Black Family in Slavery and Freedom, 1750–1925* [1976])—especially black men and white women (e.g., see Allan Kulikoff, *Tobacco and Slaves: The Development of Southern Cultures in the Chesapeake, 1680–1800* [1986])—engaged in consensual sex at all. Nevertheless, as Mechal Sobel observed in *The World They Made Together: Black and White Values in Eighteenth-Century Virginia* (1987), many persons of European and African descent developed short-term and long-term romantic relationships with each other.

As Winthrop Jordan noted in *White over Black: American Attitudes toward the Negro, 1550–1812* (1968), it was only after the institutionalization of slavery in America that several states began to pass laws prohibiting "amalgamation" or "race-mixing." As the color line was drawn within American society, many white men who wielded power over black slaves increasingly viewed black women as sexual chattel. The sexual exploitation of enslaved black women by their white captors began even before the women set foot on American soil. In *An Account of the Slave Trade on the Coast of Africa* (1788), ship physician Alexander Falconbridge described several instances of white sailors' brutalization of black women during the slave ships' trips across the Atlantic passage. Falconbridge also pointed out that many black women threw themselves overboard in order to avoid sexual abuse at the hands of their white captors.

Once they reached the United States, black female slaves often were subjected to further sexual exploitation by their white masters. Angela Davis's *Women, Race, and Class* (1983) attested to the physical and psychological abuse that many enslaved black women experienced as a result of such exploitation. Moreover, white slaveowners often enlisted black male slaves to "breed" with black female slaves, a practice described by Bryon Fulks in *Black Struggle: A History of the Negro in America* (1969). From the end of the slave trade until the beginning of the Civil War, black men's assigned role as "bucks" and black women's assigned role as "wenches" became increasingly important to the maintenance of the institution of slavery in the United States.

During the era of slavery, white racists began to concoct myths regarding African American men and women as hypersexual beings. According to Margaret Halsey in *Color Blind: A White Woman Looks at the Negro* (1946), such myths, especially regarding the potency of black men, were actually more prevalent after, rather than before, the Civil War. Nevertheless, within the antebellum South, the myths concerning black male hypersexuality had already taken hold of many white racists' imaginations.

In *Slavery, as It Relates to the Negro or African Race* (1843), Josiah Priest declared that black men and black women, as the descendants of Ham, not only possessed oversized genitalia but engaged in the most lascivious of sexual acts. As Sander Gilman noted in *Difference and Pathology: Stereotypes of Sexuality, Race, and Madness* (1985), even Thomas Jefferson, author of the Declaration of Independence, subscribed to such racist beliefs. Ironically, as is clear from a variety of sources (e.g., Bennett's *Before the Mayflower* [1993]; Toni E. Weaver's *White to White on Black/White* [1993]; Nathaniel Weyl and William Marina's *American Statesmen on Slavery and the Negro* [1971]), Jefferson not only developed a long-term romantic relationship but also had several offspring with his black slave mistress, Sally Hemmings. Winthrop Jordan's *White over Black* (1968) suggests that to the extent that Jefferson dwelled on black males' lust for black women yet kept a black slave woman as a concubine, Jefferson vividly illustrated the tendency for many white men of his era to project their own passions for black women onto black men.

According to E. Franklin Frazier in *The Free Negro Family: A Study of Family Origins before the Civil War* (1932), one tangible result of white slave-owners' rape of enslaved black women throughout the era of the "peculiar institution" was the gradual emergence of a disproportionately large number of persons with European as well as African heritage—the so-called mulattos (derivative of "mule" or half-breed)—among the free Negro class. Some white masters took favor upon the progeny of their illicit unions with black female slaves, arranging for the offspring to be freed at some specified time (e.g., upon the white masters' death). As Frazier (1932) pointed out, anti-"amalgamation" laws during the era of slavery were so stringent that the number of interracial marriages throughout the United States was too small to account for the growth of the mulatto population. According to John Hope Franklin in *From Slavery to Freedom: A History of American Negroes* (1947), the number of mulattos resulting from the illicit white male–black female unions indicated that many, if not most, white men in the South were not bound by the anti-"amalgamation" laws of the slavery era.

In *Anti-racism in U.S. History: The First Two Hundred Years* (1992), Herbert Aptheker emphasized that both within and outside of the context of marriage, white men and black women—and, to a smaller extent, black men and white women—engaged in sexual relations and produced "mixed" offspring. As Edmund S. Morgan observed somewhat ruefully in *American Slavery, American Freedom: The Ordeal of Colonial Virginia* (1975), at least some black men also operated outside the law regarding sexual relations across the color line. This is not to say, however, that black-white romantic relationships during the slavery era were devoid of love or respect. It is clear from Aptheker's work, as well as from the work of Ira Berlin (*Slaves without Masters: The Free Negro in the Antebellum South* [1974]), that many interracial romantic relationships during the era of slavery survived on the basis of mutual affection and esteem.

Once the Civil War erupted, white racists increasingly warned of the dangers that would befall the nation—particularly the South—if "social equality" were to become the law of the land. According to Forrest G. Wood in *Black Scare: The Racist Response to Emancipation and Reconstruction* (1968), an unsigned booklet entitled "Miscegenation: The Theory of the Blending of the Races, Applied to the American White Man and the Negro" was circulated in December 1863. The booklet, which eventually was found to be a hoax, was the brainchild of racists who were attempting to associate the Republican Party (i.e., Lincoln's party) with "race-mixing." Interestingly, this was the first time that the term *miscegenation* appeared in print. As Gunnar Myrdal observed in *An American*

Dilemma (1944), the term has seldom, if ever, been used outside the United States. Unlike the older term *amalgamation* (which was not in itself imbued with negative connotations), *miscegenation* carried distinctly negative overtones.

Shortly after the end of the Civil War, racist diatribes such as Hinton Rowan Helper's *Negroes in Negroland* (1868) warned that if "social equality" were to reach full fruition in the United States, then the same conditions of sexual immorality that plagued the black "race" in Africa would eventually spread from black America to white America. Similarly, in *Mongrelism* (1876), Watson F. Quimby argued that "race-mixing" would prove to be just as destructive to civilization in the United States as it had been to every previously "great" civilization that had condoned the practice. Interestingly, Naomi Friedman Goldstein noted in *The Roots of Prejudice against the Negro in the United States* (1948) that, in general, racist writings during the years immediately following the Civil War and Reconstruction tended *not* to focus upon black male hypersexuality as much as upon interracial sex per se as the primary threat to white American civilization.

In *The Southern Temper* (1959), William Peters contended that it is all too easy for intellectuals to underestimate the strong emotional appeal of anti-"miscegenation" diatribes. It is probably no accident that most of the southern state laws prohibiting intermarriage were enacted *after* the Civil War—that is, during the years in which white racists raised fears about the dire consequences of "mongrelization" to a fever pitch—as is obvious from Franklin Johnson's *Development of State Legislation Concerning the Free Negro* (1919/1979). Also, as Bennett (1993) pointed out, it was during the Reconstruction era that southern white males' fears about black male–white female sex and marriage helped give rise to the Ku Klux Klan.

From the end of Reconstruction through World War I, white segregationists' campaigns against interracial romance increasingly invoked the image of the black male as a thoroughly libidinous being whose primary object of desire was the "pure" (and, more often than not, southern) white woman. Among the most virulently racist books raising the specter of black male hypersexuality were Charles Carroll's *Tempter of Eve* (1902) and R. W. Shufeldt's *Negro: A Menace to American Civilization* (1907) and *America's Greatest Problem: The Negro* (1915). Even some European Americans who considered themselves "friends" of African Americans nonetheless invoked the image of the sexually ravenous black male, as is obvious from books by such ostensibly liberal authors as W. D. Weatherford (*Negro Life in the South* [1918]) and Mary Helm (*From Darkness to Light: The Story of Negro Progress* [1909] and *The Upward Path: The Evolution of a Race* [1909]).

As Stanford M. Lyman observed in *The Black American in Sociological Thought* (1973), white racists during the late 1800s and early 1900s created quite a dilemma for themselves. Having created the image of the black man as the sexual superior (albeit the intellectual and moral inferior) of the white man, shouldn't the Darwinian dictum "survival of the fittest" ensure that African American men would leave a disproportionately large number of progeny via mating with European American *and* African American women? In *From a Caste to a Minority: Changing Attitudes of American Sociologists toward Afro-Americans, 1896–1945* (1989), Vernon J. Williams, Jr., indicated that one strategy employed by segregationist white scholars was to depict black male–white female unions as exceptionally infertile. For example, seizing upon U.S. Census data that seemingly documented a drop in the black fertility rate during the latter part of the nineteenth century, Edward B. Eggleston contended in *The Ultimate Solution of the Negro Problem* (1913) that the black "race" was headed for extinction in the United States, thus conveniently ridding white men of their most feared sexual competitors. Unfortunately for Eggleston and like-minded social scientists of the era, as George M. Fredrickson observed in *The Black Image in the White Mind: The Debate on Afro-American Character and Destiny, 1817–1914* (1971), the U.S. Census data in question were subsequently shown to be in error.

Despite the inevitable contradictions that arose as they tried to retrofit social reality to their preconceptions, many white scholars insisted that the presumed hypersexuality of African American men would not be manifested in the reproductive conquest of white women. For example, in *The Relations of the Advanced and the Backward Races of Mankind* (1902), James Bryce asserted that, by and large, blacks and whites instinctively found each other physically repulsive. In *Totem and Taboo* (1918/1946), Sigmund Freud implicitly rejected Bryce's thesis yet went on to hypothesize that among "civilized" populations (i.e., Anglos), only neurotic individuals would harbor the same irrational desire for sexual intimacy with outgroup members that supposedly characterized "primitive" or "savage" populations (i.e., persons of color). Finally, in *A Solution of the Race Problem in the South* (1898), Enoch Spencer Simmons proposed that, regardless of race, only "insane" individuals would desire sexual relations with outgroup members.

Not all turn-of-the-century white scholars accepted such fallacious arguments against interracial sex and marriage. For example, in *Race Traits and Tendencies of the American Negro* (1896), Frederick L. Hoffman noted that the available evidence did not support the widely held claim that black male–white female unions were inherently less fertile than were white male–black female *or* white male–white female unions. Nevertheless, as I. A. Newby observed in *Jim Crow's Defense: Anti-Negro Thought in America, 1900–1930* (1973), the anti-miscegenation viewpoint pervaded American society so thoroughly that within as well as outside academia, the chorus of racist sentiments consistently drowned out opposing perspectives. In fact, among those voices contributing to the chorus (e.g., Hubert Howe Bancroft, *Retrospection, Political and Personal* [1912]; William P. Calhoun, *The Caucasian and the Negro in the United States* [1902]; Albert Bushnell Hart, *The Southern South* [1912]; Thomas N. Norwood, *Address on the Negro* [1908]; Raymond Patterson, *The Negro and His Needs* [1911/

1971]), an occasional African American (e.g., William Hannibal Thomas, *The American Negro: What He Was, What He Is, and What He May Become* [1901]) could be heard harmonizing in the background.

What did influential African American leaders of the late 1800s and early 1900s think about miscegenation? By arguing against social equality for African Americans, Booker T. Washington's *Up from Slavery* (1901) was interpreted by some segregationists as proof that Washington also opposed "race-mixing." (Given that Washington was the product of a white male–black female union, it is ironic that some white segregationists would embrace Washington as an ally.) Conversely, by arguing in favor of social equality, W.E.B. Du Bois's *Souls of Black Folk* (1903/1969) was interpreted by some segregationists as proof that Du Bois favored interracial sex and marriage. However, neither Washington's *Up from Slavery* nor Du Bois's *Souls of Black Folk* dealt specifically with black sexuality per se.

William Loren Katz's edited volume, *Proceedings of the National Negro Conference, 1909* (1969), chronicles the founding of the National Association for the Advancement of Colored People (NAACP). Among other luminaries, W.E.B. Du Bois spoke out against state anti-miscegenation laws; and Ida Wells Barnett spoke out against the epidemic of white males' lynching of black males—usually on the pretext of black males' real, imagined, or implied "advances" toward white females—throughout the United States as a whole and the South in particular. With the shift in black power from Washington's "Tuskegee machine" to Du Bois's NAACP, the opinions of African American leaders increasingly indicated that, although most African Americans were not particularly interested in marrying European Americans, most African Americans nonetheless opposed legislation that outlawed black-white marriages.

During the years between World War I and World War II, many American scholars began to reject the anti-miscegenation perspective. As Stanley O. Gaines, Jr., noted in *Culture, Ethnicity, and Personal Relationship Processes* (1997), the eugenics movement in the United States and England openly advocated involuntary sterilization of African American females.

Although the eugenics movement attracted a fairly large following, it also alienated many intellectuals by encouraging public health officials to render black women incapable of reproducing. Thus, the eugenics movement—which was allied with the anti-"mongrelization" movement in the United States—had a polarizing effect on the issue of miscegenation.

Within this sociopolitically charged context, there appeared in print many familiar segregationist refrains, such as the stereotype of black male hypersexuality (e.g., Claude G. Bowers, *The Tragic Era* [1929]; H. Champly, *White Women, Coloured Men* [1939]; John Moffatt Mecklin, *Democracy and Race Friction: A Study in Social Ethics* [1921]). An additional theme, concerning the offspring of black-white unions as intellectually (if not morally or physically) superior to "pure" blacks yet intellectually (as well as morally and physically) inferior to "pure" whites (e.g., Earnest Sevier Cox, *White America* [1923]; S. J.

Holmes, *Studies in Evolution and Eugenics* [1923]; H. S. Jennings, *The Biological Basis of Human Nature* [1930]), began to supplant the argument that whites naturally found blacks' physical appearance repulsive. However, some writers (e.g., T. T. McKinney, *All White America* [1937]) countered that "mulattos" were intellectually, physically, and morally superior to "pure" blacks *and* "pure" whites; other writers (e.g., Herbert J. Seligmann, *The Negro Faces America* [1920]) argued that white males' antipathy regarding miscegenation made them *primitive* rather than "advanced" in terms of sociolegal and sociopolitical development.

Prior to World War I, many segregationists contended that on religious as well as biological grounds, "race-mixing" was unnatural. The fact that biological determinism and theological determinism were logically inconsistent in many ways (e.g., the Darwinian concept of evolution explicitly contradicts creationists' account of the origin of humankind) appeared not to trouble segregationists. In the years between the two World Wars, however, the Catholic Church—which encouraged priests not to perform interracial wedding ceremonies in states governed by anti-miscegenation laws—nonetheless refused to condemn interracial marriage in and of itself. Francis J. Gilligan's *Morality of the Color Line* (1928) and John La Farge's *Interracial Justice* (1937) articulated the Catholic Church's position, which at that point in history was considered enlightened. Thus, both the biological and the religious underpinnings of the anti-miscegenation perspective were shaken by sociopolitical change in pre–World War II America.

Two books published during the 1930s provided perhaps the strongest evidence to date that the overtly racist version of the anti-miscegenation perspective had begun to lose favor, at least within academia. In *The Anthropometry of the American Negro* (1930), Melville J. Herskovitz's scientifically based estimate that more than 70 percent of all individuals designated as "Negroes" in the United States possessed some degree of "white" genetic heritage—and, furthermore, that more than 20 percent of all individuals designated as "Caucasian" in the United States possessed some degree of "black" genetic heritage—was cited widely as an authoritative refutation of myths concerning the biological dangers posed by miscegenation. Moreover, in *Caste and Class in a Southern Town* (1937), John Dollard argued that white segregationists' tendency to evoke black male hypersexuality and the evils of miscegenation as defenses against social equality actually concealed a more basic motive, which was to prevent blacks from having the opportunity to attain socioeconomic parity with whites.

As World War II raised the specter of "the final solution"—a specter that all but the most rabid racists found horrifying—social scientists entered a "golden era" of scholarship on sexuality and race. Otto Klineberg's edited volume, *Characteristics of the American Negro* (1944), demonstrated that prevailing myths concerning black-white marriage had essentially no basis in reality. In *Black Metropolis: A Study of Negro Life in a Northern City*, (1945) St. Clair Drake and Horace Cayton reported that progressive African American leaders typically were *not* interested in gaining access to European American women, as white segregationists had claimed for so long; rather, those leaders argued that no one should be prevented from marrying whomever one chose (and, more than 90 percent of the time, African Americans chose ingroup members as marriage partners). Finally, Gunnar Myrdal's *American Dilemma* (1944) stands as a classic account of the hypocrisy of anti-miscegenation laws and sentiments governing an ostensibly free nation.

Myrdal's (1944) impact upon the study of sexuality and race has been profound. As noted by Gordon W. Allport in *The Nature of Prejudice* (1954/1979), Toni E. Weaver in *White to White on Black/White* (1993), and the National Research Council in *A Common Destiny: Blacks in American Society* (1989), among others, Myrdal showed empirically that whites tended to assume that blacks' primary goal in striving for social equality was intermarriage with whites; whereas blacks ranked intermarriage with whites *last* among their goals in striving for social equality. As noted by Andrew Hacker in *Two Nations: Black and White, Separate, Hostile, Unequal* (1992); Hans J. Massaquoi in his contribution to Herbert Nipson's edited volume *The White Problem in America* (1966); and Doris Wilkinson in her contribution to Obie Clayton, Jr.'s edited volume *An American Dilemma Revisited: Race Relations in a Changing World* (1996), whites' commodification of black sexuality provided a powerful economic incentive for the establishment, maintenance, and expansion of slavery throughout the United States. Even after the abolition of slavery, according to Myrdal, white racists continued to equate control over the products of black physical labor with control over the products of black sexuality.

The time-honored white supremacist practice of sounding alarms concerning black sexual depravity had certainly not disappeared from the intellectual landscape during the mid-1940s, as is evident from treatises such as Ira Calvin's *Lost White Race* (1945), Archibald Coody IV's *Race Question* (1944), and J. H. Funderberg's *March of the Negro* (1945). In addition, for some white segregationists, Myrdal's *American Dilemma* (1944) represented a call to arms. Most notably, Theodore G. Bilbo's *Take Your Choice: Separation or Mongrelization* (1947) included a scathing indictment of Myrdal's work.

Nevertheless, by the late 1940s, several writers had begun to explore themes that would eventually become recurrent in post–World War II scholarship on the "Negro Question." In *Racial Pride and Prejudice* (1946), E. J. Dingwall proclaimed that it was impossible to understand the dynamics of race relations in the United States without understanding the central role of sexuality. In *Negroes in American Society* (1949), Maurice R. Davie argued that "race" was viewed most accurately as a sociological, rather than a biological, concept. In *Race Relations in a Democracy* (1949), Ira Corinne Brown maintained that many whites were under the erroneous assumption that integration was tantamount to "race-mixing." Further, in *Color and Conscience: The Irrepressible Conflict* (1946), Buell G. Gallagher concluded that institutionalized white supremacy simply could no longer be supported in the United States.

As the United States lurched toward the dawn of the civil rights era, racist appeals to white solidarity in the face of the twin threats of social equality and intermarriage (e.g., A. E. Burgess's *What Price Integration?* [1956], Powless Lanier's *Will Desegregation Desegregate the South?* [1957], and Herman E. Talmadge's *You and Segregation* [1955]) were increasingly overshadowed by scholarly exposés of sexual hysteria as endemic to white racism (e.g., Gordon W. Allport's *Nature of Prejudice* [1954], Wilbur J. Cash's *Mind of the South* [1954], Jess Walter Dees, Jr. and James S. Hadley's *Jim Crow* [1951], Oscar Handlin's *Race and Nationality in American Life* [1957], and John Bartholomew Martin's *Deep South Says "Never"* [1957]). By the 1960s, with the civil rights era in full bloom, books on sexuality and race written *by* African Americans *about* African Americans began to dominate the literature; whereas white racist warnings about the horrors of "race-mixing" were notably absent from the literature.

Some of the works by African American authors concerning sexuality and race during the heyday of the civil rights era did little to challenge prevailing racist and sexist stereotypes. For example, in *Soul on Ice* (1968), Eldridge Cleaver boasted about procuring—and sometimes raping—white women. In *Home: Social Essays* (1966), Le Roi Jones accurately called attention to white males' tendency to sexually mutilate black male lynching victims; yet Jones's homophobic musings conjured up images of the hypermasculine black male. However, the most remarkable aspect of the African American literature on sexuality and race was the infusion of new perspectives into subject matter that had been the subject of scholarly and popular inquiry predating the birth of key disciplines such as psychology and sociology.

In *The Fire Next Time* (1963), James Baldwin pointedly warned white America that a racial Armageddon could easily engulf the United States—not as a result of black men and white men competing for the affections of white women but, rather, as a result of whites' inflammatory denigration of blacks fueling blacks' smoldering resentment. In *Black Man's Burden* (1965), John Oliver Killens—who, incidentally, drew liberally upon James Baldwin's writings—noted that none of the documents of major civil rights organizations (e.g., NAACP, Urban League, SNCC, CORE) lent support to white segregationists' claims that the "real" goal of leaders in the civil rights movement was to mate with white women. In *The Wretched of the Earth* (1968), Frantz Fanon ushered in scholarship on the psychology of the oppressed. Further, in *Black Rage* (1968), William Grier and Price Cobbs described white racism as a disease that can, upon "infecting" African Americans psychologically, lead to serious sexual dysfunctionality among African Americans.

An especially vivid illustration of the changes in scholarship on sexuality and race that were precipitated by the civil rights movement was the response of African American social scientists to Daniel Patrick Moynihan's controversial treatise, *The Negro Family: The Case for National Action* (1965). Drawing upon black sociologist E. Franklin Frazier's *Negro Family in the United States* (1939), Moynihan blamed the relatively high incidence of out-of-wedlock births and father-absent homes upon the pathology presumably inherent in (and unique to) African American families as a whole. In an earlier era, Moynihan's (1965) assertions might well have gone unchallenged. By the late 1960s, however, the black power movement prompted many African American students across the nation to call for the establishment of African American studies departments and programs. Within this sociopolitical and intellectual context, Andrew Billingsley's *Black Families in White America* (1968) identified many of the adaptive (rather than maladaptive) features of African American families and communities. Furthermore, Alphonso Pinkney's *Black Americans* (1969) demonstrated that, after controlling for socioeconomic status, the gap between black females' and white females' out-of-wedlock births (and, consequently, father-absent homes) disappeared.

Perhaps the most influential book on sexuality and race published during the civil rights era was Calvin C. Hernton's *Sex and Racism in America* (1965/ 1988). Using case studies combined with his own recollections regarding interactions with white women over the years, Hernton provided an unflinching account of the subtle and not-so-subtle ways in which white racism looms as a constant threat to non-intimate as well as intimate mixed-sex, mixed-race interactions, especially those interactions involving black women and white men. Hernton (1965/1988) also described the myriad societal conventions that allow white men to regard white women *and* black women as potentially theirs for the taking, simultaneously placing the onus upon black men to conceal or deny any hint of sexual attraction toward white women. Moreover, Hernton offered insight into the ways in which many white men's fears of sexual inadequacy lead them to put overt and covert pressure on white women to conceal or deny any hint of sexual attraction toward black men.

According to Elisabeth Young-Bruehl in *The Anatomy of Prejudices* (1996), Hernton (1965/1988) gave voice to black male heterosexuality in a frank, authentic, and scholarly manner. On the one hand, Hernton did not deal with homosexuality—among black men *or* white men—to the same extent as did James Baldwin or Frantz Fanon. On the other hand, Hernton did not lapse into the homophobic prose of Le Roi Jones or Eldridge Cleaver. Hernton's (1965/ 1988) work has influenced an entire generation of scholars, black as well as white, writing on the topic of sexuality and race (e.g., Thomas Kochman, *Black and White Styles in Conflict* [1981]; Robert Staples and Leanor Boulin Johnson, *Black Families at the Crossroads* [1993]; see also Hans J. Massaquoi in *The White Problem in America* [1966]; Elisabeth Young-Bruehl, *The Anatomy of Prejudices* [1996]).

Perhaps the biggest criticism that can be made regarding Hernton's work is that Hernton, like many other African American male writers before and since, paid relatively little attention to the psychosexual experiences (whether heterosexual or homosexual) of African American women. Fortunately, post–civil rights, post–women's rights era scholarship on sexuality and race has increasingly given voice to African American women's psychosexual experiences, as is evident from books such as Joyce Ladner's *Tomorrow's Tomorrow: The Black Woman* (1971), Michele Wallace's *Black Macho and the Myth of the Superwoman* (1979), Paula Giddings's *When and Where I Enter: The Impact of Black Women on Race and Sex in America* (1984), and bell hooks's *Black Looks: Race and Representation* (1992). Within this newly developed area of the literature on sexuality and race, one primary theme is African American women's quest for affirmation of their beauty and sexuality in a society laden with images of European American women as the models of physical attractiveness.

At the present time, the literature on black male and female homosexuality is still in development. However, edited volumes such as Johnnetta B. Cole's *All American Women: Lines That Divide, Ties That Bind* (1986); John C. Fout and Maura Shaw Tantillo's *American Sexual Politics: Sex, Gender, and Race since the Civil War* (1993); and Alberto Gonzalez, Marsha Houston, and Victoria Chen's *Our Voices: Essays in Culture, Ethnicity, and Communication* (1997) provide glimpses into the psychosexual lives of black gay men and lesbians. Additional topics likely to gain prominence within the literature on sexuality and race in the years to come include "colorism" as an influence on perceptions of physical attractiveness among African Americans, as is clear from works such as Roy L. Brooks's *Integration or Separation? A Strategy for Racial Equality* (1996).

One of the most refreshing changes wrought by post–civil rights, post–women's rights era scholarship on sexuality and race is the emergence of a well-defined literature on black male-female romantic relationships. Perhaps the most influential social scientist in this area of inquiry has been Robert Staples, who has made numerous contributions as a solo author (e.g., *The World of Black Singles: Changing Patterns of Male-Female Relations* [1981]; *Black Masculinity: The Black Man's Role in American Society* [1982]) and as an editor and coauthor (e.g., *The Black Family: Essays and Studies* [1994]; see also Staples and Johnson, 1993). Staples's work consistently has shown that on average, black men and women display the same range of sexual practices and experiences as do white men and women. Thus, the image of black men and black women as would-be "studs" and "Sapphires"—immortalized in the mass media, for better or worse, as documented by Lerone Bennett, Jr.'s *Challenge of Blackness* (1972) and by Ernest Kaiser's edited volume *A Freedomways Reader: Afro-America in the Seventies* (1977)—clearly does not conform to psychosexual reality.

A related trend in the literature on sexuality and race is the attempt to eradicate the negative stereotype of black women as domineering, desexed "mammy" figures with a more positive (and accurate) portrayal of black women as sensual, sensitive, and nurturant partners in African American romantic relationships. Examples of this new scholarship include Molefi K. Asante's *Afrocentricity* (1988), Delores Aldridge's *Focusing: Black Male-Female Relationships* (1991), and Stanley O. Gaines, Jr.'s *Culture, Ethnicity, and Personal Relationship Processes* (1997). Interestingly, some of the most widely heralded post–civil rights scholarship on interracial marriages—specifically, Ernest Porterfield's *Black and White Mixed Marriages* (1978) and Paul Rosenblatt, Teri Karis, and Richard Powell's *Multiracial Couples: Black and White Voices* (1995)—also has helped eradicate the "mammy" image within the literature on sexuality and race.

Yet another emergent area of scholarly inquiry on sexuality and race is the psychosocial and psychosexual experience of biracial and multiracial individuals—the much-maligned "mongrels," as white racists commonly called them. Books such as Paul R. Spickard's *Mixed Blood: Intermarriage and Ethnic Identity in Twentieth-Century America* (1989), Lise Funderburg's *Black, White, Other: Biracial Americans Talk about Race and Identity* (1994), and edited volumes such as Maria P. P. Root's *Racially Mixed People in America* (1992) and *The Multiracial Experience: Racial Borders as the New Frontier* (1996) have helped transform the products of interracial sex and marriage into living, breathing individuals within the extant literature. Furthermore, these and other books indicate that black-white and other interracial unions need not be avoided simply because of lingering stereotypes about biracial and multiracial persons as physically, intellectually, or morally "defective."

In closing, as Staples and Johnson (1993) pointed out, the definitive book on black sexuality has yet to be written. All too often, caricatures and myths have been allowed by liberals and conservatives alike to hold sway over empirical studies as "authoritative" accounts of black men and women as sexual beings. If the state of the literature on sexuality and race at the close of the twentieth century is any indication, the literature during the infancy of the next millennium is likely to offer increasingly diverse, authentic, and accurate depictions of black male and female sexuality.

BIBLIOGRAPHY

Adams, R. *Interracial Marriage in Hawaii: A Study of the Mutually Conditioned Processes of Acculturation and Amalgamation.* New York: Macmillan, 1937.

Aldridge, Delores P. *Focusing: Black Male-Female Relationships.* Chicago: Third World Press, 1991.

Allport, Gordon W. *The Nature of Prejudice.* Cambridge, MA: Addison-Wesley, 1954/ 1979.

Aptheker, Herbert. *Anti-racism in U.S. History: The First Two Hundred Years.* New York: Greenwood Press, 1992.

Asante, Molefi K. *Afrocentricity.* Trenton, NJ: Africa World Press, 1988.

Awkward, Michael. *Negotiating Difference: Race, Gender, and the Politics of Positionality.* Chicago: University of Chicago Press, 1995.

Baldwin, James. *The Fire Next Time.* New York: Dial, 1963.

Bancroft, Hubert Howe. *Retrospection, Political and Personal.* New York: Bancroft Co., 1912.

Bell, A., and M. Weinberg. *Homosexualities.* New York: Simon and Schuster, 1978.

Belton, Don, ed. *Speak My Name: Black Men on Masculinity and the American Dream.* Boston: Beacon Press, 1995.

Bennett, Lerone, Jr. *The Challenge of Blackness.* Chicago: Johnson Publishing Co., 1972.

———. *Before the Mayflower: A History of Black America,* 6th ed. New York: Penguin Press, 1993.

Berger, Maurice, Brian Wallis, and Simon Watson, eds. *Constructing Masculinity.* New York: Routledge, 1995.

Berlin, Ira. *Slaves without Masters: The Free Negro in the Antebellum South.* New York: Pantheon, 1974.

Bilbo, Theodore G. *Take Your Choice: Separation or Mongrelization.* Poplarville, MS: Dream House, 1947.

Billingsley, Andrew, with Amy Tate Billingsley. *Black Families in White America.* Englewood Cliffs, NJ: Prentice-Hall, 1968.

Bowers, Claude G. *The Tragic Era.* Cambridge, MA: Library Guild of America, 1929.

Brooks, Roy L. *Integration or Separation? A Strategy for Racial Equality.* Cambridge, MA: Harvard University Press, 1996.

Brown, Ira Corinne. *The Story of the American Negro.* New York: Friendship Press, 1936.

———. *Race Relations in a Democracy.* New York: Harper and Row, 1949.

———. *Understanding Race Relations.* Englewood Cliffs, NJ: Prentice-Hall, 1973.

Bruce, Philip Alexander. *The Plantation Negro as a Freeman.* New York: G. P. Putnam's Sons, 1889.

Bryce, James. *The Relations of the Advanced and Backward Races of Mankind.* Oxford: Clarendon Press, 1902.

Burgess, A. E. *What Price Integration?* Dallas: American Guild Press, 1956.

Cade, Toni, ed. *The Black Woman: An Anthology.* New York: Signet, 1970.

Calhoun, A. W. *A Social History of the American Family.* New York: Barnes and Noble, 1917.

Calhoun, William P. *The Caucasian and the Negro in the United States.* Columbia, SC: Bryan, 1902.

Calvin, Ira. *The Lost White Race.* Brookline, MA: Countway-White, 1945.

Carroll, Charles. *The Tempter of Eve.* St. Louis: Adamic Publishing Co., 1902.

Case, Sue-Ellen, Philip Brett, and Susan Leigh Foster, eds. *Cruising the Performative: Interventions into the Representation of Ethnicity, Nationality, and Sexuality.* Bloomington; Indiana University Press, 1995.

Cash, Wilbur J. *The Mind of the South.* New York: Doubleday and Co., 1954.

Cassius, Elders R. *The Third Birth of a Nation.* Cincinnati: F. L. Rowe, 1920.

Centers for Disease Control. *HIV and AIDS Surveillance Report.* Atlanta: Centers for Disease Control, 1991.

Champly, H. *White Women, Coloured Men.* London: J. Long, 1939.

Cheah, Pheng, David Fraser, and Judith Grbich, eds. *Thinking through the Body of the Law.* New York: New York University Press, 1996.

Cleaver, Eldridge. *Soul on Ice.* New York: McGraw-Hill, 1968.

Cole, Johnnetta B. *All American Women: Lines That Divide, Ties That Bind.* New York: Free Press, 1986.

Coody, Archibald, IV. *The Race Question.* Vicksburg, MS: Mississippi Printing Co., 1944.

Cose, Ellis. *Color-Blind: Seeing beyond Race in a Race-Obsessed World*. New York: HarperCollins, 1997.

Cox, Earnest S. *White America*. Richmond, VA: White America Society, 1923.

Cox, Oliver C. *Race Relations: Elements and Social Dynamics*. Detroit: Wayne State University Press, 1976.

Crohn, Joel. *Mixed Matches: How to Create Successful Interracial, Interethnic, and Interfaith Relationships*. New York: Fawcett Columbine, 1995.

Daniels, Jessie. *White Lies: Race, Class, Gender, and Sexuality in White Supremacist Discourse*. Now York: Routledge, 1997.

Darwin, Leonard. *What Is Eugenics?* New York: Galton, 1929.

Davie, Maurice R. *Negroes in American Society*. New York: McGraw-Hill, 1949.

Davis, Angela. *Women, Race, and Class*. New York: Random House, 1983.

Dees, Jess Walter, Jr., and James S. Hadley. *Jim Crow*. Ann Arbor, MI: Ann Arbor Publishers, 1951.

de Tocqueville, Alexis. *Democracy in America*. New York: G. Adlard, 1838.

Deutsch, Morton, and Mary Evans Collins. *Interracial Housing: A Psychological Evaluation of a Social Experiment*. Minneapolis: University of Minnesota Press, 1951.

Dingwall, E. J. *Racial Pride and Prejudice*. London: Watts, 1946.

Dollard, John. *Caste and Class in a Southern Town*. New York: Harper and Brothers, 1937.

Dowd, Jerome. *The Negro in American Life*. New York: Century, 1926.

Drake, St. Clair, and Horace Cayton. *Black Metropolis: A Study of Negro Life in a Northern City*. New York: Harcourt, Brace and Co., 1945.

Du Bois, William Edward Burghardt. *The Souls of Black Folk*. New York: Signet, 1903/ 1969.

———. *Writings*. New York: Library of America, 1986.

Eggleston, Edward B. *The Ultimate Solution of the Negro Problem*. Boston: R. G. Badger, 1913.

Evans, Brenda J., and James R. Whitfield, eds. *Black Males in the United States: An Annotated Bibliography from 1967 to 1987*. Washington, DC: American Psychological Association, 1988.

Evans, Maurice S. *Black and White in the Southern States*. London: Longmans, Green and Co., 1915.

Falconbridge, Alexander. *An Account of the Slave Trade on the Coast of Africa*. London: J. Phillips, 1788.

Fanon, Frantz. *The Wretched of the Earth*. New York: Grove, 1968.

Fout, John C., and Maura Shaw Tantillo, eds. *American Sexual Politics: Sex, Gender, and Race since the Civil War*. Chicago: University of Chicago Press, 1993.

Franklin, John Hope. *From Slavery to Freedom: A History of American Negroes*. New York: Knopf, 1947.

Frazier, E. Franklin. *The Free Negro Family: A Study of Family Origins before the Civil War*. Nashville: Fisk University Press, 1932.

———. *The Negro Family in the United States*. Chicago: University of Chicago Press, 1939.

Frazier, Thomas R., ed. *Afro-American History: Primary Sources*. Chicago: Dorsey Press, 1988.

Fredrickson, George M. *The Black Image in the White Mind: The Debate on Afro-American Character and Destiny, 1817–1914*. New York: Harper and Row, 1971.

Freud, Sigmund. *Totem and Taboo*. New York: Vintage, 1918/1946.

Fulks, Bryan. *Black Struggle: A History of the Negro in America*. New York: Delacorte Press, 1969.

Funderberg, J. H. *The March of the Negro*. Boston: Christopher, 1945.

Funderburg, Lise. *Black White, Other: Biracial Americans Talk about Race and Identity*. New York: W. Morrow and Co., 1994.

Gaines, Stanley O., Jr., with Raymond Buriel, James H. Lui, and Diana I. Ríos. *Culture, Ethnicity, and Personal Relationship Processes*. New York: Routledge, 1997.

Gaines, Stanley O., Jr., and William Ickes. "Perspectives on Interracial Relationships." In *Handbook of Personal Relationships: Theory, Research, and Interventions*, 2nd ed., ed. Steve Duck, 197–220. Chichester: John Wiley and Sons, 1997.

Gallagher, Buell G. *Color and Conscience: The Irrepressible Conflict*. New York: Harper and Brothers, 1946.

Giddings, Paula. *When and Where I Enter: The Impact of Black Women on Race and Sex in America*. New York: Morrow, 1984.

Gilligan, Francis J. *The Morality of the Color Line*. Washington, DC: Catholic University of America Press, 1928.

Gilman, Sander L. *Difference and Pathology: Stereotypes of Sexuality, Race, and Madness*. Ithaca, NY: Cornell University Press, 1985.

Goldstein, Naomi Friedman. *The Roots of Prejudice against the Negro in the United States*. Boston: Boston University Press, 1948.

Gonzalez, Alberto, Marsha Houston, and Victoria Chen, eds. *Our Voices: Essays in Culture, Ethnicity, and Communication*, 2nd ed. Los Angeles: Roxbury Press, 1997.

Gordon, A. I. *Intermarriage*. Boston: Beacon, 1964.

Grier, William, and Price Cobbs. *Black Rage*. New York: Basic Books, 1968.

Guerrero, Ed. *Framing Blackness: The African American Image in Film*. Philadelphia: Temple University Press, 1993.

Gunther, Lenworth, ed. *Black Image: Eyewitness Accounts of Afro-American Life*. Port Washington, NY: Kennikat Press, 1978.

Gutman, Herbert G. *The Black Family in Slavery and Freedom, 1750–1925*. New York: Pantheon, 1976.

Hacker, Andrew. *Two Nations: Black and White, Separate, Hostile, Unequal*. New York: Charles Scribner's Sons, 1992.

Hall, Christine, C. Iijima, Brenda J. Evans, and Stephanie Selice, eds. *Black Females in the United States: A Bibliography from 1967 to 1987*. Washington, DC: American Psychological Association, 1989.

Haller, M. H. *Eugenics: Hereditarian Attitudes in American Thought*. New Brunswick: Rutgers, 1963.

Halsey, Margaret. *Color Blind: A White Woman Looks at the Negro*. New York: Simon and Schuster, 1946.

Handlin, Oscar. *Race and Nationality in American Life*. Boston: Little, Brown, 1957.

Harrison, Algea Othella. "Contraception: Practices and Attitudes in the Black Community." In *Black Families*, 3rd ed., ed. Harriette McAdoo, 301–19. Thousand Oaks, CA: Sage, 1997.

Hart, Albert Bushnell. *The Southern South*. New York: Appleton and Co., 1912.

Helm, Mary. *From Darkness to Light: The Story of Negro Progress*. New York: Fleming H. Nevell, 1909.

————. *The Upward Path: The Evolution of a Race*. Young People's Missionary Movement of the United States and Canada, 1909.

Helper, Hinton Rowan. *The Negroes in Negroland*. New York: G. W. Carleton, 1868.

Hendricks, Margo, and Patricia Parker. *Women, "Race," and Writing in the Early Modern Period*. New York: Routledge, 1994.

Hernton, Calvin C. *Sex and Racism in America*. Garden City, New York: Doubleday and Company, 1965.

————. *White Pages for White Americans*. Westport, CT: Greenwood Press, 1966.

Herskovitz, Melville J. *The Anthropometry of the American Negro*. New York: Columbia University Press, 1930.

Hill, Robert Bernard. *Research on the African-American Family: A Holistic Perspective*. Westport, CT: Auburn House, 1993.

Hoffman, Frederick L. *Race Traits and Tendencies of the American Negro*. New York: Macmillan, 1896.

Holmes, S. J. *Studies in Evolution and Eugenics*. London: George Boutledge and Sons, 1923.

hooks, bell. *Black Looks: Race and Representation*. Boston: South End Press, 1992.

Hopson, D. S., and D. P. Hopson. *Friends, Lovers, and Soul Mates: A Guide to Better Relationships between Black Men and Women*. New York: Fireside, 1995.

Jennings, H. S. *The Biological Basis of Human Nature*. New York: Morton, 1930.

Johnson, Franklin. *The Development of State Legislation concerning the Free Negro*. Westport, CT: Greenwood Press, 1919/1979.

Johnson, James Weldon. *Along This Way: The Autobiography of James Weldon Johnson*. New York: Viking Press, 1933.

Johnston, James Hugo. *Miscegenation in the Ante-bellum South*. Chicago: University of Chicago Press, 1939.

Jones, Le Roi. *Home: Social Essays*. New York: Morrow, 1966.

Jordan, Winthrop D. *White over Black: American Attitudes toward the Negro, 1550–1812*. Chapel Hill; University of North Carolina Press, 1968.

June, Lee N., ed. *The Black Family: Past, Present, and Future*. Grand Rapids, MI: Zondervan Publishing House, 1991.

Kaiser, Ernest, ed. *A Freedomways Reader: Afro-America in the Seventies*. New York: International Publishers, 1977.

Katz, William Loren, ed. *Proceedings of the National Negro Conference, 1909*. New York: Arno Press and the *New York Times*, 1969.

Keita, Gwendolyn Puryear, and Anne C. O. Petersen. *Blacks in the United States: Abstracts of the Psychological and Behavioral Literature, 1987–1995*. Washington, DC: American Psychological Association, 1996.

Killens, John Oliver. *Black Man's Burden*. New York: Trident Press, 1965.

Klineberg, Otto, ed. *Characteristics of the American Negro*. New York: Harper and Brothers, 1944.

Kochman, Thomas. *Black and White Styles in Conflict*. Chicago: University of Chicago Press, 1981.

Kulikoff, Allan. *Tobacco and Slaves: The Development of Southern Cultures in the Chesapeake, 1680–1800*. Chapel Hill: University of North Carolina Press, 1986.

Ladner, Joyce. *Tomorrow's Tomorrow: The Black Woman*. New York: Doubleday, 1971.

La Farge, John. *Interracial Justice*. New York: America Press, 1937.

Lanier, Powless. *Will Desegregation Desegregate the South?* New York: Exposition Press, 1957.

Lester, Julius. *Falling Pieces of the Broken Sky.* New York: Arcade, 1990.

Liebow, Elliot. *Tally's Corner.* Boston: Little, Brown, 1966.

Lincoln, C. Eric. *Race, Religion, and the Continuing American Dilemma.* New York: Hill and Wang, 1984.

Lister, L., ed. *Human Sexuality, Ethnoculture, and Social Work.* New York: Haworth Press, 1986.

Loye, David. *The Healing of a Nation.* New York: W. W. Norton, 1971.

Lyman, Stanford M. *The Black American in Sociological Thought: New Perspectives on Black America.* New York: Capricorn Books, 1973.

Mandell, Nancy. *Feminist Issues: Race, Gender, and Sexuality in the Colonial Conquest.* Scarborough, Ontario: Prentice-Hall, 1995.

Martin, John Bartholomew. *The Deep South Says "Never."* New York: Ballantine, 1957.

Massaquoi, Hans J. "Would You Want Your Daughter to Marry One?" In *The White Problem in America*, ed. Herbert Nipson, 65–78. Chicago: Johnson Publishing, 1966.

McClintock, Anne. *Imperial Leather: Race, Gender, and Sexuality in the Colonial Conquest.* New York: Routledge, 1995.

McKinney, T. T. *All White America.* Boston: Meador Publishing Co., 1937.

McPherson, James M. *The Struggle for Equality: Abolitionists and the Negro in the Civil War and Reconstruction.* Princeton, NJ: Princeton University Press, 1964.

Mecklin, John Moffatt. *Democracy and Race Friction: A Study in Social Ethics.* New York: Macmillan, 1921.

Moore, Kristin A., Margaret C. Simms, and Charles L. Betsey. *Choice and Circumstance: Racial Differences in Sexuality and Fertility.* New Brunswick, NJ: Transaction Books, 1986.

Moreno, J. L. *Who Shall Survive?* Washington, DC: Nervous and Mental Disease Publishing, 1934.

Morgan, Edmund S. *American Slavery, American Freedom: The Ordeal of Colonial Virginia.* New York: W. W. Norton, 1975.

Moynihan, Daniel Patrick. *The Negro Family: The Case for National Action.* Washington, DC: Office of Policy Planning and Research, U.S. Department of Labor, 1965.

Mura, David. *Where the Body Meets Memory: An Odyssey of Race, Sexuality, and Identity.* New York: Anchor Books, 1996.

Myrdal, Gunnar, with Richard Sterner, and Arnold Rose. *An American Dilemma: The Negro Problem and Modern Democracy.* New York: Harper and Row, 1944.

National Research Council. *A Common Destiny: Blacks and American Society.* Washington, DC: National Academy Press, 1989.

Newby, I. A. *Jim Crow's Defense: Anti-Negro Thought in America, 1900–1930.* Baton Rouge: Louisiana State University Press, 1973.

Norwood, Thomas N. *Address on the Negro.* Savannah, GA: Braid and Hutton, 1908.

Patterson, Raymond. *The Negro and His Needs.* Freeport, NY: Books for Libraries Press, 1911/1971.

Peters, William. *The Southern Temper.* Garden City, NY: Doubleday and Co., 1959.

Pettigrew, Thomas F. *A Profile of the Negro American.* Princeton, NJ: D. Van Nostrand, 1964.

Pettigrew, Thomas P. "Integration and Pluralism." In *Eliminating Racism: Profiles in Controversy*, ed. Phyllis A. Katz and Dalmas A. Taylor, 19–30. New York: Plenum, 1988.

Pickett, William P. *The Negro Problem: Abraham Lincoln's Solution*. New York: G. P. Putman's Sons, 1909.

Pierce, Julius A. *Black Tide*. Birmingham, AL: Jamax Books, 1963.

Pietropinto, A., and J. Simenauer. *Beyond the Male Myth*. New York: Quadrangle, 1977.

Pinkney, Alphonso. *Black Americans*. Englewood Cliffs, NJ: Prentice-Hall, 1969.

Porterfield, Ernest. *Black and White Mixed Marriages*. Chicago: Nelson-Hall, 1978.

Priest, Josiah. *Slavery, as It Relates to the Negro or African Race*. Albany, NY: C. Van Benthuysen, 1843.

Quimby, Watson E. *Mongrelism*. Wilmington, DE: James and Webb, 1876.

Reuter, Edward Byron. *The American Race Problem: A Study of the Negro*. New York: Thomas Y. Crowell, 1927.

———. *The Mulatto in the United States*. Boston: Richard G. Badger, 1918.

Rodgers-Rose, La Francis, ed. *The Black Woman*. Newbury Park, CA: Sage, 1980.

Root, Maria P. P., ed. *Racially Mixed People in America*. Newbury Park, CA: Sage, 1992.

———. *The Multiracial Experience: Racial Borders as the New Frontier*. Thousand Oaks, CA: Sage, 1996.

Rosenblatt, Paul C., Teri A. Karis, and Richard D. Powell. *Multiracial Couples: Black and White Voices*. Thousand Oaks, CA: Sage, 1995.

Rush, Sheila, and Chris Clark. *How to Get Along with Black People*. New York: Third Press, 1971.

Sanjek, Roger. "Intermarriage." In *Race*, ed. Steven Gregory and Roger Sanjek, 103–30. New Brunswick, NJ: Rutgers University Press, 1994.

Seligmann, Herbert J. *The Negro Faces America*. New York: Harper and Brothers, 1920.

Shufeldt, R. W. *The Negro: A Menace to American Civilization*. Boston: Gorman Press, 1907.

———. *America's Greatest Problem: The Negro*. Philadelphia: F. A. Davis Co., 1915.

Simmons, Enoch Spencer. *A Solution of the Race Problem in the South*. Raleigh, NC: Edwards and Broughton, 1898.

Simmons, William Joseph. *The Klan Unmasked*. Atlanta: Thompson Publishing Co., 1924.

Smith, Ann Marie. *New Right Discourse on Race and Sexuality: Britain, 1968–1990*. New York: Cambridge University Press, 1994.

Smith, John David, ed. *Anti-Black Thought, 1863–1925*. Vols. 6–8. New York: Garland Publishing, 1993.

Sobel, Mechal. *The World They Made Together: Black and White Values in Eighteenth-Century Virginia*. Princeton, NJ: Princeton University Press, 1987.

Spickard, Paul R. *Mixed Blood: Intermarriage and Ethnic Identity in Twentieth-Century America*. Madison: University of Wisconsin Press, 1989.

Stampp, Kenneth M. *The Peculiar Institution*. New York: Knopf, 1956.

Staples, Robert. *The World of Black Singles: Changing Patterns of Male-Female Relations*. Westport, CT: Greenwood Press, 1981.

———. *Black Masculinity: The Black Man's Role in American Society*. San Francisco: Black Scholar Press, 1982.

———, ed. *The Black Family: Essays and Studies*, 5th ed. Belmont, CA: Wadsworth, 1994.

Staples, Robert, and Johnson, Leanor Boulin. *Black Families at the Crossroads: Challenges and Prospects*. San Francisco: Jossey-Bass, 1993.

Stember, Charles H. *Sexual Racism*. New York: Harper and Row, 1976.

Stoler, Ann Laura. *Race and the Education of Desire: Foucault's History of Sexuality and the Colonial Order of Things*. Durham, NC: Duke University Press, 1995.

Talmadge, Herman E. *You and Segregation*. Birmingham, AL: Vulcan Press, 1955.

Terkel, Studs. *Race: How Blacks and Whites Think and Feel about the American Obsession*. New York: W. W. Norton, 1992.

Terry, Jennifer, and Jacqueline Urla, eds. *Deviant Bodies: Critical Perspectives on Difference in Science and Popular Culture*. Bloomington; Indiana University Press, 1995.

Tetreault, Mary Ann, ed. *Women and Revolution in Africa, Asia, and the New World*. Columbia; University of South Carolina Press, 1994.

Thomas, William Hannibal. *The American Negro: What He Was, What He Is, and What He May Become*. New York: Macmillan, 1901.

Villa, Louis Arthur. *The Sexuality of a Black American: One Man's Sexual Biography*. Oakland, CA: Ashford Press, 1981.

Wallace, Michele. *Black Macho and the Myth of the Superwoman*. New York: Dial Press, 1979.

Washington, Booker T. *Up from Slavery*. New York: Doubleday, 1901.

Washington, Joseph R., Jr. *Marriage in Black and White*. Boston: Beacon, 1970.

Weatherford, W. D. *Negro Life in the South*. New York: Association Press, 1918.

Weaver, Toni E. *White to White on Black/White*. Vandalia, OH: Voices Publishing, 1993.

Weyl, Nathaniel, and William Marina. *American Statesmen on Slavery and the Negro*. New Rochelle, NY: Arlington House, 1971.

White, Joseph L., and Thomas A. Parham. *The Psychology of Blacks: An African-American Perspective*, 2nd ed. Englewood Cliffs, NJ: Prentice-Hall, 1990.

Wilkinson, Doris. "Gender and Social Inequality: The Prevailing Social Significance of Race." In *An American Dilemma Revisited: Race Relations in a Changing World*, ed. Obie Clayton, Jr., 288–300. New York: Russell Sage Foundation, 1996.

Williams, C. W. *Black Teenage Mothers: Pregnancy and Child Rearing from Their Perspective*. Lexington, MA: Lexington Books, 1991.

Williams, Vernon J., Jr. *From Caste to a Minority: Changing Attitudes of American Sociologists toward Afro-Americans, 1896–1945*. Westport, CT: Greenwood Press, 1989.

Williamson, Joel. *New People: Miscegenation and Mulattos in the United States*. New York: Free Press, 1980.

Wood, Forrest G. *Black Scare: The Racist Response to Emancipation and Reconstruction*. Berkeley: University of California Press, 1968.

Wood, Peter H. *Black Majority: Negroes in Colonial South Carolina from 1670 through the Stono Rebellion*. New York: Knopf, 1975.

Woodson, Carter G. *The Negro in Our History*, 7th ed. Washington, DC: Associated Publishers, 1941.

Young, Carlene, ed. *Black Experience: Analysis and Synthesis*. San Rafael, CA: Lesuring Press, 1972.

Young, Lola. *Fear of the Dark: "Race," Gender, and Sexuality in the Cinema*. New York: Routledge, 1996.

Young, Wayland. *Eros Denied: Sex in Western Society*. New York: Grove Press, 1964.

Young-Bruehl, Elisabeth. *The Anatomy of Prejudices*. Cambridge, MA: Harvard University Press, 1996.

Zack, Naomi. *Race and Mixed Race*. Philadelphia: Temple University Press, 1993.

Zinn, Howard. *The Southern Mystique*. New York: Alfred A. Knopf, 1964.

XV

African American Consumerism

Robert E. Weems, Jr.

Like other groups, African Americans have been profoundly affected by the growth and entrenchment of mass consumer culture in twentieth-century America. Still, there exists a relative dearth of studies related to black consumerism, especially during the first decades of the century.

African Americans' overall subjugated position at the turn of the century helps explain the limited attention their consumption patterns attracted. Although involuntary servitude ended in 1865, a significant number of blacks remained de facto slaves (as peons and sharecroppers) in the southern agricultural economy. Moreover, any group desire for upward mobility appeared thwarted by the existence of American apartheid, popularly known as Jim Crow. Consequently, many white businesses all but dismissed the role and potential of African American consumers. This is further borne out, as documented in Marilyn Kern-Foxworth's 1994 book *Aunt Jemima, Uncle Ben, and Rastus: Blacks in Advertising, Yesterday, Today, and Tomorrow*, by the then proliferation of products whose trade names included such racially derogatory terms as *mammy, pickaninny, coon,* and *nigger.*

Notwithstanding whites' failure to consider early-twentieth-century black economic activity seriously, African American researchers did document increasing black wealth accumulation. Moreover, those blacks who amassed assets during what has been called the nadir of the postslavery African American experience formed the cornerstone of an observable black consumer market.

Booker T. Washington's 1907 book, *The Negro in Business*, provided an important window to observe turn-of-the-twentieth-century African American economic development. Among other things, Washington proudly chronicled the dramatic rise in black home ownership since 1860. Similarly, William Edward Burghardt Du Bois's 1907 book *Economic Cooperation among Negroes* and his May 1909 *World's Work* article entitled "Georgia Negroes and Their Fifty Millions of Savings" demonstrated group economic progress despite obvious obstacles.

Perhaps the most important documentation of the economic progress of early-twentieth-century black America was the *Negro Year Book and Annual Encyclopedia of the Negro*. First published in 1912 by Monroe Work, Tuskegee Institute's director of research, until its demise in the 1950s this resource provided an impressive overview of the African American experience.

The first five editions of the *Negro Year Book*—1912; 1913; 1914–15; 1916–17; 1918–19—documented such things as black ownership of 31,000 square miles of southern farmland (an area almost equal to that of Vermont, New Hampshire, Massachusetts, Connecticut, and Rhode Island); impressive post-slavery black wealth accumulation and educational achievement as compared to the wealth and education of emancipated Russian serfs; and black-owned businesses' $1.2 billion in annual sales by World War I.

In addition to witnessing the birth of the *Negro Year Book*, the second decade of the twentieth century featured the dramatic geographic relocation of African Americans known as the Great Migration. Between 1915 and 1918, coinciding with World War I, approximately 500,000 rural southern blacks migrated to northern and southern urban areas seeking employment in war-related industries. This proliferation of potential consumers in America's major markets contributed to American business' subsequent interest in reaching black shoppers.

Among the first national firms to target the embryonic black urban consumer market aggressively were record companies. Brian Rust's *American Record Label Book* (1978), Eileen Southern's *Music of Black Americans: A History* (1983), and Arnold Shaw's *Black Popular Music in America: From the Spirituals, Minstrels, and Ragtime to Soul, Disco, and Hip-Hop* (1986) discussed how such companies as OKeh, Paramount, Columbia, and the black-owned Black Swan Records developed the "Race" music genre to appeal to black lovers of blues and jazz.

. The major vehicle used by the recording industry during the 1920s to reach black consumers was the African American press. In fact, any business that sought black patronage viewed African American newspapers as a vital resource. As Frederick G. Detweiler's 1922 book *The Negro Press in America* revealed, much of the advertising in black newspapers during this period featured skin bleaches, hair straighteners, patent medicines, and dubious religious publications. Guy B. Johnson's May 1925 article in the *Journal of Social Forces* entitled "Negro Advertisements and Negro Culture" further corroborated Detweiler's earlier observations. Moreover, he asserted that much of the "respectable" advertising found in contemporary African American newspapers—placed by grocers, insurance companies, clothiers, real estate brokers, and educational institutions—were generated by black-owned businesses.

As rural southern blacks continued to stream into America's cities during the 1920s, their potential role as consumers attracted increased attention. H. A. Haring, a contributing editor to the advertising trade journal *Advertising & Selling*, emerged as one of the most notable researchers of black shoppers during this period. Significantly, his two articles, "Selling to Harlem" and "The Negro as Consumer," which appeared, respectively, in the October 31, 1928, and September 3, 1930, issues of *Advertising & Selling* were full of condescending remarks about African Americans. They nonetheless represented pioneering attempts to provide American corporations with market research about black consumers. Unlike H. A. Haring, whose conclusions regarding black consumers were often based upon anecdotal evidence tinged with condescension, Paul K. Edwards, a white professor of economics at Fisk University in Nashville, was a much more thorough and objective student of African American consumption. In fact, Edwards's 1932 book *The Southern Urban Negro as a Consumer* and his unpublished 1936 Harvard University dissertation entitled "Distinctive Characteristics of Urban Negro Consumption" represented the first truly systematic studies of African American consumers. Although Paul K. Edwards and H. A. Haring differed in their methodological rigor, they wrote for the same primary audience—the U.S. business community. Moreover, the clear thesis of the authors' publications was that the "Negro market" should be taken seriously as a source of potential corporate profits.

Among African Americans writing about the "Negro market" during the 1930s, Eugene Kinckle Jones's brief essay in the January 10, 1935, issue of *Domestic Commerce* would have a profound effect upon future black writing about black consumers. Jones, who then headed the U.S. Commerce Department's Division of Negro Affairs, consciously sought to convince white companies of the potential profits associated with courting African American consumers. Although this stance coincided with that of H. A. Haring and Paul K. Edwards, it differed considerably from that of such contemporary black writers as the National Negro Business League's Albon L. Holsey and the National Urban League's T. Arnold Hill, who discussed using black consumer dollars to enhance the black business community. Apparently, Jones and his ideological descendants believed that if U.S. corporations viewed the African American consumer market as a source of significant profits, it would enhance blacks' quest for full-fledged citizenship.

Besides a growing body of literature relating to African American consumers, the 1930s featured significant black consumer activism. A generation before the celebrated Montgomery Bus Boycott of 1955–1956, the various "Don't Buy Where You Can't Work" campaigns of the 1930s fired the imagination and initiative of the national African American community. Commencing in Chicago, this movement quickly spread to other cities. Whether blacks resided in Chicago, New York City, Cleveland, or Richmond, they suffered the same overt economic exploitation. White-owned business establishments, which all but monopolized the commercial life of African American enclaves, often refused to hire neighborhood residents.

Besides boycotting and picketing discriminatory white businesses—to force them to hire black personnel—some 1930s African American consumers ignored white businesses altogether and worked toward enhancing black business development. The Housewives' League of Detroit epitomized this trend.

As Darlene Clark Hine noted in her 1994 essay, "The Housewives' League of Detroit: Black Women and Economic Nationalism," the organization grew from 50 to 10,000 members between 1930 and 1935. To join the League, African American women pledged to support black businesses, to buy black-produced products, and to patronize black professionals. Considering that African American women generally coordinated their families' spending patterns, the League sought to mobilize this power toward community development. The evidence suggests that the Housewives' League of Detroit, along with similar organizations in Chicago, Baltimore, Washington, D.C., Cleveland, and New York City were indeed powerful forces in their respective communities.

Along with the various "Don't Buy Where You Can't Work" campaigns and the activities of local African American Housewives' Leagues, the 1930s featured growing interest in consumer cooperatives within the black community. For instance, J. G. St. Clair Drake's August 1936 *Opportunity* article entitled "Why Not Co-operate?" asserted that the widespread implementation and coordination of consumer cooperatives within the black community would substantially enhance the group's collective economic and political bargaining power.

Some of Drake's enthusiasm for black consumer cooperatives may be partially attributed to the noteworthy success of the Consumers' Cooperative Trading Company (CCTC) organized in Gary, Indiana, in 1932. Described by one observer as the "Miracle in Gary" in the September 1936 issue of *Forum & Century*, the CCTC experienced dramatic growth between 1932 and 1935. Starting as a buying club for fifteen families with initial working capital of $24, by 1935 there were more than 400 member families who coordinated a cooperative grocery store, a community credit union, and a cooperative ice cream and candy shop run entirely by children.

Stimulated by a robust wartime economy, the 1940s witnessed an acceleration of African American migration to northern, southern, and western cities as well as an acceleration of U.S. business interest in the "Negro market." Moreover, to assist those white companies interested in courting blacks, business periodicals featured an increasing number of articles related to black consumers.

David J. Sullivan, an African American pioneer in the field of market research, emerged as the country's leading expert on black consumer activity during World War II. During this period, he published several widely read articles and demographic and statistical profiles of black consumers. His most important contributions were "Don't Do This—if You Want to Sell Your Products to Negroes!" which appeared in the March 1, 1943, issue of *Sales Management*; "The American Negro—an 'Export' Market at Home," which appeared in the July 21, 1944, issue of *Printer's Ink*; and "How Negroes Spent Their Incomes, 1920–1943," a path-breaking statistical table that appeared in the June 15, 1945, issue of *Sales Management*.

Whereas Sullivan's work, like that of Harings, Edwards, and Jones, appeared to be aimed at a corporate audience, Richard Sterner and his colleagues' 1943 book, *The Negro's Share: A Study of Income, Consumption, Housing, and Public Assistance*, seemed written for government policy makers. This monograph was, in fact, part of the larger *Negro in America* research project funded by the Carnegie Corporation and coordinated by Gunnar Myrdal. Sterner's effort, which included the collaboration of other scholars, focused on racial differences related to income and consumption. The study asserted that raising the African American standard of living could be construed as altruistic and as a potentially profitable investment in human capital.

The years immediately following World War II witnessed an increasing number of American businesses, from major league baseball teams to radio stations, that actively sought the patronage of black consumers. For instance, Jackie Robinson's joining the Brooklyn Dodgers in 1947 represented both a source of pride for African Americans and a box-office bonanza for the team. Similarly, the Cleveland Indians' signing of the legendary Satchel Paige in 1948 produced profits by enhancing black attendance at Indians games. Jules Tygiel's 1984 book *Baseball's Great Experiment: Jackie Robinson and His Legacy* attempted to downplay the consumer and business implications of Jackie Robinson's entry into the major leagues. Yet, as his book made clear, Branch Rickey's signing of Robinson had relatively little to do with altruism.

The mid-twentieth century also witnessed the dramatic proliferation of "Negro-appeal" radio stations across the United States. In October 1949, *Sponsor*, the advertising trade journal of the broadcasting industry, cited only a handful of stations that carried programming aimed at blacks. By 1952, there were over 200 stations that featured this format full or part time. Three years later, there were over 600 "Negro-appeal" stations across America. Ironically, although these stations featured music and other programming of interest to blacks, most enterprises were owned by white entrepreneurs. Besides *Sponsor*, other important sources of study related to the "Negro-appeal" radio phenomenon include Norman W. Spaulding's 1981 Ph.D. dissertation, "History of Black-Oriented Radio in Chicago, 1929–1963"; Mark Newman's 1984 Ph.D. dissertation, "Capturing the 15 Billion Dollar Market"; and Nelson George's 1988 book, *The Death of Rhythm & Blues*.

One of the major news stories covered by "Negro-appeal" radio stations during the mid-1950s was the Montgomery Bus Boycott of 1955–1956. This event, besides catapulting Dr. Martin Luther King, Jr., into national prominence, demonstrated the consumer justice basis of the evolving civil rights movement. Along with Dr. King's 1958 *Stride toward Freedom: The Montgomery Story*,

Norman W. Walton's "Walking City: A History of the Montgomery Bus Boycott," which appeared in the October and November 1956 issues of the *Negro History Bulletin*, provided special insights into this important chapter in recent African American history.

The 1950s also featured an intensification of African American urbanization and simultaneous business interest in the increasingly important "Negro market." One clear manifestation of increased writing about black consumers was the first appearance of the category "Negro Market" in volume 19 of the *Reader's Guide to Periodical Literature* (April 1953–February 1955).

A number of important book-length studies relating to African American consumers also appeared during the Eisenhower era. They included Joseph T. Johnson's *Potential Negro Market* (1952); Henry Bullock's *Pathway to the Houston Negro Market* (1957); William K. Bell's *15 Million Negroes and 15 Billion Dollars* (1958); and Marcus Alexis's 1959 Ph.D. dissertation, "Racial Differences in Consumption and Automobile Ownership." Like Paul K. Edwards in his pioneering 1930s studies, Johnson, Bullock, and Alexis provided useful information to white businesses seeking their share of the "Negro market." In contrast, Bell, writing for an African American audience, decried white businesses' increased presence in the economic lives of black consumers.

The 1960s undoubtedly intensified William K. Bell's concerns. The 1960 U.S. Census revealed that for the first time in U.S. history, the percentage of black urban residents (73.2) exceeded that of their white counterparts (65.5). Consequently, more and more white businesses sought information about selling to strategically located African American consumers.

To accommodate the growing number of companies that sought insights about African American consumers, business trade journals featured a growing number of "how-to" articles concerning selling to blacks. Among the myriad publications that provided this information to their readers were *Advertising Age, Drug & Cosmetic Industry, Electrical Merchandising Week, Media-scope, Printer's Ink, Public Relations Journal, Quick Frozen Foods, Sales Management*, and *Sponsor*.

Besides relying upon trade journal articles for insights about black consumers, some corporations employed African American consultants to obtain additional information about the African American consumer market. Perhaps the two most influential black consultants to corporate America during the 1960s were John H. Johnson, publisher of *Ebony* magazine, and D. Parke Gibson, president of D. Parke Gibson Associates, Inc.

Johnson's 1989 autobiography written with Lerone Bennett, Jr., *Succeeding against the Odds*, provides detailed information about his self-described role as "special ambassador to American whites" during "the decade of the long hot summers." Likewise, D. Parke Gibson's 1969 *The $30 Billion Negro*, along with its 1978 sequel *$70 Billion in the Black: America's Black Consumers*, reflected the advice his company gave such clients as Avon Products, Coca Cola, Columbia Pictures, Greyhound, and the R. J. Reynolds Tobacco Company.

The 1970s witnessed a continued proliferation of works related to the now "black" consumer market. Articles relating to black consumers appeared in an even greater array of trade journals, including *American Druggist, Beverage World, Chemical Marketing Reporter, Chemical Week, Marketing/Communications, Product Marketing and Cosmetic & Fragrance Retailing*, and *Progressive Grocer*. Besides D. Parke Gibson's *$70 Billion in the Black*, the decade's most important books related to black consumers were George Joyce and Norman Govoni's 1971 edited work *The Black Consumer: Dimensions of Behavior and Strategy* and Alan R. Andreason's *Disadvantaged Consumer* (1975). Moreover, scholarly articles relating to black consumers appeared in such journals as the *Journal of Advertising Research, Journal of Consumer Affairs, Journal of Marketing, Journal of Marketing Research, Journal of Retailing*, and *Public Opinion Quarterly*.

Although a number of businesses used available market research to get their "share" of the 1970s black consumer market, the U.S. film industry stood out in this respect. Blacks at the time were approximately 15 percent of the U.S. population but accounted for nearly 30 percent of movie box office receipts in American cities. Consequently, in seeking to counteract the ill-effects of competition from television and foreign filmmakers, Hollywood produced a number of black-oriented movies between 1971 and 1974. Generally referred to as the "blaxploitation" film phenomenon, Hollywood's targeting of urban blacks produced huge profits for whites throughout the industry. Among the contemporary articles that examined these movies from the standpoint of marketing and consumption were Ted Angelus's July 24, 1972, article in *Advertising Age* entitled "Black Film Explosion Uncovers an Untapped, Rich Market;" James P. Murray's article "The Subject Is Money," which appeared in the winter 1973 issue of *Black Creation*; Alvin J. Poussaint's "Blaxploitation Movies: Cheap Thrills That Degrade Blacks," which appeared in the February 1974 issue of *Psychology Today*; and Renee Ward's May 1976 *Black Scholar* article "Black Films, White Profits." Books that discuss the creative and commercial aspects of 1970s blaxploitation movies include Daniel J. Leab's *From Sambo to Superspade: The Black Experience in Motion Pictures* (1975); James P. Murray's *To Find an Image: Black Films from Uncle Tom to Superfly* (1973); Donald Bogle's *Toms, Coons, Mulattoes, Mammies, & Bucks: An Interpretive History of Blacks in American Films* (1989); Ed Guerrero's *Framing Blackness: The African-American Image in Film* (1993); Nelson George's *Blackface: Reflections on African Americans and the Movies* (1994); and Jesse A. Rhines's *Black Film/ White Money* (1996).

The 1980s represented a major turning point in the history of African American consumerism. As black social and economic gains associated with the civil rights movement stalled during the ultraconservative Reagan administration, class distinctions within the African American community became much more pronounced. This "market segmentation" prompted corporate marketers to develop more class-specific advertising aimed at blacks.

Middle- and upper-class African Americans, who comprised one-third of the black community during the 1980s, found themselves actively courted by producers of upscale consumer items and financial services companies. Moreover, the nuances of this segment of black America were examined in a number of published works, including B. Drake Stelle's May 18, 1981, *Advertising Age* article, "Publishers See Segmentation in Black Market"; James C. Lawson's August 25, 1986, *Advertising Age* article, "Financial Services Target Segment within a Segment"; Robert B. Hill's essay in the National Urban League's *State of Black America 1986*, "The Black Middle Class: Past, Present and Future"; Jerome D. Williams and William J. Qualls's "Middle-Class Black Consumers and Intensity of Ethnic Identification," in the winter 1989 issue of *Psychology & Marketing*; and William O'Hare's November 1989 article in *American Demographics*, "In the Black."

The 1980s black "underclass," comprised of those individuals who did not materially benefit from the civil rights movement, also attracted the attention of writers and corporate marketers. William Julius Wilson's 1987 book, *The Truly Disadvantaged: The Inner City, the Underclass, and Public Policy* perhaps represented the decade's most-discussed book on this subject. Along with Wilson's work, the National Urban League's yearly publication, *The State of Black America*, provided detailed information about the desperate economic plight of America's inner cities during the 1980s.

Two industries that appeared especially interested in reaching the black poor during the 1980s were liquor and cigarette companies. In fact, the decade featured an accelerated marketing of alcohol and tobacco products in depressed urban black enclaves. The Center for Science in the Public Interest's widely discussed 1987 study *Marketing Booze to Blacks* represented the most detailed analysis of this phenomenon. Besides a predictable critique of beer, wine, and liquor companies, this publication criticized the government for not providing the funds necessary to counteract alcohol's growing presence in the black community. Moreover, *Marketing Booze to Blacks* blasted the acquiescence of African American businesspeople and politicians who, for personal gain, encouraged the growing relationship between the marketers of alcoholic beverages and black consumers.

Whereas purveyors of alcoholic beverages made considerable inroads among 1980s urban black consumers, the tobacco industry had a more difficult time in promoting its products among African Americans. The R. J. Reynolds Tobacco Company's ill-fated (1989) "Uptown" cigarette campaign exemplified this reality.

After extensive market research, R. J. Reynolds believed it had devised a product that would be irresistible to black smokers. Unfortunately for the company, not everyone in the black community hailed the pending appearance of "Uptown." Dr. Louis Sullivan, President George Bush's secretary of health and human services, was the most noteworthy black critic of the proposed "Uptown" cigarette. Following Sullivan's lead, other black leaders blasted R. J. Reynolds for specifically targeting blacks. Feeling the heat from this protest, R. J. Reynolds subsequently announced it would, at a loss of $5 to $7 million, withdraw "Uptown" from market consideration. Gail Baker Woods's *Advertising and Marketing to the New Majority* (1995) provides a detailed account of the "Uptown" fiasco.

By 1990, African Americans were a far different people than they had been at the dawn of the twentieth century. Once perceived as primarily a rural group with limited disposable income, blacks were a free-spending, pronouncedly urban group by the last decade of the twentieth century. Despite this reality, advertising and marketing literature continued to discuss and document an ongoing insensitivity toward black consumers. For instance, a three-year examination (1988–1991) of advertisements in twenty-seven national magazines, conducted by the New York City Department of Consumer Affairs, documented clear racial bias. Although African Americans made up 12 percent of the U.S. population and more than 11 percent of all magazine readers, black models appeared in only 4.5 percent of all magazine advertisements.

The racial nuances of contemporary television advertising has also come under scrutiny. J. Clinton Brown's February 1, 1993, *Advertising Age* article, "Which Black Is Beautiful?" discussed the clear preference shown for using lighter-skinned (versus darker-skinned) models in television ads. Moreover, he asserted that this phenomenon reflects lingering cultural values that associate lighter-skinned blacks with "attractiveness."

Besides dealing with issues related to advertising and marketing, today's black consumers are becoming increasingly concerned about using their spending power to benefit their communities and businesses. The July 1996 *Black Enterprise*, dubbed the "consumer empowerment issue," urged African Americans to make purchases that directly or indirectly positively affected black-owned businesses. Nevertheless, the evidence suggests that such sentiment, though noble, may represent the proverbial "too little, too late."

Since the passage of the Civil Rights Act of 1964, which allowed blacks to spend their money wherever they wished, black-owned businesses have witnessed declining profits. Two industries especially hard hit are black-owned insurance companies and black-owned personal care products companies.

Long before the 1990s, industry analysts questioned whether black insurance companies could survive in a desegregating society. Linda P. Fletcher's *The Negro in the Insurance Industry* (1970) and Jacob M. Duker and Charles E. Hughes's "Black-Owned Life Insurance Company: Issues and Recommendations," which appeared in the June 1973 issue of the *Journal of Risk and Insurance*, reflected this sentiment. Robert E. Weems, Jr.'s "A Crumbling Legacy: The Decline of African American Insurance Companies," which appeared in the Fall 1994 issue of the *Review of Black Political Economy*, verified the concerns of earlier scholars. Relative to the larger industry, today's black insurers are suffering from shrinking total assets, shrinking premium income, and a shrinking workforce. Moreover, between 1984 and 1997, the number of black-owned insurance companies has decreased by 64 percent (from thirty-six to thirteen).

Before the late 1960s, black-owned personal care products companies nearly monopolized the black consumer market. An overall rise of the black standard of living, however, associated with the civil rights movement, prompted white-owned companies to develop personal care products aimed at African American consumers, especially since market research revealed that blacks spent proportionately more than whites for cosmetics and hair and skin care products.

During the 1970s and 1980s, an increasing number of articles relating to the African American personal care products industry appeared in various trade journals. Some of the more important works included James P. Forkan's "Who's Who in $350,000,000 Black Grooming Market," which appeared in the November 20, 1972, *Advertising Age*; Charles Marticorena's "Ethnic Market: Biggest Potential for Growth in Cosmetics Industry," which appeared in the June 23, 1975, issue of *Chemical Marketing Reporter*; Grayson Mitchell's "Battle of the Rouge," featured in the August 1978 *Black Enterprise*; "Cosmetic Makers Explore Underdeveloped Black Market," which appeared in the December 1981 issue of *Product Marketing and Cosmetic & Fragrance Retailing*; Ellen Schultz's "Bad Times for Black Businesses," published in the May 5, 1986, issue of *Adweek*; and Laurie Freeman's "Big Marketers Move in on Ethnic Haircare," featured in the May 12, 1987, *Advertising Age*.

By the 1990s, white companies, benefiting from larger product development and advertising budgets, all but dominated the black personal care products industry. The 1993 sale of the black-owned Johnson Products Company to a white-owned company exemplified the problems faced by African American entrepreneurs in this area. Johnson Products, the originator of the popular "Ultra Sheen" and "Afro Sheen" product lines, once held a phenomenal 80 percent market share in the black hair care industry. Fierce competition from white competitors, along with domestic squabbling within this family-owned business, contributed to the demise of Johnson Products. Caroline V. Clarke's "Redefining Beautiful," which appeared in the June 1993 *Black Enterprise*, and Brett Pulley's June 15, 1993, *Wall Street Journal* article, "Johnson Products Agrees to $67 Million Ivax Buyout," provide important insights into the plight of present-day black entrepreneurs in the black personal care products industry.

Although studies of African American consumerism have increased in recent years, this phenomenon remains a relatively understudied aspect of the African American experience. This chapter, along with my 1998 book, *Desegregating the Dollar: African American Consumerism in the Twentieth Century*, may stimulate more scholarly investigations in this area.

BIBLIOGRAPHY

Abarnel, Albert, and Alex Haley. "A New Audience for Radio." *Harper's* 212 (February 1956): 57–59.

Alexis, Marcus. "Pathways to the Negro Market." *Journal of Negro Education* 28 (Spring 1959): 114–17.

———. "Racial Differences in Consumption and Automobile Ownership." Ph.D. dissertation, University of Minnesota, 1959.

———. "Patterns of Black Consumption, 1935–1960." *Journal of Black Studies* 1 (September 1970): 55–74.

Anderson, Haywood S. "Competition in the Face of Integration." *Negro Educational Review* 15 (April 1964): 51–59.

Andreason, Alan R. *The Disadvantaged Consumer.* New York: Free Press, 1975.

———. "The Differing Nature of Consumerism in the Ghetto." *Journal of Consumer Affairs* 10 (Winter 1976): 179–90.

Angelus, Ted. "Black Film Explosion Uncovers an Untapped, Rich Market." *Advertising Age* 43 (July 24, 1972): 51–53.

Bauer, Raymond A., and Scott M. Cunningham. "The Negro Market." *Journal of Advertising Research* 10 (April 1970): 3–13.

Beauford, Fred. "Black Movies Create Box Office Magic." *Black Enterprise* 4 (September 1972): 47–53.

"Beauty Chemicals: The Ethnic Market." *Chemical Marketing Reporter* 203 (June 11, 1973): 35–36.

Bell, William K. *15 Million Negroes and 15 Billion Dollars.* New York: William K. Bell, 1958.

"The Black Consumer: A New Force in the American Economy." *Black Enterprise* 4 (November 1973): 17–21.

"Black Cosmetics Market Continues to Expand." *American Druggist* 179 (April 1979): 55–56.

Blake, Rich. "Reaching the World's Ninth Largest Market." *Public Relations Journal* 41 (June 1985): 30–31.

Bogle, Donald. *Toms, Coons, Mulattoes, Mammies, & Bucks: An Interpretive History of Blacks in American Films.* New York: Continuum, 1989.

Boyenton, William H. "The Negro Turns to Advertising." *Journalism Quarterly* 42 (Spring 1965): 227–35.

Brooks, Dwight. "Consumer Markets and Consumer Magazines: Black America and the Culture of Consumption, 1920–1960." Ph.D. dissertation, University of Iowa, 1991.

Brown, J. Clinton. "Which Black Is Beautiful?" *Advertising Age* 64 (February 1, 1993): 19.

Bullock, Henry A. *Pathways to the Houston Negro Market.* Ann Arbor, MI: J. W. Edwards, 1957.

———. "Business and Government Leaders to Aid Study of Negro Market." *Sales Management* 28 (January 10, 1931): 78.

Christopher, Maurine. "CORE Intensifies Drive for Negroes in Ads; Zeroes in on Pepsi-Cola Co." *Advertising Age* 35 (November 9, 1964): 3, 71.

———. Integrated TV Ads Draw Praise of Admen." *Advertising Age* 40 (February 3, 1969): 3, 108.

Clarke, Caroline V. "Redefining Beautiful." *Black Enterprise* 23 (June 1993): 243–52.

Cohen, Dorothy. "Advertising and the Black Community." *Journal of Marketing* 34 (October 1970): 3–11.

Colfax, J. David, and Susan Frankel Sternberg. "The Perpetuation of Racial Stereotypes:

Blacks in Mass Circulation Magazine Advertisements." *Public Opinion Quarterly* 36 (Spring 1972): 8–18.

"Consumers' Cooperation among Negroes in Gary, Ind." *Monthly Labor Review* 42 (February 1936): 369–71.

"Cosmetic Makers Explore Underdeveloped Black Market." *Product Marketing and Cosmetic & Fragrance Retailing* 10 (December 1981): 1, 21, 26.

Detweiler, Frederick G. *The Negro Press in America.* Chicago: University of Chicago Press, 1922.

Drake, J. G. St. Clair. "Why Not Co-operate?" *Opportunity* 14 (August 1936): 231–34, 251.

Du Bois, William Edward Burghardt. *Economic Cooperation among Negroes.* Atlanta: Atlanta University Press, 1907.

———. "Georgia Negroes and Their Fifty Millions of Savings." *World's Work* 18 (May 1909): 11550–54.

———. "A Negro Nation within the Nation." *Current History* 42 (June 1935): 265–70.

Duker, Jacob M., and Charles E. Hughes. "The Black-Owned Life Insurance Company: Issues and Recommendations." *Journal of Risk and Insurance* 40 (June 1973): 221–30.

Edwards, Paul K. *The Southern Urban Negro as a Consumer.* New York: Prentice-Hall, 1932.

———. "Distinctive Characteristics of Urban Negro Consumption." Ph. D. dissertation, Harvard University, 1936.

Evans, W. Leonard, Jr., and H. Naylor Fitzhugh. "The Negro Market—Two Viewpoints." *Media-scope* 11 (November 1967): 70–78.

Fletcher, Linda P. *The Negro in the Insurance Industry.* Philadelphia: University of Pennsylvania Press, 1970.

Forkan, James P. "Who's Who in $350,000,000 Black Grooming Market." *Advertising Age* 43 (November 20, 1972): 96–97.

Fowler, Bertram B. "Miracle in Gary: The Negro Gropes toward Economic Equality." *Forum & Century* 96 (September 1936): 134–37.

Freeman, Laurie. "Big Marketers Move in on Ethnic Haircare." *Advertising Age* 57 (May 12, 1987): 24–28.

George, Nelson. *The Death of Rhythm & Blues.* New York : Pantheon Books, 1988.

———. *Blackface: Reflections on African-Americans and the Movies.* New York: HarperCollins Publishers, 1994.

Gibson, D. Parke. *The $30 Billion Negro.* New York: Macmillan Company, 1969.

———. *$70 Billion in the Black: America's Black Consumers.* New York: Macmillan Publishing Company, 1978.

Glaxton, Robert. "The Black Cosmetics Market." *Drug & Cosmetic Industry* 124 (May 1979): 78, 146–48.

Grayson, William P. "What the $20 Billion Negro Market Means to You." *Negro Digest* 12 (January 1962): 62–67.

Guerrero, Ed. *Framing Blackness: The African American Image in Film.* Philadelphia: Temple University Press, 1993.

Hacker, George A., Ronald Collins, and Michael Jacobson. *Marketing Booze to Blacks.* Washington, DC: Center for Science in the Public Interest, 1987.

Hare, Nathan. "How and Why Negroes Spend Their Money." *Negro Digest* 14 (May 1965): 4–11.

Haring, H. A. "Selling to Harlem." *Advertising & Selling* 11 (October 31, 1928): 17–18, 50–53.

———. "The Negro as Consumer." *Advertising & Selling* 15 (September 3, 1930): 20–21, 67–68.

Hill, T. Arnold. "The Negro Market." *Opportunity* (October 1932): 318–19.

Hill, Robert B. "The Black Middle Class: Past, Present, and Future." In *The State of Black America 1986*, edited by James D. Williams. New York: National Urban League, 1986, 43–61.

Hine, Darlene Clark. "The Housewives' League of Detroit: Black Women and Economic Nationalism." In *Hine Sight: Black Women and the Reconstruction of American History*. Bloomington: Indiana University Press, 1994, 129–45.

Hirschhorn, Adrian. "Pepsi-Cola's Campaign to the Negro Market." *Printer's Ink* 228 (September 9, 1949): 38–40.

Holsey, Albon L. "Negro in Business Aided by Racial Appeal." *Forbes* 21 (January 15, 1928): 42–48.

———. "What the Negro Is Doing in Business." *Forbes* 23 (May 1, 1929): 36–38.

Holte, Clarence L. "The Negro Market: To Profit from It, Recognize It and Service Its Needs." *Printer's Ink* 263 (April 4, 1958): 29–32.

Humphreys, Jeffrey M. "Black Buying Power by Place of Residence: 1990–1996." *Georgia Business and Economic Conditions* 55 (July–August 1995): 1–15.

Johnson, Guy B. "Newspapers Advertisements and Negro Culture." *Journal of Social Forces* 3 (May 1925): 706–9.

Johnson, John H. "Does Your Sales Force Know How to Sell to the Negro Trade? Some Do's and Dont's." *Advertising Age* 23 (March 17, 1952): 73–74.

———, and Lerone Bennett, Jr. *Succeeding against the Odds*. New York: Warner Books, 1989.

Johnson, Joseph T. *The Potential Negro Market*. New York: Pageant Press, 1952.

Jones, Eugene Kinckle. "Purchasing Power of Negroes in the U.S. Estimated at Two Billion Dollars." *Domestic Commerce* 15 (January 10, 1935): 1.

Joyce, George, and Norman Govoni, eds. *The Black Consumer: Dimensions of Behavior and Strategy*. New York: Random House, 1971.

Kassarjian, Harold H. "The Negro and American Advertising, 1946–1965." *Journal of Marketing Research* 6 (February 1969): 29–39.

Kern-Foxworth, Marilyn. *Aunt Jemima, Uncle Ben, and Rastus: Blacks in Advertising, Yesterday, Today, and Tomorrow*. Westport, CT: Praeger, 1994.

King, Martin Luther, Jr. *Stride toward Freedom: The Montgomery Story*. 1st ed. New York: Harper, 1958.

"Know-How Is Key to Selling Negro Market Today." *Sponsor (Negro Market Supplement)* 15 (October 9, 1961): 9–10, 26–27.

Lawson, James C. "Financial Services Target Segment within a Segment." *Advertising Age* 57 (August 25, 1986): S-1-S-2.

Leab, Daniel J. *From Sambo to Superspade: The Black Experience in Motion Pictures*. Boston: Houghton Mifflin, 1975.

Maggard, John P. "Negro Market—Fact or Fiction?" *California Management Review* 14 (Fall 1971): 71–80.

"Marketing to the Negro Consumer." *Sales Management* 84 (March 4, 1960): 36–44.

Marticorena, Charles. "Ethnic Market: Biggest Potential for Growth in Cosmetics Industry." *Chemical Marketing Reporter* 207 (June 23, 1975): 37–39.

McCoy, Frank. "Life-Sustaining Measures." *Black Enterprise* 28 (June 1998): 182–86.
Meier, August, and Elliott Rudwick. "The Boycott Movement against Jim Crow Street-cars in the South, 1900–1906." *Journal of American History* 55 (March 1969): 756–75.
Mitchell, Grayson. "Battle of the Rouge." *Black Enterprise* 9 (August 1978): 23–29.
Murray, James P. "The Subject Is Money." *Black Creation* 4 (Winter 1973): 26–30.
———. *To Find an Image: Black Films from Uncle Tom to Super Fly.* Indianapolis: Bobbs-Merrill, 1973.
"The Negro Consumer." *Electrical Merchandising Week* 96 (April 27, 1964): 13–26.
"The Negro Market: An Appraisal." *Tide* 21 (March 7, 1947): 15–18.
"Negro Radio Attracts Madison Ave. Attention." *Sponsor (Negro Market Supplement)* 20 (July 25, 1966): 32–39.
"Negro Radio's Prosperous Market." *Sponsor (Negro Market Supplement)* 14 (September 26, 1960): 6–10, 47–49.
"The Negro's Force in the Marketplace." *Business Week* (May 26, 1962): 76–84.
Newman, Mark. "Capturing the 15 Billion Dollar Market: The Emergence of Black Oriented Radio." Ph.D. dissertation, Northwestern University, Evanston, IL, 1984.
O'Hare, William P. "In the Black." *American Demographics* 11 (November 1989): 24–29.
Oladipupo, Raymond. *How Distinct Is the Negro Market?* New York: Ogilvy and Mather, 1970.
Petrof, John. "The Effects of Student Boycotts upon the Purchasing Habits of Negro Families in Atlanta, Georgia." *Phylon* 24 (Fall 1963): 266–70.
Pierce, Joseph A. *Negro Business and Business Education.* New York: Plenum Press, 1947, 1995.
Poussaint, Alvin F. "Blaxploitation Movies: Cheap Thrills That Degrade Blacks." *Psychology Today* 7 (February 1974): 22, 26–27, 30–32, 98.
Pulley, Brett. "Johnson Products Agrees to $67 Million Ivax Buyout." *Wall Street Journal* (June 15, 1993): B3.
Rhines, Jesse A. *Black Film/White Money.* New Brunswick, NJ: Rutgers University Press, 1996.
Rooks, Noliwe. *Hair Raising: Beauty, Culture, and African American Women.* New Brunswick, NJ: Rutgers University Press, 1996.
Rust, Brian. *The American Record Label Book.* New Rochelle, NY: Arlington House, 1978.
Sawyer, Broadus E. "An Examination of Race as a Factor in Negro-White Consumption Patterns." *Review of Economics and Statistics* 44 (May 1962): 217–20.
Schmidt, David, and Ivan Preston. "How NAACP Leaders View Integrated Advertising." *Journal of Marketing Research* 9 (September 1969): 13–16.
Schultz, Ellen. "Bad Times for Black Business." *Adweek* 27 (May 5, 1986): 16–17.
"Selling to the Black Consumer." *Black Enterprise* 4 (November 1973): 31–33, 58–60.
"Selling to the Negro Market." *Tide* 25 (July 20, 1951): 37–44.
Shaw, Arnold. *Black Popular Music in America: From the Spirituals, Minstrels, and Ragtime to Soul, Disco, and Hip-Hop.* New York: Schirmer Books, 1986.
Shepard, Juanita M. "The Portrayal of Black Women in the Ads of Popular Magazines." *Western Journal of Black Studies* 4 (Fall 1980): 179–82.
Smikle, Ken. *The Buying Power of Black America.* Chicago: Target Market News Group, 1992.

Snyder, Glenn H. " 'Black Is Beautiful' Market Bringing New Dollars to Supers." *Progressive Grocer* 51 (April 1972): 142–50.

Solomon, Paul J., Ronald F. Bush, and Joseph F. Hair, Jr. "White and Black Consumer Sales Response to Black Models." *Journal of Marketing Research* 13 (November 1976): 431–34.

"The Soul Market in Black and White." *Sales Management* 102 (June 1, 1969): 37–42.

Southern, Eileen. *The Music of Black Americans: A History*. 2nd ed. New York: W. W. Norton, 1983.

Spaulding, Norman W. "History of Black-Oriented Radio in Chicago, 1929–1963." Ph.D. dissertation, University of Illinois at Urbana-Champaign, 1981.

Stelle, B. Drake. "Publishers See Segmentation in Black Market." *Advertising Age* 52 (May 18, 1981): S6, S16.

Sterner, Richard, Lenore A. Epstein, and Ellen Winston, et al. *The Negro's Share: A Study of Income, Consumption, Housing and Public Assistance*. New York: Harper and Brothers Publishers, 1943.

Sturdivant, Frederick D., and Walter T. Wilhelm. "Poverty, Minorities, and Consumer Exploitation." *Social Science Quarterly* 49 (December 1968): 643–50.

Sullivan, David J. "Don't Do This—If You Want to Sell Your Products to Negroes!" *Sales Management* 52 (March 1, 1943): 46–50.

———. "The American Negro—an 'Export' Market at Home!" *Printer's Ink* 208 (July 21, 1944): 90–94.

———. "How Negroes Spent Their Incomes, 1920–1943." *Sales Management* 54 (June 15, 1945): 106.

———. "Why a Handful of Advertisers Dominate Negro Markets." *Sales Management* 65 (September 15, 1950): 154–60.

"Tips on Selling via Negro Radio." *Sponsor (Negro Market Supplement)* 8 (September 20, 1954): 56, 146–48.

"TV: A 'New Force' in Selling to U.S. Negroes." *Sponsor (Negro Market Supplement)* 18 (August 17, 1964): 44–49.

Tygiel, Jules. *Baseball's Great Experiment: Jackie Robinson and His Legacy*. New York: Vintage Books, 1984.

Wall, Kelvin A. "The Great Waste: Ignoring Blacks." *Marketing/Communications* 298 (February 1970): 42–50.

Walton, Norman W. "The Walking City: A History of the Montgomery Boycott Part I." *Negro History Bulletin* 20 (October 1956): 17–20.

———. "The Walking City: A History of the Montgomery Boycott Part II." *Negro History Bulletin* 20 (November 1956): 27–33.

Ward, Renee. "Black Films, White Profits." *Black Scholar* 7 (May 1976): 13–24.

Washington, Booker T. *The Negro in Business*. New York: AMS Press, 1907, 1971.

Weems, Robert E., Jr. "The Revolution Will Be Marketed: American Corporations and Black Consumers during the 1960s." *Radical History Review* 59 (Spring 1994): 94–107.

———. "A Crumbling Legacy: The Decline of African American Insurance Companies in Contemporary America." *Review of Black Political Economy* 23 (Fall 1994): 25–37.

———. "African American Consumer Boycotts during the Civil Rights Era." *Western Journal of Black Studies* 19 (Spring 1995): 72–79.

————. *Desegregating the Dollar: African American Consumerism in the Twentieth Century*. New York: New York University Press, 1998.

"Why the Negro Market Counts." *Business Week* (September 2, 1967): 64–70.

Williams, Jerome D., and William J. Qualls. "Middle-Class Black Consumers and Intensity of Ethnic Identification." *Psychology & Marketing* 6 (Winter 1989): 263–86.

Wilson, William Julius. *The Truly Disadvantage: The Inner City, the Underclass, and Public Policy*. Chicago: University of Chicago Press, 1987.

Woods, Gail Baker. *Advertising and Marketing to the New Majority*. Belmont, CA: Wadsworth, 1995.

Work, Monroe N., ed. *Negro Year Book and Annual Encylopedia of the Negro*. Vol. 1. Tuskegee, AL: Negro Year Book Company, 1912.

————. "A Half-Century of Progress: The Negro in America in 1866 and in 1922." *Missionary Review of the World* 45 (June 1922): 430–40.

Zikmund, William G. "A Taxonomy of Black Shopping Behavior." *Journal of Retailing* 53 (Spring 1977): 61–72.

Zinkham, George M., William J. Qualls, and Abhijit Biswas. "The Use of Blacks in Magazine and Television Advertising: 1946–1986." *Journalism Quarterly* 67 (Autumn 1990): 547–53.

XVI

The Civil Rights Movement

John Dittmer

The black-led struggle for freedom and equality in the middle of the twentieth century was the most important social movement the United States witnessed since the Civil War. The civil rights movement succeeded in gaining for African Americans, on paper, at least, the basic rights guaranteed them in the Constitution. It has been responsible for changes in southern society undreamed of only a few decades ago. The movement radicalized part of a generation of young black and white Americans. It was both the training ground and the inspiration for the student movement of the mid-1960s, the anti–Vietnam War crusade, and the welfare rights, gay rights, and women's liberation movements. The civil rights movement failed, however, to end poverty and racism, or to alter the process of how fundamental economic and political decisions are made in this country. Since the early 1970s scholars have been engaged in the effort to tell the story of the movement and the people who made it, and to evaluate its impact on the South and the nation.

The past two decades have witnessed an outpouring of books and essays on the civil rights movement. In many of these works scholars have challenged earlier assumptions about movement leadership and goals. The periodization of the movement also came under review. One can argue with conviction that the black freedom struggle began in 1619 when the first boatload of Africans arrived in Virginia, but most scholars saw the 1954 *Brown v. Board of Education* as the modern civil rights movement's starting point. More recent studies have found the movement's origins in the activism of black World War II veterans who "returned home fighting," or even with the white and black activists who attempted to create a "New Deal" for African Americans in the 1930s and early 1940s.

The historiography of the movement has also moved through several stages. The first group of studies were accounts by journalists and the participants themselves. By the mid-1970s, as movement archives became available, historians examined the major national civil rights organizations and their leaders, with proper attention devoted to their relations with federal officials in Washington. The decade of the 1980s saw scholars questioning this "top-down" approach and calling for more attention to the history of rank-and-file activists, the local people who made the national leaders and organizations possible in the first place. More recently, the role of women in the struggle has become an important field of research and writing.

Autobiographical accounts by civil rights activists have had a significant impact on the way that scholars later assessed the movement. Among the most influential memoirs are Student Nonviolent Coordinating Committee (SNCC) executive secretary James Forman's *Making of Black Revolutionaries* (1972), SNCC's Cleveland Sellers's *River of No Return* (1973), and Anne Moody's *Coming of Age in Mississippi* (1968). Also important are Congress of Racial Equality (CORE) leader James Farmer's *Lay Bare the Heart* (1985), Martin Luther King, Jr.'s *Stride toward Freedom* (1958), and SNCC's Mary King's 1987 memoir, *Freedom Song*. To these should be added CORE activist Tom Dent's *Southern Journey: A Return to the Civil Rights Movement* (1997), a bittersweet look at the major movement centers of the 1960s and what they have become today.

The earlier autobiographical writings provided a base for the scholarly studies, but it was not until the papers of the major civil rights organizations became available that historians were able to examine the movement in greater depth. The first study based on archival material was the work of journalists Pat Watters and Reece Cleghorn, who used the files of the Voter Education Project for their important 1967 book, *Climbing Jacob's Ladder*, which examined the "arrival" of blacks into southern politics. In *CORE: A Study in the Civil Rights Movement* (1973), historians August Meier and Elliott Rudwick mined the CORE archives to produce the definitive volume on that organization's role in the movement. The first book on SNCC was that of historian-activist Howard Zinn. His *SNCC: The New Abolitionists*, first published in 1964, was a sympathetic and moving account of SNCC's early years. Clayborne Carson's *In Struggle: SNCC and the Black Awakening of the 1960s* (1981) remains the best single volume on SNCC. Carson's major contribution here was to analyze SNCC's growing radicalism in the mid-1960s and the reasons for its demise by the end of that decade.

There is no comprehensive history of the National Association for the Advancement of Colored People (NAACP), although several accounts detail the NAACP's school desegregation efforts and lobbying activities. An impressive state history that focuses on the work of the NAACP is Adam Fairclough's *Race*

& *Democracy: The Civil Rights Struggle in Louisiana, 1915–1972* (1995). Important works in progress are Raymond Gavin's study of the NAACP in North Carolina, and August Meier's and John Bracey's provocative examination of the relationship between A. Philip Randolph and the NAACP. For the National Urban League, see Nancy J. Weiss, *Whitney M. Young, Jr., and the Struggle for Civil Rights* (1989), and Arvarh E. Strickland, *History of the Chicago Urban League* (1966).

The Southern Christian Leadership Conference (SCLC) had the largest national visibility during the 1960s, thanks to its charismatic leader, Dr. Martin Luther King, Jr. The first scholarly biography of King was David Lewis's *King*, originally published in 1970, an impressive analysis of the leader's strengths and shortcomings, written before much archival material was available. Adam Fairclough's *To Redeem the Soul of America: The Southern Christian Leadership Conference and Martin Luther King, Jr.* (1987) effectively deals with the internal politics of SCLC during King's ascendancy and after his death. Fairclough's book was overshadowed by the publication a year earlier of David J. Garrow's Pulitzer Prize–winning biography of King, *Bearing the Cross*. Garrow's King emerges as a charismatic but troubled leader who in the last three years of his life became increasingly radical and alienated from the mainstream politicians who had previously worked with him. Taylor Branch's *Parting the Waters: America in the King Years, 1954–63* (1988), which also won the Pulitzer, is the most dramatic account of the early movement years, focusing on King but also dealing in considerable detail on grassroots activity in Mississippi. Branch's second volume of a projected trilogy, *Pillar of Fire: America in the King Years, 1963–65* (1998), broadens its focus to include material on Malcolm X and the Nation of Islam, as well as the escalating war in Vietnam. Branch tries to do too much in this volume, which lacks focus.

One cannot leave King historiography without mentioning two important projects. The first is an eighteen-volume series edited by David J. Garrow, *Martin Luther King, Jr., and the Civil Rights Movement* (1989). An eclectic mix of published articles, unpublished doctoral dissertations, master's theses, and undergraduate honors essays, the collection ranges widely over the South and the movement years of the 1950s and 1960s. The second is the multivolume collection *The Papers of Martin Luther King, Jr.* (1992). Under the general editorship of Clayborne Carson, the early volumes of this series promise not only the most comprehensive look at King but also valuable information and insights into the movement as a whole.

Beginning with the publication in 1980 of William H. Chafe's *Civilities and Civil Rights: Greensboro, North Carolina, and the Black Struggle for Freedom*, scholars began to focus more on grassroots activism in southern communities and less on national leaders like King and their organizations. *Civilities* used oral history sources to uncover an activist tradition in Greensboro, tracing the local movement's origins back to its roots in the 1930s and 1940s. Chafe also examined white "moderate" leadership in North Carolina and found it lacking.

In 1985 two other important community studies were published. In *Reaping the Whirlwind*, Robert J. Norrell focuses on a fascinating group of middle-class activists in Tuskegee, Alabama. David R. Colburn examines local black protest and the angry white response in St. Augustine, Florida, in *Racial Change and Community Crisis*. These community studies emphasize the importance of a tradition of local leadership and question the efficacy of national organizations and leaders in achieving local movement goals.

The community studies also revealed that the modern civil rights movement predated the 1954 *Brown* decision. Two recent books have examined the origins of the movement in the New Deal and World War II era. John Egerton's *Speak Now against the Day* (1994) deals with southern white and black activists in the 1930s and 1940s. Patricia Sullivan's *Days of Hope* (1996) is an illuminating look at southern radicals at home and in Washington, and the Cold War red baiting that destroyed the hope of a genuine interracial movement in the South. See also Linda Reed's *Simple Decency and Common Sense* (1991), which deals with the biracial southern conference movement from 1938 to 1963; and Darlene Clark Hine's *Black Victory* (1979), which chronicles the rise and fall of the white primary in Texas. Aldon D. Morris's *Origins of the Civil Rights Movement* (1984) focuses on the 1950s and emphasizes the role of the black church in promoting social change.

The *Brown* decision was an important event in the history of American race relations. Although it formally outlawed segregation in public education, *Brown* was responsible for a new wave of activism in the South, particularly in the area of voter registration. Blacks in the South seemed to sense that the federal government was now on their side (an assumption that proved premature, to say the least). The best book on *Brown* and the cases leading up to it remains Richard Kluger's *Simple Justice* (1976). Another good analysis is Mark V. Tushnet, *The NAACP's Legal Strategy against Segregated Education, 1925–1950* (1987). Daryl Michael Scott's pathbreaking *Contempt and Pity* (1997) shows how the idea that African Americans are psychologically damaged played an important role in the plaintiffs' arguments in the *Brown* case.

Robert A. Pratt's *Color of Their Skin* (1992) is a thorough study of school desegregation in Richmond, Virginia, from 1954 to 1989. For the Little Rock crisis of 1957, see Daisy Bates's *Long Shadow of Little Rock* (1962), written by a leading black activist; and Melba Patillo Beals's *Warriors Don't Cry* (1994), a poignant memoir by one of the "Little Rock Nine." For the relatively neglected field of school desegregation after 1965, see Constance Curry's fascinating *Silver Rights* (1995), which examines the courage and determination of a black Mississippi family to integrate the public schools during the era of "Freedom of Choice"; and David S. Cecelski's *Along Freedom Road* (1994), the story of the struggle of blacks in Hyde County, North Carolina, to prevent the closing of two historically black schools in the late 1960s.

In the aftermath of *Brown*, whites organized to maintain their supremacy. Neil McMillen's excellent study *The Citizens' Council*, first published in 1971, remains the best account of the South's leading segregationist agency, the "uptown Ku Klux Klan." Other significant studies of white resistance are Numan V. Bartley's *Rise of Massive Resistance* (1969) and journalist John Barlow Martin's contemporary account, *The Deep South Says "Never"* (1957).

The Montgomery bus boycott was the most important direct action campaign of the 1950s. The biographies of King by Garrow and Branch cover the boycott in detail, as does King's *Stride toward Freedom*. Jo Ann Gibson Robinson's memoir, *The Montgomery Bus Boycott and the Women Who Started It* (1987), is an important corrective to the notion that Martin Luther King was the driving force behind the boycott's instigation. *Daybreak of Freedom* (1997), edited by Stuart Burns, is a valuable documentary history of the Montgomery boycott.

In February 1960 four black students from North Carolina A&T University sat in at the Woolworth lunch counter in Greensboro, North Carolina, initiating the direct action campaigns of the 1960s. William H. Chafe's *Civilities and Civil Rights* (1980) is the definitive account of the Greensboro sit-ins. See also Howell Raines's collection of oral history interviews, *My Soul Is Rested* (1977). Nashville quickly became a major center of the sit-in movement, and the memories of the Nashville activists (many of whom went on to work full time in the movement) are recorded in Henry Hampton and Steve Fayer's *Voices of Freedom* (1990). The interviews were done in connection with the *Eyes on the Prize* film documentary, in itself an important history of the movement era. These sources also deal with the "Freedom Rides" of 1961. A contemporary account by one of the riders is James Peck's *Freedom Ride* (1962). Meier and Rudwick's *CORE* is a valuable source here, as are the SNCC histories by Zinn and Carson. David Halberstam's *Children* (1998) examines the Freedom Rides and the Nashville sit-ins from the perspective of a journalist who covered these events.

Several scholars have examined the relationship between the federal government and the southern movement. For the Eisenhower years, see Robert F. Burk's *Eisenhower Administration and Black Civil Rights* (1984). The best analysis of the Kennedy administration's ambivalent relationship with the civil rights movement is Victor S. Navasky's *Kennedy Justice* (1971). Carl M. Brauer's *John F. Kennedy and the Second Reconstruction* (1977) is too sympathetic toward the Kennedys. Two other books, especially helpful in dealing with national policies, are Michal R. Belknap, *Federal Law and Southern Order* (1987), and Kenneth O'Reilly, *Racial Matters: The FBI's Secret File on Black America, 1960–1972* (1989). O'Reilly shows that the image of the FBI as defender of downtrodden civil rights workers, as portrayed in the film *Mississippi Burning*, is inaccurate, to say the least.

The SCLC-led direct action campaign in Birmingham in spring 1963 dominated media coverage as had no other movement event and led to passage of the Civil Rights Act of 1964. Garrow, Fairclough, and Branch all devote a chapter to Birmingham. The best book on Birmingham and the movement is Glenn T. Eskew's 1997 study, *But for Birmingham: The Local and National Movements in the Civil Rights Struggle*. See also Martin Luther King, Jr.'s *Why*

We Can't Wait (1964). For a fine account of black political power in postmovement Birmingham, Jimmie Lewis Franklin's *Back to Birmingham* (1989) chronicles Richard Arrington, Jr.'s successful struggle to become that city's first black mayor.

The campaign to win the vote in Selma, Alabama, in 1965 marked both the high point and the turning point of the civil rights movement. It resulted in the Voting Rights Act of 1965, which changed the political map of the South. Selma demonstrated both the power of the movement to mobilize a national constituency and the difficulty facing the civil rights movement once the franchise had been won. The major study on the history of the events leading to passage of the Voting Rights Act of 1965 is Steven F. Lawson's definitive *Black Ballots: Voting Rights in the South, 1944–1969* (1976). His *In Pursuit of Power* (1985) takes the story of southern black politics down to 1982. For a right-wing critique of the application of the Voting Rights Act, see Abigail M. Thernstrom, *Whose Votes Count* (1987).

On the Selma campaign itself, see David J. Garrow, *Protest at Selma* (1978), which stresses the importance of the media in advancing the movement's agenda; and Charles E. Fager's *Selma, 1965* (1974), a remembrance by an activist. Two black children, Sheyann Webb and Rachel West Nelson, were participants in the Selma campaign and featured in the "Bridge to Freedom" segment of *Eyes on the Prize*. Their book (as told to Frank Sikora), *Selma, Lord, Selma* (1980), is a warm remembrance of that monumental event seen through the eyes of two precocious youngsters. In the aftermath of Selma, SNCC organized the Black Panther Party next door in Lowndes County. Charles Eagles's *Outside Agitator* (1993) is a moving account of the life and death of a white seminarian, Jon Daniels, who worked with SNCC in Lowndes County.

No state has received more scholarly attention than Mississippi. It was, in the words of the NAACP's Roy Wilkins, "the worst state" in terms of its race relations. Young movement activists were drawn to Mississippi because of its reputation, and service there became of badge of courage. In *Mississippi: The Closed Society* (1964), published at the height of the state's racial turmoil, James W. Silver writes unflinchingly about the depth of racism in his adopted state. Notorious acts of white violence are recorded in Stephen J. Whitfield's *Death in the Delta: The Story of Emmett Till* (1988) and in Howard Smead's *Blood Justice: The Lynching of Mack Charles Parker* (1986). In her fascinating *Civil Rights Chronicle: Letters from the South* (1997) Clarice T. Campbell provides an eyewitness account of race relations in the Magnolia State during the late 1950s and early 1960s.

In summer 1964 Mississippi became the focus of attention throughout the world. Movement leaders had invited students from across the country to come to Mississippi to work on voter registration projects, in community centers, and to teach in the new freedom schools. The lynching of three workers—James Chaney, Mickey Schwerner, and Andrew Goodman—during the first week of the project cast a pall over what would later be called "Freedom Summer," but the volunteers and their hosts persevered despite the reign of terror. The best study of the murders of the three workers is Seth Cagin and Philip Dray's *We Are Not Afraid* (1988), which has made good use of the FBI's MIBURN ("Mississippi Burning") files. See also Florence Mars, *Witness in Philadelphia* (1977), an absorbing account of the events surrounding the lynchings, told from the point of view of a white moderate who believed that justice demanded the arrest and conviction of the killers, and who found few white allies in her home town.

For the summer itself, no account is more compelling than Sally Belfrage's *Freedom Summer* (1965). A journalist who was also a summer volunteer, Belfrage worked in Greenwood, and her observations on the movement and the white resistance ring true today, more than three decades after the event. Other memoirs include sections of the autobiographies of Forman, Sellers, and Mary King, along with Tracy Sugarman's *Stranger at the Gates: A Summer in Mississippi* (1966). During Freedom Summer much of the media attention focused on the white northern volunteers. An interesting collection edited by Elizabeth Sutherland, *Letters from Mississippi* (1965), provides initial impressions from the volunteers in letters home to friends and family. Historian Mary Aickin Rothschild has studied the volunteers in *A Case of Black and White* (1982), and sociologist Doug McAdam has focused on their contributions in 1964 and their lives after Mississippi in *Freedom Summer* (1988). Nicolaus Mill's *Like a Holy Crusade* (1992) exaggerates the importance of the volunteers, who at times appear to be the cavalry coming to the rescue of beleaguered black Mississippians.

In the mid-1990s two books, one by an historian and another by a sociologist, examined the civil rights years in Mississippi from a variety of perspectives. John Dittmer's *Local People* (1994) argues that the modern black freedom struggle began in the aftermath of World War II and was primarily a movement led by black Mississippians assisted by the "outside agitators" from SNCC and CORE. Charles Payne's *I've Got the Light of Freedom* (1995) is the best history of grassroots organizing in the movement. Although he looks most intently at Greenwood and the Delta, Payne examines movement activity across the state; he stresses the continuity between black organizers in the 1940s and the young activists of the 1960s.

Other important books on Mississippi include Myrlie Evers's memoir of her life with NAACP leader Medgar Evers, *For Us, the Living* (with William Peters), originally published in 1967 and recently reissued. The best book on the impact of the Voting Rights Act of 1965 on Mississippi is the late Frank Parker's *Black Votes Count: Political Empowerment in Mississippi after 1965* (1990). The most effective defender of African American voting rights in the Deep South, attorney Parker details the tactics of white supremacists in Mississippi to derail the Voting Rights Act and shows the responses of the civil rights community to keep the act intact. Of the books on local political campaigns, see Minion K. C. Morrison's *Black Political Empowerment* (1987), which focuses on black mayors in three small towns in Mississippi; and Melany Neilson, *Even*

Mississippi (1989), an interesting look at the unsuccessful 1982 and 1984 congressional campaigns of black representative Robert Clark, told by a white Mississippian who served on his staff. Frederick M. Wirt's *"We Ain't What We Was"* (1997) examines race relations today in Panola County.

Mississippi also played a role in the birth of the black power movement of the late 1960s. The Meredith march of 1966 was the last great march of the civil rights years. When James Meredith was shot after attempting to walk from Memphis to Jackson, all the major civil rights leaders and organizations joined the march. It was in the Mississippi Delta that SNCC activist Stokely Carmichael made the slogan "Black Power" a household word. Although blacks and whites continued to work together on civil rights issues, the Meredith march ushered in a new era of black nationalist thought and in effect brought an end to the integrationist phase of the movement. The Meredith march receives mention in most general studies of the movement. Dittmer's *Local People* devotes a chapter to the march, arguing that the media did much to magnify ideological and personal disputes among the marchers. A good first-person account is journalist Paul Good's *The Trouble I've Seen* (1975). See also Lawson's *In Pursuit of Power* and Milton Viorst's *Fire in the Streets* (1979).

The Autobiography of Malcolm X (1965) persuaded many young activists that traditional political involvement would not lead to black liberation. Stokely Carmichael and Charles V. Hamilton's *Black Power: The Politics of Liberation in America* (1967) was the opening manifesto of the movement, but its emphasis on voting and traditional political participation made it seem tame at a time when insurrections were rocking northern cities. Carson's *In Struggle* effectively explains the impact of black power on the transformation of SNCC, as do Meier and Rudwick for CORE. Harold Cruse provided a useful critique of black power in his *Crisis of the Negro Intellectual* (1967).

There are several general accounts of the civil rights movement, most of which focus on the period 1954–1968 and follow closely the career of Dr. Martin Luther King, Jr. The most successful of these surveys is Harvard Sitkoff, *The Struggle for Black Equality* (1981). The revised edition (1993) of this book adds much to the original account. Steven F. Lawson's *Running for Freedom* (2nd ed., 1997) is an excellent synthesis of black politics since World War II. Manning Marable's *Race, Reform, and Rebellion* (1984) is a solid interpretive essay. Fred Powledge's *Free at Last?* (1991) is an informed account of the movement years by a journalist who was on the scene. Vincent Harding's *Hope and History* (1990) is an inspirational essay on the lessons the movement can teach us today. Robert Weisbrot's *Freedom Bound* (1990) expands the treatment of the movement beyond the South and into the early 1970s, but his account of the southern struggle is not well informed.

Scholars have written numerous essays analyzing the civil rights revolution and its impact. The best early collection is Charles Eagles, ed., *The Civil Rights Movement in America* (1986), which features papers and responses by a bevy of Pulitzer and Bancroft scholars. Armstead Robinson and Patricia Sullivan's

New Directions in Civil Rights Studies (1991) includes essays by movement activists as well as scholars. See also *Have We Overcome?: Race Relations since Brown* (1979), edited by Michael V. Namorato; and John Dittmer, George C. Wright, and W. Marvin Dulaney, *The American Civil Rights Movement* (1993). Also of interest here is the documentary collection edited by Clayborne Carson and others, *The Eyes on the Prize: Civil Rights Reader* (1991).

The earliest accounts of the civil rights movement emphasize the role of the black church in identifying with and advancing the struggle. Morris's *Origins of the Civil Rights Movement* placed the church at the center of movement activity. (Later works by Dittmer and Payne show that in Mississippi, at least, black preachers often had to be dragged kicking and screaming into opening their churches to movement mass meetings.) In *Church People in the Struggle* (1993), James F. Findlay, Jr., has written an excellent study of the interaction between the National Council of Churches and the southern movement. James H. Cone's *Martin & Malcolm & America* (1991) presents a human portrait of the two legends, concluding that both men made monumental contributions to the black freedom struggle. Two recent studies are worth reading: Michael B. Friedland's *Lift up Your Voice like a Trumpet* (1998) examines the role of white clergy in the civil rights and antiwar movements. Charles Marsh has written a fascinating account of the impact of religion on civil rights activists and opponents in *God's Long Summer* (1997).

In recent years scholars have begun to devote serious attention to the roles of women in the civil rights movement. Earlier works emphasized the key contributions of Martin Luther King, Roy Wilkins, and James Farmer, along with the young men in SNCC and CORE. Yet women were a majority in the movement; they took the same risks as men and were the major local links with the young activists who came to the South in the early 1960s. The first serious treatment of women in the movement was Sara Evans's controversial *Personal Politics* (1979), which argued that women in the movement were treated as second-class citizens by their male colleagues (a point later disputed by a number of black and white women activists—see Mary King's *Freedom Song*). The first major collection of essays on women and civil rights was *Women in the Civil Rights Movement: Trailblazers and Torchbearers, 1941–1965* (1993), edited by Vicki L. Crawford, Jacqueline Anne Rouse, and Barbara Woods. Cynthia Griggs Fleming's *Soon We Will Not Cry* (1998) is a compelling biography of Ruby Doris Smith Robinson, one of the movement's most influential (yet least-known) activists.

The most famous woman activist was Mrs. Fannie Lou Hamer, the Ruleville, Mississippi, sharecropper who came to symbolize the grassroots struggle. Kay Mill's *This Little Light of Mine* (1993) is a highly readable, informative biography that gives special attention to Hamer's final years as an activist. Chana Kai Lee has written the first scholarly biography, *For Freedom's Sake: The Life of Fannie Lou Hamer* (1999), and Linda Reed is also working on a biography of the Mississippi activist.

Ella Baker's career as an activist goes back to the 1930s. She was director of branches for the NAACP during World War II and later served as SCLC's executive director. Baker was the person most responsible for the founding of SNCC and served as an advisor to that militant organization during its most activist period. Joanne Grant's biography, *Ella Baker: Freedom Bound* (1998), is a personal account written by a journalist and activist who worked with Baker. Historian Barbara Ransby is completing a scholarly biography of Ella Baker. In addition, scholars are examining group leadership among women in the southern movement. Vickie Crawford's forthcoming study on African American women in Mississippi will be an important addition to the growing literature on women in the movement.

Civil rights historiography over the past two decades has produced much impressive and important work. Yet the new scholarship raises additional questions, and some important areas remain relatively unexplored.

If civil rights scholars are guilty of stereotyping today, it is more likely to be in their treatment of whites rather than blacks. The caricature of the pot-bellied, Red-man chewing sheriff as both the symbol and the substance of white resistance oversimplifies the problems facing black activists in the 1960s, ignores the racist leadership of white businesspeople and elected officials, and can lead to sanguine conclusions about racial progress in the South over the past two decades. Dan T. Carter's important biography of Governor George Wallace, *The Politics of Rage* (1995), proves that the political tactics employed by race-baiters like Wallace in the 1960s are still effective today. As we approach the twenty-first century, with many of the gains made during the civil rights movement suddenly in jeopardy, we need to learn more about the leadership of white elites and to determine why resistance to black demands for freedom and equality remains so strong among white people of all social and economic classes in all regions of the country.

The current emphasis in civil rights scholarship on community organization has been selective; by and large it has not dealt with why the movement took hold in certain towns and counties and not in others, where conditions appeared to be equally promising. There is a need for more comparative studies on the local level and for more state studies that deal with the varieties of movement experiences in different geographical areas. To what extent did interorganizational rivalry and differences in social class inhibit the development of local movements? As noted, the impact of school desegregation in the late 1960s and 1970s needs attention, as does the impact of the War on Poverty on southern black communities. Exploring these and other questions will enrich our knowledge and appreciation of the freedom struggles of the 1950s and 1960s. It will also give us a more realistic assessment of the distance still to be traveled.

BIBLIOGRAPHY

Abernathy, Ralph David. *And the Walls Came Tumbling Down*. New York: Harper and Row, 1989.

Ashmore, Harry S. *Civil Rights and Wrongs: A Memoir of Race and Politics, 1944–1996*. Columbia: University of South Carolina Press, 1997.

Barnes, Catherine A. *A Journey from Jim Crow: The Desegregation of Southern Transit*. New York: Columbia University Press, 1983.

Bartley, Numan V. *The Rise of Massive Resistance: Race and Politics in the South during the 1950s*. Baton Rouge: Louisiana State University Press, 1969.

Bates, Daisy. *The Long Shadow of Little Rock: A Memoir*. Fayetteville: University of Arkansas Press, 1962.

Beals, Melba Patillo. *Warriors Don't Cry: A Searing Memoir of the Battle to Integrate Little Rock's Central High*. New York: Washington Square Press, 1994.

Beifuss, Joan T. *At the River I Stand: Memphis, the 1968 Strike, and Martin Luther King*. Memphis: B and W Books, 1985.

Belfrage, Sally. *Freedom Summer*. New York: Viking, 1965; 2nd ed., Charlottesville: University of Virginia Press, 1994.

Belknap, Michal R. *Federal Law and Southern Order: Racial Violence and Constitutional Conflict in the Post-Brown South*. Athens: University of Georgia Press, 1987.

Bennett, Lerone, Jr. *The Negro Mood and Other Essays*. Chicago: Johnson Publishing, 1964.

Blumberg, Rhoda L. *Civil Rights: The 1960s Freedom Struggle*. Boston: Twayne Publishers, 1984.

Branch, Taylor. *Parting the Waters: America in the King Years, 1954–63*. New York: Simon and Schuster, 1988.

———. *Pillar of Fire: America in the King Years, 1963–65*. New York: Simon and Schuster, 1998.

Brauer, Carl M. *John F. Kennedy and the Second Reconstruction*. New York: Columbia University Press, 1977.

Burk, Robert F. *The Eisenhower Administration and Black Civil Rights*. Knoxville: University of Tennessee Press, 1984.

Burns, Stuart, ed. *Daybreak of Freedom: The Montgomery Bus Boycott*. Chapel Hill: University of North Carolina Press, 1997.

Cagin, Seth, and Philip Dray. *We Are Not Afraid: The Story of Goodman, Schwerner, and Chaney and the Civil Rights Campaign for Mississippi*. New York: Macmillan, 1988.

Campbell, Clarice T. *Civil Rights Chronicle: Letters from the South*. Jackson: University Press of Mississippi, 1997.

Carmichael, Stokely, and Charles V. Hamilton. *Black Power: The Politics of Liberation in America*. New York: Random House, 1967.

Carson, Clayborne. *In Struggle: SNCC and the Black Awakening of the 1960s*. Cambridge: Harvard University Press, 1981.

———, ed. *The Papers of Martin Luther King, Jr*. Berkeley: University of California Press, 1992.

Carson, Clayborne, et al., eds. *Eyes on the Prize: America's Civil Rights Years: A Reader and Guide*. New York: Penguin Books, 1987.

————. *The Eyes on the Prize: Civil Rights Reader: Documents, Speeches, and First-hand Accounts from the Black Freedom Struggle, 1954–1990*. New York: Penguin Books, 1991.

Carter, Dan T. *The Politics of Rage: George Wallace, the Origins of New Conservatism, and the Transformation of America*. New York: Simon and Schuster, 1995.

Cecelski, David S. *Along Freedom Road: Hyde County, North Carolina and the Fate of Black Schools in the South*. Chapel Hill: University of North Carolina Press, 1994.

Chafe, William H. *Civilities and Civil Rights: Greensboro, North Carolina and the Black Struggle for Freedom*. New York: Oxford University Press, 1980.

Clark, Septima. *Echo in My Soul*. New York: E. P. Dutton and Co., 1962.

Colburn, David R. *Racial Change and Community Crisis: St. Augustine, Florida, 1877–1980*. New York: Columbia University Press, 1985.

Cone, James H. *Martin & Malcolm & America: A Dream or a Nightmare?* Maryknoll, NY: Orbis Books, 1991.

Crawford, Vicki L., Jacqueline Anne Rouse, and Barbara Woods, eds. *Women in the Civil Rights Movement: Trailblazers and Torchbearers, 1941–1965*. Bloomington: Indiana University Press, 1993.

Cruse, Harold. *The Crisis of the Negro Intellectual*. New York: William Morrow and Co., 1967.

Curry, Constance. *Silver Rights*. Chapel Hill, NC: Algonquin Books, 1995.

Dent, Tom. *Southern Journey: A Return to the Civil Rights Movement*. New York: William Morrow and Co., 1997.

Dittmer, John. *Local People: The Struggle for Civil Rights in Mississippi*. Urbana: University of Illinois Press, 1994.

Dittmer, John, George C. Wright, and W. Marvin Dulaney. *Essays on the American Civil Rights Movement*. College Station: Texas A&M University Press, 1993.

Durr, Virginia Foster. *Outside the Magic Circle: The Autobiography of Virginia Foster Durr*. Holliger F. Barnard, ed. University: University of Alabama Press, 1985.

Eagles, Charles. *Outside Agitator: Jon Daniels and the Civil Rights Movement in Alabama*. Chapel Hill: University of North Carolina Press, 1993.

————, ed. *The Civil Rights Movement in America*. Jackson: University Press of Mississippi, 1986.

Egerton, John. *Speak Now against the Day: The Generation before the Civil Rights Movement in the South*. New York: Alfred A. Knopf, 1994.

Eskew, Glenn T. *But for Birmingham: The Local and National Movements in the Civil Rights Struggle*. Chapel Hill: University of North Carolina Press, 1997.

Evans, Sara. *Personal Politics: The Roots of Women's Liberation in the Civil Rights Movement & the New Left*. New York: Alfred A. Knopf, 1979.

Evers, Mrs. Myrlie, with William Peters. *For Us, the Living*. New York: Doubleday, 1967; 2nd ed., Jackson: University Press of Mississippi, 1997.

Fager, Charles E. *Selma, 1965*. New York: Scribner's, 1974.

Fairclough, Adam. *Race & Democracy: The Civil Rights Struggle in Louisiana, 1915–1972*. Athens: University of Georgia Press, 1995.

————. *To Redeem the Soul of America: The Southern Christian Leadership Conference and Martin Luther King, Jr.* Athens: University of Georgia Press, 1987.

Farmer, James. *Freedom—When?* New York: Random House, 1965.

————. *Lay Bare the Heart: An Autobiography of the Civil Rights Movement*. New York: Arbor House, 1985.

Findlay, James F. *Church People in the Struggle: The National Council of Churches and the Black Freedom Movement, 1950–1970*. New York: Oxford University Press, 1993.

Fleming, Cynthia Griggs. *Soon We Will Not Cry: The Liberation of Ruby Doris Smith Robinson*. New York: Rowan and Littlefield, 1998.

Forman, James. *The Making of Black Revolutionaries*. New York: Macmillan, 1972.

Franklin, Jimmie Lee. *Black to Birmingham: Richard Arrington, Jr., and His Times*. University: University of Alabama Press, 1989.

Friedland, Michael B. *Lift up Your Voice like a Trumpet: White Clergy and the Civil Rights and Antiwar Movements, 1954–1973*. Chapel Hill: University of North Carolina Press, 1998.

Garrow, David J. *Bearing the Cross: Martin Luther King, Jr., and the Southern Christian Leadership Conference*. New York: William Morrow and Co., 1986.

————. *The FBI and Martin Luther King, Jr: From "Solo" to Memphis*. New York: W. W. Norton, 1981.

————, ed. *Martin Luther King, Jr., and the Civil Rights Movement*. 18 vol. Brooklyn: Carlson Publishing, 1989.

————. *Protest at Selma: Martin Luther King, Jr., and the Voting Rights Act of 1965*. New Haven, CT: Yale University Press, 1978.

Good, Paul. *The Trouble I've Seen: White Journalist/Black Movement*. Washington, DC: Howard University Press, 1975.

Grant, Joanne, ed. *Black Protest*. Greenwich, CT: Fawcett Books, 1968.

————. *Ella Baker: Freedom Bound*. New York: John Wiley and Sons, 1998.

Halberstam, David. *The Children*. New York: Random House, 1998.

Harding, Vincent. *Hope and History: Why We Must Share the Story of the Movement*. Maryknoll, NY: Orbis Books, 1990.

Hampton, Henry, and Steve Fayer. *Voices of Freedom: An Oral History of the Civil Rights Movement from the 1950s through the 1980s*. New York: Bantam Books, 1990.

Hine, Darlene Clark. *Black Victory: The Rise and Fall of the White Primary in Texas*. Millwood, NY: KTP Press, 1979.

Jacoway, Elizabeth, and David R. Colburn, eds. *Southern Businessmen and Desegregation*. Baton Rouge: Louisiana State University Press, 1982.

King, Jr. Martin Luther, *Stride towards Freedom: The Montgomery Story*. New York: Harper and Brothers, 1958.

————. *Where Do We Go from Here: Chaos or Community?* New York: Harper and Row, 1967.

————. *Why We Can't Wait*. New York: New American Library, 1964.

King, Mary. *Freedom Song: A Personal Story of the Civil Rights Movement*. New York: William Morrow and Co., 1987.

Kluger, Richard. *Simple Justice*. New York: Alfred A. Knopf, 1976.

Lawson, Steven F. *Black Ballots: Voting Rights in the South, 1944–1969*. New York: Columbia University Press, 1976.

————. *In Pursuit of Power: Southern Blacks and Electoral Politics, 1965–1982*. New York: Columbia University Press, 1985.

————. *Running for Freedom: Civil Rights and Black Politics in America since 1941*. New York: McGraw-Hill, 1991; ed., 1997.

Lee, Chana Kai. *For Freedom's Sake: The Life of Fannie Lou Hamer*. Urbana: University of Illinois Press, 1999.

Lewis, Anthony. *Portrait of a Decade*. New York: Random House, 1965.

Lewis, David Levering. *King: A Critical Biography*. New York: Praeger, 1970; rev. ed., Urbana: University of Illinois Press, 1978.

Lomax, Louis. *The Negro Revolt*. New York: Harper and Brothers, 1962.

McAdam, Doug. *Freedom Summer*. New York: Oxford University Press, 1988.

McLemore, Leslie Burl. "The Mississippi Freedom Democratic Party: A Case Study of Grass-Roots Politics." Ph.D., University of Massachusetts, 1971.

McMillen, Neil R. *The Citizens' Council: Organized Resistance to the Second Reconstruction, 1954–1964*. Urbana: University of Illinois Press, 1971.

Malcolm X, with Alex Haley. *The Autobiography of Malcolm X*. New York: Grove Press, 1965.

Marable, Manning. *From the Grassroots*. Boston: South End Press, 1980.

————. *Race, Reform, and Rebellion: The Second Reconstruction in Black America, 1945–1982*. Jackson: University Press of Mississippi, 1984.

Mars, Florence. *Witness in Philadelphia*. Baton Rouge: Louisiana State University Press, 1977.

Marsh, Charles. *God's Long Summer*. Princeton, NJ: Princeton University Press, 1997.

Marshall, Burke. *Federalism and Civil Rights*. New York: Columbia University Press, 1964.

Martin, John Barlow. *The Deep South Says "Never."* New York: Ballantine Books, 1957.

Meier, August, and Elliot Rudwick. *CORE: A Study in the Civil Rights Movement*. New York: Oxford University Press, 1973.

Mills, Kay. *This Little Light of Mine: The Life of Fannie Lou Hamer*. New York: E. P. Dutton, 1993.

Mills, Nicolaus. *Like a Holy Crusade: Mississippi, 1964—the Turning of the Civil Rights Movement in America*. Chicago: Ivan R. Dee, 1992.

Moody, Anne. *Coming of Age in Mississippi*. New York: Dial Press, 1968.

Morris, Aldon D. *The Origins of the Civil Rights Movement: Black Communities Organizing for Change*. New York: Free Press, 1984.

Morrison, Minion K. C. *Black Political Empowerment*. Albany: State University Press of New York, 1987.

Muse, Benjamin. *The American Negro Revolution*. Bloomington: Indiana University Press, 1968.

Namorato, Michael V., ed. *Have We Overcome? Race Relations since Brown*. Jackson: University Press of Mississippi, 1979.

Navasky, Victor S. *Kennedy Justice*. New York: Atheneum, 1971.

Neary, John. *Julian Bond: Black Rebel*. New York: William Morrow and Co., 1971.

Neilson, Melany. *Even Mississippi*. Tuscaloosa: University of Alabama Press, 1989.

Norrell, Robert J. *Reaping the Whirlwind: The Civil Rights Movement in Tuskegee*. New York: Vintage Press, 1985.

O'Reilly, Kenneth. *Racial Matters: The FBI's Secret File on Black America, 1960–1972*. New York: Free Press, 1989.

Parker, Frank R. *Black Votes Count: Political Empowerment in Mississippi after 1965*. Chapel Hill: University of North Carolina Press, 1990.

Payne, Charles M. *I've Got the Light of Freedom: The Organizing Tradition and the Mississippi Freedom Struggle*. Berkeley: University of California Press, 1995.

Peck, James. *Freedom Ride*. New York: Grove Press, 1962.

Powledge, Fred. *Free at Last? The Civil Rights Movement and the People Who Made It*. Boston: Little, Brown, 1991.

Pratt, Robert A. *The Color of Their Skin: Education and Race in Richmond, Virginia, 1954–1989*. Charlottesville: University Press of Virginia, 1992.

Raines, Howell. *My Soul Is Rested: Movement Days in the Deep South Remembered*. New York: G. P. Putnam's Sons, 1977.

Reed, Linda. *Simple Decency and Common Sense: The Southern Conference Movement, 1938–1963*. Bloomington: Indiana University Press, 1991.

Robinson, Armstead, and Patricia Sullivan, eds. *New Directions in Civil Rights Studies*. Charlottesville: University Press of Virginia, 1991.

Robinson, Jo Ann Gibson. *The Montgomery Bus Boycott and the Women Who Started It: The Memoir of Jo Ann Gibson Robinson*. Ed. David J. Garrow. Knoxville: University of Tennessee Press, 1987.

Rothschild, Mary Aicken. *A Case of Black and White: Northern Volunteers and the Southern Freedom Summers, 1964–1965*. Westport, CT: Greenwood Press, 1982.

Rowan, Carl T. *Go South to Sorrow*. New York: Random House, 1957.

Rustin, Bayard. *Down the Line*. Chicago: Quadrangle Books, 1971.

Salter, John R., Jr. *Jackson, Mississippi: An American Chronicle of Struggle and Schism*. Malabar, FL: Krieger Publishing, 1987.

Scott, Daryl Michael. *Contempt and Pity: Social Policy and the Damaged Black Psyche*. Chapel Hill: University of North Carolina Press, 1997.

Sellers, Cleveland, with Robert Terrell. *The River of No Return: The Autobiography of a Black Militant and the Life and Death of SNCC*. New York: William Marrow and Co., 1973; 2nd ed., Jackson: University Press of Mississippi, 1990.

Silver, James W. *Mississippi: The Closed Society*. New York: Harcourt, Brace and World, 1964.

Sitkoff, Harvard. *The Struggle for Black Equality*. New York: Hill and Wang, 1981; rev. ed., 1993.

Smead, Howard. *Blood Justice: The Lynching of Mack Charles Parker*. New York: Oxford University Press, 1986.

Strickland, Arvarh E. *History of the Chicago Urban League*. Urbana: University of Illinois Press, 1966.

Sugarman, Tracy. *Stranger at the Gates: A Summer in Mississippi*. New York: Hill and Wang, 1966.

Sullivan, Patricia. *Days of Hope: Race and Democracy in the New Deal Era*. Chapel Hill: University of North Carolina Press, 1996.

Sutherland, Elizabeth, ed. *Letters from Mississippi*. New York: McGraw-Hill, 1965.

Thernstrom, Abigail. *Whose Votes Count? Affirmative Action and Minority Voting Rights*. Cambridge: Harvard University Press, 1987.

Tushnet, Mark V. *The NAACP's Legal Strategy against Segregated Education, 1925–1950*. Chapel Hill: University of North Carolina Press, 1987.

Viorst, Milton. *Fire in the Streets: America in the Sixties*. New York: Simon and Schuster, 1979.

Watters, Pat. *Down to Now: Reflections on the Southern Civil Rights Movement*. New York: Pantheon, 1971.

Watters, Pat, and Reece Cleghorn. *Climbing Jacob's Ladder: The Arrival of Negroes in Southern Politics.* New York: Harcourt, Brace and World, 1967.

Webb, Sheyann, and Rachel West Nelson. *Selma, Lord, Selma.* University: University of Alabama Press, 1980.

Weisbrot, Robert. *Freedom Bound: A History of America's Civil Rights Movement.* New York: W. W. Norton, 1990.

Weiss, Nancy J. *Whitney M. Young, Jr., and the Struggle for Civil Rights.* Princeton, NJ: Princeton University Press, 1989.

Whitfield, Stephen J. *A Death in the Delta: The Story of Emmett Till.* New York: Free Press, 1988.

Wilkins, Roy, with Tom Matthews. *Standing Fast: The Autobiography of Roy Wilkins.* New York: Viking Press, 1982.

Wirt, Frederick. *"We Ain't What We Was": Civil Rights in the New South.* Durham, NC: Duke University Press, 1997.

Zinn, Howard. *The Southern Mystique.* New York: Alfred A. Knopf, 1964.

―――. *SNCC: The New Abolitionists.* Boston: Beacon Press, 1964.

XVII

African American Religion in the United States

Charles H. Long

INTRODUCTION

Between the sixteenth and early nineteenth centuries somewhere between 11 million and 15 million Africans were transported across the Atlantic into the Americas. There is an extensive and controversial literature on the demographics of the slave trade. Philip Curtin's *Atlantic Slave Trade* (1969) is the watershed for this discussion. One should also look at Noel Deerr's *History of Sugar* (1949–50). Counters to Curtin's position are expressed in Joseph Inikori's *Forced Migration* (1982) and also in J. Inikori, D. C. Ohadike, and A. C. Uno-mah's *Chaining of a Continent* (1992). The controversy arises over the estimates of the illegal slave trade that took place after the official abolition of slavery by various European countries and centers primarily on the importation of slaves into South America. Given these estimates, one could approximate somewhere between 2 million and 3 million Africans entering British North America and the United States. It is from this long historical event that the generations of persons of African descent became a part of North America and the United States. The problematic nature of the religion in the modern period in general and the religion of communities and persons of African descent in the United States can be located within this context.

With the coming of Africans to the Americas, the lands across the Atlantic contained three groups of people: the several aboriginal inhabitants of these lands (later called Indians); the European immigrants; and the Africans imported and enslaved by the Europeans. These three groups define different religious situations. The aboriginal inhabitants possessed no meaning of religion as a separate and identifiable aspect of life. What is called religion was for them a way of life; more precisely, the way of their life in their "nation" or tribe. The power of this meaning was present in their landscape, speech, activities of live-lihood, and all life incidental to the meaning of social existence. For example, to be Cherokee meant to live in a Cherokee landscape, to speak a Cherokee language, to eat a Cherokee diet, and to understand in a Cherokee manner those powers and forces that are other and prior to human existence—thus to have Cherokee gods and spirits.

European immigrants brought their gods and religion with them across the ocean. Most Europeans who settled in North America were Protestant reformers. The Puritans who settled in New England were religious reformers seeking a place to practice their form of Calvinism; the establishment of a religious com-munity was the theological rationale for their settlement. For many in the Middle Colonies the reason for immigration was entrepreneurial. Some Roman Catholics settled in what is now Maryland, but in the main most Europeans in North America were Protestants or dissenters in one of the variations of Protestantism. The Europeans thus imposed their religion and settlement upon the land, in most cases dispossessing the original inhabitants of the land. Few if any attempts of amalgamation or accommodation were made with the aboriginal inhabitants.

The case of the Africans brought to North America was radically different from the case of the other two groups. The aboriginal populations of the con-tinent knew this land as their home. It was the place of their ancestors and the source of their sustenance as a people. The Europeans undertook a conscious and voluntary decision to cross the ocean and to settle. From a religious point of view, the voyage across the Atlantic was sanctioned and blessed by their god. They brought with them their religion, its texts and doctrines, and attempted to recapitulate their religion in the acts of their settlement. In contrast, Africans from several different groups in Africa were forcefully brought to North Amer-ica. For the sake of control, North American enslavers tended to mix Africans from several different tribes and language groups on a single plantation. This lack of communication lessened the enslavers' fear of unity among the slaves. Given these circumstances, what can one say about the nature of African Amer-ican religion?

Although several excellent monographs exist on the interpretation of partic-ular African American denominational groups, I agree with David Wills, who is quoted by Timothy E. Fulop and Albert J. Raboteau in their edited volume *African-American Religion* (1997): "The study of African American religious history still lacks an obvious entry point for persons seeking an obvious initial orientation to the field." In the article contributed to the Fulop and Raboteau volume, Wills sets forth three models for the meaning of African American religion within an American context. These are "Pluralism and Toleration"; "The Southern Theme: The Encounter of Black and White"; and "Black and White: From the Evangelical Awakening to the Present."

Earlier, in his edited work *The Black Experience in Religion* (1974), C. Eric

Lincoln, the dean of black church studies, had commented on the difficulty of characterizing black religion. Lincoln makes clear that black religion is not simply white religion in blackface; neither is black religion a formal denomination with a structured doctrine. It is, rather, says Lincoln, "an attitude, a movement. . . . It represents the desire of Blacks to be self-conscious of black people about the meaning of their blackness and to search for spiritual fulfillment in terms of their understanding of themselves and their experience of history. . . . Black religion, then, cuts across denominational, cult, and sect lines to do for black people what other religions have not done; to assume the black man's humanity, his relevance, his responsibility, his participation, and his right to see himself as the image of God" (p. 3).

The difficulty in coming to terms with the religion of African Americans is directly related to their enslavement in North America. First, enslavement is coincidental with a lack of self-determination; Africans did not choose to be here. They were enslaved in Africa, brought in chains across the Atlantic, and sold into slavery in a distant and foreign land. African American churches did not come into being until the end of the eighteenth century and then only in limited regions. What is or could be the religious experience and expression of these enslaved Africans from the early seventeenth century until the end of the Civil War? Although most studies of African American religion identify this religion with African American religious institutions, African peoples have been free to form their own institutions in any significant manner only since 1865.

ORIENTATION AND BEGINNINGS

Seeking a point of departure for African American religion, several works set forth the African origins as this originating point. See, for example, Albert Raboteau, *Slave Religion*, (1978), Chapter 1, "The African Diaspora"; and Part 1 of Mechal Sobel's "West African Cosmos" in *Trabelin' On: The Slave Journey to an Afro-Baptist Faith* (1979) and his *The World They Made Together: Black and White Values in Eighteenth-Century Virginia* (1987). Africa as exemplary origin has been on the scene since the publication of Melville Herskovits's *Myth of the Negro Past* (1941). Before Herskovits's publication most African American intellectuals paid scant attention to the meaning of their African origins, since unlike Africans enslaved in South America, and especially in Brazil, Africans in North America had not been able self-consciously to carry on their African religious and linguistic cultures. This line of inquiry was continued by the work of the linguist Lorenzo Turner in his *Africanisms in the Gullah Dialect* (1949). Ira Berlin's *Many Thousands Gone: The First Two Centuries of Slavery in North America* (1998) places the problematic of freedom, religion, and slavery within the context of the structures of American society during its formative years. A similar comprehensive study of Virginia and the Lowcountry plantation slave cultures is undertaken in Philip D. Morgan's *Slave Counterpoint: Black Culture in the Eighteenth-Century Chesapeake & Lowcountry* (1998).

From the perspective of several active intellectuals the best option for African Americans was to achieve legitimacy within the structures of the American Republic. This position was carried forth in the program of the Chicago school of sociology, whose most prominent spokesperson was E. Franklin Frazier. This position is made clear in Frazier's *Negro Church in America* (1974). For a series of essays continuing this debate see Joseph E. Holloway's *Africanisms in American Culture* (1990).

An authentic basis for origins might be found in the conscious and unconscious memories of the many and various black communities over time. One theme that recurs over and over in African American life is the sense of water and water symbolism. This symbol is present in the spirituals such as "Roll, Jordan, Roll," and it appears prominently in sermons and in scholarly texts. The title of a major study of the religion of enslaved Africans is Eugene Genovese's *Roll Jordan, Roll* (1974). This text is matched by Vincent Harding's *There Is a River* (1981) and Sylvia Frey's *Water from the Rock* (1991). The first volume of the masterful biography of Martin Luther King, Jr., by Taylor Branch is entitled *Parting the Waters: America in the King Years 1954–63* (1989).

The instances of the meaning of water and water symbolism in the experience and expressions by and about African Americans are too numerous to mention; it is clear that this is a powerful symbol, a meaning remembered within the collective communities of African Americans. Probably W.E.B. Du Bois's *Souls of Black Folk*, first published in 1903 but has undergone numerous reprints and editions and is still in print, first adumbrated this new and different modality of religion. Du Bois sensed a depth of meaning in what he called the "Sorrow Songs." He noted the sadness, poignancy, authenticity, and creativity in this music. One might suggest two related origins for African American religion: (1) the actuality and horror of the Middle Passage, and (2) the experience of North American slavery.

This is obviously not the normal source African Americans have cited when asked about their religious experience, but it is what they remembered and from where they derived that fierce desire for freedom, judgment, and critique. Although slavery is a common background for all African Americans, the issue has to do with how one understands this tradition. From a religious point of view, there is a meaning of religion that comes into being during slavery. Sterling Stuckey in his *Slave Culture: Nationalist Theory and the Foundation of Black America* (1987) attends to some of the complexity of slave culture. Stuckey shows that since most of the enslaved Africans could not speak the same language and did not share kinship from Africa, they resorted to more generalized ritualistic modes from Africa such as the Ring Shout, a counterclockwise dance, which became the empirical and metaphorical mode employed by Africans to create a self-conscious community among slaves, a community that was not simply what it was because of their owners. Stuckey demonstrates the curious fact that, through the use of African modes, enslaved Africans remade or re-created themselves as Americans. This is an important concept, for many African Americans tend to assume along with most European Americans that the term *American* is reserved only for Americans of European ancestry.

David Brion Davis ends his book *The Problem of Slavery in the Age of Revolution, 1770–1823* (1975) with a musing about the nature and possibility of religion in the modern Western world. He says that "especially as Marx and Freud deepened the meaning of the message: that we can expect nothing from the mercy of God or from the mercy of those who exercise worldly lordship in His or other names; that man's true emancipation, whether physical or spiritual, must always *depend on those who have endured and overcome some form of slavery* [emphasis added]" (p. 564).

The tradition of enslavement of African Americans in the United States thus becomes a datum out of which various religious modalities emerge. This tradition remains a reservoir of historical memory and critique; it almost constitutes a religious tradition in itself. If it is a religious tradition or ethos, such a tradition finds expression in the continuing traditions of African American folklore and equally within the institutional forms of various denominations of African American Christianity and Islam. Although distinguishing among and between these various forms of African American religion is possible, these forms overlap and intertwine because they all emerge from a common cultural past.

Folkloric tradition in the form of oral literature may be seen in Langston Hughes and Arna Bontemps, *Book of Negro Folklore* (1958), and in Roger Abrahams and John F. Szwed, *After Africa* (1983). Synthetic accounts of an African American ethos are found in Lawrence Levine, *Black Culture and Black Consciousness* (1977). The slave tradition of religion and folklore can be seen in the interpretive work by Albert Raboteau, *Slave Religion* (1978). Sources for these interpretations have often come from narratives of slaves recorded after emancipation. One of the most valuable of these collections is *Slave Testimony* (1977), edited by John Blassingame. A smaller collection is Frederick Ramsey's *Been Here and Gone* (1960). Leon Litwack's *Been in the Storm So Long* (1979) deals with this tradition immediately after the Civil War. John Langston Gwaltney continues this tradition of oral literature in *Drylongso* (1980/1993).

For the African American music tradition three works are indispensable: Miles Mark Fisher, *Negro Slave Songs in the United States* (1953); Eileen Southern, *The Music of Black Americans* (1983); and John Lovell's *Black Song: The Forge and the Flame* (1972). Oral literature and the music tradition form the foci of expressiveness for the African American religious ethos—an ethos formed within the slavery tradition. Aspects of this tradition were incorporated within the church and in the literary and musical traditions of African Americans, but these incorporations never exhausted this tradition, which continues to exist both within and alongside the institutional religious, musical, and intellectual traditions of African Americans. Dolan Hubbard's *Sermon and the African American Literary Imagination* (1994) shows how one tradition of African American literature owes its origin to the oral literary productions of the black preacher. Bruce A. Rosenburg had explored the African American sermon as oral literature in *The Art of the American Folk Preacher* (1970). For an appreciation of the black literary style stemming from the religious tradition of folklore, see the edited work *Chant of Saints*, by Michael S. Harper and Robert B. Stepto (1979).

THE AFRICAN AMERICAN RELIGIOUS INSTITUTION

Though enslaved Africans were creating communities of identity within the structures of slavery, such communities were sociologically ephemeral, since Africans were owned by others and subject to being sold away from their communities. There was, however, a deeper meaning of their integration—this was the constitution of a person, self, soul, that bore an identity and became a mode of self-critique and the basis for a critical relationship with others. It was within this milieu that Africans heard the gospel, or as Lawrence Jones put it in the title to his forthcoming work, *They Overheard the Gospel: American Religious Experience prior to the Civil War.* During the last half of the eighteenth century the English colonists in North America were in the midst of critical assessments of their religious and political situations. These religious assessments eventuated in the Great Awakenings, evangelical Christian revivals that began in New England and extended as far south as Georgia. This was also the beginnings of the political debates and agitations that would lead to the American Revolution.

This turmoil forms the context for the beginning of African American Christian religious institutions. One of the best short discussions of this period is Albert Raboteau's "Black Religious Experience in American Evangelicalism," in Fulop and Raboteau, *African-American Religion.* For a comprehensive discussion of this period within the context of the American Revolution, see Sylvia Frey's *Water from the Rock* (1991), especially chapter 8, "The Christian Social Order: Reformulating the Master's Ideology," and chapter 9," The African-American Response: Black Culture within a White Context." This same historical terrain is traversed by Mechal Sobel's *Trabelin' On: The Slave Journey to an Afro-Baptist Faith* (1979).

George Liele and Richard Allen signal the beginnings of black institutional church Christianity. Most histories of African American religion have been limited to a study and interpretation of a Baptist or Methodist form of Christianity. According to C. Eric Lincoln and Lawrence H. Mamiya in *The Black Church in the African-American Experience* (1990), the first black Baptist churches are "generally acknowledged to have been the African Baptist or 'Bluestone' Church on the William Byrd plantation near the Bluestone River in Mecklenberg, Virginia, in 1758, and the Silver Bluff Baptist Church, located on the South Carolina bank of the Savannah River, not far from Augusta, Georgia. Although historical records indicate that the Silver Bluff Church was established by a slave named George Liele sometime between 1773 and 1775, the cornerstone of the present church building claims a founding date of 1750" (p. 23). In reference to the beginning of separate black Methodist churches, Milton C. Sernett in *Afro-American Religious History: A Documentary Witness* (1985) stated, "Though convinced that Methodism best suited the religious needs of Afro-Americans and dedicated to preserving the unity of the body of Christ, Allen led the African Methodists into a separate denomination in 1816 after many years of struggle against white control" (p. 135).

Fulop and Raboteau list the following general studies of African American churches: W.E.B. Du Bois, *The Negro Church* (1903); Carter G. Woodson, *History of the Negro Church* (1921); Benjamin E. Mays and Joseph W. Nicholson, *The Negro's Church* (1969); Ruby Johnson, *The Development of Negro Religion* (1954); and Willis D. Weatherford, *American Churches and the Negro: An Historical Study from Slave Days to the Present* (1957). Lincoln and Mamiya's historical sociological study, *The Black Church in the African-American Experience*, is the only general text that takes account of black Pentecostals and Roman Catholics, as well as the various Baptists, Methodist, Presbyterians, and other mainline denominational groups. For African American Catholics, see Cyprian Davis, *The History of Black Catholics in the United States* (1990).

We are fortunate to have Richard Allen's autobiography, *The Life Experiences and Gospel Labors of the Rt. Rev. Richard Allen* (1960/1983). The definitive biography of Allen is Charles H. Wesley's *Richard Allen, Apostle of Freedom* (1935/1969). There are several good histories of the various African American Methodists. These include David H. Bradley, *History of the A.M.E. Zion Church* (1956, 1970); James Walker Hood, *One Hundred Years of the African Methodist Episcopal Church* (1895); and John J. Moore, *History of the A.M.E. Zion Church* (1884). Bishop William J. Walls wrote a definitive history of the AME Zion Church *The African Methodist Episcopal Zion Church* (1974). Accounts of the history of the Christian Methodist Episcopal Church include Charles Henry Phillips, *The History of the Colored Methodist Episcopal Church in America* (1898), and M. C Pettigrew, *From Miles to Johnson* (1970).

Baptists have not been as prolific. General histories include Owen Pelt and Ralph Smith, *The Story of the National Baptist Convention* (1960); Leroy Fitts, *A History of Black Baptists* (1985); and Joseph H. Jackson, *A Story of Christian Activism: The History of the National Baptist Convention* (1980). For specific issues see James Melvin Washington, *Frustrated Fellowship: The Black Baptist Quest for Social Power* (1986), and Sandy D. Martin, *Black Baptists and African Missions: The Origins of a Movement 1880–1915* (1989).

African American Christians have traditionally been more numerous in either black Baptist or Methodist religious bodies. Since the 1930s, however, African Americans have been members of Pentecostal churches, and black membership in these denominations is growing. Apart from a relatively small group of African Americans who are members of the Roman Catholic, Episcopal, and Presbyterian Churches, there are a number of other religious bodies that do not fall easily into any of the above classifications. I make reference here to groups such as the Father Divine Peace Mission or the Garvey movement. Arthur Huff Fauset presents and analyses these religious groups in *Black Gods of the Metropolis*

(1944). The groups discussed include Mt. Sinai Holy Church of America, Inc., United Church of Prayer for All People, Church of God (black Jews), Moorish Science Temple of America, and Father Divine's Peace Mission Movement. Fauset refers to these groups as cults and attempts to justify his classification on the basis of a sociopsychological functional theory of religion. According to Fauset, these "cults" exist to relieve the psychological tensions of their adherents.

RELIGION, PROTEST, AND FREEDOM

Gayraud Wilmore in his *Black Religion and Black Radicalism* (1972/1998) places these religious movements (cults) in his chapter titled "The Deradicalization of the Black Church." This characterization implies a certain theological and ideological stance in the interpretation of black religion in the United States. The origin of Wilmore's stance can be seen in David Walker, *David Walker's Appeal to the Colored Citizens of the World* (rpt. 1965/1995). Walker's *Appeal* was first published in 1829. David Walker was born a legally free black person in 1785 in Wilmington, North Carolina. He moved to Boston in 1826 and became an agent and editor of an abolitionist publication, *Freedom's Journal*. Walker's *Appeal* enunciated a critical view of the situation of persons of African descent and of slavery based upon the normative traditions of Protestant Christianity and the ideals of American republicanism. It is significant to note that Walker's work is the first written form of protest that is informed by a specific religious meaning.

Vincent Harding, in his *There Is a River* (1981), places his discussion of David Walker and Nat Turner in the same chapter. Harding saw a historical relationship between the publication of the *Appeal* in Boston in 1829 and Nat Turner's revolt in Virginia in 1831. The locales of the two events are radically different; Turner is enslaved on a plantation in Virginia, whereas Walker is a free person of color living as a publisher in Boston. Given the radicality of locales, they are united by a common concern for the freedom of others enslaved and the abolition of the institution of slavery itself.

Walker's work is in the genre of accusatory and polemical publishing. It uses the rhetoric of Christian theology and Enlightenment democracy to critically assess the nature and destiny of the United States. Turner's published work is the result of an action, and his *Confessions* (transcribed by Thomas W. Higginson, 1831; reprinted in Eugene D. Genovese's, *From Rebellion to Revolution: Afro-American Slave Revolts in the Making of the Modern World* [1979]) and Herbert Aptheker's *American Negro Slave Revolts* (1943) relates the reasons and causes of his leadership of a slave revolt. Turner's *Confessions* result from an action done but not completed, whereas Walker's words are meant to posit a viable future for a free America and warn of the grave consequences from America's continuation in status quo. Both positions are critical and prophetic.

Before his revolt in 1831, Nat Turner had escaped from slavery but returned voluntarily to his master. One can surmise two reasons for this action. In the first instance, in his voluntary return to enslavement, Nat was recognizing a complex moral position. Though slavery was an evil, it was an evil to which he had submitted and through that submission had by virtue of this participation partly legitimized the institution and situation of slavery. His escape from enslavement left the institution of slavery intact. In his later revolt he expressed what he felt was a more authentic position regarding the institution of slavery. His revolt was an expression of freedom against the institution of slavery itself and thus involved the creation of a wider community of those who were enslaved. A similar position was taken by David Walker; though a free African American living in Boston, he knew he could not feel free until all slaves were free and the institution of slavery abolished.

The Problematic of African American Religion

Lincoln and Mamiya, in their *Black Church in the African-American Experience*, define six dialectical models for understandings the black church, models that might easily be extended to the understanding of black culture in general. These dialectical models are (1) the dialectic between priestly and prophetic functions; (2) the dialectic between other-worldly versus this-worldly; (3) the dialectic between universalism and particularism; (4) the dialectic between the communal and the privatistic; (5) the dialectic between the charismatic versus bureaucratic; and finally (6) the dialectic between resistance versus accommodation. Posing the issue in terms of these dialectics gives a sense of the ambiguity of black religion and culture. To be sure, a great deal of ambiguity exists in the history and culture of African Americans, but there is equally an empirical and felt sense of identity and continuity.

Lincoln and Mamiya's dialectics tend to express structural binaries undergirded by the tenacity for survival within the various black communities. Binary dialectics might be supplemented by the desire for survival that is capable of uniting what appear to be opposites into a creative wholeness, a kind of *co-incindentia oppositorium*. Both Walker and Turner died early deaths for their work on behalf of African American freedom. Although there is no conclusive proof, it is assumed that Walker was poisoned. Nat Turner was hanged. Walker died in Boston, Turner at the end of a hangman's rope in Virginia. Nat's writings, *The Confessions of Nat Turner*, are his straightforward confessions of his religious experience. Walker's *Appeal* is a well-wrought logical theological indictment composed in reflection by a thinker. Both Walker and Nat Turner speak of the judgment of God in other-worldly and apocalyptical images.

The Nature of Religion

Our English term *religion* is derived from two Latin terms, *religare* and *religio*. The former term, *religare*, means "to tie," "to fasten together," or "to collect or gather up again." The term *religio* carries the connotations "scrupulousness, conscientiousness, seriousness." The second term, *religio*, pervades all aspects of the struggle of African Americans to think, act, and imagine a new form of human bindings and relationships within the American world. It is clear that the Romans did not use the word *religion* as we now use it. As a matter of fact, a foremost scholar of Roman religion, Georges Dumezil, in *Archaic Roman Religion* (1970), asserted that "Latin does not have a word to designate religion" (vol. 1, p. 132).

These Latin terms nevertheless bear directly on the topic of African American religion. In the first sense, the issue of binding has to do with "who are those who are bound?" "to whom are they bound?" and "what are the possibilities of another form of binding?" In the most literal and historical senses, Africans were bound in chains, enslaved, and brought across the ocean to be enslaved in America. Even in slavery, Africans sought new modes of establishing a more humane binding among themselves as a source of their humanity and identity. This new binding carried with it a protest against the persons and institutions that had bound them in slavery and oppression. Given the situation of enslaved Africans in North America, the very notion of bindings or being bound carries the concomitant meaning of experience, action, and discernment. African Americans have always discerned that they desired to be bound to each other and that through this binding they would come to know a caring God who would be bound to them, sustaining their lives and identities. They have also desired a new relationship and binding to the larger entity of the American state. Such a new binding and relationship would call for a rectification of the older structures of their relationship to the American Republic.

The binaries and dichotomies stated by C. Eric Lincoln emerge within black religious communities in their attempts to come to terms with the problematical nature of the various forms of binding, unbinding, and rebinding in African American history and culture. While acknowledging the value of Lincoln's dialectics for an understanding of the dynamics of the black church as an institutional and public structure, allow me to restate the position in specifically religious terms. The fundamental issues of black religion in the United States can be stated as follows:

1. Where is the locus and what is the nature of an *otherness that can be an-other source* of meaning and value that creates and sustains black life in this place? The entire history of blacks since their removal from Africa demonstrates that American culture and its institutions have not been created for the well-being and enhancement of blacks; consequently, black communities question whether the continuation of any important structure of this country can ever come to terms with their humanity. They have thus sought a meaning and value in their lives that was never under the aegis and control of those who embody the history of those who enslaved them.

2. What is the best *entrée and access to this surplus and excess of power, meaning, salvation, and value* that is the *otherness* necessary for the humanity of the black

community? The experiential and expressive modalities of otherness lie in the realm of transcendence. The black church inherited a specific and legitimated language and performance of the *otherness* of world and being; however, within the history and culture of African Americans the definition, and the performance of this meaning, has never been limited to the arena of the church.

RELIGIOUS EXPERIENCE: CONJURING, DECIPHERING, AND DISCERNMENT

Charles H. Long's "Perspective for a Study of African American Religion in the United States," in *History of Religions* (1971), reprinted in Fulop and Raboteau, highlighted three fundamental structures in African American religion. First is the involuntary presence as a situational stance of the African American communities. This stance led to the "sense of being here," as opposed to being "over against," as the reality of one's situation. From this perspective the meaning of protest is built into the very presence of African peoples in North America. Given that North America and later the United States became significant political units in the modern period by virtue of immigrants from Europe, the involuntary situation of African Americans constitutes a unique stance within the orders of the modern world. The second element is the perduring reality of Africa as historical empirical reality and as religious image. We must remember that the word *Africa* is a Western term that refers to the entire continent of Africa. Africans who were enslaved were unfamiliar with the term *Africa*. They knew themselves to be Yorubas, Ibos, Ibibios, Ashantis, Dogon, Bambaras, and so on. These individual peoples came to be designated in the slave trade and the colonizing missions of European countries by the general term *Africans*.

Coming as they did from several different groups from West Africa and Angola, unable to communicate in a common language, and finding themselves under the common yoke of enslavement, these peoples found the designation of those who enslaved them, "Africans," to be itself a mark of their commonality. Furthermore, it allowed them to know that they came from *another* place—that this place of enslavement was not their home. Thus through their enslavement, *Africa*, a term foreign to them, became a term loaded with the familiarity of the intimacy of home and homeland—a place where they could be humanly known.

That place was not only the other land from which they had come; it was equally a future land to which they would return. African American folklore contains images of "flying back to Africa." Later, biblical imagery of Ethiopia is a metaphor for all Africa, and Africa appears as the eschatological savior of all black persons. Africa had to do with being black in a land that had through the empirics and symbolism of the color white turned "whiteness" into an ordinary and extraordinary designation for tyranny. Blackness thus became, not simply the color of one's skin, but a sign of oppression and the possibility for a meaning of life and existence freed from the tyranny of whiteness as the normality of oppression. The various traditions of African Americans have never forgotten Africa. Especially in the movements and protest for freedom, some meaning of Africa will emerge as part of the literal and symbolic power of the movement.

The third element of Long's discussion is the meaning of God for African Americans. For the most part, Africans derived their meaning of God from their experience rather than from abstract doctrines of theology. During the period of slavery most enslaved Africans were not permitted to learn to read or write; they lived in a nonliterate oral culture. Meanings, values, thought, and thought processes take on different modes in such an oral tradition. For enslaved Africans, the context for all meanings and thought processes was the situation of enslavement where the work and awareness of their work and their bodies was under the domination of others. The understanding of God and the world of spirits had to be deciphered through these circumstances. Whether the enslaved Africans used religious language derivative from the tradition of the slaveowners, deciphered from the nature, or remembered from Africa, their notions of God were existentially related to their existence and yet defined the locus of *otherness and transcendence*—a structure of value that was not created by the slaveowners and could not be determined by them. James Washington's *Conversations with God: Two Centuries of Prayers by African Americans* (1994) is a most important text that bears directly on this point. The prayers reveal the depth and variety of the ways in which various African Americans have acknowledged and addressed the ultimate mystery of their existence.

It was through modes of divination that enslaved Africans recognized another and more accessible world of the ultimate values during their enslavement. Divination and deciphering were techniques by which enslaved Africans found an entrée into a world that they experienced and imagined. The experience and practice of divination and deciphering was called "conjuring." The conjured world existed alongside and behind the world that had been created for them by their slave masters. Not only did enslaved Africans divine the weightier issues of god and the spirits; they also interpreted the wide range of chance, luck, and spontaneity. Conjure played a very important role in healing traditions; through conjure aspects of African healing were continued in North America. Several versions of conjure are to be found in Hughes and Bontemps's *Book of Negro Folklore*. The largest collection of instances of conjure is Newbell Niles Puckett's *Folk Beliefs of the Southern Negro* (1926/1969). Other collections related to conjuring and divination are Harry M. Hyatt, *Hoodoo—Conjuration—Witchcraft—Rootwork*, 4 vols. (1970–75); Richard M. Dorson, *American Negro Folktales* (1967); Guy and Candie Carawan, *Ain't You Got a Right to the Tree of Life?* (1966); Georgia Writers' Project, *Drums and Shadows* (1940/1973); and Alan Dundes, *Mother Wit from the Laughing Barrel: Readings in the Interpretation of Afro-American Folklore* (1973).

James Weldon Johnson and Langston Hughes began a literary tradition based upon this strata of African American culture. The most prominent examples are James Weldon Johnson, *God's Trombones* (1927); Roy Decarava and Langston

Hughes, *The Sweet Flypaper of Life* (1955/1967); and Hughes, *The Weary Blues* (1926/1939). This tradition was continued by Zora Neale Hurston in her *Mules and Men* (1935). Sterling Stuckey, in his *Going through the Storm: The Influence of African American Art in History* (1994), traces the impact of this tradition on black nationalism and political movements.

Yvonne Chireau's dissertation, "Toward a History of Conjure and Black Folk Religion" (1994), is the best treatment of the meaning of conjure and conjuring as a perennial structure of African American religion. Theophus H. Smith has shown how conjure and the conjuring mode constitutes a hermeneutical epistemology of religion in African American religion in his *Conjuring Culture: Biblical Formations of Black America* (1994).

The theologian who has consistently made use of and worked out of this tradition has been Howard Thurman. His major works include *The Negro Spiritual Speaks of Life and Death* (1947); *Jesus and the Disinherited* (1949/1969); *Deep River. Reflections on the Religious Insight of Certain of the Negro Spirituals* (1955); *Deep Is the Hunger* (1951); and *The Luminous Darkness: A Personal Interpretation of the Anatomy of Segregation and the Ground of Hope* (1965).

BLACK POWER AND BLACK THEOLOGY

Prior to the advent of black theology in the 1960s the major moral discourse by black intellectuals took place within the sociological tradition of scholarship. Black sociologists, beginning with W.E.B. Du Bois's *Philadelphia Negro* (1899) to the Chicago school of sociologists, which included E. Franklin Frazier, Robert Hill, and Allison Davis, this tradition brought the empirical investigations of the social scientists as the basis for analysis and alleviation of the American "race problem."

Sociologists undertook investigations of the black church and black ministers but were "lukewarm" or even cold to any meaning that affirmed the efficaciousness of the "Negro's God." Even the work of black scholars of religion reflected the power of sociological analysis. Benjamin E. Mays has this to say about the idea of God among the masses of blacks in his *Negro's God as Reflected in His Literature* (1938/1968): "It is conceivable that the literature of the period would be laden with the other-worldliness and ideas of God that serve as an opiate to deaden one's sensitivity to slavery and other social problems. As strange as it may seem this is not the case. The Negro ministers of that period were keenly aware of *social questions and they used God to support their claim that social righteousness shall be established*" (emphasis added) (p. 59). The continuing moral element in this tradition may be seen in Allison Davis's *Leadership, Love, and Aggression* (1983). In this work Davis undertakes a psychological study of black leadership as expressed in the lives of Frederick Douglass, W.E.B. Du Bois, Richard Wright, and Martin Luther King, Jr. This work parallels the earlier

University of Chicago dissertation by the religious scholar Carleton L. "Patterns of Leadership in Race Relations" (1951).

There has been an expression of black religious themes both within and out side the black church, and, in the case of Howard Thurman, a specific theolo arising from the tradition of black peoples. In addition, the black church, throug its ministers, produced a body of sociotheological literature carrying on th abolitionist emancipatory protest from the perspective of the black church and communities. Benjamin E. Mays in chapters 3 and 4 of *The Negro's God*, deals with this tradition from Jupiter Hammond's "An Evening Thought: Salvation by Christ" to Kelly Miller's writing in *Race Adjustment* (1908).

This same territory is explored in a different way by Gayraud Wilmore in his *Black Religion and Black Radicalism*. Wilmore sees the black church fluctuating between several positions. The black church, as well as all black people, is destined to deal with the issue of freedom and identity. Various styles and modes have found historical expression during and since the time of slavery. The church has been at the forefront of the freedom movement; it has at various times espoused forms of black nationalism and at other times has been content to seek salvation apart from social-historical conditions. At other periods the expression of freedom has been devoid of religious elements.

Although one may read a meaning of "black theology" into the history of black religious action, thinking, and writing, the first self-conscious genre of a distinctively black theology must be dated from the publication of James Cone's *Black Theology and Black Power* (1969). This little book, which launched the black theology movement, was both polemical and analytical. In its early statements it made clear that black theology as conceived by Cone was definitively on the side of black radicalism. Cone states, on page 1 of this text, that "if, as I believe, Black Power is the most important development in American life in this century, there is a need to begin to analyze it from a theological perspective. In this work an effort is made to investigate the concept Black Power, placing primary emphasis on its relationship to Christianity, the Church, and contemporary American theology."

Cone's first text appears at the height of a major upheaval in American culture. The civil rights movement, growing out of the Supreme Court desegregation decision of 1954, had escalated since the Montgomery bus boycott led by Martin Luther King, Jr. The Montgomery boycott was the initial stage of a nationwide movement by black people to end American oppression. The Montgomery boycott led to the organization of the Southern Christian Leadership Conference (SCLC) and brought hundreds of young people into the struggle for civil rights.

Martin Luther King, Jr., himself a holder of a Boston University Ph.D. in theology, wrote serious reflective theological statements growing out of the existential situations of the movement itself. His works and the movement are synchronic and simultaneous. King wrote *Stride toward Freedom: The Mont-*

gomery Story (1958), *Strength to Love* (1963/1981), *Why We Can't Wait* (1964), and *Where Do We Go from Here?* (1967). The best biographies of King are David J. Garrow, *Bearing the Cross: Martin Luther King, Jr., and the Southern Christian Leadership Conference* (1986), and two volumes by Taylor Branch, *Parting the Waters: America in the King Years, 1954–63* (1989) and *Pillar of Fire: America in the King Years, 1963–65* (1998).

Martin Luther King's movement, the Southern Christian Leadership Conference, grew out of the black church tradition and made use of the resources of this tradition for its rhetoric, organization skills, and meeting places. For a thorough discussion of this relationship as well as the involvement of non-SCLC groups in the movement, see Aldon D. Morris, *The Origins of the Civil Rights Movement: Black Communities Organizing for Change* (1984).

Although Cone claims to undertake a theological meaning of black power, it is clear that by implication he presupposes a Christian theological interpretation and an apologetic theology for the meaning of freedom for black persons and communities in the United States. In his position as a senior theology professor at Union Seminary in New York, one of the most prestigious Christian theological seminaries in the country, Cone has carried on a systematic study of black theology and has not only produced a distinguished genre of work himself but also trained two generations of black scholars of theology.

Cone's works cover *A Black Theology of Liberation* (1970), *The Spirituals and the Blues* (1972), *God of the Oppressed* (1975/1997), *My Soul Looks Back.* (1982), and *Speaking the Truth* (1986). Cone and Gayraud Wilmore have documented the relationship of the black theology movement to other aspects of black religious thought and community in two volumes; *Black Theology: A Documentary History* (1993). In *Revolution in Zion* (1990) Charles Shelby Rooks provides an account of the black theological ferment as it affected the training of ministers and scholars of religion. Rooks had been director of the Fund for Theological Education, president of the Chicago Theological Seminary, and executive vice president for Homeland Ministries of the United Church Board; in all these capacities he effectively promoted the cause of theological education in the church and the academy.

Cone's work spawned a theological renaissance among scholars of black religion. In conversation with his work several important volumes ensued. One of the most provocative was William R. Jones's *Is God a White Racist?* (1973). A philosopher of religion, Jones raised the question of the biblical presuppositions of black theology. He pointed to the fact that biblical salvation was always premised on the actuality of God's love and care; the promise emerged from a prior fulfillment. He wondered whether there had ever been that fulfillment in the case of African Americans. Other works extended the range of black theology. Most notable is the work of J. Deotis Roberts, who raised more concrete issues regarding black theology in *Liberation and Reconciliation* (1974/1994), *A Black Political Theology* (1974), and *Roots of a Black Future* (1980).

Robert E. Hood, a New Testament Scholar, challenged Greek modes of thought within the Christian community in his *Must God Remain Greek?* (1990). James H. Evans, Jr., set forth the structure of a systematic black theology in his *We Have Been Believers* (1992). Cornel West explored the possibility of an activist philosophy of religion based upon Marxist analysis and the Christian mythos in *Prophesy Deliverance!* (1982).

It quickly became apparent that to be viable, black theology must include the constructive and creative voices and minds of black women. From the days of Harriet Tubman—see *Harriet Tubman: Negro Soldier and Abolitionist* edited by Earl Conrad (1942)—through the participation of black women in various church and black cultural movements, black women have played a major if not majority role in the creation and maintenance of black culture and the black church. Bettye Collier-Thomas has also given us profiles of Harriet Tubman and Sojourner Truth in her *Black Women in America: Contributors to Our Heritage* (1983). Deborah Gray White deals with the situation of African American women slaves in *Ar'n't I a Woman* (1985); Trudier Harris describes the creative meaning of domestic workers in *From Mammies to Militants: Domestics in Black American Literature* (1982). The work of an early woman evangelist is treated in *An Autobiography: The Story of the Lord's Dealings with Mrs. Amanda Smith, the Colored Evangelist* (1893). In her insightful *Righteous Discontent: The Women's Movement in the Black Baptist Church, 1880–1920* (1993) and her article "The Black Church: A Gender Perspective," Evelyn Brooks Higginbotham, along with Cheryl Townsend Giles in her article "The Roles of Church and Community Mothers: Ambivalent American Sexism or Fragmented African Familyhood," sets the stage and agenda for continued historical and sociological studies of this too often neglected meaning of African American religion. These articles are found in the Fulop and Raboteau volume.

Black womanist theology is represented by the following: Katie Cannon, *Black Womanist Ethics* (1988); Delores S. Williams, *Sisters in the Wilderness: The Challenge of Womanist God-Talk* (1993); Cheryl Sanders, ed., *Living the Intersection: Womanism and Afrocentricism in Theology* (1995); and Jacquelyn Grant, *White Woman's Christ and Black Women's Jesus* (1989). Ella Mitchell deals with the traditions of black women preachers in *Those Preaching Women* (1985–1996).

Black scholars of the Bible have dealt with two major issues: the presence of Africa and Africans in the biblical text and the presence, situation, and theological significance of women in the Bible. Cain Felder has produced two critical volumes: *Troubling Biblical Waters* (1989) and *Stony the Road We Trod* (1991). Felder also served as general editor of an Afrocentric edition of the biblical text, *Original African Heritage Study Bible* (1993). Renita Weems, a biblical scholar, has explored the implications of a womanist theological interpretation of the Bible in *Just a Sister Away: A Womanist Vision of Women's Relationship in the Bible* (1988).

BACK TO AFRICA AND THE MISSIONARY MOVEMENT

One aspect of the northern abolitionist movement was the emergence of the American Colonization Society. Although Abolitionists desired the destruction of the institution of slavery, some felt that the United States should be a country for white people only. Thus, they believed, once slavery is abolished, the freed slaves should be transported to another place, preferably Africa. This view appealed to the sentiments of various black nationalists, many of whom also felt that this country, under its Constitution, could never treat an African person as a human being.

Other African American members of African American Episcopal and other Methodist and Baptist denominations were intent upon bringing the Gospel of Jesus Christ to their brothers and sisters in Africa. Sometimes, as in the case of Bishop Henry MacNeal Turner, the black nationalist sentiment combined with a missionary zeal for the salvation of Africa.

Milton C. Sernett in chapter 4 of *Afro-American Religious History*, "Freedom's Time of Trial: 1865–World War I," gives examples of this nationalist position in Alexander Crummel's "The Regeneration of Africa" and in Henry MacNeal Turner's "Emigration to Africa." MacNeal made four trips to Africa—three to West Africa, and one to South Africa. Edward Blyden, a Presbyterian African American missionary to West Africa, had fueled the fires of the back-to-Africa movement in his treatise, *Christianity, Islam and the Negro Race* (1967). In this work, Blyden suggested that Islam seemed to be a religion better suited to African peoples.

Sylvia Jacobs's edited volume *Black Americans and the Missionary Movement in Africa* (1982) discusses several missionary situations of black Americans in Africa. James T. Campbell's *Songs of Zion: The African American Methodist Episcopal Church in the United States and South Africa* (1995) is an exhaustive study of the A. M. E. missionary movement in South Africa. The impact of African American missionaries on the religious and political situation in colonial central Africa is dealt with in Karen E. Fields's *Revival and Rebellion in Colonial Central Africa* (1985).

ISLAM, BLACK RELIGION, AND OTHER RELIGIOUS ORIENTATIONS

The ferment in American culture of the 1960s and 1970s not only produced the leadership of Martin Luther King, Jr., and the Southern Christian Leadership Conference but also brought into prominence the Nation of Islam through its gifted spokesperson Malcolm X. James Cone has written an intriguing book *Martin & Malcolm: A Dream or a Nightmare* (1991), discussing the religious and theological differences between the two men, but also placing them within the context of the common fight for the human rights of African Americans in the United States. C. Eric Lincoln's early work, *The Black Muslims in America*

(1961), was somewhat prophetic in that it predicted the important role that this group would play on the American scene. E. U. Essien-Udom's *Black Nationalism: A Search for Identity in America* (1962) is an anthropologist's interpretation of the Black Muslims. Allan D. Austin in *African Muslims in Antebellum America* (1984) identifies sources and traces the extent of Islam among enslaved Africans. Alex Haley's *Autobiography of Malcolm X* (1965) is becoming a classic American text. The latest interpretation of African American Islam is Richard Brent Turner's *Islam in the African American Experience* (1997). Aminah Beverly McCloud's *African American Islam* (1995) is a useful guide and compendium of the basic teaching and practices of Islam for African Americans.

Since the 1950s among African Americans there has been a steady rise of religious orientations that are not identified with the mainline African American Christian denominations. These religious have resulted from travel by African Americans to other parts of the world and to the immigration of other cultures into the United States. Leonard Barrett, in his *Soul-Force: African Heritage in Afro-American Religion* (1974), presents a scholarly history of the Rastafarians. He provides a sequel with *The Rastafarians* (1977). Robert Faris Thompson traces the influence of Africa in African American art and performance in his *Flash of the Spirit: African and Afro-American Art and Philosophy* (1983). Joseph M. Murphy explores the African elements in African American religions of Vodou, Candomble, Santeria, Revival Zion, and the Black American Church in his *Working the Spirit: Ceremonies of the African Diaspora* (1994). Similar ground is covered in Anthony Pinn's *Varieties of African American Religious Experience* (1998). Tracey Elaine Hucks's Harvard University dissertation, "Approaching the African God: An Examination of African American Yoruba History from 1959 to the Present" (1998), traces the history of the Oyotunji African Village, a Yoruba religious site in South Carolina. Karen McCarthy Brown in *Mama Lola: A Vodou Priestess in Brooklyn* (1991) describes the activities of a Yoruba religious functionary in New York. Finally, John Patrick Deveney's *Paschal Beverly Randolph: A Nineteenth Century Black American Spiritualist, Rosicrucian, and Sex Magician* (1997) is the biography of one of the most famous American theosophists and spiritualists of nineteenth-century America.

BIBLIOGRAPHY

Abrahams, Roger D., and John F. Szwed, eds. *After Africa: Extracts from British Travel Accounts and Journals of the Seventeenth, Eighteenth, and Nineteenth Centuries concerning the Slaves, Their Manners, and Customs in the British West Indies.* New Haven, CT: Yale University Press, 1983.

Allen, Richard. *The Life Experience and Gospel Labors of the Rt. Rev. Richard Allen: To Which Is Annexed the Rise and Progress of the African Methodist Episcopal Church in the United States of America: Containing a Narrative of the Yellow*

Fever in the Year of Our Lord, 1793: with an Address to the People of Color in the United States. Bicentennial ed. Nashville: Abingdon Press, 1983.

Andrews, William L., ed. *Sisters of the Spirit: Three Black Women's Autobiographies of the Nineteenth Century.* Bloomington: Indiana University Press, 1986.

Aptheker, Herbert. *American Negro Slave Revolts.* New York: Columbia University Press, 1943.

Austin, Allan D., ed. *African Muslims in Antebellum America: A Sourcebook.* New York: Garland Pub., 1984.

Baer, Hans A. *The Black Spiritual Movement: A Religious Response to Racism.* Knoxville: University of Tennessee Press, 1984.

Barrett, Leonard E. *The Rastafarians: Sounds of Cultural Dissonance.* Boston: Beacon Press, 1977.

———. *Soul-Force: African Heritage in Afro-American Religion.* Garden City, NY: Anchor Press, 1974.

———. *The Sun and the Drum: African Roots in Jamaican Folk Tradition.* Kingston, Jamaica: Sangster's Book Stores in Association with Heinemann, 1976.

Berlin, Ira. *Many Thousands Gone: The First Two Centuries of Slavery in North America.* Cambridge, MA: Belknap Press of Harvard University Press, 1998.

Blassingame, John, ed. *Slave Testimony: Two Centuries of Letters, Speeches, Interviews, and Autobiographies.* Baton Rouge: Louisiana State University Press, 1977.

Blyden, Edward Wilmot. *Christianity, Islam and the Negro Race.* Edinburgh: Edinburgh University Press, 1967.

Bradley, David. *A History of the A.M.E. Zion Church.* 2 vols. Nashville: Parthenon Press, 1956, 1970.

Branch, Taylor. *Parting the Waters: America in the King Years, 1954–63.* New York: Simon and Schuster, 1989.

———. *Pillar of Fire: America in the King Years, 1963–1965.* New York: Simon and Schuster, 1998.

Brown, Karen McCarthy. *Mama Lola: A Vodou Priestess in Brooklyn.* Berkeley: University of California Press, 1991.

Campbell, James T. *Songs of Zion: The African Methodist Episcopal Church in the United States and South Africa.* New York: Oxford University Press, 1995.

Cannon, Katie G. *Black Womanist Ethics.* Atlanta: Scholars Press, 1988.

Carawan, Guy, and Candie Carawan. *Ain't You Got a Right to the Tree of Life?: The People of Johns Island, South Carolina, Their Faces, Their Words, and Their Songs.* New York: Simon and Schuster, 1966.

Chireau, Yvonne. "Toward a History of Conjure and Black Folk Religion." Ph.D. dissertation, Princeton University, 1994.

Collier-Thomas, Bettye. *Black Women in America: Contributors to Our Heritage.* Washington, DC: Bethune Museum-Archives, 1983.

———. *Daughters of Thunder: Black Women Preachers and Their Sermons, 1850–1979.* San Francisco: Jossey-Bass, 1998.

Cone, James H. *Black Theology and Black Power.* New York: Seabury Press, 1969.

———. *A Black Theology of Liberation.* Philadelphia: Lippincott, 1970.

———. *For My People: Black Theology and the Black Church.* Maryknoll, NY: Orbis Books, 1984.

———. *God of the Oppressed.* Rev. ed. Maryknoll, NY: Orbis Books, 1991.

————. *Martin & Malcolm: A Dream or a Nightmare.* Maryknoll, NY: Orbis Books, 1991.

————. *My Soul Looks Back.* Nashville: Abingdon, 1982.

————. *Speaking the Truth: Ecumenism, Liberation, and Black Theology.* Grand Rapids, MI: W. B. Eerdmans Pub., 1986.

————. *The Spirituals and the Blues: An Interpretation.* New York: Seabury Press, 1972.

Cone, James H., and Gayraud S. Wilmore, eds. *Black Theology: A Documentary History.* 2nd ed, rev. 2 vols. Maryknoll, NY: Orbis Books, 1993.

Conrad, Earl. *Harriet Tubman, Negro Soldier and Abolitionist.* New York: International Publishers, 1942.

Curtin, Philip D. *The Atlantic Slave Trade: A Census.* Madison: University of Wisconsin Press, 1969.

Daniel, Walter C. *Images of the Preacher in Afro-American Literature.* Washington, DC: University Press of America, 1981.

Davis, Allison. *Leadership, Love, and Aggression.* San Diego: Harcourt Brace Jovanovich, 1983.

Davis, Cyprian. *The History of Black Catholics in the United States.* New York: Crossroad, 1990.

Davis, David Brion. *The Problem of Slavery in the Age of Revolution, 1770–1823.* Ithaca, NY: Cornell University Press, 1975.

Decarava, Roy, and Langston Hughes. *The Sweet Flypaper of Life.* New York: Hill and Wang 1955/1967.

Deerr, Noel. *The History of Sugar.* 2 vols. London: Chapman and Hall, 1949–50.

Deveney, John P. *Paschal Beverly Randolph: A Nineteenth-Century Black American Spiritualist, Rosicrucian, and Sex Magician.* Albany: State University of New York Press, 1997.

Dixie, Quinton Hosford, and Cornel West, eds. *The Courage to Hope: From Black Suffering to Human Redemption.* Boston: Beacon Press, 1999.

Dorson, Richard Mercer. *American Negro Folktales.* Greenwich, CT: Fawcett Publications, 1967.

Du Bois, W.E.B. *The Negro Church: Report of a Social Study Made under the Direction of Atlanta University; Together with the Proceedings of the Eighth Conference for the Study of the Negro Problems, Held at Atlanta University, May 26th, 1903.* Atlanta: Atlanta University Press, 1903.

————. *The Philadelphia Negro: A Social Study.* Philadelphia: Published for the University of Pennsylvania, 1899.

————. *The Souls of Black Folk: Essays and Sketches.* Chicago: McClurg and Company, 1922.

Dumezil, Georges. *Archaic Roman Religion,* with an appendix on the Religion of the Etruscans. Trans. Philip Krapp. 2 vols. Chicago: University of Chicago Press, 1970.

Dundes, Alan. *Mother Wit from the Laughing Barrel: Readings in the Interpretation of Afro-American Folklore.* Englewood Cliffs, NJ: Prentice-Hall, 1973.

Essien-Udom, Essien Udosen. *Black Nationalism: A Search for an Identity in America.* Chicago: University of Chicago Press, 1962.

Evans, James H., Jr. *We Have Been Believers: An African-American Systematic Theology.* Minneapolis: Fortress Press, 1992.

Fauset, Arthur Huff. *Black Gods of the Metropolis: Negro Religious Cults of the Urban North*. Philadelphia: University of Pennsylvania Press, 1944.

Felder, Cain Hope, ed. *The Original African Heritage Study Bible: King James Version*. Nashville: James C. Winston Publishing Company, 1993.

——, ed. *Stony the Road We Trod: African American Biblical Interpretation*. Minneapolis: Fortress Press, 1991.

——. *Troubling Biblical Waters: Race, Class, and Family*. Maryknoll, NY: Orbis Books, 1989.

Fields, Karen E. *Revival and Rebellion in Colonial Central Africa*. Princeton, NJ: Princeton University Press, 1985.

Fisher, Miles Mark. *Negro Slave Songs in the United States*. Ithaca, NY: Cornell University Press for the American Historical Association, 1953.

Fitts, Leroy. *A History of Black Baptists*. Nashville: Broadman Press, 1985.

——. *Lott Carey: First Black Missionary to Africa*. Valley Forge, PA: Judson Press, 1978.

Frazier, Edward Franklin. *The Negro Church in America*, New York: Schocken Books, 1974.

Frey, Sylvia R. *Water from the Rock: Black Resistance in a Revolutionary Age*. Princeton, NJ: Princeton University Press, 1991.

Frey, Sylvia R., and Betty Wood. *Come Shouting to Zion: African American Protestantism in the American South and British Caribbean to 1830*. Chapel Hill: University of North Carolina Press, 1998.

Fulop, Timothy E., and Albert J. Raboteau, eds. *African-American Religion: Interpretive Essays in History and Culture*. New York: Routledge, 1997.

Garrow, David J. *Bearing the Cross: Martin Luther King, Jr., and the Southern Christian Leadership Conference*. New York: W. Morrow, 1986.

Genovese, Eugene D. *From Rebellion to Revolution: Afro-American Slave Revolts in the Making of the Modern World*. Baton Rouge: Louisiana State University Press, 1979.

——. *Roll, Jordan, Roll: The World the Slaves Made*. New York: Pantheon Books, 1974.

Georgia Writers' Project. Savannah Unit. *Drums and Shadows: Survival Studies among the Georgia Coastal Negroes*. Westport, CT: Greenwood Press, 1940/1973.

Grant, Jacquelyn. *White Woman's Christ and Black Women's Jesus: Feminist Christology and Womanist Response*. Atlanta: Scholars Press, 1989.

Gwaltney, John Langston, ed. *Drylongso: A Self Portrait of Black America*. New York: New Press, 1980/1993.

Harding, Vincent. *There Is a River: The Black Struggle for Freedom in America*. New York: Harcourt Brace Jovanovich, 1981.

Harper, Michael S., and Robert B. Stepto, eds. *Chant of Saints: A Gathering of Afro-American Literature, Art, and Scholarship*. Urbana: University of Illinois Press, 1979.

Harris, Trudier. *From Mammies to Militants: Domestics in Black American Literature*. Philadelphia: Temple University Press, 1982.

Hayes, Diana I., and Dyprian Davis, eds. *Taking down Our Harps: Black Catholics in the United States*. Maryknoll, NY: Orbis Books, 1998.

Herskovits, Melville J. *The Myth of the Negro Past*. New York: Harper and Brothers, 1941.

Higginbotham, Evelyn Brooks. *Righteous Discontent: The Women's Movement in the Black Baptist Church, 1880–1920*. Cambridge, MA: Harvard University Press, 1993.

Holloway, Joseph E., ed. *Africanisms in American Culture*. Bloomington: Indiana University Press, 1990.

Hood, James Walker. *One Hundred Years of the African Methodist Episcopal Church; or The Centennial of African Methodism*. New York: A.M.E. Zion Book Concern, 1895.

Hood, Robert E. *Begrimed and Black: Christian Traditions on Blacks and Blackness*. Minneapolis: Augsburg Fortress, 1994.

———. *Must God Remain Greek?: Afro Cultures and God-Talk*. Minneapolis: Fortress Press, 1990.

Hubbard, Dolan. *The Sermon and the African American Literary Imagination*. Columbia: University of Missouri Press, 1994.

Hucks, Tracey Elaine. "Approaching the African God: An Examination of African American Yoruba History from 1959 to the Present." Ph.D. dissertation, Harvard University, 1998.

Hughes, Langston. *The Weary Blues*. New York: A. A. Knopf, 1926/1939.

Hughes, Langston, and Arna Bontemps, eds. *The Book of Negro Folklore*. New York: Dodd, Mead, 1958.

Hurston, Zora Neale. *Mules and Men*. Philadelphia: J. B. Lippincott Company, 1935.

Hyatt, Harry Middleton. *Hoodoo—Conjuration—Witchcraft—Rootwork: Beliefs Accepted by Many Negroes and White Persons, These Being Orally Recorded among Blacks and Whites*. Hannibal, MO: Western Pub., 1970–75.

Inikori, J. E., ed. *Forced Migration: The Impact of the Export Slave Trade on African Societies*. New York: Africana Pub., 1982.

Inikori, J. E., D. C. Ohadike, and A. C. Unomah. *The Chaining of a Continent: Export Demand for Captives and the History of Africa South of the Sahara, 1450–1870*. Mona, Jamaica: Institute of Social and Economic Research, University of the West Indies, 1992.

Jackson, Joseph H. *A Story of Christian Activism: The History of the National Baptist Convention, U.S.A., Inc*. Nashville: Townsend Press, 1980.

Jacobs, Sylvia M. *Black Americans and the Missionary Movement in Africa*. Westport, CT: Greenwood Press, 1982.

Johnson, James Weldon. *God's Trombones: Seven Negro Sermons in Verse*. New York: Viking Press, 1927.

Johnston, Ruby Funchess. *The Development of Negro Religion*. New York: Philosophical Library, 1954.

———. *The Religion of Negro Protestants: Changing Religious Attitudes and Practices*. New York: Philosophical Library, 1956.

Jones, Lawrence. *They Overheard the Gospel: American Religious Experience prior to the Civil War*. Durham, NC: Duke University Press, forthcoming.

Jones, William R. *Is God a White Racist?: A Preamble to Black Theology*. Garden City, NY: Anchor Press, 1973.

King, Martin Luther, Jr. *Strength to Love*. Philadelphia: Fortress Press, 1963/1981.

———. *Stride toward Freedom: The Montgomery Story*. New York: Harper, 1958.

———. *Where Do We Go from Here: Chaos or Community?* New York: Harper and Row, 1967.

————. *Why We Can't Wait*. New York: Harper and Row, 1964.

Lee, Carleton L. "Patterns of Leadership in Race Relations." Ph.D. dissertation. University of Chicago, 1951.

Levine, Lawrence W. *Black Culture and Black Consciousness: Afro-American Folk Thought from Slavery to Freedom*. New York: Oxford University Press, 1977.

Lincoln, C. Eric., ed. *The Black Church Experience in Religion*. Garden City, NY: Anchor Press, 1974.

————. *The Black Muslims in America*. Boston: Beacon Press, 1961.

————. *Race, Religion, and the Continuing American Dilemma*. New York: Hill and Wang, 1984.

Lincoln, C. Eric, and Lawrence H. Mamiya. *The Black Church in the African-American Experience*. Durham, NC: Duke University Press, 1990.

Litwack, Leon F. *Been in the Storm So Long: The Aftermath of Slavery*. New York: Knopf, 1979.

Loewenberg, Bert James, and Ruth Bogin, eds. *Black Women in Nineteenth-Century American Life: Their Words, Their Thoughts, Their Feelings*. University Park: Pennsylvania State University Press, 1976.

Long, Charles H. "Perspective for a Study of African American Religion in the United States." *History of Religions* 11 (August 1971): 54–66.

Lovell, John. *Black Song: The Forge and the Flame: The Story of How the Afro-American Spiritual Was Hammered Out*. New York: Macmillan, 1972.

Martin, Sandy D. *Black Baptist and African Missions: The Origins of a Movement, 1880–1915*. Macon, GA: Mercer University Press, 1989.

————. *For God and Race: The Religious and Political Leadership of AMEZ Bishop James Walker Hood*. Columbia: University of South Carolina Press, 1999.

Mays, Benjamin E. *The Negro's God as Reflected in His Literature*. New York: Russell and Russell, 1938; reprint 1968.

————. *Seeking to Be Christian in Race Relations*. New York: Friendship Press, 1957.

Mays, Benjamin E., and Joseph W. Nicholson. *The Negro's Church*. New York: Negro Universities Press, 1969; reprint of 1933.

McCloud, Aminah Beverly. *African American Islam*. New York: Routledge, 1995.

Miller, Kelly. *Race Adjustment: Essays on the Negro in America*. New York and Washington, DC: Neale Pub., 1908.

Mitchell, Ella Pearson. *Those Preaching Women*. 3 vols. Valley Forge, PA: Judson Press, 1985–1996.

Moore, John J. *History of the A.M.E. Zion Church in America*. York, PA: Teachers Journal Office, 1884.

Morgan, Philip D. *Slave Counterpoint: Black Culture in the Eighteenth-Century Chesapeake and Lowcountry*. Chapel Hill: Published for the Omohundro Institute of Early American History and Culture by the University of North Carolina Press, 1998.

Morris, Aldon D. *The Origins of the Civil Rights Movement: Black Communities Organizing for Change*. New York: Free Press; London: Collier Macmillan, 1984.

Moses, Wilson Jeremiah. *Black Messiahs and Uncle Toms: Social and Literary Manipulations of a Religious Myth*. University Park: Pennsylvania State University Press, 1982.

Murphy, Joseph M. *Santeria: An African Religion in America*. Boston: Beacon Press, 1988.

————. *Santeria: African Spirits in America*. Boston: Beacon Press, 1993.

————. *Working the Spirit: Ceremonies of the African Diaspora*. Boston: Beacon Press, 1994.

Murray, Andrew E. *Presbyterians and the Negro: A History*. Philadelphia: Presbyterian Historical Society, 1966.

Pelt, Owen D., and R. L. Smith. *The Story of the National Baptist*. New York: Vantage Press, 1960.

Pettigrew, M. C. *From Miles to Johnson: One Hundred Years of Progress, 1870–1970, of the Christian Methodist Episcopal Church*. Memphis: C.M.E. Publishing House, 1970.

Phillips, Charles Henry. *The History of the Colored Methodist Episcopal Church in America; Comprising Its Organization, Subsequent Development, and Present Status*. Jackson, TN: Publishing House, C.M.E. Church, 1898.

Pinn, Anthony B. *Varieties of African American Religious Experience*. Minneapolis: Fortress Press, 1998.

————. *Why, Lord?: Suffering and Evil in Black Theology*. New York: Continuum, 1995.

Puckett, Newbell Niles. *Folk Beliefs of the Southern Negro*. Chapel Hill: University of North Carolina Press, 1926; reprint, New York: Dover Publications, 1969.

Raboteau, Albert J. *A Fire in the Bones: Reflections on African-American Religious History*. Boston: Beacon Press, 1995.

————. *Slave Religion: The "Invisible Institution" in the Antebellum South*. New York: Oxford University Press, 1978.

Ramsey, Frederic. *Been Here and Gone*. New Brunswick, NJ: Rutgers University Press, 1960.

Roberts, J. Deotis. *A Black Political Theology*. Philadelphia: Westminster Press, 1974.

————. *Black Theology in Dialogue*. Philadelphia: Westminster Press, 1987.

————. *Black Theology Today: Liberation and Contextualization*. New York: E. Mellen Press, 1983.

————. *Liberation and Reconciliation: A Black Theology*. Maryknoll, NY: Orbis Books, 1994.

————. *The Prophethood of Black Believers: An African American Political Theology for Ministry*. Louisville: Westminster/John Knox Press, 1994.

————. *Roots of a Black Future: Family and Church*. Philadelphia: Westminster Press, 1980.

Rooks, Charles Shelby. *Revolution in Zion: Reshaping African American Ministry, 1960–1974; A Biography in the First Person*. New York: Pilgrim Press, 1990.

Rosenberg, Bruce A. *The Art of the American Folk Preacher*. New York: Oxford University Press, 1970.

Sanders, Cheryl Jeanne. *Living the Intersection: Womanism and Afrocentrism in Theology*. Minneapolis: Fortress Press, 1995.

Sernett, Milton C., ed. *Afro-American Religious History: A Documentary Witness*. Durham, NC: Duke University Press, 1985.

Shannon, David T., and Gayraud S. Wilmore, eds. *Black Witness to the Apostolic Faith*. Grand Rapids, MI: W. B. Eerdmans Publishing Company for Commission on Faith and Order, National Council of the Churches of Christ in the U.S.A., 1985/1988.

Smith, Amanda. *An Autobiography: The Story of the Lord's Dealings with Mrs. Amanda Smith, the Colored Evangelist: Containing an Account of Her Life Work of Faith and Her Travels in America, England, Ireland, Scotland, India, and Africa, as an Independent Missionary.* Chicago: Meyers and Bros., 1893.

Smith, H. Shelton. *In His Image, but . . . Racism in Southern Religion, 1780–1910.* Durham, NC: Duke University Press, 1972.

Smith, Theophus Harold. *Conjuring Culture: Biblical Formations of Black America.* New York: Oxford University Press, 1994.

Sobel, Mechal. *Trabelin' On: The Slave Journey to an Afro-Baptist Faith.* Westport, CT: Greenwood Press, 1979.

———. *The World They Made Together: Black and White Values in Eighteenth-Century Virginia.* Princeton, NJ: Princeton University Press, 1987.

Southern, Eileen. *The Music of Black Americans: A History.* 2nd ed. New York: W. W. Norton, 1983.

Stuckey, Sterling. *Going through the Storm: The Influence of African American Art in History.* New York: Oxford University Press, 1994.

———. *Slave Culture: Nationalist Theory and the Foundation of Black America.* New York: Oxford University Press, 1987.

Thompson, Robert Farris. *Flash of the Spirit: African and Afro-American Art and Philosophy.* New York: Random House, 1983.

Thurman, Howard. *Deep Is the Hunger.* New York: Harper and Row, 1951.

———. *Deep River: Reflections on the Religious Insight of Certain of the Negro Spirituals.* Rev. and enlarged, New York: Harper, 1955.

———. *Jesus and the Disinherited.* Nashville: Abingdon Press, 1949/1969.

———. *The Luminous Darkness: A Personal Interpretation of the Anatomy of Segregation and the Ground of Hope.* New York: Harper and Row, 1965.

———. *The Negro Spiritual Speaks of Life and Death.* New York: Harper, 1947.

Tucker, David M. *Black Pastors and Leaders: Memphis, 1819–1972.* Memphis: Memphis State University Press, 1975.

Turner, Lorenzo Dow. *Africanisms in the Gullah Dialect.* Chicago: University of Chicago Press, 1949.

Turner, Richard Brent. *Islam in the African-American Experience.* Bloomington: Indiana University Press, 1997.

Walker, David. *David Walker's Appeal, in Four Articles, Together with a Preamble, to the Coloured Citizens of the World, but in Particular, and Very Expressly, to Those of the United States of America.* New York: Hill and Wang, 1965/1995.

Walls, William J. *The African Methodist Episcopal Zion Church: Reality of the Black Church.* Charlotte, NC: A.M.E. Zion Publishing House, 1974.

Ward, Hiley H. *Prophet of the Black Nation.* Philadelphia and Boston: Pilgrim Press, 1969.

Washington, James Melvin, ed. *Conversations with God: Two Centuries of Prayers by African Americans.* New York: HarperCollins Publishers, 1994.

———. *Frustrated Fellowship: The Black Baptist Quest for Social Power.* Macon, GA: Mercer University Press, 1986.

———, ed. *A Testament of Hope: The Essential Writings of Martin Luther King, Jr.* San Francisco: Harper and Row, 1986.

Weatherford, Willis D. *American Churches and the Negro: An Historical Study from Early Slave Days to the Present.* Boston: Christopher Publishing House, 1957.

Weems, Renita J. *Just a Sister Away: A Womanist Vision of Women's Relationships in the Bible.* San Diego: LuraMedia, 1988.

Weisbrot, Robert. *Father Divine and the Struggle for Racial Equality*. Urbana: University of Illinois Press, 1983.

Wesley, Charles H. *Richard Allen, Apostle of Freedom*. 2nd ed. Washington, DC: Associated Publishers, 1969.

West, Cornel. *Prophesy Deliverance!: An Afro-American Revolutionary Christianity*. Philadelphia: Westminster Press, 1982.

White, Deborah Gray. *Ar'n't I a Woman?: Female Slaves in the Plantation South*. New York: W. W. Norton, 1985.

Williams, Delores S. *Sisters in the Wilderness: The Challenge of Womanist God-Talk*. Maryknoll, NY: Orbis Books, 1993.

Williams, Ethel L., and Clifton L. Brown, comps. *Afro-American Religious Studies: A Comprehensive Bibliography with Locations in American Libraries*. Metuchen, NJ: Scarecrow Press, 1972.

Wilmore, Gayraud, ed. *African American Religious Studies: An Interdisciplinary Anthology*. Durham, NC: Duke University Press, 1989.

———. *Black Religion and Black Radicalism: An Interpretation of the Religious History of African Americans*. 3rd ed., rev. and enlarged. Maryknoll, NY: Orbis Books, 1998.

Woodson, Carter G. *The History of the Negro Church*. Washington, DC: Associated Publishers, 1921.

X, Malcolm. *The Autobiography of Malcolm X*. With the assistance of Alex Haley. New York: Grove Press, 1965.

Index

Abbott, Robert S., 221–22, 296–97
Abbott's Monthly, 223
Abdul, Raoul, 154
Abiding Courage (Lemke-Santangelo), 12, 82
Abolitionists: black, 190, 219; black women, 79; emigration to Africa, 168; literature, 118–19; movement, 190
Abolitionist Sisterhood (Yellin and Van Horne), 79
Abolition's Axe (Sernett), 99
Abrahams, Roger, 372
An Account of the Slave Trade on the Coast of Africa (Falconbridge), 317
"Accumulation of Wealth by Black Georgians, 1890–1915" (Hornsby), 293
"Acquisition and Loss on a Spanish Frontier" (Landers), 288
Adam Clayton Powell, Jr. (Hamilton), 202
Address on the Negro (Norwood), 320
"An Address to the Slaves of the United States" (Garnet), 119, 191
Adeleke, Tunde, 169
Advertising and Marketing to the New Majority (Woods), 344

Affirmative Action and Black Entrepreneurship (Boston), 298
Affirmative Action and the Constitution (Chin and Finkelman), 298
Affirmative Action and the Stalled Quest for Black Progress (Holsworth), 298
The Affirmative Action Debate (Curry), 298
African-American Business Leaders (Ingham and Feldman), 281–82
"African-American Business Leaders in the South, 1810–1945" (Ingham), 293
African American Economic Development and Small Business Ownership (Kijakazi), 298
"African American Entrepreneurship" (Levenstein), 296
African American Entrepreneurship in Richmond (Plater), 296
"The African American Financial Industries" (Kwolek-Follands), 291
"African American Gospel of Success" (Friedman), 295
African American in the Union Navy, 1861–1865 (Valuska), 237
African American Islam (McCloud), 385

African-American Religion (Fulop and Raboteau), 369, 373

"African Americans in the City" (Trotter), 296

"African Americans in the City since World War II" (Kusmer), 10

African American Soldiers in the National Guard (Johnson), 240

"African American Women and Competitive Sport" (Gissendanner), 266

African American Women and the Struggle for the Vote, 1850–1920 (Terborg-Penn), 171

African American Women in Congress (Gill), 85

"African American Women Olympians" (Gissendanner), 266

"African-American Women's History and the Metalanguage of Race" (Higginbotham), 42

Africana Womanism (Hudson-Weems), 135

The African Colonization Movement, 1816–1865 (Staudenraus), 3, 168, 192

African Communities League, 174

African Folklore (Dorson), 117

Africanisms in the Gullah Dialect (Turner), 370

The African Methodist Episcopal Zion Church (Walls), 374

African Music (Beby), 149

African Music (Gray), 149

African Music in Ghana (Nketia), 149

African Music in Perspective (Merriam), 149

African Musicology (DjeDje), 149

African Muslims in Antebellum America (Austin), 385

Africans and Creek (Littlefield), 3

Africans and Seminoles (Littlefield), 3

Africansims in American Culture (Holloway), 283, 371

Africans in Colonial Louisiana (Hall), 283

African Women South of the Sahara (Hay and Stritcher), 283

Afro-American (Baltimore), 219, 221

Afro-American and the Second World War (Wynn), 244

Afro-American Classical Music (Barbour), 154

Afro-American Literature (Stepto and Fisher), 135

The Afro-American Periodical Press, 1838–1909 (Bullock), 219

The Afro-American Press and Its Editors (Penn), 220

Afro-American Religious History (Sernett), 155, 374, 384

The Afro-American Woman (Harley and Terborg-Penn), 42, 73

The Afrocentric Idea (Asante), 136, 178

Afrocentricity, 102–3, 136, 178, 326

Afrocentricity (Asante), 178, 326

"Afrocentrism" (Early), 102

"Afrocentrism" (Wiley), 103

Afro-Yankees (Cottroll), 4

After Africa (Szwed), 372

"Against the Consensus" (Fletcher), 99

Agents of Repression (Churchill and Hall), 177

Ain't I a Woman (hooks), 85

Ain't You Got a Right to the Tree of Life? (Carawan), 379

Air Force Integrates, 1945–1964 (Gropman), 244

Alabama Federation of Labor, 34

Aldridge, Delores, 326

Alexander, Adele Logan, 78

Alexander, John H., 239

Alexis, Lucien, 262

Alexis, Marcus, 341

Ali, Muhammad, 261, 264

Alkalimat, Abdul, 178

All American Women (Cole), 326

Allen, Anthony D., 288

Allen, Richard, 77, 190, 373–74

Allen, William Francis, 149

All God's Dangers (Rosengarten), 35–36

Allport, Gordon W., 323–24

All That We Can Be (Moskos and Butler), 246

All White America (McKinney), 322

Along Freedom Road (Cecelski), 355

Altoff, Gerard T., 234

Amalgamation, 316, 319
Ambiguous Lives (Alexander), 78
A.M.E. churches, 219, 374, 384
A.M.E. Church Review, 219
American Apartheid (Massey and Denton), 13
The American Civil Rights Movement (Dittmer et al.), 360
American Colonization Society (ACS), 3–4, 384
An American Dilemma (Myrdal), 9, 97, 279, 318–319, 323
An American Dilemma Revisited (Clayton), 323
The American Enlisted Man (Moskos), 244
American Federation of Labor (AFL), 26
American Hunger (Wright), 130
My American Journey (Powell), 246
The American Negro (Thomas), 321
"The American Negro—an Export Market at Home" (Sullivan), 340
American Negro Folktales (Dorson), 117, 379
"American Negro Literature" (Reddings), 129
The American Negro Revolution (Muse), 198
American Negro Slave Revolts (Aptheker), 190
American Opera and Its Composers (Hipsher), 151
American Record Label Book (Rust), 337
American Sexual Politics (Fout and Shaw), 326
American Slavery (Kolchin), 3
American Slavery, American Freedom (Morgan), 318
American Women in Jazz (Placksin), 153
America's Black Congressmen (Christopher), 202
America's Black Musical Heritage (Brooks), 148
America's First Black General (Fletcher), 243
America's First Black Town (Cha-Jua), 294

America's Greatest Problem (Shufeldt), 94, 319
Ammons, Lila, 292
Amongst My Best Men (Altoff), 234
Amos, Alcione M., 235
An Analysis of Black Business Enterprises (Handy), 298
The Anatomy of Prejudices (Young-Bruehl), 325
"Anatomy of Scientific Racism" (Miller), 268
Anderson, E., 64
Anderson, James D., 100–101
Anderson, James P., 97–98
Anderson, Karen Tucker, 83
Anderson, Robert, 155
Andreason, Alan R., 342
Andrew Durnford (Whitten), 287
Andrews, William L., 77, 118
"Andrew Young and the Georgia State Elections of 1990" (Davis and Willingham), 203–4
"And the Truth Shall Make You Free" (Patton), 102
Angela Davis (Davis), 203
Angelou, Maya, 132, 134
Angelus, Ted, 342
Annie Allen (Brooks), 129
Another Country (Baldwin), 131
"Antebellum Black Coeds at Oberlin College" (Henle and Merrill), 99
Antebellum Black Newspapers (Jacobs), 218
"The Antebellum 'Talented Thousandth'" (Lawson and Merrill), 99
Anthology of Art Songs by Black American Composers (Patterson), 154
"Anthony D. Allen" (Scruggs), 288
The Anthropometry of the American Negro (Herskovitz), 322
Anti-racism in U.S. History (Aptheker), 318
Anvil, 128
Appeal (Walker), 78, 119, 190–91, 219, 375–76
"Approaching the African God" (Hucks), 385
Aptheker, Herbert, 93, 190, 237, 318

Ardrey, Saundra C., 203
"And Aren't I a Woman?" (Truth), 119
Aristocrats of Color (Gatewood), 293
Army Life in a Black Regiment (Higginson), 235
Arnesen, Eric, 5, 39
Ar'n't I a Woman? (White), 74, 383
Arrington, Richard, Jr., 357
"The Arrival and Ascendence of Black Athletes in the Southeastern Conference" (Paul), 263
"The Articulation of Difference" (Davis), 268
"The Art of Fiction" (Ellison), 129
The Art of Ragtime (Schafer and Riedel), 152
The Art of the American Folk Preacher (Rosenburg), 373
Asante, Molefi Kete, 102, 136, 178, 326
Ashbaugh, Carolyn, 80
Ashe, Arthur, Jr., 255
Assata (Shakur), 84
Assault at West Point, 239
Association for the Study of African American Life and History (ASALH), 282
Association for the Study of Negro Life and History, 124
Athearn, Robert G., 5, 172
Athletic experience, 255–68; baseball, 258–59, 262–63, 340; basketball, 259, 263; black superiority, 268; boxing, 264–65; college sport, 262–64; elite athletes, 260–61; football, 259, 263–64; general reviews, 255–56, 259–60, 266–67; integration, 262–64; post–Civil War, 257; pre–Civil War, 256–57; protests, 265; women, 260, 265–66
"Athleticism among American Blacks" (LeFlore), 267
Atlanta Life Insurance Company (Henderson), 291
Atlantic Slave Trade (Curtin), 2, 368
"At Noon, Oh How I Ran" (Schwartz), 75
Atwood, Rufus B., 99
Aunt Jemima, Uncle Ben, and Rastus (Foxworth), 336

Austin, Allan D., 385
The Autobiography of a Black Activist, Feminist, Lawyer, Priest & Poet (Murray), 83
The Autobiography of an Ex-coloured Man (Johnson), 120, 124
The Autobiography of Malcolm X, 132, 359, 385
The Autobiography of My Mother (Kincaid), 134

Back to Birmingham (Franklin), 357
Bad Nigger (Gilmore), 260
Bailey, Anne J., 236
Bailey's Cafe (Naylor), 134
Baker, David, 154
Baker, Ella, 83–84, 361
Baker, Gordon, 197
Baker, Houston, Jr., 118, 135
Baker, Liva, 98
Baker, Tod A., 198
Baker, William J., 261
Baldwin, James, 129–31, 324
Bambara, Toni Cade, 134
Bancroft, Frederick, 2
Bancroft, Hubert Howe, 320
Banker, Stephen, 258
Banks, William Venoid, 292
Banner-Haley, Charles T., 167
Baraka, Imamu Amiri, 132–33, 154, 324
Barbara Jordan (Jordan and Hearon), 203
Barbeau, Arthur E., 242
The Barber of Natchez (Davis and Hogan), 287
Barbour, Glenn, 154
Bareknuckles (Brailsford), 257
Barker, Lucius, 202
Barksdale, Richard K., 116, 125, 136
Barnes, Claude W., Jr., 201
Barnett, Ida Wells, 321. See also Wells, Ida B.
Barrett, Leonard, 385
Barrow, Lionel C., Jr., 218
"Bars Fight" (Terry), 118–19
Bartley, Numan V., 356
Barton, Rebecca C., 120

Baseball's Great Experiment (Tygiel), 263, 340

"Baseball's Reluctant Challenge" (Davis), 263

Bass, Charlotta, 85

Bass, Jack, 198

Bates, Daisy, 203, 355

Bates, Leonard, 262

Bates, Timothy, 282

Bauer, Carl M., 196

Beale, Frances, 84

Beals, Melba Patillo, 355

Bearing the Cross (Garrow), 354, 382

Beby, Francis, 149

Bederman, Gail, 80

Bee (Washington, D.C.), 219

Been Here and Gone (Ramsey), 372

Been in the Storm So Long (Litwack), 79, 237, 372

Before the Ghetto (Katzman), 6

Before the Mayflower (Bennett), 192, 316, 317

Beggs, John J., 298

"The Beginnings of Insurance Enterprise among Negroes" (Browning), 290

Behee, John, 262

Behind Ghetto Walls (Rainwater), 11

Behind the Mule (Dawson), 202

Behind the Scenes (Keckley), 73, 120, 290

Behold the Promised Land (Shick), 4, 192

Belfrage, Sally, 358

"Be Like Mike?" (Dyson), 267

Belknap, Michal R., 356

Bell, Derrick, 198

Bell, Philip, 218

Bell, William K., 341

Beloved (Morrison), 134

Belt, Lida, 154

Benjamin O. Davis (Davis), 243

Benneker, Benjamin, 118

Bennett, Gwendolyn, 128

Bennett, Lerone, Jr., 167, 192–93, 316, 326

Bentley, George, 192

Beoku-Betts, Josephine, 74

Berea's First Century, 1855–1955 (Peck), 98

Berkeley, D., Jr., 285

Berlin, Edward, 152

Berlin, Ira, 4, 31–32, 170, 232, 284, 287, 318, 370

Berry, Mary Frances, 191, 235

Berryman, Jack W., 257

Bethel, Elizabeth Rauh, 168

Bethune, Mary McLeod, 83, 102

"Beyond Either/Or" (Bennett), 167

Beyond the Melting Pot (Glazier and Moynihan), 281

Beyond the Ring (Sammons), 261

"Beyond the Sound of Silence" (Higginbotham), 72

Bibliography of Black Music (De Lerma), 154

Bickel, Alexander, 197

Big Bands (Simon), 153

Bigglestone, W. E., 99

Big Steel (Greer), 12

Bilbo, Theodore G., 323

Billingsley, Andrew, 57–58, 325

Billington, Monroe L., 240

Binga, Jesse, 292

Binion, V. J., 66

Biographical Dictionary of Afro-American and African Musicians (Southern), 154

A Biography of Colonel Charles Young (Chew), 239

The Biological Basis of Human Nature (Jennings), 322

Birrell, Susan, 265

Birth of a Nation (Griffith), 316

Bitter Fruit (Grimshaw), 12

Bittle, William E., 5

Black Abolitionists (Quarles), 3, 99, 168, 190, 218

The Black Aesthetic (Gayle), 131

Black Aesthetics, 131–32

The Black American (Fishel and Quarles), 190

The Black American in Sociological Thought (Lyman), 319

Black American Music (Roach), 148

Black Americans (Pinkney), 325

Black Americans and the Missionary Movement in Africa (Jacobs), 384

Black Americans and the White Man's Burden, 1893–1903 (Gatewood), 239–40

Black Americans in Congress (Ragsdale and Treese), 202

Black American Writing from the Nadir (Bruce), 120, 123

"Black and Hispanic Socioeconomic and Political Competition" (McClain and Karnig), 200

"Black and Indian Cooperation and Resistance to Slavery" (Katz), 235

"Black and White" (Wills), 369

Black and White Mixed Marriages (Porterfield), 327

Black and White Styles in Conflict (Kochman), 325

Black Arts Movement, 131–33

The Black Athlete (Henderson), 255

Black Ballots (Lawson), 197–98, 357

Blackball Stars (Holway), 258

"Black Benefit Societies in Nineteenth Century Alabama" (Spencer), 290

Black Bostonians (Horton and Horton), 4

Black Bourgeoisie (Frazier), 280–81

"Black Business Community in Post–Civil War Virginia" (Kenzer), 293

Black Business in the Black Metropolis (Weems), 292

Black Business in the New South (Weare), 291

"Black Businessmen in Post–Civil War Tennessee" (Kenzer), 293

"Black Business Ownership in the Rural South" (O'Hare), 294

"Black Capitalism and Black Inequality" (Beggs), 298

Black Cargoes (Mannix), 2

"Black Chaplains in the Union Army" (Redkey), 237

Black Charlestonians (Powers), 4

Black Chicago (Spear), 9

"The Black Church" (Higginbotham), 383

The Black Church in the African American Experience (Lincoln and Mamiya), 373–74, 376

Black Coal Miners in America (Lewis), 41

The Black Composer Speaks (Baker et al.), 154

Black Confederates and Afro-Yankees in Civil War Virginia (Jordan), 236

Black Congressional Reconstruction Orators and Their Orations, 1869–1879 (McFarlin), 193

"Black Consciousness and Olympic Protest Movements" (Spivey), 265

Black Conservatism (Eisenstadt), 178

The Black Consumer (Joyce and Govoni), 342

"Black Control of Central Cities" (Friesema), 201

Black Culture and Black Consciousness (Levine), 123, 154, 167, 372

Black Culture and the Harlem Renaissance (Wintz), 174

Black Diamonds (Banker), 258

Black Eagle (McGovern), 246

Black Education in New York State (Mabee), 99, 101

Black Educators in White Colleges (Moore and Wagstaff), 99

Black Enterprise (Graves), 297

Black Entrepreneurship in America (Green and Pryde), 298

"Black Entrepreneurship in the National Pastime" (Lomax), 258

Black Entreprise Titans of the B.E. 100s (Dingle), 297

Blackett, R.J.M., 235

Black Exodus (Redkey), 5, 172

The Black Experience in Religion (Lincoln), 369–70

Black Faces, Black Interests (Swain), 202

"Black Faculty at White Institutions before 1900" (Dorsey), 99

Black Families at the Crossroads (Staples and Johnson), 325

Black Families in White America (Billingsley), 57, 325

The Black Family in Slavery and Freedom, 1750–1925 (Gutman), 4, 30, 170, 316

Black Feminist Thought (Collins), 85

"Black Film Explosion Uncovers an Untapped, Rich Market" (Angelus), 342
"Black Films, White Profits" (Ward), 342
Black Fire (Neal and Baraka), 132
Black Folktales (Lester), 117
The Black Ghetto (Meister), 11
Black Gods of the Metropolis (Fauset), 374
"The Black Hessians" (Jones), 234
Black History and the Historical Profession, 1915–1980 (Meier and Rudwick), 6, 95
Black Hymnody (Spencer), 155
The Black Image in the White Mind (Fredrickson), 320
Black Images of America, 1784–1870 (Sweet), 166
Black in Blackface (Sampson), 151
"Black-Indian Interaction in Spanish Florida" (Lander), 233
Black Infantry in the West 1869–1891 (Fowler), 238
"Black Intellectual and Iconoclast, 1877–1897" (Wright), 102
Black Jacks (Bolster), 234
Black Journalists in Paradox (Wilson), 225
Black Laborers and Black Professionals in Early America (Perdue), 286
Black Labor in the South (Rachleff), 5, 36
Black Literature and Literary Theory (Gates), 135
Black Literature in America (Baker), 118
Black Lodge in White America (Fahey), 291
Black Looks (hooks), 326
Black Macho and the Myth of the Superwoman (Wallace), 326
Black Majority (Wood), 2, 316
Black Man, 223
"The Black Man in Military History" (Marszalek), 232
Black Man's Burden (Killens), 324
Black Man's Dreams, the First 100 Years (Lovett), 296
"Black Markets and Future Superstars" (Jordan), 268

Black Masculinity (Staples), 326
Black Masters (Johnson and Roark), 287
"Black Mayoral Leadership in Atlanta" (Jones), 201
"Black Mayoralty Campaigns" (Pettigrew), 199
"Black Mecca Reconsidered" (Barnes), 201
Black Metropolis (Drake and Cayton), 8, 279, 322
"The Black Midshipman at the U.S. Naval Academy" (Field), 239
Black Migration (Henri), 9
Black Migration and Poverty (Pleck), 6
Black Migration in America (Johnson and Campbell), 10–11
"Black Migration to the Urban Midwest" (Hine), 82
The Black Military Experience (Rowland), 232
Black Military Experience in the American West (Carroll), 238
Black Milwaukee (Trotter), 9, 37
Black Music in America (Haskins), 148
Black Music in the Harlem Renaissance (Floyd and Reisser), 153
Black Music in Two Worlds (Roberts), 148
The Black Muslims in America (Lincoln), 384
Black Nationalism, 131–32, 154, 190–91, 385
Black Nationalism (Essien-Udom), 385
Black Nationalism and the Revolution in Music (Kofsky), 154
Black Nationalism in America (Bracey et al.), 190
A Black National News Service (Hogan), 221–22
Blackness and the Adventure of Western Culture (Kent), 126
Black New Orleans (Blassingame), 5, 193
Black Ohio and the Color Line, 1860–1915 (Gerber), 9
Black over White (Holt), 171, 193
"Black-Owned Life Insurance Company" (Duker and Hughes), 344
Black Panther Party, 177, 198, 357

The Black Phalanx (Wilson), 234–35

Black Poet (Walser), 119

Black Political Empowerment (Morrison), 358

Black Political Mobilization (Morrison), 198

Black Political Parties (Walton), 203

A Black Political Theology (Roberts), 382

Black Politics (Walton), 192, 195, 203

Black Popular Music in America (Shaw), 155, 337

Black Power (Carmichael and Hamilton), 177, 200, 359

Black Power (Wright), 130

The Black Power Imperative (Cross), 217

"Black Power—Nixon Style" (Kotlowski), 298

Black Power U.S.A. (Bennett), 193

Black Presidential Politics in America (Walters), 202

Black press. *See* Press, African American

The Black Press (Dann), 219

The Black Press and the Struggle for Civil Rights (Senna), 225

The Black Press in Mississippi, 1865–1985 (Thompson), 220

The Black Press in the Middle West, 1865–1985 (Suggs), 220

The Black Press in the South, 1865–1979, 220

The Black Press, U.S.A. (Wolseley), 218

"Black Pride and Negro Business in the 1920's" (Tucker), 295

Black Property Owners in the South, 1790–1915 (Schweninger), 287, 293

Black Protest (Dick), 168

Black Protest Thought in the 20th Century (Meier), 198

Black Rage (Grier and Cobbs), 324

Black Reconstruction in America (Du Bois), 94–95, 170, 193

"The Black Regulars" (Phillips), 238

Black Religion and Black Radicalism (Wilmore), 172, 375, 381

Black Sailors (Putney), 234

Blacks and the Military in American History (Foner), 232

Black Savannah (Johnson), 286

Black Scare (Wood), 194, 318

Black Scholar (Urban), 95

Black Seminoles (Porter), 235

Blacks in Canada (Winks), 3

Blacks in Classical Music (Abdul), 154

Blacks in Classical Music (Gray), 154

Blacks in Southern Politics (Baker), 198

Blacks in the American Armed Forces, 1776–1983 (Davis and Hall), 232

Blacks in the City (Parris), 194

Blacks in the Marine Corps (Shaw and Donnelly), 244

Blacks in the United States Armed Forces (MacGregor and Nalty), 232

Blacks in the West (Savage), 238

Blacks in Topeka, Kansas, 1865–1915 (Cox), 5

Black Slaveowners (Koger), 287

Black Soldier, White Army (Bowers et al.), 244

Black Soldier and Officer in the United States Army, 1891–1917 (Fletcher), 239

Black Soldiers in Jim Crow Texas, 1899–1917 (Christian), 241

"Black Soldiers on the White Frontier" (Schubert), 240

Black Song (Lovell), 150, 372

Black State Legislators (Bositis), 202

Black Struggle (Fulks), 317

"Blacks Who First Entered the World of White Higher Education" (Slater), 99

Black Theology (Cone and Wilmore), 382

Black Theology and Black Power (Cone), 381

A Black Theology of Liberation (Cone), 382

Black Tide (Pierce), 316

Black Towns (Crockett), 5

Black Towns and Profit (Hamilton), 5, 294

Black Troopers (Lynck), 239

"The Black Urban Regime" (Reed), 201

Black Valor (Schubert), 238

Black Victory (Hine), 355

Black Violence (Button), 199

Black Votes Count (Parker), 198, 358

Black Wealth through Black Entrepreneurship (Wallace), 299
The Black West (Katz), 238
Black, White and Southern (Goldfield), 194
Black, White, Other (Funderburg), 327
Black Woman (Cade), 73, 85
Black Womanist Ethics (Cannon), 383
Black Woman's Civil War Memoirs (Taylor), 237
A Black Woman's Odyssey (Prince), 77
Black Women Abolitionists (Yee), 79
Black Women in America (Collier-Thomas), 383
Black Women in America (Hine), 221
"Black Women in Colonial Pennsylvania" (Sonderlund), 75
"Black Women in Politics and Government" (Williams), 203
"Black Women in the Era of the American Revolution in Pennsylvania" (Newman), 75
Black Women in the New World Order (Hemmons), 85
Black Women in White America (Lerner), 73
The Black Worker (Spero and Harris), 25
"Black Workers and Labor Unions . . ." (Worthman), 34
Black Writers of America (Barksdale and Kinnamon), 116, 125
Black Writers of the Thirties (Young), 175
Blake (Delaney), 191
Blassingame, John W., 3, 5, 31, 170, 191, 193, 372
Blaustein, Albert P., 197
"Blaxploitation Movies" (Poussaint), 342
Blesh, Rudi, 152–53
"Blocked Shot" (Gems), 259
Blockson, Charles L., 3
Blood (Terry), 245
Blood Justice (Smead), 357
Blood on the Border (Clendenen), 240
Blood Relations (Watkins-Owens), 82
"Bloods in the Nam," 245
"A Blueprint for Negro Authors" (Ford), 130

"Blueprint for Negro Writing" (Wright), 129
Blues Fell This Morning (Oliver), 151
Blues for Mr. Charlie (Baldwin), 129, 131
Blues Ideology and Afro-American Literature and Criticism (Baker), 135
The Blues Line (Sackheim), 151
Blues People (Baraka), 154
The Bluest Eye (Morrison), 134
Blyden, Edward, 384
Bolster, W. Jeffrey, 234
Bond, Horace Mann, 95–96, 101
Bond and Free (Howard), 120
Bone, Robert, 82, 127
Bonner, Marita, 126
Bontemps, Arna, 118, 372, 379
Booker T. Washington (Harlan), 173, 220, 295
Book of American Negro Poetry (Johnson), 126
Book of Negro Folklore (Hughes and Bontemps), 372, 379
Boone, Dorothy DeLoris, 221
Bositis, David, 202
Bosman, William, 283
Boston, Thomas D., 282, 298
"Bottled" (Johnson), 126
Bowers, Claude G., 321
Bowers, William T., 244
"Boxing as a Reflection of Society" (Sammons), 261
"Boxing's Sambo Twins" (Wiggins), 260
Boyd, Melba Joyce, 219
Boyd, Richard Henry, 296
Boyd, Robert L., 282, 290, 296, 298–99
Boyett, Cheryl Race, 235
Bracey, John, 169, 190, 354
Bradley, David H., 374
Bradley, Tom, 204
Brailsford, Dennis, 257
Branch, Taylor, 354, 371, 382
Branches without Roots (Jaynes), 32
Brashler, William, 258
Brauer, Carl M., 356
Brawley, Benjamin, 119, 153
Brazeal, Brailsford R., 194

Breaking Ice (McMillan), 134
Breaking the Ice (Pennington), 263–64
Breen, T. H., 286
Brewer, James H., 286
Brier, Stephen, 34–35
Brimmer, Andrew F., 292–93
"To Bring the Race Along Rapidly" (Miller), 260
Broadcasting industry, 340
Broken Promises (Lapchick), 265
Brooks, Gwendolyn, 129–30
Brooks, Maxell R., 224
Brooks, Roy L., 326
Brooks, Tilford, 148
Brotherhood of Sleeping Car Porters (BSCP), 36, 194–95
The Brotherhood of Sleeping Car Porters (Brazeal), 194
Brothers (Goff and Sanders), 245
Brown, Elaine, 84, 203
Brown, Elsa Barkley, 42, 80, 170, 291
Brown, Ira Corinne, 323
Brown, J. Clinton, 344
Brown, John, 192
Brown, Karen McCarthy, 385
Brown, Letitia Woods, 4
Brown, Sterling, 125–29
Brown, Warren, 220, 221
Brown, William Wells, 119–20
Brownies' Book (Du Bois), 222
Browning, James, 290
Browning, Rufus, 199, 201
Brownsville Affair (Lane), 241
Brownsville Raid (Weaver), 241
Brown v. Board of Education, 98, 197, 352, 355
Bruce, Dickson D., Jr., 120, 123
Bruce, Janet, 258
Bryan, Carter R., 218
Bryce, James, 320
Buckmaster, Henrietta, 3
"Buffalo Soldier Chaplains" (Lamm), 238
The Buffalo Soldiers (Leckie), 238
Buffalo Soldiers, Braves, and the Brass (Schubert), 240
Bullock, Charles S., III, 199
Bullock, Henry, 98, 101, 341
Bullock, Penelope I., 219

Bunche, Ralph J., 195
Buni, Andrew, 297
Burgess, A. E., 324
Burk, Robert Frederick, 196, 356
Burns, Stuart, 356
Bush, Barbara, 75
Bush, Rod, 199
Business history, 278–99; African commercial background, 283; black entrepreneurs, 296–98; black towns, 294; black women, 283, 288–90; Booker T. Washington, 294–95; emergence, 279–82; financial institutions, 290–93; free blacks, 286–88; insurance companies, 290–93, 344–45; post–civil rights era, 298–99, 344; post–Civil War, 293–96; profiles of single businesses, 293; under slavery, 283–86
Bussey, Charles M., 244
Butchart, Ronald E., 100–101
Butcher, Margaret Just, 153
But for Birmingham (Eskew), 356
Butler, John Sibley, 246, 282, 296
But Some of Us Are Brave (Hull et al.), 224
Button, James, 199
Bynum, Victoria E., 76

Cade, Toni, 73, 85
Cages to Jump Shots (Peterson), 259
Cagin, Seth, 358
Cahn, Susan, 266
Calhoun, William P., 320
Calista, Donald J., 295
Call and Response (Hill), 118, 124, 130, 135–36
Calvin, Ira, 323
Campbell, Clarice T., 357
Campbell, Bishop Jabex, 218
Campbell, James Edwin, 122
Campbell, James T., 384
Campbell, Johnny, 203
Campbell, Rex R., 10–11
"Camp William Penn and the Black Soldier" (Wert), 237
Cane (Toomer), 125, 127
Cannon, Katie, 383

Can We All Get Along? (McClain and Stewart), 200

Capeci, Dominic J., Jr., 11, 261

Capitalism and Slavery (Williams), 2

Captain, Gwendolyn, 260, 265

"Capturing the 15 Billion Dollar Market" (Newman), 340

Carawan, Candie, 379

Carawan, Guy, 154, 379

Carlisle, Rodney, 169

Carmichael, Peter A., 194

Carmichael, Stokely, 133, 177, 198, 200, 359

Carnegie, Andrew, 96, 340

Carnival of Fury (Hair), 5

Caroling Dust (Cullen), 126

Carroll, Charles, 319

Carroll, John M., 238, 262

Carson, Clayborne, 353–54, 356, 359–60

Carter, Dan T., 361

A Case of Black and White (Rothschild), 358

Cash, Wilbur J., 324

Caste and Class in a Southern Town (Dollard), 322

Castel, Albert, 236

Catholic Church, 322

The Caucasian and the Negro in the United States (Calhoun), 320

Caucasians Only (Vose), 195

"Caught in the Web of the Big House" (Clinton), 74

Cayton, Horace R., 8, 27, 279, 322

Cazenave, N., 64, 66

Cecelski, David S., 355

Celia, a Slave (McLaurin), 74

A Century of Negro Migration (Woodson), 6–8

Chadbourn, James H., 194

Chadwick, Bruce, 258

Chafe, William H., 11, 354, 356

Chained to the Rock of Adversity (Gould), 289

Chaining of a Continent (Inikori et al.), 368

Cha-Jua, Sundiata Keita, 294

Challenge, 128

Challenge of Blackness (Bennett), 326

Chalmer, David M., 194

Champion (Mead), 261

Champly, H., 321

Chaney, James, 357

"Changing Patterns in Black School Politics" (Plank and Turner), 100

Chant of the Saints (Harper and Stepto), 373

Characteristics of the American Negro (Klineberg), 322

Charters, Samuel, 150

Chase, William Calvin, 219

Chavers, P. W., 292

Chavers-Wright, Madrue, 292

Check List of Negro Newspapers in the United States, 1827–1946 (Brown), 221

Chen, Victoria, 326

Chester, Thomas Morris, 235

Chestnutt, Charles Waddell, 121–24

Chew, Abraham, 239

Chicago Defender, 221, 297

Chicago Divided (Kleppner), 12

Chicago Metropolitan Assurance Company, 292

Children (Halberstam), 356

Children, slave, 60

Childress, Alice, 129, 131–32

Chin, Gabriel J., 298

The Chinaberry Tree (Fauset), 82

Chireau, Yvonne, 380

Chisholm, Shirley, 84, 203

Christian, Garna L., 241

Christianity, Islam and the Negro Race (Blyden), 384

Christopher, Maurine, 202

Christopher, Nehemiah M., 98

"Christopher McPherson, Free Person of Color" (Berkeley), 285

Churchill, Ward, 177

Church People in the Struggle (Findlay), 360

Cimprich, John, 236

The Citizens' Council (McMillen), 355

Civilities and Civil Rights (Chafe), 11, 354, 356

"Civilization, the Decline of Middle-Class Manliness" (Bederman), 80

Civil Rights and the Presidency (Graham), 196

Civil Rights Chronicle (Campbell), 357

Civil rights movement, 352–61; actions, 356; black businesses and, 298; black unionism and, 40; black women in, 83–84; churches and, 360; Freedom Summer, 357–58; gender equity, 84; general accounts of, 359–60; government and, 356; historiography, 353; intellectual and political thought, 176; Meredith march, 359; migration and, 11; Montgomery Bus Boycott, 84, 203, 341, 356, 381; music, 155; NAACP, 124, 173, 194–95, 222, 321, 353–54; Negro-appeal radio stations, 340; organizations, 353–54; origins, 196, 355; politics of, 196–98; voting rights, 357–58; women in, 83–84, 360–61. *See also* Voting rights

The Civil Rights Movement in America (Eagles), 359

"Civil Rights on the Gridiron" (Smith), 263

"The Civil War in Kentucky" (Howard), 79

Claiming Earth (Madhubuti), 136

Clark, Herbert L., 295

Clark, Kenneth, 11

Clark, Michael J., 240

Clark, Robert, 359

Clarke, Caroline V., 345

Clarke, John Henrik, 174

"Claude McKay" (Hudson-Weems), 126

Clay, William L., 202

Clayton, Obie, Jr., 323

Cleaver, Eldridge, 132, 198, 324

Cleghorn, Reese, 196, 353

Clement, Rufus E., 94

Clendenen, Clarence C., 240

Climbing Jacob's Ladder (Cleghorn), 196, 353

Clinton, Catherine, 74–75, 79

Clotel (Brown), 119–20

Coal, Class, and Color (Trotter), 10, 37

Cobbs, Price, 324

Cody, Cheryl, 74

Coffin, Levi, 3

Coffman, Edward M., 238, 242

Cohassey, John, 290

Cohen, William, 4

"Coincoin" (Mills), 75, 287, 289

COINTELPRO, 177

Colburn, David R., 355

Cole, Johnetta B., 326

Cole, Robert A., 292

Coleman Young and Detroit Politics (Rich), 201

The College Bred Negro (Du Bois), 94

Collier-Thomas, Bettye, 102, 167, 383

Collins, Patricia Hill, 85

"Colonel Charles Young" (Heinl), 239

"Colonial Militia and Negro Manpower" (Quarles), 233

Color, Sex, and Poetry (Hull), 83

Color and Conscience (Gallagher), 323

Color Blind (Halsey), 317

The Color Curtain (Wright), 130

Colored American (Cornish, Bell and Ray), 218

"The Colored American and *Alexander's"* (Schneider), 295

Colored American Magazine (Wallace), 222

The Colored Cadet at West Point (Flipper), 239

Colored Patriots of the American Revolution (Nell), 233

Color of Their Skin (Pratt), 355

The Color Purple (Walker), 134

Comedy: American Style (Fauset), 82

Coming of Age in Mississippi (Moody), 83, 203, 353

Coming on Strong (Cahn), 266

A Common Destiny (NRC), 323

Communist Party, 175

Complete History of the Negro Leagues, 1884 to 1995 (Ribowsky), 258

"The Conceptualization of Deracialization" (McCormick and Jones), 200

Condition, Elevation, and Destiny of the Colored People of the United States (Delany), 119

Cone, Carl B., 257

Cone, James H., 176, 360, 381–82

The Confessions of Nat Turner, 119, 375–76

Congressional Black Caucus (CBC), 202

Congressional Black Caucus in the 103rd Congress (Bositis), 202

Congress of Industrial Organizations (CIO), 27–28, 40–41, 175

Conjure Woman (Chestnutt), 122

Conjuring Culture (Smith), 380

Conrad, Earl, 383

"The Conservative Aims of the Militant Rhetoric" (Finkle), 244

Consumerism, African American, 336–45; alcohol marketing, 343; black consumer activism, 339, 344; black market consultants, 341; blaxploitation movies, 342; current perception, 344; early twentieth century, 336–37; market segmentation, 342–43; personal care products, 345; post–World War II, 340; press and, 337; in the 1970s and 1980s, 342–43; tobacco companies, 343–44; during World War II, 339–40; writings about Negro market, 338–41

Consumers' Cooperative Trading Company (CCTC), 339

Contempt and Pity (Scott), 355

Contending Forces (Hopkins), 124

"A Contextual Analysis of Black Self-Employment . . . " (Boyd), 298

"Controversy" (Asante), 102

Conversations with God (Washington), 379

Converse, Elliott V., III, 246

Coody, Archibald, IV, 323

"Cool Pose" (Majors), 267

Cooper, Anna Julia, 72, 124

Coppin, L. J., 219

CORE (Meier and Rudwick), 353, 356, 359

Cornell's Three Precursors (Wright), 99

Cornish, Dudley, 235

Cornish, Samuel, 216, 218

Corregidora (Jones), 134

Cose, Ellis, 167

Cottroll, Robert, 4

The Country Blues (Charters), 150

Country Place (Petry), 131

Courier (Pittsburgh), 221–22

Courlander, Harold, 151

Court-Martial (Marszalek), 239

Court-Martial of Lieutenant Henry Flipper (Robinson), 239

Cowan, Robert S., 288

Cox, La Wanda, 192

Cox, Thomas C., 5

Craft, Ellen, 79

Crawford, Vicki L., 360–61

Creel, Margaret Washington, 170

Cresswell, Nicholas, 149

The Crisis, The Opportunity (Thurman), 126

The Crisis, 124, 222

The Crisis of the Negro Intellectual (Cruse), 167, 224, 359

"Critical Theory and Problems of Canonicity in African American Literature" (Barksdale), 136

Crockett, Norman L., 5

Cross, Theodore, 217

The Crucible of Race (Williamson), 121

"A Crumbling Legacy" (Weems), 292–93, 344

Crummell, Alexander, 121

Crusade for Justice (Wells), 220

Cruse, Harold, 167, 173, 224, 359

The Cry Was Unity (Solomon), 175

Cuffe, Paul, 3, 168, 190–91, 287

Cullen, Countee, 125–26

Cultivation and Culture (Berlin and Morgan), 284

Culture, Ethnicity, and Personal Relationship Processes (Gaines), 321, 326

Curry, Constance, 355

Curry, George E., 298

Curry, Leonard P., 4, 287

Curtin, Phillip D., 2, 368

Curtis, Susan, 152

Cutler, James E., 194

Dabney, Lillian G., 98

Dailey, Maceo C., 295

Daily World (Atlanta), 221

Dalfiume, Richard M., 244

Dance, Stanley, 153

Dancing to a Black Man's Tune (Curtis), 152

Dan Emmett and the Rise of Early Negro Minstrelsy (Nathan), 151

Daniels, Jon, 357

Dann, Martin E., 219

Dark Ghetto (Clark), 11

Darwin's Athletes (Hoberman), 268

Daughters of Sorrow (Guy-Sheftall), 81

Davidson, Chandler, 198

David Walker's Appeal, 78, 119, 190–91, 219, 375–76

Davie, Maurice R., 323

Davis, Allison, 380

Davis, Angela, 73, 84–85, 203, 317

Davis, Arthur P., 129

Davis, Benjamin O., Sr., 243

Davis, Cyprian, 374

Davis, David Brion, 372

Davis, Edwin A., 287

Davis, Frank Marshall, 128

Davis, Jack E., 263

Davis, Laurel R., 268

Davis, Lenwood G., 194, 232

Davis, Marilyn, 203

Davis, Richard L., 28, 41

Dawson, Michael, 202

Dawson, William, 195–96

Daybreak of Freedom (Burns), 356

Day of Absence (Ward), 132

Days of Hope (Sullivan), 355

Death in the Delta (Whitfield), 357

The Death of Rhythm & Blues (George), 340

Debating the Civil Rights Movement, 1945–1968 (Lawson and Payne), 176

Decarava, Roy, 379

The Declining Significance of Race (Wilson), 12

Deep Is the Hunger (Thurman), 380

Deep like the Rivers (Webber), 101, 103

Deep River (Thurman), 380

The Deep South Says Never (Martin), 324, 356

Deerr, Noel, 368

Dees, Jess Walter, Jr., 324

Delaney, Martin R., 119, 169–70, 191, 218–19

De Lerma, Dominique-René, 154

dem (Kelley), 132

Democracy and Race Friction (Mecklin), 321

"Democracy in the Foxhole," 245

"Demographic Change and Entrepreneurial Occupations" (Boyd), 296

Dent, Tom, 353

Denton, Nancy A., 13

Desegregating the Dollar (Weems), 282, 298, 345

Desegregation and the Law (Blaustein and Ferguson), 197

"Desegregation in New Orleans Public Schools during Reconstruction" (Harlan), 97

Desegregation of the U.S. Armed Forces (Dalfiume), 244

"De Sun Do Move" (Jasper), 121

Detweiler, Frederick G., 221, 337

The Development of Segregationist Thought (Newby), 194

Development of State Legislation Concerning the Free Negro (Johnson), 319

Deveney, John Patrick, 385

The Devil Finds Work (Baldwin), 131

DeVries, Walter, 198

Dick, Robert C., 168

Dickerson, Dennis, 38, 41

Dickson, Amanda America, 74

Dickson, L., 65

Dicksworth, Selika Marianne, 244

Dictionary of Afro-American Performers (Turner), 154

Dictionary of Negro Biography (Logan and Winston), 239

Difference and Pathology (Gilman), 317

"The Dilemma of Black Banking" (Brimmer), 292–93

Dilemmas of Black Politics (Persons), 199

Dill, Augustus, 26

Dingle, Derek, 297

Dingwall, E. J., 323

Disadvantaged Consumer (Andreason), 342

Disappearing Acts (McMillan), 134

Discarded Legacy (Boyd), 219

"Discontented Black Feminists" (Terborg-Penn), 85

Discovering the Women in Slavery (Morton), 74

Disfigured Images (Morton), 81

Dittmer, John, 358–60

Divided Skies (Jakeman), 243

Dixon, Phil, 258

DjeDje, Jacqueline Cogdell, 149

Doby, Larry, 263

Documents Illustrative of the History of the Slave Trade to America (Donnan), 2

Dollard, John, 322

Donnan, Elizabeth, 2

Donnelly, Ralph W., 244

Don't Buy Where You Can't Work campaigns, 338–39

"Don't Do This . . . " (Sullivan), 339–40

Don't Look Back (Ribowsky), 259

Don't Make No Waves, Don't Back No Losers (Rakove), 195

Dorsey, Carolyn, 99

Dorson, Richard M., 117, 379

"Double Bonds of Race and Sex" (Gundersen), 75

Double V (Scott and Womack), 243

Douglas, Davison M., 98

Douglas, Robert, 259

Douglas, William, 192

Douglass, Frederick, 103, 117, 120, 169–70, 191, 218–19

Dove, Rita, 134

Down by the Riverside (Joyner), 170

Downey, Dennis, 43

Drake, Avon W., 298

Drake, St. Clair, 8, 279, 322, 339

Dray, Philip, 358

Dreaming Emmett (Morrison), 134

Dream Makers, Dream Breakers (Rowan), 98

Dred Scott decision, 169

Drums and Shadows (Georgia Writers' Project), 379

Drylongso (Gwaltney), 167, 372

Du Bois, W.E.B.: being black in America, 123–24, 167, 178; black business, 295; black education, 93–95; black families, 57–58; black labor, 25–27; black press, 222; Booker T. Washington and, 173, 295; business history, 279–80, 291; economic progress, 337; Harlem Renaissance, 125; interracial marriage, 316, 321; on Jessie Fauset, 82; on John Brown, 192; migration and urbanization, 6–8; Pan-Africanism, 175; Reconstruction, 170, 193; religion, 371; the slave trade, 2

du Cille, Ann, 85–86

Duker, Jacob M., 344

Dulaney, W. Marvin, 360

Dunbar, Paul Laurence, 121–24

Dundes, Alan, 379

Dunmore, Lord, 233–34

Durnford, Andrew, 287

Du Sable, Jean Baptiste Point, 288

Dutchman (Baraka), 132

Dvorak, Antonin, 151

Dye, Ira, 234

Dyson, Michael, 267

Eagles, Charles W., 244, 357, 359

Early, Charity Adams, 243

Early, Gerald, 102, 264, 297

"Early Black Leadership in Collegiate Football" (Berryman), 257

The Early Black Press in America, 1827–1860 (Hutton), 218

Early Jazz (Schuller), 153

Early Negro American Writers (Brawley), 119

Early Negro Education in West Virginia (Woodson), 95

Eaton, Clement, 285

Ebony, 297

Economic Cooperation among Negro Americans (Du Bois), 279, 291, 337

Economic Detour (Stuart), 279, 291

Economic Perspectives on Affirmative Action (Simms), 298

Economics. *See* Business history; Consumerism, African American

"Economic Status of the Town Negro in Post-Reconstruction North Carolina" (Logan), 293

Economy and Material Culture of Slaves (McDonald), 283

Edley, Christopher F., 298

Edmonds, Anthony O., 261

Edmunds, George, 41

Education, 93–103; Afrocentrism, 102–3; black education history, 99–102; black professors, 99; *Brown* decision, 98, 197, 352, 355; college, 98–99; desegregation, 196–97, 355; Du Bois and Washington on, 93–94; move for equality, 96–97; publications on, 94–95

"The Educational Outlook in the South" (Washington), 94

The Education of Black People (Du Bois), 93

The Education of Negroes in New Jersey (Wright), 96

The Education of the Negro in the American Social Order (Bond), 95, 101

The Education of the Negro prior to 1861 (Woodson), 94–95

Edward, Paul, 117

Edwards, Harry, 265

Edwards, Paul K., 338

"The Edwards Family and Black Entrepreneurial Success" (Lehman), 294, 297

Egerton, John, 355

Eggleston, Edward B., 320

Eight Men (Wright), 130

The Eisenhower Administration and Black Civil Rights (Burk), 196, 356

Eisenstadt, Peter, 178

Eisinger, Peter K., 200–201

Eitzen, D. S., 59–61, 63

Electing Black Mayors (Nelson and Meranto), 199

Elevating the Game (George), 259, 263

Elizabeth Potter (Dean), 289

Ella Baker (Grant), 83–84

Ellison, Ralph, 127, 129–30, 223

Emancipation, 29–33, 61–63, 76, 192

The Emancipation Proclamation (Franklin), 192

"Emancipators, Protectors, and Anomalies" (Schwarz), 287

Emerging Influentials in State Legislatures (Nelson), 202

Emigration vs. Assimilation (Kinshasa), 219

Emmett Till (Hudson-Weems), 130

Employment of Negro Troops (Lee), 242

Encyclopedia of African American Business History (Walker), 282

Encyclopedia of Educational Research, 96

"End Jim Crow in Sports" (Spivey), 262

Engerman, Stanley, 30, 32

"Enter Ladies and Gentlemen of Color" (Captain), 260

Enterprising Southerners (Kenzer), 293

Entrepreneurs (Wright and Viens), 286

Entrepreneurship and Self-Help among Black Americans (Butler), 296

Epstein, Dena, 149

Equiano, Olaudah, 117–18, 148, 283

Escape, or Leap to Freedom (Brown), 119

Eshleman, J. P., 62–63

Eskew, Glenn T., 356

Essien-Udom, E. U., 385

"Esther and Her Sisters" (Gilbert), 289

Ethnic and Racial Politics in California (Jackson and Preston), 200

"Ethnic Market" (Marticorena), 345

Eugenics, 316, 321–22

Evans, James H., Jr., 383

Evans, Sara, 360

Eva's Man (Jones), 134

"An Evening Thought" (Hammon), 119

Even Mississippi (Nielson), 358–59

Evers, Myrlie, 358

"Everybody's Protest Novel" (Baldwin), 129

"The Evolution and Impact of Biracial Coalitions and Black Mayors . . . " (Perry), 202

"The Evolution of Black-Owned Banks . . . " (Ammons), 292

The Exchange Economy of Pre-colonial Tropical Africa (Sundstrom), 283

The Exclusion of Black Soldiers for the Medal of Honor in World Wars (Converse et al.), 246

Exodusters (Painter), 5, 31, 172

"Experiment in Interracial Education at Berea College, 1858–1908" (Nelson), 98

"The Exploitation of an African-American Inventor on the Fringe" (Fouche), 294

Eyes on the Prize (Williams), 196, 356–57, 360

Facing up to the American Dream (Hochschild), 167

The Facts of Reconstruction (Lynch), 193

Fager, Charles E., 357

Fahey, David, 291

Fairclough, Adam, 353–54

Fair Dealing and Clean Playing (Lanctot), 258

Fair Employment Practice Committee (F.E.P.C.), 195

Falconbridge, Alexander, 317

Families, 55–67; African influences, 59; after emancipation, 61–63; after the Civil War, 4, 30; culturally equivalent/deviant models, 56–58; cultural relativity school, 57; cultural variant model, 57; ecology approach, 58; as economic unit, 284; future of, 64–67; historical overview, 59–64; holistic approach, 58; marriage, 64–65; Moynihan Report, 30, 56, 81, 281, 324–25; sharecropping, 32; single-parent, 63–64; slavery and, 30, 59–60, 75; stereotypes, 55–56, 59, 81

Fanon, Frantz, 324

Farewell—We're Good and Gone (Mark), 9

Farmer, James, 353

Farrakhan, Louis, 177, 203

Father of the Blues (Handy), 150

Fauset, Arthur Huff, 374

Fauset, Jessie, 82, 125

Fayer, Steve, 196, 356

Feagin, Joe R., 199, 299

Feather, Leonard, 153

Federal Government Policy and Black Business (Yancy), 298

Federal Law and Southern Order (Belknap), 356

Federal Writer's Project, 127–28

Felder, Cain, 383

Feldman, Lynne B., 281

The Female Economy (Gamber), 290

Feminists movement, 84–85, 135

Feminist Theory (hooks), 135

Fences (Wilson), 134

Ferguson, Clarence, Jr., 197

Fernett, Gene, 153

Field, R. L., 239

Fields, Karen E., 384

15 Million Negroes and 15 Billion Dollars (Bell), 341

Fight for Freedom (Hughes), 195

Film industry, 342

Finch, Minnie, 195

Findlay, James F., Jr., 360

Fine, Sidney, 12

Finkelman, Paul, 298

Finkle, Lee, 244

Fire!! (Thurman), 126

Firefight at Yechon (Bussey), 244

Fire in the Streets (Viorst), 359

The Fire Next Time (Baldwin), 131, 324

"First Kansas Colored" (Fisher), 236

Fishel, Leslie, Jr., 190

Fisher, Dexter, 135

Fisher, Mark, 372

Fisher, Mike, 236

Fisher, Miles Mark, 150

Fisher, Rudolf, 125

Fisher, William H., 194

Fisk Jubilee Singers, 151

Fitzpatrick, Michael Andres, 295

Five Minutes to Midnight (Lapchick), 267

Flash of the Spirit (Thompson), 385

Fleet Walker's Divided Heart (Zang), 258

Fleming, Cynthia Griggs, 360

Fletcher, Juanita D., 99

Fletcher, Linda P., 344

Fletcher, Marvin E., 239, 243

Fletcher, Robert S., 98

Flight and Rebellion (Mullin), 3

Flight to Canada (Reed), 133

Flipper, Henry O., 238–39

Flipper's Dismissal (Johnson), 239

Florence (Childress), 129

Floyd, Samuel, Jr., 148–49, 153

Flynn, Sarah, 196
Focusing (Aldridge), 326
Fogel, Robert William, 30, 32, 285
Folk Beliefs of the Southern Negro (Puckett), 379
Foner, Eric, 170–71, 191, 237
Foner, Jack D., 232, 238
Forced Migration (Inikori), 368
for colored girls who have considered suicide when the rainbow is enuf (Shange), 134
Ford, Nick Aaron, 130
For Freedom's Sake (Lee), 360–61
Forged in Battle (Glatthaar), 236
Forging Freedom (Nash), 4
The Forgotten People of Color (Mills), 287
Forkan, James P., 345
Forman, James, 353
For My People (Walker), 128
Forrest, Nathan Bedford, 236
Forten, Charlotte, 76, 79
Forten, James, 191, 287
"Fort Pillow, Forrest, and the United States Colored Troops in 1864" (Moore), 236
"The Fort Pillow Massacre" (Castel), 236
"Fort Pillow Massacre" (Mainfort), 236
"Fort Pillow Revisited" (Mainfort), 236
Fortune, T. Thomas, 172
Forty Years in Politics (McCain et al.), 220
For Us, the Living (Evers), 358
Fouche, Rayvon, 294
The Fourteenth Amendment (Schwartz), 193
Fout, John C., 326
Fowke, E., 154
Fowler, Arlen, 238
Fox, Stephen R., 173, 222
Fox-Genovese, Elizabeth, 75
Francis, Charles E., 243
Franklin, Jimmie Lewis, 5, 357
Franklin, John Hope, 192–93, 218, 232, 285, 318
Franklin, Vincent P., 96, 100, 102
Franks, Gray, 202
Fraser, George C., 299

Fraternal orders, 292
Frazier, E. Franklin, 8, 56, 61, 280–81, 318, 324, 371
Frederick Douglass (McFeely), 219
Frederick Douglass (Quarles), 191, 218
Fredrickson, George M., 320
"Free African-American Women in Savannah, 1800–1860" (Johnson), 76–77
Free at Last? (Powledge), 359
The Free Black in Urban America, 1800–1850 (Curry), 4, 287
Freedom (Berlin), 32–33
Freedom Bound (Weisbrot), 359
"Freedom of the Press and Black Publications" (Snorgrass), 225
Freedom Ride (Peck), 356
At Freedom's Edge (Cohen), 4
Freedom's Journal, 216, 218, 375
Freedom's Lawmakers (Foner), 171
Freedom Song (King), 353, 360
Freedom Summer (Belfrage), 358
Freedom Train (Sterling), 191
A Freedomways Reader (Kaiser), 326
Free Frank (Walker), 287
Freeman, Laurie, 345
Free Negroes in the District of Columbia (Brown), 4
The Free Negro Family (Frazier), 318
Free Speech and Headlight, 219
"Free Women of Color" (Lebsock), 289
Free Women of Petersburg (Lebsock), 4, 75, 78
Freud, Sigmund, 320
Frey, Sylvia, 371, 373
Friedland, Michael B., 360
Friedman, Walter, 295
Friesema, Paul, 201
Fritz Pollard (Carroll), 262
From a Caste to a Minority (Williams), 320
From Brown to Bakke (Wilkinson), 101
From Darkness to Light (Helm), 319
"From Enforced Segregation to Integration" (Puth), 291
From Jazz to Swing (Hennessey), 153
From Mammies to Militants (Harris), 383
From Miles to Johnson (Pettigrew), 374

From Plantation to Ghetto (Meier and Rudwick), 192

"From Protest to Politics" (Rustin), 198

From Protest to Politics (Tate), 179, 202

From Race Riots to Sit-Ins, 1919 and the 1960s (Waskow), 196–97

From Set Shot to Slam Dunk (Salzberg), 263

From Slavery to Freedom (Franklin and Moss), 192, 218, 232, 318

From Slavery to Public Service (Uya), 192, 237

From Sundown to Sunup (Rawick), 170

The Fruits of Integration (Banner-Haley), 167

Frustrated Fellowship (Washington), 171

Fuchs, Richard L., 236

Fulani, Lenora B., 203

Fulks, Bryon, 317

Fuller, Hoyt, 132

Fullinwider, S. P., 166–67

Fulop, Timothy E., 369, 373–74

Funderberg, J. H., 323

Funderburg, Lise, 327

Fundi, 84

Funnyhouse of a Negro (Kennedy), 132

"The Future of College Athletics Is at Stake" (Wiggins), 265

Gaines, Kevin K., 174

Gaines, Stanley O., Jr., 321, 326

Gallagher, Buell G., 323

Galster, George C., 12

Gamber, Wendy, 290

Gansta (Ro), 155

"Gantt *versus* Helms" (Wilson), 204

Gara, Larry, 3

Gardell, Mattias, 177

Garfinkel, Herbert, 175, 195

Garland, Phyl, 155

Garnet, Henry Highland, 119, 191, 219

Garofalo, Reebe, 155

Garrison, Lucy McKin, 149

Garrison, William Lloyd, 168, 190

Garrow, David J., 196, 198, 203, 354, 357, 382

Garvey movement, 44, 126, 174, 223

Gaspar, David Barry, 75

Gaston, Arthur G., 297

Gates, Henry Louis, 73, 135

Gatewood, Willard B., 239, 293

Gavin, Raymond, 354

Gayle, Addison, Jr., 131

Gazette (Cleveland), 219

Geis, Gilbert, 5

Gems, Gerald R., 259, 263

"Gender Conventions, Ideals, and Identity . . . " (Stevenson), 75

Genovese, Eugene, 30, 32, 59, 170, 371

George, Carol, 4

George, Nelson, 259, 263, 340

"Georgia Negroes and Their Fifty Millions of Savings" (Du Bois), 337

Gerber, David A., 9

Ghettoization, 37, 296

Ghetto model, 6, 8, 10, 34

Ghetto Revolts (Feagin and Hahn), 199

A Ghetto Takes Shape (Kusmer), 6, 9

Gibbs, Mifflin W., 218

Gibson, D. Parke, 341

Gibson, Josh, 258–59

Giddings, Paula, 326

Gifts of Power (Jackson), 77

Gilbert, Judith A., 289

Giles, Cheryl Townsend, 383

Gill, Gerald R., 85

Gill, La Verne McCain, 85

Gillette, William, 193

Gilligan, Francis J., 322

Gilman, Sander, 317

Gilmore, Al-Tony, 260

Giovanni, Nikki, 133

Giovanni's Room (Baldwin), 131

Gissendanner, Cindy Himes, 266

Glasco, Laurence, 296

Glatthaar, Joseph T., 236

Glazier, Nathan, 281

Glory, 236

Gloster, Hugh, 129

God of the Oppressed (Cone), 382

God's Long Summer (Marsh), 360

God's Trombones (Johnson), 379

Goff, Stanley, 245

Going through the Storm (Stuckey), 380

Going to the Territory (Ellison), 130

Gold, Michael, 128

Goldberg, Joe, 153
Golden, Harry, 196
The Golden Age of Black Nationalism
  (Moses), 169
Goldfield, David R., 194
Goldin, Claudia D., 4
Goldstein, Naomi Friedman, 319
Gomillion v. Lightfoot, 197
Gonzalez, Alberto, 326
Good, Paul, 359
Goodman, Andrew, 357
Goodman, Michael H., 257
Goodwin, M. B., 94
Gordon, Charles, 132
Gordy, Berry, 297
Gore, George, Jr., 221
Gorn, Elliott J., 257, 264
Gosnell, Harold F., 195
Gospel Music Encyclopedia (Anderson
  and North), 155
Gospel Sound (Heilbut), 155
Go Tell It on the Mountain (Baldwin),
  131
Gottlieb, Peter, 10, 38
Gould, Virginia Meacham, 289
Govoni, Norman, 342
"Gracia Real de Santa Teresa de Mose"
  (Landers), 288
Graham, Hugh Davis, 196
Graham, Shirley, 119
A Grand Army of Black Men (Redkey),
  236
Grant, Jacquelyn, 383
Grant, Joanne, 83–84, 361
Graves, Earl G., 297
Gray, John, 149, 154
Gray, Linda C., 294
"A Great Agitation for Business" (Fitz-
  patrick), 295
*The Great Migration in Historical Per-
  spective* (Trotter), 6, 10
"The Great Migration to the North . . . "
  (Boyd), 290, 296
Great Slave Narratives (Bontemps), 118
"Great Speed but Little Stamina" (Wig-
  gins), 268
Green, Constance McLauglin, 9
Green, Shelley, 298

Greenberg, Jonathan D., 297
Greene, Lorenzo J., 2, 233, 286, 288–89
Greene, Michael, 295
Greene, Percy, 222
Greenlee, Gus, 259
Green Power (Gaston), 297
Greer, Edward, 12
Gregory, Sheila T., 292
Gridley, Mark, 153
Grier, William, 324
Griffith, D. W., 316
Grim, Valerie, 294
Grimshaw, Allen D., 199
Grimshaw, William J., 12
Grofman, Bernard, 198
Gropman, Alan L., 244
Gross, James A., 23
Grossman, James R., 10, 38
Grundman, Adolph, 265
The Guarantee (Chavers-Wright), 292
Guardian (Boston), 221
The Guardian of Boston (Fox), 173, 222
Guinier, Lani, 197
Gullah Statesman (Miller), 237
Gundersen, Joan R., 75
Guralnick, Peter, 155
Gurin, Patricia, 201
Gutman, Herbert G., 4, 28–29, 30, 34–35,
  60, 170, 316
Guy-Sheftall, Beverly, 81
Guzman, Jessie Parkurst, 222
Gwaltney, John Langston, 167, 372

Hacker, Andrew, 323
Hadden, Jeffrey K., 199
Hadley, James S., 324
Hadlock, Richard, 153
Hahn, Harlan, 197, 199
Hail to the Victors! (Behee), 262
Hair, William Ivy, 5
Hairdresser's Experience in the High Life
  (Potter), 76
Halberstam, David, 356
Haley, Alex, 132, 359, 385
Half Sisters of History (Clinton), 79
Hall, George, 232
Hall, Gwendolyn Midlo, 283
Halpern, Rick, 40

Halsey, Margaret, 317
Hamer, Fannie Lou, 83–84, 203, 360
Hamilton, Alexander, 81
Hamilton, Charles V., 177, 198, 200, 202, 359
Hamilton, Kenneth M., 5, 294
Hamilton, Thomas, 218
Hammer and Hoe (Kelley), 41–42
Hammon, Briton, 117
Hammon, Jupiter, 118–19, 381
Hammond, William M., 244
Hampton, Henry, 196, 356
"The Hampton Model . . . " (Anderson), 101
Handley, Lisa, 198
Handlin, Oscar, 324
Handy, John, 298
Handy, William C., 150
Hanger, Kimberly S., 288
Hanks, Lawrence J., 198
Hannigan, Patrick J., 258
Hansberry, Lorraine, 129
Happy in the Service of the Lord (Lornell), 155
Haralambos, Michael, 155
Hardaway, Roger Dale, 232
Hard Fight for We (Schwalm), 80
Harding, Vincent, 176, 190–91, 219, 359, 371, 375
Hard Trials (Simpson), 151
Hare, Maude Cuney, 151
Hargis, Peggy G., 294
Haring, H. A., 338
Harlan, Louis R., 97–98, 101, 173, 220, 295
Harlem (Osofsky), 9
Harlem (Thurman), 126
Harlem Gallery (Tolson), 127
Harlem Renaissance, 82–83, 124–27, 147, 152–53, 174
Harlem Renaissance (Huggins), 127, 174
The Harlem Renaissance in Black and White (Hutchinson), 174
The Harlem Renaissance Remembered (Sato), 82
The Harlem Riot of 1943 (Capeci), 11
Harley, Sharon, 42, 73, 102
Harmon, J. H., 279

Harmon-Martin, Sheila F., 203
Harper, Francis Ellen Watkins, 119–20, 219
Harper, Michael S., 373
Harriet Tubman (Conrad), 383
Harris, Abram L., 25–27, 279–80, 292
Harris, Carl V., 101
Harris, Fred R., 13
Harris, Joel Chandler, 121
Harris, Michael, 155
Harris, Robert, 197
Harris, Sheldon H., 168
Harris, Trudier, 383
Harris, William H., 35–36
Hart, Albert Bushnell, 320
"Harvard and the Color Line" (Miller), 262
Haskins, James, 148
Hatchett, Shirley, 201
Hauser, Thomas, 264
Have We Overcome? (Namorato), 197, 360
Hay, Margaret Jean, 283
Hayden, Robert, 130
Haygood, Wil, 202
Haynes, Robert V., 241
He, Too, Spoke for Democracy (McGuire), 243
Hearon, Shelby, 203
Hedden, Margaret K., 220
Heilbut, Anthony, 155
Heinl, Nancy G., 239
Helm, Mary, 319
Helper, Hinton Rowan, 319
Hemmings, Sally, 318
Hemmons, Willa Mae, 85
Henderson, Alexa Benson, 291–92
Henderson, Edwin B., 255
Henle, Ellen, 99
Hennessey, Thomas, 153
Henri, Florette, 9, 242
Henry Highland Garnet (Schor), 219
"Heritage" (Cullen), 126
"Herman E. Perry and Black Enterprise in Atlanta, 1908–1925" (Henderson), 292
Hermann, Janet Sharp, 294
Herndon, Alonzo F., 291

Hernton, Calvin C., 325
Herskovits, Melville, 370
Hickey, Joseph V., 294
Higginbotham, Evelyn Brooks, 71–72, 383
Higginbotham, Leon, 189
Higginson, Thomas Wentworth, 235
Hill, Edward W., 12
Hill, Herbert, 40
Hill, Patricia Higgins, 118, 124, 130, 136
Hill, Robert A., 174
Hill, T. Arnold, 338
Himes, Chester B., 128
Hine, Darlene Clark, 73, 75, 77, 80, 82, 85, 100, 197, 221, 339, 355
Hipsher, Edward, 151
"Hiram Young" (O'Brien), 288
Hirsch, Arnold, 11
"The Historical Development of Public Education . . . " (Mann), 98
"A Historical Review and a Bibliography of Selected Negro Magazines, 1910–1969," 221
History of Black Business in America (Walker), 282, 286, 299
The History of Black Catholics in the United States (Davis), 374
"History of Black-Oriented Radio in Chicago" (Spaulding), 340
"A History of Gammon Theological Seminary" (Taylor), 98
History of Negro Education (Bullock), 101
"History of Negro Education in North Carolina " (Clement), 94
A History of Negro Education in the South (Bullock), 98
"The History of Negro Education of Florida" (Lanier), 94
"The History of Negro Public Education in Texas, 1865–1900" (Christopher), 98
History of Negro Slavery in Colonial New York (McManus), 2
A History of Oberlin College (Fletcher), 98
"A History of Public Education and

Charitable Institutions . . . " (Williams), 94
"The History of Schools for Negroes in the District of Columbia . . . " (Dabney), 98
History of Sugar (Deerr), 368
History of the A.M.E. Zion Church (Bradley), 374
History of the Chicago Urban League (Strickland), 195, 354
The History of the Colored Methodist Episcopal Church in America (Phillips), 374
A History of the Freedmen's Bureau (Bentley), 192
The History of the Negro Race in America (Williams), 93, 121
History of the Negro Troops in the War of the Rebellion, 1861–1865 (Williams), 120, 121, 235
"History of the Schools for the Colored Population in the District of Columbia" (Goodwin), 94
"A History of the Twenty-fourth United States Infantry Regiment in Utah, 1896–1900" (Clark), 240
Hochschild, Jennifer L., 101, 167
Hoffman, Frederick L., 320
Hogan, Lawrence D., 221
Hogan, Lloyd, 217
Hogan, William R., 287
Holden, Matthew, Jr., 203
Holding Aloft the Banner of Ethiopia (James), 175
Hollandsworth, James G., 236
Holloway, Harry, 198
Holloway, Joseph E., 283, 371
Holmes, S. J., 322
Holsey, Albon L., 338
Holsworth, Robert D., 298
Holt, Thomas, 171, 193
Holway, John, 258
Home (Jones), 324
Home Girls (Smith), 85
Home to Harlem (McKay), 126
Homosexuality, 131, 135, 326
Honey, Michael, 40
Hood, Robert E., 383

Hooded Americanism (Chalmer), 194

Hoodoo—Conjuration—Witchcraft—Root-work (Hyatt), 379

hooks, bell, 85, 135, 326

Hope, Lugenia Burns, 80

Hope and History (Harding), 176, 359

Hopkins, Pauline E., 124

Horizon, 222

Horne, Frank R., 94

Hornsby, Annie R., 293

Horse, John, 235

Horton, James Oliver, 4, 286

Horton, Lois E., 4, 286

Hot Jazz (Panassié), 152

House behind the Cedars (Chestnutt), 124

"The Housewives' League of Detroit" (Hine)

Houston, Marsha, 326

Houston Riot, 241

Howard, James H. W., 120

Howard, Victor B., 79

"How Negroes Spent Their Incomes, 1920–1943" (Sullivan), 340

How Stella Got Her Groove Back (McMillan), 134

How the NAACP Began (White), 195

How to Succeed in Business without Being White (Graves), 297

"How We Got Over" (Trimiew and Greene), 295

Hubbard, Dolan, 372

Hucks, Tracey Elaine, 385

Hudson, Herman, 154

Hudson, Hosea, 35–36

Hudson, Larry E., Jr., 74, 284

Hudson, Lynn M., 290

Hudson-Weems, Clenora, 126, 130, 135

Huggins, Nathan, 153, 174

Huggins, Nathaniel Irvin, 127

Hughes, Charles E., 344

Hughes, Langston, 82, 125–27, 174, 195, 222, 372, 379–80

Hull, Gloria T., 82–83

Hunter, Charles N., 45

Hunter, Tera, 42, 80

Hunton, Addie W., 242

Hurston, Zora Neale, 82, 125, 127–28, 380

Hutchinson, George, 174

Hutton, Frankie, 218

Hyatt, Harry M., 379

Hyser, Raymond, 43

The Ideological Origins of Black Nationalism (Stuckey), 169

If He Hollers Let Him Go (Himes), 128

"If We Must Die" (McKay), 125

I Know Why the Caged Bird Sings (Angelou), 132, 134

"Image of Intercollegiate Sports and the Civil Rights Movement" (Grundman), 265

Imani, Nikitah, 299

The Impact of Reapportionment (O'Rourke), 197

Incidents in the Life of a Slave Girl (Jacobs), 73, 119

Incomes, 65

"Independence Day Speech" (Douglass), 119

Independent Black Leadership in America (Pleasant), 203

Indians, Settlers, & Slaves in a Frontier Exchange Economy (Usner), 284

Industrial Workers of the World (IWW), 26

"I Never Want to Take Another Trip like This One" (Lamb), 263

Infants of the Spring (Thurman), 126

"The Influence of William Alexander Leidesdorff on the History of California" (Savage), 288

Ingalls, Robert P., 5

Ingham, Frank, 41

Ingham, John N., 281, 293

Inikori, Joseph, 368

In Love and Trouble (Walker), 134

Innes, Stephen, 286

Innovation and Growth in an African American Owned Business (Todd), 299

In Pursuit of Power (Lawson), 357, 359

"In Remembrance of Mira" (Powell), 75

In Search of Canaan (Athearn), 5, 172

In Search of Our Mother's Gardens
(Walker), 85, 135
Inside Bebop (Feather), 153
In Struggle (Carson), 353, 359
"Insurance Business among Negroes"
(Woodson), 291
Insurance companies, 290–93, 344–45
"Integrating New Year's Day" (Martin),
264
"Integration and Race Literature" (Davis),
129
"The Integration of Intercollegiate Athlet-
ics in Texas" (Marcello), 264
Integration of the Armed Forces (Mac-
Gregor), 244
*Integration of the Negro into the United
States Navy, 1776–1947* (Nelson), 244
Integration or Separation? (Brooks), 326
Intellectual and political thought, 166–79;
black nationalism, 168–70, 191; black
power, 176–77, 198; blacks as chosen
people, 166–67; black studies, 178;
civil rights movement, 176; during the
Depression, 175; Du Bois and Wash-
ington, 172–73; integration or separa-
tion, 167; the New Negro, 173–74;
Pan-Africanism, 3, 102, 126, 131, 169;
post-Civil War, 170–71; return to Af-
rica, 3–5, 168, 172, 174, 191–92, 219,
384; skin color, 167
"Intercollegiate Athletic Servitude"
(Jones), 262
*The Interesting Narrative of the Life of
Olaudah Equiano, or Gustavus Vassa,
the African* (Equiano), 117–18, 148
Interracial Justice (La Farge), 322
"Interracial Organizing in the West Vir-
ginia Coal Industry" (Brier), 34
In Their Own Interests (Lewis), 37
*In The Matter of Color, Race and the Le-
gal Process* (Higginbotham), 189
In the Name of Elijah Muhammad (Gar-
dell), 177
Invisible Empire (Fisher), 194
Invisible Man (Ellison), 127, 129–30
"Invisible Men" (May), 235
Invisible Men (Rogosin), 258
Invisible Politics (Walton), 202

Iola Leroy (Harper), 120
Is God a White Racist? (Jones), 382
Islam in the African American Experience
(Turner), 385
*Issues and Trends in Afro-American
Journalism* (Tinney and Rector), 225
I've Got the Light of Freedom (Payne),
358

*J. E. Springarn and the Rise of the
NAACP, 1911–1939* (Ross), 195
Jackie Robinson (Rampersad), 263
"Jack Johnson as Bad Nigger" (Wiggins),
260
Jackson, Bryan O., 200
Jackson, James S., 201
Jackson, Jesse, 202–3
Jackson, Kenneth T., 194
Jackson, Peter, 257
Jackson, Rebecca Cox, 77
Jacobs, Donald, 218
Jacobs, Harriet, 73, 119
Jacobs, Sylvia, 384
Jakeman, Robert J., 243
James, Gen. Daniel "Chappie," 246
James, Winston, 175
Janiewski, Dolores E., 83
Janis, Harriet, 152
Jasper, John, 121
Jaynes, Gerald David, 32
Jazz (Morrison), 134
Jazz Era (Dance), 153
Jazz Exiles (Moody), 154
Jazz Masters of the Fifties (Goldberg),
153
Jazz Masters of the 20s (Hadlock), 153
Jazz Styles (Gridley), 153
"Jean Baptiste Point Du Sable, the First
Chicagoan" (Meehan), 288
Jefferson, Robert Franklin, 243
Jefferson, Thomas, 118, 317–18
Jencks, Christopher, 13
Jennings, Elizabeth, 78–79
Jennings, H. S., 322
Jennings, James B., 201
Jennings, Thelma, 74
The Jesse Jackson Phenomenon (Reed),
203

"Jesse Jackson's Campaigns for the Presidency" (Tryman), 202

Jesse Jackson's 1984 Presidential Campaign (Barker and Walters), 202

Jesse Owens (Baker), 261

Jesus and the Disinherited (Thurman), 380

Jewell, Malcolm, 197

JFK and the Second Reconstruction (Bauer), 196

Jim Crow: athletics, 264; black churches, 172; black workers, 24, 42; enactment, 62; migration, 5; miscegenation, 318–21; politics, 193–94; reaction to, 12

Jim Crow (Hadley), 324

"Jim Crow in the Gymnasium" (Martin), 264

Jim Crow's Defense (Newby), 194, 320

Joe Louis (Edmonds), 261

John Brown (Du Bois), 192

John F. Kennedy and the Second Reconstruction (Brauer), 356

"John Hanks Alexander of Arkansas" (Gatewood), 239

Johnson, Abby Arthur, 126

Johnson, Ann, 289

Johnson, Anthony, 286

Johnson, Barry C., 239

Johnson, Bruce, 240

Johnson, Charles, Jr., 240

Johnson, Charles S., 8, 97, 134, 222–23

Johnson, Daniel M., 10–11

Johnson, Franklin, 319

Johnson, Guy B., 337

Johnson, Helene, 125–26, 128

Johnson, Jack, 260

Johnson, James Weldon, 120, 124–26, 379

Johnson, John H., 223, 297, 341

Johnson, Joseph T., 341

Johnson, Katherine M., 242

Johnson, Leanor Boulin, 325

Johnson, Michael P., 4, 78, 287

Johnson, Ronald Maberry, 126

Johnson, Whittington B., 76, 286

"Johnson Products Agrees to $67 Million Ivax Buyout" (Pulley), 345

Joint Center for Political Studies, 200–201

Jones, A. M., 149

Jones, Charles E., 200

Jones, Edward A., 99

Jones, Eugene Kinckle, 338

Jones, Gayl, 85, 134

Jones, George Fenwick, 234

Jones, Jacqueline, 83, 101

Jones, Lawrence, 373

Jones, LeRoi (Imamu Amiri Baraka), 132–33, 154, 324

Jones, Mack H., 201

Jones, Thomas Jesse, 97

Jones, Tom, 262

Jones, Virginia L., 99

Jones, William R., 382

Joplin, Scott, 152

Jordan, Barbara, 203

Jordan, Daniel P., 34–35

Jordan, Ervin L., Jr., 236

Jordan, Larry E., 267–68

Jordan, Michael, 267

Jordan, Winthrop, 189, 317, 318

Josh Gibson (Brashler), 258

Journalism. *See* Press, African American

Journal of a Residence on a Georgian Plantation in 1838–1839 (Scott), 76

Journal of Negro History, 102, 223

Journal of Nicholas Cresswell, 149

Journal of Urban History, 6

Journey Back (Baker), 135

Journey toward Hope (Franklin), 5

Joyce, George, 342

Joyner, Charles W., 170

Jubilee (Walker), 132, 190

The Jubilee Singers and Their Campaign for Twenty Thousand Dollars (Pike), 151

Jupiter Hammon and the Biblical Beginnings of African-American Literature (O'Neale), 119

Just a Sister Away (Weems), 383

Just before Jazz (Riis), 151

Just Permanent Interests (Clay), 202

Just Schools (Kirp), 101

Kaiser, Ernest, 326
Kansas City Monarchs (Bruce), 258
Kaplan, Sidney, 294
Karenga, Maulana, 177
Karis, Teri, 327
Karnig, Albert, 200
Katz, Michael B., 13
Katz, William Loren, 235, 238, 321
Katzman, David M., 6
Keckley, Elizabeth, 73, 120, 290
Keeling, John, 122–23
Keeping the Faith (Harris), 35
Keil, Charles, 151
Kelley, Don Quinn, 295
Kelley, Robin D. G., 41–42, 44
Kelley, William Melvin, 132
Kellogg, Charles Flint, 173
Kellor, Margaret M. R., 75
Kemble, Frances Anne, 76
Kennedy, Adrienne, 132
Kennedy, John F., 196, 356
Kennedy, Louise V., 8
Kennedy, William J., 291
Kennedy Justice (Navasky), 356
Kent, George, 126
Kenzer, Robert C., 293
Kerner Commission report, 12
Kern-Foxworth, Marilyn, 336
Key, V. O., 198
Kijakazi, Kilolo, 298
Killens, John Oliver, 129, 324
Kincaid, Jamaica, 134
King, Martin Luther, Jr.: biographies, 371;
    black theology, 381–82; civil rights,
    11, 132–33, 176, 340, 353–54, 356;
    voting rights, 198–99
King, Mary, 353, 360
King, Wilma, 75–77, 80, 85, 257
King of Ragtime (Berlin), 152
King of the Cats (Haygood), 202
Kinnamon, Kenneth, 116
Kinshasa, Kwando M., 219
Kirp, David L., 101
Kiser, Clyde Vernon, 8
KKK, 194, 315, 319
KKK (Davis), 194
KKK in the City, 1915–1930 (Jackson),
    194

Klein, Herbert S., 2
Kleppner, Paul, 12
Klineberg, Otto, 322
Kluger, Richard, 98, 101, 197, 355
Knights of Labor, 26, 34–35, 37
Kochman, Thomas, 325
Kofsky, Frank, 154
Koger, Larry, 287
Kolchin, Peter, 3, 31
Korstad, Robert, 39–40
Kotlowski, Dean, 298
Kraditor, Eileen, 190
Ku Klux Klan (KKK), 194, 315, 319
Kulikoff, Allan, 317
Kusmer, Kenneth L., 6, 9, 10
Kwanzaa (Karenga), 177
Kwolek-Follands, Angel, 291

Labor. *See* Workers, African American
Labor of Love, Labor of Sorrow (Jones),
    83
Labor unions, 24–29, 34–35, 39–41, 45
Ladner, Joyce, 326
La Farge, John, 322
Lamb, Chris, 263
Lamm, Alan K., 238
Lamont, Thomas D., 168
Lanctot, Neil, 258
Lander, Jane, 233
Landers, Jane G., 288
Land of Hope (Grossman), 10, 38
The Land Where the Blues Began (Lo-
    max), 151
Lane, Ann J., 241
Lane, Lunsford, 285
Lane, Roger, 6
Langley, Harold D., 234
Lanier, O'Hara R., 94
Lanier, Powless, 324
Lapchick, Richard, 265, 267
Larsen, Nella, 82, 125
"Last Hired, First Fired" (Anderson), 83
"The Last Quatrain in the Ballad of Em-
    mett Till" (Brooks), 130
Lawd Today (Wright), 130
Lawson, Bill E., 13
Lawson, Ellen, 99

Lawson, Steven F., 176, 197–98, 357, 359
Lay Bare the Heart (Farmer), 353
Layered Violence (Wilkerson), 11
Leadership, Love, and Aggression (Davis), 380
Lebsock, Suzanne, 4, 75, 78, 289
Leckie, William H., 238
Lee, Carleton L., 381
Lee, Chana Kai, 360
Lee, George Washington, 295
Lee, Ulysses, 242
LeFlore, James, 267
Legacy of Dreams (Gregory), 292
The Legacy of the Blues (Charters), 150
Lehman, Paul, 294, 297
Leidesdorff, William, 288
"The Leidesdorff-Folsom Estate" (Cowan), 288
Lemann, Nicholas, 11–12, 82
Lemke-Santangelo, Gretchen, 12, 82
Lerner, Gerda, 72–73
Lesbians, 135
Leslie, Kent Anderson, 74
Lester, Julius, 93, 117
Let My People Go (Buckmaster), 3
"Letter from Birmingham Jail" (King), 176
Letters from Mississippi (Sutherland), 358
"Letter to the editor" (Dorsey), 99
"Letter to the Editor" (Titcomb), 99
"Letter to Thomas Jefferson" (Banneker), 118
Levenstein, Margaret, 296
Levine, Lawrence, 123, 154, 167, 372
Lewis, David Levering, 125, 174
Lewis, Earl, 37, 45
Lewis, Edward E., 8
Lewis, Reginald, 298
Lewis, Ronald, 41, 44
Lewis, Rupert, 174
Liberation and Reconciliation (Roberts), 382
Liberia, 168, 172, 192
Liberty Line (Gara), 3
"Libretto for the Republic of Liberia" (Tolson), 130
Lichtenstein, Nelson, 39–40

Liebow, Elliot, 11
Liele, George, 373
Life and Public Services of Martin R. Delaney (Rollin), 219
Life and Times of Frederick Douglass (Douglass), 120
Life and Writings of Frederick Douglass (Foner), 191
Life behind a Veil (Wright), 5
Life for Us Is What We Make It (Thomas), 10
Life in Black and White (Stevenson), 170
The Life of Fannie Lou Hamer (Lee), 361
"Lift Every Voice and Sing" (Johnson), 125
"Lifting the Veil, Shattering the Silence" (Hine), 73
Lift up Your Voice like aTrumpet (Friedland), 360
Like a Holy Crusade (Mill), 358
Lincoln, Abraham, 192
Lincoln, C. Eric, 369–70, 373–74, 376–77, 384
Lincoln and Black Freedom (Cox), 192
Lincoln and the Negro (Quarles), 192
Linden Hills (Naylor), 134
Lindsay, Arnett G., 279, 292
Literary Garveyism (Martin), 126
Literary tradition, 116–36; Chicago Renaissance, 128; Civil War, 119–20; contemporary, 133–36; dialect poetry, 122; early 1930 to 1950, 127–31; Harlem Renaissance, 124–27; oral tradition, 116–17, 121, 145, 372; post–Civil War, 120–24; protest, 128–29; in the 1960s, 131–33; slavery and antislavery, 116–19; structuralists and deconstructionists, 135–36; women writers, 77–78, 82–83, 134–35
Littlefield, Daniel, 3
Litwack, Leon F., 4, 79, 237, 372
Living the Intersection (Sanders), 383
Local People (Dittmer), 358–59
Locke, Alain, 125–26, 173
Logan, Frenise A., 293
Logan, Rayford W., 129, 234, 239
Loggins, Vernon, 118
Lomax, Alan, 151–52

Lomax, Michael E., 258
Lonely Warrior (Ottley), 296
Long, Charles H., 378–79
The Long Dream (Wright), 130
The Longest Way Home (Bittle and Geis), 5
Long Memory (Berry and Blassingame), 191
Long Shadow of Little Rock (Bates), 203, 355
"Loose, Idle and Disorderly" (Olwell), 75, 289
Lornell, Kip, 155
Lost White Race (Calvin), 323
Louis, Joe, 260–61
Louisiana Native Guard (Hollandsworth), 236
Lovell, J. R., 150, 372
Lovett, Bobby L., 296
"Lucy Diggs Slowe" (Perkins), 102
Lucy Parsons (Ashbaugh), 80
The Luminous Darkness (Thurman), 380
Lyman, Stanford M., 319
Lynch, John R., 193
Lynching and the Law (Chadbourn), 194
Lynchings: civil rights movement and, 130, 357–58; Ida B. Wells campaign against, 80, 120, 124, 194, 321; in labor conflict, 43; NAACP crusade against, 194
Lynch Law (Cutler), 194
Lynck, Miles V., 239
Lyrics of Lowly Life (Dunbar), 122
Lyson, T., 66

Mabee, Carleton, 99, 101
MacGarrigle, George L., 244
MacGregor, Morris J., Jr., 232, 244
Machine Politics (Gosnell), 195
Mack, Raymond W., 98, 197
Madgett, Naomi Long, 129, 224
Madhubuti, Haki, 133, 136, 223
Magazines, 222–23. *See also* Press, African American
Magriel, Paul, 257
Mainfort, Robert C., Jr., 236
Majority Finds Its Past (Lerner), 72
Majors, Richard, 267

Major Taylor (Ritchie), 258
The Making of A Fringe Candidate, 1992 (Fulani), 203
Making of Black Revolutionaries (Forman), 353
"Making of Negro Mayors" (Hadden et al.), 199
Making Their Own Way (Gottlieb), 10, 38
"Making the Men of the 93rd" (Jefferson), 243
Making the Second Ghetto (Hirsch), 11
Malcolm X, 132–33, 176–77, 354, 384
Mallas, Aris A., Jr., 220
Mama (McMillan), 134
Mama Day (Naylor), 134
Mama Lola (Brown), 385
Mamiya, Lawrence H., 373–74, 376
The Manly Art (Gorn), 257
Mann, George L., 98
Mannix, Daniel R., 2
"Manumission by Purchase" (Matison), 285
Many Thousands Gone (Berlin), 170, 370
Marable, Manning, 196, 359
Marcello, Ronald E., 264
March of the Negro (Funderberg), 323
Marcus Garvey (Lewis), 174
Marcus Garvey and the Vision of Africa (Clarke), 174
The Marcus Garvey and Universal Negro Improvement Association Papers (Hill), 174
Marina, William, 317
Mark, Carole, 9
Marketing Booze to Blacks (Center for Science in the Public Interest), 343
Marriage, 64–65, 78. *See also* Families
The Marrow of Tradition (Chestnutt), 122
Mars, Florence, 358
Marsh, Charles, 360
Marshall, Dale Rogers, 199, 201
Marshall, Paule, 129
Marshall, Ray, 26
Marszalek, John F., 232, 239
Marticorena, Charles, 345
Martin, Charles H., 264
Martin, John Barlow, 356

Martin, John Bartholomew, 324
Martin, Larry, 282
Martin, Tony, 126, 174, 175
Martin, Waldo E., Jr., 169
Martin Luther King, Jr. and the Civil Rights Movement (Garrow), 354
Martin & Malcolm & America (Cone), 176, 360, 384
Martin R. Delany (Ullman), 170
"Mary McLeod Bethune and the National Youth Administration" (Ross), 83
"Mary McLeod Bethune's 'Last Will and Testament'" (Smith), 102
Mason, Charlotte Osgood, 126
Massaquoi, Hans J., 323, 325
Massey, Douglas S., 13
Massoti, Louis, 199
Matison, Summer E., 285
Matzeliger, Jan Earnst, 294
Maxey, Samuel Bell, 236
May, Robert E., 235
Mays, Benjamin E., 172, 380–81
McAdams, Doug, 199
McCain, Rea, 220
McClain, Paula D., 200
McCloud, Aminah Beverly, 385
McConnell, Roland C., 234
McCormick, John M., 200
McDonald, Roderick A., 283
McDonnell, Lawrence T., 284
McDougald, Elise, 126
McFarlin, Annjeannette, 193
McFeely, William S., 219
McGovern, James R., 246
McGuire, Phillip, 243
McKay, Claude, 125–26
McKenzie, Edna Chappell, 285
McKinney, T. T., 322
McLaurin, Melton A., 74
McManus, Edgar J., 2
McMillan, Terry, 134
McMillen, Neil R., 243, 355
McNeil, Genna Rae, 100
McPherson, Christopher, 285
McPherson, James M., 235
Mead, Chris, 261
Means and Ends in American Abolitionism (Kraditor), 190

The Measure of Bondage in the Slave States (Morris), 285
Mecklin, John Moffatt, 321
Medical History of a Civil War Regiment (Steiner), 237
Meehan, Thomas A., 288
Meeting the Croson Standard (Boston), 298
Meier, August, 6, 40, 95, 97, 168, 172, 192, 198, 295, 353–54, 356, 359
Meister, Richard J., 11
Memphis since Crump (Tucker), 195
Men, African American: families and, 64; hypersexuality myth, 316–17, 319–20; marriage and, 64–66; peer groups, 64; sexuality, 325. *See also* Sexuality and race
The Men of Brewster Place (Naylor), 134
Men of Mark (Simmons), 220
Meranto, Philip J., 199
Meredith, James, 359
Mergen, Bernard, 257
Meridian (Walker), 134
Merriam, Alan, 149
Merrill, Marlene, 99
The Messenger, 223
Messner, Michael A., 265
Metalanguage of race, 71
Metoyer, Marie Theresa, 287
The Metropolis in Black and White (Galster and Hill), 12
Mfume, Kweisi, 202
Middle Class Blacks in a White Society (Muraskin), 291
"Middle Passage" (Hayden), 130
Middle Passage (Johnson), 134
Middle Passage (Klein), 2
Migration, 1–13; black consumerism and, 337–38; causation, 7–9; education and, 95, 102; to Harlem, 125; involuntary, 1–3; to Kansas, 172; labor and, 38–39; post-Civil War, 4–6, 62, 194–96; post–World Wars, 10; poverty, 11–12; race relations approach, 6–10; return to Africa, 3–5, 168, 172, 174, 191–92, 219, 384; self-determination, 3; women, 82
Military, African Americans in, 231–47; in the American Revolution, 233–34;

bibliographies, 232–33; black chaplains, 237–38; Civil War, 235–37; in the colonial period, 233; desegregation, 244–47; Jim Crow, 237–41; Korean War, 244; omission from history books, 231; pre–Civil War, 234; during Reconstruction, 237; Seminole Wars, 234–35; Spanish-American War, 239–41; Vietnam War, 245; West Point, 238–39; World War I, 241–42; World War II, 242–43

Military Necessity and Civil Rights Policy (Berry), 235

Mill, Nicolaus, 358

Miller, Edward A., Jr.

Miller, Floyd J., 3, 168, 192

Miller, Kelly, 381

Miller, Patrick B., 260, 262, 268

Mills, Gary B., 75, 287, 289

Mills, Kay, 203, 360

Mills, Kaye, 84

The Mind and Mood of Black America (Fullinwider), 166–67

The Mind of Frederick Douglass (Martin), 169

The Mind of the Negro (Thorpe), 166

Mind of the South (Cash), 324

Miners, 24, 28, 34–35, 37, 41, 43–44

Mingo War, 34–35

"The Mingo War" (Brier), 34

Minnie's Sacrifice (Harper), 77

Minority Politics in Black Belt Alabama (Hamilton), 198

Minority Representation and the Quest for Voting Equality (Grofman et al.), 198

Minority Vote Dilution (Davidson), 198

Mirror of Liberty, 218

Mirror of the Times, 218

Miscegenation, 318–21

Mis-education of the Negro (Woodson), 95

Mississippi (Silver), 357

Mr. Kennedy and the Negroes (Golden), 196

Mr. Lincoln and the Negroes (Douglas), 192

Mister Jelly Roll (Lomax), 152–53

Mitchell, Ella, 383

Mitchell, George, 27

Mitchell, Grayson, 345

Mixed Blood (Spickard), 327

The Mobility of the Negro (Lewis), 8

The Modern Encyclopedia of Education, 96

Moitt, Bernard, 75

Molineaux, Tom, 257

"The Molineaux-Cribb Fight, 1810" (Cone), 257

"Money Knows No Master" (McDonnell), 284

Mongrelism (Quimby), 319

Montage of a Dream Deferred (Hughes), 127

Montgomery, Benjamin, 285

Montgomery, William E., 171

Montgomery Bus Boycott, 84, 203, 341, 356, 381

The Montgomery Bus Boycott and the Women Who Started It (Garrow), 84, 203, 356

Moody, Anne, 83, 203, 353

Moody, Bill, 154

Moon Illustrated Weekly, 222

Moore, Brenda L., 243

Moore, Jesse T., 173

Moore, John Hebron, 285

Moore, Joseph T., 263

Moore, Kenneth Bancroft, 236

Moore, William, 99

"The Moor *vs.* Black Diamond" (Goodman), 257

Morality of the Color Line (Gilligan), 322

Moreland, Laurence, 198

"More Myth than History" (Vertinsky and Captain), 265

More than Chattel (Gaspar and Hine), 75

Morgan, Edmund S., 318

Morgan, Philip D., 31, 284, 370

Morris, Aldon D., 196, 355, 360, 382

Morris, Lorenzo, 202

Morris, Milton, 189

Morris, Richard B., 285

Morris, Robert C., 101

Morrison, Minion K. C., 198, 358

Morrison, Toni, 85, 134
Morton, Patricia, 74, 81
Moses (Hurston), 127
Moses, Wilson J., 169
Moskos, Charles C., Jr., 244–46
Moss, Alfred A., Jr., 192, 218, 232
Moss, James Allen, 99
"Most Invisible of All" (Scott), 80
Mother Wit from the Laughing Barrel (Dundes), 379
Motley, Willard, 129
Mound Bayou, Mississippi, 294
Moynihan, Daniel P., 30, 56, 81, 281, 324–25
Muhammad, Elijah, 177
Muhammad Ali (Gorn), 264
Muhammad Ali (Hauser), 264
Muhammed Ali Reader (Early), 264
Mulattos, 318, 322
Mules and Men (Hurston), 127, 380
Mullin, Gerald W., 3
"Multifarious Hero" (Capeci and Wilkerson), 261
Multiracial Couples (Powell), 327
The Multiracial Experience (Root), 327
Mumbo Jumbo (Reed), 133
Muraskin, William, 291
Murphy, Carl, 219
Murphy, Isaac, 257
Murphy, Joseph M., 385
Murray, James P., 342
Murray, Pauli, 83–84
Murray, Richard, 199
Muse, Benjamin, 197–98
Music, 144–56; African traditions, 144–45, 148–50; blues and ragtime, 150–52, 155; chosen people, 167; classical, 154; contemporary, 153–55; European traditions, 145–46, 151; folk, 145, 151–52; Harlem Renaissance, 152–53; oral tradition, 145, 149; overview, 148; post–Civil War, 150–52; record companies, 337; religious, 117, 149, 151–52, 155, 372–73
Music and Some Highly Musical People (Trotter), 151
Music in Primitive Culture (Nettl), 149
Music of Africa (Warren), 149

Music of Black Americans (Southern), 337, 372
The Music of Black Americans (Southern), 148
Music & Politics (Sinclair), 154
Must God Remain Greek? (Hood), 383
"My Fear Is for You" (Westheider), 245
My Larger Education (Washington), 94
Myne Owne Ground (Breen and Innes), 286
Myrdal, Gunnar, 9, 97, 279, 318–19, 323
My Soul Is Rested (Raines), 356
My Soul Looks Back (Cone), 382
Mystery, 218
"The Myth, Legend and Folklore of Joe Louis" (Gilmore), 261

NAACP, 124, 173, 194–95, 222, 321, 353–54
NAACP (Kellogg), 173
The NAACP (Finch), 195
"The NAACP and a Federal Anti-lynching Bill, 1930–1940" (Zangrando), 194
"The NAACP Crusade against Lynching, 1909–1950" (Zangrando), 194
The NAACP's Legal Strategy against Segregated Education, 1925–1950 (Tushnet), 195, 355
Nalty, Bernard C., 232
"The Names of Negro Newspapers" (Pride), 222
Namorato, Michael V., 197, 360
"Nannie Helen Burroughs" (Harley), 102
Napier, James Carroll, 295
A Narrative Bibliography of the African-American Frontier (Hardaway), 232
Narrative of Hosea Hudson (Painter), 35
The Narrative of Lunsford Lane, 285
Narrative of the Life of Frederick Douglass (Douglass), 117, 119, 219
A Narrative of the Negro (Pendleton), 233
Narrative of the Uncommon Sufferings, and Surprising Deliverance of Briton Hammon (Hammon), 117
The Narrows (Petry), 131
Nash, Gary B., 4

Nash, Horace D., 241

Nathan, Hans, 151

National Association for the Advancement of Colored People (NAACP), 124, 173, 194–95, 222, 321, 353–54

National Labor Tribune, 28

National Negro Congress, 175–76

National Organization for Women (NOW), 84

National Reformer, 218

National Survey of Black Americans, 1979–1990 (Jackson and Gurin), 201

National Urban League, 173, 195, 354

The National Urban League, 1910–1940 (Weiss), 173, 195

Native Son (Wright), 128

The Nature of Prejudice (Allport), 323–24

Navasky, Victor S., 356

Naylor, Gloria, 134

Neal, Larry, 132–33

"Negotiating and Transforming the Public Sphere" (Brown), 80, 170

Negro (Shufeldt), 319

"Negro Advertisements and Negro Culture" (Johnson), 337

The Negro and His Needs (Patterson), 320

The Negro and Organized Labor (Marshall), 26

The Negro and Reconstruction of Florida (Richardson), 193

"The Negro and the American Labor Movement," 23

The Negro Artisan (Du Bois), 25, 279

"The Negro Artist and the Racial Mountain" (Hughes), 126, 174

Negro as a Businessman (Harmon et al.), 279

Negro As Capitalist (Harris), 279–80, 292

"The Negro as Consumer" (Haring), 338

The Negro Author (Loggins), 118

Negro Baseball Leagues (Dixon and Hannigan), 258

Negro Business and Business Education (Pierce), 279–80

Negro Church in America (Frazier), 371

The Negro College Graduate (Johnson), 97

The Negro Common School (Du Bois), 94

Negro Digest, 223

Negro Education (Jones), 97

Negro Education in Alabama (Bond), 95–96, 101

Negroes and the Great Depression (Wolters), 196

Negroes in American Society (Davie), 323

Negroes in Negroland (Helper), 319

"Negroes on White College Faculties" (Jones and Jones), 99

The Negro Faces America (Seligmann), 322

The Negro Family (Moynihan), 30, 56, 81, 324–25

Negro Family in the United States (Frazier), 324

Negro Folk Music (Courlander), 151

The Negro Genius (Brawley), 153

Negro in American Culture (Butcher), 153

Negro in American Fiction (Brown), 126

"The Negro in Banking" (Lindsay), 292

The Negro in Business (Du Bois), 279

Negro in Business (Washington), 279, 336

The Negro in Chicago (Chicago Commission on Race Relations), 8

Negro in Colonial New England (Greene), 233, 286, 288

The Negro in Colonial New England (Greene), 2

The Negro in Congress (Smith), 202

The Negro in Depression and War (Sternsher), 196

The Negro in Music and Art (Patterson), 154

Negro in Sports (Henderson), 255

Negro in the American Rebellion (Brown), 119

Negro in the American Revolution (Quarles), 233

"The Negro in the Armed Forces of the United States" (Greene), 233

The Negro in the Civil War (Quarles), 192, 235

The Negro in the Insurance Industry (Fletcher), 344

The Negro in the Military Service of the United States (Woodward), 232

"The Negro in the Political Life of the U.S." (Bunche), 195

"The Negro in the Quasi War, 1798–1800" (Logan), 234

"The Negro in the Union Navy" (Aptheker), 237

Negro in Third Party Politics (Walton), 192, 203

Negro in World War II (Silvera), 242

Negro Journalism (Gore), 221

Negro Journalism in America before Emancipation (Bryan), 218

Negro Labor (Weaver), 25–26

Negro Labor in the United States (Wesley), 25

Negro Life in the South (Weatherford), 319

Negro Migration (Woofter), 8

Negro Migration during the War (Scott), 8

Negro Migration in 1916–1917, 8

Negro Militia and Reconstruction (Singletary), 237

Negro Musicians and Their Music (Hare), 151

The Negro Newspaper (Oak), 221

Negro Novels in America (Bone), 82, 127

Negro on the American Frontier (Porter), 234

The Negro on the American Frontier (Porter), 233

The Negro Peasant Turns Cityward (Kennedy), 8

Negro Poetry and Drama (Brown), 127

"The Negro Policy of the United States Army, 1775–1945" (Reddick), 238

Negro Politics (Wilson), 195

The Negro Press in America (Detweiler), 337

The Negro Press in the United States (Detweiler), 221

The Negro Press Re-examined (Brooks), 224

"Negro Property Owners in Seventeenth-Century Virginia" (Brewer), 286–87

Negro Quarterly, 223

Negro's Adventure in General Business (Oak), 280

The Negro's Civil War (McPherson), 235

"Negro Secret Societies" (Palmer), 291

The Negro's God as Reflected in His Literature (Mays), 172, 380–81

Negro's Image in the South (Nolen), 194

Negro Slave Songs in the United States (Fisher), 150, 372

Negro Soldiers in World War I (Williams), 242

The Negro Spirituals Speak of Life and Death (Thurman), 380

The Negro's Share (Sterner), 340

"Negro Teachers in Northern Colleges and Universities . . . " (Atwood et al.), 99

"Negro Teachers in White Colleges" (Taylor), 99

Negro Thought in America (Meier), 172, 295

Negro Troops of Antebellum Louisiana (McConnell), 234

Negro Workaday Songs (Odum), 150

Negro World (Garvey), 126

The Negro Year Book, 1941–1946 (Guzman), 222

Negro Year Book (Work), 221, 279, 337

Neilson, Melany, 358

Nell, William C., 233–34

Nelson, Albert J., 202

Nelson, Bruce, 41

Nelson, Dennis Denmark, 244

Nelson, Paul D., 98

Nelson, Rachel West, 357

Nelson, William E., 199

Nettl, Bruno, 149

New American Dilemma (Hochschild), 101

A New and Accurate Description of Guinea (Bosman), 283

The New Black Vote (Bush), 199

Newby, Idus A., 194, 320

New Day in Babylon (Van Deburg), 177, 265

New Directions in Civil Rights Studies (Robinson and Sullivan), 360

New Era, 219

Newman, Debra, 75

Newman, Mark, 340

New Masses, 128

New Mexico's Buffalo Soldiers, 1866–1900 (Billington), 240

The New Negro (Locke), 126, 173

New Negro on Campus (Wolter), 101

The New Negro Thirty Years Afterward (Logan et al.), 129–30

New Perspectives on Black Educational History (Franklin and Anderson), 100

Newspapers. *See* Press, African American

Newton, Huey P., 177

New York Age (Fortune), 219

"New York Central College" (Short), 99

Niagra movement, 124, 173

Niemi, Richard G., 198

Nigger Heaven (Van Vechten), 126

Night of Violence (Haynes), 241

Nipson, Herbert, 323

Nixon, Richard M., 298

Nketia, Joseph H. Kwabena, 149

Nobody Knows My Name (Baldwin), 131

No Chariot Let Down (Roark and Johnson), 4

No Free Ride (Mfume), 202

Nolen, Claude H., 194

No Place to Be Somebody (Gordon), 132

Norrell, Robert J., 11, 40, 197, 355

North, Gail, 155

North Carolina Mutual Story (Kennedy), 291–92

Northern Schools, Southern Blacks, and Reconstruction (Butchart), 101

Northern Teacher in the South, 1862–1870 (Swint), 96

A Northern Woman in the Plantation South (King), 76

North of Slavery (Litwack), 4

Northup, Herbert R., 26–27

Norwood, Thomas N., 320

Notable Black American Women (Smith), 224

Not All Black and White (Edley), 298

Notes of a Native Son (Baldwin), 131

"The Novel as Social Criticism" (Petry), 130

Oak, Vishnu, 221, 280

"Oberlin College and the Negro Student, 1865–1940" (Bigglestone), 99

O'Brien, Claire, 294

O'Brien, William Patrick, 288

Odum, Howard Washington, 150

Ogden, Frederic D., 197

Ohadike, D. C., 368

O'Hare, William P., 294

Old Army (Coffman), 238

Oliver, Paul, 151

Olwell, Robert, 75, 289

"On Being Young—a Woman—and Colored" (Bonner), 126

O'Neale, Sondra, 119

One Nation under a Groove (Earley), 297

One Woman's Army (Early), 243

On Lynchings (Wells-Barnett), 194

Only the Ball Was White (Peterson), 258

On the Trail of the Buffalo Soldier (Schubert), 239

Operation PUSH, 178

"Opportunities Found and Lost" (Korstad and Lichtenstein), 39

Opportunity (Johnson), 222

Oral tradition, 116–17, 121, 145, 149, 171

O'Reilly, Kenneth, 356

Orfield, Gary, 101

Organized Labor and the Negro (Northup), 26–27

"Organized Labor and the Struggle for Black Equality in Mobile during World War II" (Nelson), 40–41

Original African Heritage Study Bible (Felder), 383

Origins of the Black Press (Tripp), 218

Origins of the Civil Rights Movement (Morris), 196, 355, 360, 382

Origins of the New South, 1877–1913 (Woodward), 193

O'Rourke, Timothy, 197

Osgood, Henry, 152

Osofsky, Gilbert, 9, 117
Osthaus, Carl R., 292
Ottley, Roi, 296
Our Children's Burden (Mack), 98, 197
Our Nig (Wilson), 77, 119
"Our Own Cause" (Barrow), 218
Our Time Has Come (Barker), 202
Our Voices (Gonzalez et al.), 326
Out of the Crucible (Dickerson), 38
"Out of the Shadow of Tuskegee"
    (Rouse), 102
"Out of the Shadows" (Weems), 281
Outside Agitator (Eagles), 357
The Outsider (Wright), 130
"Outside the Pale" (Smith), 263
"Outthinking and Outflanking the Owners
    of the World" (Butchart), 100
Overton, Anthony, 292
Owen, Chandler, 223
Owens, Jessie, 260–61
Owens, Leslie Howard, 3, 170
"The Ownership of Property by Slaves"
    (Morgan), 284

Pagan Spain (Wright), 130
Paige, Satchel, 259, 340
Painter, Nell Irvin, 5, 31, 35–36, 78, 172,
    191
Palmer, Edward Nelson, 291
The Pan-African Connection (Martin),
    175
Pan-Africanism, 3, 102, 126, 131, 169,
    174–75
Panassié, Hughes, 152
Papa Jack (Roberts), 260
The Papers of Martin Luther King, Jr.
    (Carson), 354
"Pap Singleton's Dunlap Colony"
    (Hickey), 294
Paradigms in Black Studies (Alkalimat),
    178
Park, Rosa, 130
Parker, Frank R., 198, 358
Parker, Mack Charles, 357
Parris, Guichard, 194
Parting the Waters (Branch), 354, 371,
    382

Paschal Beverly Randolph (Deveney),
    385
Passing (Larsen), 82
Paterson, Paul E., 13
Pathway to the Houston Negro Market
    (Bullock), 341
"Patronage, Property and Persistence"
    (Hanger), 288
Patterns of Interracial Politics (Eisinger),
    200
"Patterns of Leadership in Race Rela-
    tions" (Lee), 381
Patterson, Lindsay, 154
Patterson, Raymond, 320
Patterson, Willis, 154
Patton, Gerald W., 242
Patton, June O., 100, 102
Patton, Phil, 81
Paul, John, 263
Paul Cuffe (Harris), 168
Paul Cuffe (Thomas), 287
"Paul Dunbar and the Mask of Dialect"
    (Keeling), 122–23
Payne, Charles M., 176, 358
Pearson, Hugh, 177
Pease, Jane H. and William H., 168
Peck, Elisabeth S., 98
Peck, James, 356
The Peculiar Institution (Stampp), 3
A Peculiar People (Creel), 170
Pelham, Ben, 220
Pendleton, Leila Amos, 233
Penn, I. Garland, 220
Pennington, Richard, 263
Perdue, Robert E., 286
Perkins, Linda M., 100, 102
Perry, Herman E., 292
Perry, Huey L., 200, 202
Perry, Oliver Hazard, 234
Personal Politics (Evans), 360
Persons, Georgia, 199
"Perspective for a Study of African
    American Religion in the United
    States" (Long), 378–79
Peters, William, 319
Peterson, Robert W., 258, 259
Petry, Ann, 128, 130–31
Pettigrew, M. C., 374

Pettigrew, Thomas F., 199, 204
"Phallus(ies) of Interpretation" (du Cille), 85
The Philadelphia Negro (Du Bois), 6–7, 295, 380
Phillips, Charles Henry, 374
Phillips, Tom, 238
Phylon, 222
Piano Lesson (Wilson), 134
Pierce, Joseph, 279–80
Pierce, Julius A., 316
Pike, Gustavus, 151
Pillar of Fire (Branch), 354, 382
Pinkney, Alphonso, 64, 325
Pinn, Anthony, 385
"Pioneer Slave Entrepreneurship" (Walker), 285
Placksin, Sally, 153
Plaindealer, 221
Plank, David N., 100
Plantation Mistress (Clinton), 75
Plater, Michael A., 296
Play and Playthings (Mergen), 257
Playing in the Dark (Morrison), 134
"The Play of Slave Children in the Plantation Communities . . . " (Wiggins), 257
Plays and Pageants of Negro Life (Richardson), 126
Pleasant, Mary Ellen, 290
Pleasant, William, 203
Pleck, Elizabeth, 6
Plessy v. Ferguson, 169, 193, 239
Plum Bun (Fauset), 82
Plunkitt of Tammany Hall (Riordan), 195
Plural but Equal (Cruse), 173
"Pluralism and Toleration" (Wills), 369
Poems on Miscellaneous Subjects (Harper), 119
Poems on Miscellaneous Subjects (Watkins), 77
Poison Spring massacre, 236–37
"Political Behavior of American Black Women" (Prestage), 203
Political experience, 189–204; biracial coalitions, 200; black officeholders, 199–204; black power movement, 198–200; civil rights movement, 196–98; Constitutional rights, 193; empowerment, 201; during FDR's administration, 195; Great Migration, 194–96; machine politics, 195–96; modern, 200–204; Reconstruction, 192–93; sectional division, 191–92; during slave period, 189–90; voting rights, 197–98; women, 203
Political Process and the Development of Black Insurgency (McAdams), 199
The Political Status of the Negro in the Age of F.D.R. (Bunche), 195
Politics and Policy (Sundquist), 196
Politics and the Warren Court (Bickel), 197
Politics in Black and White (Sonenshein), 200
The Politics of Black America (Morris), 189
The Politics of Black Empowerment (Jennings), 201
The Politics of Displacement (Eisinger), 201
Politics of Minority Coalitions (Rich), 200
The Politics of Rage (Carter), 361
The Politics of Reapportionment (Jewell), 197
Politics of the Southern Negro (Holloway), 198
Pollard, Fritz, 262
The Poll Tax in the South (Ogden), 197
Populists, 34
Porter, Dorothy Burnett, 287
Porter, Kenneth W., 233–35
Porterfield, Ernest, 327
Posey, Cum, 259
Possessing the Secret of Joy (Walker), 134
Potential Negro Market (Johnson), 341
Potter, Elizabeth, 76, 289
Potter, Vilma Raskin, 218
Poussaint, Alvin J., 342
Powell, Adam Clayton, Jr., 195–96, 202
Powell, Carolyn J., 75
Powell, Gen. Colin, 246
Powell, Richard, 327
Power and the Darkness (Ribowsky), 259

The Power of Black Music (Floyd), 148–49

Powers, Bernard E., Jr., 4

Powledge, Fred, 359

Praisesong of Survival (Barksdale), 136

Prather, Leon H., Sr., 5

Pratt, Robert A., 355

Prentice, William, 41

"The Present Status of Negro Education . . . " (Horne), 94

The Presidency and Black Civil Rights (Wolk), 196

Press, African American, 216–25; biographies of press leaders, 222; black consumerism and, 337; book publishing companies, 223; economic realities, 216–18, 223; magazines, 222–23; mass media, 224, 340; post–Civil War, 219–21; post–World War I, 221; post–World War II, 223–25; protest, 222; during slavery, 218–19

Prestage, Jewell L., 203

Preston, Michael B., 200

Pride, Armistead Scott, 222

Pride against Prejudice (Moore), 263

Priest, Josiah, 317

Prince, Nancy, 77

Principles of Black Political Economy (Hogan), 217

"Prized Performers but Frequently Overlooked Students" (Wiggins), 262

The Problem of Slavery in the Age of Revolution (Davis), 372

Proceedings of the National Negro Conference, 1909 (Katz), 321

Proletarianization, 46–47

"The Promised Land" (Walker), 297

The Promised Land (Lemann), 11, 82

The Promising Years, 1750–1830 (Johnson), 286

"Promoting Black Entrepreneurship and Business Enterprise . . . " (Walker), 288

Propaganda and Aesthetics (Johnson and Johnson), 126

"Property Owning Free African–American Women" (Schweninger), 77, 289

Prophesy Deliverance! (West), 383

"Protected Markets and African American Professionals . . . " (Boyd), 296

Protest at Selma (Garrow), 198, 357

Protest Is Not Enough (Browning et al.), 199

Pryde, Paul, 298

Puckett, Newbell Niles, 379

Pulley, Brett, 345

"The Punitive Expedition" (Johnson), 240

Pursuit of a Dream (Hermann), 294

Puth, Robert C., 291

Putney, Martha S., 234, 243

Puttin' on Ole Massa (Osofsky), 117

Quarles, Benjamin, 3, 99, 168, 190, 192, 218, 233, 235

The Quest for Equality (Harris), 197

The Quest for Equality (Wesley), 217

Quicksand (Larsen), 125

Quiet Revolution in the South (Davidson and Grofman), 198

Quiet Riots (Harris and Wilkins), 13

Quimby, Watson F., 319

R. I. Reynolds Tobacco Company, 343–44

Rabinowitz, Howard N., 4–5, 193

Raboteau, Albert J., 369, 370, 372–74

Race and Nationality in American Life (Handlin), 324

"Race and Sport" (Sammons), 256

"Race and the Negro Writer" (Gloster), 129

Race, Class, Nationality and Color (Collier-Thomas), 167

Race, Class and Culture (Smith and Seltzer), 201

Race & Democracy (Fairclough), 353

Race First (Martin), 174

Race for Success (Fraser), 299

Race-ing Justice, En-Gendering Power (Morrison), 85, 134

Race, Jobs and Politics (Ruchames), 195

Race, Politics, and Governance in the United States (Perry), 200, 202

Race, Politics and Culture (Reed), 199

Race Question (Coody), 323

Race, Racism and the Law (Bell), 198

Race, Reform, and Rebellion (Marable), 196, 359
Race relations approach, 6–10, 24–27
Race Relations in a Democracy (Brown), 323
Race Relations in the Urban South, 1865–1890 (Rabinowitz), 5
Race Relations in Transition (Vander Zanden), 194
Race Riot (Tuttle), 9
Race Traits and Tendencies of the American Negro (Hoffman), 320
Rachleff, Peter J., 5, 36–37
"Racial Barriers to African American Entrepreneurship" (Feagin and Imani), 299
"Racial Change and Big-Time College Football in Georgia" (Martin), 264
Racial Change and Community Crisis (Colburn), 355
"Racial Crossover Voting and the Election of Black Officials" (Bullock), 199
"Racial Differences in Consumption and Automobile Ownership" (Alexis), 341
Racial discord, 11–12
Racially Mixed People in America (Root), 327
Racial Matters (O'Reilly), 356
Racial Politics in American Cities (Browning et al.), 201–2
Racial Pride and Prejudice (Dingwall), 323
Racial Violence in the U.S. (Grimshaw), 199
"Racial Voting Patterns in the South" (Murray and Vedlitz), 199
Racism: apartheid, 13; Jim Crow laws, 62; KKK, 194; labor, 26, 31, 34, 38, 41; literature and, 123; minimization of, 12; moral indignation over, 97; race relations approach, 7; scientific, 100, 268; slavery and, 60–61. *See also* Jim Crow
"Racism, Slavery, and Free Enterprise" (Walker), 287
The Rage of a Privileged Class (Cose), 167
Ragsdale, Bruce, 202
Railroad Brotherhoods, 26, 194–95

Raines, Howell, 356
Rainwater, Lee, 11
A Raisin in the Sun (Hansberry), 129
Rakove, Milton, 195
Rampersad, Arnold, 263
Ramsey, Frederick, 372
The Ram's Horn, 218
Randall, Dudley, 223
Randolph, A. Philip, 175, 195, 223, 354
Randolph, Paschal Beverly, 385
Range, Willard, 98
Ransby, Barbara, 361
Rap (Stanley), 155
Raper, Arthur F., 194
Rap on Rap (Sexton), 155
Rap Whoz Who (Stancell), 155
The Rastafarians (Barrett), 385
Rawick, George P., 73, 170
Ray, Charles B., 218
Reading, 'Riting, and Reconstruction (Morris), 101
Reading, Writing, and Race (Douglas), 98
Reagon, Bernice, 155
Reaping the Whirlwind (Norrell), 11, 197, 355
The Reapportionment Revolution (Baker), 197
Reconstruction (Foner), 170, 237
Reconstruction after the Civil War (Franklin), 193
Rector, Justine J., 225
Reddick, L. D., 238
Reddings, Saunders, 119, 129
"Redefining Beautiful" (Clarke), 345
Redkey, Edwin S., 5, 172, 236–37
Reed, Adolph, Jr., 199, 201, 203
Reed, Ishmael, 133
Reed, Linda, 75, 77, 80, 85, 355, 361
A Reference Guide to Afro-American Publications and Editors, 1827–1946 (Potter), 218
"Reflections on the Black Woman's Role in the Community of Slaves" (Davis), 73
Regime Politics (Stone), 201
"A Register and History of Negro Newspapers . . . " (Scott), 218–19
Reidy, Joseph P., 232

Reisser, Marsha, 153

The Relations of the Advanced and the Backward Races of Mankind (Bryce), 320

Religion, 368–85; African American churches, 373–75; African origins, 369–73, 378–79; Baptists, 374; black theology, 380–83; Catholic Church, 322; civil rights movement and, 360; conjuring, 379–80; dialectical models, 376; enslavement and, 370; European immigrants, 369; folk, 121; Islam, 384–85; Methodists, 219, 374, 384; music, 117, 149, 151–52, 155; Native American, 368–69; nature of, 376–78; Pentecostals, 374; poetry, 119; post–Civil War, 171–72; protest and, 375–78; Rastafarians, 385; religious experience, 378–80; return to Africa, 384; slavery and, 372; water symbolism, 371; women, 383

Remaking Dixie (McMillen), 243

"Remember Poison Spring" (Fisher), 236

Reminiscences of Levi Coffin (Coffin), 3

Remond, Sarah Parker, 79

"The Remonds of Salem, Massachusetts" (Porter), 287

The Report of the National Advisory Commission on Civil Disorders, 12

Retrospection, Political and Personal (Bancroft), 320

Revival and Rebellion in Colonial Central Africa (Fields), 384

The Revolt of the Black Athlete (Edwards), 265

Revolution in Zion (Rooks), 382

"Rewards of Daring and the Ambiguity of Power" (Holden), 203

Ribowsky, Mark, 258, 259

Rich, Wilbur C., 200–201

Richardson, Joe, 193

Richardson, Willis, 126

Riedel, Johannes, 152

Righteous Discontent (Higginbotham), 383

Rights of All, 218

Right to Vote (Gillette), 193

Riis, Thomas, 151

Riordan, William L., 195

The Rise and Fall of the White Primary in Texas (Hine), 197

The Rise and Progress of Negro Colleges in Georgia, 1865–1949 (Range), 98

Rise of Gospel Blues (Harris), 155

Rise of Massive Resistance (Bartley), 356

Rise to Be a People (Thomas), 3, 168, 190

Rishell, Lyle, 244

Rising Wind (White), 242

Ritchie, Andrew, 258

River of No Return (Sellers), 353

Ro, Ronin, 155

Roach, Hildred, 148

Roark, James L., 4, 78, 287

Roberts, J. Deotis, 382

Roberts, John Storm, 148

Roberts, Randy, 260

Robeson, Paul, 262

Robinson, Armistead, 32, 359

Robinson, Charles, M., III, 239

Robinson, Eddie, 259

Robinson, Jackie, 262–63, 340

Robinson, Jo Ann Gibson, 84, 203, 356

Robinson, Ruby Doris Smith, 360

A Rock in a Weary Land (Walker), 171

Rockin' the Boat (Garofalo), 155

Rogosin, Donn, 258

"The Roles of Church and Community Mothers" (Giles), 383

Roll, Jordan, Roll (Genovese), 170, 371

"The Roller-Coaster Ride of Black Students at Berea College" (Nelson), 98

Rollin, Frank A., 219

Rooks, Charles Shelby, 382

Roosevelt, Theodore, 240–41

Root, Maria P. P., 327

Roots of a Black Future (Roberts), 382

The Roots of African-American Identity (Bethel), 168

The Roots of Black Nationalism (Carlisle), 169

The Roots of Prejudice against the Negro in the United States (Goldstein), 319

Roots of Violence in Black Philadelphia (Lane), 6

Rosenblatt, Paul, 327

Rosenburg, Bruce A., 372
Rosengarten, Theodore, 35–36
Ross, B. Joyce, 83
Ross, Barbara J., 195
Rothschild, Mary Aickin, 358
Rouse, Jacqueline Anne, 80, 102, 360
Rowan, Carl T., 98
Rowland, Leslie S., 232
Rubin, R. H., 57
Ruchames, Louis, 195
Ruck, Rob, 259
Rucker, David M., 295
Rudman, William S., 267
Rudwick, Elliott, 6, 40, 95, 97, 168, 192, 353, 356, 359
Ruggles, David, 218
Running for Freedom (Lawson), 198, 359
Russwurm, John B., 216, 218
Rust, Brian, 337
Rustin, Bayard, 198

The Sable Arm (Cornish), 235
Sabo, Donald F., 265
Sackheim, Eric, 151
St. Helena Islanders, 8
"Sale and Separation" (Cody), 74
The Salt Eaters (Bambara), 134
Salzberg, Charles, 263
Sammons, Jeffrey T., 256, 261
Sampson, Henry, 151
Sanders, Cheryl, 383
Sanders, Robert, 245
Sandler, Stanley, 243
Sandlot Seasons (Ruck), 259
Sanger, Kerran, 155
Saperstein, Abe, 259
Sato, Hiroko, 82
Savage, W. Sherman, 238
Savage, William S., 288
Savage Holiday (Wright), 130
Savannah Syncopators (Oliver), 151
Saville, Julie, 33
Schafer, Judith, 76
Schafer, William, 152
Schattsneider, E. E., 197
Schechter, Patricia, 31
Schneider, Mark R., 295
Schnittman, Suzanne, 31

The Schomburg Library of Nineteenth-Century Black Women Writers (Gates), 73
Schooling for the New Slavery (Spivey), 101
Schor, Joel, 219
Schubert, Frank N., 238–40
Schuller, Gunther, 153
Schultz, Ellen, 345
Schwalm, Leslie, 80
Schwartz, Bernard, 193
Schwartz, Marie Jenkins, 75
Schwarz, Philip J., 287
Schweninger, Loren, 77, 287, 289, 293
Schwerner, Michey, 357
Scott, Anne Firor, 72, 80
Scott, Armistead, 218
Scott, Daryl Michael, 355
Scott, Emmett J., 8, 242
Scott, John, 76
Scott, Laurence P., 243
Scott, R. C., 296
Scott's Official History of the American Negro in the World War, 242–43
Scruggs, Marc, 288
"Seafarers of 1813" (Dye), 234
Sea Island to City (Kiser), 8
Seale, Bobby, 177, 198
The Search for a Black Nationality (Miller), 3, 168, 192
A Search for Equality (Moore), 173
Searching for the Promised Land (Franks), 202
Second Battle of New Orleans (Baker), 98
"Second Louis-Schmeling Fight" (Edmonds), 261
The Secret City (Green), 9
Segregated Sabbaths (George), 4
Segregated Skies (Sandler), 243
Segregation. *See* Jim Crow
Seize the Time (Seale), 198
"Self-Hire among Slaves" (McKenzie), 285
Seligmann, Herbert J., 322
Seller, Cleveland, 353
"Selling to Harlem" (Haring), 338
Selma (Fager), 357

Selma, Lord, Selma (Webb and Nelson), 83, 357

Seltzer, Richard, 201

"The Seminole-Black Alliance . . . " (Boyett), 235

Senechal, Roberta, 43

Senna, Carl, 218, 225

Senter, Thomas P., 235

Separate and Unequal (Harlan), 97–98, 101

Sermon and the African American Literary Imagination (Hubbard), 372

Sernett, Milton C., 99, 155, 373, 384

Services of Colored Americans in the Wars of 1776 and 1812 (Nell), 234

The Seventh Son (Lester), 93

$70 Billion in the Black (Gibson), 341

Sex and Racism in America (Hernton), 325

Sexton, Adam, 155

Sexuality and race, 315–27; black fertility rate, 320; civil rights era, 323–27; eugenics, 316, 321–22; homosexuality, 131, 135, 326; hypersexuality, 316–17, 319–20; interracial marriage, 316–18, 322, 327; miscegenation, 318–22; mixed offspring, 318, 322; post–Civil War, 319–20; post–World War II, 322–23; recent scholarship, 316; sexual exploitation of black women, 74, 317; slavery and, 315–17

Shadow and Act (Ellison), 130

The Shadow of the Panther (Pearson), 177

Shakers, 77

Shakur, Assata, 84

Shange, Ntozake, 134

Sharecropping, 32, 36, 62

Sharpton, Al, 203

Shaw, Arnold, 155, 337

Shaw, Henry I., Jr., 244

Shaw, Stephanie, 80

"She Make Funny Flat Cake She Call Saraka" (Beoku-Betts), 74

Shick, Tom W., 4, 192

Shining Trumpets (Blesh), 153

"Shooting Stars" (Gems), 263

Short, Kenneth R., 99

Shufeldt, R. W., 94, 319

Siebert, Wilbur, 190

The Signifying Monkey (Gates), 135

Silver, James W., 357

Silvera, John D., 242

Silver Rights (Curry), 355

Simmons, Enoch Spencer, 320

Simmons, Jake, 297

Simmons, William J., 220

Simms, Margaret, 298

Simon, George, 153

"Simon Gray, Riverman" (Moore), 285

Simons, William, 262

Simple Decency and Common Sense (Reed), 355

Simple Justice (Kluger), 98, 101, 197, 355

Simpson, Ann, 151

Sinclair, John, 154

Sinful Tunes and Spirituals (Epstein), 149

Sing for Freedom (Carawan), 154

Singletary, Otis, 237

Sisterhood Denied (Janiewski), 83

Sisters in the Wilderness (Williams), 383

Sisters of the Spirit (Andrews), 77

Sitkoff, Harvard, 359

Slater, Robert Bruce, 99

Slave and Soldier (Voelz), 233

The Slave Community (Blassingame), 3, 170

Slave Counterpoint (Morgan), 370

Slave Culture (Stuckey), 118, 167, 371

"Slave-Hiring in the Upper South" (Eaton), 285

Slave Religion (Raboteau), 370, 372

Slavery: emancipation, 29–33, 76; families, 59–60; food traditions, 74; gender ratio, 71; illegal slave trade, 368; importance of work in, 29–31, 33; literary tradition, 116–19; narratives, 73–74, 117–18, 285; recreation, 257; sexual abuse, 74; transition from, 32–33, 170; women, 30–31, 75–76

Slavery, as It Relates to the Negro or African Race (Priest), 317

Slavery in Colonial Georgia (Wood), 2

Slavery in the Cities (Wade), 4

Slaves' Economy (Berlin and Morgan), 284

Slave Songs of the United States (Allen et al.), 149

"'Slaves Virtually Free in Ante-bellum North Carolina" (Franklin), 285

Slaves without Masters (Berlin), 4, 287, 318

Slave Testimony (Blassingame), 372

Slave Trading in the Old South (Bancroft), 2

Smalls, Robert, 192, 237

Smead, Howard, 357

Smith, Amanda, 383

Smith, Barbara, 85, 135

Smith, Elaine M., 102

Smith, Graham, 243

Smith, H. S., 99

Smith, James Webster, 239

Smith, Jessie Carney, 224

Smith, Robert C., 201

Smith, Ronald A., 262

Smith, Samuel D., 202

Smith, Theophus H., 380

Smith, Thomas G., 263

Smith, Wendell, 262

Smith, Yvonne, 266

Smith v. Allwright, 197

Smoked Yankees (Gatewood), 239–40

SNCC (Zinn), 353, 356

Snorgrass, J. William, 224–25

Sobel, Mechal, 317, 370, 373

"Social and Economic Influences on the Public Education of Negroes . . . " (Bond), 95

The Social and Political Implications of the 1984 Jesse Jackson Presidential Campaign (Morris), 202

"Social Change and the Negro Press, 1860–1880" (Brown), 220

Social Reform in the United States Navy, 1798–1862 (Langley), 234

Sojourner Truth (Painter), 78, 191

Soldiers of Light and Love (Jones), 101

Solomon, Mark, 175

A Solution of the Race Problem in the South (Simmons), 320

Somebody's Calling My Name (Walker), 155

Some Efforts for Social Betterment among Negro Americans (Du Bois), 291

Sonderlund, Jean R., 75

Sonenshein, Raphael J., 200

Song in a Weary Throat (Murray), 83

Song of Solomon (Morrison), 134

Songs of Work and Protest (Fowke), 154

Songs of Zion (Campbell), 384

Soon We Will Not Cry (Fleming), 360

So This Is Jazz (Osgood), 152

Soul-Force (Barrett), 385

Soul Music (Haralambos), 155

Soul on Ice (Cleaver), 132, 198, 324

The Souls of Black Folk (Du Bois), 93, 123, 167, 173, 295, 316, 321, 371

The Sound of Soul (Garland), 155

The South and Segregation (Carmichael), 194

Southern, Eileen, 148, 154, 337, 372

Southern Black Leaders of the Reconstruction Era (Rabinowitz), 193

Southern Christian Leadership Conference (SCLC), 354, 356, 382

"Southern Horrors" (Wells), 120

Southern Journey (Dent), 353

Southern Politics in State and Nation (Key), 198

The Southern South (Hart), 320

The Southern Temper (Peters), 319

"The Southern Theme" (Wills), 369

The Southern Urban Negro as a Consumer (Edwards), 338

Southern Workman, 121

Sowing and Reaping (Harper), 77

Spaulding, Charles Clinton, 291

Spaulding, Norman W., 340

Speaking the Truth (Cone), 382

Speak Now against the Day (Egerton), 355

Spear, Allan H., 9

Special Problems of Negro Education (Wilkerson), 97

Spencer, Anne, 125

Spencer, C. S., 290

Spencer, Jon, 154, 155

Spero, Sterling, 25–27
Spickard, Paul R., 327
The Spirituals and the Blues (Cone), 382
Spivey, Donald, 101, 262, 265
Sponsor, 340
Sport, Men, and the Gender Order (Messner and Sabo), 265, 267
"Sport and Popular Pastimes" (Wiggins), 257
"Sport Mystique in Black Culture" (Rudman), 267
Sport of the Gods (Dunbar), 124
Sports. *See* Athletic experience
"Sportswomen in Black and White" (Williams), 266
"Stability and Change in Discrimination against Black Public Schools" (Harris), 101
Staking a Claim (Greenberg), 297
Stampp, Kenneth M., 3
Stancell, Steven, 155
Stanley, Harold W., 198
Stanley, Lawrence, 155
Staples, Robert, 325, 326
Stark, Inez Cunningham, 129
Star of Zion, 219
The State of Black America (NUL), 343
Statesmen on Slavery and the Negro (Marina), 317
Staudenraus, Philip J., 3, 168, 192
Steed, Robert P., 198
Steelworkers, 38–41, 175
Stein, Judith, 40
Steiner, Paul E., 237
Stepto, Robert B., 135, 373
Sterling, Dorothy, 79, 191, 289
Sterner, Richard, 340
Sternsher, Bernard, 196
Stevenson, Brenda, 75, 170
Stewart, Joseph, 200
Stewart, Maria W., 78–79
Stokely Speaks (Carmichael), 198
Stolen Childhood (King), 257
Stone, A. H., 24
Stone, Clarence, 201
Stony the Road We Trod (Felder), 383
Story of Christian Music (Wilson-Dickson), 155

Story of Phillis Wheatley (Graham), 119
The Story of the Lord's Dealings with Mrs. Amanda Smith (Smith), 383
The Strange Career of Jim Crow (Woodward), 194, 237
Stranger at the Gates (Sugarman), 358
The Street (Petry), 128, 131
Strength for the Fight (Nalty), 232
Strength to Love (King), 382
Strickland, Arvarh E., 195, 354
Stride toward Freedom (King), 11, 340–41, 353, 381
Stritcher, Sharon, 283
"The Strivings of the Negro People" (Du Bois), 123
Strother, Horatio T., 3
The Struggle for Black Equality (Sitkoff), 359
Struggle for Black Political Empowerment in Three Georgia Counties (Hanks), 198
Struggle for Equality (McPherson), 235
Stuart, Merah S., 279, 291
Stuckey, Sterling, 118, 167, 169, 371, 380
Student Nonviolent Coordinating Committee (SNCC), 84, 353, 357, 359, 361
Studies in African Music (Jones), 149
Studies in Evolution and Eugenics (Homes), 322
"The Subject Is Money" (Murray), 342
Succeeding against the Odds (Johnson), 297, 341
Success Runs in Our Race (Fraser), 299
"Success Story" (Moskos), 245
Sugarman, Tracy, 358
Suggs, Henry Lewis, 220
Sula (Morrison), 134
Sullivan, David J., 339–40
Sullivan, Louis, 343
Sullivan, Patricia, 355, 359
Sundquist, James, 196
Sundstrom, Lars, 283
Suppression of the African Slave Trade to the United States, 1638–1870 (Du Bois), 2
Surface, George T., 24
Sutherland, Elizabeth, 358

Swain, Carol, 202
Sweet, Leonard I., 166
The Sweet Flypaper of Life (Hughes), 380
Sweet Soul Music (Guralnick), 155
Swing Out (Fernett), 153
Swint, Henry L., 96
Szwed, John F., 372

T. Thomas Fortune (Thornbrough), 172, 220
Tabb, David H., 199, 201–2
"Taft" (Gray), 294
Take Your Choice (Bilbo), 323
"Taking Care of Business" (Glasco), 296
Talking Back (hooks), 85
Tally's Corner (Liebow), 11
Talmadge, Herman E., 324
Tantillo, Maura Shaw, 326
Taps for a Jim Crow Army (McGuire), 243
Tar Baby (Morrison), 134
"The Task of Negro Womanhood" (McDougald), 126
A Taste of Power (Brown), 84, 203
Tate, Katherine, 179, 202
Taylor, Arnold H., 220
Taylor, Major, 258
Taylor, Prince A., 98
Taylor, Susie King, 79, 237
Temple of My Familiar (Walker), 134
Tempter of Eve (Carroll), 319
Ten Years of Prelude (Muse), 197
Terborg-Penn, Rosalyn, 42, 73, 85, 171
Terry, Lucy, 118–19
Terry, Wallace, 245
Their Eyes Were Watching God (Hurston), 82, 125, 128
There Is a River (Harding), 190, 219, 371, 375
There Is Confusion (Fauset), 82
Thernstrom, Abigail M., 357
They All Played Ragtime (Blesh and Janis), 152
They Overheard the Gospel (Jones), 373
They Who Would Be Free (Pease and Pease), 168
Thiesson, Victor, 199

Thinking Black (Wickham), 224
The Third Life of Grange Copeland (Walker), 134
The $30 Billion Negro (Gibson), 341
This Little Light of Mine (Mills), 84, 203, 360
This Species of Property (Owens), 3, 170
Thomas, Lamont D., 3, 190
Thomas, Richard W., 10, 37
Thomas, William Hannibal, 321
Thomas and Beulah (Dove), 134
Thomas Morris Chester (Blackett), 235
Thompson, Charles H., 97
Thompson, Julius E., 220
Thompson, Robert Faris, 385
Thornbrough, Emma Lou, 172, 220
Thorpe, Earl E., 166
Those Preaching Women (Mitchell), 383
Thurman, Howard, 380–81
Thurman, Wallace, 126, 128
Till, Emmett Louis "Bobo," 130, 357
Time on the Cross (Fogel and Engerman), 30
Tinney, James S., 225
Titcomb, Caldwell, 99
Toast of the Town (Wilson and Cohassey), 290
Tobacco and Slaves (Kulikoff), 317
Tobacco companies, 343–44
To Be Loved (Gordy), 297
Todd, Gwendolyn Powell, 299
To Have and to Hold (Hudson), 284
"To 'Joy My Freedom" (Hunter), 80
Tolson, Melvin B., 127, 130
To Make a Poet Black (Reddings), 119
Tom Bradley's Campaigns for Governor (Pettigrew), 204
"Tom Molineaux" (Magiel), 257
Tomorrow's Tomorrow (Ladner), 326
Toomer, Jean, 125, 127
To Redeem the Soul of America (Fairclough), 354
To Serve My Country, to Serve My Race (Moore), 243
To Tell a Free Story (Andrews), 118
Totem and Taboo (Freud), 320
"Toward a Black Feminist Criticism" (Smith), 135

"Toward a History and Bibliography of the Afro-American Doctorate ..." (Anderson), 98

"Toward a History of Conjure and Black Folk Religion" (Chireau), 380

"Town and Sword" (Nash), 241

Trabelin' On (Sobel), 370, 373

"Trade and Markets in Precolonial West and West Central Africa" (Walker), 283

Tragedy of Lynching (Raper), 194

The Tragic Era (Bowers), 321

Trail and Triumph (Harper), 77

Transformation of Southern Politics (Bass and DeVries), 198

Travail and Triumph (Taylor), 220

Treese, Joel, 202

Trelease, Allen N., 194

Tribune (Philadelphia), 219

Tribune (Savannah), 219

Trimiew, Darryl M., 295

Tripp, Bernell E., 218

Trotter, James, 151

Trotter, Joe William, Jr., 6, 9–10, 37, 296

Trotter, William Monroe, 124, 173, 221–22

The Trouble I've Seen (Good), 359

Troubling Biblical Waters (Felder), 383

The Truly Disadvantaged (Wilson), 12, 343

Truman, Harry S., 196, 244

Truth, Sojourner, 119, 191, 383

Tryman, Mfanya Donald, 202

Tubman, Harriet, 79, 190, 383

Tucker, David M., 195

Turner, Bishop Henry MacNeal, 384

Turner, James, 167

Turner, Lorenzo, 370

Turner, Marcia, 100

Turner, Nat, 375–76

Turner, Patricia, 154

Turner, Richard Brent, 385

Tushnet, Mark V., 195, 355

Tuskegee Airmen (Francis), 243

Tuttle, William M., Jr., 9, 43

"Two Choices" (Wilson), 77

Two Colored Women with the American Expeditionary Forces (Hunton and Johnson), 242

"Two Double V's" (Eagles), 244

Two Nations (Hacker), 323

Tygiel, Jules, 263, 340

The Tyranny of the Majority (Guinier), 197

Ullman, Victor, 170

The Ultimate Solution of the Negro Problem (Eggleston), 320

UnAfrican Americans (Adeleke), 169

Unbought and Unbossed (Chisholm), 203

The Uncalled (Dunbar), 122

"Uncle Julius" (Chestnutt), 122

"Uncle Remus" (Harris), 121

Underclass Debate (Katz), 13

Underclass Questions (Lawson), 13

Underground Railroad, 3, 190

Underground Railroad (Blockson), 3

The Underground Railroad from Slavery to Freedom (Siebert), 190

Underground Railroad in Connecticut (Strother), 3

Under Their Own Vine and Fig Tree (Montgomery), 171

Unerring Fire (Fuchs), 236

Unions, labor, 24–29, 34–35, 39–41, 45

United Automobile Workers (UAW), 40

United Mine Workers of America, 28–29, 34–35, 39, 41

United States Soldier between Two Wars (Foner), 238

Universal Negro Improvement Association (U.N.I.A.), 44, 126, 174, 223

Unknown Soldiers (Barbeau and Henri), 242

Unomah, A. C., 368

Unruly Women (Bynum), 76

Up from Slavery (Washington), 120, 123, 321

Uplifting the Race (Gaines), 174

The Upward Path (Helm), 319

Urban, Wayne J., 95–96

Urban Blues (Keil), 151

Urbanization, 1–13; black workers, 34; post–Civil War, 5, 62; poverty, 11–12; pre–Civil War, 4; race relations

approach, 6–10; recent, 10–11; urban
slavery, 4
"Urbanization and Reapportionment"
(Schattsneider), 197
Urban-Rural Conflict (Hahn), 197
*Urban Slavery in the American South,
1820–1860* (Goldin), 4
The Urban Underclass (Jencks and Pater-
son), 13
Urban Vigilantes in the New South (In-
galls), 5
Urwin, Gregory J., 236
"Us Colored Women Had to Go through
a Plenty" (Jennings), 74
Usner, Daniel H., 284
Uya, Oden Edet, 237
Uya, Okon, 192

Valuska, David L., 237
Van Deburg, William L., 177, 265
Vander Hall, Jim, 177
Vander Zanden, James W., 194
Van Horne, John C., 79
Vann, Robert L., 221, 222, 297
Van Vechten, Carl, 126
*Varieties of African American Religious
Experience* (Pinn), 385
Vaughan, Catherine O., 99
Vaughn, William P., 239
Vedlitz, Arnold, 199
Vertinsky, Patricia, 265
Viens, Katheryn P., 286
Villa, Pancho, 240
Villemez, Wayne J., 298
"Vindicating the Race" (Franklin and
Collier-Thomas), 102
Violence in the Model City (Fine), 12
Viorst, Milton, 359
Voelz, Peter, 233
Voice from the South (Cooper), 72
*Voices from the Great Negro Baseball
Leagues* (Holway), 258
Voices from the Harlem Renaissance
(Huggins), 153
Voices of Freedom (Hampton et al.), 196,
356
Vose, Clement E., 195

*Voter Mobilization and the Politics of
Race* (Stanley), 198
Voting rights: black women, 171; court
cases, 98, 197, 352, 355; effect of, 198;
Freedom Summer, 357–58; gerrymandering, 197; primaries, 355; Voter Education Project, 353; Voting Rights Act
of 1965, 197, 357–58

Wade, Richard C., 4
Wagstaff, Lonnie H., 99
Waiting to Exhale (McMillan), 134
Walker, A'Lelia, 126
Walker, Alice, 85, 134, 135
Walker, Clarence G., 171
Walker, David, 78, 119, 190–91, 219,
375–76
Walker, Juliet E. K., 282–83, 285–88,
297, 299
Walker, Maggie Lena, 291
Walker, Margaret, 128, 132, 190
Walker, Wyatt Tee, 155
Walker, Zachariah, 43
Walker's Appeal in Four Articles (Wal-
ker), 78, 119, 190–91, 219, 375–76
"Walking City" (Walton), 341
Wallace, George, 361
Wallace, Michele, 326
Wallace, Robert L., 299
Wallace, Walter W., 222
Walls, Bishop William J., 374
The Walls Came Tumbling Down
(White), 195
Walrond, Eric, 128
Walser, Richard, 119
Walters, Ronald W., 202
Walton, Hanes, 192, 195, 202–3
Walton, Norman W., 341
War. *See* Military, African Americans in
War and Race (Patton), 242
Ward, Douglas Turner, 132
Ward, Renee, 342
Ware, Charles Pickard, 149
Warren, Fred, 149
Warriors Don't Cry (Beals), 355
War to End Wars (Coffman), 242
Washington, Booker T.: black businesses,
294–95, 336; criticism of, 172–74; on

education, 93–94; literature, 120, 123; miscegenation, 321
Washington, James M., 171, 379
Waskow, Arthur I., 196
"Was There a Massacre at Poison Spring" (Bailey), 236
Water from the Rock (Frey), 371, 373
Waterfront Workers of New Orleans (Arnesen), 5, 39
Watkins, Frances Ellen, 77
Watkins-Owens, Irma, 82
Watters, Pat, 196, 353
We Ain't What We Was (Wirt), 359
Weare, Walter, 291
We Are Not Afraid (Cagin and Dray), 358
"We Are Not What We Seem" (Kelley), 44
We Are Your Sisters (Sterling), 79, 289
The Weary Blues (Hughes), 380
Weatherford, W. D., 319
Weaver, John D., 241
Weaver, Robert, 25–26
Weaver, Toni E., 317, 323
Webb, Sheyann, 83, 357
Webber, Thomas, 101, 103
"We Cannot Treat Negroes . . . as Prisoners of War" (Urwin), 236–37
The Wedding (West), 125
Weekly Anglo-African, 218
Weems, Renita, 383
Weems, Robert E., Jr., 281–82, 292, 298, 344–45
We Have Been Believers (Evans), 383
We Have Taken a City (Prather), 5
Weisbrot, Robert, 359
Weiss, Nancy J., 173, 195, 354
Wells, Ida B., 80, 120, 124, 194, 219, 321
Wells-Barnett, Ida B., 194
We'll Understand It Better By and By (Reagon), 155
"Wendell Smith, the Pittsburgh Courier-Journal, and the Campaign to Include Blacks in Organized Baseball" (Wiggins), 262
Wert, Jeffrey D., 237
We Shall Overcome (Garrow), 196

Wesley, Charles H., 24–26, 217, 374
We Specialize in the Wholly Impossible (Hine, King, and Reed), 75, 77, 80, 85
West, Cornel, 383
West, Dorothy, 125, 128
West, Rachel Nelson, 83
West, Togo, 244
Westheider, James Edward, 245
"West Point and the First Negro Cadet" (Vaughn), 239
Weyl, Nathaniel, 317
What a Woman Ought to Be and to Do (Shaw), 80
"What Hour of the Night" (Ducksworth), 244
"What is Africa to Me" (Cullen), 126
Whatley, Warren, 44–45
What Price Integration? (Burgess), 324
Wheatley, Phillis, 118
When and Where I Enter (Giddings), 326
When Harlem Was in Vogue (Lewis), 125, 174
When Hell Froze Over (Yancey), 203
When Jim Crow Met John Bull (Smith), 243
When Negroes March (Garfinkel), 175, 195
When the Game Was Black and White (Chadwick), 258
When the Nation Was in Need (Putney), 243
"When the Spirit Says Sing" (Sanger), 155
Where Do We Go from Here (King), 199, 382
"Which Black Is Beautiful?" (Brown), 344
Whipper, William J., 218
White, Deborah Gray, 30, 74, 81, 383
White, Mary O., 195
White, Walter, 128, 242
White America (Cox), 321
White Man, Listen! (Wright), 130
White over Black (Jordan), 189, 317, 318
The White Problem in America (Nipson), 323, 325
White Terror (Trelease), 194

White to White on Black/White (Weaver), 317, 323

White Woman's Christ and Black Women's Jesus (Grant), 383

White Women, Coloured Men (Champly), 321

Whitfield, Stephen J., 357

Whitman, T. Stephen, 31

Whittaker, Johnson Chesnut, 239

Whitten, David O., 282, 287

Whose Votes Count (Thernstrom), 357

"Who's Who in $350,000,000 Black Grooming Market" (Forkan), 345

"Why It Worked in Dixie" (Orfield), 101

"Why Not Cooperate?" (Drake), 339

"Why Should White Guys Have All the Fun?" (Lewis and Walker), 298

Why We Can't Wait (King), 357, 382

Wickham, DeWayne, 224

The Wife of His Youth and Other Stories of the Color Line (Chestnutt), 122

Wiggins, David K., 257, 262, 265, 268

Wiggins, William H., 260

Wilder, L. Douglas, 203

Wiley, Ed, III, 103

Wilkerson, Doxey A., 97

Wilkerson, Martha, 11, 261

Wilkins, Roger W., 13

Wilkins, Roy, 222

Wilkinson, Doris, 323

Wilkinson, J. Harvie, 101

Will Desegregation Desegregate the South? (Lanier), 324

The William Grant Still Reader (Spencer), 154

Williams, Charles H., 242

Williams, Delores S., 383

Williams, Eddie N., 203

Williams, Eric, 2

Williams, George Washington, 93, 119–21, 235

Williams, Henry Sylvester, 175

Williams, Juan, 196

Williams, Lillian, 100

Williams, Linda, 266

Williams, Richard T., 94

Williams, Vernon J., Jr., 320

Williamson, Joel, 121

Willingham, Alex, 203

Wills, David, 369

Wilmore, Gayraud S., 172, 375, 381–82

Wilson, August, 133

Wilson, Clint C., II, 225

Wilson, Harriet, 77, 119

Wilson, James Q., 195

Wilson, Joseph T., 234–35

Wilson, Sunnie, 290

Wilson, William Julius, 12, 343

Wilson, Zaphon, 204

Wilson-Dickson, Andrew, 155

Winch, Julie, 287

Wine in the Wilderness (Childress), 132

Winks, Robin, 3

Winston, Michael R., 239

Wintz, Cary, 174

Wirt, Frederick, 359

With a Black Platoon in Combat (Rishell), 244

Within the Plantation Household (Fox-Genovese), 75

"With One Mighty Pull" (O'Brien), 294

Without Consent or Contract (Fogel), 285

Witnesses for Freedom (Barton), 120

Witness in Philadelphia (Mars), 358

Woke Me Up This Morning (Young), 155

Woler, Raymond, 101

Wolk, Allen, 196

Wolseley, Roland E., 218

Wolters, Raymond, 196

Womack, William M., Sr., 243

Womanism, 135

"Womanist Consciousness" (Brown), 42, 291

Woman of Color (Leslie), 74

Women, African American, 71–86; abolitionists, 79; athletes, 260, 265–66; in business, 283, 288–90; civil rights movement, 83–84, 360–61; feminist movement and, 84–86, 135; food traditions, 74; free, 78; gender role views, 66; journalists, 221, 224; labor history, 42; migration, 82; in the military, 237, 242–43; paucity of resources on, 72; political activism, 80, 85–86; in politics, 203; religion, 383; sexual abuse, 74; sexuality, 325–26; slave narratives, 73–74; slave studies, 74–75; stereotypes, 81; suffrage, 171; transition from slavery, 79–80; voluntary clubs, 81; white women and, 75–76; writers, 77–78, 82–83, 134–35

Women, Race, and Class (Davis), 85, 317

Women, Sport, and Culture (Birrell and Cole), 266

Women in the Civil Rights Movement (Crawford et al.), 84, 360

The Women of Brewster Place (Naylor), 134

"Women of Color, Critical Autobiography, and Sport" (Birrell), 265

Women's Work, Men's Work (Woods), 284

Wood, Betty, 2

Wood, Forrest G., 194, 318

Wood, Peter, 2

Woods, Barbara, 360

Woods, Betty, 284

Woods, Gail Baker, 344

Woods, Granville T., 294

Woods, Peter H., 316

Woodson, Carter G., 6–8, 94–95, 124, 223, 279, 291

Woodward, C. Vann, 193, 237

Woodward, Elon A., 232

Woofter, Thomas J., Jr., 8

Work, Monroe, 221, 279, 337

"Work and Culture" (Morgan), 284

Workers, African American, 23–47; agricultural, 31–32; discrimination, 40–41; gaps in knowledge, 43–47; in the industrial age, 33–43; new labour history, 28–29; old labor history, 24–28; proletarianization, 46–47; sharecropping, 32, 36, 62; slaves as, 29–32; stereotypes of, 24–25; transition from slavery, 32–33, 39; urban studies, 42–43; women, 42. *See also* Labor unions; Slavery

Working the Spirit (Murphy), 385

Working toward Freedom (Hudson), 74, 284

The Work of Reconstruction (Saville), 33

World (Indianapolis), 219

The World of Black Singles (Staples), 326

The World They Made Together (Sobel), 317, 370

Worthman, Paul B., 34–35

The Wretched of the Earth (Fanon), 324

Wright, Albert H., 99

Wright, Conrad E., 286

Wright, George C., 5, 360

Wright, Marion M. Thompson, 96

Wright, Richard, 82, 102, 128, 129–30

Wynn, Neil A., 244

Yancey, Dwayne, 203

Yancy, Robert, 298

"Yardbird" (Hayden), 130

"The Year of Awakening" (Wiggins), 265

Yee, Shirley, 79

Yellin, Jean Fagan, 79

You and Segregation (Talmadge), 324

"You Know I Am a Man of Business" (Winch), 287

Young, Alan, 155

Young, Alexander J., 261

Young, Andrew, 203

Young, Charles, 239

Young, Coleman, 201

Young, Hiram, 288

Young, James O., 175

Young, P. B., 222

Young, Whitney M., Jr., 354

Youngblood (Killens), 129

Young-Bruehl, Elisabeth, 325

Zang, David W., 258

Zangrando, Robert L., 194

Zieger, Robert, 36

Zinn, Howard, 353, 356

Zinn, M. B., 59–61, 63

About the Editors and Contributors

EDITORS

ARVARH E. STRICKLAND is Professor Emeritus of History at the University of Missouri–Columbia. His major publications include *History of the Chicago Urban League* (1966) and two volumes of the Lorenzo J. Greene diaries, *Working with Carter G. Woodson, the Father of Black History: A Diary, 1928–1933* (1989) and *Selling Black History for Carter G. Woodson: A Diary, 1930–1933* (1996).

ROBERT E. WEEMS, JR., is Professor of History at the University of Missouri–Columbia. He is the author of *Black Business in the Black Metropolis: The Chicago Metropolitan Assurance Company, 1925–1985* (1996) and *Desegregating the Dollar: African American Consumerism in the Twentieth Century* (1998).

CONTRIBUTORS

JOHN DITTMER is Professor of History at DePauw University. He is the author of *Black Georgia in the Progressive Era, 1900–1920* (1977) and the award-winning *Local People: The Struggle for Civil Rights in Mississippi* (1994).

CAROLYN A. DORSEY is Associate Professor Emeritus of Educational Leadership and Policy Analysis at the University of Missouri–Columbia. She has published widely in the areas of blacks and higher education and black faculty at white institutions.

STANLEY O. GAINES, JR., is Assistant Professor of Psychology and Black Studies at Pomona College. He has published numerous articles and is the author of *Culture, Ethnicity, and Personal Relationship Processes* (1997).

ROBERT L. HARRIS, JR., is Associate Professor of History and Africana Studies and is Special Assistant to the provost at Cornell University. He has published widely in the field of African American history, including *Teaching African American History* (1992).

CLENORA HUDSON-WEEMS is Professor of English at the University of Missouri–Columbia. Her numerous publications include *Toni Morrison* (1990), *Africana Womanism: Reclaiming Ourselves* (1993), and *Emmett Till: The Sacrificial Lamb of the Civil Rights Movement* (1994).

WILMA KING is the Arvarh E. Strickland Distinguished Professor of African American History and Culture at the University of Missouri–Columbia. Her major publications include *A Northern Woman in the Plantation South: Letters of Tryphena Blanche Holder Fox, 1856–1876* (1993) and *Stolen Childhood: Slave Youth in Nineteenth Century America* (1995).

CHARLES H. LONG is Professor Emeritus of Religious Studies at the University of California–Santa Barbara. A founding member of the American Society for the Study of Religion and a founding editor of the journals *History of Religions* and *Studies in Religion*, Long's major publications include *Alpha, The Myth of Creation* (1963), *The History of Religions: Essays in Understanding* (1967), and *Significations: Signs, Symbols, and Images in the Interpretation of Religion* (1987).

JOHN F. MARSZALEK is the William L. Giles Distinguished Professor of History at Mississippi State University. He is coeditor of the *Encyclopedia of African American Civil Rights* and has authored several books on American race relations.

MINION K. C. MORRISON is Professor of Political Science at the University of Missouri–Columbia. Morrison's interests are in African American politics and African politics. He has authored three books and numerous articles in the professional journals of political science.

HORACE D. NASH is Adjunct Professor of History at San Antonio College. He is the author of articles, encyclopedia entries, and book reviews related to American race relations and African Americans in the military.

JOHN A. TAYLOR is Associate Director of the North Central Association of Colleges and Schools' Commission on Institutions of Higher Education. He previously worked at Lincoln University (Missouri) in a variety of capacities, including Head of the Department of Fine Arts and Vice-President for Academic Affairs. He was also a member of the Jefferson City Symphony, starting as a trumpeter and eventually becoming conductor.

AARON THOMPSON is Associate Professor of Sociology and Coordinator for Academic Success at Eastern Kentucky University. He has published in the areas of educational attainment, African American fatherhood, divorce in the black family, and black and white differences in marital expectations. Much of his research and publications surrounds the life aspects of race, gender, and African American families.

JULIUS E. THOMPSON is Director of Black Studies and Associate Professor of History at the University of Missouri–Columbia. His major publications include *The Black Press in Mississippi, 1865–1985: A Directory* (1988); *The Black Press in Mississippi, 1865–1985* (1993); *Percy Greene and the Jackson Advocate: The Life and Times of a Radical Conservative Black Newspaperman, 1897–1977* (1994); and *Dudley Randall, Broadside Press, and the Black Arts Movement in Detroit, 1960–1995* (1999).

JOE WILLIAM TROTTER, JR., is Mellon Bank Professor of History and Director of the Center for African American Urban Studies and the Economy at Carnegie Mellon University. His numerous publications include *Black Milwaukee: The Making of an Industrial Proletariat, 1915–1945* (1985); *Coal, Class, and Color: Blacks in Southern West Virginia, 1915–1932* (1990); *The Great Migration in Historical Perspective: New Dimensions of Race, Class, and Gender* (1991); and *River Jordan: African American Urban Life in the Ohio Valley* (1998).

JULIET E. K. WALKER is Professor of History at the University of Illinois at Urbana-Champaign. Her numerous publications include *Free Frank: A Black Pioneer on the Antebellum Frontier* (1983) and the award-winning study *The History of Black Business in America: Capitalism, Race, Entrepreneurship* (1998).

DAVID K. WIGGINS is Professor of Health, Fitness, and Recreation Resources at George Mason University. He is author of *Ethnicity and Sport in North American History and Culture* (1994), *Sport in America: From Wicked Amusement to National Obsession* (1995), and *Glory Bound: Black Athletes in a White America* (1997). He is currently editor of the *Journal of Sport History*.

SHARON D. WRIGHT is Assistant Professor of Political Science and Black Studies at the University of Missouri–Columbia. She has written extensively on black mayoral politics, black political behavior, black women in politics, and rural economic development. She is also the author of *Race, Power, and Political Emergence in Memphis* (1999).